THE NOBLE SAVAGE

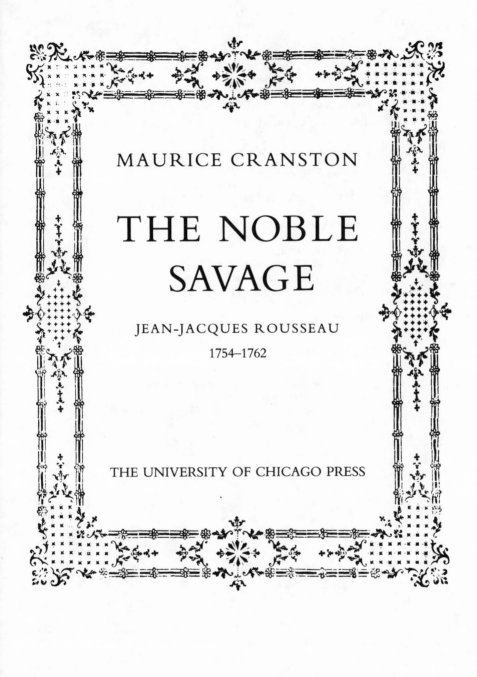

MAURICE CRANSTON

THE NOBLE SAVAGE

JEAN-JACQUES ROUSSEAU

1754–1762

THE UNIVERSITY OF CHICAGO PRESS

The University of Chicago Press, Chicago 60637
Viking/Penguin, Ltd., London
© 1991 Maurice Cranston
All rights reserved. Published 1991
Printed in the United States of America

00 99 98 97 96 95 94 93 92 91   5 4 3 2 1

Library of Congress Cataloging-in-Publication Data

Cranston, Maurice William, 1920–
    The noble savage: Jean-Jacques Rousseau,
    1754–1762 / Maurice Cranston.
      p.   cm.
    Includes bibliographical references and index.
    ISBN 0-226-11863-0 (cloth). — ISBN
    0-226-11864-9 (paper)
    1. Rousseau, Jean-Jacques, 1712–1778—Biography.
2. Authors, French—18th century—Biography.
I. Title.
PQ2043.C73 1991
848'.509 — dc20
[B]   90–28111
                                                           CIP

CONTENTS

LIST OF PLATES

PREFACE

This book continues the biography which began with the publication in 1983 of *Jean-Jacques: The Early Life and Work of Jean-Jacques Rousseau*. In writing the present volume I have again tried to keep close to the evidence, so as to allow the reader to hear as often as possible the voices of Rousseau and his contemporaries, voices so often distorted or lost amid the din of interpretation, commentary and analysis. There is no lack of material for research. Rousseau's manuscripts in institutional libraries have at last been so well assembled and catalogued, and the papers that remain in private collections so generously opened to study that there is no longer any excuse for traditional caricatures of Jean-Jacques to be allowed to stand as portraits.

Rousseau's work has been widely reassessed since the Second World War, and its value recognized anew. This book takes a fresh look at his life in the years when he wrote several of his most important books: the *Letter to M. d'Alembert*, *Julie, or the New Heloise*, *Émile*, and *The Social Contract*. My purpose is less critical than explanatory, and since I believe that explanation in biography, as in history, *se trouve dans les détails*, it is on details that this biography concentrates. The epistemology I invoke is that of Locke.

A reviewer of the first volume of this biography protested that with this method of impartial pursuit of the facts I had made Rousseau seem 'almost normal'. The Rousseau who appears in the present volume may strike readers as less normal, as he grows increasingly fretful, anxious, suspicious – and often physically ill, the predictable effects, in the opinion of his literary friends in Paris, of his leaving the city to live in unhealthy rustic solitude. The first philosopher of the Greens was not necessarily at his best when he was closest to Nature. However, those readers who cannot imagine Rousseau as anything other than thoroughly paranoid must wait for the third volume of this biography, which will trace the last tormented years of his life.

In writing this book I have become indebted to many individuals and institutions for their help in allowing me access to research materials. I must first thank Her Majesty the Queen of the Netherlands for graciously allowing me to make use of the correspondence, preserved in her library at The Hague, between Rousseau and his publisher Marc-Michel Rey. I am also grateful to Dr B. Woelderink, Director of the Koninklijk Huisarchief, for giving me access to the Dutch royal archives. The richest source of manuscript material for the present volume is the Bibliothèque Publique et Universitaire at Neuchâtel, and I am greatly indebted to the Director, Monsieur Jacques Rychner, and Mme Maryse Schmidt-Surdez, Conservatrice des Manuscrits, for their unfailing help and cooperation. The Bibliothèque Publique et Universitaire of Geneva contains an almost equally important Rousseau archive and I have to thank the Librarian and Monsieur Philippe Monnier, Conservateur des Manuscrits, for allowing me access both to their own collections and to those of the Société Jean-Jacques Rousseau, by arrangement with its Secretary, Charles Wirz, to whom I am also indebted for many kindnesses in his capacity as Director of the Institut Voltaire at Geneva. I must also record my gratitude to the Speaker of the Assemblée Nationale and to the Librarian of the Palais Bourbon in Paris for allowing me once again to work on the manuscript of the *Confessions* and the several original letters of Rousseau which are housed in that library.

Acknowledgements are also due to numerous other librarians and archivists who have given me access to their Rousseau holdings, notably those of the Bibliothèque Nationale, the Archives Nationales, the Bibliothèque de l'Arsenal, the Bibliothèque Mazarine, the British Library, the British Library of Political Science and Economics, the University of London Library, the Bodleian Library and the Taylorian Library, Oxford, the London Library, the Zentralbibliothek, Zurich, the Burgerbibliothek, Berne, the Central University Library of the University of California, San Diego, the Huntington Library, Pasadena, The Library of Congress, Washington, the Morgan Library, New York, the New York Public Library, the Widener Library and the Houghton Library, Cambridge, Massachusetts, The Beinecke Library, Yale University, New Haven, the Saltykov-Shchedrin Library, Leningrad, the Bibliothèque de Versailles, the Musée Rousseau, Montmorency, the Musée Jacquemart-André, Chaalis, the Wisbech Literary Institute, the Riksarkivet, Stockholm, the Bayerische Staatsbibliothek, Munich, the Bibliothèque de la Ville, Poitiers the Bibliothèque de la Ville, Nancy, the Bibliothèque Municipale, Besançon, the University Library, Leyden, the Archives Municipales, Bordeaux.

For permission to consult material which still reposes in private collections, I am especially indebted to the Vicomtesse de Montmagner de

Loube, whose father, the late Comte Maximilien de Foy, conserved at his château at Chérigny letters written by Rousseau to Mme d'Houdetot.

Many friends and Rousseau scholars have helped me. My greatest debt is to the late Ralph Leigh, whose knowledge of the Rousseau archive was only matched by his generosity over the years in helping me find my way in it. I am also particularly grateful to my friend and former pupil Robert Wokler, who, with his deep erudition and lively sympathy for Rousseau's thought, has taught me much. Other friends and Rousseau specialists who have helped me in one way or another include Jean Starobinski, Robert Derathé, James MacAdam, Roger Masters, Bernard Gagnebin, Bronislaw Baczko, Paul Edwards, Benjamin Barber, Grace Roosevelt, Sanford A. Lakoff, Mira Morgenstern, Athanasios Moulakis, Victor Gourevitch, Howard Cell, Raymond Polin, Harvey Mansfield, Guy Lafrance, Jean Roy, Aubrey Rosenberg, Lucien Jaume, Gita May, Carol K. Blum, Shirley Letwin, Robert Thiéry, Tanguy L'Aminot, Terence Marshall, Anne de Herdt, Josiane Ayoub-Boulade, Joel Schwartz, Judith N. Shklar, John Charvet, Mortimer J. Adler, Patrick Riley, John Gray, John Hope Mason, Philip E. J. Robinson, Douglas G. Creighton, John W. Chapman, Frederick Rosen, Arthur M. Melzer, Maurizio Viroli and André Reszler.

Some paragraphs in Chapter 11, 'Two Social Contracts', originally appeared in *The Great Ideas Today, 1985* (Encyclopaedia Britannica, Chicago) and are reproduced by permission of the publishers.

For financial support over the eight years during which I have been working on this book I am indebted to the Leverhulme Foundation, the Central Research Fund of the University of London, the Suntory-Toyota International Centre, the Fulbright Commission, and the British Academy. I am also pleased to place on record my gratitude to my research assistant Mrs June Burnham and my secretary Miss Kate Redmond.

INTRODUCTION

Rousseau's early life was that of a wanderer, an adventurer, the life of a hero of a picaresque novel. Orphaned by the early death of his mother and the defection of his father, he had run away from his native Geneva at the age of sixteen to escape the life of a plebeian engraver's apprentice, and found refuge as a Catholic convert in Savoy. Making his own way in the world as a footman in Turin, a student at a choir school in Annecy, the steward and the lover of a Swiss baroness in Chambéry, the interpreter to a Levantine mountebank, an itinerant musician, a private tutor in the family of Condillac and Mably in Lyons, secretary to the French Ambassador in Venice and research assistant to the Dupins at Chenonceaux, he set out with his great friend and contemporary Denis Diderot to conquer Paris as a writer, and, much to his own surprise, did so almost overnight at the age of thirty-eight with the publication of his *Discourse on the Sciences and Arts*.

He had already started writing articles for Diderot's *Encyclopédie*, that monumental compendium of the ideas of the Enlightenment; but paradoxically his *Discourse* not only rejected the central message of the Enlightenment – that science and technology could save mankind – it argued that all such advances of knowledge were deleterious, taking men farther and farther away from their original innocence towards corruption.

Rousseau went on to achieve more fame in a field where his ideas were close to those of Diderot and the Encyclopédistes, music. When he first reached Paris he had offered the Academy of Sciences a new scheme of musical notation and he composed the score of an opera. The scheme was politely rejected, and the opera rudely damned by the leading French composer, Rameau. A year or two later, Rousseau had his sweet revenge as the champion of the new Italian music against the conservative French music of Rameau. Rousseau produced a philosophy of melody which captured fashionable as well as liberal and intellectual support against

Rameau's metaphysics of harmony; and he fortified his credentials as a musicologist by writing an opera, *Le Devin du village*, which was performed to the delight of everyone at Fontainebleau and Paris.

However, by this time Rousseau was so convinced by the argument of his own first *Discourse* that he refused to accept the rewards of worldly success and declared himself determined henceforth to live on the frugal earnings of a music copyist and a *moraliste*. The more he listened to his conscience, the less he liked the conversation of the Encyclopédistes, who seemed to enjoy nothing better than mocking God, notwithstanding their nominal attachment to the established Catholic Church. Looking inward, Rousseau realized that he believed no more than they did in the teachings of the Catholic Church; but he loved and needed God. He could only identify himself as a Protestant; and so at the age of forty-two he went back to Geneva to secure readmission to the Calvinist Church into which he had been baptized as an infant.

1

PARIS

Rousseau's visit to Geneva in the summer of 1754 was seen by him as an important moment in the history of his 'reform'. Some of his friends assumed he had rejoined the Protestant Church only in order to recover his rights and privileges as a citizen of Geneva, outward observance of religious forms without inner adherence to creeds being a commonplace thing in an age when nonconformity was everywhere severely penalized. But Rousseau saw himself as having become a true believer in the Reformed religion, at least as he understood it, which was a religion reformed to the point where there was little left of familiar Christian teaching beyond the propositions that God is love and the soul of man immortal.

His 'reform', moreover, was not simply a matter of faith; he had resolved that all his actions should conform to the laws of morality; he would lead a thoroughly virtuous life. Again he was himself the judge of what virtue entailed. He did not feel impelled either to marry his mistress, Thérèse Levasseur, or to stop living with her; but he did conscientiously pursue a life of austerity, in which Thérèse, with her mother, shared, still enacting the roles of *gouvernantes*, or housekeepers. For some eighteen months between the autumn of 1754 and the spring of 1756, the three of them lived together in Paris in a modest flat on the third floor of a house in the rue de Grenelle-St Honoré, where Mme Levasseur grumbled constantly about the policy of frugal living, and encouraged her relations to scrounge what little there was to be scrounged from her daughter's celebrated lover. It is not easy to see how Rousseau managed to run even so Bohemian a household, as he said he did, on his earnings as a music copyist at ten sous a page,* but he certainly did not get much in the way of royalties for his literary and musical compositions, and he always refused brusquely any gift

---

*In 1764 Rousseau said his outgoings for 'the past twenty years' had been about 'sixty louis a year':[1] sixty louis equalled 1,440 livres or 28,800 sous.

from private benefactors – to whom, however, Mme Levasseur furtively proffered, whenever possible, a greedy palm.

In the *Confessions* Rousseau says he was planning at this time in Paris to return to Geneva and live permanently there, but other evidence shows that he cannot seriously have intended to do so. Whenever an opportunity of going there arose, he always found a new reason for refusal. They were all such sound reasons that they make it hard to believe that he ever really meant to go. Even so, he went out of his way to make himself agreeable to the Genevese. He scoured Paris for a copy of the Bible of Sixtus for the State Library of Geneva and although he could not find one, he discharged other commissions in the bookshops, and made a present to the library of a manuscript record of the trial of Joan of Arc, for which he is said to have paid one louis.[2] He was not overwhelmed with gratitude for these efforts; it was five years before the Librarian of Geneva got round to thanking him for the manuscript.[3]

In Paris he resumed the life of a fashionable writer regularly attending the *salons*, where the hostesses vied with each other in entertaining the stars of the literary, artistic and scientific worlds. Although he speaks often in the *Confessions* of his extreme shyness and his gauche behaviour in polite society, others testify to the charm of his personality and the brilliance of his conversation.[4] The leading Philosophes of the Enlightenment were still his closest friends. He declared on his return from Geneva to Paris[5] that the only people worth seeing there were Diderot, Duclos, Grimm and d'Alembert; and he soon fell again into the company of these Encyclopédistes despite the fact that he was now officially a Protestant and Christian and they were as irreligious as ever, if not more so. Indeed he began to frequent again the most aggressively atheistic of them all, the Baron d'Holbach. Mme d'Holbach had died while Rousseau was in Geneva, and Rousseau's *lettre de condoléance* expressed such tender sympathy that the widower made special efforts to lure him back to his *salon*. In principle, Rousseau objected to the luxury and splendour of Holbach's hospitality; in practice he enjoyed it.

He accepted no less eagerly the hospitality of Helvétius* who was both as rich as Holbach and as generous a host. Rousseau reported, in February 1755,[6] attending a carnival ball put on by Mme Helvétius and witnessing there a most agreeable sight: 'It was the worthy Fontenelle who opened the ball with a young lady of four. I advised the mother to point out to

---

*Claude-Arien Helvétius (1715–71) had in 1750 given up the office of tax-farmer to devote himself to writing and research. The following year he married Mme de Ligniville-d'Autricourt, a witty and lavish hostess. It was not until 1758 that he made himself notorious by the publication of his materialist, atheist treatise, *De l'esprit*, which he was forced three times to recant.

the girl the singularity of the occasion, something she will look back on in her old age with pleasure.' Fontenelle, at that time, was no less than ninety-eight years old and besides being a famous author himself had known all the literary figures of the age of Louis XIV; his partner,* who was in fact only two and a half years old, would be able to boast in the age of Chateaubriand and Byron that she had danced with a friend of Racine and Corneille.

The festivity at the Helvétius house was remembered as a *'très-beau bal'*,[8] and Rousseau was evidently happy enough to be among the guests. If he was afterwards to utter many harsh words about the smart bright life of Paris, he could also appreciate its advantages. He once wrote to a Genevese friend: 'In Paris there is a certain purity of taste, a certain rightness of style that you will never find in the provinces.'[9] He has St-Preux in the novel *Julie* say: 'There is no country in the world where the women are as enlightened as they are in Paris, or generally talk more sensibly and judiciously or know how to give better advice when it is needed.'[10] When d'Alembert was elected to the Académie Française in November 1754, Rousseau was among the friends who celebrated the event, a victory for an Encyclopédiste over three Catholic candidates. Writing[11] to Jean Jallabert,† the Genevese physicist and mathematician, Rousseau reported: 'M. de Buffon came back at last to Paris for the election of M. d'Alembert. We dined together last week and drank your health.' As soon as he learned that Voltaire was installed in Geneva, Rousseau urged his friend Pastor Jacob Vernes‡ to make a point of meeting the man he described[14] as 'the finest writer of his century', adding 'he is not simply the greatest wit but the most likeable man socially ... No one could portray the charms of virtue and the sweetness of friendship as he does without having a heart that can feel both.'

Rousseau also wrote[15] to Jallabert about Voltaire's decision to live in Geneva with his niece – and mistress – Mme Denis:§ 'With a large measure of genius, and even more wit, and the finest pen of his century, that man has a heart prone to generate his own misfortune and sometimes that of others. As for Mme Denis, I once made her acquaintance, and took her to be a woman of merit and good sense, but they say that her mania to be a wit has made her rather disputatious, a defect which the society of her uncle is hardly likely to correct. Their stay can only confer honour on our

*The future Comtesse de Mun.[7]

†Jean Jallabert (1713–68), a noted scholar and a staunch supporter of Rousseau against his critics in Geneva.[12]

‡Jacob Vernes (1728–91), Genevese pastor of literary ambitions.[13]

§Rousseau's acquaintance with Mme Denis could well have dated from her first appearance at Mme Dupin's salon; he mentions in the *Confessions* having met her with François Mussard at Passy.[16]

city; may they not disturb the peace that reigns among our men of letters.'

If these remarks betray any uneasiness about Voltaire, there is nothing approaching hostility. It is, however, instructive to compare them with Rousseau's unqualified praise for Montesquieu, as expressed in a letter[17] to Pastor Perdriau,* written a few weeks later:

You will regret as I do the death of the illustrious Montesquieu. He had no need of so long a life to become immortal; but he ought to have lived for ever to teach people their rights and duties. I was in the country when he died, and I am told that of all the men of letters with whom Paris teems, M. Diderot alone walked in the funeral *cortège* – fortunately, he was also the one whose presence would make the absence of the others less noticeable.

A shared admiration for Montesquieu was one of the bonds that sealed the friendship of Rousseau and Diderot at a time when Montesquieu was somewhat out of favour with the avant-garde of the Enlightenment; his form of liberalism, which proposed to secure political freedom through the separation and counterbalancing of the several institutions of government, was attacked by Voltaire and other champions of enlightened absolutism as an ideology of the aristocratic interest, seeking to recover for the various noble orders in France the share in sovereignty they had enjoyed in the feudal past. The dominant political conflict in France throughout the eighteenth century was between the *noblesse de robe*, established in the so-called sovereign courts or *parlements*, struggling to enlarge their powers at the expense of the prerogatives of the monarch, and a royal government at Versailles determined to maintain as much as it could of its absolute authority. While Montesquieu's political philosophy justified the claims of the *parlements*, Voltaire provided arguments in support of the royalists – reproducing substantially the thesis of Francis Bacon, that only a strong, centralized, unified government could further the policy of rational progressive reorganization and scientific planning to solve the problems of the nation. The younger intellectuals of the Enlightenment tended either to be indifferent to the quarrels between the Crown and the *parlements*, or to support the absolutism of Voltaire, which seemed indeed to be the political doctrine best suited to the Baconian aim of the salvation of mankind through science.

If Diderot at this phase of his intellectual development was closer to Voltaire in his political sentiments, he recognized in Montesquieu a more

---

*Jean Perdriau (1712–86), pastor of Saconnex, elected in 1756 Professor of Literature at the Académie de Genève.

profound thinker, and was to come in time to subscribe to Montesquieu's theory of freedom.[18] Rousseau, whose own republican ideology set him apart from both the liberalism of Montesquieu and the royalism of Voltaire, admired Montesquieu above all as a social scientist, a pioneer in a field where he himself had worked as the author of the *Discourse on Inequality* and was to work again as the author of *The Social Contract*. Had Rousseau been in Paris at the time of the funeral, Diderot would not have been alone among the Philosophes in mourning publicly the death of Montesquieu.

In the autumn of 1754 Rousseau had been lucky enough to find as a publisher for his *Discourse on Inequality* a compatriot established in the book trade of Amsterdam, Marc-Michel Rey,* who was to prove as honest, capable and friendly a man of business as any writer could desire. Rousseau, for his part, was by no means the easiest of authors, constantly complaining to Rey about misprints, delays and lost deliveries, demanding what was due to him, but refusing to be put under obligation to anyone. Rey tried at one point to placate Rousseau by offering a present to Thérèse – a dress. Rousseau was none too pleased by this ploy, and still less pleased when the dress failed to arrive.

He had asked Rey for 25 louis for rights of *Inequality* and Rey paid him promptly;[20] but Rey did not get the book into print as quickly as Rousseau had hoped and indeed expected. He kept badgering Rey to speed up the publication, and by May 1755 he could control his impatience no longer: 'Having heard, Monsieur, nothing about my book nor any of your news,' he wrote,[21]

I ask you kindly to accept mine for the last time. When you took charge of my manuscript you knew that an earlier promise had made me give it to you rather than to M. Bousquet [a Lausanne publisher], who offered me much better terms than I had demanded or received from you, believing ours to be a good bargain. You received the manuscript last October and undertook to publish it in January at the latest. You assured me also in reply to my insistent beseeching that the printing would be faultless. At the end of eight months this work, which should have been ready in six weeks, has yet to be published, and, moreover, the proofs of the text bristle with misprints . . . I shall not speak of your idle promise to Mlle Levasseur. Your letter drove her wild. I had to calm her by buying her another dress to take the place of the one you led her to expect.

*Marc-Michel Rey (1720–80), born in Geneva, had by his own account little schooling, and earned his living in the book trade from the age of seventeen, first with Marc-Michel Bousquet in Geneva and Lausanne, and then on his own in Amsterdam, where, in 1747, he married Elizabeth Bernard.[19]

Rey's present did eventually arrive, and Rousseau's anger diminished, but he showed little understanding of a publisher's problems, although he knew that Rey needed to secure government consent before *Inequality* could be sold in France. In March[22] Rey had tried to accelerate the process by sending to Paris an almost complete text of the book with a request for an import licence for two bales of copies for the French market. He addressed the request directly to Malesherbes, the Director of Publications, a magistrate who was to play an important role in Rousseau's destiny. Although he was responsible for the censorship in France, Malesherbes* was in practice a good friend of literary freedom; he did much to protect, at occasional risk to his own career, Diderot's great *Encyclopédie* and other works which challenged religious orthodoxy.[23] His methods were necessarily devious, and he was far too cautious to give Rey the answer he wanted; he explained[24] to Rey that he would need to see the entire text before he said anything about permission, and also to know how many copies would be included in each bale. Later in that same month, April,[25] Rey sent Malesherbes some further pages of *Inequality* – they contained the footnotes which add so much to the interest of that discourse – adding that there were still more pages to come. As for the number of copies he proposed to send to France, Rey said these would be 1,500. He explained that the publication had entailed a substantial investment, so that it would be a serious loss for him if the permission were denied; he said that his intention was to come to Paris to negotiate the sale in person with the booksellers there.

When Rey suggested that Rousseau himself should intervene with Malesherbes to smooth the procedures, Rousseau refused:[26] 'I regard myself in France as a man who has nothing to do with the book you are printing. Act as if I did not exist.' Nevertheless, Rousseau urged Rey[27] to advertise *Inequality* in England – 'the only country where, in my opinion, the book, if it is any good, will be esteemed for what it is worth'. At the same time he implored Rey to beg Malesherbes not to let the copy he had out of his hands lest it fall into those of pirate publishers.

On 24 April[28] Rey was able to send Malesherbes the last three sheets of *Inequality* and he offered to provide as many copies, printed on superior paper, as the magistrate would like to have for himself and his friends. However, at this stage Rousseau became alarmed at the thought of the book being read in Paris before it reached Geneva, and he decided after all to intervene personally with Malesherbes. He wrote[29] begging him not

*In 1755 Chrétien-Guillaume de Lamoignon de Malesherbes was aged only thirty-four, and probably owed his position to his being the son of M. de Lamoignon, Chancellor of France: he rose to be Secretary of State under Louis XVI, defended that King at his trial and perished on the guillotine in 1794.[23]

to allow the sheets of the book to leave his office: 'Since the work is dedicated to the Republic of Geneva it would be an offence to my sovereigns and greatly displeasing to me personally to see it circulating in other quarters before arriving at its destination.'

Malesherbes did more than Rousseau asked; he sent him all the sheets of *Inequality* he had received from Rey; and finally, on 12 May,[30] he authorized Rey to sell the book in France, instructing him to send a hundred advance copies to the bookseller Guérin,* and to release the rest of the edition eight or ten days later. Rey, however, needed time to organize deliveries, and Rousseau still found occasion to complain about delays in publication. He protested[31] that despite Malesherbes having returned his sheets of *Inequality* to him, the book had been read by others in Paris and news of it had reached Geneva, where people were rightly indignant that a work dedicated to them should be offered to foreigners first. At the same time Rousseau pointed out that rumours of the edition being held up in Rey's warehouse only led the French to suppose that the book was so bad that the author was having to rewrite and improve it endlessly.

Rousseau had been hoping that *Inequality* would receive a rapturous welcome in Geneva. He confessed[32] to Jallabert: 'I desire passionately that it should be approved of there and I do not doubt that the zeal of my friends will do more to that end than any merit of the book itself. Besides, it is written for a very small number of readers, and if it proves not unworthy of their suffrage, it need only be read by them in order to be useful to everyone.'

When Rousseau was able at last to send a copy of the *Inequality* to the authorities of Geneva, the first syndic, Jean-Louis Chouet wrote[33] to acknowledge the gift:

M. Saladin has sent me on your instructions the new work which you have just had printed. I made a report to the Council of the Dedication as you wished. The sentiments of virtue and patriotic zeal that you express so eloquently were noted with pleasure. It is always a matter of great satisfaction to the fathers of the Republic when their fellow citizens acquire fame, as you have done, through works which can only be the product of rare merit and distinguished talents. Allow me personally, Monsieur, to declare how much I have been touched by the beauties of your essay, and believe me to be, with all the esteem that you deserve, your very humble and obedient servant, Chouet.

---

*Hippolyte-Lucas Guérin (1698–1765), bookseller and publisher in partnership with his son-in-law Louis-François de La Tour.

This was certainly not a hostile reception, as even Perdriau, who had led Rousseau to expect one, had to admit. He assured him some months later[34] that the Dedication had been properly appreciated by the people of Geneva: 'I blush when I think of the efforts I made to dissuade you from publishing it.' Moreover, Chouet's letter was followed by another[35] from the former first syndic of Geneva, Jean-Louis Du Pan, praising *Inequality* as the product 'of a virtuous man and a zealous patriot', a work 'which confirmed the idea I have had of you since I first had the honour of knowing you'. Du Pan went on to say, 'In the Dedication you have followed the movements of your heart, and I fear you will be thought to have flattered us too much. You have depicted us as we ought to be, and not as we are.'

This last phrase may well betray a certain reserve about Rousseau's description, in the Dedication, of Geneva as a 'well-tempered democracy' when in truth Geneva was an hereditary oligarchy with only the residual trappings of a lost democracy, but Du Pan's praise of *Inequality* is obviously as sincere as that of the syndic Chouet, and indeed at the time Rousseau seems to have been well enough pleased with the reception of the book in Geneva. 'I cannot express the joy with which I learned that the Council had accepted in the name of the Republic the Dedication of the *Discourse*,' he wrote to Jacob Vernes in July,[36] 'and I am conscious of all the kind indulgence and graciousness there is in their statement.'

By the time he came to write his *Confessions*, he no longer considered that *Inequality* had been well received in Geneva. He speaks there of Chouet's letter as 'polite but very cold', and while he admits having received a few compliments about the book from friends, he adds, 'I did not notice that a single Genevese recognized the heartfelt zeal there was in the book.'[37] 'This indifference,' he goes on to say in the *Confessions*, 'shocked everyone who was aware of it. One day at a dinner given by Mme Dupin* at Clichy for M. de Crommelin, diplomatic representative of Geneva, another guest, M. de Mairan,† declared to everyone present that the Genevese Council owed me an award and public honours for the book and that it would disgrace itself if it failed to do both. Crommelin, who was a dark and deeply evil little man, dared not reply in my presence, but he put on a terrible grimace, which made Mme Dupin smile.'

In the *Confessions* Rousseau speaks of the 'ill success' of the book in Geneva as one of the factors that made him change his mind about retiring there, together with the presence in that city of Voltaire. In letters written in 1755 there is no evidence of strong feeling on either score. Indeed, in

---

*Louise-Marie-Madeleine Dupin (1706–99), the notably beautiful hostess and feminist for whom Rousseau had worked as a secretary in the 1740s.[38]

†J.-J. Dortous de Mairan (1678–1771), mathematician.

the summer of that year Rousseau sent a copy of *Inequality* to Voltaire at the villa Robert Tronchin had found for him in Geneva, and which is today the Institut et Musée Voltaire; Voltaire named it Les Délices. Rousseau received in acknowledgement a letter[39] which began with words he might well have thought offensive:

I have received, Monsieur, your new book against the human race, and I thank you for it ... Never has so much intelligence been deployed in an effort to make us beasts. One wants to walk on all fours after reading your book, but since I lost the habit more than sixty years ago, I fear I cannot recover it.

The letter went on to offer more polite and reasoned objections to Rousseau's argument, although they were directed more to that of the *Discourse on the Science and Arts* than to that of *Inequality*. 'Literature,' Voltaire suggested, 'nourishes the soul, corrects it and consoles it. Literature is indeed the source of your own glory at the very moment that you write against it. You are like Achilles, taking up arms against fame, or Malebranche, exercising his brilliant imagination against imagination.'

Voltaire went on to urge Rousseau to join him in Geneva: 'I am happy to be a peaceful savage in the solitude I have chosen in your republic, where you ought also to be ... You must come here and restore your health in your native air ... enjoy freedom, join me in drinking the milk of our cows and nibbling our vegetables.'

Rousseau's reply[40] was cordial:

It is I, Monsieur, who have you to thank in every way. In offering you the sketch of my melancholy reveries, I did not think I was sending something worthy of you, but simply discharging a duty and rendering a homage that we writers all owe you as our leader. Besides, being sensible of the honour you have done my country, I share the gratitude of my fellow citizens, which I hope will be all the greater when they have profited from the instruction which you are able to give them ... All who come near you ought to learn from you the path to glory and immortality.

Far from displaying any displeasure at Voltaire's remarks about resuming the posture of the beast, Rousseau responded with uncharacteristic joviality: 'Don't attempt to go back to walking on all fours; no one would be less likely to succeed. You teach us too well how to stand on our own two feet to stop standing on yours.' Rousseau went on to defend the argument of his first *Discourse*: history, he said, showed that progress had increased men's corruption, but he agreed that a time arrived when the cause of that corruption, namely culture, was itself 'needed to prevent its becoming worse ... it is a case of leaving the weapon in the wound for fear that the victim would die if it were pulled out.' He ended his letter with thanks to Voltaire for his invitation to Geneva: 'if this winter leaves me fit enough to come next spring, I shall take advantage of your kindness, but I would rather drink the water of your fountain than the milk of your cows.'

Both Voltaire and Rousseau may have written these letters with an eye to publication. Rousseau agreed promptly enough when Voltaire suggested that they should be published[41] and neither may have really felt any of the warmth their words declare, yet there is no indication of actual hostility between them at that period,* nor is there any ground for believing that Voltaire's presence was what kept Rousseau away from Geneva.

A more plausible reason for Rousseau's decision to stay in France is given in a letter[43] he wrote to Jallabert in November 1755. He says that even if his health improved enough to allow him to come to Geneva, he could not expect that his trade as a music copyist, 'which hardly gives me enough to live on in Paris', could be exercised in Geneva or that 'I should practice among my fellow citizens the frivolous activities that I condemn'. He could fairly claim that there was nothing inconsistent in his criticizing French music and participating in musical life in Paris, since according to his theory, the kind of advanced art that would be injurious to the uncorrupted Swiss was positively beneficial to the sophisticated Parisians.

He told Jallabert: 'I have absolutely not a sou to live on apart from what I earn by my copying.'[44] Diderot urged Rousseau to earn money, as he himself did, by literary journalism; but Rousseau had set his mind against any sort of commissioned work. When Jacob Vernes invited him to contribute to a new journal he was starting in Geneva, Rousseau expressed[45] only disapproval of the project: 'What is a periodical? An ephemeral work, without merit or utility, the reading of which is neglected and despised by scholarly people, and only serves to give women and fools vain ideas without knowledge; a thing designed to shine in the morning on the dressing-table and die in the evening in the waste-paper basket.' However, Rousseau added that if Vernes persisted with his foolish scheme, he would do his best 'to send you a piece to fill a gap for better or worse'.[46]

Rousseau had spent time in the early months of 1755 preparing his

---

*Although there are harsh words about Rousseau written by Voltaire in the margin of his copy of Inequality, there is no reason to believe that they were written in 1755. Indeed Voltaire always referred kindly to Rousseau in his letters of this period. When the Jesuit Castel published in February 1756 a pamphlet against Inequality entitled L'Homme moral opposé à l'homme physique de Monsieur R, Voltaire wrote to Pierre Pictet saying, 'Castel is the cynic of the Philosophes. But Rousseau has never spoken harmfully of anyone, and he writes much better than Castel does – two great merits.'[42]

Dictionary of Music for the press, but as that was not published until several years later, it did nothing to improve his immediate financial situation. In these straitened circumstances his health deteriorated, although he was inclined to put the blame for that on the bad air of Paris. His friends thought he needed a good doctor. Jacques-François Deluc, whose son Guillaume-Antoine, or 'Guillot', stayed with him in Paris on his way to England,* begged[48] Rousseau to consult the Genevese physician Dr Théodore Tronchin, who had made a great name for himself by innoculating against smallpox the children of the French royal family. Rousseau refused, even when Dr Tronchin himself wrote[49] offering his services. Rousseau explained[50] that for the past three years he had ceased consulting doctors altogether: 'long experience has taught me the uselessness of medical science in my case'. The worse part of his problem, he explained, was the retention of urine – due, he believed, to a malformation of the urethra; the leading physicians and surgeons of Paris had treated him from time to time with *bougies*, probes and other such instruments, which produced agony without relief. He told Dr Tronchin he was enjoying his life rather more since he had given up efforts to prolong it.

In November 1755, the fifth volume of Diderot's *Encyclopédie* came out, and despite the efforts of the clergy and others to have it suppressed, it was able, with the blessing of Malesherbes, to survive the storm. It contained an important contribution by Rousseau; the entry on 'Political Economy', which can be seen as a sort of bridge between his *Discourse on Inequality* and his *Social Contract*. In this article he explains that the expression 'political economy' means the administration of the state, on the analogy of 'domestic economy' or the management of the family, but he takes care to dissociate himself from those who try to represent the state as a family writ large, with the king ruling as its patriarch like a father ruling in the home. Instead he depicts the state as a society composed of individual citizens united by choice; a society where men can be free if they make the laws they live under. Each individual member of the society has a private will, but as a citizen he also has – and must have – what Rousseau calls a 'general will'. He takes that expression from Diderot and refers the reader to the article '*Droit naturel*' written by Diderot himself elsewhere in the *Encyclopédie*.[51] The significance of the term is not difficult to grasp. We can understand how a man who obeys his own will is free; but how can a group of men be free if each has only a private will tending towards his personal interest and competing perhaps with those of his neighbours? If the group as a whole is to rule itself, there must be a shared or public

---

*Rousseau offered him 'a bed and a little room where he can snore and play music as he pleases undisturbed'.[47]

will directed towards the common interest. *La volonté générale*, a concept of which Rousseau was to make rather different use in *The Social Contract*,★ is introduced in this article as part of his account of why a political society is *not* a family, but an artificial body similar to a man:

The body politic is a moral being which has a will; and this general will, which tends always to the conservation and the well-being of the whole and of each part, and which is the source of the laws for every member ... is also the regulator of what is just and unjust.[53]

The economic doctrine Rousseau encapsulates in this article is that of Locke and Diderot rather than that of the physiocrats and Adam Smith: it is a form of 'mercantilism' in which the government is called upon to supervise the economy and intervene in trade and industry to protect the interest of the nation rather than rely on the workings of the market. He cites as a model the nationalized granaries of the Republic of Geneva, where wheat bought by the state is held for sale at a fair price in every season, so that the people of Geneva neither starve nor pay excessively for bread when harvests fail.

At the same time Rousseau opposes heavy taxation to finance the activity of the state. He favours a simple economy, mainly agricultural in character, where there are no extremes of poverty and riches, where taxes are adjusted to the means of the contributor and national service or a *corvée* is an alternative to financial payments. Property, which is named in *Inequality* as the source of conflict and injustice in human relations, is here described, much as it is in the writings of Locke, as 'the most sacred of all the rights of citizens, and more important in some respects than liberty itself'.[54] Nevertheless, Rousseau will not allow this right to property to be used as a charter for the rich. He repeats, with only a little variation of language, what is said in *Inequality* about the nature of the social pact which institutes the state. The rich man says to the poor: 'You have need of me, as I am rich and you are poor: let us then reach an agreement between us. I will permit you to have the honour of serving me on condition that you give me the little you have for the trouble I will take to command you.'[55]

Rousseau's antipathy to the rich is no less evident in his private correspondence. One day, for example, a basket containing a gift of butter for Mme Levasseur was delivered by mistake to the house of the Comte

---

★Wokler points out that Rousseau's use of the concept of *la volonté générale* in the 'Économie politique' is close to Diderot's, in being identical with the collective expression of particular wills. In his later writings, Rousseau's concept of *la volonté générale* 'does not assimilate or conjoin but rather excludes particular wills'.[52]

de Lastic,★ who promptly took possession of it. An indignant Rousseau drafted a heavily ironical protest:[56]

Although I have not the honour, Monsieur, of being known to you, I hope my letter will not be unwelcome, since it offers you both apologies and money.

I understand that Mlle de Cléry sent a basket from Blois to a good old woman named Mme Levasseur, who is so poor that she lives in my house, and that this basket, which contained among other things a twenty-pound jar of butter, turned up mysteriously in your kitchen. The old woman was naïve enough to send her daughter, with the consignment note, to ask for her butter, or the cost of it, to which you and Madame your wife responded by having your servants drive her away.

I have tried to console the good woman in her distress by explaining the rules of high society and superior culture. I have shown her that there would be no point in having servants if they were not employed to drive away the poor when they come to claim their rights; I have explained to her that 'justice' and 'humanity' are words understood only in the common people's language; I have made her realize at last that it is an honour for her to have her butter eaten by a count. She, therefore, instructs me, Monsieur, to express her appreciation of the honour you have done her and her regret for any inconvenience she may have caused you, together with the hope that her butter proved to your taste.

If, by any chance, you had to pay any delivery charges, she offers to reimburse you, as is only just. I await your orders in the matter.

In the end, Rousseau did not mail the letter, but he read it aloud to friends in the *salons* to show what he thought of the behaviour of French noblemen. It was Mme d'Épinay who persuaded him against sending it. 'What you wish, Madame, must be done,' he wrote to her.[57] 'The letter will not be sent and Monsieur le Comte de Lastic may henceforth rob all the good women of Paris of their butter without any protest from me.'

Rousseau's more measured attack on the rich, his *Discourse on Inequality*, was finally on sale in August. The author grumbled (in a letter[58] to Jallabert) about the 'inconceivable laxness' of his publisher in organizing deliveries to Paris, but at least this meant that the book was read first, as Rousseau wanted, in Geneva. It consolidated his reputation as a writer and philosopher, although it did not provoke such immediate controversy in print as did his *Discourse on the Sciences and the Arts*. He was himself aware of its subversive tendencies, and of a certain pessimistic tone which he afterwards

---

★François, Comte de Lastic (b.1729), a colonel in the Grenadiers de France.

attributed to the influence of Diderot. Whatever his influence may have been, it is of all Rousseau's writings the one closest to Diderot's way of thinking, at once scientific and radical. Diderot did not share Rousseau's belief that human societies were contractual in origin, but, if there had to be a contract, he would readily accept the account Rousseau gives of it in *Inequality* as a fraudulent covenant imposed by the rich on the poor, whereby, in order to secure peace, which is advantageous to everyone, the poor agree to change all *de facto* possession into lawful ownership which is of advantage only to the rich. One of Rousseau's central themes, that human servitude originates in the oppression of the poor by the rich rather than of the weak by the strong, is in accord with Diderot's own social philosophy. Although Rousseau complains in the *Confessions* about Diderot's efforts to dominate him, in a fragment[59] he wrote at about the time *Inequality* was published, he speaks of Diderot as 'that virtuous Philosopher whose friendship . . . is the glory and the joy of my life; that astonishing genius, universal and perhaps unique, which his own century does not understand, but which the future will hardly fail to recognize'.

If Rousseau joined Diderot in attacking the rich, he was rather closer to the rich in his friendships than was Diderot, who led the model bourgeois life of long office hours in his editorial job and of domesticity with a wife and daughter and mistress. Rousseau alternated the frugality of his Bohemian existence in the rue de Grenelle with the luxury of rich friends' châteaux and *hôtels particuliers*. He saw less of Mme Dupin after his return from Geneva, but a great deal more of Mme d'Épinay, who had, like Mme Dupin, married a man who had made an enormous fortune as a farmer of taxes. It was at Mme d'Épinay's château of La Chevrette, north of Paris in the valley of Montmorency, that Rousseau enjoyed a holiday in the autumn of 1755 after his illness in the summer. Their relationship was one of mutual solicitude, Rousseau being troubled in his health, Mme d'Épinay in her heart. She had discovered – or was perhaps informed by the notoriously indiscreet Charles Duclos – that her lover, Dupin de Francueil,* was unfaithful to her, and, what was worse, was having an affair with Mlle Rose, sister of the actress who was her husband's mistress.

Francueil, the stepson of Mme Dupin, had long been Rousseau's friend, and Rousseau may well have tried to effect a reconciliation. But even when Francueil offered to give up Mlle Rose, Mme d'Épinay refused to have him back on anything other than a platonic basis. Being a woman of great emotional intensity, she consoled herself for the absence of love by increasing the pressure of friendship. She targeted her attention on Rousseau. He had comforted her on the death of her first child some eight

*Charles-Louis Dupin de Francueil (1716–80).[60]

years earlier[61] and he was called upon to comfort her again.

Inevitably, the gossips[62] said they were lovers, but there is no evidence whatever for this, and every reason to believe that theirs was a chaste *amitié amoureuse*. This did not, however, preclude on either side strong feelings of possessiveness and jealousy. Mme d'Épinay called Rousseau her 'bear' – by reason of his cuddliness rather than his clumsiness – and although she called other friends her 'bears' as well, Rousseau was the first of them, and that precedence meant much to him.

Mme d'Épinay was no beauty; the best efforts of such portraitists as La Tour and Liotard fail to disguise her plainness – a marked contrast to the ravishing looks of Mme Dupin – but she was intelligent, lively, cultured and, what was more important for Rousseau, hospitable.* For all his insistence on his independence and his resistance to patronage, he accepted her benefactions almost as eagerly as her affection; almost, but not quite, for she had sometimes to overcome vigorous refusals and Italian-style *complimenti* before he agreed to be helped.

When he refused Dr Tronchin's offer of medical treatment in December 1755,[64] Rousseau sought it on behalf of Mme d'Épinay, though he can hardly have rendered it more efficacious by telling her that he was very suspicious of Dr Tronchin: 'He has so much of a reputation that he could well be just a charlatan.'[65] What was Mme d'Épinay's affliction? On the evidence of her autobiographical novel *Madame de Montbrillant* we may assume that she had caught from her husband a venereal disease which continued to undermine her health, but there are also suggestions that she had a stomach ulcer.[66]

Some small excitement was caused in the winter of 1755–6 by the performance at Lunéville in the presence of King Stanislas of a play by Charles Palissot called *Les Originaux*, a satire on the Encyclopédistes in which Rousseau in particular was mocked. The King, who had done Rousseau the honour of writing for publication a reply to his *Discourse on the Sciences and Arts*, was displeased, and he instructed[67] his Grand Marshal, the Comte de Tressan, to inform Rousseau that he was having the dramatist expelled from his academy. D'Alembert, as Rousseau's friend, was delighted at this news,[68] but Rousseau himself decided to show magnanimity, and pleaded[69] for Palissot to be pardoned by the King: 'If his only crime is to have exposed my absurdities, that is simply the privilege of the theatre, and I see nothing at all reprehensible in a gentleman for doing that – indeed, I can even see merit in the author's choosing such an excellent

---

*In *Mes moments heureux*, Mme d'Épinay describes herself thus: 'I am not at all pretty; however, I am not ugly. I am small, thin, very well made. I have a youthful air, without freshness; noble, sweet, vivacious, witty and interesting ... I am true without being candid ... Timidity often gives an appearance of falseness.'[63]

target.' Rousseau also urged d'Alembert to drop the affair; and d'Alembert agreed. 'As M. Rousseau's friend,' he wrote[70] to Tressan, 'I should urge you to demand justice for him; as a philosopher he himself desires that the one who insulted him be forgiven, and I am entirely of his opinion.'

Palissot showed little gratitude for all this magnanimity.* He wrote a grovelling apology to King Stanislas, but in a letter[72] to Jacob Vernes, he complained: 'This new method of rectifying an imaginary offence by demanding pardon for the accused is a very cunning stratagem, and wholly typical of the wiles of the Philosophes.' Palissot continued to use his *droit du théâtre* to mock Rousseau and the Philosophes in further plays. Rousseau was not surprised; as he wrote to Vernes: 'I doubt if M. Palissot will easily forgive the good turn I have done him.'[73]

During his autumn holiday as the guest of Mme d'Épinay at La Chevrette, Rousseau was taken to inspect the improvements that her extravagant husband was making to the estate. In a remote corner of the grounds, towards the forest of Montmorency, they came upon an old hunting lodge, newly transformed into a bright new house. Mme d'Épinay reminded him that he had admired it on an earlier occasion when he had seen it in its former dilapidated state. He did remember: 'In my delight, I had blurted out, "Ah, Madame, what an enchanting building; it's a refuge made for me." She did not then react at once to my words, but now I saw in place of the old ruin, a small house, entirely new, very well laid out and very convenient for a household of three.'[74] Mme d'Épinay told him that she had restored the building at small cost by diverting men and materials from the works on the château, and she offered it to him there and then: 'My bear, here is your refuge. You chose it yourself and it is offered you out of friendship.'[75]

Rousseau's response was characteristic. He was 'deeply, deliciously moved', he 'moistened her generous hands with tears',[76] and he said no. Mme d'Épinay continued to press him, both in conversation and in letters, pointing out that if he accepted the house he would not only enjoy the solitude and the beauty of the countryside he loved, but be near her. He liked the idea of being near her. Once, when they were both confined to sick-beds, he wrote[77] to say how unhappy he was at not being well enough to visit her: 'Let me have your news, and take care of your health. As for myself, my only desire is to pass the rest of my life near you.'

In *Madame de Montbrillant*, Mme d'Épinay depicts herself making the offer of the Hermitage to Rousseau lightly, by no means pressing him to accept it. She describes him as being unhappy with his life in Paris, but

---

*Palissot drafted, but did not send, a letter to Rousseau himself declaring: 'Your procedures, Monsieur, show the true philosopher that I do not always see in your writings.'[71]

unable to make up his mind about retiring to Geneva. In her version Rousseau says he would like to accept, but does not know what to do about his two *gouvernantes*.[78] Mme d'Épinay represents herself as urging prudence: 'It is hardly possible, my friend, to make up your mind in two hours upon so serious a matter. Give yourself time to think it over and we shall see.'[79] Again, according to the novel, she offers to take care of the *gouvernantes* if he decides to go to Geneva. But she reminds him that there would be no lack of space at the Hermitage, where there are five rooms, a kitchen, a cellar, a kitchen garden of an acre, a spring of running water, and a whole forest for its grounds. She also offers him an annuity. 'We can add to the sale of your last work the amount required to make up the hundred pistoles you say you need to live on ... In this manner the service is reduced to such small proportions that you cannot make any objection to it.'*[80]

The original letter from Mme d'Épinay to Rousseau, on which this text is based, has disappeared, but she must have written in some such terms, as we can judge from Rousseau's reply:[81]

You have consulted your heart more than your pocket or my disposition in the arrangement you propose to me. This offer has chilled my heart. How ill you understand your own interests in wishing to make a valet of a friend, and how little you understand my character if you think that such arguments can persuade me ...

As for what concerns you personally, I do not doubt that your heart is sensible of the value of friendship, but I have reason to believe that your friendship is more necessary to me than is mine to you, for you have consolations which I lack and which I have renounced for ever.

Mme d'Épinay evidently reproached Rousseau for being annoyed at a proposal dictated by friendship and protested that she did not know what he meant by 'consolations'. She must, however, have realized that Rousseau was referring to her new intimacy with his old friend Grimm. Ever since her break with Francueil, Grimm had been paying court to Mme d'Épinay. If *Madame de Montbrillant* is to be believed, Charles Duclos was constantly warning her against Grimm but only making him more interesting to her by describing him as villainous. Grimm, who had once earned notoriety by falling sick with love for Mlle Fel, had much to recommend him to the intensely emotional Mme d'Épinay; the social climber and ambitious journalist was simply the perfect German romantic

*A hundred pistoles was equal to a thousand livres.

in her eyes.* He clinched his conquest by actually fighting a duel to defend her honour. Unkind rumours had spread in Paris that Mme d'Épinay had seized an opportunity in sorting out the affairs of her dead sister, Mme de July,† to destroy papers which proved her husband to owe a large sum of money to Mme de Jully's heirs. At a dinner given by Grimm's employer, the Comte de Friese, a certain baron had repeated this slander, whereupon Grimm, declaring himself to be a friend of Mme d'Épinay, challenged the baron to a duel, in which both were wounded, if only slightly.

Grimm was promptly rewarded; he became Mme d'Épinay's 'cavalier' and her lover. Duclos was banished from her *salon* and Francueil disappointed for ever in his hopes of a return to her favour. Rousseau, too, was plainly displeased; hence his bitter words to Mme d'Épinay about her 'consolations'. He grew more indignant as Grimm took an increasingly prominent place in Mme d'Épinay's life. The death in that same year of the Comte de Friese left Grimm with more time on his hands, and a greater need of such an influential friend as Mme d'Épinay in his search for another patron.

Grimm was already on the way to his transformation from a friend of Rousseau into an enemy. In his *Correspondance littéraire* he wrote a long review of *Inequality*, in which, after various polite words of praise, he denounced what he called its declamatory style, its chimerical ideas, its defective logic and its lack of just measure.[83] If Grimm was envious of Rousseau's fame, Rousseau was also perhaps a little jealous of Grimm, not because he wished to be Mme d'Épinay's lover, but because her love-affair with Grimm had diminished the importance of her friendship for him.

Charles Duclos, at any rate, believed this: 'Rousseau,' he said,[84] 'was supplanted by Grimm and thought himself betrayed and sacrificed for his friend, and never ceased to feel it.'

Writing to Mme d'Épinay sometime in March 1756[85] Rousseau tried to assure her that he was not annoyed with her, even when he accused her of trying to make him her valet. He had used the word 'valet', he explained, only to indicate the sense of humiliation into which the abandonment of his principles would throw his soul. He was determined, he said, to preserve his independence: 'The independence I have in mind is not freedom from work. I do indeed want to earn my living. I enjoy doing it, but I do not wish to be bound by any other obligation if I can help it.'

---

*In *Montbrillant*[82] she describes his character as 'a mixture of truthfulness, gentleness, reserve, melancholy and high spirits. The society of his friends adds to his happiness, but is not essential to it ... This sort of solitary, shut-in streak in him, coupled with considerable indolence, has the effect of giving a certain ambiguity to his public utterances. He never says openly what he does not believe, but he leaves what he does believe vague.'

†She died at the age of twenty-three of smallpox.

In the same letter he referred to her offer of the Hermitage:

I will gladly listen to your proposals, but you must expect me to refuse to entertain them for either they are charity or there are conditions attached to them, and I desire neither the one nor the other ...

Study my dictionary, my good friend, if you wish us to understand one another. Believe that my words rarely have the ordinary meaning; it is always my heart that speaks to yours, and perhaps you will understand one day that it does not speak as others do.

Having uttered this admonition, Rousseau informed her curtly that he had decided to accept the offer of the Hermitage. In an unpublished autobiographical fragment he wrote: 'Mme d'Épinay spared no solicitations, no pains, no inducements – even to my housekeeper – to make me change my mind and agree to stay in France. Finally, seeing me determined to live no longer in Paris, she had the Hermitage got ready and made me promise to go and live there.'

Thérèse, who had no liking for the country, needed more persuading to fall in with the project; her mother's agreement was even less enthusiastic, but since Rousseau had arranged a place for old M. Levasseur in a workhouse (where he promptly died), she could find no excuse for refusing,[86] nor could she afford to do so. Rousseau himself, once he had agreed to go, became impatient to leave Paris.

Grimm scolded Mme d'Épinay for letting Rousseau have the Hermitage, and warned her that she was doing him an ill service, and herself a worse one, since solitude would poison Rousseau's mind and make him an unbearable neighbour. Mme d'Épinay claims in *Madame de Montbrillant* that she defended Rousseau to Grimm: 'In my house he will meet with nothing but indulgence; we shall consider it a duty and a pleasure to make his life happy.'[87]

Grimm was not alone in thinking that country life would be bad for a character already prone to melancholy. Holbach and his friends said the same thing. In the *Confessions*, Rousseau writes: 'I was too eager to get to the Hermitage to wait for the good weather, and as soon as the house was ready, I hurried there amid cries from Holbach's coterie, who protested loudly that I would not be able to endure three months' solitude.'[88]

Rousseau must have heard these cries a few days before he left, since he wrote to Mme d'Épinay[89] on 18 March, saying: 'I am dining today with the Baron ... I cannot tell you how much pleasure I get from the thought of seeing no one but you.' In the same letter he told her of the preparations he was making for the move from Paris to the Hermitage, selling every-

thing that was no longer of use, 'my music even more than my books'.
He asked her help in finding buyers.

In the event, he put Mme d'Épinay to a good deal of trouble, both in
arranging the move and the settling of his affairs in Paris. This involved
her sending domestic staff to the rue de Grenelle to collect books,
mattresses, papers and other objects, and paying on his behalf rent and
taxes owed to his landlady after he had left: 'Your servants,' he suggested,
'should take the small precaution of opening proceedings by paying Mme
Fabi what I owe her lest she should take fright at seeing them stripping
my rooms before mention is made of the quarter's rent which is now
due.'[90]

However, Rousseau watched carefully to make sure that Mme d'Épinay
did not use these various commissions to pay the cost of his move. 'I have
spotted two mistakes in the bill attached to the money you sent me [for
the sale of books or music]', he reported in one of his letters[91] to her. 'They
are both mistakes in my favour, and they prompt me to believe that you
have made others of the same kind; this is something that must not go
on.'

Despite this warning, Mme d'Épinay found various ways of subsidizing
Rousseau while he was at the Hermitage, besides providing the house rent
free. When Grimm warned her that he would bite the hand that fed him,
Mme d'Épinay assured her lover: 'He will cost me little; he will be
comfortable; and he will not know what I intend to do to help him; he
will not even suspect it.'[92]

THE HERMITAGE

'It was on 9 April 1756 that I left Paris,' Rousseau writes in the *Confessions*,[1] 'never to live in a city again.' In *Émile*[2] he bids farewell to 'Paris, city of noise, smoke and mud, where women no longer believe in honour or men in virtue. Farewell Paris. In our search for love, happiness and innocence, we can never be far enough away from you.' Rousseau was convinced that his own character changed for the better as soon as he left the corrupt metropolis; he no longer looked down on his fellow-men, but became tolerant, mild, timid and good: 'I recovered my own true nature.'[3]

He was undoubtedly happy in that first spring in the valley of Montmorency. Some years later he declared in a letter[4] to Malesherbes that he 'did not begin to live' until 9 April 1756, although in the *Confessions* he dates his awakening to life from a much earlier period, as the young lover of Mme de Warens,[5] and he complains elsewhere of the Hermitage that 'it was *not* Les Charmettes'.[6]

In many respects, however, the Hermitage resembled Les Charmettes, the house near Chambéry where Rousseau had spent idyllic months with Mme de Warens. It was only marginally smaller, and had been handsomely rebuilt. Although it was demolished in the nineteenth century, the fame of its tenant attracted the attention of several artists, whose drawings show us its shape and proportions, not a Gothic cottage but a dignified and symmetrical house, with good-sized rooms, an elegant door and windows, with both ornamental and kitchen gardens and an orchard, surrounded by fields and the forest. Mme d'Épinay had even had a series of pipes installed so that the whole house could be heated by the fire in the living-room. In its modest way, it was a spacious and comfortable dwelling which satisfied Rousseau's taste for rusticity as well as his Swiss insistence on the spick and span. It did not make too much work for his *gouvernantes*; if anything, it left them with too much time to brood on their discontentments and their nostalgia for Paris. The Hermitage was undoubtedly an isolated place, a mile from the nearest neighbour and farther still from a decent road.[7]

The *Confessions* gives a cheerful picture of the move. Rousseau recalls[8] how Mme d'Épinay came with her carriage to fetch him and his house-keepers from the rue de Grenelle, while her farmer came to load their few belongings on to a cart, so that all were installed at the Hermitage in one day: 'I found it delightful to be the guest of my friend in a house of my own choosing which she had specially prepared for me.'

Mme de Épinay herself in *Madame de Montbrillant*[9] gives a less ecstatic account of the proceedings. She describes the road to the Hermitage as being so thick with mud that the last part of the journey had to be done on foot. The older housekeeper, a woman of seventy,* heavy, stout and almost helpless, could not walk through the mud, so that servants from the château had to carry her in an armchair nailed to planks. In the scene of their arrival Mme d'Épinay describes the old woman weeping with gratitude while Rousseau remains aloof, despite the fact that his bene-factress is almost fainting from exhaustion. Mme d'Épinay even accuses him of continuing to ignore her distress, but there is in existence a letter[10] written by him to her expressing his concern: 'I shall reproach you for having come out when you were ill, and going to the trouble of installing me here without thinking of yourself or me.'

Although there was snow as well as mud on the ground in the valley of Montmorency, spring was already burgeoning; there were violets and primroses in bloom, and the buds on the trees were breaking. On his very first night at the Hermitage, Rousseau says he 'awoke from a light sleep to hear the first song of the nightingale'.[11] Ornithologists suggest that he is more likely to have heard that sound while dreaming, since nightingales had never been known to sing in that part of France as early in the year as 9 April. At all events, Rousseau was up and about soon after daybreak. Even before he had unpacked and arranged his belongings in the house, he started wandering around the grounds, so that there was 'not a path, not a copse, not a wood, not a book' he had failed to explore that day: 'The more closely I examined this charming retreat, the more I felt it was made for me.'[12]

His letters to Mme d'Épinay expressed his pleasure and gratitude. On 13 April[13] he assured her that he had spent 'the most peaceful and the happiest three days of my life' at the Hermitage, even though the weather had been bad. A week later[14] he wrote to her saying, 'You will be pleased to know, Madame, that my sojourn here delights me more and more. You and I must exchange visits, or I shall never leave this place.'

Mme d'Épinay could not visit him just then because she did not feel

*Mme Levasseur was closer to eighty.

well. She had returned to Paris, and put herself in the care of Dr Tronchin, thanks to an introduction from Rousseau, which he was afterwards to regret having given. To Rousseau, Paris seemed a world away.

'No one suddenly put down at the Hermitage,' Rousseau writes,[15] 'could believe himself only four leagues from Paris'. A league, in the measurements of the *ancien régime*, was less than three miles, but unless the paths that led to the Hermitage were frozen by the winter cold or dried by the summer sun, they were not easily traversed, even by a traveller who shared Rousseau's own passion – so singular at that time – for walking. Unfortunately for Rousseau, Diderot, the friend he loved most, and whose company he missed more than others, was the least inclined to relish a hike in the mud. Wistfully Rousseau remarked in one of his letters[16] to Mme d'Épinay: 'Walking this morning in a charming place, I imagined Diderot by my side, and by describing all the pleasures of my walk to him, I noticed that they became all the greater for myself.'

But Diderot did not appear. A despairing Rousseau even suggested[17] to Mme d'Épinay that Grimm, installed at La Chevrette as her lover, should intervene to persuade Diderot to come to the Hermitage: 'Perhaps he can and will procure for me a visit from a friend I procured for him, and share with me the pleasure I should have in welcoming him here.' Diderot, however, seems to have had reasons for keeping his distance at that time from Mme d'Épinay and her château, and Rousseau had to wait for the summer weather to receive a visit from the man he still considered his best friend.

Another visitor Rousseau tried to lure to the Hermitage in the spring was the Genevese exile Lenieps.* He suggested[18] to him that the journey was not really arduous: a coach ran from Paris to Saint-Denis, from which place there were 'less than five miles to be covered on foot', something 'easily done on a good path in good weather'. It is not clear whether Lenieps was persuaded to go; but he was plainly in no mood to respond to Rousseau's suggestion that he should make his peace with the patrician regime in Geneva, or accept the intervention of Deluc, as Rousseau himself had done, to secure the restoration of his rights as a citizen. Lenieps remained a stalwart of the ideal of republican government in Geneva, and regarded Deluc as 'a traitor to their cause'[19] for he had accepted the settlement imposed in 1737 by the French mediator, which made only cosmetic changes to the oligarchic system. Far from Lenieps yielding to Rousseau's arguments, it was Lenieps who opened Rousseau's eyes to the realities of Genevese politics; but that process was to take some time,

*Toussaint-Pierre Lenieps (1694–1774), a radical opponent of the patrician Genevese regime, who had prospered in exile in Paris as a banker.

since Rousseau was not a man to be easily stripped of his illusions.

One Genevese visitor to the Hermitage had invited himself – a bank clerk aged twenty-two named François Coindet, who cultivated the acquaintance of celebrities and was only too willing to walk five miles to meet one. When Rousseau received Coindet's first fan letter, he warned[20] him that it was his policy generally to discourage visitors, 'in order to make free use of the little time that remains to me', but he added gracefully, 'my compatriots, and you in particular, will always be welcome'.

Once Coindet had his foot in the door, he went on to ingratiate himself with Rousseau by doing all sorts of useful services for him over the years without, however, fully overcoming Rousseau's doubts about a young man he described at various times as 'ignorant, self-satisfied, greedy and grasping',[21] as 'cunning'[22] and as 'enterprising and bold to the point of effrontery'.[23] Even so, Coindet took advantage of the fact that Rousseau was often neglected by his older friends in Paris to make himself increasingly indispensable. If he was disappointed at Rousseau's unwillingness even to pretend to show much affection for him, he was consoled by meeting through Rousseau other literary celebrities as well as fashionable hostesses who invited him to their salons.

In *Madame de Montbrillant*,[24] Mme d'Épinay describes Rousseau as being in a fretful mood in his first four weeks at the Hermitage, although she was hardly there often enough to observe it at the time. Solitude, she suggests, made him cantankerous, and she speaks of his complaining about such friends as Diderot, Grimm and Holbach having neglected him, and being remembered only by his old Genevese friend Gauffecourt* and herself. She concludes that there was only one way to deal with Rousseau, 'and that is to pretend to leave him alone entirely but actually to be fussing over him all the time'.

Mme d'Épinay's reference to Gauffecourt being in favour with Rousseau is confirmed by Rousseau's correspondence of the time, although it accords ill with Rousseau's claim in the *Confessions*[26] that he had lost all faith in Gauffecourt's friendship after Gauffecourt tried to seduce Thérèse with the aid of pornographic drawings on their journey to Chambéry in 1754. Gauffecourt was, indeed, one of the very few people for whom Rousseau brought himself to leave the Hermitage to visit in Paris.

However much Rousseau may have missed human company, his few years in the valley of Montmorency were immensely productive in literary work. He quickly developed a daily routine, almost as regular as that of

*Victor Capperonner de Gauffecourt (1691–1766), having made a small fortune from the salt monopoly of Geneva and other financial activities, cultivated in France the society both of tax-farmers such as M. d'Épinay and of intellectuals in Diderot's circle. Rousseau called him '*papa*'.

Immanuel Kant, spending the mornings copying music, taking a walk in the afternoon, and writing in the evening. Thérèse, who did not like the walks, soon ceased to accompany him. So as not to lose time while alone with his thoughts he carried, like Hobbes, a little notebook and pencil to jot down ideas that came into his head: 'The forest of Montmorency became my study.'[27]

One of the literary tasks he undertook was to edit and abridge for publication the writings on peace of the Abbé de St-Pierre, who had already been dead twelve years. Rousseau did this, he claims,[28] mainly to please his former employer, Mme Dupin, even though it meant lugging to the Hermitage the seventeen volumes of the printed *Oeuvres* and five cartons of manuscripts which were given him by the Abbé's nephew the Comte de St-Pierre. Mme Dupin's enthusiasm for the Abbé de St-Pierre's political ideas seems odd, since he was a champion of a form of *la thèse nobiliaire* (expounded in his *Polysydonie*),* akin to that of his friend Montesquieu, and Mme Dupin had previously employed Rousseau to help her and her husband to draw up a hostile critique of Montesquieu's aristocratic politics from the perspective of a more commercial or bourgeois form of liberalism.

However, there are no elements of a *thèse nobiliaire* in St-Pierre's *Project for Perpetual Peace*, and since Mme Dupin was something of a pacifist as well as a feminist, and had a high regard for an author she had often entertained in her *salon*, she wanted to see his plans for ending war given a wider diffusion than he himself – a notoriously long-winded writer – had been able in his lifetime to achieve. Rousseau says in the *Confessions* that it was only out of respect for the author and the nobility of the cause of peace that he agreed to undertake such a 'painful labour'.[30] It must be said, however, that he did it very much in his own way.

St-Pierre was a reader of Thomas Hobbes, and he diagnosed the recurrent condition of war which prevailed between nations as being analogous to the condition of war which existed among individuals in the Hobbesian state of nature. His solution to the problem of war was similar to Hobbes's: a covenant through which the separate states would agree to unite under the rule of a universal sovereign, who would keep peace among them by holding them all in awe. However, St-Pierre did not conceive this universal sovereign as a single being on the Hobbesian model, but as a 'confederal government',[31] a council or diet on which the ruling princes of each member-state would sit. While he admits that his scheme would entail a surrender of some measure of sovereignty on the part of each prince, he claims that all would gain more than lose by joining the confederation,

---

*Rousseau drafted a summary and a fragmentary commentary on the *Polysydonie*.

for in return for what he surrendered, every prince would receive the manifest benefits of an assured peace, becoming more free to devote his energies to increasing the happiness of his subjects, and so acquire the greatest glory to which any prince could aspire, that of a just ruler doing good. St-Pierre does not exclude the possibility of force being used to bring his confederation into being, for if once the great majority of states have come together voluntarily, it would be legitimate, he suggests, for them to use their joint power to bring the stragglers into the fold. If his argument is laboured, the whole spirit of St-Pierre's *Projet* is in tune with that of the Enlightenment, both in the confidence in human progress it expresses and the utilitarian values it invokes, peace being glorified because it secures the greatest happiness of the greatest number and princes being told to see that their true interest lies not in conquest but in '*bienfaisance*', a word St-Pierre is said to have introduced into the French language. Moreover, St-Pierre proclaims a characteristically Enlightenment belief that trade furthers peace; he suggests that commercial exchanges are mutually advantageous and, by promoting mutual understanding, diminish the likelihood of war; he even predicts the emergence of an international economic community together with the universal political confederation.

Given that St-Pierre held such views, it is hard to think of a more unsuitable person to act as his editor than Jean-Jacques Rousseau. For while Rousseau may have shared St-Pierre's belief that peace was a noble ideal, his opinions were at odds with St-Pierre's at almost every stage of the argument. First, Rousseau rejected the Hobbesian doctrine that the state of nature is a state of war of each against all, and its corollary that anarchy and peace are incompatible. Since Rousseau held that the state of war between individuals begins only after the introduction of society among individuals, he could not be expected to subscribe to the idea of St-Pierre that the formation of a society of nations would lead to peace between states. Rousseau's position on this subject, made clear enough in *Inequality*, where he says that peace reigned between individuals before they formed societies, is made even more explicit in his short essay entitled: 'That the State of War Originates in the Social State'.[32] Hence on Rousseau's premises, St-Pierre's 'society of nations' would be a formula not for peace, but for war.

Furthermore, Rousseau could not accept St-Pierre's suggestion that since peace was in the interests of princes, princes could be expected to seek it. Rousseau agreed that princes 'pursue their interest', but that interest was what they believed to be their interest, which was the glory of victory and the enlargement of their dominions, and not what the Abbé de St-Pierre conceived to be their interest, the glory that attended works of *bienfaisance*. Princes measured their satisfaction by their own standards; and

St-Pierre's reasoning, which took no account of that, was bound to fall on deaf ears or, worse, to sound absurd.

Indeed in his abridgement of St-Pierre's project, Rousseau can hardly hide his own opinion that the project is absurd. He ends that text with the remark that the whole scheme rests on the unproven assumption that princes have enough reason to see what is truly useful and enough courage to work for their own happiness; if St-Pierre's argument fails, it is because men are senseless and 'it is a sort of madness to be wise in a world of fools'.[33]

Rousseau's more detailed criticisms of St-Pierre are set down in a separate commentary which he entitled 'Jugement sur le projet de paix perpetuelle'.[34] This essay is our main source of knowledge of Rousseau's own thoughts on the subject of war and peace. He rejects St-Pierre's claim that history provides evidence in support of his idea that peace could be achieved through a confederation of states, arguing that all known associations of states have been alliances for war against a common enemy. He also rejects St-Pierre's suggestion that trade breeds peace, insisting instead that commerce furthers competition between states, and that competition leads to war. If countries which trade together form a society, then it is at best like that of the beau monde of Paris, a society of rivals and enemies posing as friends. Rousseau also objects to the idea of force being used to introduce the unwilling members, St-Pierre having admitted it might be necessary: 'If wars and revolutions are needed to establish a confederation,' Rousseau writes, 'then a confederation is more to be feared than desired.'[35]

Having thus expressed disagreement with St-Pierre on almost every point, Rousseau was left with a certain duty of suggesting an alternative approach to the question of peace and war. He was not an optimist. He did not believe that perpetual peace would ever be achieved in the relations between kingdoms, since monarchs, he maintained, were by nature belligerent. Peace could only be expected to prevail between republics and then only between republics satisfied with the dimensions of their territory. Rousseau repeatedly asserted that for a state to be free, it must be small, so that every citizen could personally participate in the making of its laws; here he argues that for peace to prevail, each state must be content to stay small.

Rousseau nevertheless acknowledges that the small size of his ideal republic must make its defence difficult, so he goes on to advocate 'defensive alliances' or 'leagues' between such small republics as instruments of peace. But he distinguishes his 'leagues' in several fundamental aspects from the 'confederation' proposed by St-Pierre; first there will be no surrender of sovereignty by each state, since the popular retention of sovereignty is for

Rousseau a defining characteristic of an authentic republic; secondly, there will be no economic interdependence, since Rousseau considers economic self-sufficiency a necessary condition of political liberty; and, thirdly, no state will be forced to join the league. His league would be one of willing neighbours. As one commentator has expressed it, for Rousseau, 'the ideal international society would be like pearls juxtaposed, but not on a string'.[36]

Even his conception of Switzerland was that of a league of autonomous cantons, not a true confederation, still less a nation state. In a certain sense of the word Rousseau himself was Swiss,[37] and thought of himself as such, although his *patrie* was the republic of Geneva, which was not at that time a canton in the Swiss confederation; he could also speak of Switzerland as a 'country', and one which could command – as in the case of St-Preux, the Vaudois protagonist of his novel *Julie* – intense patriotism, notwithstanding the fact that the canton of Vaud was ruled by the alien patriciate of Berne.

Rousseau did his work on St-Pierre's writings – abridging the *Projet* and drafting the *Jugement* – in the summer of 1756, a somewhat inopportune time, since the Seven Years War was just beginning, and people were, perhaps, too excited by the promise of battle to want to hear of schemes for perpetual peace. The Abbé's *Projet* had to wait for five years of the Seven Years War to elapse before it found a publisher; Rousseau's '*Jugement sur le projet de paix perpetuelle*' remained in manuscript form until after his death.[38]

Rousseau claims in the *Confessions*[39] that he became more genial in his manner as a result of living in the country, contradicting the assertion of Mme d'Épinay and others that solitude made him cantankerous. He says he shed the haughty and scornful pose that he had picked up in Paris and became his own true self. At home with Thérèse he found a new intimacy, and even though she would not join him on his walks, he 'spent many delightful hours with her under the trees', when 'she seemed happier than she had ever been' and 'opened her heart as never before'.[40] In the same chapter he makes two faintly incongruous assertions: first that 'the day which united me with my Thérèse was the one that determined my moral being', and then that 'I have never felt the least glimmering of love for her'.[41] He goes on to declare that he had no more desired to possess her emotionally than he had desired as a young man to possess Mme de Warens: 'the needs I satisfied with Thérèse were purely sexual, and had nothing to do with her as a person'.[42]

It may well be that Thérèse had already ceased to be his mistress in the fullest sense. In Geneva, two summers earlier he had pretended that she shared his bedroom solely in the capacity of a nurse, and that pretence seems soon to have become a reality. In 1761 he said he had for several years been living with her as 'brother and sister', which suggests they were already doing so at the Hermitage in 1756, although the word 'sister', entailing at least equality of class, is hardly appropriate, for Thérèse was treated more and more as a servant, as well as being increasingly in demand as nurse, washing out Rousseau's catheters and carrying trays up the stairs to his bedroom when he did not feel well.

If Rousseau could say of Thérèse that she had never looked happier than at the Hermitage, he could not say the same of her mother. Mme Levasseur was now too old to discharge the secretarial duties with which she had once supplemented the domestic services of her illiterate daughter, and she grew more disagreeable as she became less useful. She lent herself very readily to Mme d'Épinay's schemes of subsidizing Rousseau's living expenses without his knowledge, and she also solicited money for herself and Thérèse behind Rousseau's back from Diderot and Grimm, whose ears she regaled with lamentations about the poverty to which Rousseau had reduced her, together with such scraps of scandal and gossip that she supposed (in the case of Grimm correctly) might render her conversation more interesting.

In the summer of 1756 Voltaire sent Rousseau, through Charles Duclos, a copy of a poem[43] he had written about the earthquake which had happened at Lisbon the previous November, a disaster which, in causing the deaths of several thousand innocent people, had radically shaken Voltaire's faith in the good ordering of the universe. Voltaire had always been – and he remained – a deist; the systematic design of the universe convinced him that God exists, that 'there is a being who exists necessarily of himself from all eternity and is the origin of all other beings'.[44] Lisbon prompted Voltaire to doubt the benevolence of that Supreme Being, to suspect that he had either gone to sleep or allowed some fallen angel to take over the direction of the universe. Although Voltaire declares in one single stanza:

> Je ne m'élève point contre la Providence[45]

the whole poem calls into question the goodness of God:

> Élements, animaux, humains, tout est en guerre
> Il le faut avouer, le MAL est sur la terre.[46]

Rousseau was disturbed by what he understood, not unreasonably, to be an attack on the sort of religious faith to which he himself had come to attach such importance, and he felt it his duty[47] to defend Providence against Voltaire's bitter rhymes. He drafted,[48] and then carefully rewrote, a long letter[49] to Voltaire on the subject. This letter was clearly designed with an eye to eventual publication, but having no wish at this stage to antagonize the poet, Rousseau took the precaution of sending[50] it first to Dr Tronchin, with the request that he should vet it: 'If there is too much indiscretion in the zeal which inspired the letter, please suppress it and send it back to me without showing it to M. de Voltaire'. In the same letter Rousseau assured Dr Tronchin that he had by no means renounced his project of 'ending my days in Geneva'.

Dr Tronchin found no reason to suppress the letter, and was, in any case, only too likely to have been pleased to see the fur flying between his two friends; he forwarded the letter promptly to Voltaire at Les Délices. It was a very personal, heartfelt sort of letter. The faith that Voltaire derided as 'optimism', Rousseau said was what 'consoles me in bearing the very sorrows that you describe as unbearable'. He went on to argue in detail that God could not be held responsible for the miseries of man's life on earth: 'most of our physical ills are of our own making'. As for the deaths in the earthquake at Lisbon, he pointed out that it was not Providence which had built twenty thousand houses of six or seven storeys in that small space: 'If the population had been dispersed over a wider area, and housed in different sorts of buildings, there would have been less damage, and perhaps none at all.' He suggested that the earthquake was evidence in favour of his own teaching that men ought not to build large cities rather than evidence which supported Voltaire's assertion that Providence was indifferent to human suffering. 'Is Nature to submit to *our* Laws,' he demanded, 'and forbid an earthquake in a certain place just because people have built houses there?' He insisted that man, not God, is the true author of human suffering.

Towards the end of the letter, Rousseau's tone becomes more impassioned as he addresses Voltaire directly: 'Crowned with glory as you are, and rid of empty grandeur, you live as a free man amidst abundance; you philosophize peacefully about the nature of the human soul; and yet you can see nothing but evil on earth, while I, an obscure, poor and solitary man, tormented by an incurable affliction, meditate with pleasure in my retreat and I observe that all that is, is right.'*

Rousseau apologized for the fervour of his utterance, explaining that his own faith in the goodness of God meant everything to him: 'I have suffered too much in this life not to look forward to another. The subtleties of metaphysics may increase my sorrows but they cannot shake my faith in the immortality of the soul. I feel it; I believe it; I desire it, I hope for it; I will defend it to my last breath.'

Dr Tronchin, informing Rousseau that he had passed the letter to

---

*Although Rousseau had criticized Alexander Pope's doctrine of the Great Chain of Being when he borrowed a French translation of *The Essay on Man* from M. de Conzié,[51] we find him here repeating Pope: 'Whatever is, is right.'

Voltaire, congratulated[52] him on his defence of Providence and declared that he himself had 'urged Voltaire to burn the Lisbon poem', without, of course, any success, and he warned Rousseau that Voltaire would be unlikely to welcome his criticism. On this last point Dr Tronchin predicted correctly. Voltaire chose not to answer Rousseau's argument, and simply apologized[53] in a brief, bright note of acknowledgement for not doing so:

My dear Philosopher,
You and I may in the intervals of our illnesses argue together in verse and prose, but at the present moment you will forgive me if I leave aside all those metaphysical discussions, which are only pastimes. Your letter is very fine, but at the moment I have with me one of my nieces, who is dangerously ill. I am a sick-nurse, and I am sick myself.

Again Voltaire urged Rousseau to join him in Geneva, and he ended with affectionate words: 'No one is more disposed to love you tenderly. I begin by suppressing all ceremony. V.'

The friendly tone of this note was not altogether false, to judge from favourable references to Rousseau in other letters Voltaire wrote at that period of his life, but Voltaire never found time to write to Rousseau on the various points he had made in his letter. Rousseau afterwards came to consider Voltaire's novel *Candide* a reply to his letter, as indeed it was; he told the Prince of Württemberg in 1764: 'My letter gave birth to *Candide*; *Candide* was his answer to it. I wanted to philosophize with Voltaire; in return he made fun of me.'[54] By that time, as will be seen, all talk of friendship between the two philosophers had ended.

Besides the assurances Rousseau gave to his Genevese friends that he was still planning to retire to Geneva, he was discussing with Gauffecourt a visit to Switzerland to collect material for a short history of the Valais.[55] Rousseau had been outraged by an article in Diderot's *Encyclopédie* where the mountain folk of that somewhat underdeveloped Swiss canton were described as 'cretins', and by way of amends Diderot invited him to write an article on the Valais for a later volume. Rousseau undertook some preliminary research,[56] but in the end he discarded the project, although he introduced some colourful descriptive passages about the scenery of the Valais into his novel *Julie*.

Rousseau started work on this book, as well as much else, including *The Social Contract*, during his first summer months at the Hermitage. He was half-ashamed of spending his time on something as frivolous as a novel, but *Julie* – afterwards better known by its second title, *La Nouvelle Héloïse* – became the most popular of all his books with the reading public. It was a love-story prompted by the absence of love in his life: 'How can it be explained that I, with such warm affections, such inflammable senses, and a heart designed for love, had not even once felt its flame burn for one determinate object? . . . I saw myself approaching death without having lived.'[57]

For lack of someone real to love, he recalls in the *Confessions*, he allowed imaginary creatures to enter his mind, and keep him company 'in the delightful month of June, in cool shades, amid the songs of the nightingales and the babbling of brooks'.[58] He thought of the sweet joy of the day he spent as a young man in the cherry orchard at Thônes with Mlle de Graffenried and Mlle Galley; as he felt himself 'surrounded in imagination by a seraglio of houris from my past acquaintances',[59] he was transported with erotic excitement. He says he was not such a fool as to believe he might still, as a grave, grey-haired citizen of Geneva, inspire love in the real world, but in the realm of fantasy, where he was perhaps rather more at home, everything was possible: 'In my continual ecstasy I intoxicated myself with the most delicious feelings that ever entered the heart of man. Entirely forgetting the human species, I invented societies of perfect beings, whose virtues were as celestial as their beauty, tender and faithful friends such as I had never found here below.'[60]

It was these creatures of his dreams who became the characters of his novel:

I conjured up love and friendship, the two idols of my heart, under the most ravishing images. I amused myself by giving them all the charms of the sex that I had always adored. I imagined two female friends rather than two of my own sex, because although such friendships are less common, they are more pleasing. I endowed my heroines with two personalities, different but matching, with two faces, not perfectly beautiful, but in accord with my own taste, and animated with benevolence and sensibility. I made one dark the other fair, one lively the other languid, one wise the other weak, but of so touching a weakness that it seemed to add a charm to virtue. I gave to one of the two a lover, of whom the other was a tender friend, and sometimes more than a friend, but I did not admit rivalry, quarrels or jealousy . . . Smitten with my two charming models, I drew my own portrait as the lover and the friend, as much as it was possible to do so, but I made him attractive and young and gave him at the same time the virtues and the defects which I felt in myself.[61]

Rousseau wrote the novel in the form, then fashionable, of letters exchanged between the leading protagonists. The central character is Julie, her friend Claire, and the lover, based on himself, St-Preux. It is a pastoral novel, although its setting is not the valley of Montmorency, where it was written, but the shores of Lake Geneva, in that part of Switzerland forever associated in Rousseau's mind with Mme de Warens, his first mistress.

St-Preux is a tutor in the service of a Vaudois nobleman, Baron d'Étange, just as Rousseau himself had once been in that of M. de Mably at Lyons, except that, whereas Rousseau had demanded an adequate salary, St-Preux is unpaid. Nevertheless St-Preux is a bourgeois, and he offends against the law of class by falling in love with his aristocratic pupil, Julie. When he finally reveals his love to her in a letter, he admits his effrontery in doing so, and begs her to punish him by sending him away. Julie replies briefly telling him to stay. But when St-Preux protests that he cannot bring himself to stay knowing that she despises him, even adding a threat of suicide, Julie is forced to reveal that she loves him too: 'I must confess at last the fateful and all-too-little-hidden secret ... What can I say? How can I break the painful silence? Or have I not already said everything? And have you not understood me too well?'[62]

She gives him in the presence of Claire the 'first kiss of love', and faints, but afterwards she contrives to be alone with him in a chalet which serves as a convenient *nid d'amour*. It cannot be said that St-Preux seduces Julie, or rather it ought not to be said, though it was in fact said by Voltaire[63] when he read the book. It is Julie who seduces St-Preux, and she exercises over him what Rousseau confessed he had always wanted from his ideal woman, domination. 'My Julie,' he tells her, 'you were made to rule. Your empire is the most absolute I know. It extends to my very will ... You impose your will on mine. You overwhelm me, your spirit crushes mine. I am nothing in your presence.'[64]

But if Julie is able to thrill St-Preux with her 'adorable and powerful sway',[65] she is in turn dominated by her father, and the Baron d'Étange will not tolerate any suggestion of marriage between Julie and a bourgeois, for the Baron d'Étange, reduced like the rest of the Vaudois nobility by the Bernese conquest to the possession of a title without any other vestiges of aristocratic privilege, is obsessed with rank. He forbids the marriage even when, miraculously, an English nobleman named Bomston offers to set up St-Preux with a substantial estate and fortune. The Baron's reaction to this is to lose his self-control entirely. He strikes his daughter and even though her mother intervenes, he continues to beat her mercilessly. A subsequent fall causes her to miscarry the child she has conceived with St-Preux. Nevertheless, Julie forgives her father, and seeing remorse in his bearing, throws her arms around him and covers his face with kisses and tears: 'Only a sweet and potent innocence was lacking in my heart to make this natural scene the most delightful in my life,' she writes in a letter afterwards.

It is a curious avowal, for Julie, like Rousseau himself, is dedicated to an ideal of virtue which is not ordinary virtue, and yet she feels guilty because she has offended conventional morality by her sexual union with St-Preux, her 'loss of innocence'. On the other hand, she does not accept the remedy profferred by conventional wisdom and marry her lover. Instead she obeys her father's orders, not only rejecting St-Preux, but agreeing to marry the suitor of her father's choice, a fellow nobleman named Wolmar. It is then that by enacting the role of the perfect wife and mother – not in love with her husband, but esteeming him, and concentrating her energies on the upbringing of her children – she recovers her purity. Fortified by her faith in Providence, she becomes a paragon of virtue, while her husband, Wolmar, an atheist, proves to be, in his own cold way, a model of rectitude.

St-Preux, heart-broken, goes into exile, only to return some years later to live in chaste and fraternal harmony with Julie and her husband as tutor to their children on their lakeside estate, an ideal domestic community of family and guests and servants, a small Utopia, if more feudal than egalitarian.*

At one point Wolmar decides – presumably in order to put the fidelity of his wife to the test – to leave her alone with St-Preux for some time. One day the former lovers take a boat-trip together on the lake; a storm drives them ashore, and they find refuge on the rocks of Meillerie. There, against a background of high mountains and stormy skies, a scene of emotional tension unfolds. Julie's love for St-Preux, we discover, is not dead after all, nor his for her. Their bodies almost touch; almost but not quite. Chastity triumphs. The novelist chose to pause at this point in his narrative – he could not decide what was to happen next.

Rousseau had begun the book without any clear design for its plot, relying on the creative power of his imagination to carry him forward. After the reunion of his lovers at Meillerie he had reached a certain impasse, and admitted as much to his friends. Nevertheless he was pleased with what he had written. He bought gold-edged paper on which to make a fair copy, azure and silver powder to dry the ink, and blue ribbon to tie the sheets together.

Julie is not only a story of love and virtue, it is also a picture of rustic life in Switzerland – no less idealized – with graphic descriptions of mountains and forests and lakes, of a world where violent passions excite or torment the leading characters, while the humble folk are at peace with themselves and with nature. The success of the novel was such as to modify prevailing tastes radically, to elevate romantic love and *sensibilité* to new

---

*Should a servant ever forget himself, even during the grape harvest, 'he is sacked, without appeal, next day'.[66]

heights, give new charm to all things rustic, and transform Alpine scenery from an object of dread into a source of aesthetic pleasure.

The book also challenged, in a more ambiguous way, established notions of sexual morality; not at all a story of the conflict of reason and passion, but a steamy mixture of sensuous feeling and moralistic thoughts, and from Rousseau's point of view the one redeemed the other: 'My voluptuous imaginings would have lost all their grace if they had lacked the gentle colours of innocence.'[67] Even so, he could see that readers might fail to understand the message. Could the upper classes of eighteenth-century France, which tolerated infidelity in a wife while judging sexual activity in an unmarried daughter scandalous, be persuaded that a girl could allow herself to be conquered by love before marriage and then regain her virtue as a faithful and dedicated wife?

Yet it was just this public to whom the novel was addressed. In the first of two prefaces he wrote for the published text, where he posed as the 'editor' of the letters brought together in *Julie* rather than the author, Rousseau wrote: 'There must be theatres in large cities and novels for corrupt peoples. I have observed the morals of my time, and I have published these letters. Would that I had lived in a century when my duty would have been to throw them in the fire.'[68]

To judge from the correspondence Rousseau received, it was not only fashionable – or corrupt – people who read the novel and not only those lacking moral sense who were baffled by its message. Several scrupulous readers wrote to say that they could not understand how virtue was attained by a girl's refusal to marry a bourgeois she loved and had slept with, to become the wife of a nobleman she did not love. Indeed they suggested that her story could be seen as the triumph of snobbery over decency rather than that of virtue over vice. Rousseau himself, when challenged, insisted that Julie's motive for marrying Wolmar was love for her father, who would have died of grief if she had followed her heart's desire and married St-Preux. The field of moral experience for Rousseau was not a conflict of passion and reason, but of one feeling against another; in *Julie* romantic love is defeated by filial love, and virtue shares its victory with conjugal fidelity, friendship and good works.[69] Indeed Rousseau has his heroine assert that love and marriage never go well together: 'Love is accompanied by continual uneasiness over jealousy or loss, little suited to marriage, which is a state of enjoyment and peace.'

In the *Confessions*, Rousseau says he was 'so fond of soaring in the empyrean' with his imaginary creatures at the Hermitage that he gave any 'wretched mortal' who came to disturb him a 'reception so brusque that it might justly be termed brutal'.[70] But in letters he wrote at the time, he complained that he did not have enough visitors, and all his visitors speak of being welcomed warmly, and indeed of being regaled with readings from Rousseau's unfinished novel. The *Mémoires*[71] of the economist and Encyclopédiste, the Abbé Morellet, offer testimony of this:

We often went, Diderot and I, from Paris to Rousseau's Hermitage near Montmorency to pass entire days. There under the great chestnut tree beside his little house, I heard him read long excerpts from his *Julie*, which enthralled me as it did Diderot, and we each expressed in our way our genuine admiration for the novel, sometimes adding little criticisms which can only have made him realize how well we thought of the rest of the book.

The word 'often' is very probably inexact here, for Rousseau in his correspondence was constantly reproaching Diderot for the paucity of his visits. Diderot seems to have managed to get to the Hermitage only once or twice, when the summer weather made the journey less of an ordeal. Besides, we know from other evidence that Rousseau never had unqualified feelings of friendship towards the Abbé Morellet. Nevertheless there is no doubt that Rousseau enjoyed reading aloud from the manuscript of *Julie* and, when there was no better audience, he read to his housekeepers. Thérèse, he recalls, was moved to tender emotions as she listened and mingled her sighs with his; her mother, who understood very little of what the novel was all about, was content to say from time to time, 'Monsieur, that's very fine.'[72]

Another who heard readings from *Julie* that summer, a young man who was always welcome at the Hermitage, and to whose whims Rousseau extended an unusual measure of tolerance, was Alexandre Deleyre, who served among other things as an intermediary with Diderot when Diderot was more than usually elusive. Born in 1726, and thus fourteen years younger than Rousseau and Diderot, Deleyre had established for himself a modest literary reputation with a book about the philosopher who was regarded as the first prophet of Enlightenment, Francis Bacon. After writing one or two articles for the *Encyclopédie*, Deleyre had tried to set up as an editor himself, assuming the direction of a review, *Le Journal étranger*, without in the end enjoying much success. Even as a contributor to the *Encyclopédie* he had some difficulty in pleasing Diderot, who rejected his article 'Fortune' and made him rewrite his article 'Fanaticism'. Rousseau, on the other hand, liked Deleyre's work well enough to compose music for one or two of his lyrics,[73] and he liked Deleyre personally well enough to put up with his jokes, for Deleyre's numerous letters are spiced with raillery of a kind which Rousseau had generally too little sense of humour to appreciate.

As early as July 1756 we find Deleyre writing[74] to Rousseau on terms of easy intimacy, calling him Mme d'Épinay's 'first bear', and promising 'to join her menagerie one day'. He adds: 'Was it Minerva or Cybele who attached lions to her chariot? If only our Pallas could be seen drawn in her carriage along the boulevards by her bears! ... Amuse yourself, my dear Hermit, in all the activities that have driven you into solitude. And try to laugh a little – moaning is too exhausting.' Deleyre asked whether Rousseau had received a visit from their 'illustrious friend Diderot', declaring that he was not unjust enough to claim a quarter of an hour of Diderot's time if Diderot could not spare a day to go to the Hermitage. He went on to express disapproval of Diderot's article '*Autorité*' in the *Encyclopédie*, which he had only just read, an article which began by suggesting that submission and prayer were a subject's only answers to injustice and violence on the part of a monarch. Deleyre did not fail to observe that Diderot, in his characteristically dialectical style, took back at the end of the article the doctrine of passive obedience he had asserted at the beginning, but that did not make Deleyre think any better of an author whose contradictions, as he put it, 'destroyed his own work'. Since Deleyre had had to endure Diderot's editorial criticism of his own writing, it is hardly surprising that he should be so critical of Diderot's, although not perhaps to Diderot's face.

One person who did not often disturb Rousseau's tranquillity at the Hermitage that summer was Mme d'Épinay herself. This was partly because her health was still indifferent and partly because building works at the château of La Chevrette obliged her either to stay in Paris or put up in smaller quarters at La Briche. Even when she did visit Rousseau, they found little to talk about, and passed the time playing chess. Rousseau noticed that while Mme d'Épinay might sparkle in society, her conversation was dull in private, and that he had to make tiring efforts to 'enliven our meetings en *tête-à-tête*'.[75] Since she had no sexual attraction for him, there was no element of gallantry in these efforts, at most 'a few fraternal little kisses'.[76]

In her own house Mme d'Épinay was usually surrounded by her retinue of favourite guests. Thus one Wednesday in August 1756[77] we find Rousseau writing to excuse himself from visiting her because he did not feel strong enough to endure the midday sun, and asking her to apologize for his absence to the whole company, his '*prétendus confrères*' who had become her 'bears'. Those 'bears' were his '*prétendus confrères*' by reason of the literary aspirations which every one of them, save Gauffecourt, cherished: Joseph Desmahis was a poet as well as an *Encyclopédiste*, Adrien Quiret de Margency, the lover of Mme de Verdelin, had published a few verses, and Grimm, of course, was well established as a literary journalist. Even so, the scornful expression '*prétendu confrère*' could have been aimed as much at Grimm as at anyone, for although Grimm had a good claim to be considered a fellow writer, Rousseau no longer liked him. As for Deleyre, he had not achieved the status of a 'bear', so he, '*prétendu confrère*' that he undoubtedly was, could not have been in Rousseau's mind. Deleyre was, in any case in Paris at the time, and he wrote[78] from there to complain that Rousseau's silence was 'more rigorous than that of La Trappe or La Grande Chartreuse'. Deleyre protested that he, for his part, never forgot Rousseau even in his sleep. 'Last night I dreamt that you made me embark for one of your islands – all because the King had spoken well of you, which you did not like.'

Rousseau was unwell again towards the end of the summer but he refused[79] to accept Mme d'Épinay's offer to send a carriage to bring him to see her: 'I shall come proudly on foot, since that machine of a carriage makes me imagine I do not have legs to carry me to you.' He duly paid the visit, but as a result of walking both ways in bad weather he reached home 'soaked to the skin at one o'clock in the morning'.[80] He had evidently spent the evening in the company of Grimm as well as of Mme d'Épinay, because in writing to thank her he sends greetings to 'The Tyrant'. Grimm had been given this nickname by Gauffecourt, 'Tyran le Blanc' – or 'The White Tyrant' – being a character in a Spanish novel popular at the time. Grimm earned the name not only by his dictatorial manner but by his newly acquired habit of applying white powder to his face.

In the fullness of time Grimm was to be made a Baron of the Holy Roman Empire, a dignity secured for him – and paid for – by a German mistress. But that did not happen until 1772. He turned into a dandy in 1756 while still climbing the lower rungs of the social ladder. Rousseau observed this and disapproved of it: 'I could not believe he used powder, but decided that a man who spent two hours every morning polishing his fingernails could well spend a few moments filling in the lines on his face with powder.'[81] Grimm used scent as well, as a result of which he was sometimes referred to by Rousseau as a 'perfumed philosopher'. Mme d'Épinay's son, Louis-Joseph Lalive, recalled years later how Grimm had 'given up his old black *râpé* suits and old socks and started to wear an embroidered suit, white silk stockings, court shoes and a sword'.[82] Lalive dated this transformation from Grimm's appointment, following the death of his old employer, the Comte de Friese, to the position of secretary to the much grander Duc d'Orléans, cousin of the King, but Lalive's dislike of Grimm seems to have dated, as did that of Rousseau, from Grimm's installation as Mme d'Épinay's lover.

One night that summer, Rousseau caught one of Mme d'Épinay's gardeners stealing peaches from the walled orchard near the Hermitage in order to sell them in the market at Montmorency. Since the supervision of the orchard, together with the kitchen garden which provisioned the household at La Chevrette, was one of the duties which Rousseau discharged in lieu of rent, he reported the matter to the château. He was instructed to dismiss the gardener, and engage a new one, which he did. However, 'the old rogue of a gardener', as he called him, continued 'to prowl round the Hermitage at night, armed with an iron-tipped stick like a club, and accompanied by other vagabonds of his kind'.[83] Mme Levasseur and her daughter became so thoroughly frightened that Rousseau decided to arm himself. He told[84] Mme d'Épinay that he needed a gun or a pistol, 'but I can find no one who is willing to lend me either, and it would not be reasonable for me to buy one'. The problem was solved when one of the other gardeners at La Chevrette lent him a shotgun.

When Deleyre heard this story he could not restrain his impulse to tease Rousseau about it. 'Even in Paris,' he declared,[85]

I can hear the sound of your firearms. Now you will agree with me that it is not good for you to be shooting. Is it worth running away from mankind if only to be afraid of men? . . . You have weapons that are better than a gun. First, there is the poverty which is your glory. Then there is your hope of a future life. And what could anyone steal from you now? . . . If there is a Providence, you are safe: if there is not, come and make war here, my dear and well-loved Citizen.

Rousseau's replies to Deleyre have not been traced, but it seems that he did not mind being teased in this way. Indeed he says as much in the *Confessions*,[86] where he recalls that Deleyre's letters were full of pleasantries which might have offended him if he had been disposed to be offended, but as his heart was at that time 'bathed in fond and tender sentiments', he 'saw nothing in Deleyre's bitter sarcasms but matter for laughter, and simply found amusing what anyone else would have thought outrageous'. On his copy[87] of Deleyre's letter of 13 October, Rousseau noted at a later date:* 'All his raillery arose from the fact that in order to reassure my housekeeper and her mother, I secured a gun from the gardener, and I sometimes amused myself by shooting at the dormice which ate M. d'Épinay's fruit.'

In the *Confessions*, Rousseau speaks of 'laughing together' with Deleyre about his 'military precautions' when Deleyre visited him that autumn, and then goes on to say: 'When Deleyre returned to Paris, he tried to amuse Diderot with the story, and that was how the Holbach coterie

*Probably in 1769.

learned that I intended to spend the winter at the Hermitage.'[88] This, he adds, reinforced all their 'devious efforts to lure me back to Paris',[89] because 'they were frightened that I might be happy in the country, and be mad enough to stay there'.[90]

In spite of this Rousseau forgave Deleyre. Years later he added these words to his note on Deleyre's letter: 'He lent himself at first to the manoeuvres of the Philosophes, but he became ashamed in the end, and detached himself from them.'[91] There was, in any case, nothing 'devious' about Deleyre's efforts to persuade Rousseau to return to Paris: 'M. Diderot and I will come to lay siege to you,' he threatened in his letter of 13 October,[92] 'and since we have an intense desire to hold you captive in Paris, please believe that we shall spare nothing to force you.'

At the beginning of November, Deleyre reported[93] to Rousseau that Diderot, who had been laid up with colic, was better and that he hoped to bring him to the Hermitage; but later in the month Deleyre had to apologize[94] for not coming; he said he had been kept in Paris by work on his review *Le Journal étranger* and 'today the rain postpones yet further the consoling prospect of a visit to you'. Deleyre reminded Rousseau of his promise to write an article for the review, adding that he had already received contributions from Diderot and d'Alembert, and was expecting something from Grimm:* 'Have you got to the end of your novel,' he asked with reference to *Julie*, 'and your people, are they drowned? You would do well to dispose of them that way, for this world is not fit to possess them as you have depicted them. And where there are no great rewards to give to virtue, one must cover it in misfortune, in order to make it interesting.'

Rousseau must have told Deleyre how he was thinking of ending *Julie*; in the final form of the novel the heroine dies from an illness caught trying to rescue her drowning child from the lake, but at one stage Rousseau considered having Julie and St-Preux drown together. That would have made a romantic ending. The bright cynicism of Deleyre's advice may have prompted Rousseau to work out another denouement. In any case, his work on *Julie* was nowhere near the final chapters in the winter of 1756–7, when he chose to allocate much of his writing time to what he thought of as more serious work.

Mme d'Épinay had also embarked on literary activity, much to Rousseau's irritation. He accuses her in the *Confessions* of writing more for the pleasure of reading aloud than of seeing her work in print: 'if she managed to scribble two or three pages, she had to be sure of at least the same number of appreciative listeners at the end of her labours'.[95] However, at

---

*Evidently Rousseau had not revealed to Deleyre his growing antipathy towards Grimm.

the end of the autumn, Mme d'Épinay returned to Paris, where she had a house in the rue St Honoré opposite Les Capucins, and Rousseau was spared the ordeal of further readings from her various unfinished 'novels, letters, plays, stories and other trash'.

At that time Rousseau took care to dissimulate his contempt for Mme d'Épinay's essays into authorship. Indeed in *Madame de Montbrillant* she says he was enthusiastic in his praises of her writing, and a letter[96] he wrote her in November 1757 plainly encourages her to continue with it: 'take care,' he urges, 'of your health, your happiness and your plays'. The same letter [97] reveals that he must have been reading aloud to her from his own novel, for having mentioned that silence now reigned in the woods around his house, he declares that 'the name of Julie and your own are the only sounds that echo there'. Mme d'Épinay, as we shall see, did not much admire *Julie*; but doubtless she concealed her opinions from him as he concealed his from her.

The weather worsened in the valley of Montmorency as winter advanced, and Rousseau complained of rheumatism, a word then applied to all sorts of aches and chills connected with the cold and damp. Mme d'Épinay, nursing her own rheumatism in Paris, with advice by letter from Dr Tronchin,* sent Rousseau one of her flannel petticoats that could be turned into a warm waistcoat for him. In the *Confessions* Rousseau says the gift moved him to tears: 'I kissed the letter and the petticoat twenty times as I wept.'[99] His expressions of thanks[100] to Mme d'Épinay at the time were less emotional, even somewhat ungracious: 'I'm afraid your garment will make me rather too hot, since I am not used to being so well covered.' Mme d'Épinay also sent Rousseau a present of some salt, so that next time he wrote[101] he thanked her for offering him 'prudence as well as warmth', but again his thanks were by no means effusive: 'In the end,' he warned her, 'your gifts will put me in a bad temper.'

The transformation of the flannel petticoat into a waistcoat was presumably to be effected by Thérèse, since her mother had gone to Paris for the marriage of her granddaughter. Rousseau had told Mme d'Épinay that he hoped Mme Levasseur would bring him her news when she returned;† later he was to regret encouraging such contacts between the two women, since they led to Mme Levasseur begging Mme d'Épinay as well as Diderot and Grimm to persuade Rousseau to leave the Hermitage and return to Paris, and also to 'borrow' money from her in Thérèse's name. He already

---

*Dr Tronchin was by this time on fairly intimate terms with Mme d'Épinay, addressing her as '*ma bonne amie*'.[98] He told her that in cases where there was no cure an opiate against pain was the only treatment.

†Mme Levasseur returned to the Hermitage in the company of Deleyre on 29 November 1756.

knew that the old woman was regularly seeing Grimm behind his back: 'Had I been more clear-sighted I should from that moment have realized that I was nourishing a serpent in my bosom. But my blind confidence, which nothing had yet diminished, was such that I could not imagine she could want to injure the person she ought to love.'[102]

What hurt Rousseau most when he discovered that Mme Levasseur was cadging money was that Thérèse had known about it and not told him: 'How could she, from whom I have never kept a secret, keep one from me? Can one conceal anything from a person one loves?' He noticed that the secrets Thérèse shared with her mother bound the two of them together and left him feeling isolated and alone. Far from forming 'a society of three' at the Hermitage he soon ceased even to form with Thérèse a society of two: 'I was under constraint in my own house ... We had an intimate relationship without living in intimacy.'[103]

In his letter[104] to Mme d'Épinay of 1 December, Rousseau had asked whether she had yet met Diderot. As a literary lionizer she had long desired to make the acquaintance of the celebrated editor of the *Encyclopédie*, but he continued to stay clear of her. Rousseau warned her:

I think that the Diderot of the morning will always wish to visit you and the Diderot of the evening will not appear ... You know that his rheumatism sometimes keeps him indoors, and when he is not soaring on his two great wings towards the sun, you will find him on a bed of grass with his four claws closed up in pain. Believe me, if you have another spare petticoat, you would do well to send it to him.

Diderot was actually with Rousseau on the day he wrote this letter to Mme d'Épinay, and he showed him what he had written. On Diderot's prompting, he appended a further message saying both that Diderot had a great esteem for her and that he would not come to see her. Soon afterwards, however, Mme d'Épinay met Diderot at Holbach's *salon*, and promptly coralled him into her little circle.

The week after Diderot's visit to Rousseau, another old friend went to spend the day at the Hermitage, his one-time pupil, Mme de Chenonceaux,* who had rented a house in the neighbouring parish of Deuil; she stayed so long that she had to leave by torchlight. Despite such visits, Rousseau undoubtedly felt lonely in the long winter evenings, and he wrote again to Mme d'Épinay in December[106] urging her to leave Paris and return to her château: 'My dear and lovable friend, I do wish you

*Marie-Alexandrine-Sophie Dupin de Chenonceaux, née Rochechouart-Ponville (1730–76) gave Rousseau as much satisfaction as her husband, Jacques-Armand, gave him little.[105]

were here at my fireside. We would chat sweetly together and it seems to me that heart would speak to heart.'

Mme d'Épinay must have told Rousseau she was worried about the upbringing of her daughter, Angélique, because Rousseau's letter offers her his opinion on the subject. 'Is there any sense,' he asks,

in these anxieties about a child of six, when it is impossible to know her character? What one's children do when they are in the care of other people proves nothing, because one can never know who is responsible for their faults. It is when they are no longer under nurses, governesses and tutors that one can see what nature has made them, and it is then that their real education begins. Besides, I am not sure you are wise to have your daughter so far from your own supervision. I do know that she ought not to be as happy away from you as she is with you, although I do not see how you could ever be sure of that. Think of it; this precaution is even more important for the future than for the present.

In the same letter, Rousseau reported to Mme d'Épinay that he had 'a terrible stomach-ache lately as result of having tried to live like a peasant and feed on cabbage and bacon'. Later in the month, however, he told Lenieps:[107] 'Since I have been here I see neither books nor papers, and I delight in living like a peasant, which I feel is my true vocation.'

Deleyre challenged this self-image of Rousseau's in a letter[108] he wrote in mid-December to apologize for not coming to the Hermitage: 'You have a mischievous spirit which likes noise, drama and trouble. How can you survive amid all that repose and peace you have had for the past eight months? It is odd to see how solitude civilizes you. You have never been so sociable as you are in the woods.'

Several of Rousseau's letters* to Mme d'Épinay from this period express concern about the health of 'Papa Gauffecourt' who had had a stroke. Rousseau was afraid that the doctors of Paris would kill his old friend if the effects of the stroke did not: 'For the love of God get rid of that lot,' he implored her,[109] and when he heard that Gauffecourt was worse, he overcame his aversion to Paris to visit him on his sickbed.† He was reassured to find that Gauffecourt was recovering from the stroke, even though he was still experiencing difficulties with his memory and speech, and, in Rousseau's opinion, was being attended 'by three doctors too many'.[110]

As soon as he got back to the Hermitage at the beginning of January, Rousseau collapsed into bed: 'We are all ill here with colds and fever,' he

---

*In *Montbrillant*, Mme d'Épinay distorts these letters to make Rousseau appear totally indifferent to his friend's illness.

†He offered if necessary to stay with Gauffecourt to the end.

complained[111] to Mme d'Épinay, and he was startled to receive from her a week or two later a message that Gauffecourt wanted to see him again in Paris. Reluctantly he offered to go.

'We are three sick people here,' he told[112] Mme d'Épinay:

and I do not know which one has the least need of nursing. I have to leave in the middle of winter the persons I brought here with the promise never to abandon them. The roads are frightful and one sinks up to the knees in mud. Of the two hundred and more friends that M. de Gauffecourt has in Paris, it is strange that a poor invalid, overwhelmed with his own ills, should be the only one he needs. I leave you to reflect on all that. I shall allow two more days for my health to improve and the roads to dry. Then I shall leave on Friday, if it does not rain or snow.

He asked Mme d'Épinay to arrange for a carriage to take him from Montmorency to Paris, but only on condition that she should let him pay for it – 'if not, I shall never forgive you'. He told her that he would like to dine with her while he was in Paris but to sleep at Diderot's house, and at the same time he asked her to forward a letter to Diderot (doubtless informing him of his forthcoming visit) and a 'packet'. The 'packet' contained a fair copy of the first two parts of *Julie*, which Rousseau wanted Diderot to read and review as an editorial critic.

In Paris Rousseau spent much of his time with the afflicted Gauffecourt: 'I left his sickroom only to sleep,' he told[113] Lenieps, with some measure of exaggeration, in explaining why he did not come to see him while he was in Paris. A letter Rousseau wrote to Dr Tronchin[114] at the time shows that Gauffecourt was far from critically ill, and was actually planning to leave Paris within a fortnight for Lyons. 'Your letter,' Rousseau informed the doctor, addressing him as *mon philosophe*, 'has done him almost as much good as your prescriptions.' He went on to impart less cheerful news of Mme d'Épinay's health: she had been in bed for two days with pains in her legs, headaches and a fever that did not cease: 'she ought to live, not only for the sake of her children and her friends, but because of her confidence in you and her obedience in following your orders'.

In the same letter to Dr Tronchin Rousseau referred again to his project of retiring to Geneva, but explained that he could not do so until Mme Levasseur had found another resting-place and unless he himself could earn some kind of livelihood in Geneva. He asked Dr Tronchin if he had 'spoken to any bookseller in Geneva' about him, at the same time imploring him not to let Mme d'Épinay know he was contemplating leaving the Hermitage to settle in his native city. Rousseau also mentioned Voltaire, but only in the most cordial terms; Voltaire's short letter of acknowledgement of his long defence of Providence had, Rousseau said, 'added to the admiration I have always felt for his writing and to my esteem and friendship for his person'.

Rousseau was undoubtedly worried about Mme d'Épinay's health, especially as Tronchin, the only doctor in whom he had any sort of faith, was in Geneva while she was in Paris. Once he had returned to the Hermitage, he fretted at not hearing from her. In mid-February he wrote[115] begging for reassurance, and swearing that he would gladly have her shut up in the Bastille in order to spend six months together with her there. He was less enthusiastic, however, about a suggestion that was actually put to him; namely that of accompanying Mme d'Épinay to Geneva so that she could be treated by Dr Tronchin in person. 'I have not yet made up my mind about the journey to Geneva,' he informed her.

He seems to have been hardly more enthusiastic about the short trip to Geneva than about going there to settle, and subsequent developments were to make him less eager still. Dr Tronchin, however, did not relax his efforts to persuade Rousseau to return on a permanent basis and he offered to help overcome the obstacles that Rousseau said hindered his doing so. He asked[116] the Duc de La Rochefoucauld to sponsor the admission of Mme Levasseur to an old people's home and then tried to have Rousseau appointed a librarian by the city of Geneva.

Rousseau promptly rejected[117] this proposal: 'Where should I find the qualifications for such a job? I do not know anything about books; I have never been able to tell which were the good editions of any work; I have no Greek, very little Latin, and no memory at all. Would that not make me an illustrious librarian?'

As usual, when any scheme was suggested to Rousseau that might facilitate his return to Geneva, he immediately found fault with it. He even found a reason for scepticism about the project of bringing Mme d'Épinay to Geneva for treatment by Dr Tronchin, namely that her problems were not all of a medical kind: 'As for Mme d'Épinay, her heart and her body are in need of the journey; the difficulty is that she feels her physical ills, and will be docile; but she clings to the moral principles of the fine-scented philosophers, and I do not think you will easily cure her of those.' He went on to deplore the fact that Mme d'Épinay, 'a sensible woman, an excellent mother, who loves justice and virtue', should 'allow her inclinations to overcome her reason'.

The reference to 'fine-scented philosophers' suggests the name of Grimm, and it is clear from what Rousseau wrote later in the *Confessions* that he must have had Grimm in mind: 'I remembered the summary of Grimm's principles which Mme d'Épinay had given me, and which she had adopted. It consisted of one single article – that the only duty of man

is to follow in everything the inclinations of his heart.'[118] In the letter to
Tronchin, Rousseau declared: 'There is not a single man in the world who
in doing everything his heart proposed to him would not soon become
the worst of scoundrels.'

Dr Tronchin, a more orthodox Calvinist* than Rousseau, would
undoubtedly have agreed with this last sentiment; he also had ideas at
variance with those of the medical establishment about the interaction of
the moral and the physical in matters of health; he ascribed Gauffecourt's
stroke, for example, both to the immediate cause, 'arthritic humour carried
to the brain', and to its more distant cause, the whole life-style of a sensual
man 'who confused desire with strength'.[120]

If Grimm's influence had the deleterious effect on Mme d'Épinay that
Rousseau suspected, his physical presence, at least, was soon to be removed
by wartime duties, his new patron, the Duc d'Orléans, having secured
him the job of secretary to the Maréchal-Duc d'Estrées, who was just then
preparing his army for the campaign in Westphalia.

Mme d'Épinay's projected visit to Geneva was postponed and in mid-
February she left Paris only to go to her country estate, where Rousseau
joined her for dinner on Shrove Tuesday, 22 February. He had been
expecting a visit from Diderot that day, but once again Diderot disappointed him. The weather was so bad at that season that Rousseau
himself advised[122] Lenieps to put off a visit he had promised to make to
the Hermitage until the spring: 'then I shall make a real festivity of seeing
you and showing you my delightful dwelling amid the first burgeoning
of new vegetation ... I shall have wine and rustic foodstuffs, and if my
picnic does not suit you, you may bring your own ... Come on a
pilgrimage to visit a devout hermit and kiss him as a relic.'

With Mme d'Épinay installed nearby and giving him much of her
attention, Rousseau seems to have been less impatient to entertain his
friends from Paris. On the other hand, he complains in the Confessions –
written, it must be remembered, long after he had ceased to be a friend
of Mme d'Épinay – that she was an importunate bore. As soon as she
found that he preferred to see her alone or in petit comité rather than in
large social gatherings, she suggested that she should signal him when it
would be opportune for them to meet:

The result was that I no longer visited her at my own time, but at hers;
and I was never certain of being master of myself for a single day. This
constraint greatly diminished the pleasure I had in seeing her. I found that

---

*Rousseau said to him apropos of Julie, 'Oh, how you would despise me if you knew
what kind of book I am writing, and, what is worse, writing with pleasure.'[119]

that freedom which she had so frequently promised was given me on
condition that I should never enjoy it, and when, once or twice, I tried to
do so there were so many messages, notes and alarms about my health that
I saw I could only escape running in response to her first summons by
retiring to a sick-bed.[122]

When Grimm was called away on military duties, Mme d'Épinay was
more than ever demanding of Rousseau's attention, but at least Grimm
himself was no longer there to get on Rousseau's nerves. His patience,
however, was tested by another, and much closer, friend, Diderot. In
February, Diderot sent him a copy of his new play *Le Fils naturel*, in which
Rousseau read with dismay a remark made by one of the characters,
Constance, to another, Dorval, who, like Rousseau, has decided to withdraw from society to live in rustic solitude: 'Only the bad man is alone.'
  Rousseau addressed what he says in the *Confessions* was a restrained
protest to his old friend.[124] Wounded as he was by the cruel remark,
coming as it did on top of Diderot's stubbornness in opposing him in all
his tastes and inclinations – 'I was revolted by the spectacle of a man
younger* than myself trying to manage me like a child' – Rousseau insists
that he reproached Diderot in such mild and affectionate language that
'the letter was soaked with my tears' and 'ought to have drawn tears from
him'.[124]
  In the event, Diderot's reply[125] was cheerful, even flippant: 'I am glad
my work has pleased you, and touched you. You do not share my opinion
of hermits; say what good you will about them, you are the only one in
the world of whom I shall think it true. There is still a lot to be said on
the subject, if one could only say it without making you cross. A woman
of eighty years!'† Diderot added a postscript, however, in which he wrote:
'I ask your forgiveness for what I said about the solitude in which you
live,' an apology somewhat weakened by the signing-off line 'Adieu,
Citizen – and yet a hermit makes a very peculiar citizen.'
  Rousseau reproduces in the *Confessions*[126] a paragraph from Diderot's
letter, but not the postscript in which Diderot apologized. Nor does he
reproduce the first part of the letter, in which Diderot invited him to visit
him in Paris and spend two days there *incognito*, working on the manuscript
of his novel *Julie* and settling 'the business of the Baron's manuscript'.
  The 'Baron's manuscript' was a work about chemistry which Holbach
had translated and then presented the copyright to Rousseau so that he
might enjoy the royalties, an act of charity which Rousseau says he

---

*Diderot was in fact only a year younger than Rousseau.
†A reference to Mme Levasseur.

accepted only because Diderot forced him to do so.[127] We do not have the text of his reply to Diderot's letter, but he evidently wrote angrily, spelling out several grievances he had been harbouring against his old friend – the broken promises to come to the Hermitage, the failure to keep appointments, and his general bullying ways. Rousseau may well have mentioned in that letter, as he does in the *Confessions*, those occasions when he had 'gone all the way to Saint-Denis to meet Diderot, and dined alone after waiting all day in the rain for him'.[128] He must, at all events, have written in the letter: 'I do not want to come to Paris. I will not come. This time I am determined,' for those words are quoted and underlined in Diderot's reply.[129]

If Rousseau had been willing to overlook the remark that 'Only the bad man is alone', he would not forgive the reference to 'a woman of eighty years' followed by an exclamation mark, because he saw those words as a renewal of the accusation that he was 'committing a crime in keeping old Mme Levasseur at the Hermitage, far away from the kind of assistance she might need'.[130] Rousseau revealed his feelings about Diderot in a letter[131] to Mme d'Épinay, who had returned to Paris to look after her sick mother:*

I should suffocate if I could not pour out my sorrows in the bosom of friendship. Diderot has written me a letter which has pierced my soul. He has given me to understand that it is only through indulgence that he does not regard me as a scoundrel and that *'there is still a lot more to be said on the subject'* – these are his words. And all this – do you know why? – because Mme Levasseur is with me. And, good God, what would they say if she were *not* here? I took them off the street, her and her husband, when they were no longer of an age to earn a living, and she has never given me more than three months' service in the ten years during which I have taken the bread out of my own mouth to feed her. I bring her here to this clean air where she lacks nothing. I give up returning to my homeland for her sake. She is her own absolute mistress, coming and going as she pleases, without accounting to me. I take as much care of her as if she were my own mother. All this means nothing, and I am made out to be a scoundrel if I don't sacrifice my happiness and my life, if I don't go and die in Paris in order that she should be amused there. Alas, the poor woman does not wish it, she is very content where she is.

Rousseau went on to suggest – unwisely in view of Mme d'Épinay's

---

*Florence-Angélique Tardieu d'Esclavelles, née Proveur, had for many years been an impoverished widow.

attachment to her lover – that Grimm was behind Diderot's efforts to have
him take Mme Levasseur back to Paris.*

Philosophers of the city – if these are your virtues, you console me when
you judge me a bad man. I was happy in my retreat; solitude is no hardship
for me; I am not afraid of poverty; I am indifferent to the world's neglect;
I endure my pains with patience; but to love and receive only ingratitude
in return is the one thing I cannot bear! Forgive me, my dear Friend, my
heart is burdened with grief and my eyes are swollen with the tears I
cannot shed. If only I could see you and weep, how I should be comforted!
But I shall not set foot again in Paris. I have sworn I will not!

Diderot himself replied[132] promptly to Rousseau's letter, suggesting that
he was being unreasonable in refusing absolutely to come to Paris,
especially as he did not know the business matter which he, Diderot, had
wished to put to him there. He needed to talk to him about his 'book'
(presumably *Julie*): 'You don't want to come to Paris? Very well, on
Saturday morning, whatever the weather, I shall come to the Hermitage.
I shall come on foot. My engagements will not allow me to travel sooner.
My fortune will not allow me to travel otherwise;† and it is high time I
requited all the pains you have given me for the past four years.'
    Diderot assured Rousseau that however far he tried to run away from
his friends, their friendship would follow him; Diderot then spoiled the
conciliatory effect of those words by adding: 'nor would you escape the
interest they take in Mme Levasseur. Live, my friend, live, and do not fear
that she will die of hunger.'
    Mme d'Épinay had in the meantime received Rousseau's account of his
grievances against Diderot, and she wrote[133] back saying that his letter had
filled her with grief. She was sure he had misunderstood Diderot's meaning;
she herself had heard it said at Holbach's house that Diderot was going to
visit Rousseau the following Saturday:

But what can I say to you? I know nothing except that you and Diderot
love each other tenderly. If perhaps some misconstrued words have
wounded you, take care, my dear friend, not to let the seeds of bitterness
take root. Perhaps you started out by being in the right, but be careful
not to end up by being in the wrong ... Finally, it seems to me that thirty
complete proofs are needed to justify suspicion of a friend turning against
one.

*He also accused Grimm of trying to take all his friends away from him.
†Despite his straitened circumstances, Diderot was, according to his daughter, regularly
handing, without Rousseau's knowledge, money to Mme Levasseur.

As for Rousseau's accusation against Grimm, Mme d'Épinay refused to comment: 'I shall try to forget as soon as I can that it is you who suspect him of an infamy of which only a scoundrel could be capable.' She promised Rousseau she would come to see him as soon as possible. 'For God's sake,' she implored him, 'Calm yourself ... I embrace you tenderly with all my heart.'

Rousseau followed Mme d'Épinay's advice to the extent of sending her, for her approval, the letter he proposed to send to Diderot. He hesitated to send it, he explained[134] to her, because he feared he was 'too embittered and too violently indignant to think rationally'. In this letter[135] Rousseau urged Diderot to call off the visit to the Hermitage he intended to make the following Saturday, unless, Rousseau added sarcastically, he wished to catch some illness 'so as to be able to blame me for it'. He accused Diderot of having been the aggressor in all their quarrels and of wanting to spoil the happiness he had found in his solitude: 'You say "Only the bad man is alone" and then to justify your assertion at whatever cost, things must be such that I actually become bad. Philosophers! Philosophers!'

As for old Mme Levasseur, Rousseau declared that he was beginning to agree with Diderot; she would be happier in Paris, and although he could not keep her there in luxury, he would give her everything he earned and live alone on bread and water if need be. He only insisted that he would not give up the liberty of his own person or become a slave. At the end of the letter, Rousseau declared that he had never written to Diderot without tenderness in his heart – 'I moistened with tears my last letter to you' – but Diderot's own asperity had at last infected him: 'My eyes are dry; my heart is hardened as I write to you. I am in no state to see you. Do not come, I beseech you.'

In his covering letter[136] to Mme d'Épinay, Rousseau reported that he had informed Mme Levasseur of his friend's opinion that the Hermitage was no place for a woman of her age, and that he had offered to give her everything he possessed so that she could live with Thérèse and her children in Paris. This had prompted the daughter to burst into tears, and protest that she would never leave him, while the old woman simply treated the offer as a ploy to get rid of her, saying that having endured the winter at the Hermitage it was unfair that she should be sent away in the spring. 'A fortnight ago,' Rousseau wrote, 'we were living peacefully together, and in perfect harmony. Now you see us all alarmed, agitated, weeping, and forced to separate.'

In a postscript added that evening, he told Mme d'Épinay of further reproaches being hurled at him by Thérèse's mother: 'You see I cannot avoid being a monster. I am one in the eyes of M. Diderot if Mme Levasseur stays here; and I am one in her eyes if she does not stay here.

Whatever I do, I am a bad man in spite of myself.'

On the same day[137] Mme d'Épinay wrote from Paris begging Rousseau once again not to destroy his friendship with Diderot:

In truth, my dear good friend, I have read and reread M. Diderot's letters, and I cannot find a word that ought to put you in the state you are in. I see the first letter, full of friendship and the desire to see you; he makes a remark to you which is not in the least offensive, which does not say a word which, even on the most severe interpretation, is other than the kind of observation made between friends about the disadvantages that have to be weighed against the advantages of a course of action. He has the delicacy to blame himself, and to beg you in the end to forgive him. Yet on the strength of this, you believe that he regards you as a scoundrel and you behave to him as if he had actually treated you as one. I cannot hide from you that you are very wrong. I declare that I love you with all my heart, and for that reason I do not hesitate to tell you what I think. You are wrong. Dear God, if only I had wings I would fly to you and then fly back to my mother. I would bring you, perhaps, some comfort in your sorrows.

As for the second letter from M. Diderot, I cannot say anything; it depends on what you wrote in reply to his first. I do not wish to forward your latest letter to him. He shall not have it, and I insist that you do not send it. I shall take it upon myself to send him a message by my son,* who is seeing him tomorrow, to urge him not to go to the Hermitage because of the bad weather. This does not mean, my dear friend, that I do not consider it very essential for M. Diderot and you to see each other soon, but there is a real likelihood that he would get ill if he made such a journey on foot in this terrible weather we are having. Write him a letter dictated by your heart. I am sure your heart will speak for him as mine speaks for you ...

As for Mme Levasseur, her business seems to be easy to arrange. Does she want to stay with you, or doesn't she? If she does, all is said: if she does not, I will take charge of her ... Adieu, my dear and unhappy friend, how I love you and how I feel for you.

Rousseau accepted Mme d'Épinay's advice. He promised[138] her that he would not send the letter to Diderot and that he would say no more about his quarrel with him, but added bitterly, 'The Gospel tells us to turn the other cheek, not to ask for forgiveness.' He ended his short missive by

---

*Louis-Joseph Lalive, nicknamed 'Le Lettré' by reason of his total inaptitude for literary studies.

repeating his vow not to return to Paris: 'I bless Heaven for having made me a bear and a hermit and an obstinate fellow rather than a philosopher.' Despite these assertions he did visit Paris and he did say more about the quarrel, both to her and to Diderot himself.

Diderot wrote[139] to Rousseau as soon as he received from Mme d'Épinay's son the message that he should put off his visit to the Hermitage; he had been told the reason was that Rousseau was coming to see him in Paris, and he said he had waited in all day to welcome him. Now he realized that Mme d'Épinay had told a white lie, and he could understand why:

You would have abused me; you would have slammed your door in my face, and she wanted to spare us both a scene which would have hurt me and given you cause to blush. My friend, do not lock yourself up in your sanctuary with injustice. She is a bad companion. Once and for all, ask yourself who thought of your health when you were sick, who took your part when you were attacked, who has sustained a lively interest in your fame and who has rejoiced in your success? Answer sincerely, and recognize those who love you ... Oh Rousseau, you are getting to be bad, unjust, ferocious, and I weep with sorrow.

Diderot ended his letter on a less emotional note: 'M. d'Holbach asks you to make an arrangement with a printer or bookseller so that the book on chemistry you know about may be published.'*

Rousseau replied[141] promptly to Diderot's letter:

I would like to sum up in a few words the history of our quarrel. You sent me your play. I wrote to you about it in the most tender and decent words that I have ever written in my life, protesting, with all the sweetness of friendship at a most dubious maxim – 'only the bad man is alone' – which people might apply, very hurtfully, to me. In reply I received a very dry letter, in which you appeared to grant me the indulgence of not considering me a dishonourable man – and that solely because I had under my roof a woman of eighty, as if the country air were deadly at that age, and as if there were no woman of eighty outside Paris. My reply had all the intensity of an honest man insulted by a friend. Your rejoinder to that was an abominable letter. I defended myself again very forcefully, but

---

*It was not perhaps the most opportune time to remind Rousseau that he was accepting the charity of the Baron d'Holbach. However, Rousseau's reaction was entirely practical. He put the matter in the hands of Mme d'Épinay and asked her to organize the publication of the book in Paris, with the injunction not to publish it herself: 'That is a way of forcing people to buy a book, and making one's friends contribute. I don't want that.'[140]

distrusting myself in the fury that you had provoked, and fearing to put myself while I was in such a state in the wrong with a friend, I sent my letter to Mme d'Épinay, making her the judge of our difference. She sent the letter back to me, imploring me to suppress it. I did suppress it. You now write me another letter in which you call me bad, unjust, cruel and ferocious. That is a summary of what has happened between us ... Who is the aggressor in the affair? Unfeeling and hard-hearted man, two tears of yours shed on my breast would mean more to me than the throne of the world, but you refuse me them, and are satisfied only to make me weep. Well, keep all your tears. I want nothing more from you.

It is true that I persuaded Mme d'Épinay to prevent your coming here last Saturday. We were both of us angry ... It would have been dangerous for us to meet in such a state of mind.

Having written all this, Rousseau calmed down, and Diderot seems not to have been provoked to a further rejoinder. Deleyre joined Mme d'Épinay in trying to bring about a reconciliation, and the quarrel was patched up at the beginning of April. A letter from Deleyre to Rousseau dated 31 March 1757[142] reported that he had met Diderot the day before: 'You would have seen him on Sunday, dear Citizen, if he had not had a chemistry lesson on Saturday with M. Rouelle. You and he will soon be of one mind again; your last letter has calmed him. Make him tell you everything he has in his heart. It is only by openness that your friendship can be calmed.'

In the *Confessions*[143] Rousseau says he took the initiative towards reconciliation when he was made to understand that Diderot was in trouble. Not only was another storm being stirred up by the Church against the *Encyclopédie*, but Diderot was being accused of having plagiarized, in his *Le Fils naturel*, a play by Goldoni, *Il vero amico*. Moreover, Mme de Graffigny had, according to Rousseau, 'maliciously spread the rumour that the plagiarism was the reason why I had broken with Diderot. It seemed only fair and generous to demonstrate the contrary to the public and to spend two days not only with him in Paris but at his house.'[144]

Diderot in turn visited Rousseau at the Hermitage at the beginning of April, although the wounds seem not to have been entirely healed at that time, to judge from a remark of Rousseau's in a letter to Jacob Vernes dated 4 April:[145] 'Your letter came to console me at a moment when I believed I had much to complain of friendship, and I have never felt so keenly how dear yours is to me.' Once again Rousseau spoke of his intention to return to Geneva, saying that the only impediment was an old housekeeper of eighty for whom he had not yet found a home.

His letter to Mme d'Épinay, however, gives no hint of his leaving the Hermitage. She herself returned to La Briche in April to arrange the furnishings of the château at La Chevrette, where building works had been completed, and she was able to prepare the place in readiness for spending the summer there. From time to time Rousseau would dine with her at La Briche, but the weather was bad that spring and heavy rains made the road more difficult than ever, so they still had to communicate by letter. In one such letter, dated 23 April,[146] he recalled that it was just a year since she had brought Grimm to dine at the Hermitage, and he asked her if she had heard from him, for Grimm, newly appointed to the staff of the Maréchal-Duc d'Estrées, was now in the thick of the war in Westphalia.

One might have imagined that since Rousseau had come so heartily to dislike Grimm, he would have been pleased to have him out of the way; but that was not the case. He only regretted an absence that left Mme d'Épinay with time on her hands, and a greater need for the consolation of his friendship, which he was in no position just then to provide. For in the month of May 1757 something happened which banished all other concerns from Rousseau's mind: he fell in love.

3

SOPHIE

It was not love at first sight. Rousseau had known Élisabeth-Sophie-Françoise, Comtesse d'Houdetot, for several years, at La Chevrette* as the sister-in-law of Mme d'Épinay, and in the milieu of the *Encyclopédie* in Paris as the mistress of his friend, Jean-François de St-Lambert. She was twenty-six years old, the mother of three children and the wife of a Norman count of ancient lineage, Claude-Constant-César d'Houdetot, an army officer with a commission in the gendarmerie, a husband she had never loved.

She was not especially beautiful. Rousseau noted that her face was marked with smallpox and that her complexion was rather coarse, that she was short-sighted and had eyes that were 'too round',[1] but he also observed that she had beautiful, thick black naturally curling hair that reached down her back to her waist, and he was taken with the expression on her face, which was 'soft, lively and caressing'.[2] Above all, he was impressed by her sweetness of nature, which everyone recognized and which had earned her the nickname at La Chevrette of '*Le Parfait*' – 'The Perfect One'. She radiated goodness. If she had none of Mme d'Épinay's sharp sophisticated wit, she was intelligent in her own scatter-brained way; she danced well, and played the harpsichord and even wrote what Rousseau considered 'rather pretty verses'.[3]

She was *petite*, and shaped as Rousseau liked a woman to be shaped; far from being 'flat-chested' like her sister-in-law, she had the ample bosom of Rousseau's Julie – a feature of his heroine on which he had insisted when instructing the artist who provided illustrations for his novel. St-Preux tells Julie in a letter of somewhat indecorous candour that the sight of her breasts excites him, and Rousseau was to make a similar avowal to

*At the age of eighteen she had acted with Rousseau in an amateur performance of his play *L'Engagement téméraire*.

Mme d'Houdetot.[4] Indeed, he admits that the chief reason why he fell in love with her is that he came to see her as his imaginary Julie brought to life, as in the myth of Pygmalion and Galatea, itself a subject of one of his operatic fragments.[5]

Before he had invented his Julie, he had hardly noticed Mme d'Houdetot; but the day came, as he puts it, when 'I saw my Julie in Mme d'Houdetot, and soon I saw nothing but Mme d'Houdetot, invested with all the virtues with which I had endowed the idol of my heart.'[6]

The revelation came to him after a visit paid to the Hermitage by Mme d'Houdetot, at the suggestion of St-Lambert,* to bring him news of the health of Gauffecourt in January 1757:† this visit, Rousseau explains[10]

had somehow the air of the beginning of a novel. She had lost her way, and her coachman, leaving the winding road, tried to drive straight across from the mill at Clairvaux to the Hermitage. The carriage became stuck in mud at the bottom of the valley, so she decided to get down and complete the journey on foot. Her delicate shoes were soaked; she sank up to the knees in the mire; her servants had all the trouble in the world to pull her out and in the end she arrived at the Hermitage wearing boots, piercing the air with peals of laughter – to which I added my own when I witnessed her appearance. She had to change everything. Thérèse provided fresh clothes, and I persuaded her to forget her dignity, and join us in a rustic meal, which she very much enjoyed.

As soon as she got home to Paris,‡ Mme d'Houdetot sent back the clothes she had borrowed from Thérèse, together with a very friendly

---

*In the *Confessions* Rousseau writes: 'She had married very young and against her wishes a man of vanity and a good soldier, but a gambler and a trickster. She found in M. de St-Lambert the good qualities of her husband, with others more agreeable: brains, virtue and talent ... it was partly from inclination, as I like to think, but much more to please St-Lambert that she came to see me. He had urged her to do so, and there was reason to believe that the friendship that was beginning between us would make our relationship agreeable to all three.'[7]

According to Mme d'Épinay, St-Lambert had more friendship for Rousseau than Rousseau for him. She records St-Lambert saying to Rousseau: 'I take a delight in my need for you – but you are sometimes embarrassed by your need for me.'[8]

†In the *Confessions* Rousseau confuses the occasion of the visit with that of another, which took place in June 1756, when Mme d'Houdetot brought him news of the welfare of St-Lambert. But evidence from the time proves that the visit in question must have taken place in January 1757; for example, a letter to Mme d'Épinay of 11 January 1757, expresses concern about 'the excessive fatigues Mme d'Houdetot endured in coming here'.[9] In any case, the road to the Hermitage would not have been deep in mud in June.

‡Her house was in the rue de l'Université in the Faubourg St-Germain.

letter[11] thanking Rousseau for his hospitality and telling him that on her
return she had found a much better road to the Hermitage –

a discovery which pleases me because it opens the possibility of visiting
you again. I am really sorry to have seen so little of you. Stay in your
woods if you like it there, but allow us to protest that you like it too
much! I should have less to complain of if I were more free, and always
sure of not being a nuisance to you. Adieu, my dear Citizen, and please
thank Mlle Levasseur for the care she took of me.

The tone of her letter borders on the flirtatious; evidently while Rousseau was beginning to look on her with different eyes, she was beginning
to take a new interest in him. One reason for this, perhaps, was that she
was now very much alone. First her husband had gone off to the war – a
departure which, according to malicious testimony of Mme d'Épinay had
left her 'drunk with joy';[12] then St-Lambert was called to the colours as
well, and his mistress was disconsolate, 'desperate'[13] according to Mme
d'Épinay. The war thus deprived both sisters-in-law of the company of
their lovers; and Mme d'Épinay, who had hoped to find in Rousseau
consolation for the absence of Grimm, was none too pleased to discover
that Mme d'Houdetot had chosen him to console her for the absence of
St-Lambert.

There was already a certain element of jealousy in Mme d'Épinay's
attitude towards Mme d'Houdetot, for while she had married somewhat
beneath her into the moneyed bourgeoisie, her sister-in-law* had married
upwards into the higher ranks of society, and as a member of the *noblesse
de race* could be received at the court of Versailles; moreover, while Mme
d'Épinay's current lover was a mere literary journalist making his way in
the world, Mme d'Houdetot's was a marquis, at any rate considered a
marquis then, even though later genealogists claimed that St-Lambert was
not entitled to higher rank than that of a chevalier. Mme d'Épinay knew
all too well that as a *bourgeoise* she was judged in her private morals by
different standards from those applied to the nobility; her *liaisons* with
Francueil and Grimm were disapproved of, while that of Mme d'Houdetot
with St-Lambert was accepted as natural and normal, and the *complaisance*
of the count, her husband, more or less a duty, a jealous husband in the
monde of the *ancien régime* being regarded, as Montesquieu puts it in *Les
Lettres Persanes*, as a 'selfish fellow who wants to enjoy the sun to the
exclusion of all other men'.[14]

---

*Born Élisabeth-Sophie-Françoise Lalive de Bellegarde on 18 December 1730, she was
sister of Mme d'Épinay's husband.

Mme d'Épinay, however, was richer than Mme d'Houdetot, even though her husband was less generous to her than he was to his actresses and was running into grave financial difficulties as a result of over-spending on the refurbishment of La Chevrette. As its *châtelaine* Mme d'Épinay could feel herself to be a woman of importance. There was a park of thirty hectares designed by Le Nôtre, and the château itself was of feudal dimensions – 'sad and magnificent' according to Diderot,[15] and even the smaller manor-house at La Briche, where the family took refuge while the château was being renovated, had a tower and a chapel. By contrast, Mme d'Houdetot was housed in modest quarters* rented cheaply some three miles from La Chevrette at Eaubonne. According to *Madame de Montbrillant*,[16] M. d'Houdetot had wanted his wife to go back to his family seat in Normandy while he was away at the war, but was persuaded by Mme d'Épinay to let her sister-in-law stay near her in the valley of Montmorency. Mme d'Épinay, who may well have regretted this kind deed, described the house at Eaubonne as 'ugly';[17] Rousseau, who had sweeter memories of the place, called it 'rather pretty'.[18]

Mme d'Houdetot's mud-stained arrival in January was the beginning of their *amitié amoureuse*, but Rousseau dated his falling in love with her from a second unexpected visit she paid him in the spring, after St-Lambert had gone off to the war and she had installed herself in the house at Eaubonne: 'This time she came on horseback,' Rousseau recalls[19] 'and in men's clothes. Although I do not much care for such masquerades, I was captivated by the romantic air of this one, and this time it was love ... the first and only love of my whole life.'[20]

'Romantic'? This is one of the rare occasions when Rousseau uses the word so often associated with his name. But how could he, the ailing, ageing, penniless little hermit, compete as a romantic lover with St-Lambert, that dashing Byronic figure, just forty years old, tall and handsome, with dark seductive eyes, a nobleman, poet, soldier, a hero of the battle of Coni and a notorious conqueror of women's hearts, including that of Voltaire's mistress, who died giving birth to his child? Yet Rousseau did compete, and he did so by inventing out of himself another model of the romantic hero – or, as we might now say, anti-hero – which he introduced to the world in his novel *Julie* in the person of St-Preux, a lonely outsider who lives for love: 'You are surrounded by people who cherish and adore you,' St-Preux[21] tells his Julie, 'but I, alas, am a wanderer, with no family and almost no country. I have you alone in the whole world, and love takes the place of everything for me. So do not be surprised

---

*Quarters which had, however, the advantages of being near a property owned by her lover, St-Lambert.

that while your soul may be more sensitive, mine knows better how to love, and while I yield to you in many other things, I take the prize for love.'

Rousseau had also one advantage which St-Preux did not have; he was a literary celebrity, and as such he enjoyed in eighteenth-century France an undoubted sex appeal. Mme d'Houdetot did nothing to discourage his attentions to her. Indeed, we find her writing to him on the Sunday[22] after her visit:

If you have nothing better to do, my dear Citizen, you must come and dine with me on Tuesday. I shall be absolutely alone, as my sister-in-law [Mme de Blainville] has business that day in Paris. I had the intention of suggesting that we meet at Mme d'Épinay's, or to invite her here, but she won't be back that day. I hope you have discovered a shorter way here. I will show you around this neighbourhood. If M. Deleyre is with you, and he would like to come, I should be pleased for you to bring him. Adieu, my dear Citizen.

Rousseau accepted the invitation to dine on the appointed day* and he did not take Deleyre with him. He spent his time with his hostess *tête-à-tête* and soon afterwards, he declared his love to her. She did not rebuff him. She told him she was in love with St-Lambert, but Rousseau did not allow that to be reason to withdraw. Indeed the more she talked to him about St-Lambert the more he 'felt', as he puts it, 'the contagion of love'.[23] He encouraged her to unburden her heart: 'As I listened, I felt myself with her; I was seized by a delicious trembling that I had never experienced with any other woman ... She inspired me with all the feelings for herself that she had expressed for her lover.'[24]

Rousseau says he made his own feelings known to her in a confused, blushing way,† but that she put him at his ease in a manner that was at once 'prudent and generous'.[26] As events developed, however, there was more generosity than prudence in her behaviour. She stimulated his ardour, and clearly enjoyed the admiration of a celebrated writer. She had the temperament of an *allumeuse* as well as of an angel. When his advances went too far, she scolded him: 'She did not spare me, when necessary, the harsher reproaches I thoroughly deserved,' Rousseau recalls.[27] The trouble

---

*Tuesday, 24 May 1757.

†He came near to betraying his secret in a letter to Mme d'Épinay, written the following Sunday: 'I went on Tuesday to dine at Eaubonne and was caught on my return by rain and confusion which have both continued to the present. Good day, Madame, love me as a hermit as you love me as a bear. Otherwise I shall take off my hermit's habit and put on my fur.'[25]

was that such gestures of female domination only served to inflame still further his erotic passions.

Rousseau assures the readers of his *Confessions* that he also reproached himself. At his age – forty-five – he thought it was disgraceful to be consumed with illicit desire for a young woman whose heart was already engaged. Confused by his sense of guilt, he admits he became suspicious, and sometimes wondered whether Mme d'Houdetot was not mocking him, and acting in cahoots with St-Lambert 'to turn my head completely and then make fun of me'.[28] But he soon convinced himself that both she and her lover were 'too honourable to indulge in so barbarous an amusement'[29] and he decided to make the most of Mme d'Houdetot's willingness to let him court her: 'She continued to pay me visits which I was not slow to return. She liked walking as I did, and we went for long walks in that delightful countryside ... She refused me nothing that the most tender friendship could offer; she granted me nothing that could render her unfaithful.'[30]

He began to address her as 'Sophie' – her middle Christian name, and one closer to 'Julie' than the 'Mimi' by which she was known to other intimates. When they did not meet they wrote letters to each other – letters so intimate that Sophie took care afterwards that they should not be seen by St-Lambert. Thérèse was employed to carry their correspondence to and fro.

Having suggested in the *Confessions*[31] that Sophie did not feel a spark of the fires that burned in his own senses, Rousseau qualifies the remark:

I am wrong to speak of an unrequited love – mine was in a way returned. There was equal love on both sides, even if it was not reciprocal. We were both drunk with love, she for her lover, I for her; our sighs, our sweet tears mingled ... yet even at the height of our dangerous intoxication, she never forgot herself for a moment. As for myself, I protest that if sometimes I was misled by my senses and tried to make her unfaithful, I loved her too much to wish to possess her.

Evidence apart from the *Confessions* shows that Rousseau's efforts 'to make her unfaithful' were rather more determined than these words would have us believe. Since Sophie d'Houdetot was still alive when Rousseau wrote his *Confessions*, he had good reason to minimize the extent of that intimacy in writing his autobiography. She, for her part, clearly relished the fame she enjoyed after the publication of the book as a romantic heroine, more chaste (by the standards of the time) than Julie. She lived to a great age, dying in 1813, with St-Lambert as her companion until his death in 1803, a quarter of a century after the death of Rousseau.

People who met her in her old age remarked both on her lack of physical beauty and the charm of her personality. One such witness was the Anglo-Irish novelist Maria Edgeworth,[32] writing from Paris in January 1803:

We drove to the excellent Abbé Morellet's,* where we were invited to meet Mme d'Ouditot [*sic*], the lady who inspired Rousseau with the idea of Julie. Julie is now seventy-two years of age, a thin woman in a little black bonnet; she appeared to me thoroughly ugly, she squints so much that it is impossible to tell which way she is looking, but no sooner did I hear her speak than I began to like her ... I asked her if Rousseau was grateful for all the kindness shown to him. 'No, he was ungrateful: he had a thousand bad qualities, but I turned my attention from them to his genius, and the good he had done to mankind.'

At the age of twenty-six, Mme d'Houdetot was neither thin nor thoroughly ugly, and there is manifest evidence that she was interested in Rousseau for other reasons besides his genius. She allowed him to caress her as well as to talk to her, and to spend nights in her bedroom as well as days in the countryside, and evenings in an arbour in the park.†

'One evening,' he writes in the *Confessions*,[35]

after having supped *en tête-à-tête*, we went for a walk in the garden by the light of a beautiful moon. At the end of the garden was a rather large copse through which we passed to a pretty grove, adorned with a waterfall which she had had installed at my suggestion. Immortal memory of innocence and bliss! It was in that grove, sitting on a bank of grass beneath an acacia in blossom that I found words to match the emotions of my heart. It was the first and only time in my life, but I was sublime, if such a word can express all that is lovable and pleasing in the feelings that the most tender and ardent passion can breathe into a man's heart. What intoxicating tears I shed at her feet, and drew from her despite herself! Finally, in an involuntary transport she exclaimed: 'No, never was a man so lovable, and never a lover loved like you. But your friend St-Lambert hears us, and my heart cannot love twice.' Silent, I sighed. I kissed her. What a kiss! But that was all.

Such is Rousseau's avowal in the *Confessions*. However, even in what

---

*André Morellet was one of the very few leading Encyclopédistes to live through the Revolution; by keeping his head down, he kept it on.

†'It is almost a league from the Hermitage to Eaubonne, and it happened on my frequent excursions that I sometimes slept there.'[33] In a letter to Sophie he speaks not just of sleeping at Eaubonne ('*y coucher*') but of being 'in your bedroom' ('*dans ta chambre*').[34]

remains of the love-letters there is much to suggest that a kiss was not all. Perhaps the kiss was all on that particular occasion, but there were other meetings under the same acacia tree* beside the waterfall. In a letter to Sophie which Rousseau wrote in October 1757, but which he did not send, and which he probably had in front of him as he wrote the passage about the moonlit night, we find these words: 'How many times was your heart, filled with love for another, moved by the transports of mine? How many times did you say to me in the grove beside the waterfall, "You are the most tender lover I could imagine; no, never a lover loved like you!".'[37]

In writing his *Confessions* Rousseau used artistry as well as discretion, and condensed those 'many times' into one dramatic occasion, even tempting several of his biographers[38] to try to work out, on the basis of the moon being bright and the acacia in blossom, the exact date of the kiss.

In the course of the summer Rousseau and Sophie met in several places. The house at Eaubonne had only a modest garden, but Mme de Verdelin lent Sophie the key to the neighbouring park of Margency, the property of her lover Adrien Cuyret de Margency, which she had persuaded her husband to rent, and there Sophie and Rousseau could meet and walk in privacy. There was also the forest of Montmorency. Sometimes Sophie would have her servants drive her in a mule-cart towards the Hermitage, and meeting Rousseau on the road, go off on foot with him alone in the woods. Sometimes she took with her her sister-in-law, Mme de Blainville,† only to leave her to rest on her own, while she disappeared into the trees on the arm of her admirer. Rousseau says they made no effort to conceal their intimacy, because 'it was not of a nature to require any concealment'.[40]

It was far from a tranquil relationship. How much so we can judge from a letter to Sophie which can be read in draft form in his letter-book[41] conserved at Neuchâtel. Evidently written at the height of their relationship in late June or early July, it tells Sophie about the terrible agitations she has made him endure. He is worn out, tortured by the deprivations which follow the sweetest pleasures; but in his state of annihilation he still thinks of her:

Do you remember having reproached me once for very refined cruelties?

---

*According to the Vicomtesse d'Allard, Mme d'Houdetot showed her the acacia tree at Eaubonne thirty years after the summer of her romance with Rousseau and said, 'It was under that acacia, beside that waterfall, that he read me his *Julie* in instalments as he wrote it.'[36]

†Anne-Charlotte-Simonette, Marquise de Blainville, née d'Houdetot, was the sister of Sophie's husband, and considered by Mme d'Épinay to be a monumental bore: 'a fat little woman, very high and mighty, very nice to her sister-in-law, very difficult with other people ... I love the Countess with all my heart, but when she is accompanied by her dogs and the Marquise, I could wish for someone else.'[39]

Ah, to judge from the fatal impression which your words have not failed to produce in me, it is you who should be reproached for cruelties. For my own repose, I shall refrain from looking deeply into the meaning that those words might have in the circumstances in which they were spoken – but whatever meaning they can have to make me guilty they can never make me a seducer.

No, Sophie, I may die of my frenzies, but I shall never defile you. If you were to betray any sign of weakness, I would succumb that very instant. While you remain in my eyes what you are, though I betray my friend in my heart, I shall restore to him his charge as pure as I received it. A hundred times I have willed the crime. If you have willed it too I shall consummate it, and become the most treacherous and the most joyful of men, but I cannot corrupt the woman I idolize. Let her stay faithful and I will die – or let me read in her eyes that she is guilty, and nothing will hold me back.

It is obvious that Sophie set the stage for their love-scenes by taking Rousseau into the lonely grove by moonlight and receiving him in her bedroom, much as Julie captures St-Preux by inviting him to meet her alone in the chalet. Even if Sophie had occasion to reproach Rousseau for the 'cruelty' of his love-making, even if he had carried her to the peak of excitement and denied her the ultimate satisfaction, she must have found in the experience something that moved her in a strange new way. St-Lambert, like many another successful womanizer, treated his mistress with a certain offhand, brisk *machismo*; he was not interested in the exploration of her soul or his own. Rousseau talked to her all the time about spiritual and moral things, even as he pressed himself upon her person. The urbane and accomplished St-Lambert might know all about sex, but Rousseau offered something less common in the *beau monde* of the eighteenth century, the thrilling and deeply flattering homage of romantic love.

What did Sophie give in return? Whatever it was, it was enough to cast him in the deepest despair when it was withdrawn. The evidence of this is a letter[42] Rousseau wrote to her in the autumn, but decided not to send:

Come, Sophie, so that I can torment your unjust heart, that I may be in my turn as pitiless as you are. Why should I spare you when you deprive me of reason, honour, life? Why should I let your days slip peacefully by when you have made mine unbearable? It would have been far less cruel if you had driven a dagger in my heart, instead of the deadly arrow which is killing me . . .

Oh Sophie, I implore you, do not be embarrassed about the friend you sought. It is for your own honour that I ask you to value me. Am I not yours? Did you not take possession of me? You can never take that away, and because I belong to you, in spite of myself and of yourself, let me at least be not unworthy of belonging to you ... I shall not remind you of what happened in your park or in your bedroom; but in order to understand how much the impact of your charms prompted in my senses the desire to possess you, just remember Mont Olympe. Remember those words pencilled under an oak tree; I could have written them with my undiluted blood ...

Oh Sophie, after such sweet moments, the idea of eternal deprivation is too terrifying for someone who is trembling because he cannot merge his identity with yours. What! Your eyes would never again grow tender and look down with that sweet modesty which thrills me with exquisite delight? What! My burning lips would never again lay my soul on your heart with my kisses? What! I would never again experience that heavenly tremor, that swift all-devouring fire, which, quicker than lightning ... that moment, that inexpressible moment? What heart, what man, what God could have experienced you and then given you up? ...

Sophie, cruel Sophie, give me back the friend who is so dear to me. You offered her to me; I received her; you no longer have the right to deprive me of her ...

Rousseau mentions 'Mont Olympe' in the *Confessions*,[43] explaining that it was a 'pleasant terrace' on the road from the Hermitage to Eaubonne where he used to meet Sophie; after his death and the publication of the book his admirers believed they had traced the spot and created a monument to him there. He also mentions the 'notes' he pencilled under the oak tree – he says he did so to occupy his mind while he waited impatiently for her there. He admits they were seldom legible, although he did leave for her, in the niche they had agreed on, one note that could not fail to make her understand the deplorable state he was in. He recalls that in his love affairs with Mme de Warens and Thérèse, his passion had left him relatively undisturbed: but with Sophie, he was not only inspired with love but 'with love in all its energies and furies'.[44] Even the thought of her in his imagination, the prospect of the kiss she would give him when he met her, inflamed him physically as he walked across the hills of Audilly to the rendezvous at Eaubonne. He tells the reader of his *Confessions*, with remarkable frankness, that he used to pause on these journeys to relieve the tension and that he 'never made this little excursion alone with impunity'.[45]*

---

*What he means by 'impunity' is made explicit in an earlier chapter of the *Confessions*:[46] 'Naturally what I had most to fear in awaiting the possession of a woman I loved so dearly [Mme de Warens] was to anticipate it, and to be unable to control my desires and imagination

In a word, he masturbated. As a result he arrived at Eaubonne 'weak, exhausted, worn out and scarcely able to stand up'.[47] However: 'The moment I saw her, everything was repaired; all I felt in her presence was the importunity of inexhaustible and useless vigour'.[48]

Useless? According to the testimony of Thérèse, Rousseau was an accomplished lover. When James Boswell went to bed with her – ten years after the romance between Rousseau and Sophie – Thérèse informed him that his youthful strength did not make him 'a better lover than Rousseau'. She told Boswell he had virility but lacked art, 'and of the two she preferred art'. She 'asked him as a man who had travelled much if he had not noticed how many things were achieved by men's hands', and she instructed him *in arte amoris*, such as she had experienced as the mistress of Rousseau.[49]

We can believe that Rousseau tells the truth when he says he did not make Sophie unfaithful to St-Lambert in the strict sense of that word, but we can hardly doubt that he employed his hands about her person with that same skill to which Thérèse bore witness, and excited her with his caresses. If nothing of this kind had happened, it would be hard to understand the guilt she afterwards betrayed.

In the early stages of their romance, Sophie and her admirer had behaved with ostentatious indifference to the opinion of others, acting on Rousseau's conviction that they had nothing to hide. They not only went for walks in the park at La Chevrette, but strolled arm in arm* under Mme d'Épinay's window. At the time neither seems to have given any thought as to what Mme d'Épinay might be thinking. 'I was so taken up with my passion,' Rousseau admits,[51] 'that I had eyes for nothing but Sophie.' Mme d'Épinay, for her part, pretended to be unconcerned, although Rousseau noticed that while she redoubled her attentions to him, 'she overwhelmed her sister-in-law with unpleasant behaviour and signs of contempt'.[52]

Mme d'Épinay was in fact both angry and jealous, angry that the man she had brought to the Hermitage should forsake her so completely when she most needed his company, and jealous because her scatter-brained sister-in-law had captivated the philosopher she herself, the bluestocking

so as not to forget myself. It will be seen that at a more advanced age, the very idea of some light favours I had to expect from the person I loved inflamed me so much that I could not endure with any degree of patience to traverse the short space that separated us.'

*In the unposted letter to Sophie Rousseau wrote: 'Anyone would have thought by your eagerness to see me that you missed me when you did not see me. Your eyes did not avoid mine, and their gaze was not that of coldness. You took my arm when we went out walking; you did not take pains to conceal from me the sight of your charms, and when my lips dared to press yours, sometimes at least I felt them respond. You did not love me, Sophie, but you let yourself be loved and I was happy.'[50]

of the family, had failed to enthral. She tried to comfort herself by thinking of the whole thing as a grotesque joke, a joke in which her mirth was joined by that of the Baron d'Holbach on one of his rare visits to La Chevrette – Mme d'Épinay had invited him in the hope that he might agree to rent the smaller house at La Briche.*

Rousseau realized he was being mocked. He noticed that Holbach no longer looked at him 'with his usual moroseness', but 'made a hundred jovial remarks without my knowing what he meant. I answered not a word. Mme d'Épinay shook her sides with laughing.'[53]

She was not really amused and her curiosity was deadly earnest. Thérèse told Rousseau some time after the event that Mme d'Épinay was so determined to see the letters which she, Thérèse, carried between Rousseau and Sophie that she put her hand in her bodice to see if she had a letter hidden there.[54] Mme d'Épinay herself told a different story. In a letter[55] written in early June, she informed her lover Grimm:

Mlle Levasseur has just been to see me. She says that Rousseau's temper gets more difficult every day and that since he was last here at La Chevrette he has spent his days and nights weeping, and neither her mother nor she can understand why. He talks to himself at night. The other day he cried out: 'Poor Madame d'Épinay – if only you knew.' And they have no idea what he meant. He says he is coming to spend a fortnight here and that he has a lot to tell me, and that he always feels better for my advice. But what seems inconceivable to me is that Mlle Levasseur claims that Mme d'Houdetot goes to see the hermit every day. She leaves her servants in the forest, and comes alone, and returns alone. Little Levasseur is jealous, but I think she is telling lies.

In another letter[56] to Grimm, Mme d'Épinay asserted that Thérèse and her mother tried to make her listen to gossip about Rousseau as they scrounged money from her: 'I had to put a stop to their confidences, which are really scandalous. They said they had found a letter! I don't know what it was all about, since I would not allow them to give me any details. I said to Mlle Levasseur: "My child, you should either throw any letter you find into the fire or return it to the owner."'

Thérèse, as can be imagined, had no recollection of this episode. On the contrary, she told Rousseau that Mme d'Épinay had come to the Hermitage one day when he was out for a walk and boldly demanded to be shown the letters he had received from Sophie. Rousseau's comment on this was that if Mme Levasseur had known what the letters were, they

*The project fell through, largely, Mme d'Épinay suspected, because Charles Duclos persuaded the Baron against it.

would have been handed over, but 'fortunately only the daughter knew and she denied that I had kept any'.[57]

It is by no means certain that Rousseau was correctly informed. In a little book of reminiscences that Mme d'Épinay had privately printed in Geneva in 1758 under the title *Mes moments heureux*[58] she wrote about the predicament of a 'friend', who is clearly Mme d'Houdetot, being courted by an admirer, who is clearly Rousseau, and knowing 'from several letters which fell into my hands' that 'she had had her head turned'. This clue is all the more revealing in that Mme d'Épinay had the references to 'several letters that fell into my hands' deleted from the second edition of *Mes moments heureux*.[59]

The likelihood is that neither Mme d'Épinay nor Thérèse told the truth, that Mme d'Épinay had never refused to look at a letter Thérèse offered her to read, and that Thérèse had not resisted every effort of Mme d'Épinay to see a letter. Rousseau himself seems to have been perversely blind to the possibility of Thérèse being just as jealous as Mme d'Épinay. It is clear from what he says in the *Confessions* that he gave no consideration to the poor woman having any feelings at all. Although he continues to refer to her, even in this same passage of the *Confessions*, as 'my companion', he had obviously come to look upon her as a mere servant whose only role in the drama was that of a go-between in the *amours* of her superiors. However, Thérèse said nothing at the time about Mme d'Épinay's efforts to read his letters and Rousseau continued throughout the summer to behave as normally as he could in his dealings with his benefactress at La Chevrette. He even found time to offer her a copy of the first chapters of *Julie* which she read aloud on the occasion of Holbach's visit. She did not enjoy the novel: 'It was wonderfully written,' she remarked in a letter[60] to Grimm. 'But the writing is overblown, and seems to me to lack truth and warmth. The characters do not say a word they ought to say. It is always the author who speaks.'

Grimm was rather more interested in what she had to report about Rousseau and Mme d'Houdetot: In a letter[61] to her from his army GHQ in Germany he wrote: 'What you tell me about Rousseau seems most extraordinary, and those mysterious visits of the Countess even more so. He is a poor devil who torments himself and does not dare admit the real cause of his misery, which is in his own damned head and his pride.'

In the same letter Grimm informed Mme d'Épinay: 'I was interrupted yesterday by the arrival of St-Lambert. I spent the evening with him ... It will be a great consolation for me to be able to spend the rest of the campaign in his company. He spoke of Rousseau's hostility to me; he thinks Rousseau has been in love with you for some time past, and that is why I am his *bête noire*. Why is the Countess so cheerful?'

The problem which arises from this letter* is to know how much of Mme d'Épinay's news of the relationship between Rousseau and Sophie was transmitted by Grimm to St-Lambert. He evidently told him enough to make him uneasy, but he seems not to have told him all he had heard from Mme d'Épinay. And every letter brought fresh news from her of the romance.

'Rousseau hardly ever comes to see me,' she wrote to Grimm some time in June.[62] 'He is always with Mme d'Houdetot: he came only once during the visit of the Baron d'Holbach.' In another letter[63] she reported:

They say that the Countess and Rousseau continue their mysterious rendezvous in the forest. Three days ago he sent me word by the gardener that he could not come to see me because he was indisposed. The same evening I went to the Countess's house, and there he was seated en tête-à-tête and he stayed for two days. It is so bizarre and so comical that I believe I am dreaming. He came to spend the day yesterday. He seemed embarrassed, but I pretended to know nothing and to see nothing.

To Grimm's question as to why Mme d'Houdetot was so 'cheerful' without St-Lambert, Mme d'Épinay replied with artful ambiguity, asserting both that the Countess was really distressed by the absence of her lover, and that she had never allowed sorrow to prevent her being gay: 'She cries and laughs at the same time.'

Very soon afterwards – on Monday, 11 July, to be precise – the laughter ended abruptly, as Mme d'Épinay reported[64] to Grimm. On the day before she had taken Margency and the Marquis de Croismare,† a new friend she had roped into her circle, to dine with Rousseau at the Hermitage, and then brought Rousseau back with her party to stay at La Chevrette. Rousseau, she said, 'was in the best of humours', and remained so until the following day. Then he had a shock: St-Lambert made an unexpected

---

*Which may, of course, have been doctored, like so much else in *Montbrillant*.

†Marc-Antoine-Nicolas, Marquis de Croismare (1694–1772). Grimm had encouraged Mme d'Épinay to cultivate the friendship of Croismare. She described him as 'a man of sixty years of age, although he does not look it. He is of average height, and his face must have been handsome; it is still distinguished by an air of nobility and grace which lends appeal to his whole personality ... Intellectually he strikes one as having more charm than solidity, but I think it would be unjust to call him frivolous.'[65] Rousseau had met Croismare some years earlier in Paris through Diderot, and enjoyed a certain friendship with him on the basis of a shared interest in music. He does not mention him in the *Confessions*, but in a letter to Massard, written in March 1753,[66] he suggests that Croismare should be one of a party, and in a letter written in December 1762[67] to Mme Alissan de La Tour, who had inquired about 'a man with a wart', Rousseau asks if it is the Marquis de Croismare, 'who in truth is very intelligent, but who is neither young nor good-looking, and upon whom I would certainly not have intruded with good advice'.

appearance at the château, recalled from the front.

Mme d'Épinay resumed her letter[68] to Grimm just before she retired for the night:

I am petrified. Just as I was about to write to you the Marquis de St-Lambert came in. I cannot get over it. If only you knew how we welcomed him and how we talked of you ... The Countess appeared an hour after St-Lambert arrived to find him here. Alas, some people have all the luck. I hope she still appreciates it. But each of them seemed to me to look pretty coolly at the other. And I see one who is visibly in bitter misery. I pity him, if misery which is neither honourable nor reasonable should be pitied. The effect of the arrival of the Marquis on Rousseau has left me in no doubt at all that he is in love with the Countess.

St-Lambert was not on leave; he had been summoned to Versailles on a short military mission, and both Sophie and Rousseau seem to have hoped that they might keep the true extent of their intimacy concealed from him until his return to the front. Their efforts were not altogether adroit. The day after St-Lambert's appearance at La Chevrette Rousseau wrote Sophie a letter[69] worded in such an unnaturally stilted and formal style that it was all too obviously designed to be read by St-Lambert and allay any suspicions he might have about the relationship between his mistress and the writer. Heading his letter 'At La Chevrette, Tuesday morning', Rousseau announces that he is going to Paris to visit Diderot and apologizes for the fact that he will not have time to call on Mme d'Houdetot: 'But you know, Madame, how eager I would be to embrace M. de St-Lambert. If you could persuade him to come to Diderot's house* tomorrow some time during the day he would find me there and I should be delighted to see him.' Rousseau even took pains to refer to his walks with Sophie, knowing that St-Lambert would inevitably be told about them: 'Ah, Madame,' he asks, 'what will become of those *promenades charmantes* during which we discussed everything that could interest honourable and sensitive souls? There are no walks here at La Chevrette like those at Eaubonne, and even the Hermitage seems a solitary place since you no longer come here.' He sends word of Sophie's daughter, having seen her at Deuil 'sleeping soundly and apparently in splendid form', and the letter ends with coolly correct 'assurances of my respect'.

According to Mme d'Épinay[70] Rousseau had suddenly decided on St-Lambert's return to go to see Diderot in Paris. He was in a 'highly

*Diderot lived in the rue Taranne close to Mme d'Houdetot's house in the rue de l'Université.

emotional state', she noted, and told her that he 'wanted to throw his arms round Diderot's neck' and 'swear eternal friendship, after their recent quarrel'. A more likely motive* is that Rousseau wanted to unburden on his oldest friend his feelings about Sophie and St-Lambert. At all events, Rousseau told Diderot that he was passionately in love with the Countess and had been seeing her daily in St-Lambert's absence. Diderot says he advised Rousseau to be absolutely frank with St-Lambert, tell him everything, and give up seeing the Countess.† Diderot also claims that Rousseau promised to follow his advice, but if Rousseau did make such a promise, he did not keep it.

It seems that Rousseau must have met St-Lambert briefly on the occasion of this visit to Paris, because a letter[72] from Mme d'Épinay inviting Rousseau to dine at La Chevrette reminds him to bring the manuscript he has promised the Marquis to read to him. She adds, 'I imagine it's a question of your *Julie*.' In this last conjecture she was mistaken; the manuscript in question was the letter to Voltaire on Providence, and Rousseau records in his *Confessions*[73] the occasion of his reading from it, an occasion which was not a success:

Appearances were against me. Shame, always pronounced in me, gave me in the presence of St-Lambert a guilty look, and he took advantage of this in order to humble me. I read to him after dinner the letter I had written to Voltaire, and about which he had heard reports. While I was reading he fell asleep, and I, who had once been so proud, had now become so foolish that I dared not stop, and continued to read while he continued to snore.

Mme d'Épinay's account[74] of the evening does not, on this occasion, contradict Rousseau's: 'Mme d'Houdetot has just dined with us. She brought with her St-Lambert and Rousseau. The Marquis de Croismare said that she made an entry like a princess in a stage tragedy at the moment of disaster. I asked him what he meant by that, but he told me that he always spoke without thinking. Personally, I am convinced that he made the remark intentionally. St-Lambert and the Countess both looked very worried, and Rousseau was no more cheerful. I decided to leave them alone as soon as dinner was over, with the excuse that I needed to rest.'

---

*He also wanted to discuss his unfinished novel with Diderot, and took the manuscript of *Julie* with him. Diderot afterwards complained that, although Rousseau spent hours discussing his own literary work, he had not time to talk to Diderot about his.

†Diderot tells this story in his *Tablettes*: 'I advised him to write telling all to M. de St-Lambert, and to keep away from Mme d'Houdetot. This advice pleased him, and he promised to follow it.'[71]

Mme d'Épinay was thus not present to hear either the reading or the snoring.

Rousseau must have been further unnerved by a letter[75] from Deleyre, dated 22 July 1757, which began, in his usual tone of raillery, with the words: 'They say in Paris that the hermit runs from château to château visiting all the nymphs of the neighbourhood. I would laugh to see him captured by the charms of one of them.' If such rumours were current in Paris, could Rousseau reasonably expect to keep St-Lambert in ignorance? Would he not have done well to follow Diderot's advice, and make some kind of confession? As it was, St-Lambert returned to the front in Germany at the beginning of August little better informed than he had been when he arrived, but evidently more suspicious. What he seems specifically to have suspected was that Rousseau had been preaching to the Countess about the wickedness of adultery, and the supreme virtue of marital fidelity, which was indeed an article of Rousseau's published credo and one of the themes of his novel *Julie*. St-Lambert suspected, in other words, that Rousseau was trying to detach his mistress from him by moralizing, and not that he was trying to steal her from him by love-making. It is even possible that Rousseau's artificially stilted letter of 12 July reinforced this suspicion, for Rousseau enclosed with it a draft copy of some '*Lettres*', most probably his *Lettres morales*,[76] which, in the finished form[77] at any rate, make an eloquent plea for chastity, modesty and conscience against the corrupt sexual morality of Paris.

The departure of St-Lambert did not signal a return to the old intimacy between Rousseau and Sophie: there were to be no more close embraces under the acacia tree and no more rendezvous in her bedroom at Eaubonne. Rousseau was profoundly disappointed.

'After St-Lambert's return to the army', he writes in the *Confessions*,[78] 'I found Mme d'Houdetot greatly changed in her attitude to me. I was more surprised by this than I ought to have been; it upset me more than it should have done; it caused me considerable pain ... I resolved to conquer myself, and do everything to change my foolish passion into a pure and lasting friendship ... But when I tried to speak to her, I found her distracted or embarrassed. She asked me to give her back her letters, which I did with a scrupulousness which she did me the insult of calling into question.'

Rousseau goes on to say that Sophie was afterwards ashamed of doubting his word and that 'that gave me a small advantage with her.' And yet he admits that he himself doubted Sophie's word when she told him she could not return the letters he had written to her because she had burned them: 'No. Letters such as mine are never put in the fire. The letters in *Julie* have been considered passionate. Heavens, what would have been said of these?

No. No woman capable of inspiring such love would have the courage to burn the proof of it.'[79]★

There is conflicting testimony as to what Mme d'Houdetot did with the letters; but clearly she had a very strong motive for burning them at the time she said she did. She was deeply attached to St-Lambert, and was perceptibly terrified at the thought of antagonizing him. Rousseau, however, tried to keep up his meetings with Sophie as frequently as before, if on a more platonic basis.

On the other hand, with Sophie less attentive to him, Rousseau had more time for Mme d'Épinay. She no longer admired him as she had once done, to judge from a remark of hers in a letter to Grimm:[82] 'Rousseau has ceased to be anything in my eyes but a moral dwarf on stilts.' But she was still fond of him and in the same letter she informed Grimm that, after a tearful scene provoked by her reproaching Rousseau for overplaying the part of an 'homme singulier', they had parted as very good friends. They were even on warm enough terms in August to want to exchange their portraits. Rousseau promised her the copy that Maurice-Quentin de La Tour had made of the celebrated portrait exhibited in the Salon of 1753[83] and which the artist was planning to bring to the Hermitage at the end of the month. Rousseau would not allow Mme d'Épinay to pay for it, as she offered,† but he agreed[85] to accept a portrait of her 'as a form of remuneration'.

Rousseau was once again unwell: 'I left you too ill a man not to be worried about you,' Mme d'Épinay said in her letter[86] of 11 August, written from Paris, where she had gone for the accouchement of Mme d'Holbach, second wife of the philosopher, with whom Mme d'Épinay had succeeded in forging a friendship despite her failure to persuade the Holbachs to rent the house at La Briche.

Rousseau replied[87] assuring Mme d'Épinay that he bore his afflictions with patience although he questioned the traditional theory that philosophy cures sorrow: 'I have the feeling that philosophy causes sorrow.' He added graciously: 'The good things that come to me from you are almost the only ones that remain to me,' and he expressed his eagerness to see her again at La Chevrette. 'Good-day, Mother of bears,' he wrote a few days later,[88] 'You are wrong not to be here, for I have a fresh clipped muzzle.' Again he asked her for news of her health and that of Mme

---

★The actual fate of the letters is uncertain. Mme Broutain, a neighbour of Mme d'Houdetot, once claimed to have heard from her that she burned all the letters except one, 'a masterpiece of eloquence and passion', but on another occasion the same Mme Broutain said Mme d'Houdetot spoke of burning all the letters save four.[80] Mme de Vintimille, a niece of Mme d'Houdetot, is reported to have said that Mme d'Houdetot kept the letters, and that they were burned by her granddaughter Mme de Bazancourt.[81]

†'We could make him a little present, passing through your hands.'[84]

d'Holbach: he added that he was feeling sad, but made no reference to Mme d'Houdetot, whose coolness, we can hardly doubt, was the cause of that sadness.

Mme d'Holbach gave birth to her child on 21 August, and a few days later Mme d'Épinay returned to La Chevrette. Rousseau was there to welcome her. He seemed no longer to be unwell; he greeted her affectionately and promised to come again regularly from the Hermitage to spend time with her. When he failed to reappear or send any message Mme d'Épinay grew anxious. Something, she believed, must have happened to him, and it had.

One day in the last week of August Rousseau visited Sophie at Eaubonne to find that she had been weeping. She told him the reason: 'Your follies will cost me the repose of the rest of my days.' He reports in the *Confessions*[89] her saying to him: 'St-Lambert has been informed, and ill-informed. He does me justice, but he is angry; and what is worse he hides a part of his anger.' Sophie assured Rousseau that she had always told her lover of her friendship with him and only kept silent about Rousseau's 'extravagant passion' for her – a passion she had hoped to cure, but which 'St-Lambert now imputes to me as a crime.'

It is not altogether clear from this account what St-Lambert had written in his letter to Sophie, or in what manner he had been 'ill-informed'. But we cannot doubt that Rousseau's memory is exact when he says that Sophie warned him that there must either be a clear break between them or he must behave correctly in future: Rousseau says – and again we can believe him – that his heart was filled with 'rage against the vile slanderers'. He suspected Mme d'Épinay and Grimm of guilt in the matter, and his suspicions were confirmed soon afterwards, when Thérèse told him, for the first time, that Mme d'Épinay had tried to intercept his correspondence with Mme d'Houdetot and – perhaps less truthfully – that she had successfully prevented her from doing so. 'On hearing this,' says Rousseau,[90] 'my rage and indignation are not to be described.'

On Wednesday 31 August[91] Rousseau received from Mme d'Épinay a friendly message[92] to which he sent an unfriendly answer. 'I am worried about you,' she wrote, in what was to be the first of five letters they exchanged in a single day. 'If you had not told me you were in good health I should believe you were ill. I was expecting you here the day before yesterday and again yesterday but you did not come. What is wrong?'

Rousseau replied:[93] 'I cannot tell you anything yet. I am waiting to be better informed, and sooner or later I shall be. In the meantime, be assured that outraged innocence will find a zealous champion to make slanderers repent, whoever they may be.'

'Your letter frightens me,' she wrote back.[94]

What can it mean? I have read it more than twenty-five times and honestly I cannot understand a word. I only see that you are anxious and tormented, and are waiting until you are no longer in that stage before you speak to me. My dear friend, is that what we agreed? What has happened to our friendship, to our trust? How have I come to lose it? ... If you are not here by six o'clock this evening, I shall come to the Hermitage tomorrow whatever the weather and whatever my state of health.

'No,' answered[95] Rousseau, 'I cannot come to see you nor can I receive you here as long as my uneasiness continues ... In the difficulty you pretend to have in understanding my letter I recognize your usual cunning. But do you think me such a dupe as to believe that you really failed to understand it? No. I shall answer your deviousness with frankness, and overcome it.'

He then went on to reveal what was on his mind:

Two lovers happily united and worthy of each other's love are dear to me. I imagine you will not know of whom I speak unless I tell you their names. I assume that someone has tried to separate them, and that I have been made use of to provoke jealousy in one of them. The choice of me is none too clever, but it might fit neatly into a malicious design, and of that design I suspect you.

It is clear from what Rousseau says next that he had been accused of trying to detach Mme d'Houdetot from St-Lambert by preaching against adultery:

I have not hidden from you or from her how much I disapprove of certain liaisons, but I have only expressed the wish that they end as honourably as they begin, and that an illegitimate love should be transformed into an eternal friendship.

Rousseau did not exclude the possibility that his suspicions of Mme d'Épinay were unfounded: 'if so,' he added, 'I shall have a great wrong to repair and never in my life shall I do anything more wholeheartedly'.*

Mme d'Épinay assured him that he had indeed done a great wrong. In her third letter[96] she protested her own innocence and promised him: 'I

---

*However he adds menacingly, 'I shall atone for my errors ... by telling you frankly what the world thinks of you, and what fences you have to mend in your reputation.'

shall be only too pleased to forgive you, and you shall have a better reception here than your suspicions deserve.'

According to the *Confessions*,[97] this offer of Mme d'Épinay's made him feel he must either go to see her or leave the Hermitage forthwith, so he decided to go to see her. In his version of this meeting, she greeted him by throwing her arms round his neck and bursting into tears, while he, on his side, wept no less copiously; the quarrel ended with no explanation being given or received.

Mme d'Épinay gives[98] a rather different account of the episode. She says that Rousseau came to La Chevrette, threw himself on his knees with every sign of the most violent despair, blaming himself for his wrongs and declaring: 'My life will be too short for me to make amends.' He said he had been misled, she claims, by reports that she herself was hopelessly in love with St-Lambert and she reproached him for believing such a tale and for thinking that she could have stooped to slander-mongering through jealousy of Mme d'Houdetot. In the end, she says, Rousseau was more or less pardoned.

Mme d'Épinay's version of the episode appears in a letter to Grimm, whose comment[99] on it is to warn her to be more prudent in her dealings with Rousseau: 'You know madmen are dangerous, especially if one panders to them as you have sometimes done to that poor devil through your ill-judged pity for his insanity.'

In another letter[100] to Grimm, Mme d'Épinay reported a rumour that Mme d'Houdetot had forbidden Rousseau to see her. This rumour was not true, but a letter[101] from Rousseau to Mme d'Épinay does suggest that Sophie had told him he would have to see her less often: 'I went to Eaubonne yesterday, hoping that the walk and Mme d'Houdetot's gaiety would have a soothing effect on me. I found her ill, and I returned worse than I set out. It is absolutely essential for me to abstain from all society and live in solitude until this state of affairs ends one way or another. Rest assured that on the first day of respite I shall not fail to see you.' He added that he had never felt so ill as he had in the past few days: 'I cannot stand the company of anyone – starting with myself.'

A letter[102] from Mme d'Épinay to Grimm suggests that Mme d'Houdetot was also in a bad way: 'The Countess spent a minute or two here yesterday for the first time in ages. Her eyes are swollen as big as fists and she had a terrible headache and she never stopped bemoaning the unfairness of men.'

In his despair Rousseau finally decided that the best way to deal with the situation created by St-Lambert's 'alarming' letter to Sophie was to write to St-Lambert directly – not the kind of letter Diderot had advised him to write, confessing to being in love with St-Lambert's mistress, but an audacious letter[103] of complaint, demanding an explanation of why St-Lambert's mistress had suddenly become so cool towards him:

'From the time I first came to know you,' he wrote,

I have wanted to be your friend. I have seen nothing of you that has not increased that desire. At a time when I was forsaken by everyone dear to me, I was indebted to you for a friend who consoled me in everything, and to whom I grew the more attached the more she spoke to me about you.

You must realize, my dear St-Lambert, that I have good reasons for loving you both and also that my heart is not made of stone. Why, then, is it that you both cause me such suffering? Let me relieve my soul at once of the weight of your wrongs. As I have complained to her about you, I now complain to you about her.

Rousseau went on to remind St-Lambert that the Countess originally sought his company, not he hers, and that once they had made friends, St-Lambert was always present in their conversations: they 'made plans for the time when we should be able, all three of us, to form a delightful society together'. Now 'all has changed except in my heart. Since your departure, Mme d'Houdetot has received me without warmth, she hardly speaks to me, not even about you. She finds all sorts of pretexts for avoiding me ... I do not know what such a sudden change can mean. If I have deserved it, let it be told, and I shall consider myself dismissed.'

Rousseau had evidently made a very shrewd guess at what St-Lambert had suspected, and he decided to rebut the unspoken accusation. He did not apologize for turning to St-Lambert for an explanation of his mistress's behaviour:

Yes, it is from you that I ask it. Do not all her feelings come from you? And who knows this better than I ... Tell me, then, where does her coldness originate? Could you have feared that I might prejudice her against you, and a distorted love of virtue make me perfidious and deceitful? A remark about me in one of your letters prompts me to think you may suspect me of that; but you are mistaken. No, no, St-Lambert. The breast of Jean-Jacques Rousseau will never hold the heart of a traitor and I would despise myself more than you think if I had ever tried to detach her from you.

While Rousseau admitted that he disapproved in principle of adulterous unions, he said he recognized the value of the great love that united St-Lambert and his mistress; indeed he felt that he himself 'had almost become its accomplice'. He ended the letter by saying that he was every day more and more withdrawn from human society. The only company he now cared for, he assured St-Lambert, was that of Mme d'Houdetot and himself: 'if that is denied me I shall die alone and abandoned in my solitude'.

In truth Rousseau was far from withdrawn from human society. Having patched up his quarrel with Mme d'Épinay, he spent more time than ever with her and her friends, as he admits in the *Confessions*:[104] 'While awaiting the effect of my letter I threw myself into amusements that I ought to have looked for sooner.' He even became a house guest at La Chevrette where festivities were planned for the annual fête of the local village and the dedication of the refurbished chapel at the château. Rousseau composed a motet for the last occasion, partly, as he says in the *Confessions*[105] to vindicate his competence as a musician which, despite the continued fame of *Le Devin du village*,* had been called into question 'even at La Chevrette', with the result that 'M. d'Épinay himself was not exempt from doubts about it'. Rousseau offered to provide music for any words M. d'Épinay chose to commission and his son's tutor Jean de Linant produced a text beginning *Ecce sedes hic tonantis*, which Rousseau afterwards discovered he had cribbed from Santeul. The composer was pleased with his work: 'annoyance had inspired the richest music to flow from my pen'.[107]

M. d'Épinay engaged a sizeable orchestra to accompany the soloist Mme Bruna, although he could ill afford such extravagance, and the performance was a resounding success in the composer's own judgement.[108] Rousseau also wrote music for a theatrical entertainment – half play, half mime – with words by Mme d'Épinay herself, which was put on at La Chevrette to celebrate her husband's name-day, the feast of St Denis.†

The consolation Rousseau found as a house guest at La Chevrette for the coolness of Mme d'Houdetot was diminished towards the end of September by the return from the front of Mme d'Épinay's lover. Grimm seemed not at all improved in Rousseau's eyes as a result of his experiences of war, rather to be even more arrogant, pompous and vain than ever. To make way for Grimm, Rousseau was removed from the bedroom next to Mme d'Épinay's and installed in one in a far corner of the château. In the *Confessions*[109] he says he embarrassed his hostess by protesting to her: 'Such is the way that newcomers turn old inhabitants out', adding that Mme d'Épinay was still pretending to him that she was not having an affair with Grimm, although it was obvious to everyone.

Rousseau makes no effort to deny that he was annoyed by the precedence

---

*In the same month of August this little opera of Rousseau's was performed in the theatre of Carouge, at the gates of Geneva.[106]
†9 October. M. d'Épinay's Christian names were Denis-Joseph.

which Mme d'Épinay accorded to Grimm and which Grimm loftily assumed. He mentions an occasion when she invited him to join her for supper beside the fire in her bedroom: 'Grimm followed us up, and seeing a little table set up with only two places, he promptly sat down opposite Mme d'Épinay, opened his napkin and began to eat without saying a word to me.'[110] Rousseau maintains that this gesture was typical of Grimm's new behaviour towards him: 'he did not treat me as his inferior; he simply looked on me as a nonentity'.[111]

Rousseau says he was also put off by Grimm's new foppishness – 'he spent two hours every morning polishing his nails'; his conceit – 'despite his fleshy face and huge dull eyes, he fancied himself with the ladies';[112] his falseness – 'at the death of the Comte de Friese he wept copiously every morning in public, and stopped immediately he thought no one could see him';[113] and his unwillingness to introduce any of his friends to Rousseau while taking advantage of every friend Rousseau introduced him to. The snubbing in front of Mme d'Épinay was just too much, and Rousseau informed her that he had decided to have nothing more to do with Grimm.

Mme d'Épinay begged him to change his mind. 'Why do you harden yourself against a friend,' she asked in a long letter[114] she wrote to him instead of speaking to him on the subject. She reminded him that he had been a friend of Grimm's for years, and known him 'as a man with the most lovable qualities of heart beneath a cold exterior'; she suggested that Grimm needed to be understood as a man who 'was born melancholy', 'extremely sensitive', 'reserved', and had a soul that was 'true and upright'. She urged Rousseau not to let his judgement be swayed by bitterness.

Rousseau says he allowed himself to be persuaded: 'I went to Grimm,' he recalls,[115] 'to apologize for the injuries he had done me ... I acted on the false belief that there is no hatred that cannot be disarmed by gentleness and decent behaviour ... He greeted me like a Roman emperor, with a haughtiness I have seen in no one else ... He gave me the kiss of peace with a light embrace, which was rather like the accolade conferred by a king on new-made knights.'

Mme d'Houdetot was pleased to hear of their reconciliation. She wrote[116]* to express her satisfaction: 'I cannot say how happy I am to see you reunited with your friends; you are not made to be separated from them; they are worthy of you, and you are worthy of them.' She wanted the four friends – St-Lambert, Grimm, Diderot and Rousseau himself – always to remain together. As for herself, she declared that she would never cease to wish Rousseau well and be concerned for him: 'that feeling is as true in my heart as any sincere friendship for you'. But she also

---

*This is the earliest surviving letter from Sophie to Rousseau written after May 1757 – letters from the intervening period having been returned by him to her.

reminded him that her great love for St-Lambert had filled the best part of her heart for the past five years: 'Respect and do not condemn a passion to which we have been able to join so much honesty; and please, from the sublime plane to which virtue lifts you, forgive two hearts who will never forsake their love of virtue.'

This last injunction suggests both that Sophie had been infected with the rhetoric of virtue by Rousseau's novel *Julie* and that Rousseau really had been going on and on to her about the immorality of adulterous unions notwithstanding his efforts to push her to the brink of one with himself. His reply,[117] written from the Hermitage on 1 October, struck a disconsolate note: 'Winter approaches: I am getting weaker; I am going to cease seeing you, and I have no hope of living to see either the spring or my homeland ... They say you are in the country very far from here.* I hope very much that you will find someone there whose company will prove less tedious than mine and who will be able to restore your taste for walks that I was unlucky enough to make you lose.' With equal bitterness he asked whether her wish to give him to other friends meant that she wanted to rid herself of him; he promised he would never be a nuisance. However, he expressed the hope of seeing her at La Chevrette for the festivity in honour of M. d'Épinay, which was only nine days ahead.

This last hope was not disappointed. Sophie came to the party, but Rousseau found little opportunity of conversation with her. The music he had written for Mme d'Épinay's theatrical show was well received, although the hero of the occasion, her husband, was probably too worried about his financial problems to enjoy himself wholeheartedly; he knew he was about to be dismissed from the lucrative office of tax farmer. M. d'Épinay had also the humiliation of seeing that his wife's lover Grimm had become the effective master of the house. There was dancing as well as the entertainment, and Rousseau squirmed as he watched Sophie take the floor with other partners.

When the *fête* was over he wrote her the long letter[118] which has already been quoted, the letter he did not send, and which, in the absence of earlier letters which he did send her, tells us much about the extent of his feelings for her. In the first four paragraphs he addresses her as '*tu*', then changes to the formal '*vous*':

'What has become of that time, that happy time?' he demands.

All our conversations are now going to be marked by coldness and embarrassment, sadness or silence. Two enemies, even two strangers, would treat each other with less reserve than our two hearts, which were

*Probably on her husband's estates in Normandy.

made to love one another. My heart, constricted by fear, no longer dares give life to the flames that devour it. My frightened soul sinks and draws in on itself. All my feelings are weighed down by pain, and this letter, damp from my cold tears, has nothing left of the sacred fire which used to flow through my pen in sweeter times ... it is easier for you to change, O Sophie, than it is for you to hide that change from my eyes ...

Help me, for pity's sake, to deceive myself; my tormented heart could not ask for anything better. I try all the time to imagine that you still have the tender concern for me that you no longer have. I twist everything you say to me so as to interpret it in my favour ... and as I cannot obtain any real sign of affection from you, a mere trifle is enough to inspire some figment of my imagination. The last time our eyes met, when you unveiled new charms to kindle new fires in me, you looked at me twice while you were dancing. All your movements are printed in the depths of my soul. My hungry eyes followed all your steps; not one of your gestures escaped my observation, and in the splendour of your triumph, this soft heart was simple enough to believe that you deigned to concern yourself with me. Sophie, cruel Sophie, give me back the friend who is so dear to me.

A day or two after he had finished this effusion, and thought better of sending it, Rousseau wrote Sophie a more measured letter[119] expressing concern about her health. Having heard that she had lost weight and was not eating, he reproached her for rejecting her food as well as her friends. As for himself, he said his illnesses and the bad weather were likely to confine him to his house until the spring. 'I feel alone, forgotten by everyone dear to me. I have ceased to live, and yet I breathe. That is enough to tell you how I am.'

Sophie's reply[120] was sweetness itself: 'I implore you, my dear Citizen, not to give yourself up to the black melancholy which obsesses you: that is the first entreaty of my friendship and the most urgent. Do not imagine yourself to be alone in the world; you have friends and you must not do them the wrong of thinking they could forget you or forsake you.'

She informed Rousseau that she was going to La Chevrette the following Friday and hoped she would find him there. He went, and they met, and Rousseau seems to have undertaken the improbable mission of reconciling her with Grimm after some sort of misunderstanding. On that occasion Sophie invited Rousseau to visit her at Eaubonne the following Thursday. It promised to be a sad visit since Sophie was going there to close the house, and 'say farewell to the valley'.[121]

In the event Rousseau went there in the highest of spirits. For at long last he had received a reply to his bold letter to St-Lambert. Diderot claimed that St-Lambert had told him Rousseau had written him a letter that 'could only be answered with a stick';[122] in fact St-Lambert's answer[123] was a model of cordiality. It was written from Wolfenbuttel on 11 October. In it he begged Rousseau not to accuse 'our friend' (Mme d'Houdetot) of 'fickleness or coldness'; he assured him that she was capable of neither: 'Her heart has not changed towards you; she loves you, she honours you; but she has seen less of you because she wanted to spare me the pains you should not have caused me, but have in fact caused me; and it is my own fault. It is I who tried to bring you together, and it is certainly not for that that I reproach myself.'

St-Lambert went on to explain that he had noticed a certain change in Mme d'Houdetot when he had seen her in Paris in the summer; he had felt that change cruelly and he added frankly that he had suspected that Rousseau was responsible for it. Although he had every confidence in Rousseau's austere moral principles, all sorts of stupid fears had troubled his mind. But now he regretted having entertained such thoughts and he went on to apologize both for having 'made three people unhappy' and for having done an injustice to Rousseau. He assured him 'We have neither of us ceased to love and esteem you.'

Having read* this letter, Rousseau wrote[124] at once in joyful mood to Sophie: 'I shall come to dine with you tomorrow. I shall bring an entirely new heart that will please you – and I shall have in my pocket an invincible charm [St-Lambert's letter] that will guarantee your friendship.'

Mme d'Houdetot was less exhilarated. She had just learned that St-Lambert was ill;† he had had a stroke which left him paralysed in an arm and a leg, and he was being sent to Aix for treatment. She had always been worried that he might once again be wounded – or worse – in battle, even though she had been assured that he would not be sent to where the action was.[125] He was unscarred in the war; instead, at the age of forty-one he was struck with the same paralysis which had affected Gauffecourt at the age of sixty-five.

Rousseau expressed polite concern about the health of Sophie's lover, but he was too pleased to find himself still on good terms with both of them to realize the full implications of St-Lambert's changed status. Reduced from the virile role of the soldier-poet to that of an invalid in need of loving care, St-Lambert was henceforth to claim that part of Sophie's heart which she had given to Rousseau himself, as the ailing and

---

*In the *Confessions* Rousseau writes, 'St-Lambert's reply brought consolation of which I had much need just then, with the assurances of friendship and esteem with which it was filled, and which gave me the courage and the strength to deserve them. From that time forth I did my duty, but it is a fact that if St-Lambert had been less sensitive, less generous, less honourable a man, I should have been lost without hope.'

†As indeed had Rousseau: St-Lambert mentioned in his letter from Wolfenbuttel that he had a stroke.

ill-used outsider. If Rousseau had formerly been St-Lambert's rival for Sophie as a mistress, St-Lambert was now Rousseau's rival for Sophie as a mother-figure; and against such competition Rousseau could not hope to win.

The joy of his restored friendship with Sophie was marred by trouble that developed from another quarter, a trivial event in itself, but one which was to lead to a breach between Rousseau and Mme d'Épinay and her whole circle of friends at La Chevrette, even with one who had not yet joined that circle, Diderot. The crisis arose from Mme d'Épinay's plan to go to Geneva to consult Dr Tronchin in person about certain problems connected with her health. She invited Rousseau to accompany her, and he refused.

In October 1757 Rousseau had two strong reasons for not wishing to accompany Mme d'Épinay to Geneva, neither of which he wished at the time to avow. Even in the *Confessions* he only hints at them, but in a note he added years later to the copy he kept of one of his letters to Sophie[126] he reveals that those reasons were, first, 'the horrible crime of being in love with Mme d'Houdetot and being unable to drag himself away from her', and, secondly, 'a reason I could not speak of to Mme d'Épinay'. This second reason was that he did not wish to put himself in a position where he could be assumed to be Mme d'Épinay's lover. On the testimony of servants' gossip,[127] Rousseau believed that Mme d'Épinay was pregnant by her actual lover, Grimm, and that her sudden desire to consult Dr Tronchin in person was prompted by anxiety about her condition.* Rousseau thought, but could not say, that Grimm was the man who should accompany her to Geneva. He did not want to be 'trapped'[131] into taking Grimm's place.

Grimm by this time had come back from the war, a veteran more puffed up than ever with his own importance. 'I congratulate you on the return of Grimm,' wrote Deleyre in a letter[132] to Rousseau on 20 October. Rousseau saw no grounds for congratulation. Indeed he soon found a new reason for disliking Grimm. He learned that Grimm was trying to rob him of his livelihood by saying that he was no good at the work of a music copyist.[133]

According to the *Confessions*, Rousseau had not at first taken too seriously Mme d'Épinay's suggestion that he should go with her to Geneva. He did not even believe that she intended him to: 'I simply laughed at the fine figure I should cut if I had been so foolish as to agree to the proposal.'[134]

---

*Leigh[128] suggests that Rousseau was mistaken in thinking that Mme d'Épinay was pregnant, but Bernard Gagnebin and Marcel Raymond[129] argue that the possibility is not excluded, especially in view of the fact that Mme d'Épinay suffered an unspecified 'accident' (a miscarriage?) at Châtillon on 6 November 1757.[130]

Besides, he was never well at the onset of winter: 'and what use would one invalid be to the *cortège* of another?'[135] The whole idea was lightly brushed aside. What made it take on a more serious and disturbing aspect was an unwelcome letter from Diderot, a letter all the more cruelly timed in that it followed swiftly on the good letter that Rousseau had received from St-Lambert, spoiling his joy with an access of fury.

'I am made to love you and to bring you sorrow,' Diderot's letter[136] began.

I learn that Mme d'Épinay is going to Geneva, but I have not heard whether you will accompany her. My friend, if you are happy with Mme d'Épinay you must go with her, and if you are not, you must do so with all the more alacrity. Are you overwhelmed by the weight of your indebtedness to her? Then here is a chance to repay a part of it, and ease your conscience. Will you find in the rest of your life another opportunity to prove to her your gratitude? She is going to a place where she will be a total stranger. She is ill, and she will need amusement and distraction. The winter! Look, my friend, your health may be a stronger impediment to travel than I realize. But are you any worse today than you were a month ago or than you will be at the beginning of spring? Will you make the journey in three months' time more easily than today?

For myself, I declare that if I could not stand travelling in a carriage, I would take up my walking-stick and follow her. And, then, are you not afraid that your behaviour will be misunderstood? You will be suspected of ingratitude or some other secret motive. I know very well that whatever you do, you will have the approval of your own conscience to support you, but is that approval enough on its own? Is it permissible to ignore the judgement of others? At all events, I write this letter to discharge an obligation towards you and towards myself. If it displeases you, throw it in the fire ... Farewell, I am your friend and I embrace you.

One can well believe Rousseau when he says[137] he trembled with rage and amazement as he read this letter and could hardly get to the end of it, short as it was. Why should Diderot, who had only recently made friends with Mme d'Épinay after avoiding her for years, intervene in this fashion? What were these 'suspicions of a secret motive' Diderot spoke of? Rousseau asserts in the *Confessions*[138] that the letter was sent to La Chevrette, so that Mme d'Épinay would be aware of it, and that Diderot had folded it in an unusual way, so that its contents could easily be read. The letter itself, which is preserved at Neuchâtel, does not confirm this recollection. It is addressed, 'To Monsieur Rousseau, At the Hermitage or La Chevrette', and it is not folded in an unusual way.*

As soon as he had calmed down enough to write, Rousseau drafted a reply to Diderot; then, still in 'a blind rage'[140] he set off to La Chevrette to read it aloud, together with Diderot's original, to Mme d'Épinay. This was his letter:[141]

My dear friend,

You cannot know either the magnitude of my indebtedness to Mme d'Épinay or the extent to which it obliges me; you cannot know if she really needs me on her journey, if she seriously wishes me to accompany her, if it is possible for me to do so, or what reasons I might have for not doing so. I do not refuse to discuss all these matters with you at leisure, but in the meantime, you must agree that for you to prescribe so categorically what I should do, without your putting yourself in a position to judge, my dear philosopher, is to talk like a fool. What is even worse, as I see it, is that the advice you offer is not your own. Apart from the fact that I am in no mood to let myself be bullied in your name by some third or fourth party, I detect in all these manoeuvres a certain deviousness which does not suit your open character, and from which you would do well, for your sake and mine, to abstain in future ...

When Rousseau arrived at La Chevrette, he found Mme d'Épinay in the company of Grimm, so he read the letter aloud to the pair of them. He had the impression that they were 'amazed at the audacity of a man who was usually so timid', and although they did not make any comment at the time, Rousseau observed that Grimm, 'that arrogant man', lowered 'his eyes to the ground and dared not lift them to meet mine'.[142] Only later did Rousseau come to suspect that all three of them – Grimm, Mme d'Épinay and Diderot – were plotting together to get him out of France.[143]

Having read the two letters to Mme d'Épinay and her lover at La Chevrette, Rousseau took them next to Eaubonne to read to Mme d'Houdetot. She was more vocal, but less encouraging than he had hoped. She told him she wished he would agree to go to Geneva with Mme d'Épinay, lest she herself might be compromised by his refusal. Not only did she suspect, correctly, that Rousseau's chief motive for refusing to go to Geneva was his desire to remain near her, she also feared that other people – including St-Lambert – would entertain the same suspicion and assume that something was still going on between Rousseau and herself. She

*As Leigh observes, 'It would have been impossible to read it without breaking the seal.'[139]

seems, however, not to have pressed Rousseau very energetically to accept Diderot's advice; she simply implored him to take care 'to avoid scandal at any price'.[144]

Rousseau was by this time so displeased with Mme d'Épinay that he was on the point, he told Sophie, of leaving the Hermitage altogether; but again she dissuaded him from a course of action which could only give rise to unfortunate gossip and conjectures.

Tuesday 25 October was the appointed day for the departure of Mme d'Épinay for Geneva. Grimm was not in the large party she planned to take with her. Rousseau, feeling it was Grimm's duty to go but unable to say so openly, decided to write a long letter to Grimm in the hope that he would agree that at least it was not his, Rousseau's, duty to go. At the time Rousseau did not think that Grimm had had any share in Diderot's decision to intervene as he had, although it is more than likely that it was Grimm who had prompted Diderot to write the offending letter.[145] So Rousseau wrote,[146] in all innocence:

Tell me, Grimm, why do all my friends think that I ought to accompany Mme d'Épinay? Am I wrong or are they all bewitched? Do they all share that base prejudice which is always ready to help the rich and saddle the poor with a hundred useless duties which only make their poverty greater and more inescapable? I wish to refer this matter to you alone. Although no doubt you are as prejudiced as the others, I still believe you are fair enough to be able to put yourself in my place and decide where my duty lies. Hear then, my friend, what I have to say, and tell me what I ought to do, for whatever you advise, I promise to do at once.

What is it that makes it a duty for me to accompany Mme d'Épinay? Friendship, gratitude, or the help I could offer her? Let us examine these points in turn. If Mme d'Épinay has shown me friendship, I have shown her more. Attentions have been mutual and not least as great on my side as on hers. Since we are both invalids, I am no more obliged to wait on her than she is obliged to wait on me, unless it is the duty of the greater invalid to nurse the lesser. Just because my afflictions are incurable, is that a reason for disregarding them? I will add one more word. She has friends who are not so ill, not so poor, not so jealous of their liberty, and less pressed for time; friends of whom she is just as fond as she is of me, and I cannot see why some of them should not consider it their duty to accompany her.* By what bizarre reasoning am I singled out, I who am the least fitted to undertake the duty? If I loved Mme d'Épinay enough to

---

*In this sentence, at least, Rousseau comes close to suggesting to Grimm that it was his duty to go.

sacrifice myself to amuse her, how little would she love me if she wanted to purchase the services of such a clumsy courtier as myself at the price of my health, my life, my pain, my repose and every soul I possess? I do not know whether I ought to have offered to go with her, but I do know that she could not have accepted the offer unless she had the usual hard heart of the rich, which I have always believed her to be very far from having.

As for kindnesses, I do not like them, I do not want them, and I do not feel grateful to those who force me to accept them, as I explained clearly to Mme d'Épinay before I received any from her. It is not that I object any more than anyone else to the sweet chains of friendship – but once the chain is pulled too tight, it breaks, and I am free. What has Mme d'Épinay done for me? You know better than anyone else, and I can speak frankly to you on the subject. She had a little house built for me at the Hermitage, and persuaded me to live there, and I add with pleasure that she did her utmost to make it a pleasant and safe habitation for me.

What have I done, on my side, for Mme d'Épinay? At a time when I was thinking of returning to my native city, and wished very much to do so, and ought to have done so, she moved heaven and earth to keep me here. With her pleas, with intrigues even, she overcame my very proper and prolonged resistance. My will, my tastes, my preferences, the disapproval of my friends all yielded in my heart to the voice of my friendship for her, and I allowed myself to be dragged to the Hermitage. Since that time I have always felt myself to be in another person's house; and that moment of weakness has already caused me bitter repentance. My loving friends, bent on disturbing me, have never left me a minute in peace, and I have often wept with regret at not being a thousand miles away from them ... Mme d'Épinay, often alone at her château, wanted me to keep her company. Indeed that is why she got me to the Hermitage in the first place. So after making a sacrifice to friendship, I had to make another to gratitude. One needs to be poor, to have no manservant, to hate fuss and to have my kind of soul to know what it means to live in the house that belongs to another person.

However, I have lived for two years in Mme d'Épinay's house, in constant subjection while listening all the time to high-flown discourses on liberty ... Well, then, take one hour of a man's time and consider what it represents in money, and then take Mme d'Épinay's kindnesses and balance them against the sacrifice of my design to return to my own country and my two years of slavery* here and then tell me which of us, she or I, has the greater obligation to the other.

*It is interesting to contrast this protest at 'two years of slavery' with Rousseau's avowal

Next, there is the question of the help I might offer Mme d'Épinay on her journey to Geneva. She is setting off in a good post-chaise, accompanied by her husband, her son, his tutor, and five or six servants. She is going to a populous city where there is no lack of social life, and she will only have difficulty in choosing which people to meet. She is going to Dr Tronchin, her physician, an intelligent man, much admired and much sought after. She will be living with a distinguished family, where she will find all the necessary resources for the restoration of her health, for friendship and for amusement. Then consider my situation, my ill health, my disposition, my means, my tastes, my way of life ... and tell me, I beg you, what sort of help I could offer Mme d'Épinay on her journey, and what sort of agonies I should have to endure to be of any use to her whatever. Could I bear the post-chaise? Could I expect to travel so far, and at such speed without a mishap? Should I have to make them stop every five minutes for me to get down* or should I have to accelerate my sufferings and my death by containing myself? Let Diderot make light of my life and my health as he will, but my affliction is well known and the most celebrated surgeons of Paris can certify it, and considering how much I suffer, I am hardly less tired of being alive than others are tired of seeing me living so long.

Mme d'Épinay would have the prospect of repeated inconvenience, a sorry spectacle, and perhaps some misadventure on the journey ... of course I could follow her carriage on foot, as Diderot wants me to, but the mud, the rain and the snow would hold me up at this time of year. However well I ran, how could I cover sixty miles a day? And if I let the carriage go on without me, what help would I be to the person inside it?

Moreover, Rousseau added, he could be of no use to Mme d'Épinay if he ever got to Geneva, since his acquaintances there would not suit her nor hers him. He would not have the clothes to accompany her in polite society, although he adds bitterly, 'If I were better dressed, I might pass for a footman.' What is more, he suggests that even if he did agree to go, Diderot would soon find new grounds for criticism and would doubtless accuse him of neglecting Mme Levasseur and her daughter in order to amuse himself with a rich friend. He expressed his dismay at the fact that neither Diderot nor his other friends understood him:

No one seems to be able to put himself in my place, and they all refuse to

to Malesherbes some years later, that 'I did not begin to live until I arrived at the Hermitage on 9 April 1756'.[147]

    *As Rousseau explained on another occasion he needed to 'use a chamber-pot every five minutes'.

see that I am a creature apart, having neither the character and principles nor the resources of other people, so that I must not be judged by their standards. If anyone comments on my poverty, it is not to notice what consoles me for it, but only to make that poverty harder for me to bear. And so we see the philosopher Diderot, sitting in his study by a cosy fire, wrapped in his fur-lined dressing-gown, wanting me to travel sixty miles a day in winter on foot in the mud, following a post-chaise, because, after all, running along in dirty clothes is the poor man's destiny. But the truth is that Mme d'Épinay, rich as she is, does not deserve such an insult from Jean-Jacques Rousseau. Do you imagine that the philosopher Diderot, for all his talk, would even dream of actually running behind someone's carriage if he was too unwell to ride inside?

Rousseau ended the letter by asking Grimm squarely what he thought he ought to do. He explained that his inclination was to leave the Hermitage, but felt it his duty not to do so in a spirit of discontent that would give the appearance of a quarrel with Mme d'Épinay. Besides, it would be difficult for him to leave just as winter was beginning, and he would prefer to wait for the spring when his departure would be more natural. He ended on a note of renewed bitterness: 'I am determined then to seek a retreat unknown to all these barbarous tyrants that are called one's friends.'

No sooner had Rousseau sent this letter to Grimm than he began to regret it. He admitted to Sophie that he had written it in heat and indignation and that it was full of things that were better left unsaid. On her side, she made it clear to him in a letter dated 26 October[148] – the same day on which he was writing the long letter[149] to Grimm – that he must not make people think he was refusing to go to Geneva just in order to stay near her: 'I am waiting impatiently for news of your journey,' she wrote, 'whether you make it or not, and I wish earnestly that you will not be thought to be in the wrong; I am sure that you will not feel yourself to be, whatever you decide; but, my friend, I am very anxious that others should not do so, because I want your friends to consider you to be as irreproachable as I believe you are in fact.'

In the same letter she assured him that he was of all her friends the one she cherished most, but she was careful to draw a distinction between love and friendship, between her feelings for St-Lambert and those she had for Rousseau: 'My heart is satisfied that the goodness it receives from a lover such as he and a friend such as you leaves nothing to be desired.'

In the *Confessions*[150] Rousseau says he had by this time resigned himself to seeing in Sophie nothing more than 'my friend and the mistress of my friend'; and on the occasion of his reconciliation with her he says, 'we formed the charming project of an intimate society of three'. At Sophie's suggestion, Rousseau[151] wrote to St-Lambert to let him know that he had been to see her – she having evidently told him that nothing henceforth should be hidden from her lover. After expressing a proper concern about St-Lambert's health, Rousseau wrote:

I passed a sad and deplorable half-day at Eaubonne on Tuesday. Our hearts held you between them, and our eyes were never dry as we spoke of you. I told our beloved friend that her attachment to you was henceforth a virtue; she was so touched that she wanted me to write to you, and I gladly obey. Yes, my children, be friends for ever; there are no longer souls like yours, and you both deserve to love each other unto death.

It is not altogether clear what St-Lambert was meant to understand by certain words in this paragraph. Was the occasion 'sad' because Mme d'Houdetot was about to leave Eaubonne to spend the winter in Paris, or 'sad' because so many tears were shed over St-Lambert's suffering the effects of a stroke? As for the word 'henceforth', could St-Lambert's suspicions that Rousseau had been preaching to Sophie about the sinfulness of her adultery be eased by the assurance that Rousseau would henceforth consider it virtuous? And what could St-Lambert have felt on being addressed, with his mistress, as 'my children' by a man who was only four years older than he was?

In the same letter, Rousseau informed St-Lambert that his friendship with Grimm had been restored by Mme d'Épinay's efforts, but that Diderot was still angry with him because of his refusal to accompany Mme d'Épinay to Geneva. He then went on to explain why he had refused, again no doubt to satisfy Sophie's urgent wish that St-Lambert should not think that he was staying behind to be near her. He emphasized his incapacity and his inadequate means; he even added a rhetorical flourish: 'Ah! St-Lambert, it seems to me that my heart is prouder because you love me. Tell me, should your friend exhibit his poverty and slavery in his native land in the *cortège* of a tax-farmer's wife?'

Rousseau ended the letter with a disturbing account of Mme d'Houdetot's health: 'It is getting worse and worse; she is losing weight; she has stomach pains and indigestion; she has no appetite, and she only eats unhealthy foods.' He mentioned that she was going to take the waters at Passy, but suggested that what she really needed was to consult a good doctor and adopt a sound diet, and he begged St-Lambert to use his influence with her to make her follow this sensible course of action.

Mme d'Épinay's departure for Geneva was delayed because her son was taken ill. Grimm, in a first 'interim' reply[152] to Rousseau's long letter, suggested that there was still time for him to offer to accompany her, and he urged him to do so 'in the sure knowledge of what her answer would be'. Such a move, Grimm suggested, would enable Rousseau to tell his friends — 'since you seem so very anxious to reply to them' — that the reason why he was not going was that he had offered and been refused.

Rousseau regarded this as a trap: 'I did not fall into it,' he asserts in the *Confessions*,[153] 'I simply wrote to Mme d'Épinay on the subject of her son's illness a letter as polite as it could be.' The actual text[154] of the letter is far from polite. Having expressed his sympathy in one short sentence over her son's illness, Rousseau goes on to complain at length to Mme d'Épinay about the 'manoeuvres' behind the efforts of Diderot and Mme d'Houdetot to persuade him to accompany her to Geneva: 'they lead me to suspect a conspiracy of which you are the motivator ... I find in it all an air of tyranny and intrigue which makes me very angry.' He closes the letter with the words: 'I do not know how all this will end, but whatever happens, rest assured that I shall never forget your kindness to me, and when you no longer want me as a slave you will always have me as a friend.'

Rousseau realized that his long letter to Grimm might produce, as he put it to Sophie,[155] 'a quarrel among friends', but he seems not to have considered how much he had himself done to provoke the quarrel. He told Sophie that he consoled himself with the knowledge that at least his friendship with her was secure; but again he wrote without much tact, 'Perhaps one day, knowing my antipathy to rank and fortune, people will say "She was noble and rich, and yet he loved her unto death."'

For once, he underestimated the cynicism of the public, which was rather disposed to suspect that being noble and rich was just what made Sophie d'Houdetot so attractive to him. He was to see less of her in the weeks that followed, for with the approach of winter, she closed down the household at Eaubonne and returned to Paris. He contemplated her departure in the lowest of spirits: 'Can I ever hope to see spring again?' he asked her in his next letter.[156] 'And even to see you again?' He tried not to yield to depression. 'Although I am ill and melancholy,' he wrote, 'my life is not without pleasure; I am sheltered here from tedious company; I continue my work on ethics; and I think about you. I believe more than ever that sublime virtue and sacred friendship are the sovereign good of man, which he must always strive to achieve if he is to be happy.'

These elevated reflections were soon interrupted by Grimm's 'definitive' reply[157] to Rousseau's letter. If very little longer, it was decidedly more unpleasant than his 'provisional' one:

'I have done my best,' Grimm wrote,

to avoid a positive answer to the horrible apologia you addressed to me. You press me for one, and I shall consider only my duty to myself and my friends, whom you insult, in giving it to you.

I never thought it your duty to have gone to Geneva with Mme d'Épinay. If your first impulse had been to offer to do so, it would have been for her to forbid you, by reminding you of what you, in your situation, have to consider – your health, and the women you have dragged into your retreat. That is my opinion. You did not feel any such impulse, and that does not shock me. It is true that on my return from the army, I learned that despite all the objections I had pointed out to you, you had been planning to return to Geneva for some time past, and therefore it did not surprise me that my friends should be surprised at your lingering here when such an honourable opportunity of going to Geneva presented itself.

I never understood your monstrous system; now it simply makes me shudder with indignation as I contemplate such odious principles, such baseness and duplicity. You dare to speak of your 'slavery' to me – to me, who have for two years been the daily witness of all the marks of the most tender and genuine friendship that you have received from Mme d'Épinay. If I could make myself forgive you, I should consider myself unfit to have a friend. I will never set eyes on you again for as long as I live, and I shall consider myself fortunate if I can expunge the memory of your deeds from my mind. I beg you to forget me and not to trouble my soul again.

Rousseau's rejoinder[158] was short: 'I resisted my own better judgement; I have learned too late what you are. So here is the letter you took so long to think out. I return it to you.[159] It is not for me. You may show mine to the whole world, and display your hatred openly. That will be one falsehood the less on your part.'

Sophie had in the meantime received a copy of Grimm's 'interim' letter to Rousseau, and she tried to persuade him not to be offended by it; not having seen Grimm's second letter, she may even have expected to succeed.

'My dear Citizen,' she wrote from Paris,[160] 'I see nothing in Grimm's letter of what you seem to fear. It seems to me simply that he does not attach as much importance as Diderot and I do to your going to Geneva, and he thinks you do not need to be so vigorous in justifying yourself when you are not in the wrong.' In any case, she informed Rousseau, Mme d'Épinay had already departed, so there was nothing left for him to do but control himself and moderate his passions. She herself still dreaded being a victim of the storm, and longed for it all to die down. However, by the time her message reached Rousseau, he had received Grimm's second letter and his indignation was greater than ever, as he hastened to explain to Sophie:[161]

'I have just received from Grimm a letter which has made me tremble, and I have sent it back to him at once from fear of reading it a second time. Madame, all those I loved now hate me, and you know my heart so well that that will tell you enough. Everything I learned about Mme d'Épinay is only too true – and I have discovered more ... I am going to leave the Hermitage.'

Sophie was not only distressed by Rousseau's news, but alarmed, and alarmed for herself. She again urged Rousseau to calm down, and to tell her more: 'Am I involved in all this?' she asked[162] repeatedly. 'I know you suspected Mme d'Épinay of a strange piece of mischief. Has there been any development of that?'

Sophie was presumably referring to what Rousseau had told her about Mme d'Épinay's efforts to intercept the love-letters that Thérèse had carried between them, and it appears that Thérèse had just told him more about that episode. Clearly, however, Rousseau was too agitated to give Sophie the precise information she needed to be reassured. He interpreted[163] her injunctions to him to calm himself as a sign that she was forsaking him: 'I could be abandoned by all the world, and endure it ... but you ... you hate me! ... You despise me! ... you who know my heart. Good God, am I a scoundrel? A scoundrel, I? I learn it very late ... Ah, if I am wicked, how evil is the whole human race!'

He went on to say that he would like to write to St-Lambert in order to calm his troubled soul and he asked Sophie for his address on the assumption that she would agree to his doing so. Far from agreeing, Sophie was appalled at the prospect: 'I forbid you to write to anyone at all in the state you are now in ... not even to my friend.' She repeated the interdiction three times in the same short letter.[164]

Sophie was still not well,* and still very afraid that Rousseau's quarrels would lead to St-Lambert learning more than she wanted him to know. Rousseau, for his part, became increasingly disturbed, and when Sophie's letters did not reach him as quickly as he expected, he assumed that she was deliberately leaving his letters to her unanswered. He sent her a bitter protest[165] on All Souls' Day, 'the day of mourning and affliction', saying that her neglect was making him 'die of sorrow', and the following day[166] he wrote to accuse her of 'barbaric' neglect: 'This silence is a refinement of cruelty. You will be told of the wretched state I have been in for the past eight days.'

Rousseau proposed to have Thérèse take the letter to Sophie in Paris and to bear witness to his distress.

*She told Rousseau in her letter of 1 November (see above) that her stomach was still upset, and that her health was affected by worry about that of St-Lambert, although her news of him was better; he had recovered some feeling in his paralysed limbs.

'And you too,' the letter continued, 'you too, Sophie, think me wicked! Oh God, if you believe it – to whom can I appeal?' He went on to talk of throwing himself in front of her carriage and being crushed by its wheels so that he might 'at least drag from you some regret for my death'. He assured her that she and St-Lambert were the last attachments of his heart: 'I shall think of you constantly. I can detach myself from you only by renouncing life itself.' He added, without much conviction, 'I ask of you no sign of remembrance; speak of me no more; do not write to me, forget that you have ever honoured me with the name of friend.'

Two letters from Sophie then reached Rousseau at the Hermitage before he had finished this extravagant missive, and the following day he posted it to her with the addition of a more moderately worded note:[167] 'this fragment will show you a soul which belongs to you in a situation which is new to it'. He admitted to her that he had not altogether recovered his composure: 'One is reborn little by little: serenity, alas, does not return to the soul as promptly as sorrow ... the storm has calmed, but the sea is still turbulent.'

He explained that he had still received no word from Diderot, and said he did not know whether Grimm had shown Diderot the letter in which he called him a monster. He only hoped Diderot would judge him on the basis of sixteen years of friendship rather than of one day's anger.

Rousseau at this stage wanted to repair his friendship with Diderot, and even asked Sophie to intervene with him on his behalf, to go and appeal to Diderot to have 'some pity for a heart so tormented'. Rousseau added that he was, in any case, eager to further Sophie's own acquaintance with Diderot: 'I would have as much satisfaction in seeing Diderot in your company as I would have repugnance in seeing Grimm there.'

He ended his letter by informing her that he was about to leave the Hermitage: 'I must drag my bed through the mud to the village of Montmorency to a hole* I have found there in which to pass the winter.'

Sophie, on learning of his plan to move to Montmorency, implored[169] him once again not to leave the Hermitage. She pointed out that by doing so he would only be giving Mme d'Épinay a new reason to take offence; he had, after all, nothing to reproach Mme d'Épinay for other than her failure to reply to a somewhat aggressive letter he had written to her. It was not Mme d'Épinay herself, Sophie reminded him, who was responsible for his present trouble, but the 'all-too-ardent zeal of your friends'.

As for Rousseau's request for her to intervene with Diderot, Sophie urged him instead to write to Diderot himself 'in a spirit of tenderness and

---

*In a letter to Coindet he called it a 'barn', saying he was too busy packing up to receive any visitors.[168]

in the fullness of your heart'. Her news of St-Lambert ('my dear heart') was that he was beginning thermal treatment at Aix-les-Bains, but had not yet recovered the use of the affected limbs. With her lover still in mind, she added: 'I have a favour to ask you. Do not burn my letters, so that I can let my friend read them, if need be.' Sophie was obviously hoping to remedy past secretiveness with future demonstrative openness.

A day or two later[170] she renewed her plea to Rousseau not to leave the Hermitage – 'I ask it as a favour to me.' Her letter was full of sweet words, no doubt intended to make her appeal the more persuasive, for she was still afraid that too open a breach between Rousseau and Mme d'Épinay would confirm suspicions about his relations with herself.

Rousseau followed her advice on the subject of Diderot, and although the manuscript of his letter to his old friend cannot be traced, it must have been worded as Sophie wished, because it elicited from Diderot a reply[171] which was affectionate and sincere, despite a somewhat ominous beginning: 'It is certain that you have no friend left except me; but it is equally certain that you still have me.' Diderot went on to assert that there had been no conspiracy to make Rousseau go to Geneva. He reproached him gently for taking the letter he had written him on the subject to Mme d'Épinay and reading it aloud to her together with his reply. Rousseau should have known better than to do that: 'For God's sake, my friend, let your heart lead your head, and you will always do the best it is possible to do, and never allow your head to impose its sophisms on your heart.'

All the fuss over Mme d'Épinay's journey, Diderot protested, had become tedious. As for Rousseau's plan to leave the Hermitage for Montmorency, Diderot could see no reason for an action that would only make a bad impression. The letter ended: 'I have been your friend for a long time, I am still your friend. If your troubles are due to some doubts about my feelings, have them no longer. My feelings are unchanged.'

Sophie, for her part, while disappointing Rousseau's request to intervene with Diderot in person, did write to him offering to take him in her carriage to the Hermitage, so that he could visit Rousseau while she went on to Eaubonne. Diderot, in thanking her, explained[172] that he was not able, as he had hoped, to visit Rousseau, because pressing family duties were keeping him in Paris; all he could find time for was to write to Rousseau, and to join Mme d'Houdetot (at her prompting) in urging Rousseau to stay where he was.

Rousseau was not to be persuaded that he had no real grievance against Mme d'Épinay. He recalled in a letter[173] to Sophie, dated 10 November, that Mme d'Épinay's attitude to him had changed the previous summer as a result of her jealousy:

My visits to Eaubonne were not forgiven. Being used to having me entirely at her disposal, she could not endure sharing with you even a part of my attentions ... she swore to separate us; she boasted of it, and her very words were 'it will end one way or another'. Unmindful of honour, love, trust and sacred friendship, she dared to soil with calumnies something worthy of the highest esteem, and to cast shameful suspicions on two people she ought most to respect. Her sister! Her friend! ... She stirred up trouble and discord in my modest household, where peace is the one consolation for poverty. She even dared to urge a person attached to me to storm out of here and take refuge with her.*

Having written all this, however, Rousseau expressed his willingness to forgive Mme d'Épinay: 'If she were to write me a decent letter asking me to stay on at the Hermitage, I would agree.' The truth was, as he admitted, that he was beginning to dread the thought of having to move house in the depths of winter.

Sophie was pleased to observe that his resolution was weakening. Once again[174] she implored him: 'My dear Citizen, do not leave the Hermitage, at least for the moment; you are in no state to face a removal. Do calm down.' She offered to write to Mme d'Épinay, presumably to get her to urge Rousseau to remain at the Hermitage. To Rousseau himself, she wrote three days later[175] defending her sister-in-law against Rousseau's accusations, and suggesting again that the over-energetic language he had used in writing to Mme d'Épinay might be responsible for the discord between them. She had not changed her mind, she said, over the advice she had given him to stay at the Hermitage, but if his quarrel with Mme d'Épinay persisted, she suggested he should leave the next spring, quietly and with some decent pretext, so that his departure would not 'have the air of a rupture and of dissatisfaction'.

Sophie's letters from Paris continued to take longer to reach Rousseau than he could understand, and he went on pestering her with reproaches for the delays.

'Try, my friend, not to be so impatient,' she implored him on 15 November.[176] 'Learn not to feel neglected if one does not reply instantly ... Keep calm; keep yourself occupied – otherwise your imagination will devour itself and torture you.'

Even before he received this scolding, Rousseau had to admit[177] to Sophie that he was becoming importunate. He excused himself by saying that he was in a state of crisis – suspended between two lodgings, not

*This reference is to Mme d'Épinay's alleged offer to shelter Thérèse when Thérèse's jealousy of Mme d'Houdetot made life at the Hermitage intolerable, according, that is, to Mme d'Épinay's own interpretation of Thérèse's feelings.

knowing whether to remain where he was or go to Montmorency. But
no sooner had he written this, than he received her letter of the previous
Sunday urging him to stay at the Hermitage until the following spring
and he promised her: 'I will obey.'

At the same time he reproached her, saying that her letters to him were
delayed by her policy of franking them in advance in order to save his
paying the charge for delivery:

The letter you wrote me on Sunday and posted on Monday could not
calm me on Tuesday because today is Thursday and it has still not arrived.
By franking the letter you found an excellent method of making it vanish,
and by the time it does reach me I shall have endured eight days of torment,
and saved five sous. May heaven preserve me from such economies! Time –
time – Madame – that's the thing one should save; for time passed in
happiness is the true wealth of mankind.

Rousseau went on to admonish Sophie for writing to Diderot:

As soon as I heard you had done that, I saw you had spoiled everything
. . . if you had left it to me I would have delivered him to you bound hand
and foot in less than a fortnight. He is a man one must take by force or
catch him on the wing. For the rest, I do not know if he has been able to
write to you, but I am much mistaken if there is a woman in the world
he esteems and honours more than you. If he comes to see me, I will show
him your letter and tell him what I must.

Rousseau was, however, gracious enough to express in this letter some
interest in Sophie's health. He urged her to make a practice of going to
bed earlier at night and rising earlier in the morning, for such, he said, was
the natural way to live, since the cool hours of the night afforded the
healthiest sleep. He particularly advised her against sitting up late at night
at her writing table, because that 'must in the long run inflame the blood'.

Since it was largely in order to write the letters that Rousseau demanded
of her so insistently that Sophie sat up late at night, she may well have
regarded this last piece of advice as singularly inopportune. However, her
sweetness of nature did not fail her, and she answered[178] Rousseau's series
of lamentations and exhortations with words of tenderness. She explained
that her only intention in proposing to bring Diderot to the Hermitage
was to 'get him to you sooner, because you needed to see him; and
whatever the success of that effort and whatever the outcome, I cannot
reproach myself for a project which friendship alone dictated'. She added
that while no one admired Diderot more than she did, or would be happier

to make his acquaintance, she would never importune, or impose herself upon him.

She reported that St-Lambert, who was still on crutches in Aix, had promised to send her a letter for Rousseau. As for her own letters, she undertook not to frank them in future since that caused displeasure: 'But, my friend, learn that friendship should not take such offence at trifles.' She admitted that the continued absence of St-Lambert did nothing to restore her own health, although she had been rather better in the last few days and 'the opiate does its usual good'.

Sophie was not unnaturally disappointed by St-Lambert's decision to go from Aix, after his treatment there, to join his family at Nancy, rather than return to her; he did not in fact reach Paris until March 1758. But he kept his promise to send a letter[179] for Rousseau together with one of his letters to Sophie. In it he explained that as a result of the stroke it was still difficult for him to use a pen, and also that in any case he had things to say that he did not wish to dictate. He assured Rousseau that he considered it perfectly simple and straightforward that he had not accompanied Mme d'Épinay to Geneva, but if he had gone he, St-Lambert, would not have visualized him as someone 'exhibiting his poverty and slavery in his native land in the *cortège* of a tax-farmer's wife', but as a good friend helping a benefactress.

'Permit me to say,' he continued, 'that you are both the maddest of us all, and the least culpable ... Do not break with Mme d'Épinay; she has friendship for you, I feel sure; she has done wrong, but allow yourself the pleasure of forgiving her ... The misfortune of being born too sensitive to what goes on around one kills all the talents, and makes them useless.'

St-Lambert, feeling guilty, perhaps, at leaving Sophie alone in Paris while he went to Nancy, urged Rousseau to visit 'our friend': 'Make a little journey to Paris; her sweetness, her tenderness for you, her honesty will do your soul good. She thinks as I do, except that I insist more than she does that you should stay friends with Mme d'Épinay.'

St-Lambert's insistence came too late. That friendship had already ended. From Geneva Mme d'Épinay wrote to Rousseau on 12 November:[180]

You make me pity you. If you are sane, your conduct horrifies me on your behalf, because I do not think it straightforward. It is not natural to spend one's life suspecting and wounding one's friends. There are incomprehensible things in all this. What I will say to you once more is that you abuse the patience which my friendship for you has so far given me.

Rousseau replied to her on 23 November:[181]

If one died of grief I should no longer be alive. But at least I have made up my mind what to do. Friendship is dead between us, Madame, but I know how to respect the rights of the dead. I have not forgotten your kindness to me, and you can count on my being as grateful as anyone can be to a person one no longer loves. Further explanations would be useless. My conscience is my judge, and I refer you to yours. I wanted to leave the Hermitage, and I should have done so already. But I am told I ought to stay here until the spring, and since my friends want it, I shall stay here if I have your permission.

Having fired this shot at Mme d'Épinay, Rousseau wrote on the same day[182] to Sophie to tell her that he had recovered his equilibrium: 'I have peace of mind and I begin to be happy again. I have nothing worse than ill-health to put up with.' He was even in sufficiently good spirits to enact once more the role of moral counsellor to Sophie. He thought of her alone in Paris, with her husband still away at the war, and her lover on his way to his family. He did not find the strength to go to Paris to visit her as St-Lambert had suggested, which is perhaps a sign that he was no longer as much in love with her as he had been. Instead he wrote to her to warn her not to be seduced by anyone else; a lonely, attractive *femme du monde*, he reminded her, was at risk in the life of the city:

You have neither your husband nor your lover to occupy your heart and your attentions, and you do not have your friend to express and nourish the feelings that are so dear to you. Alas, what will become of you? You will be surrounded both by the boredom of solitude and dangers which make solitude desirable. You are so young still – of how many mistakes might a heart at once honest and tender yet simple and open fall victim?

He went on to warn Sophie against the wiles by which a clever, dishonourable man might snare a vulnerable woman, suggesting that it was better to take a thousand useless precautions to preserve virtue than to neglect one that might save it.

In the same letter he reported that he had received a visit from his publisher, Marc-Michel Rey from Amsterdam, to discuss the printing of *Julie*, and he promised to tell her at a later date about a new literary work he had just embarked upon. This latter was probably *Émile*. We learn from another letter, however, that Rousseau settled nothing with Rey on this occasion. 'Rey,' he informed Sophie on 5 December,[183] 'has no money and I did not want to entrust my manuscript to him, especially after his meanness at Montmorency in paying for his carriage: that did not give me a high opinion of him.'

In the meantime, Sophie had received from St-Lambert a letter which distressed her, and she sent it on to Rousseau with the comment[184] that her lover was

more reasonable about you than he is about me; I am more compromised than you are by what Mme d'Épinay has done; I doubt that she is so much my friend. Farewell my friend, I cannot write any more today. I was getting a little better, but this cursed letter has upset everything. I tell myself this storm will pass like the others. All is well, dear Citizen, when one has the support of one's conscience and one's heart; one must always have them on one's side; that is the right and only way to overcome the troubles of life.

Rousseau did not know the reason for St-Lambert's anger with Sophie, and this time it was his turn to tell her to calm down: 'Will you torment yourself for ever over chimeras,' he asked,[185]

and will you never learn to be happy when you have so many reasons for being happy? Your friend loves you; what more do you want of him? If he is sometimes uneasy, can a man be really in love without being so? And if he is sometimes angry when he is well, think how he must be when he is ill. Are you looking for a perfect man? Where will you find him? And what fault in your lover ought to displease you less than one which shows that he is always concerned about you? You yourself have discovered why you should console yourself; the reason is sound and gratifying and it suits you better than anyone. Your own heart justifies you, and mine honours you, and that could not be if his reproaches were justified. But they are too unjust to be lasting. Can a soul like his be deaf to the united voices of innocence and love? Calm yourself, then, I beseech you ... continue to deserve your self-respect and I will answer for it that you will never lose his.

Sophie promptly thanked[186] Rousseau for the way in which he had entered into her sorrows and for what he had said to help diminish them; she also expressed regret at his decision not to come to Paris to see her. She assured him that she was doing her best to take care of her health, if only for the sake of those she loved. 'O love, O friendship,' she wrote in an access of romantic ardour,

while you exist for me, you enhance my days and make them precious. Don't ask me what life I lead. I fulfil with indifference the duties of a society to which I do no more than lend my time. I see my two women friends for my particular satisfaction. I go to the theatre for amusement and distraction, but the most constant and most delightful of my occupations is giving myself up to the feelings of my heart, meditating on them, nourishing them, and expressing them to those who inspire them. That is what fills my real life and what makes me feel the joy of living.

Reading this, Rousseau may well have fancied he was reading his own *Julie*.

One day in December he received the long-delayed visit from Diderot. According to *Madame de Montbrillant*[187] the visit took place on 5 December, and since Diderot had a hand in writing that book, scholars have generally been willing to accept the date, but a letter[188] Rousseau wrote to Sophie and dated 5 December 1757 makes no mention of Diderot, and while it reports other comings and goings, says nothing of Diderot, expected or arrived. This letter's chief lament is over the diminished volume of correspondence from Sophie, of whom Rousseau speaks in the third person: 'She used to write me two or three times a week, then once; soon it will be once a fortnight and then she will write no more.' Rousseau adds in a different voice: 'I have no longer any contact with the world except with you alone; I am attached to no one in the world besides you; but while that state of affairs lasts it will be the happiest time of my life.'

He goes on to speak of the slow progress he is making with the copying he is doing for her, about the reflections on ethics he is writing for her, and about his arrangements for publishing *Julie*, which he says he contemplates with 'a sort of repugnance'. Nevertheless he asks her to help with his project of commissioning a set of illustrations for the novel, by asking her brother, Lalive de Jully,* a noted collector, to recommend an artist. Rousseau mentions that he has in mind François Boucher for the job, in spite of his being 'very mannered'.†

The same letter informed Sophie that M. Cahouet, steward at La Chevrette, had received from Mme d'Épinay instructions concerning the disposal of the furniture at the Hermitage once Rousseau had left. Sophie nevertheless continued to advise him to stay. 'Do not leave the Hermitage,' she wrote on 6 December,[189] in a letter which brought Rousseau assurances of her continued friendship for him: 'Even at this stage I still believe you will make a great mistake if you go.'

By this time, however, the situation had changed. Mme d'Épinay settled the matter. She wrote to Rousseau from Geneva on 1 December:[190]

---

*Ange-Laurent Lalive de Jully (1727–75), amateur painter and art collector, appointed Introducteur des Ambassadeurs in 1757.

†Sophie's own opinion was that Van Loo was the artist best qualified to do the illustrations.

After having shown you every possible mark of friendship and sympathy for several years, there is nothing left for me but to pity you. You are most unfortunate! I wish your conscience were as easy as mine. Such may be necessary for the repose of your life. Since you want to leave the Hermitage, and since you ought to do so, I am surprised that your friends are keeping you there. Personally, I never consult my friends about my duty, and I have nothing further to say to you about yours.

Rousseau promptly informed[191] Sophie of what Mme d'Épinay had written: 'This time I think her opinion is preferable to yours ... Finally, honour demands that I go, and when that speaks I must listen to no other voice. I have taken a new lodging at Montmorency, and but for the bad weather I should be there already; whatever happens, within eight days I shall no longer be at the Hermitage.'

Sophie could hardly wish him to act differently. 'I shall not argue any more about the decision you have taken,' she wrote on 14 December.[192] 'I believe you to be an honourable man because you are one of my friends, and in this case you do well to follow your conscience.'

Even so, she suggested it would have been wise for him, on quitting the Hermitage, to go to stay with his friend Diderot, and to do so quietly, without advertising the fact that he wanted to leave Mme d'Épinay's house. She asked whether Diderot had yet paid his projected visit to the Hermitage: 'You do not say whether you have seen your friend.'

If that visit had not already taken place it must have done so before 15 December, because on that day Rousseau left the Hermitage for good. There is a radical difference between Rousseau's account of what happened during Diderot's visit and that of his visitor. In the *Confessions*[193] Rousseau describes a wholly agreeable occasion: the visit – 'so often promised and cancelled' – could not, he writes,

have been more opportune. Diderot was my oldest friend, almost the only one left, and the pleasure I felt in seeing him in such circumstances can be readily imagined. My heart was full, and I poured it out to him. I explained to him a number of facts that had either not come to his knowledge or had been distorted or fabricated. I informed him, as far as I could do so with propriety, of all that had happened. I did not attempt to hide from him that which he already knew too well – that a mad and ill-fated passion had been the cause of my undoing. But I never admitted that Mme d'Houdetot knew of it or that I had declared it to her. I told him about Mme d'Épinay's unworthy manoeuvres to intercept the very innocent letters that her sister-in-law wrote to me. I wanted him to hear the details from the very persons she had tried to suborn. Thérèse gave him an exact account; but my astonishment may be imagined when the mother's turn came to speak and I heard her swear and declare that she had no knowledge of anything of the kind. That was her testimony and she never modified it. Only four days earlier she had told the same story as Thérèse, and now in the presence of my friend she contradicted me to my face.

This is all Rousseau has to say in the *Confessions* about Diderot's visit, and his correspondence from the time is totally silent on the subject. Diderot's accounts of the visit not only contradict Rousseau's; they also contradict themselves, and, as will be seen, disprove some of Diderot's subsequent avowals.

In his *Tablettes*,[194] notes written about a year after the event, and after his final breach with Rousseau, Diderot asserts:

Having gone to the Hermitage to find out whether he was mad or bad, I accused him of having maliciously desired to provoke a quarrel between M. de St-Lambert and Mme d'Houdetot. He denied it, and to exculpate himself he produced a letter* from Mme d'Houdetot which proved that he had played the very game I accused him of. He blushed; then he became angry when I pointed out that the letter confirmed what he had just denied.

A letter[195] Diderot is supposed to have written to Grimm on the evening after he had visited Rousseau at the Hermitage is more detailed:

That man is insane. I have seen him. And with all the energy that comes with honesty and the concern that remains in the heart for one who has been a friend for a very long time, I reproached him for the enormity of his conduct. His tears at Mme d'Épinay's feet were shed at the very moment he was making to me the gravest accusations against her. That odious *apologia* he sent to you (and in which there was not one decent excuse); the letter he proposed to send to St-Lambert, intended to ease his conscience about feelings for which he blamed himself, and which, in reality, far from being an admission of love born despite himself in his heart, was a letter of excuse for having made Mme d'Houdetot uneasy about her own love. And even now, what do I know? I was never satisfied with his answers. I had not the courage to tell him so. I preferred to leave

*The only letter from Sophie that Rousseau is likely to have produced is the one dated Sunday, 13 November 1757. Rousseau told her (in his letter of 17 November) that he would show it to Diderot. But this letter is almost wholly taken up with Sophie's plea to Rousseau to mend his quarrel with Mme d'Épinay; it makes no reference to her relations with St-Lambert, and contains no proof whatever of Rousseau's trying to spoil them.

him the consolation of thinking he had deceived me. Long may he live! He stood up to me with a cold fury which has distressed me. I fear he is utterly hardened.

Farewell, my friend. Let us be, and continue to be, men of honour; the state of those who cease to be terrifies me. Farewell, my friend. I embrace you tenderly ... I throw myself into your arms like a frightened man. I try in vain to write verse; but that man keeps appearing to me across my work, and it is as if I have beside me a damned man. He is damned, that is certain ... Oh, my friend, what a spectacle is this of a wicked and tormented man. Burn, tear up this paper! Don't let it come again in front of your eyes. May I never see that man again. He would make me believe in devils and hell. If I am ever forced to return to his house again, I am sure I shall tremble throughout the journey.

Diderot was never forced to return to Rousseau's house. The friendship between them was doomed, but Diderot still felt able to say when the final rupture came that Rousseau was responsible for ending it.

4

MONTLOUIS

The 'hole' at Montmorency to which Rousseau moved some two miles up the hill from the Hermitage was a cottage known as the Petit Montlouis and can still be seen today, enlarged and incorporated into the Musée Rousseau. It was in a dilapidated state in that cold December of 1757 and had to be thoroughly repaired and restored a year or two later, but it provided at short notice a tolerable shelter for a household of two, Rousseau having seized the opportunity of the removal to send Mme Levasseur to live *en pension* with relations in Paris.[1]*

If smaller and less well-appointed than the Hermitage, the Petit Montlouis was larger than the average cottage, and it was cheap – fifty livres a year, ten livres less than the amount Rousseau paid to the gardener at the Hermitage in lieu of rent to Mme d'Épinay. It stood in the grounds of a larger house named Montlouis, owned by Jacques-Joseph Mathas, procureur-fiscal to the Prince de Condé, a bourgeois property on the edge of the village. The Mathas family had been established in Montmorency for many generations, rising from the ranks of trade – as butchers – to the dignity of lawyers and magistrates. Rousseau writes kindly of his landlord in the *Confessions*:[3]

M. Mathas had heard about my predicament. He offered me a little house he had in his garden ... I accepted eagerly and gratefully. The deal was quickly done. I hastened to buy a few sticks of furniture for Thérèse and me to sleep on. I had my things removed from the Hermitage with great difficulty and at much expense. In spite of the ice and the snow, the move was accomplished in two days.

*Rousseau says he undertook to pay for her board. Mme d'Épinay[2] says Grimm supported her because she had been abandoned by Rousseau.

Rousseau was quick to appreciate the advantages of the cottage which had a little garden of its own, with a high terrace commanding a view of the valley of Montmorency, together with a row of lime trees and at the bottom of the garden a small square tower, which he called a *donjon* and used as a room to work in. These features of the place are still much as they were when he was there; at the time they consoled him for a leaking roof and broken floorboards.

As soon as he had installed himself at the Petit Montlouis, Rousseau wrote a short, harsh letter to Mme d'Épinay:

Nothing could be simpler, Madame, nor more necessary than leaving your house, since you do not approve of my being there. Following your refusal to agree that I should pass the winter at the Hermitage, I left on 15 December. My destiny was to live there against my will and the will of my friends, and to leave it against my will and theirs. I thank you for a stay you made me undertake, and I would thank you more heartily if I had paid less dearly for it. For the rest, you are right to consider me unfortunate, for nobody in the world knows better than you just how unfortunate I must be. It is unfortunate to be mistaken in the choice of one's friend, and it is no less cruel to have to acknowledge such a sweet error. Your gardener is paid up to January.

This is all Rousseau had to say to Mme d'Épinay, but, feeling that some sort of acknowledgement was due for the hospitality he had enjoyed at the Hermitage, he wrote what he calls a 'very decent letter of thanks'[5] to her husband, and received in reply one 'equally decent'.[6] It is clear from the *Confessions* that Rousseau was anxious to keep the good opinion of M. d'Épinay and liked to think that he had done so.

In the first letter[7] he wrote from Montlouis to Sophie, he spoke of his relief at being there: 'At last I am free to recover the frank and independent character with which nature endowed me. Had I always adhered to it, everybody would have been pleased with me and I would have been more pleased with myself. My whole fault is to have yielded to false and deceptive friendship. I resisted it for a long time. It ought always to be resisted.'

In the spirit of this 'frankness' he went on to complain about the disgrace of being thrown out of the Hermitage in the midst of winter, with an implied reproach to Sophie for having made him stay there longer than he had wished. He also protested against a remark in one of her letters to him, in which she had said she believed him to be an honourable man because he was one of her friends. He assured her that whatever price he put on friendship, he put an even greater one on virtue. Moreover, he did not want to be *one* of her friends, but simply her friend: 'since you yourself conferred that title on me, I believe I have deserved it enough not to lose it. I must yield the first place to the one who is dear to you: you warned me of that, and I agreed. But except for him, a second place after any other is unworthy of my heart, and I refuse it.'

He tried to explain to Sophie that friendship to him meant a sharing of feelings, not a rendering of services:

Devoured as I am by the need to love and be loved, and caring little about anything else, I do not want my friends to worry more than I do about my poverty; I want them to love me as I am, and not to express their attachment in patronage but in affection ... Oh my friend, whoever you are, if there is a heart in the world born for friendship and capable of feeling all that a friend can inspire in me, put aside all this show of services and simply love me. Do not build me a house on your estate where you will never visit me and only tell yourself you have me in your power and cherish my friendship no longer. Build me a house in the depths of your heart – for it is there that I will make my home; it is there that I will dwell for the rest of my life, with no more inclination to leave it than you will have to dismiss me from it.

He begged her to console him in his sufferings by pouring out her own woes on his breast so that 'our very sorrows may become a source of pleasure, and our shared life a woven thread of mutual aid and a testimony of friendship'. At the same time Rousseau urged Sophie not to take up his defence against his accusers: for if she did so, he warned her, she would do it alone, and only make enemies for herself.

In the *Confessions*[8] Rousseau says that as soon as he was settled in his new house he began to suffer from more frequent and violent attacks of his urinary complaint, an affliction complicated by a newly acquired hernia, which he ascribed to the emotional agitation of his relationship with Sophie. He was in such pain that he overcame his deep mistrust of doctors, and summoned to his bedside his old friend Dr Thierry, who gave him the usual treatment: 'Probes, catheters, bandages – all the paraphernalia of the infirmities of age assembled around me only made me painfully aware that one cannot have a young heart with impunity when one has an old body.'[9]

Notwithstanding these sufferings, Rousseau did a great deal of work at Montlouis that winter, and in spite of the harsh weather, he did most of it in the unheated *donjon* he had made his study. He had been spurred to literary activity by an article which had appeared in the seventh volume of Diderot's *Encyclopédie*, an article he had read with more dismay than pleasure: d'Alembert on 'Geneva'. Rousseau seems not to have voiced the obvious question: why had Diderot not asked him, the one citizen of Geneva among his regular contributors, to write the article, and indeed Rousseau found no faults with the general outline that d'Alembert provided of the history and general character of the city, but two thoughts that d'Alembert expressed, almost as asides, made him so indignant that he took up his pen and wrote, for publication, a reply that was ten times as long as d'Alembert's original text.

The offending remarks were, first, that the clergy of Geneva had discarded the old dogmas of Calvinism to such an extent that 'many of them have no religion beyond a complete Socinianism';[10] and further that the city of Geneva, which had hitherto banned dramatic performances, ought to institute a theatre to elevate the culture and morals of its citizens and so 'add the urbanity of Athens to the prudence of Sparta'.[11]

Rousseau detected in both these observations the prompting of Voltaire, under whose roof at Les Délices d'Alembert had stayed while preparing the article, and whose particular interest in the project for a theatre in Geneva was that of a dramatist eager to have a stage for his own plays. Voltaire's unabashed promotion of this vested interest evidently overcame Rousseau's earlier reluctance to offend the great man; if Rousseau was peeved by Voltaire's failure to reply in any detail to his letter on Providence, there was still between them a certain friendship, however cool, that he thought worth preserving. But Rousseau felt so deeply and strongly on both the subjects d'Alembert had raised that he decided to risk an open breach.

It is not immediately obvious why. The theological liberalism – or 'Socinianism' – which d'Alembert ascribed to the Genevese clergy was what had enabled them to bend the rules to re-admit Rousseau to their communion in 1754; in an ever more extreme form, it was the only kind of Christianity to which Rousseau himself subscribed, as he was to make manifestly clear in 'The Profession of Faith of the Savoyard Priest' which he incorporated in *Émile*. Why, then, should he protest?

As for the introduction of a theatre to Geneva, Rousseau could only be expected to welcome it. He was a dramatist himself. He had written both plays and operas, and had for many years been, on his own admission, an avid theatre-goer. When d'Alembert's article was in the press, Rousseau's *Le Devin du village* was performed in Carouge, the Savoyard town at the gates of Geneva which housed a theatre for a largely Genevese audience. Had he not the same interest as Voltaire in seeing a theatre established in Geneva itself? He did not think so.

Rousseau was, as he freely admitted, a 'man of paradox', and he promptly proclaimed his dissent from the views expressed in d'Alembert's article by means of a work he published under the title *A Letter to Monsieur d'Alembert on the Theatre*. It is one of his most eloquent and, apart from certain lapses, well-reasoned contributions to political and social theory, and one which distinguishes him, no less categorically than does his *Discourse on the Sciences and the Arts*, as a man of the Enlightenment at war with the Enlightenment, a dramatist against the stage.

He does not devote much space to the question of the Socinianism of the Genevese clergy. It is chiefly the word to which he takes exception. Like Locke, who vigorously denied that he was a Socinian while all the time adhering to the doctrine of Fausto Socino which reduced Christianity to deism, Rousseau repudiated an appellation which had become pejorative. He claimed, somewhat disingenuously, that he did not know what Socinians actually taught, but he knew that they were sectarian; and he held that 'every sectarian name is always odious'.[12] Moreover, he pointed out that any imputations of sectarianism were bound to be injurious to the clergy of Geneva, however harmless to laymen.

Rousseau was well aware that the more liberal pastors of Geneva, who included some of his personal friends, were already regarded with suspicion by the rigid Calvinist faction; and it was they, he feared, who would suffer from the charge of Socinianism. He demanded of d'Alembert how any observer could possibly know what faith another man entertained in his heart, since all one could see was external behaviour. While he was in accord with d'Alembert in recognizing the spirit of philosophy and humanity which prevailed among the Genevese clergy, he reminded him that 'because they are philosophers and tolerant, it does not follow that they are heretics'.[13] What Rousseau did not say, but what he thought, was that Voltaire had put up d'Alembert to make mischief among the Genevese clergy by ascribing to them the opinions which agreed with his own.

Again, in turning to the subject of the stage, Rousseau chose not to avow his belief that Voltaire was behind d'Alembert's proposal that a theatre be introduced to Geneva, or his knowledge that Voltaire had for some time been battling with the authorities of that city over interdictions on performances of plays in his own villa. Indeed, with a measure of cunning which matched Voltaire's, Rousseau suggested that if it was absolutely essential for Geneva to have a theatre, then 'M. de Voltaire should be commissioned to write plays for it – fill it with his genius and live as long as his plays'[14] – on the grounds that native Genevans would never have any talent for dramaturgy 'and it will be a bad sign for the republic to see its citizens, disguised as wits, setting themselves to composing French verses and plays'. Once again, Rousseau seems to have forgotten that he himself had done that very thing.

Nevertheless, his criticism of the drama from the perspective of morality is sharp, serious and systematic. He argues at length against d'Alembert's belief, well-rooted in tradition, that the theatre changes people's morals for the better. He claims, on the contrary, that the theatre can only follow and embellish existing morals. An author who set himself against the prevailing taste of his audience would soon write for himself alone. The old argument that 'the theatre purges the passions', Rousseau suggests, is false; for 'the only instrument that can serve to purge passions is reason, and reason has no effect in the theatre'.[15] If the theatre can be said, in any sense, to 'purge passions', it purges us of the passions we do not have, and inflames those that we do have. As for the idea of the theatre 'making virtue lovable, and vice hateful', Rousseau argues that it will more likely have the opposite effect. He gives the example of tragedies about Phaedra and Medea, and suggests that someone who was told about the crimes of these persons before he had seen the plays would actually hate them more than he would after he had witnessed them enacted by their interesting, even thrilling protagonists.

Can men learn justice from observing the conflicts of good and evil on the stage? Rousseau claims that we already love justice in what concerns the quarrels of others; it is only where our own interest is involved that we are tempted to prefer injustice. We do not need the theatre to teach us that virtue and honesty in other men are beautiful; we think that already because we hope to profit from it; what we do not want is virtue and honesty in ourselves, because that is too costly, and the theatre does nothing to make us want it.

People enjoy the theatre, he argues, precisely because it is a temple of illusions and falsehood. The heart is more readily touched by feigned misfortunes than by real ones; we weep more over disasters on the stage than over disasters in the world, because those events entail no anxiety for ourselves: 'In shedding our tears for fiction, we satisfy all the duties of humanity without having to give up anything further of ourselves.'[16] The theatre does not bring virtue closer to us; it takes it farther from us; on the stage feelings are inflated and morality is exalted to a level where it is as unreal and as alien as the language that is spoken and the costumes that are worn: 'We say to ourselves that none of that magnificence is suitable for people like us, and we would think it as absurd to adopt the virtues of the heroes as to speak in verse or to put on Roman costumes.'[17]

Rousseau admits that in tragedies on the stage crimes are always punished, but he points out that the punishment is effected by means so extraordinary that nothing similar is to be expected in everyday life, and therefore they have no deterrent effect on ordinary people. The effect tragedies do have is the reverse of beneficial. For what happens in tragedies accustoms the eyes of the people to horrors that they might never have imagined for themselves. Far from murder and parricide being made hateful, they are made fascinating, even rendered permissible and pardonable: 'At the French theatre ... it is hard not to excuse Phaedra, when she is incestuous and shedding innocent blood. Syphas poisoning his wife, the young Horatius stabbing his sister, Agamemnon sacrificing his daughter or Orestes cutting his mother's throat do not fail to be attractive characters.'[18]

Apart from pointing to these unintended consequences of seeing tragedies on the stage, Rousseau also criticizes the central message of Racine and his imitators: 'What do we learn from *Phèdre* and *Oedipe* if not that man is not free and that heaven punishes him for the crimes which it makes him commit?'[19]

Comedy Rousseau claims to be even more harmful than tragedy, for comedy uses ridicule, and ridicule is 'the favourite arm of vice'.[20] To illustrate this argument Rousseau analyses the work of the greatest exponent of comedy in French literature, Molière. He says that Molière's plays make fun of goodness and simplicity, while treachery and falsehood become attractive and appealing. 'Molière and his imitators mock vice without making virtue loved.'[21] Indeed Rousseau claims that Molière's true intention as a dramatist – apart from his first purpose, which was to please the public – was not to correct the vicious but to condemn the ridiculous. Rousseau gives as an example of this, Molière's acknowledged masterpiece, *Le Misanthrope*, a play which he says holds up to mockery and derision 'a virtuous man', Alceste.

Since Rousseau was already beginning to acquire the reputation of being himself a misanthrope, some readers would not have been surprised to find him taking up the cudgels for a character in whom he might see more than a little of himself. In fact Rousseau proclaims his sympathy for Alceste by arguing that Alceste is not a real misanthropist at all. Alceste is 'an upright man, sincere, and worthy, a truly good man'.[22] Far from being an enemy of mankind, which is what a misanthropist is, Alceste is a man whose very love of his fellow creatures makes him detest the evils they do to one another and the vices that ensue. Rousseau points out that it is the scoundrels and the flatterers that Alceste hates; were it not for them, he would love all mankind. If Alceste has little failings one can fairly laugh at, Rousseau insists that he is the one really admirable character in the whole play. Even so, he notes that Molière clearly set out to make Alceste ridiculous, and does so by contrasting him with another character, Philinte, who is presented as a model of excellent normality, which indeed he is according to the standards of Paris. That is to say, he is, as Rousseau puts it, 'one of those very gentle, moderate people who consider that everything is well in the world because it is in their interest that nothing should be

better, and who are always pleased with everyone because they care about
no one'.[23] Philinte is a typical gentleman who endures with calm fortitude
the misfortunes of others, a character that Molière wants us to admire just
as he wants us to laugh at Alceste.

What, then, is the moral of the play? Its purpose, Rousseau suggests, is
to amuse the audience, that is, to please corrupt souls. As a result, it upholds
a preference for the practice and principles of fashionable society over
those of strict honesty and truth. It teaches us that wisdom lies in a certain
mean between vice and virtue and it 'comforts the audience by persuading
them that to be an honourable man it is enough not to be a total scoundrel'.[24]

Rousseau compares all the plays of modernity unfavourably with those
of antiquity. The dramatists of the ancient world, he observes, wrote on
heroic themes; the favourite subject of contemporary authors is love. Even
though love is often sacrificed to duty and virtue in modern plays, or
punished when it is impure, Rousseau maintains that such plays still
provoke in the audience a desire for love: 'If these plays do not exactly
generate love, they prepare the way for it to be experienced.'[25] Thus even
innocent love depicted on the stage can lead to guilty love in the real world.
The very atmosphere which prevails inside a theatre, the heightening of
emotions people feel when the curtain rises, the shared excitement all
diminish, he argues, the power of reason to resist the triumph of passion.

From these carefully argued criticisms of the drama Rousseau passes to
a blanket condemnation of actors and actresses, without denying that while
doing so he is adhering to an age-old prejudice. He defends the prejudice
on the grounds that 'in general the estate of the actor is one of licence, bad
morals and disorder'.[26] Actors, he notes, have everywhere been excom-
municated and despised, except among the ancient Greeks, and that was
only because the Greek theatre was a sacred institution and actors close to
priests. As for actresses, Rousseau suggests that a profession which calls for
a woman to exhibit herself in public is inherently inimical to modesty and
morality. A woman who 'sets herself for sale in performance is only too
likely to do the same off stage'.[27] Rousseau goes on to paint a lurid picture
of the effect actresses would have on the life of Geneva if a theatre were
to be established there; they would have the menfolk of the city at their
feet, so that candidates for public office would have to seek their patronage
and 'elections would take place in the dressing-rooms of actresses'.[28]

One of the more curious arguments Rousseau employs against the
actor's art is that it is a form of deceit:

What is the talent of the actor? The art of counterfeit, of assuming a
personality other than his own, of appearing different from what he is, of

simulating passion when his blood is cold, of saying something he does not believe as naturally as if he really believed it, and finally, of forgetting his own place by dint of taking another's ... What, then, at bottom is the spirit that an actor receives from his estate? A mixture of abjectness, duplicity, absurd conceit and shameful abasement which renders him fit for all sorts of roles except the most noble of all – that of a man, which he forsakes.[29]

This attack on the actor seems even more bizarre as Rousseau goes on to praise the political orator whose estate he sees as being as noble as that of the actor is ignoble:

The difference between them is very great. When the orator presents himself to the public it is to make a speech, and not to show himself off; he represents no one but himself; he fills only his own role; he speaks in his own name alone; he does not say, nor should he say, anything except what he thinks; the man and the *persona* being identical, he is where he should be; he is in the situation of any other citizen who discharges the duties of his station. An actor on the stage, however, displaying feelings other than his own, saying only what he is made to say, often representing a non-existent being, annihilates himself, so to speak, and disappears into his hero.[30]

The reader cannot fail to be struck by the contrast between Rousseau's uncharitable description of the actor and his lavish encomium of the orator and indeed by the sheer unfairness of his blaming as 'counterfeit' an imitation plainly declared to be an imitation, coupled, as that charge is, with a description of the orator drawn wholly from an ideal image of 'the orator' and not from actual observation of the insincerity, the hyperbole, and the tricks of persuasion used by actual orators, men often more fairly accused of deception than any actor.

The worst that Rousseau can justly say against the actor is that the habit of continually impersonating other characters on the stage might leave the actor somehow drained of any solid personality of his own; but evidently Rousseau was far too hostile towards actors to be able to exercise the kind of psychological insight into their condition that he was able to show towards others. Moreover, like his most ardent critic, Edmund Burke, Rousseau the philosopher could sometimes be carried away by his own eloquence as a pamphleteer. He seems almost to be aware of this himself, for towards the end of the *Letter* he inserts a note[31] to his readers warning them that they will be mistaken if they conclude from his remarks that he dislikes the theatre and is the enemy of actors; he declares that he 'loves the drama passionately' and has every reason to be pleased with actors, even if he has 'only one as a personal friend'.* He stresses the point that he does not advocate the abolition of the theatre in large – and corrupt – cities such as Paris; his only purpose, he says, is to oppose the introduction of it to Geneva, a republic with other forms of cultural activity, which a theatre would interrupt and undermine.

In many ways the most important paragraphs of Rousseau's *Letter to Monsieur d'Alembert* are those where he outlines these alternative forms of entertainment which are appropriate to a society of good citizens and conducive to republican virtue. His emphasis is on participatory arts as opposed to spectator amusements, and on Swiss as opposed to French traditions. He recalls having seen in his youth a community on a mountainside near Neuchâtel, where the people in their leisure time made all sorts of musical instruments and played them, and practised, as hobbies, all sorts of crafts, such as sketching, painting, dancing and singing. 'These arts were not taught there by masters, but were passed down from generation to generation by tradition.'[33] Such folk arts, Rousseau claims, are superior to the arts of advanced societies not only for the reasons set forth in his first *Discourse* – that they are uncorrupted by sophistication – but because they are practised by the people themselves, who put to use the talents that nature has given them, instead of delegating the arts to artists, and watching performers perform.

Rousseau looks also to Geneva's own traditions. He recalls having seen as a child a drill of the local militia which was followed by feasting and dancing, and being told by his father to observe their happiness and fellowship and patriotic pride; he suggests that such military parades and open-air festivities, public balls, athletics, games and competitions should be developed in order to entertain the people and cultivate the sort of civic spirit that a republic needs: 'The only true joy is public joy.'[34]

Rousseau also proposes a re-animation of two Genevese institutions which were at that time falling into disfavour, notably in the eyes of the clergy: the men's clubs and the women's societies. The men's clubs were alternatives to taverns as places where men could meet to drink and smoke together and play games of skill or chance; the women's societies met in private homes for coffee, needlework and conversation. Rousseau believed it was good to keep the sexes apart; for men to fortify their manliness in the company of men, and for women to enjoy appropriate amusements in feminine society. His experience of the *salons* in Paris had persuaded him that when men were too much in the company of women they

*The reference is probably to Joseph-Baptiste Sauvé, known as Lanoue, who produced Rousseau's *Narcisse* and to whom Rousseau donated the royalties for the improvement of his theatre.[32]

became effeminate. This does not mean that Rousseau, in his own life, ceased to seek the company of women more often than that of men; he simply wanted the Genevese citizenry to avoid the fate of the Parisians, and to live, as republicans, republican lives.

Disapproval of the clubs and societies was expressed in Geneva, he recognized, for what might seem sound puritanical reasons: that the clubs encouraged drunkenness and gambling and the societies facilitated gossip. Rousseau believed, however, that these evils were relatively trivial; if intemperance was vicious, the taste for wine was no crime; and although gambling was folly, it was more easily regulated in a club than in a private house. Moreover, gossip was not always harmful – fear of being talked about might lead people to eschew scandalous behaviour. In a similar vein, Rousseau argues that the clubs keep the citizens of Geneva out of mischief of a sexual kind: 'let us allow them to spend the night drinking lest, without it, they spend nights doing something worse.'³⁵

But for all his appeal to Swiss experience and Genevese traditions, Rousseau admits that his ideal model of republican culture is taken from the ancient world: 'Sparta, which I have never cited often enough as the example we ought to follow,' he writes at the end of his *Letter to Monsieur d'Alembert*, 'cultivated its citizens with modest games and simple festivals.'³⁶ Rousseau was far from willing to adopt d'Alembert's suggestion that Geneva should add the urbanity of Athens to the prudence of Sparta. He never abandoned the opinion proclaimed in his *Discourse on the Sciences and the Arts* that Athens owed its decline to the sophistication of its culture, and he supported this judgement with the authority of the great Athenian philosopher Plato, who had stipulated that there should be no artists in his ideal republic.

It is possible that Rousseau discussed his idea of replying to d'Alembert's article with Diderot when he saw him in December and the publication of it with Rey when Rey came to the Hermitage; at all events, as soon as it was finished, he sent the manuscript of it to Amsterdam to be printed.

Despite the work he put into his literary activity that winter and the dislocation of the move from the Hermitage to Montlouis, Rousseau found time and energy to write letters to Sophie in such numbers that she could not keep up with them. She begged³⁷ him to understand that if her letters became shorter and less frequent, it was not because of any lessening of her affection for him, but because of the pressure of other duties. For a while, he seemed willing to accept this explanation: 'Your letter has restored me to life,' he wrote from Montlouis on 26 December,³⁸ urging her to think only of protecting her own health. 'The mind and body are kept well on the same principles, and it is by dominating one's fantasies that one learns to conquer one's passions ... Remember, above all, that good morals are the best medicine for healthy living.'

Unfortunately, Rousseau was not altogether successful at dominating his own fantasies, for he became increasingly irritable and suspicious, and, however good his own morals, they did not prove an effective remedy either for his new hernia or his old urinary complaint.

It was a bad time for others as well. In Paris, Diderot was facing renewed harassment from the authorities in the wake of the publication of the seventh volume of the *Encyclopédie*. His collaborators, d'Alembert, Duclos and Marmontel, withdrew from the enterprise for their own safety's sake, and Voltaire implored Diderot to remove himself and his encyclopaedia from French territory. Diderot, as brave in such matters as he was stubborn, refused to move or capitulate. Deleyre sent[39] Rousseau news of these developments: 'Our philosophers are attacked on all sides, and they do not get on too well among themselves.'

In the same letter Deleyre told Rousseau that he was going to visit old Mme Levasseur in Paris, where Rousseau had undertaken to provide for her keep. Deleyre also inquired about Rousseau's new life at Montlouis: 'Is your niche – or your grotto – warm? Your pigeons, your chickens, your cats, your dogs – where do they all live? I am impatient to see your brood all together. Forgive my jokes. I do not know if they amuse you; but I laughed a lot the other day when I heard that you had refused a hundred louis from the Prince de Clermont when you had not even paid your laundress.'

Rousseau's reply to this letter has not been traced, but he had described his new home in writing[40] to Sophie: 'My present hermitage is less beautiful than the other, but as I pay rent, it is mine. The truth is that I am not rich enough to live rent-free.'

The domestic animals Deleyre mentions were, if not already installed, soon to become a prominent feature of Rousseau's household at Montlouis. The less he found to love in his fellow men, the more he became attached to his pets. The story about the 'Prince de Clermont' is probably apocryphal, since the reference must be to Louis de Bourbon-Condé, Comte de Clermont, who is unlikely to have offered money to Rousseau since it was he who said to Louis XV, when that monarch threatened to put Rousseau in jail, that he would do better to have him flogged.[41]

Sophie sent Rousseau a New Year greeting from Paris on 30 December:[42] 'My dear Citizen, I wish you more tranquillity in the coming year if it is possible; and also that you will be better pleased with your own heart and those of your friends.' Her own health, she reported, was fairly good, and with care, she hoped it would continue to be. She urged Rousseau to press on with the manuscript copy of *Julie* he was making for her, and promised to send him a fresh supply of paper. She reproached him gently for regarding as 'chains' the benefactions that friendship bestowed.

Rousseau's reply, which has been lost, must have informed her that he was sick and agitated, because she wrote back on 3 January 1758[43] saying:

I am anxious about you in every way. In God's name, my dear Citizen, calm yourself about everything, and do not surrender yourself to illusions, as you do, but use your reason to sustain you in your sorrows and avoid mistakes; remember that without it, everything can mislead us; take care of yourself ... Be reasonable and you will be content with yourself and everyone else.

Rousseau was not at all pleased with this advice, and hurriedly drafted an angry reply:[44]

Since your heart has nothing more to say to mine, I would rather assume alone the burden of a correspondence which can only be onerous for you and to which you can contribute nothing but words. It is a contemptible pretence to substitute civilities for real feelings and to be honest only on the surface. He who has the courage to appear always what he is will sooner or later become what he ought to be, but there is nothing to be hoped from those who develop an outward show of character. If I forgive you for having no more friendship for me, it is because you no longer show me any. I love you a hundred times better that way than in these cold letters which try to be friendly but which reveal in spite of yourself that you are thinking of something else as you write them. Frankness, Sophie; that alone elevates the soul, and sustains through respect of oneself the right to the respect of another ...

I believe you are naturally good. It is this belief which draws me to you still, but great wealth coupled with recent adversities must have hardened your heart. You have too little experience of misfortune in your life to feel the misfortune of others, so the sweetness of compassion is unknown to you, and having never shared in the sufferings of others, you are less able to endure suffering yourself.

It seems that Rousseau, having written this cruel letter, thought better of sending it; and instead went on to write another, equally bitter and reproachful, but marginally less offensive, which he dated and posted on 5 January:[45]

I will begin by telling you that the equivocal and ambiguous style of your latest letters has not escaped my notice. I have done everything to give you an opportunity to explain yourself. I have asked you for clarification. I have begged you to ask the same of your friend [St-Lambert]. You have evaded everything. The only frankness of your polite society is never to say what you think except with qualifications, civilities, double-meanings and half-truths. My own crude candour, as you please to call it, is to translate all that into my own homespun language and to reply squarely to what is expressed to me deviously. So then, instead of being proud of my friendship, you are ashamed of it. I will take it back, to save you blushing any longer. Despise me henceforth, if you wish. I will not go on taking offence. I declare to you that from now on, I shall see you only as Madame la Comtesse and him, with all his genius, as Monsieur le Marquis – and that means you have come down lower than you think.

Ah, you used not to be 'The Countess!' You seemed to me to be, for all your weaknesses, an angel sent from heaven to inspire me with your constancy and virtue. How you have changed! But my heart, which is treated as ungrateful by base and venal minds, never changes. If a man must forget those who despise him, he knows how to respect and honour merit, and will never lose the tender memory of kindness received. Finally, although I am resolved not to try to see you, gratitude alone is such a sweet feeling that even if I never see you again, I shall have that to console me.

Rousseau went on to suggest – cruelly and surely unjustly – that since money was the thing to which Sophie attached the highest price,* he would refuse to accept any payment for the copy of *Julie* he was making for her: 'it is a very sweet debt I owe you, for allowing me to use my time in your service.' His last sentence was almost an ultimatum: 'Either you accept my copies as a present, or you find another copyist.'

Sophie's soft answer[46] to this unpleasant tirade proved once again how well she deserved the title of the Perfect One:

I would accept your copies as a proof of your trust and as a souvenir of an old friendship, but please allow me to pay you for the copies, because otherwise I would be robbing you of the time you have employed on the work, and it is only just that every man should live on the trade he has chosen. I would not think of the copies as 'bought' and my gratitude would be the same. I beg you to agree to this, and also to believe, despite your withdrawal of friendship, and the ending of a relationship to which I could not give as much as you could, and which had become altogether

---

*'I see clearly from your letters that the thing to which you attach this highest price in the world is money.'

too stormy, but which you alone have forced me to break off, that I have
no reproaches to make.

Sophie wrote again two days later[47] to assure Rousseau that she was not
angry and that she had agreed to terminate their correspondence only
because he had proposed it: 'I break off without acrimony or bitterness a
relationship in which I could never make you happy.' The same letter,
however, indicates that Sophie had reasons of her own for ending their
correspondence. She said that the forthcoming presence in the house of
her husband – soon to return to Paris from his military duties – would
leave her little time for letter-writing, and it was embarrassing for her to
receive letters she had to hide.

No sooner had Sophie posted this letter than she began to regret it, and
the next day[48] she sent Rousseau, by express messenger, an apology: 'I
repent, my dear Citizen, of what I have done and I am not ashamed to
beg your forgiveness. I am too severely punished if I have added to the
sufferings of an unfortunate being who is my friend. Answer me at once,
my dear, and tell me that you have forgotten my petulance as I have
forgotten yours.' Sophie added that she had sent the letter by express
messenger so that she might receive his reply before her husband returned.

Her letter crossed one[49] from Rousseau in which he pointed out, bitterly,
that she seemed able to find time for writing letters that made him wretched
but not for writing letters that would bring him comfort. But when, next
day, he received her express letter with its heartfelt apology, he was ecstatic:
'Your letter,' he told her,[50]

has given me the purest, truest pleasure I have ever experienced in my life.
Ah, if only you could always have written to me in this way, what
torments you would have spared me! ... Believe me, my heart is made to
love you. It is worthy of doing so and to me you will always be, after
virtue itself, the most precious thing in the world. So let us be friends, for
the sake of my happiness, and perhaps of yours as well, for unless my heart
is mistaken we shall both be the better for it. I shall conform to all you
require of me, I shall not write you any more without having permission
from you and then only in the way you indicate to me ... The crisis is
past; the unworthy things I suffered in myself have brought about the
reformation I needed. Now you see me restored to myself and my principles. Three years of slavery had demeaned my soul. I had unwittingly
been infected by the prejudices of the world. Thank God they are now
banished, and I can offer the few friends I have left a heart that is worthy
of their respect and is never false to itself.

Rousseau's exhilaration did not last. A few days later[51] we find him writing to Sophie:

Heaven is my witness that, far from seeking a quarrel with you, I am touched and moved by your goodness, and I shall resist with all my strength the fear that still torments me, and should I ever believe it well founded I would grieve over my misfortune without complaining of your having changed.

He went on to say:

There is a word in your previous letter that troubles me cruelly. You speak of our correspondence as something you must hide from your husband. Why? Has slander about me reached his ears? Has he forbidden you to see me? If this is so, I know my duty and I honour you too much to hide yours from you ... If our relationship is disapproved of by your husband, we must renounce it.

In further pages to this letter, added two weeks later, Rousseau complained to Sophie about Diderot.

He says he loves me, but he forgets me; I would rather he said nothing, but he is a weak man dominated by everyone around him, and he dares to love me only in secret. I shall never change in my feelings for him, and I shall go on awaiting patiently his next visit to me.

It is surprising that Rousseau should thus speak of Diderot as a weak man at a time when he appeared to others to be foolishly courageous – continuing to edit the *Encyclopédie* when d'Alembert and others wanted to capitulate to its enemies.[52] But both Rousseau and Diderot were rapidly moving towards a position where neither could be altogether fair about the other.

The winter at Montmorency proved to be exceptionally cold, and the hours Rousseau spent writing in his unheated *donjon* exposed him to the worst of its rigours. But, as he explained[53] to Sophie, work was the one thing that afforded him relief in his pains. He did nothing, however, to disguise from Sophie that he felt really ill, and her letters, which became more frequent again, if never frequent enough to satisfy him, expressed her anxiety about his health. By the end of January,[54] she was able to tell him that her own health, at least, was better, and even to report that, while she did not really care for carnival festivities, she was enjoying herself at the theatre and in dancing. She mentioned that she had seen Diderot at a party at the Holbachs, but that he had run away from her; she imagined that her diamonds and crinoline had driven him off.

In another letter[55] Sophie tried to soothe Rousseau's uneasiness about her husband's attitude. She explained that the Count was prejudiced against him only because of what he had heard about him and because he had no means of knowing his true worth. That was why she had not told him about their friendship. However, she insisted that there had been no 'slanders' reaching her husband's ears and she was sure that he respected her too much to listen to any.

In a letter[56] written the same day to Sophie, Rousseau told her how much he suffered from the fact that people were making him out to be a scoundrel, and he complained once again about the 'long intervals' between her letters. As for Diderot, he said he was disturbed by the new measures which were being taken by the government against the *Encyclopédie*: 'My imagination has been filled with the dungeons of Vincennes, where I once went to see Diderot at the cost of many tears and many footsteps. I wrote to implore him to give up the editorship of the *Encyclopédie* if d'Alembert decided to do so, but he has not condescended to answer my letter, neglecting the distress of the friend who helped him in his.'*

Rousseau was able to tell Sophie that he had finished copying for her Part II of *Julie*, but he explained that the manuscript was too big for the messenger's bag. He also feared it might be soiled if it was examined by the municipal customs at the gates of Paris. He suggested therefore that Sophie should 'take the air' in her carriage as far as Saint-Denis, where he might, if it was fine, meet and give her the manuscript in person.

He may well have contemplated going to Saint-Denis on foot. Even though he told François Coindet[58] that he was far too ill to receive any guests at Montlouis, Rousseau probably exaggerated his condition in order to keep that importunate compatriot away. He still proved himself capable of walking twenty miles in a day, as he often did, although he could easily have taken a coach from Montmorency to Saint-Denis, for M. Mathas's estate, unlike the inaccessible Hermitage, was on a good road, and well served by transport. Sophie, however, turned down the idea of a rendez-vous at Saint-Denis. She informed Rousseau that she would send one of her servants to collect the manuscript of *Julie*, declaring, candidly, that because of the presence of her husband she would not be able to meet

---

*Presumably the 'distress' Rousseau felt to be comparable to Diderot's imprisonment was his illness and imminent (as he believed) death. Rousseau's effort to persuade Diderot to give up the *Encyclopédie* was identical to that of Voltaire. And if Rousseau's letter remained unanswered, Diderot wrote to Voltaire: 'To abandon the work is to turn one's back on the breach and do what the scoundrels who persecute us desire. We should do what is suitable to a man of courage. Despise our enemies, pursue them, and take advantage, as we have done, of the inbecility of our censors.'[57]

Rousseau even when she came herself to visit Eaubonne later that week. In the same letter she urged him not to be so hard on Diderot for his delay in answering letters, and in general not to be so suspicious, intolerant and unforgiving towards his friends.

In a note he added some years later to his copy[59] of this letter, Rousseau suggested that people had started to call him 'misanthrope' at just the time when he had ceased to have any such defect. He was ready to admit that some things he had written in Paris were marked by a certain black humour,* but he claimed that everything he had written since he had moved to the country proclaimed his new-found serenity, and that the author of *Julie* and the *Letter to M. d'Alembert* was no longer in any sense a misanthrope.

Rousseau was not, however, in a particularly loving mood when he received in mid-February a friendly letter from Mme d'Épinay in Geneva opening the door to a reconciliation. She suggested that their quarrel was due to 'a misunderstanding' and she begged him to accept a reimbursement of the money he had paid as wages to the gardener at the Hermitage. Rousseau reproduces this letter[60] *in extenso*, in the *Confessions*, where he also asserts that since he no longer trusted Mme d'Épinay, he did not answer it. In fact, he did answer it with a letter that Mme d'Épinay prints in a modified form in *Montbrillant*.[61] He answered rudely:[62] 'I will not attempt to explain to you what you have made up your mind not to understand, and can only admire so much wit being combined with so little intelligence, but I ought not to be surprised, since you have long praised the same defect in me.' He went on to specify the details of what he had owed her gardener and what he had paid. As for the rest of her letter, he had nothing to offer in reply, he said, other than silence, patience and integrity: 'If you have any more torments to inflict on me, do so quickly, because I do not think you will be able to have that pleasure much longer.'

In the *Confessions*,[63] Rousseau says that Mme d'Épinay was conspiring in Geneva at that time with Voltaire and others to do him harm, and that Grimm, who joined her there, abetted her efforts: 'Dr Tronchin, whom they had no difficulty in recruiting, gave them powerful support and soon became the most furious of my persecutors, without my giving him any more cause for complaint than I had given Grimm.'

These words were written in 1765. In the early months of 1758, however, Rousseau had no reason to think of Dr Tronchin as an enemy. Indeed, Rousseau's *Letter to M. d'Alembert*, which alienated Voltaire when it was published some months later, received from Dr Tronchin nothing but

*He was thinking presumably of *Inequality*.

praise and commendation. D'Alembert's article had already been read in
Geneva and caused some consternation, largely, as Rousseau expected, by
reason of its suggestion that the Genevese clergy had reduced their Calvinism to a pure Socinianism. Jacob Vernes, as one of the Genevese pastors
who felt himself a victim of this embarrassing compliment, seems to have
asked Rousseau to intervene with d'Alembert in Paris to secure some sort
of retraction, for we find Rousseau writing to Vernes on 18 February[64]
saying he has been unable to 'execute' his 'commission': 'As M. d'Alembert
and I hardly ever meet, we never write to each other, and being confined
to my solitude, I have not kept up any sort of connection with Paris. It is
as if I were at the furthest end of the earth, so that I know no more of
what is going on there than in Pekin.' Rousseau did not tell Vernes that
he had himself just written a reply to d'Alembert's article; indeed he even
tried to persuade Vernes that the subject was best ignored: 'Even if the
article you mention is indiscreet and deplorable, it is surely not offensive.'
Rousseau agreed that since the clergy of Geneva found it harmful, they
might do well to reply to it, but he said he detested the sort of detailed
theological arguments that would have to be dragged into any such
refutation:

I dislike anyone's conscience being subjected to formulas in matters of
faith. I have a religion, my friend, and it is good for me. I do not believe
there is any man in the world who has as much need of it as I. I have
passed my life among unbelievers without allowing my faith to be shaken.
I loved them, and respected them greatly, but I could not endure their
doctrine. I have always told them that while I did not know how to
refute them, I would not believe them.* Philosophy, which has neither
foundations nor boundaries, and lacks primary ideas and first principles,
is a sea of uncertainty and doubt, from which the metaphysician never
drags himself out. So I have abandoned reason and consulted nature, that
is, the inner feeling which directs my belief independently of reason ...

My friend, I believe in God, and God would not be just if my soul were
not immortal. There, it seems to me, you have everything that is essential
and useful in religion. Let us leave the rest to theologians. As for eternal
punishment, that could not be reconciled with man's weakness or God's
justice, so I reject it. It is true there are some souls so evil that I cannot
conceive how they could ever enjoy eternal blessedness, the sweetest feeling
of which, I think, must be contentment with oneself. This makes me
suspect that wicked souls may simply be annihilated at death, and that

---

*In his *Reveries* Rousseau writes: 'The philosophers did not persuade me but they
disturbed me. Their arguments shook me, without ever convincing me.'[65]

existence and consciousness are the first rewards of a good life. However that may be, the future of the wicked does not worry me. It is enough for me, as I approach the end of my life, that I do not see the end of my hopes, but await a happier life to come after having suffered so much in this world. Even if I am mistaken in this hope, it is good in itself because it has enabled me to bear all my sufferings more easily.

In the winter of 1757–8, Rousseau wrote a series of letters to Sophie on the subjects of morality and happiness. Since she had forbidden him to post letters to her because of the presence of her husband, and as he was unable to contrive any other way of delivering them to her, they accumulated on his desk, and in the end they were not sent. It was perhaps as well for her that she did not receive them, for they contained references to the triumph of virtue over passion in his relations with her which could readily give an unfortunate impression to a husband or lover or indeed any reader prone to the sort of suspicions that are prompted by jealousy or hostility or psychoanalytic theory.

Rousseau began by assuring Sophie that his 'blind passion' for her had given way to 'a thousand clear-sighted feelings', which had left him with 'the delightful duty of loving you all my life',[66] so that she was now more dear to him than she had been when he was in love with her. He did not, however, omit to describe what it had felt like to be in love with her:

Remember the beautiful days of that charming summer, so short and so unforgettable. Remember the solitary walks we loved to repeat in those shady slopes where the most fertile valley in the world spread the beauties of nature before our eyes. Remember those delightful conversations when the effusions of our souls mutually eased our sorrows, and you cast the peace of innocence over the sweetest feelings that the heart of man has ever tasted. Without being united by the same bond, without burning with the same desire, some strange celestial flame inspired us with its ardour and made us sigh together for unknown pleasures that we were born to enjoy together.[67]

How terrible it would be, he suggested, if they could not both

recall with joy the moment when, sitting together at the foot of an oak tree, your hand was in mine and your eyes, fixed tenderly on mine, shed tears that were purer than the rain from heaven. No doubt, an evil and corrupt observer would interpret from a distance our conversation by the measure of his own base heart; but the innocent witness, the eternal eye which is never mistaken, would perhaps look with approval upon two sensitive hearts mutually encouraging each other towards virtue and nourishing with generous effusions all the pure feelings with which their hearts were filled.

For the most part, however, these six letters to Sophie represent Rousseau in the role of the moral philosopher instructing the woman he has ceased to approach as a *galant*. In the first letter he invokes such names as Descartes, Locke and Newton, but goes on to make it clear how far his thinking has departed from that of the Enlightenment and its idols. He denies that knowledge is to be attained by the great empiricist enterprise of studying the external universe and its workings. He claims that human understanding can best be achieved by looking inward; it must begin with a study of oneself. And far from subscribing to the Baconian ideal of conquering nature, he protests that men deceive themselves if they think that all nature is there for human beings to make use of and exploit. He tells Sophie that he is not going to appeal to metaphysical reasoning but 'to draw from the depths of your own heart the only arguments that will convince you'.[68] He then suggests that he is able by looking into his own heart to know what she will find in hers. He claims to be able to do this because he possesses an extremely sensitive soul, and since he has been subjected by fate to every imaginable psychological experience, nothing human is strange to him. It is his nature, he explains, to find inner strength in times of adversity and to feel anxious when things go well; and the solitary life he now leads has enabled these dispositions of his soul to develop usefully: 'I believe I can feel in myself a seed of goodness which compensates me for ill fortune and a seed of nobility which enables me to rise above good fortune.'

In a later letter, he tries to persuade Sophie of the value of solitude: 'I do not want to impose on a *femme du monde* the life of an anchorite.'[69] It was less a matter, he explained, of closing her door to company than of closing her soul 'to alien passions that assail it every second'.[70] He urged her to learn to be alone in the midst of worldly company: 'Avoid objects that might distract you until you reach a point where their presence can no longer distract you.'[71] He did not wish her to give up society and its empty pleasures, but he did want her to know how to be alone without being bored: 'You will gain doubly by such a contemplative life; you will find a deeper attachment to that which is dear to you while you have it and less sorrow in losing it when you have it no longer.'[72]

In these letters to Sophie Rousseau first adumbrated the ideas about morals and happiness which he expounded at length in *Émile*, and especially the 'Profession of Faith of the Savoyard Priest'. Indeed when he says to Sophie: 'I claim less to be giving you lessons than making my own profession of faith,'[73] he entitles us to at least regard what is afterwards ascribed to the 'Savoyard Priest' as his own personal testimony. There is an invocation of conscience as the supreme source of moral guidance in the first letter to Sophie,[74] which was to be repeated, almost word for word, in *Émile*.[75]

'Conscience, conscience, divine instinct, immortal and celestial voice, sure guide of an ignorant and limited but intelligent and free mind, infallible judge of good and evil, sublime emanation of the eternal substance which renders man similar to the gods – it is thee who maketh the excellence of my nature.'

Thus, while Rousseau never sent these six letters to Sophie, the material in them was not wasted. He put the ideas into the mouth of a dissident Catholic curate and gave them to the world. He wrote the letters over a period when he was much distracted, by other work, by the move to the Petit Montlouis, and by ill health. At the time he wrote the later letters he had the further chagrin of knowing that Sophie was very near to him at Eaubonne, but unwilling to visit him simply because of the presence of a husband to whom she had been systematically and publicly unfaithful for several years. Sophie tried to make her behaviour less wounding by sending a servant to the Petit Montlouis with an occasional note. One such she wrote on 22 February[76] saying: 'Believe me it hurts me greatly to be so near and not be able to see you.' She begged for news of his health and asked him to give her messenger the parts of *Julie* that he had copied out for her.

Rousseau handed the manuscript to the servant together with a mournful message:[77] 'I am no better in my health; that is all I can tell you. I have no consolations and no testimonies of friendship except from you alone ... Whatever happens, remember, I implore you, that you have never had and will never have a friend as sincerely and as purely attached to you as I am.' He asked her not to let the copy of *Julie* he was sending her go to a bindery or allow it out of her hands in any other way. He also asked her to keep the secret of the *Letter to M. d'Alembert* that he was planning to publish. 'Farewell, once again. I await your news. It is my only pleasure in this world.'

In this note Rousseau told Sophie that she was his only contact with the world, but the next mail brought a letter[78] from Deleyre in Paris promising to come to Montlouis at the end of the week, the last Saturday in February, together with Diderot, who had suggested joining him: 'Whether he decides to come or not, I shall come.' Once again, Diderot failed to keep his word, and Deleyre went to Montlouis alone. He found Rousseau in a more wretched state than he had expected; sick, very short of money, and depressed.

'I came away shocked by your situation, dear citizen of a world that treats you so badly,' Deleyre wrote[79] to Rousseau when he returned to Paris. 'You lack only a wife to resemble the prophet Job.' In a none-too-convincing effort to cheer Rousseau up, Deleyre suggested that he should seek comfort in Nature and find joy in the rebirth of spring; even suggesting (writing in February), 'The nightingale will sing again to sweeten your sleepless nights.'

Deleyre reported that he had seen Diderot again, and he urged Rousseau to appreciate that the editor of the *Encyclopédie* had been very busy and much distracted by worries. He assured Rousseau that even though Diderot had not been able to come to Montlouis, 'he thinks of you with tenderness'. Deleyre also asked Rousseau to understand that Diderot was an embattled man, resisting a savage campaign against the *Encyclopédie*: 'There are wolves in Paris, my dear friend. They howl in the pulpits, in the schools, and the innocent doe wanders in the forest. Amid all your woes, count it a blessing that you do not see what goes on here.'

Deleyre's attempt to make Rousseau forgive Diderot was unavailing, and in that same week Rousseau wrote Diderot an extraordinarily bitter, angry letter,[80] weeping (according to Thérèse)[81] as he did so. Once again he referred to the remark of a character in Diderot's play *Le Fils naturel* that 'only the bad man is alone', and he treated it again as an accusation aimed at himself:

I am a bad man, am I not? You have the surest proof of it; it is well attested to you ... I am a bad man, but why am I? Take care, my dear Diderot, for this deserves your attention. One is not bad for nothing. If there had been such a monster, he would not have waited forty years to satisfy his depraved inclinations. Consider, then, my life, my passions, my tasks, my preferences. If I am bad, ask what interest could have led me to be bad? What would I – who have always had such a sensitive heart – gain from breaking with everyone dear to me? To what place, to what patronage and what honours have I been seen to aspire? What rivals do I have that I could wish to harm?

Rousseau demanded that Diderot should explain how a man who sought only peace, solitude and idleness could have any motive for doing bad things. He then challenged Diderot to examine his own character: 'You pride yourself on your natural goodness, but do you realize how far it can be corrupted by bad examples and error? Have you never feared being surrounded by clever flatterers who avoid crude praise only in order to appear more sincere in their efforts to ingratiate themselves with you?' Rousseau suggested to Diderot that he had been seduced and deceived by the people with whom he associated. As for himself, Rousseau said, he shivered in his solitude, forgotten by all who were dear to him: 'It is possible that proofs of your friend's innocence will reach you in the end, and that you will be forced to honour his memory, and that the image of your dying friend will leave you no more peaceful nights. Think about it, Diderot. I will not speak to you about it again.'

It seems that Rousseau really did believe he was a dying man at that time. Not only did he summon once again Dr Thierry to Montmorency to attend to him, but he drafted on 8 March, in place of a will, a declaration[82] that all the furniture and effects in the cottage at Montlouis belonged to his 'servant, Thérèse Levasseur' to whom he also admitted owing thirteen years' unpaid wages, or 1,950 livres. The inventory attached to the declaration specifies beds, tables, cupboards, carpets, curtains, chairs, stoves, crockery, linen, cutlery and other items worth altogether 300 livres. The declaration was notarized at Enghein on 22 March 1758.

Rousseau was evidently eager to protect Thérèse from any effort by his creditors to distrain on his goods, his poverty at that time being as wretched as his health. Even so, when his Genevese friend Deluc[83] tried to come to his aid with a present of six louis, Rousseau refused it,[84] together with Deluc's offer to pay for the cost of his returning to Geneva with Thérèse. Rousseau explained that his health would not allow him to travel: 'I suffer in my poor bladder, and I would only accept your offer if I thought that a golden catheter would help me piss better than another one.'

The crisis of Rousseau's illness had by this time passed, and we find Deleyre speaking in a letter dated 17 March[85] of Dr Thierry 'consoling me a little about your present state of health, and by the hopes he gives us for your future'. A letter[86] from Rousseau himself to Dr Thierry, written some weeks later, gives some indication of the nature of his illness and the treatment prescribed. Rousseau reports that the lime water he has been ordered has done him no good, so he has given up taking it. The milk, too, which suppressed the urine completely, has also been abandoned:

A swelling has developed in the lower body in the left groin. The swelling is in a straight line, in an oblique direction. One might take it for a continuation of the penis. It disappears when I lie down and reappears when I get up. It is not a hernia. It only produces the sort of dull, light pain which has been with me for years in that part of the body. For the rest, the urine diminishes daily, and emerges with great difficulty, except when it is altogether plain and the colour of clear water – then it flows with a little more abundance and ease. But whatever the state of the urine, I must press the lower belly to make it come out.

Having thus described his symptoms, Rousseau assured Dr Thierry that
he had no expectation of finding any remedy.

Work, again, was his one means of keeping his mind off the pain. By
9 March he had almost finished his *Letter to M. d'Alembert* and he offered[87]
it to Rey in place of a book on the rights of war which he had promised
the publisher, but decided to abandon. He asked thirty louis for the
copyright of the *Letter*, and he implored Rey to 'keep the secret' of it. In
another letter,[88] announcing that the manuscript was ready, Rousseau
again begged Rey to take care to keep the secret of it until the very
moment of publication and, above all, not to let it fall into the hands of
Diderot or Deleyre. Rousseau had no wish, however, for the book to be
published anonymously. It was a work he was proud of: 'It is my favourite
book,' he is said to have declared years later. 'It is the one I produced
without effort, at one go, and in the most lucid moments of my life.'[89]
Rey followed Rousseau's instructions, and printed his name, in red, on
the title page:

J.-J. Rousseau, Citizen of Geneva, to M. d'Alembert of the French
Academy, the Royal Academies of Science of Paris and of Prussia, the
Royal Society of London, the Royal Literary Academy of Sweden, and
the Institute of Bologna, on his article 'Geneva' in the seventh volume of
the *Encyclopédie* and in particular on the project to establish a dramatic
theatre in that city: *Dii meliora piis, erroremque hostibus illum.*★

Besides his efforts to keep the manuscript out of the hands of Diderot
and Deleyre, Rousseau also kept Pastor Vernes in the dark about his
forthcoming publication, although he corresponded with him on the
subject of d'Alembert's article. He realized that his attitude to the article
was not the same as Vernes's. Rousseau's purpose in his *Letter* was to
challenge d'Alembert's remarks on the theatre; and, while he was willing
to defend the Genevese clergy against the charge of Socinianism, he did
not wish to be drawn into any debate as to what was and what was not
Christianity. He made this clear in his letters to Vernes, when Vernes tried
to secure his agreement with his own formulation of sound Protestant
teaching.

'We are in agreement on so many points,' Rousseau wrote[90] to Vernes,

that it is not worth the trouble of arguing about the rest. I have told you
many times that no man in the world has more regard than I for the

---

★'May heaven grant a better lot to the pious, and madness to our enemies' (Virgil,
Georgics, III, 513).

Gospel. In my opinion it is the most sublime of books; when all others tire me, I take it up with new pleasure and when all human comfort fails me, I have never had recourse to the Gospel in vain. And yet, after all, it is only a book – a book unknown to three quarters of the human race. Am I to believe that a Scythian or an African is less precious to our common Father than you and I, and why should I suppose that He has deprived them more than us of the necessary means to knowledge of Him? No, my honoured friend, it is not in some few scattered pages that we must seek God's law, but in the hearts of man, where His hand has deigned to inscribe it.

In March St-Lambert returned from Nancy to Paris, where he was reunited with Sophie, who had ended her visit to Eaubonne without seeing Rousseau. On 23 March[91] she sent a messenger to Montlouis with a note asking Rousseau for his news, and telling him how well and happy she was now that she was together again with her beloved; she was eagerly awaiting the full text of *Julie* to read it to him.

Rousseau's reply[92] did not dissimulate his chagrin: 'I am very pleased that you still remember me,' he remarked, reporting of his own health that he was still fit enough to keep going, however feebly, and 'to take advantage of every fine day to go into the forest of Montmorency, where the spring is beginning to break through and the birds to sing.' He expressed pleasure at the news of her good health, but ended on a somewhat priggish note: 'I congratulate you on your pleasures; may you one day come to know those which bring true happiness.'

Sophie was perceptibly hurt by these words, but wrote[93] back at once to assure Rousseau that he could count on 'a friendship which does not break because of injuries, which forgives injustices and pities faults and weaknesses – a friendship to the progress of which you yourself have always been the greatest obstacle, but which will always be yours, whatever you are, unless there is crime and infamy, of which I believe you incapable'.

Although she tried to soften the blow by saying that she always believed him to be better than he sometimes chose to appear, her letter produced, as can be imagined, an outraged reaction: 'You tell me,' Rousseau replied next day,[94]

that I am the greatest obstacle to the progress of your friendship. First, let me tell you that I do not ask that your friendship should progress; only that it should not diminish, and certainly I have not been the cause of its diminution. When we parted after our last conversation at Eaubonne [in October], I swore to you that we were the two people in the universe who had the greatest esteem and friendship for one another, and the most mutual respect. It seemed to me that it was with these assurances of shared feelings that we parted, and it was still in the same spirit that you wrote to me a few days later.

Imperceptibly your letters changed their style. Your declarations of friendship became more reserved, more circumspect, more qualified. At the end of the month, it turned out that your friend was no longer your friend. I asked you several times the reason for this change, and now you oblige me to ask it again. I do not ask why your friendship has not increased, but why it is extinct. Do not blame it on my breach with your sister-in-law and her worthy friend. You know what happened; and all the time you must have been aware that there cannot be any peace between J.-J. Rousseau and the wicked.

You speak to me, in a reproachful tone, of faults and weaknesses. I am weak, it is true; my life is full of faults, because I am a man. But what distinguishes me from all the other men I know, is that with all my faults, I have always reproached myself for them, and that my faults have never made me despise my duty or trample on virtue; and, moreover, that I have struggled for virtue and conquered at times when everyone else has forgotten it. May you always find men as criminal as that . . .

Imagine my situation. Why do you make your letters add sadness to a heart that you know to be afflicted enough with its own sorrows? Is it so necessary to your own repose that you should disturb mine? Can you not understand that I have a greater need for consolation than reproaches? Spare me what you know I do not deserve, and show some respect for my misfortune. I ask three things of you: change your style or justify it or stop writing to me. I would rather do without your letters altogether than receive any more wounding ones. I can do without your respect, but I need to respect you, and I do not know how to do that if you let me down.

Sophie hesitated before answering this impassioned letter. Then something happened which put an end to their correspondence for ever. St-Lambert learned from Diderot the secret that Sophie had tried to keep from him: that Rousseau had been in love with her, and had declared his love during their numerous rendezvous of the previous summer. St-Lambert, who had previously suspected Rousseau of nothing more than undermining Sophie's attachment to him by preaching against adultery, was furious when he learned the truth, and subjected his mistress to angry scenes. Thereupon, on 6 May 1758,[95] Sophie wrote Rousseau her definitive *lettre de rupture*:

It is a long time since you have heard from me, and it is right that you should know the reason for it and for my future conduct towards you. I have to complain of your indiscretion and that of your friends. I would have kept all my life the secret of your unfortunate passion for me. I kept it from the man I love to prevent his being estranged from you. You spoke of it to persons who have made it public and also made insinuations against me which could ruin my reputation. These rumours have already reached the ears of my lover, who is angry that I should have made a mystery to him of a passion which never pleased me, and which I kept from him in the hope that you would become reasonable and be our friend. I have seen in him a change which has nearly killed me. The justice he has finally done me, in recognizing the honesty of my character, and his return to me, has restored my peace of mind, but I do not wish to risk upsetting him or to expose myself again. I owe as much to my reputation to end all relations with you. . . .

Rousseau immediately realized that it was Diderot who had revealed his secret to St-Lambert, because Diderot was the only person to whom he had confided it. Indeed Diderot admitted he had discussed Rousseau's passion for Sophie with St-Lambert, but claimed he was not aware that in doing so he was betraying a secret. 'I spoke to St-Lambert of that adventure as of something he must know more about than I,' Diderot writes in his *Tablettes*.[96] Once Rousseau had promised to take his advice to write a letter confessing all to St-Lambert, Diderot says he believed he had done so, trusting Rousseau to keep his word. 'Thus,' Diderot continues, 'as a result of Rousseau's deceitfulness, I fell into an indiscretion.'[97]

This explanation of Diderot's is patently false. He himself knew in December 1757 that Rousseau had *not* taken his advice about writing a letter to St-Lambert admitting being in love with Mme d'Houdetot. In the pseudo-memoirs of Mme d'Épinay, which Diderot edited together with Grimm,[98] Diderot is represented as informing Grimm on 5 December 1757 that Rousseau has not written to St-Lambert the letter that he had been advised to write but a totally different one: 'Far from being a confession of involuntary passion [for Mme d'Houdetot], it was a string of excuses for having made her uneasy about an adulterous love.' Even in the *Tablettes*[99] itself, Diderot admits to knowing that Rousseau had not taken his advice, for among the 'seven crimes' he ascribes to Rousseau is the following: 'Instead of writing to M. de St-Lambert in the manner we had agreed, he wrote him an atrocious letter, to which M. de St-Lambert said one could only reply with a stick.'

5

AN EVEN AND TRANQUIL LIFE

Friendship with Diderot ended at the same time as Rousseau's correspondence with Sophie. His life now entered a new phase. The man who had for years been his closest friend, the contemporary from the provinces with whom he had shared his conquest of the literary world of Paris, the man whose genius most closely matched his own, and in conversation with whom he had made himself a philosopher, was soon to be a bitter enemy. The one woman with whom he had known the experience of being in love was henceforth to be a mere acquaintance: Sophie was once more Mme d'Houdetot.

Even that distant relationship with Sophie continued only because of the intervention of her lover. As Rousseau tells the story in the *Confessions*,[1] St-Lambert undertook 'an act worthy of his generosity' when, conscious of the distress Rousseau must be feeling at the way he had been treated by Diderot and other friends, he went several times to visit him at the Petit Montlouis. On one occasion when Rousseau was out, St-Lambert stayed to talk for more than two hours with Thérèse. In the course of that conversation, Rousseau later learned, several unexpected disclosures were made. St-Lambert revealed both that he believed and that it was universally believed that Rousseau had been Mme d'Épinay's lover, and was amazed to learn from Thérèse that the rumour was false. 'As for Sophie, St-Lambert told Thérèse many things which neither she nor Sophie herself knew, but which I had confided under the seal of friendship to Diderot, from whom alone St-Lambert could have learned them. This finally decided me. Resolved to break with Diderot once and for all, I had only to settle the manner of doing it.' Settling that question took Rousseau another month.

As the weather improved at Montmorency, so did Rousseau's health; the *Confessions*[2] even suggests that he found a new kind of happiness:

After I had shaken off the yoke of my tyrants I led a tolerably even and tranquil life; deprived of the charm of attachments that were too intense, I was also free from the weight of their chains. Disgusted with patronizing friends who wanted to have the absolute disposal of my destiny and make me the slave, despite myself, of their so-called benevolence, I was determined henceforth to have only those relationships that were prompted by simple goodwill, relationships which, putting no constraint on freedom, make for the enjoyment of life and are based on a footing of equality. I had enough connections of that kind to be able to enjoy the pleasures of society[3] without suffering the loss of independence.

Rousseau did not give other people the impression of experiencing much pleasure in their society. For example, one visitor to Montlouis that May was the Venetian adventurer Giovanni-Giacomo Casanova with his mistress, Mme d'Urfé, who took some music they wanted Rousseau to copy. Casanova in his autobiography[4] says they went because they had heard that 'Rousseau copied music marvellously well', but their real motive was probably curiosity, and they were not warmly received: 'We thought Rousseau a simple man who was fair enough, who lived simply and modestly, but was in no way distinguished in his person or his mind. We did not consider him to be what is called a likeable man. He was not very polite.'

In a letter to Coindet[5] Rousseau had complained of someone who kept him in day after day awaiting a promised visit, and if that person was Casanova, it might explain the brusque welcome Casanova and his mistress received; but there can be denying that Rousseau was becoming less and less urbane in his manners and general deportment.

Rousseau also wrote[6] in a somewhat ungracious way at about this same time to Rey, complaining that he had had no answer to his offer of the completed manuscript of the *Letter to M. d'Alembert*, which, however, he had arranged to have a messenger bring to Amsterdam by hand. He told Rey he would give him twenty-four hours to decide whether to accept the work, after which time Rey should either return the manuscript to the messenger or keep it to publish, agreeing to do so with the utmost celerity and also, if possible, entrusting the author's fee of 30 louis to the same messenger.

Rey did not hand over any money, but he accepted the manuscript, promising Rousseau on 24 May[7] that he would pay the fee through a bank in Paris. He explained that he had arranged with his printer to complete the impression by the end of July, but was anxious to obtain from M. de Malesherbes before that date a licence for the sale of the book in France to prevent its being counterfeited by French pirate publishers. Rey added graciously that he was proud to be the publisher of Rousseau's *Letter*, and said he heartily agreed with what was written in it: 'I have always considered the theatre as very prone to corrupt the young.'

Rey's bank draft reached Paris within a week, but in writing[8] to thank him for it, Rousseau declared that he would rather Rey were less punctual in paying him,* and more punctual in writing to him: 'waiting and uncertainty are the torments of my life'. He said he was particularly anxious to ensure that the proofs of the *Letter to M. d'Alembert* were properly corrected, and he asked Rey to have them sent to him at regular intervals through the office in Paris of M. Dupin. He said he did not count on Malesherbes granting the import licence Rey wanted, but hoped that as that magistrate had done so against his expectations for the *Discourse on Inequality*, he might do so again. Rousseau had not yet become aware of the extent of Malesherbes's goodwill towards him. It was, in general, part of his misfortune to be less sensible of the existence of friends than of enemies, although it will be seen that when he did come to believe in Malesherbes's friendship, he was to put rather too much trust in it.

Rey in his next letter[10] to Rousseau explained that he needed Malesherbes's import licence in order to sell the *Letter to M. d'Alembert* on the most profitable market, that of France. He also reported that the printer had made good progress with the setting of the text, and by mid-June[11] he was already sending Rousseau proofs for correction, intimating as tactfully as he could his hope that the author would not delay things by making too many amendments. Rousseau assured Rey on 17 June[12] that he would not hold up proofs, but asked him to make only one correction, or rather an important addition, to the Preface. Rousseau had finally decided how to make public his break with Diderot; he would do it by denouncing him with the aid of a quotation from Scripture.

In the main text of the Preface,[13] Rousseau inserted (in French) the words: 'I had an Aristarchus, severe and judicious. I have him no longer and wish for him no more, but I shall regret him incessantly and he will be missed, more in my heart than in my writings.'[14] The reference here to Diderot is obvious, but the wounding words were those contained in a footnote: a quotation from Ecclesiasticus which read (in Latin): 'If you have drawn a sword against your friend, do not despair, you may be reconciled; if you have allowed a hostile word to escape you, do not fear, your friendship may still be restored; but there can be no reconciliation if there has been outrage, reproach, insolence or the betrayal of a secret

---

*Nevertheless, Rousseau wrote at once to Coindet asking him to have the draft exchanged for gold.[9]

or the injury of treason, for then your friend will depart from you' (Ecclesiasticus, xxii, 26–7).[15]

In the *Confessions*[16] Rousseau explains why he decided to break publicly with Diderot in this manner. He recalled that Montesquieu, a philosopher he greatly admired, had informed the world about his breach with Father de Tournemine, and had been praised for his candour in doing so. Rousseau felt it was equally a duty for him to make known his breach with Diderot, although he hoped that by not actually naming him, he might make the rupture less brutal. He did not succeed either in softening the blow or escaping the wrath of the public. 'The behaviour which won Montesquieu admiration,' Rousseau writes, 'earned me only blame and reproaches.'[17]

By veiling his denunciation of Diderot, Rousseau had made it all the more exciting to his readers' curiosity, and all the more likely to be talked about. Even women readers, who might not be formidable Latinists, could scent intrigue in a reference to '*mysterii revelatione*', and the identity of Rousseau's former 'Aristarchus' was instantly apparent to a society where the private lives of celebrated writers were subject to constant scrutiny. Rousseau had, moreover, chosen an unfortunate moment to publish his denunciation. Diderot's defence of the *Encyclopédie* almost alone against its Catholic and conservative adversaries had won him widespread respect as a courageous, intelligent, selfless champion of radical ideas, and he was also much liked as a good-natured and modest man. In betraying Rousseau's secret to St-Lambert, he had undoubtedly done a vile disservice to an old friend, but very few people would readily believe it of him. It was far easier to assume that the anchorite of Montmorency was subject to yet another delusion of an unhinged mind.

On the other hand, d'Alembert, against whose article in the *Encyclopédie* Rousseau's *Letter* was addressed, was among the first to praise it. His own relations with Diderot were not particularly warm since he had withdrawn from the co-editorship of the *Encyclopédie* rather than court the risks of imprisonment. There was no emotional element in his relationship with Rousseau, which had never been more intimate than that of two literary colleagues united by a shared enthusiasm for music. D'Alembert seems to have paid scant attention to the Preface, but was sufficiently impressed by the *Letter* itself to intervene personally with Malesherbes to ask for a licence to be granted for its sale in France. In his note[18] to Malesherbes, d'Alembert wrote: 'I have read M. Rousseau's book against me. It gave me great pleasure; I do not doubt it will please the public as well, and I find nothing in it that should impede its entry into France.' To Rousseau himself, d'Alembert wrote:[19] 'Very far, Monsieur, from being offended by your criticisms of my article "Geneva", I am on the contrary, very flattered and honoured that you should have chosen to write about it.'

Rousseau continued[20] to complain to Rey about misprints in his edition of the *Letter*, but was ready to concede that Rey had done his best. He asked him to send twenty-five complimentary copies of the book to Geneva, with one on superior paper for Pastor Vernes to present to the State Library. To Vernes himself, Rousseau wrote[21] informing him, at last, that he was publishing a reply to d'Alembert's article:

The suggestion that we should establish a theatre at Geneva seemed to me pernicious. It provoked my zeal and made me all the more indignant because I could see clearly enough that M. d'Alembert did not scruple to pay court to M. de Voltaire at our expense. There you have our authors and philosophers! Some private interest is always their motive, and the public good is always their pretext. My dear Vernes, let us be men and citizens to our last breath. Let us dare to speak for the good of all, even if it is prejudicial to our friends and to ourselves.

In the same letter Rousseau replied to an inquiry from Vernes about *Julie*: 'Far from being a philosophical novel,' he explained, 'it is about personal relations. If you come here, I will show it to you, and if you would like to take it in hand, I would gladly submit it to your direction.'

Rousseau had in the meantime found time to copy out 251 pages of *Julie* for Sophie. St-Lambert acknowledged the manuscript on her behalf on 23 June[22] with a payment of two louis. He told Rousseau that he was on his way to visit his family in Nancy, and asked him to send him there the copy he had promised of his forthcoming *Letter to M. d'Alembert*. He ended affectionately: 'Rest assured that there are two people in the world who will never let you down.'

The first edition of the *Letter to M. d'Alembert* reached Geneva in August 1758, at a time when controversy was still rife among the citizens over the suggestion in the *Encyclopédie* that they should build a theatre. The patrician class and other smart people who looked to France for cultural inspiration were in favour of the proposal; the clergy and the puritans against. Voltaire remained the leading champion of the theatre, and Marcet de Mézières,* Rousseau's father's friend, was one of Voltaire's supporters. A dramatist of sorts himself, Marcet wrote a play, *Le Diogène à la campagne*, in which the free citizens of Athens are represented as defending the drama against the attacks of the priests of Minerva. The play was performed at the gates of Geneva in the theatre at Carouge. Marcet later produced a printed version of his play with a preface attempting to refute Rousseau's *Letter*.

---

*Isaac-Ami Marcet de Mézières (1695–1763). Rousseau had visited him at the start of his summer in Geneva in 1754.

More, however, was written in Geneva in support of Rousseau's case than against it, and official representations were even made to the court at Turin to have the theatre at Carouge closed, on the grounds that, being so near to Geneva, it was attracting, and corrupting, the Genevese public.

The *Letter to M. d'Alembert* enjoyed almost as much success in France as in Geneva, for although it did not suggest that theatres should be suppressed in Paris or other places where they existed already, it contained such an eloquent and original critique of the traditional French belief that drama purifies morals that it immediately captured the attention of French readers. D'Alembert himself was largely responsible for their being able to read it. He intervened with a second letter[23] to Malesherbes in September, at the behest of Rey,[24] urging him to authorize the entry of 1,600 copies of the *Letter* into France, and he mentioned Turgot's name as another who would recommend approval of the book. It is perhaps ironical that Turgot, the most prominent exponent of Voltairian ideas of enlightened absolutism in French politics, should speak up for Rousseau; yet he was then, and remained, a solid admirer of Rousseau's work. In this he was in a minority among the intellectuals of the Enlightenment, as Rousseau knew well.

Voltaire saw Rousseau's aggression as directed personally against himself and his pet project to have a theatre built in Geneva where his own plays could be performed among others that he wanted to see staged, and perhaps act in himself, and he was furious. Like Marcet, Voltaire called Rousseau 'Diogène', and he warned[25]* d'Alembert that Rousseau was 'a Diogène barking against the theatre from the depths of his barrel . . . There is a double ingratitude in him. He attacks an art which he practises himself, and he has written against you, who have overwhelmed him with praises.'

Rousseau was aware of Voltaire's hostility, and told[27] Rey that Paris was swarming with 'irreconcilable enemies, all the more dangerous for wearing a mask of friendship in order to destroy me; and never forgiving me for the harm they have done me'. He suggested that these enemies were plotting to undermine the sales of his book in France, and was grieved that Rey might be 'the victim of the blows designed for me'.

In fact Rey had no grounds for anxiety about the sales of any book by Rousseau, and was already pressing[28] him to let him publish his collected works, a project about which Rousseau was not at first enthusiastic, but later suggested[29] he might put together in the form of a 'general edition' in four volumes of his most successful published pieces together with some unpublished ones: 'For I tell you that being no longer well enough to

---

*Voltaire had not yet read Rousseau's book, but he had heard about what it contained. To Thieriot, Voltaire wrote on 17 July: 'What about Jean-Jacques's book against the theatre? Has he become a priest of the church?'[26]

work, I have the sweet idea of leaving behind when I die a good collection
of what I have done.'

For all these protestations of incapacity and approaching death, Rousseau
continued at the Petit Montlouis to produce more literary work than ever
before; he was finishing off *Julie*, writing the opening chapters of *Émile*,
making notes for what was eventually to be published as *The Social
Contract*, and tinkering with his *Dictionary of Music*. There was little
interruption caused by social life of any kind. Even the few friends he did
still see were kept at a certain distance. For example, we find him writing
to François Coindet that autumn[30] warning him not to expect friendship
to ripen quickly; for friendship, he argued, 'is something that must mature
slowly over the years, so that true friends are friends long before they use
the word "friend"'. Rousseau suggested that what Coindet really wanted
was familiarity rather than friendship, and for that their situation, he said,
was not appropriate: 'you are young and vigorous; I am poorly and
grizzled. You have the tastes of your age, and I have those of mine.'
Nevertheless, Rousseau assured Coindet that he was writing to him as to
something more than a friend – it was as to a son: 'Enough people take
the title of friend without fulfilling the duties of a friendship. Let me do
the opposite.'

Rousseau was as good as his word when a few days later[31] he sent Coindet
a letter of introduction[32] to his former pupil Mme de Chenonceaux,
commending him to her for his 'straightforwardness, candour and simplicity'. The letter accompanied a gift to Mme de Chenonceaux of the
Letter to M. d'Alembert, Rey having already sent a batch of advance copies
to Paris. Coindet, as ever the social climber, readily seized this opportunity
to make the acquaintance of the only daughter of the head of the most
ancient noble family in France, the Vicomte de Rochechouart, and
ingratiate himself with her to a point where he was, to Rousseau's irritation,
welcomed as an intimate friend.

Rousseau showed rather more warmth at that time towards that other
young friend, Alexandre Deleyre. Replying[33] to a letter from Deleyre
(which has disappeared), Rousseau expressed his sympathy once again
with Deleyre at the death of the Comte de Gisors, who had provided him
with a comfortable secretarial job, adding, with somewhat brutal candour,
that he was all the more sorry because it meant that Deleyre was returning
to journalism. Rousseau said he trembled at the prospect of Deleyre
making simple souls unhappy by his writings:

My dear Deleyre, beware of your satirical wit, and above all, learn to
respect Religion. Simple humanity calls for such respect. The great, the
rich, the fortunate few of our century would be delighted if there were

no God, but the expectation of another life consoles the common people and the wretched of the earth for the miseries of this life. What cruelty to rob them even of that hope!

In the same letter Rousseau mentioned Helvétius, Deleyre having evidently commented on the predicament of that author, whose materialist treatise *De l'esprit* had landed him in serious trouble. The clergy had launched such a vigorous campaign that the book, originally licensed by Malesherbes, was withdrawn from circulation in August 1758[*] and Helvétius forced to publish a grovelling recantation of his opinions in order to avoid criminal charges.[34][†] The *Journal encyclopédique*, to the editing of which Deleyre returned, published in Liège that same year a series of articles on Helvétius's book, which were unique in taking a sympathetic view of Helvétius's argument. It is a reasonable conjecture that Deleyre wrote the articles himself, and had admitted as much in the missing letter to Rousseau.

Rousseau's comment was: 'M. Helvétius has written a dangerous book and made humiliating retractions, but he has quit his office as a tax-farmer, married an honest girl and made her happy, and often helped people in need. His actions are worth more than his writings. My dear Deleyre, let us try to have as much said of ourselves.'

Rousseau had not at that stage read *De l'esprit*, as he informed Vernes later that month[35] – 'I like and esteem the author, but I hear terrible things about the book' – but he read it soon afterwards[36] and was to incorporate some arguments against it into the 'Profession of Faith of the Savoyard Priest',[37] again accompanied by a friendly word about Helvétius as a man.[‡]

Rousseau received from Deleyre[38] a promise that he would not attack religion in his journalism: 'I respect public opinion, and I know the usefulness of it up to a certain point, but you give the game away to the unbelievers when you assert that one cannot be virtuous without religion.'[§] Rousseau was probably more pleased to learn from the same letter that Deleyre was giving up journalism – in which he could not make a living – to look for a place in the diplomatic service. Deleyre was indeed soon to be appointed to a secretaryship at the French Embassy in Vienna.

---

[*]In February 1759 it was burned by the public executioner.

[†]Diderot, another victim of the same campaign, stood his ground, and escaped prosecution.

[‡]Helvétius in *De l'homme* (1772) published a rejoinder to *Émile*, arguing that since men's characters were formed by the external environment, any man could be educated to do anything.

[§]In a note in the *Letter to M. d'Alembert*, Rousseau writes: 'I do not mean one can be virtuous without religion; for a long time I thought so; now I am disillusioned.' In *Julie*, M. de Wolmar is described as a virtuous atheist.

The *Letter to M. d'Alembert* had in the meantime been published. Since it contained nothing to offend the pious, Rousseau was spared the hostility which was currently targeted at Helvétius and Diderot and the *Encyclopédie*. Indeed the *Letter* was regarded by many Encyclopédistes as being itself a contribution to the new wave of reaction and censorship in France. Rousseau himself was more concerned to have the book well received in Geneva, and while he asked Coindet[39] to present copies of the book to d'Alembert, to his Spanish friend from Venice days, Carrión, and to members of the Dupin family, he sent Vernes a longer list[40] of people in Geneva to whom he wanted him to distribute copies. These included Voltaire and the French Resident Monpéroux,* two of the republic's syndics, Saladin† and Mussard,‡ together with several professors of the Académie de Genève who had shown friendship towards Rousseau in Geneva in the summer of 1754 – Jallabert, Perdriau, Vernet§ and Sarasin the Elder.‖ Others listed were Dr Théodore Tronchin and two younger friends, Louis Necker,* professor of mathematics, and Daniel de Rochemont,† a pastor. Rousseau also instructed Vernes to give a copy to his steadfast friend Jean-François Deluc,‡ together with a second copy for Deluc to deliver to his aunt in Nyon, Mme Gonçerut,§ and in the same way to give a second copy to Marc Chappuis‖ so that he could pass one on to Gauffecourt. Others listed were Rousseau's two cousins, Jean-François* and Gabriel,† together with the confectioner Donzel,‡ in whose modest premises in St-Gervais Rousseau had dined happily during his summer in Geneva in 1754, and David

*Étienne-Jean Guimard de Rocheretz, Baron de Monpéroux, French Resident in Geneva from 1750 to 1765.
†Jean-Louis Saladin (1701–84), noted as a diplomat in the service of France and England as well as Geneva, was first elected syndic in 1750.
‡Pierre Mussard (1690–1767) as Ambassador of Geneva had negotiated the Treaty of Turin which in 1754 finally settled border disputes between the Genevese republic and the Savoyard monarchy of Sardinia. Rousseau had witnessed his swearing-in as syndic in 1754.[41]
§Jacob Vernet (1698–1789), one of the most influential theologians of the republic. Although he had published an attack on the *Discourse on the Sciences and the Arts*, Rousseau made successful efforts to cultivate his friendship.[42]
‖Jean Sarasin, known as the Elder (1693–1790) one of the examining pastors who voted for Rousseau's readmission to the established Church.[43] Not to be confused with Jean Sarasin the Younger, who emerged as one of Rousseau's most bitter enemies in 1762.
*Louis Necker (1730–1804), brother of the celebrated financier and minister to Louis XVI.
†Daniel de Rochemont (1720–69) had been promoted to be a pastor in 1756, although Rousseau named him simply as a minister.
‡Jean-François Deluc (1698–1780).[44]
§Suzanne Gonçerut, née Rousseau (1682–1775) Rousseau's 'Tante Suzon'.[45]
‖Marc Chappuis (1714–79), a good friend to Rousseau but a less than loyal protégé of Gauffecourt, whose salt monopoly in Geneva he usurped.
*Jean-François Rousseau (1685–1763), son of Noë Rousseau.
†Gabriel Rousseau (1715–80), son of David Rousseau.
‡Jean Donzel (1695–1768).[46]

Rival,* the old family friend who had accompanied Rousseau's father on his half-hearted attempt to recover Jean-Jacques when he had run away from Geneva at the age of sixteen.

Rousseau had planned to send a copy of the *Letter* to St-Lambert in Lorraine, but by this time the ailing veteran had returned from his visit to his mother and was once more with Mme d'Houdetot at Eaubonne. From that address, which was so near the Petit Montlouis, St-Lambert wrote on 9 October,[47] 'We have been here two days, Monsieur, and we have each of us the most tender friendship for you. I will come to assure you of it if you will tell me at what time you can generally be found at home. Mme d'Houdetot is impatient to see what you have done with *Julie*, and I am just as eager, and if the weather were not so bad you would have seen me today.'

Rousseau promptly sent a presentation copy of the *Letter to M. d'Alembert* to St-Lambert at Eaubonne. St-Lambert opened it and began to read it. When he saw the denunciation of Diderot he was shocked, horrified, disgusted. He sent the book back with a harsh reproachful letter:[48]

In truth, Monsieur, I cannot accept the present you have just offered me. When I came upon the page in the Preface where you quote Eclesiastes [*sic*],† the book fell from my hands. After our conversations this summer you seemed convinced that Diderot was innocent of the supposed indiscretions you had imputed to him. He may have done you some wrong that I do not know about but I do know that this does not give you the right to insult him publicly. You take no account of the persecutions he has now to endure, and you add the voice of an old friend to the cries of his enemies. I confess, Monsieur, that I cannot hide from you how much that atrocity revolts me. I am not close to Diderot, but I honour him, and I feel deeply the sorrow you are giving to a man whom, in my presence, you have only accused of a minor fault. Monsieur, we differ too much in our principles for us ever to agree. Forget my existence; it ought not to be difficult ... I promise you that I, for my part, will forget your person, and remember only your talents.

It is understandable that St-Lambert should feel protective towards Diderot at a time when Diderot was being harassed by the Church and state; he was ideologically in sympathy with the *Encyclopédie* and all it stood for, and, having been invalided out of the army as a result of his stroke, he was no longer a part-time poet, but a full-time writer in the

*David Rival (1696–1759), watchmaker and father of the celebrated actor, Jean Rival (1728–1805).

†He means Ecclesiasticus.

service of the Enlightenment, a Philosophe of liberal principles and high intellectual ambitions. It is only strange that his breach with Rousseau was not permanent.

Rousseau sent only a curt reply[49] to St-Lambert's rebuke: 'Monsieur, in reading your letter I paid you the compliment of being surprised at it, and I was stupid enough to be upset by it, but I think it unworthy of an answer.' He went on to say that he no longer wished to go on making a copy of *Julie* for Mme d'Houdetot, and asked her to return the prospectus she had been sent for the set of illustrations to that novel which was about to be published separately. His letter ended: 'Adieu, Monsieur.'

According to Rousseau's interpretation[50] of events, this letter 'caused St-Lambert to reflect'; stirred by a generous heart, the Marquis 'came to be sorry' for having written the *lettre de rupture*, and then contrived a way to reconciliation by having M. d'Épinay invite Rousseau to a dinner at La Chevrette when both he and Mme d'Houdetot would be fellow guests.

Whether St-Lambert prompted him or not, M. d'Épinay did invite[57] Rousseau to dine at La Chevrette, where, in the continued absence of Mme d'Épinay in Geneva, he lived alone in a style much beyond his diminished means. M. d'Épinay's invitation to Rousseau indicated that he was having to dinner on the following Sunday, 29 October, the Dupins, St-Lambert, Francueil and Mme d'Houdetot, 'who would all be charmed to spend a part of the day with you'. In the *Confessions*[52] Rousseau writes:

This invitation made my heart beat horribly. After having been the talk of Paris for a year, the idea of going to exhibit myself face to face with Mme d'Houdetot made me tremble, and I could hardly summon up the courage to sustain the ordeal. However, since she and St-Lambert desired it, and since M. d'Épinay spoke in the name of all those who had been invited, and mentioned no one I should not be glad to meet, I decided that I would not be compromising myself by accepting an invitation which was sent me, so to speak, by all the guests. So I promised to go.

Rousseau had seen the Dupin family a few days earlier, having dined with them at Clichy on Saturday, 14 October,* together with Francueil who had written to him that same week[53] to thank him for the copy of the *Letter to M. d'Alembert* he had sent him. In his letter Francueil reproached Rousseau for the unkind things he had said about Mme d'Épinay, but assured him of the fidelity of his own friendship. He said he had enjoyed reading as much as he had been able to read – since he was not feeling very well – of the *Letter to M. d'Alembert*, but made no mention of the

---

*He dined with them again at Clichy on 1 November.

denunciation of Diderot in the Preface, and may well not have deciphered it.

The weather was bad on the Sunday of the dinner at La Chevrette, so M. d'Épinay sent his carriage to the Petit Montlouis to fetch Rousseau, who was nevertheless the last to arrive.

In the *Confessions*,[54] he says that his arrival at the château 'caused a sensation', and also that he received the most affectionate welcome of his life: 'One would have said that all the company felt how much I needed reassurance. Only French hearts know this kind of delicacy.' Rousseau was not altogether pleased to see among the guests two people that his host had not mentioned in the invitation – the Comte d'Houdetot and his sister Mme de Blainville, for Rousseau knew that Sophie's husband (whom he had not met before) was prejudiced against him, and that Mme de Blainville had disliked him ever since the days when Sophie had left her sitting alone in the mule-cart when she went for long walks with Rousseau in the forest of Montmorency. 'Mme de Blainville nourished her resentment against me throughout the dinner,'[55] Rousseau asserts; but he adds that despite her malicious sarcasms 'the dinner did me a world of good and I was very pleased I had not refused the invitation'.

After the midday dinner, the company withdrew to the *grand salon*. There, as Rousseau recalls, 'I was delighted to see St-Lambert and Mme d'Houdetot approach me, and we chatted together for a good part of the afternoon – about trivial things it is true, but with the same familiarity as before my infatuation. Their friendliness was not lost on my heart, and if St-Lambert could have seen into it, he would surely have been happy. I could swear that although the first sight of Mme d'Houdetot almost made me faint with palpitations, I had scarcely a thought of her when I left. I could think only of St-Lambert.'[56]

Rousseau was happy to reflect that reports of the dinner at La Chevrette reaching Paris would scotch the rumour that he had quarrelled with everyone there, when in fact he had only quarrelled with Mme d'Épinay and Grimm. He also felt that the 'gentleness of soul' which was evident in the *Letter to M. d'Alembert* would disprove the myth that he was 'devoured by ill-humour in his retreat'.[57] If, as it turned out, some readers were more struck by the bitterness of Rousseau's denunciation of Diderot in the Preface than by the 'gentleness of soul' exhibited in the text, Rousseau felt able to say in the *Confessions*[58] that the *Letter to M. d'Alembert* 'met with a great success' and 'taught the public to mistrust the insinuations of the Holbachian clique'. He mentions having made only one enemy with the book – the dramatist and editor of the *Mercure*, Marmontel, who took offence, Rousseau says,[59] because he inscribed his copy to him *not* as an editor of the *Mercure* but as 'Monsieur Marmontel'. It may well be that

Rousseau misunderstood Marmontel's motive – that it was simply that, as a man who had risen from poverty to fame by writing plays, Marmontel hated everything that was said against the theatre in the *Letter to M. d'Alembert.*

Rousseau also received some criticisms of the *Letter* from several of his correspondents. His pious Catholic friend, the widowed Marquise de Créqui,[60] suggested to him, after she had turned aside from her usual devotional literature to read it, that the moral teaching of the *Letter to M. d'Alembert* was only suited to Calvinist Geneva. But several Genevese correspondents complained that it was not Calvinist enough. One such critic was Lenieps, who appears to have discussed the book when he visited the author at the Petit Montlouis that October. Writing to Lenieps on the twenty-sixth of that month,[62] Rousseau said he realized 'after our last conversation' that Lenieps did not agree with everything he had argued in the *Letter to M. d'Alembert*: 'I will not defend it against you, you know the true state of morals in our Republic better than I, provided you recognize the honest man in the writer, the good citizen and sentiments that are worthy of your friend.'

Another friend whose admiration for the *Letter to M. d'Alembert* was somewhat qualified was Alexandre Deleyre. He wrote from Liège on 29 October[63] saying that while he did not find 'any bitterness against the human race' in the book, 'I did feel the anguish which reigns in your heart ... What a passage of Scripture you quote! It seems you do not want any more friends, since you renounce the best friend you have, according to your own avowal. It makes me sad and hurt and leads me to think about you with a sort of sorrow – and yet I cannot stop myself thinking about you.'

Deleyre at this period was still close to Diderot, still modelling his life as editor of the *Journal encyclopédique* in Liège on that of Diderot as editor of the *Encyclopédie* in Paris. But it is fair to note that when the time came for him to choose between Rousseau and Diderot, he chose Rousseau. Deleyre said to Girardin[64] after Rousseau's death in 1778, 'I do not know who told you Diderot was my friend. I did undoubtedly love Diderot in my youth with a sort of blind passion ... but twenty years ago when he undeceived me, I broke with him for good.' Of Rousseau, Deleyre said on the same occasion: 'I always loved him even when living among his enemies ... It is enough to read his books to feel the virtue, the goodness, the humanity which each line breathes.'

Correspondents who agreed with Rousseau's arguments against introducing a theatre to Geneva often objected to what he proposed as alternatives – clubs, festivals and balls. Lenieps was one such critic, and Rousseau wrote[65] to him in November to defend his proposals:

Public balls may not be suited to Geneva ... but when you condemn dancing in general, you are surely much mistaken. Dancing is an inspiration of nature and nature is never wrong; it is only a matter of regulating nature, which is what I have proposed to do. Why, you ask, should girls and boys be taught what they will be forbidden to do when they are married? Why, because sons and daughters must necessarily live differently from husbands and wives; because when they are married they will have no further need of getting married; because the tastes of each age demand different amusements; because reasons of health prescribe that we should allow the young the exercise that nature demands. There is a time to be young; the Author of Nature has willed it ... Why, you ask, should we divert the minds of boys and girls from their work and their duties? It is one of their duties to marry. Answer what I have said about that in my book. Then, will you allow no kind of amusement to the young? Dear Lenieps, that seems very hard, and I warn you that if you take all things away from them, they will find something for themselves, despite you, and what they choose will be rather worse than what I allow them.

In the same letter Rousseau expressed the hope that Lenieps would come to Montmorency on 12 December to celebrate the Genevese National Day, commemorating the 'Escalade', when an attempt by Savoyard troops to invade the city in 1602 by scaling the walls was frustrated: 'if it is necessary for me to agree to your bringing your own dish of food, I do so with pleasure. Come both of you, you and your meal – the one will be embraced, the other eaten.'

Another minister of religion in Geneva wrote[66] to congratulate Rousseau on a book that was a 'rallying cry to all citizens', and lamented the decay of morals in the city: 'The rich, long since corrupt, have begun to corrupt the poor by degrading them. Virtues can only be found in the middling men, because republican virtues can only exist in such a class ... but there are people among us who are trying to replace the austere virtues of citizens with the brilliant vices of monarchies.' The author of this letter, destined to become one of Rousseau's most intimate friends, was Paul-Claude Moultou,* the one Genevese pastor he continued to trust and who did not let him down.

Dr Theodore Tronchin wrote[67] suggesting that the morals of the Genevese were less pure than Rousseau realized, but also to suggest that the cultural activities Rousseau had proposed in his *Letter to M. d'Alembert* as an alternative to a theatre would only make things worse. In particular the men's clubs, which once seemed good, had become a source of

---

*Paul-Claude Moultou (1731–87), consecrated as pastor in 1755.

dissipation and wasted time, and were injurious to family life. He reminded Rousseau that the Genevese were not Greeks; they were a people of artisans, not warriors, and Rousseau's idea of imitating Sparta and introducing state education, gymnastics, and military training was unsuited to children destined to earn their living in trades and industries. Moreover, if Rousseau's policy of separating the sexes was adopted, Dr Tronchin pointed out that children would spend all their time with their mothers, and be deprived of the discipline of a father's hand. 'Geneva no more resembles Sparta,' he continued, 'than the white glove of an opera girl resembles the gauntlet of an athlete.'

Another Genevese correspondent, Professor Perdriau, also wrote[68] to express at the same time his approval of Rousseau's attack on the theatre and his dissent from Rousseau's positive proposals. He, too, described the men's clubs as centres of drunkenness and idleness. As for public balls, that idea, said Perdriau, was 'the dream of man awake'. He suggested that such balls would encourage in the young romantic feelings inimical to domestic tranquillity and add to the already heavy burdens of Genevese mothers the work of dressing up their daughters for display, and also sow seeds of rivalry and jealousy throughout the female population.

Professor Vernet was less critical; while he expressed some doubts about the value of the men's clubs, his letter[69] of thanks for Rousseau's presentation copy of the *Letter to M. d'Alembert* was one of the most wholeheartedly enthusiastic. He thanked Rousseau for defending the Genevese clergy against the charge of Socinianism, and he expressed appreciation of the distinction drawn in the book between large corrupt cities, where the drama could mitigate evil, and small innocent towns, where it could only do harm. He was pleased to note that whereas fashionable writers spoke only of money, glory and pleasure, Rousseau invoked such noble objects as God, virtue and *patrie*. 'Your generous writing seems to me very well designed, Monsieur, to rekindle in the hearts of our citizens the masculine virtues of our fathers.'

Rousseau defended his proposal for the encouragement of men's – and separate women's – clubs in his reply[70] to Dr Tronchin. He agreed that some experience of them had been unfortunate, but claimed that even greater abuses would follow if they did not exist. He accepted Dr Tronchin's observation that Geneva was not Greece, but argued that this did not preclude the introduction of state education in their city. The Genevese already had experience of public elementary schools, with the result that there was a great difference between their artisans and foreign ones:

A watchmaker of Geneva is presentable anywhere; a watchmaker of Paris is only fit to talk about watches. The education of a worker tends to develop his fingers, nothing more. The *citizen*, however, remains; for better or worse his head and his heart develop; there is always time for that, and that is just what an educational system should provide. Here, Monsieur, I have an advantage over you, as you have over me in general observations. The estate of the artisan is my own, the one into which I was born, in which I ought to have lived, and which I quit only to bring misfortune on myself. I received that public education, not directly, but through the traditions and precepts which, passing from age to age, give the young in good time the knowledge that is fit for them and the feelings they ought to have. At twelve I was a Roman; at twenty I had wandered around the world and was nothing better than a young rogue.

Rousseau also defended to Dr Tronchin his proposal to separate the sexes: boys, he said, should be reared by their fathers, girls by their mothers: 'That is precisely the moderate education which suits us, the mean between the public education of the Greek republics and the domestic education of monarchies, where every subject remains isolated and has nothing in common with others except obedience to the sovereign.' Rousseau added that the gymnastic exercises he recommended were not intended to be professional, as they were for the Greeks, but recreational – to be practised in the leisure hours of working people. He noted with pleasure that Dr Tronchin shared his views on the drama and expressed the hope that 'your authority and your wisdom will prevent both the introduction of a theatre into the city and the continued existence of one at its gates', the latter being of course, a reference to the theatre at Carouge, which Tronchin and others were trying to have closed.

In writing[71] to Deluc, Rousseau spoke less solemnly about the Carouge theatre. He told him he had read Marcet's play *Le Diogène à la campagne*, which mocked him as an enemy of the drama and which had been performed at Carouge that summer: 'If they were to act plays like that in Geneva,' he remarked, 'I would have no fears of actors.' In the same letter Rousseau replied to a suggestion that Deluc had made after meeting Mme d'Épinay in Geneva, that the time was opportune for a reconciliation with his former benefactress:

There was a time when Mme d'Épinay felt friendship for me and gave me every possible testimony of it; on my side, that friendship was precious enough to make me sacrifice living on my own homeland, something she did not achieve without effort. I was for Mme d'Épinay the best and perhaps the only true friend she will ever have ... That time is still dear to me, but it is past and cannot return. For the rest I shall always be pleased to learn that Mme d'Épinay is happy and that everyone respects and honours her. I would do the same if it were possible.

There was one person in Geneva to whom Rousseau sent a copy of his *Letter to d'Alembert* who did not thank him for it, and that was Voltaire, who was evidently too indignant even to write the kind of mocking acknowledgement he had sent Rousseau for the *Discourse on Inequality*. For this time Voltaire saw that he personally was as much the target as was the theatre itself. There was, indeed, a quotation in Latin from Plato as clearly aimed at him as was the quotation in Latin from Scripture aimed at Diderot: in a footnote Rousseau had cited the passage in *Republic*[72] where Plato says that if a poet comes to the city 'making a display of himself and his poems' we should 'send him away pouring myrrh over his head and crowning him with wool'. Voltaire could not fail to see that these words held a message to the Genevese: that they should expel him from their territory. At the time, however, Voltaire restrained the expression of his anger and in a letter to Vernes[73] he simply observed that it was a pity that Rousseau did not write against the tragedy that was then engulfing the theatre of Europe – the Seven Years War, as it was afterwards known – rather than against the idea of a theatre of comedy in Geneva.

Voltaire may well have felt invulnerable to Rousseau's attacks. He suggested to Thieriot:[74] 'As for Jean-Jacques, he can well write against the theatre. All Geneva goes there in droves. I do not go to Geneva, but Geneva comes to me.' Voltaire was in the process of establishing himself outside the city gates as *châtelain* of Tournay, with a private theatre where he could put on whatever plays he pleased.

Rousseau had none the less succeeded in making yet another implacable enemy. He had also won new admirers, for the *Letter to M. d'Alembert* was widely read among the artisans of Geneva and stimulated popular support for the cultural innovations Rousseau had recommended: soon after its publication, patriotic festivities, parades of the citizens' militia and other such activities were organized in response to his inspiration.

On 12 December Rousseau celebrated Geneva's *fête nationale* at the Petit Montlouis with his two compatriots, Lenieps and Coindet, and his French landlord, M. Mathas, whom he invited to join them for dinner. The occasion seems to have been a success, but Rousseau was in a melancholy mood when he lamented a few days later:[75] 'Having been long stuck in a great city where morals were incorrigible and then isolated in my solitude among a few wretched peasants, all I can do is offer my neighbours a few empty consolations, or write books, and you know very well that books serve no other purpose than amusing idle people.'

The cold winter weather, coupled with the damp in the *donjon* and the inadequate heating of his dilapidated draughty cottage, had once more undermined his health.

New Year greetings from Mme de Créqui[76] reached Montmorency together with a present of four chickens. She congratulated Rousseau on the success in Paris of his *Letter to M. d'Alembert*: 'You cannot write four lines without creating a sensation.' Rousseau accepted the compliment graciously, but he told[77] his old friend that he was less ready to thank her for the chickens. 'I have already passed two of them on to people I hardly care for.' He explained that while he welcomed tokens of friendship he did not want gifts: 'Oh, Madame, if you had sent me your greetings without sending me anything else, you would have made me both rich and grateful! Instead, now that the chickens are eaten, the best thing I can do is to forget them. So let us say no more about them: that is your reward for making presents to me.'

In her letter Mme de Créqui had said that she had been sick for a week and that she was anxious about her son in the army, who was wasting his entire fortune. In his reply[78] Rousseau expressed his approval of her maternal feelings, but reproached her for ruining herself to keep her son in money. He suggested that the son needed none of 'the ridiculous trappings, which cause your French armies to be defeated and your officers to be despised ... Where luxury is universal, it is by simplicity that a man distinguishes himself ... If your son does not shine in his equipage, he will have to do so by his merits, and in that way he can acquire honour and repay your care for him.'

Rousseau went on to say that he was developing some ideas about education – a sign that he was working on *Émile* – and he invited Mme de Créqui, 'as a mother and philosopher (albeit a Christian)', to write down for him her reflections on the subject. He ended his letter by offering the Marquise some dubious comfort in the sickness she had complained of: 'I detest healthy people – it seems to me that I have only lived since I have felt half-dead.'

Mme de Créqui did not take up Rousseau's invitation to communicate her thoughts on education. She assured him[79] that she was incapable of the kind of philosophical reflection he proposed; all she could say was that the kind of good education she believed in was impossible while men had no conception of the great and the small, and while their heads were full of false received opinions; a son such as hers would not be allowed to listen to a mother's advice which went against the world's own ways. She commented on Rousseau's ingratitude for her chickens with good humour: 'those poor beasts came from Le Mans, and had a certain reputation on account of their origin' – Le Mans chickens being then regarded by connoisseurs as the best in France. As for her own health – her digestive troubles, she reported, seemed to have calmed down, 'but for how long?'

Another invalid friend from whom Rousseau heard that January was Gauffecourt, who was still in Lyons, and still suffering after two years from the effects of a stroke. However, he informed Rousseau[80] that he was ashamed to complain of his afflictions to a younger man who was suffering much more, and that his purpose in writing was to offer Rousseau financial help through his Paris banker in what he knew to be a time of need. He urged Rousseau to accept: 'Think of us as two companions on a journey. It does not matter whether one or the other pays the bill at the inn.'

Rousseau's reply to this letter has not been traced, but one can imagine that his reaction to an offer of money was no warmer than that to a gift of chickens. But in a letter written six months later[81] we find him expressing his appreciation of Gauffecourt's generous impulses, and offering in his turn to help Gauffecourt in financial difficulties caused by the sudden loss of his monopolies in Geneva. Rousseau expressed dismay that 'you, who offered me your purse out of the goodness of your heart, should be reduced to sharing mine'. The situation was all the more shocking in that Gauffecourt had been robbed of the monopolies by his own assistant and protégé Marc Chappuis, but Rousseau urged Gauffecourt not to be embittered: 'Let the ungrateful fellow have the wretched place. He will accumulate money in his coffers and remorse in his heart. He is more to be pitied than you are.'

In Geneva, in January 1759, Pastor Vernes married, at the age of thirty, a French girl of sixteen named Marie-Françoise Clarenc. In congratulating him, Rousseau asserted[82] that 'marriage is a condition of conflict and trouble for the corrupt, but heaven on earth for good people. Dear Vernes, you are going to be happy. Perhaps you are, already.' Unfortunately Vernes was not destined to enjoy more than a short-lived happiness in his marriage; before the end of the year his young wife was dead.

In the same letter to Vernes, Rousseau said, in apparent reference to Voltaire's failure to acknowledge the *Letter to M. d'Alembert* which he had sent him: 'He puts me entirely at ease; I am not at all upset about it.' Vernes had been pressing Rousseau to contribute a piece to his literary review, *Choix littéraire*, and this prompted Rousseau to point out that he could not afford to do such work unpaid:

If I am to dine, I must earn; if I rest, I have to fast ... The miserable fees that my books have produced gave me the leisure to be ill and to put a bit of fat in my soup, but that money is all used up, and now I am more than ever tied to my work. On top of this I have to answer fifty thousand letters, receive a thousand importunate visitors and offer them hospitality. Time passes and needs remain.

Even so, Rousseau promised Vernes that he would finish the article he was writing for him on the subject of Plato and the theatre; something 'hardly to the taste of your readers or the new philosophy'.

The reference to 'the new philosophy' may have contained a barb, for Rousseau knew well that Vernes was in close contact not only with Voltaire but also with Diderot, whose achievements as an editor had perhaps inspired his ambitions in the field much as they had those of Alexandre Deleyre.* Indeed in the same week that Rousseau wrote to Vernes from Montmorency, Diderot wrote[84] to him from Paris saying how much he pitied 'that man who is buried in the depths of the forest'. Diderot spoke of Rousseau as the 'torment' of his mind, and he did not forgive him: 'It is a monstrous thing to denounce publicly an old friend, even if that friend is guilty. And what name do you give the action if the friend is innocent?'

Diderot's difficulties with the French authorities did not diminish in 1759. On 23 January the Parlement of Paris condemned the *Encyclopédie* together with Diderot's *Pensées philosophiques* and other writings. La Condamine† mentioned these events in a letter to Rousseau dated 27 January,[85] acknowledging the copy he had sent him of the *Letter to M. d'Alembert*. La Condamine noted that the *Encyclopédie* had still kept its royal privilege, but said he had heard that Malesherbes might lose the post of Director of Publications. He added that he himself was having difficulties with the French authorities; despite the success of his first *Mémoire* on smallpox, hostility to inoculation had become so intense that he was being forced to publish his second *Mémoire* on the subject in Geneva.

Rousseau himself had, as yet, no experience of the menace of censorship; it was only his dealings with publishers which unnerved him from time to time. In Geneva that winter his old friend Jacques-François Deluc wanted to arrange the publications of Rousseau's collected works, and Rousseau had to explain to him that he had already discussed the project with Rey, who wanted to publish them in Amsterdam without paying him any more money. 'Rey accuses me of wanting to sell my writings twice over,' Rousseau wrote[86] to Deluc. 'He flatly refuses the royalty I ask ... and also claims that I have no right to offer the collection to another publisher, and that having once bought my copy he is the sole proprietor of any further editions ... I would have thought in view of my own

---

*In the end Rousseau did not keep his promise to send Vernes his article about Plato and the theatre. It was published independently in 1764 as '*De l'imitation théâtrale: essai tiré des Dialogues de Platon*'. This time Voltaire had to buy a copy. He told his bookseller 'if M. Cramer wishes me to have the latest vomitings of Jean-Jacques against the theatre, I shall be pleased to receive them'.[83]

†Charles-Marie de La Condamine (1701–74), astronaut, explorer, Encyclopédiste, remained one of Rousseau's few friends in Parisian scientific circles.

moderation and of the profits he has made out of me, that I might have received a more decent treatment.'

A few weeks later Rousseau was writing in a very different spirit about Rey's character as a publisher. He informed Lenieps[87] that he had always found Rey 'exact, attentive and honest' in all things. 'I asked him for twenty-five louis for my *Discourse on Inequality* and he gave it me on the spot and what is more he gave a dress to my housekeeper. I asked him for thirty louis for my *Letter to M. d'Alembert* and he paid me at once.'

Part of the motive behind this elogium of Rey to Lenieps was Rousseau's desire to demonstrate the iniquity of his other publisher, Pissot, who had not given him a sou for his *Discourse on the Sciences and the Arts*, nor kept his word in any other dealings they had had. Rousseau hoped Lenieps would understand that he wished neither to be robbed of the little money he earned nor to be given charity: 'The public has long since created a Jean-Jacques Rousseau in its own imagination and lavished upon him generous gifts which Jean-Jacques Rousseau of Montmorency never sees. An invalid, sick for nine months of the year, I must earn with the work of the other three enough to provide for the whole year. Only those who earn their living by honest toil know the cost of their bread.'

For all his indignation against the unscrupulous Pissot, Rousseau's greatest agitation on the subject of copyright in the year 1759 was occasioned by a less clear-cut grievance. His opera *Le Devin du village*, which had not been performed for five years, was revived at the Paris Opera, staged no less than fifty-two times, and very favourably received by the critics and public alike.[88] All this made Rousseau very angry.

As soon as he heard of the revival, Rousseau submitted a petition[89] to the Comte de St-Florentin, Minister for the Arts, claiming that the copyright of *Le Devin du village* belonged to him and not to the Paris Opera, and asking the Minister to forbid any further performance of it. He recalled that he had already made the same demand in the past and been ignored; he had moreover been paid no royalties on the performances given five years before, and had even had his pass to the Opera House rescinded by the municipality of Paris. Rousseau took the precaution, as a Genevese citizen, of having this petition presented to St-Florentin by the diplomatic representative of Geneva in France, Jean-François Sellon; and he also asked Charles Duclos,[90] who had originally persuaded the Paris Opera to put on *Le Devin du village*, and to whom it was dedicated, to intervene to have it stopped. According to the *Confessions*,[91] 'M. de St-Florentin promised a response, but made none.'

Rousseau next expounded his grievances at length to Lenieps,[92] asking him also to intervene on his behalf. Besides the matter of *Le Devin du village*, which the Paris Opera had performed in breach of contract with him, and the score of which they refused to return, there was his earlier composition *Les Muses galantes*, which he had asked Philidor★ to return to him, without success: 'It is a detestable piece composed before I had any idea of music, but which, however bad, is mine.'

Then there was the matter of his pass to the Opera House. The present directors, François Rebel and François Francoeur, had offered to restore it, and pleaded that they were not responsible for his having been deprived of it; but Rousseau told Lenieps that their offer was worthless: 'What about the five years that have passed since I had it taken from me?' Lenieps may well have thought that Rousseau was being less than reasonable on this point, in asking for something that could no longer be of any use. Indeed Rousseau informed Lenieps that even a pass for future admission to the Opera would be useless to him: 'Do not Revel and Francoeur realize that I have neither the means nor the inclination to take advantage of their offer? ... What I want is justice, strict justice,' he said, only to add bitterly, 'It is clear that I am in the wrong, because I cannot get justice, and the directors of the Paris Opera are in the right because they are stronger.'

Rousseau could sensibly, and fairly, have asked for payment of royalties for the performances of *Le Devin du village*, just as he could reasonably demand of Philidor the return of the score of *Les Muses galantes*, but in his letter to Lenieps he chose to complain, bitterly and eloquently, about injuries it was too late to put right. Conceivably his chief purpose in writing as he did was to have Lenieps circulate his letter in Paris, so that grievances which could not be remedied could at least be made known, and the public made to understand that Jean-Jacques Rousseau really was a victim of injustices.

Quarrelling with publishers and producers in Paris, Rousseau made a fresh effort to improve his relations with Rey in Amsterdam. In order to find a mutually satisfactory basis for the publication of his collected works, he suggested[94] to Rey that he, Rousseau, should repay the money he had received from Rey for the *Discourse on Inequality* and the *Letter to M. d'Alembert* and that Rey should then make him an offer for the whole contents of the collected works 'in such a way that you will neither underpay me nor think me unfair towards you.' Rey did not like this proposal and simply urged[95] Rousseau to do whatever he wished with the copyrights he retained: 'I ask nothing of you but your friendship.' Rey did, however, express the hope that Rousseau still had enough friendship for him to let him publish his novel *Julie*.

★Philidor (François-André Danican) had collaborated in a small way with Rousseau in the preparation of *Les Muses galantes*,[93] and it was rumoured in Paris that Rousseau was only the part author of the work. In his letter to Lenieps Rousseau explained that Philidor had made only a few *retouches* in a session of two hours: 'I did all the rest absolutely alone.'

Rousseau responded[96] with equal warmth, assuring Rey that he would not contemplate publishing his collected works without an understanding with him, and also that he would keep his promise to let him have *Julie*. His only stipulation with regard to the novel was that no copies should on any account be sent for sale in Geneva. Rousseau was manifestly uneasy as to what his Calvinist compatriots would think of a novel about love being written by the author of the *Letter to M. d'Alembert*, which attacked the depiction of love in plays on the grounds that 'in admiring decent love one abandons oneself to criminal love'.[97]

Rey explained[98] that he could not accept this stipulation, because the Geneva market was economically necessary: 'Think, my dear friend, I need to sell ... and to sell everywhere on the same day if possible.' For the rest, he agreed to do whatever Rousseau wished in the publication of *Julie* and to pay him ninety louis during the current year for the six completed parts of the book, while leaving the author the copyright in the Preface.

Accordingly, in April Rousseau sent Rey the final version of the text[99] with the full title: *Julie, ou la moderne Héloïse*; only later did he change the subtitle to *la nouvelle Héloïse*. Rousseau still hoped to have a set of illustrations to the novel drawn by François Boucher. Whatever Rousseau's fears about the depiction of decent love on the stage leading to criminal love, he clearly did not disapprove, with Diderot,* of Boucher's erotic rococo in art. He was only worried about Boucher's fees. Well aware of Rey's thrifty disposition, Rousseau warned[101] Coindet, who was negotiating with Boucher on his behalf, not to offer him cash on completion of the work: 'You must understand that I do not have fifty louis to give him.' Boucher was to be asked to accept payment six weeks after publication or even later.† Believing Boucher would refuse, Coindet also approached the artist Gravelot.‡

As for Rey, far from having the funds to engage Mme de Pompadour's favourite artist to illustrate *Julie*, he informed the author in a letter dated 18 April[102] that his coffers were empty. He could not even afford to pay Rousseau his promised fee until later in the year: 'You have no idea, my dear friend, how difficult it is for us publishers to collect what is owed to us.' Rey nevertheless spoke of reprinting Rousseau's *Discourse on the*

---

*Diderot had an almost Stalinist attachment to social realism in art. Of Boucher's paintings Diderot wrote, 'That man has everything, except truth.'[100]

†'If M. Boucher has to be paid in cash, withdraw my project, and we shall say no more about it.'

‡Hubert-François Bourguignon, known as Gravelot (1699–1773). A very much less fashionable artist than Boucher, he could be expected to accept more modest fees. His original drawings for *Julie* are in the copy preserved in the Palais Bourbon library.

Sciences and the Arts and of bringing out his collected works after he had published *Julie*.

At the Petit Montlouis Rousseau received a fair number of visitors – if fewer than the 'thousands' he complained of to Vernes,[103] considerably more than ever came to the Hermitage. The Petit Montlouis was near the top of a fairly steep hill, but only a few yards from the centre of the village of Montmorency and easily reached. The publication of his *Letter to M. d'Alembert* had advertised to the world that Rousseau was very much alive; the controversial nature of its argument against the drama and the *frisson* of scandal afforded by the denunciation of Diderot all helped to inflame public curiosity about the author. In the early winter months, he did not venture far from his cottage,* so that friends – and others – who wished to see him had to make the journey to find him. In the *Confessions*[105] he recalls the names of some of his visitors. Among others there were three whose acquaintance he had first made during his short 'diplomatic' career in Italy: François-Xavier de Carrio, his colleague from the Spanish Embassy in Venice, now elevated in the Spanish nobility as the Chevalier de Carrión and promoted secretary of the Spanish Embassy at Versailles; M. Le Blond, the French Consul in Venice who had been a stalwart ally against Rousseau's intolerable employer, the French Ambassador; and François Chaillou de Jonville, French Minister-Plenipotentiary to the Genoan Republic, who had given him a warm welcome when he had first landed in Italy in the summer of 1743. None of these friendships, however, seems to have ripened further.

Rousseau could only blame himself for the cooling of intimacy with Le Blond. The former consul rented a house near Montmorency at La Briche, so that it would have been easy enough to exchange visits with him, but Rousseau confesses that he was intimidated by the presence there of other guests and that he kept putting off a visit until he was too ashamed to appear at all: 'My worst faults are such faults of omission.'[106]

He saw more of M. de Jonville, but only to become bored with his company: 'He had not much intelligence; he was handsome, and proud of his looks, and pretty dull.'[107] However, Rousseau says he continued to see Jonville until one day when, without providing any explanation, Jonville gave him a frosty welcome. Thinking about it afterwards, he attributed Jonville's coldness to the fact that after attending a supper party which Jonville had given for some Foreign Office clerks and some girls, Rousseau had left 'without,' as he puts it, 'giving the girls an opportunity to earn any money'.[108] This episode must have taken place on one of

*He told Mme Dupin in a letter dated 25 January 1759 that he was not well enough to leave home but hoped to visit her at Clichy in the summer.[104]

Rousseau's rare visits to Paris, and one can readily imagine how Rousseau must have alienated Jonville by his disapproving demeanour at the supper party, no less than by his failure to engage the services of one of the harpies. At all events, the occasion marked the end of another friendship.

Even so, Rousseau speaks in the *Confessions* of making new friends after he moved to Montmorency; notably Loyseau de Mauléon,* a young lawyer who had a house in the neighbourhood at Saint-Brice and was attached to the Parlement of Paris, where he was already noted for the eloquence of his pleas at the Bar. Rousseau claims[109] to have predicted a great future for him provided he used his talents only to defend the cause of justice and virtue: 'He took my advice, and has felt the benefit of it.' Another new friend Rousseau mentions was Antoine Maltor,† the *curé* of a nearby parish in the valley, Groslay, but a man more fitted, Rousseau suggested,[110] to be a statesman than a country priest; 'of all my permanent neighbours he was the one whose society was the most agreeable to me'. Guérin, the bookseller and publisher who lived at Saint-Brice, was another visitor at the Petit Montlouis. But if Rousseau appreciated his 'wit, learning and likeable personality',[111] he blew hot and cold in his feelings towards him, as he did towards publishers in general. He formed a no less wary attachment to another neighbour, Father Berthier, an Oratorian and a professor of physics. Rousseau says that while he was attracted by Berthier's geniality, he was repelled by his pedantry, his 'sardonic smile' and his adroitness in thrusting himself everywhere – 'cultivating the great men, the *femmes du monde*, the pious people and the philosophers, he was everything to everybody'.[112]

The only eminent *philosophe* in Paris with whom he remained on intimate terms was Charles Duclos, although he also kept in touch with d'Alembert, with the two half-brothers, Condillac and Mably, and, more uneasily, with Morellet. He could have met such people on his visits to Mme Dupin at Clichy, but those visits became less frequent. He explains in the *Confessions*[113] that quarrels between Mme Dupin and her daughter-in-law, Mme de Chenonceaux, made his relations with both increasingly embarrassing. It was only when Mme de Chenonceaux rented a house 'almost next door to mine' at Deuil and 'came to see me fairly often', that he was on easy terms once more with his former pupil.

In the spring of 1759, however, it was difficult for Rousseau to receive any visitors at all at the Petit Montlouis. The floorboards were collapsing and, as he expressed[114] it to Coindet, 'I shall soon end up sleeping in the

---

*Alexandre-Jérome Loyseau de Mauléon (1728–71), advocate, later celebrated as defender at the Bar of Calas and other victims of injustice.

†Antoine Maltor (1689–1767) had been secretary to the French Ambassador in Switzerland, the Comte Du Luc, before retiring to his country benefice.

cellar or the street.' It was just at this inopportune time that he received an unexpected visit from the most illustrious personage in the valley, the Maréchal-Duc de Luxembourg, who had come from Versailles to spend the Easter vacation at his country estate, the château of Montmorency.

AT THE CHÂTEAU

Charles-François-Frédéric de Montmorency-Luxembourg,★ Duc de Lux-embourg and Maréchal de France, was head of the ancient family of Montmorency, and his splendid château, designed by Crozat le Cadet and Le Nôtre, dominated the countryside where Rousseau lived. A close friend of the King's and one of his chief military advisors, with many duties at Versailles, especially since the country was at war, the Maréchal could spend only a few weeks of the year at his country seat. As soon as he heard that Rousseau was living on the edge of his estate, he sent a servant to Montlouis to invite him to dine. The grandest of French grandees in the eighteenth century still prized the company of writers and philosophers, but Rousseau, suspecting that the invitation was prompted by curiosity rather than goodwill, and fearing that he would be expected to dine in the servants' hall, declined. The invitation was repeated, and again Rousseau refused. Then the Comtesse de Boufflers,† who was a close friend of Mme de Luxembourg, and a guest at the château, sent an emissary, the Chevalier de Lorenzy, to Montlouis to urge Rousseau to accept.

'I did nothing,' he writes in the *Confessions*.[1] 'Finally one afternoon, altogether unexpectedly, I saw the Maréchal-Duc de Luxembourg himself arriving at my house with an entourage of five or six people. There was no way of escape. I could not, without being considered arrogant and ill-bred, avoid returning his visit and paying my respects to the Maréchale, his wife, in whose name he overwhelmed me with kind messages.'

Rousseau admits he was rather afraid of Mme de Luxembourg. He had

★Born 1702, and thus aged fifty-seven at the time of his first meeting with Rousseau, he was the grandson of an earlier Maréchal de Luxembourg who had received his baton from Louis XIV. M. de Luxembourg succeeded his father as Governor of Normandy while still a minor, but did not become a Maréchal de France until 1757.

†Not to be confused with the Marquise de Boufflers, mistress of the King of Poland, or the Duchesse de Boufflers, the title of Mme de Luxembourg before her marriage to the Maréchal, and subsequently that of her daughter-in-law.

already met her in the salon of Mme Dupin ten or twelve years before, when, as he puts it, 'she still possessed her youthful and radiant beauty',[2] but she had a reputation for spitefulness which, he says in the *Confessions*, 'made me tremble'.[3] The Maréchale had another reputation, that of a *grande horizontale*, notoriously unfaithful to her first husband, the Duc de Boufflers.* Her second marriage was unclouded by scandal, but she could still bewitch a man. She possessed a stately beauty, tall and elegant, with an ample bosom of the kind that Rousseau admired. Mme Du Deffand said of her that her gestures had so much grace, were so natural and so much in harmony with what she said, that one was easily persuaded to think and feel as she did: 'she dominates wherever she is, and she can make whatever impression she wants to make'.[4]

Rousseau says that the moment he saw her again at the château of Montmorency he was her slave; she was over fifty, but she had, as he puts it, 'a charm that is proof against time'.[5] Her conversation, far from being, as he expected, barbed and ironical, proved to be simple, natural, spontaneous. Her compliments all sounded sincere. For a short time, Rousseau says, when her daughter-in-law, the Duchesse de Montmorency† seemed to vie with her in coquetry, he suspected that they were both making fun of him, but in the end, the Maréchal's 'extraordinary kindness' convinced him that the whole family was pleased to have him at the château.

Rousseau was deeply reassured by the fact that neither the Maréchal nor his wife expressed any concern about or interest in his financial situation; they did not assume the role of patrons; they never offered to help him with appointments or preferments, although Mme de Luxembourg did once suggest proposing him for the Académie Française, an honour he told her he would have to decline since he had already refused nomination to the Académie Royale of Lorraine. What Rousseau did not decline, once the ice was broken, were invitations to visit the château, where he spent a great deal of time not only in the company of the Maréchal and his family, but of other such socially exalted persons as the Comtesse de Boufflers, the Duc de Villeroy, the Prince de Tingry, the Marquis d'Armentières and the Comtesse de Valentinois. Grimm[6] remarked bitterly that Rousseau had forsaken the company of literary men for that of society women, and he was not entirely wrong. Diderot,[7]

---

*Mme de Luxembourg was born in 1707, Madeleine-Angélique de Villeroy, granddaughter of the Maréchal de Villeroy. As Duchesse de Boufflers, her affairs were considered scandalous even by the standards of Versailles. A young widow, she married in 1750 her principal lover the Maréchal de Luxembourg, himself a widower after the death of his first wife, Marie-Sophie Colbert de Seignelay.

†Louise-Françoise-Pauline de Montmorency-Fosseux, b.1734, married in 1752, Anne-François de Montmorency, the son of M. de Luxembourg by his first wife.

with rather sharper wit, said that Rousseau had found a remedy for his bile in sucking the milk from the breasts of Mme de Luxembourg. Given her reputation, this sally was good for a laugh; but there was no suggestion, this time, that Rousseau had fallen in love. What he had done was to find a genuine friend and admirer. Mme de Luxembourg could claim to have some knowledge of men, and she could see Rousseau's true worth as well as his originality; she was not put off by his somewhat brutal honesty; indeed she appreciated his naturalness and candour. She also admired his books, and in her presence he was happy.

He was rather more at ease, however, with the Maréchal. For although Rousseau sometimes played the part of the plebeian outsider, he felt more at home with members of the highest ranks of the nobility than with members of the moneyed bourgeoisie; he did not despise them in the way that he despised the rich, and with his conversation he often struck a sympathetic chord in their hearts. For Rousseau believed himself to be a man of superior merit, yearning for a society ruled by an aristocracy of virtue, and he found a certain affinity with the kind of French nobleman who looked back sadly to the feudal world which the absolutist monarchy had destroyed, the world of chivalry and *châteaux forts* and shining honour, where the *noblesse d'épée et de race* was answerable to no one but God. Between their obscure memory of a lost world and Rousseau's dream of a world unborn there was much in common, a shared capacity to imagine something better than the prevailing alliance of despotic government with materialistic culture.

When M. de Luxembourg paid that first unexpected visit during his Easter holiday in 1759, Rousseau had felt unable to entertain him and his entourage in the cottage, fearing that the floorboards were too rotten to hold their weight. He explained the reason to his guests and took them to the unheated *donjon* in the garden, and it was there that he had his first conversation with the Maréchal. Soon afterwards, when M. Mathas proposed to have the cottage repaired, the Maréchal offered Rousseau and his *gouvernante* hospitality while the work was being done. He suggested that they should use a house that was known as the Petit Château in the grounds of his estate.

The Petit Château was an architectural jewel which had been designed and decorated by the painter Charles de Brun for his own use – a classical villa in miniature, with a façade of double columns, Ionic and Doric, supporting a central pediment.* It was situated in the grounds of the château between the pond of the orangery and a large ornamental lake, so that Rousseau, when he first looked at it, was reminded of the Isola Bella

*The Petit Château was demolished in 1792; the main château in 1818.

on Lake Maggiore, a building entirely surrounded by water.[8] He fell in love with the place, and promptly accepted the Maréchal's invitation. Of the four apartments that the Petit Château contained, Rousseau chose the 'smallest and simplest', above the kitchen, which was also placed at his disposal.

In writing on 30 April[9] to thank the Maréchal for his offer, Rousseau tried to reassure his future host that while he addressed him, as he did all his friends, in the informal language of familiarity, he was very conscious of the difference in rank between them. He liked to believe that since the Maréchal had honoured him with a visit, and 'sat on a cane chair among my broken pots' it was because of 'some reputation for probity' that he had acquired, and in which he could take pride.

The Maréchal replied[10] at once explaining, on behalf of his wife and himself, that it was their desire to have Rousseau nearer to them and their fear that he might perish in the crumbling ruins of Montlouis which had prompted them to offer him the apartment in the Petit Château. They were delighted, he said, by his acceptance, and he promised him that when they were better acquainted, Rousseau would never doubt the sincerity either of his own friendship for him or that of his wife.

At about the same time[11] Rousseau informed Rey – to whom he was sending the second part of *Julie* – 'I am moving to the house of a neighbouring peasant [sic] while they repair my cottage.' Within a week he was installed with Thérèse in his elegant refuge, and we find him writing[12] to Mme de Luxembourg:

The Petit Château of Montmorency,
6 May 1759

Madame, my whole letter is in the address. How that address does me honour! I shall not praise you. I shall not thank you. But I inhabit your house. Everyone has his own language, and I have said all in mine. Deign to receive, Madame la Maréchale, my profound respects.

J.-J. Rousseau.

Mme de Luxembourg, who had by that time returned to Paris, replied,[13] saying graciously that it was for her and her husband to thank him rather than he them. She said she was impatient to return to Montmorency so that she could enjoy Rousseau's company, but promised that she would not disturb his tranquillity.

On the day of his installation at the Petit Château, Rousseau also wrote[14] to Mme Dupin to inform her that he would be staying there while his cottage was being repaired – 'when it is finished it will be very attractive and comfortable'. In contrast to the winter of 1757 when he was homeless, he would soon be able to boast of having two of the prettiest apartments in the world: 'Such are the vicissitudes of things. I am enjoying a good life, but I will not allow myself to get accustomed to it.'

In the same letter he begged Mme Dupin not to ask him to copy out for her his abridgement of the Abbé de St-Pierre's *Project for Perpetual Peace*: 'In working on the project, I knew it was impractical, and if it was not so in itself it became so in the form I gave it. But I write for the public and not for ministers of state. I hope I shall never write for those people in all my life.'

Despite the confusion of his move to the Petit Château, Rousseau found time to write[15] another long letter to Lenieps about his grievances against Philidor, who had failed to return his *Muses galantes*, and against the directors of the Paris Opera, who had failed to halt performances of *Le Devin du village*: 'I am not in a hurry to obtain justice,' he explained; 'it is enough to have demanded it.' Having heard from Lenieps that the directors of the Opera had proposed a fee of 50 louis d'or for the rights of *Le Devin du village*, Rousseau's only comment was, 'That would be 50 louis fit to throw in their faces if they dared offer it to me.'

The wording of this letter suggests that Rousseau was almost enjoying his grudge against the Paris Opera, and a few weeks later,[16] when Lenieps reported further efforts to recover the score of *Les Muses galantes* from Philidor, he could only express doubts about the use of having it back, since Philidor had had ample time to pillage the work at leisure: 'You will see me henceforth very familiar with the ways of scoundrels.'

In general, however, Rousseau was blissfully happy during his stay at the Petit Château. He adored his apartment, with its blue and white furnishings, the gardens, the park, the lake – where he fed the carp from his hand as he had fed the fish in Lake Geneva in the summer of 1754. He relished the singing of the birds and the scent of orange blossom.

'With what eagerness,' he writes in the *Confessions*,[17] 'did I get up every morning at sunrise to breathe the perfumed air in the peristyle. What excellent coffee I drank there with my Thérèse. My dog and cat were our company. This retinue would have been enough for me throughout my life and given me not a moment of boredom. I lived in innocence and I tasted happiness.'

To M. de Luxembourg himself Rousseau wrote:[18] 'Your house is charming; my stay here is delightful ... You know, Monsieur le Maréchal, that solitary beings all have a romantic spirit. I am full of that spirit, and I do not grieve over it. Why should I seek to cure such a sweet folly if it helps to make me happy? Men of the world and of the court – do not think you are wiser than I; we only differ in our illusions.'

Rousseau went on to suggest to the Maréchal the principles that should govern their friendship, since 'you dictated that word to me': 'You must not try to be my patron and I promise not to be your panegyrist.' He hoped to see the Maréchal without his hangers-on from time to time, 'so that I may earn your esteem and learn from you how to deserve it'. But again Rousseau insisted that he should not be asked to sacrifice his solitude.

In the prompt reply[19] he sent from Paris, M. de Luxembourg promised Rousseau that he would not be disturbed in his new refuge, but he said he looked forward to being, on his return to Montmorency in July, 'a witness of the tranquillity and the solitude you have found at the Petit Château'. He added: 'I accept with great pleasure the proposition you make about the principles that shall govern our association. When you know me, you will understand that I do not deserve, and that I cannot endure, praises. So, Monsieur, let us confine ourselves to friendship.'

The friendship – if it can be called a friendship – between Rousseau and Théodore Tronchin came to an end that summer. On 23 March[20] Rousseau wrote to the doctor in Geneva asking for medical advice for two of his neighbours at Montmorency, one suffering from a disease that could not be diagnosed and another from severe gingivitis he suspected to be cancerous. Dr Tronchin answered promptly[21] with a prescription for the gingivitis, explaining that he could not suggest any diagnosis for the other patient without more information. However, he upset Rousseau by reproaching him for not writing more often, and what was worse, by asking 'how is it that the friend of humanity is hardly any longer the friend of men?'

To this last question Rousseau replied[22] indignantly:

You accuse me of indifference to men, and you use the sweetest of words to name me. In order to answer you, Monsieur, I must ask you in turn by what standards you judge me. Your manner of questioning me resembles that used in the interrogation of the wretched victims of the Inquisition. If I have secret accusers, tell me who they are, and of what they accuse me; then I will answer you. In the meantime, of what do I accuse myself? If since my birth I have done the least harm to anyone on earth, may the evil fall on my head.* If I refuse to do anyone any good I might do, or any service I could render without harming another, then let me suffer the same refusal in my time of need! ...

I congratulate you heartily on your good life, on your health, on your

*Rousseau was clearly in no mood to admit to Dr Tronchin the misdeeds he avows in the *Confessions*.

friends, and if I have none of these things, it is a misfortune and not a crime. Such as I am, I complain neither of my fate nor of my condition. I am the friend of the human race, and men are found everywhere. The friend of truth also finds ill-wishers everywhere, and I do not need to come far to meet them ... I prefer to live among the French rather than seek out enemies in Geneva. In a place where smart wits are fêted, J.-J. Rousseau will hardly be fêted, and if he were, he would hardly glory in it.

O worthy Tronchin. Let us both stay where we are. You may still honour your country. For me, it remains only to weep for it.

Rousseau's reference to 'smart wits' was plainly aimed at Voltaire. He suspected that however much Dr Tronchin might share his views about the evils of the stage, he was in close and regular contact with Voltaire in Geneva, and, if forced to choose between them, would choose Voltaire. These suspicions proved to be amply justified.

Nevertheless Tronchin claimed to be a loyal and devoted friend of Rousseau. To Rousseau's letter he replied:[23] 'You have wounded my soul, and my soul did not deserve the least injury from you.' He then went on to make matters worse by suggesting that if Rousseau's health were better his 'ink would be less black'. He repudiated Rousseau's insinuation that he himself honoured 'smart wits' and declared his commitment to the belief that 'the most profound humility is the only state suited to man: the philosophers are absurd'. He added: 'I pity clever men.'

Having written this, Tronchin immediately passed Rousseau's letter to Voltaire, who had asked to read what Tronchin had received from the 'descendant of Diogenes's dog'.[24] Voltaire's brief comment[25] was: 'Extreme insolence is extreme stupidity, and nothing is more stupid than a Jean-Jacques talking about "the human race and I".'

Again, Rousseau wrote[26] to Tronchin assuring him that he had no wish to offend him, but only to defend himself against the doctor's charge of misanthropy. What was the basis of that charge? He suggested to Tronchin that he should not play games with words, but judge men by what they did and not by what they said. Faced with this challenge, Tronchin chose to justify his accusation, in his next letter,[27] by pointing out that Rousseau had cut himself off from all his friends. He brought up the case of Rousseau's denunciation of Diderot, saying that even if Diderot had faults, 'no one is perfect in this world'. He also deplored Rousseau's declared preference for the French and his criticism of Geneva, in which city, Tronchin claimed, the voice of the people was the voice of God, virtue prevailed under the rule of wise magistrates and clergy, an academy took care of education and a court of morals watched over private conduct.

Living in such an excellent republic, he declared, 'makes us pity those who live in Montmorency'.

Rousseau's answer[28] to this was to express relief that Tronchin's charge of misanthropy had so little foundation, and he suggested to him that a preference for a few select friends over all mankind was injurious to humanity: 'three or four persons concentrating on each other easily forgot the rest of the universe'. On the other hand, 'a heart which is pleased to reach out to all his fellow men is less prompt to form attachments to individuals and more moderate in those attachments'. As for the republic of Geneva, Rousseau added: 'Judging from your letter, I cannot expect much sympathy there.'

While Voltaire was setting the tone in Geneva, this conjecture was not unreasonable. For Voltaire had by this time become almost obsessional in his hatred of Rousseau. 'What!' Voltaire exclaimed to d'Alembert in May 1759,[29] 'Are you replying seriously to that fool Rousseau, that bastard of Diogenes's dog?'

In fact, despite the severity of his denunciation of Diderot, Rousseau became mellower after leaving the Hermitage; less bitter in some of his judgements. For instance, in a letter[30] to a young theology student named Jean-Edmé Romilly, who had expressed some radical opinions to him, Rousseau wrote:

You seem to me to judge the rich too harshly. You do not realize that having contracted in their childhood a thousand needs that we do not have, they cannot be reduced to the condition of the poor without making them more wretched than the poor. One must be just towards everybody, even to those who are not just to us ... One more word. To have the right to despise the rich, one must be thrifty and prudent oneself, so as not to have any need for riches.

But Rousseau was not always so tolerant. When Deleyre visited the Petit Château towards the end of May to say farewell to Rousseau on his appointment to the French Embassy in Vienna, he took with him his fiancée, Caroline-Alexandrine Loiseau. Rousseau did not like the girl, or the intrusion, and although Deleyre had broken with Diderot out of loyalty to Rousseau, and given up literary journalism, as Rousseau had wished, for diplomacy, Rousseau received the visit without warmth. Deleyre did not, however, falter in his devotion to him.

Rousseau's other young admirer, François Coindet, who continued to make himself useful in various business matters, was a more frequent visitor to the Petit Château. Among other things, Coindet, who had only recently been appointed to a senior post in his bank, agreed to deal with the royalties Rousseau received from Rey. These royalties were slow to appear. Having received in May the second part of *Julie*, Rey informed[31] the author that he would pay him the first instalment of 400 livres in that same month and the rest of the 2,160 livres due to him before the end of the year. When the promised advance had not reached Rousseau by the end of May, he wrote an acid letter[32] to the publisher saying, 'If M. Rey makes me any more promises I shall die of hunger', and asking him to return the two parts of *Julie* he had sent him. However, by 11 June,[33] Rousseau was able to inform Coindet that the letter of credit from Rey for the 'grand sum of 400 livres' had been sent through a merchant in Rouen, and he asked Coindet to bring the money to Montmorency the following Sunday when he came to dinner with his 'engraver'.

This engraver was a young man named Jean Houel,* whom Rousseau probably wanted to meet in connection with the illustrations he planned to have made for *Julie*; Houel could have been engaged to engrave the plates. In the end Houel did not do the work, but he did make a drawing of Rousseau, which was afterwards engraved by Parelle and published.[34] On the back of the original drawing, Houel himself noted: 'This drawing represents Jean-Jacques Rousseau, citizen of Geneva, at Montmorency, in the little house of the orangery of the Maréchal de Luxembourg near his château'.[35] According to a story told by the artist's great-nephew, Rousseau dozed off after dining with Houel and Coindet and 'Houel took advantage of that sleep to make a sketch'.[36] The published version shows Rousseau in a dressing-gown and cap brooding in the kitchen at the fireplace, with a candle burning at his elbow, his cat Minette la Doyenne on his lap and his dog Turc at his feet.

It is an attractive sketch, but it does raise a certain problem. The dinner took place on Sunday, 17 June – one of the longest days of the year – so why should Rousseau be seen sitting between a lighted candle and a fire? Since he received the Hungarian Count Teleki† in the same outfit, we cannot, however, be surprised that Rousseau should be wearing a cap and dressing-gown when entertaining guests for dinner. He dressed as an invalid, and had not yet adopted the Armenian caftan. A note in Houel's hand on the same side of the sheet as the drawing reads: 'J.-J. Rousseau of Geneva, done at Montmorency in 1764, by J. Houel, after dining with him.' The date '1764' is clearly a simple mistake, for the dinner must have taken place during the only summer that Rousseau spent at the Petit Château, that of 1759; but it is possible that Houel worked over the sketch after the event, and added features not drawn from life.

*Jean Houel (1735–1813) a painter and engraver from Rouen then working in Paris.
†See p. 270.

A day or two after Houel's visit, Rousseau wrote[37] to Rey about the illustrations he wished to have made for *Julie*. He said he envisaged twelve plates, of which 'the subjects are charming and suitable to be treated in a superior way by François Boucher, a celebrated painter in this country. I have calculated that the drawings and the engravings done with the perfection that the enterprise demands would be an affair of a hundred louis. Truly that would make an admirable and sought-after collection. The plates alone would ensure the success of the book.' Rousseau said he realized it was 'useless' to make the proposal to Rey, but he still urged him to agree to it. Boucher had given his consent, the choice of engraver could soon be made, and there 'would not be a more pleasing and interesting set of plates produced this century'. Rousseau did not mention Gravelot, and may not have known that Coindet was in touch with him.

In Paris Mme de Luxembourg had been unwell ever since her Easter holiday at Montmorency, and in early June[38] Rousseau wrote urging her to return to the château: 'The air of your park, which is so good for invalids, should be no less good for convalescents, and I feel too well here not to recommend it to you.'

For once, Rousseau was both fit and happy. His days were well filled. In the comfort of the Petit Château – a dry house, despite the fact that it was surrounded by water – he did a great deal of writing. In the park, he enjoyed his daily walks. Unlike the grounds of Mme d'Épinay's château, which were flat and uninteresting, the estate of Montmorency had been landscaped, as Rousseau noted,[39] among hills and valleys, so that there were woods and meadows and streams as well as the gardens which Le Nôtre had laid out with terraces, groves, parterres and ornaments. This fusion of the romantic and the classical seems to have appealed to him almost as strongly as the majestic landscape of the Alps.

Mme de Luxembourg, announcing[40] their return to the château for the summer, assured Rousseau that he need fear no intrusion into his privacy; but once the Maréchale and her husband arrived, Rousseau, by his own admission, chose to be constantly in their company. 'I scarcely ever quitted them,' he writes in the *Confessions*, 'I went in the morning to pay my court to Madame la Maréchale; I dined with them, and after dinner I took a walk with the Maréchal'. He explains that he did not stay for supper in the evening, because the hour was too late for him, and because there were too many other guests, but otherwise he lived on almost equal terms both with the Luxembourgs and their exalted friends; 'I kept all the usual familiarity of my manners, while they kept in theirs all the politeness to which they had accustomed me.'

With Mme de Luxembourg herself Rousseau was still somewhat ill at ease, still afraid of boring her with his silences in conversation. Then he hit upon the expedient of offering to read *Julie* aloud to her, and she accepted. He went to her bedroom at ten o'clock every morning, and with the Maréchal in a chair beside him, he sat at the side of her bed and held her spellbound until the hour when she had to rise.

'The success of these readings exceeded my expectations,' he recalls.[41]

Mme de Luxembourg was captivated by Julie and her author. She spoke of nothing but me, thought of nothing but me, said kind things to me from morning to night, and embraced me ten times a day. She insisted on having me placed by her side at the table, and whenever some nobleman wanted it, she told him the place was mine and made him sit somewhere else. The impression these charming attentions made on someone overwhelmed, as I am, by the least mark of affection, may easily be judged. I became attached to her in proportion to the attachment she showed to me.

In spite of all this, there remained what Rousseau called 'a natural opposition' between his mind and that of Mme de Luxembourg, which created a certain tension between them. He continued to prefer the company of the Maréchal. There were others, too, among the habitués of the château with whom he enjoyed an easy friendship. One was the Chevalier de Lorenzy,* an Italian and a former officer who was employed as aide-de-camp by the Prince de Conti, and spent much of his time looking after, and occasionally sleeping with, the Prince's mistress, the Countess of Boufflers, being, according to Rousseau, 'the most passive instrument in her hands'.[43] In the *Confessions*[44] Rousseau says Lorenzy professed to be his friend while actually being more the friend of d'Alembert 'under whose protection he passed among women as being a great geometrician', but the correspondence of the time bespeaks a genuine cordiality on both sides. Although Lorenzy's efforts to persuade Rousseau to visit the château had been unavailing until the Maréchal appeared in person, Rousseau liked Lorenzy, regularly kept in touch with him by letter, and even sent Coindet in search of him when he feared his letters went astray. As soon as he had moved to the Petit Château, Rousseau invited Lorenzy to visit him, as we learn from Lorenzy's letter of acceptance:[45] 'Yes, Monsieur, I shall certainly give myself the pleasure of coming to see you ... your invitation has a considerable value since it is pro-

---

*Orlando de Lorenzy (1712–84) was the son of a Tuscan family of French origin, and as an army officer had fought with St-Lambert in the Minorcan campaign of 1756. He never learned correct French, and was generally considered to be remarkably unworldly and unsophisticated. An English traveller writes of him: 'Indeed he was esteemed an absurd sort of character, and some stories he told of himself, very sufficiently proved him to be so.'[42]

portionate to the esteem I attach to your friendship.' Rousseau had evidently told Lorenzy he preferred walking to reading, since we find Lorenzy saying he approved of that preference, but Rousseau nevertheless found Lorenzy very useful in lending him or finding for him certain books he needed. Lorenzy lived in a tower attached to the Luxembourgs' mansion in Paris, and he was often able to transmit in his letters to Rousseau greetings and fond messages from the Maréchal and Maréchale.

In Geneva Dr Tronchin had been talking about Rousseau's disaffection from his native city, according to Pastor Vernes. Rousseau tried[46] to persuade Vernes that his attitude had been misunderstood:

When Dr Tronchin tells you that I have made up my mind not to come to Geneva he has put his own wrong interpretation on my words. There is a great difference between not deciding to come and deciding not to come or never to come. I am so far from having decided the latter that if I knew I could be of the least service to anyone there or even be sure of being received with pleasure by everyone, I would set off tomorrow. But, my good friend, do not make any mistake; the Genevese do not all have for me the affection of my friend Vernes. Every friend of truth has enemies everywhere, and it is less painful for me to find them abroad than in my own country ... Besides, my beloved Genevese, you have become too civilized for me. You are so elegant, so polished. What would you make of my strange figure and my Gothic principles? What should I do among you when you all have a master-jester who teaches you so well?

The reference to Voltaire is obvious. Rousseau was evidently as willing now to show his antipathy for Voltaire as Voltaire was willing to show his for Rousseau; only Rousseau expressed his less aggressively. Dr Tronchin, for his part, tried to keep on good terms with both, writing[47] to Rousseau in somewhat extravagant language, and underlining the words: '*I want to share the sweetness of life with you.*' Rousseau was unmoved by this hyperbole, and there their correspondence ended.

Vernes sent a vigorous denial[48] of Rousseau's assertion that a 'master-jester' was instructing the Genevese; Voltaire influenced, Vernes said, 'only a few young men who are in Geneva but do not have a Genevese soul'. He begged Rousseau not to judge a whole city in the light of a frivolous minority: 'Come back to us. I will arrange a circle of friends among whom your heart will be at ease.' Pastor Roustan[49] reinforced this plea: 'It was to live among us that Heaven had you born among us,' he wrote, if only to add, somewhat tactlessly, that Rousseau should come back to die in Geneva, 'so that we can build a mausoleum to your glory'.

With that other Genevese friend, Toussaint-Pierre Lenieps, the radical exile and bitter critic of the Genevese regime, Rousseau's friendship seemed to ripen as his illusions about his native land diminished. Not only did Rousseau look to Lenieps to help in his fight with the directors of the Paris Opera, he found in him a ready listener to all his grievances. From the Petit Château, Rousseau wrote[50] in July urging Lenieps to come with his daughter and grandson, who both had been unwell, to visit him, advising him that the way to find his present refuge in M. de Luxembourg's park was to leave one's carriage at the gardener's gate and then take just four steps on foot. Later in the year,[51] Rousseau thought it necessary to add to an invitation to Lenieps a warning against bringing any other visitor with him: 'I do not like new acquaintances, whoever they are, and a strange face disturbs all the pleasure I have in seeing old friends.'

Rousseau seems to have addressed some frosty words to other prospective visitors, to judge from a remark in a letter[52] from Deleyre: 'How shall I be received if I knock on your door? Will you point your gun at me? One of your letters gives me that idea.' Deleyre was writing from Vienna, where he had just started his duties at the French Embassy. He told Rousseau he envied his garden at the Petit Château: 'Here one sees only fortifications and canons.'

Rousseau's letter to Deleyre has disappeared, but it is clear that he had continued to criticize Deleyre for his attachment to Mlle Loiseau, the fiancée he had taken to Montmorency to introduce to Rousseau. At all events, Deleyre had to go on defending his love for her in further letters: 'Cruel friend,' he demanded,[53] 'how do you want me to receive – I do not say the affront – but the mortal blow you deliver in describing as a "gossip" the young woman to whom, I have told you, I have pledged eternal love? What greater injury could one do to one's worst enemy than despise the object of his love?' The truth was, he explained, that he had sworn with his blood to marry this girl that Rousseau regarded as 'one of the most despicable members of her sex'. If she knew what Rousseau thought of her, he added, she would die of sorrow.

Rousseau's heart was unmoved by this plea. 'You are decidedly mad, my dear Deleyre,' were the opening words of his reply.[54] 'Fortunately there are madnesses that come to an end, and when they are healed they leave only shame for a scar.' Rousseau went on to say that he had assumed that Deleyre's love-affair had ended with his departure for Vienna; he had certainly had no wish to offend Deleyre by what he wrote. Even so, he did not think it a 'terrible insult' to call a girl a 'gossip', although he admitted it was not a respectful appellation.

He asked Deleyre to consider his own predicament. He was tormented in his home by importunate visitors, and if Deleyre's beloved had been a discreet and modest person she would not have made him bring her to

Montmorency to satisfy her curiosity, but would have refused to disturb a writer's solitude. Rousseau apologized for the word 'gossip', but he warned Deleyre 'for the last time' that no woman or girl who behaved as Mlle Loiseau had behaved would be liked by him. As for Deleyre's promise to marry the girl, Rousseau was no less harsh:

You have done a stupid thing ... I see that love makes children of philosophers as it does of everyone else. Dear Deleyre, without being your friend I have friendship for you, and I am alarmed at the state you are in. Ah, for heaven's sake remember that love is only an illusion, and that one never sees things as they are when one loves, and if you have a scrap of reason left in your head, do nothing without consulting your parents.

Having read Rousseau's *Julie* in manuscript, Deleyre could not have been surprised to be enjoined to consult his parents, which is precisely what the heroine of that novel does before rejecting St-Preux in favour of Wolmar; but equally Deleyre must have been startled by the contrast between the exaltation of love in that novel and the denigration of it in Rousseau's letter to him. As it was, he reacted to Rousseau's hard words with remarkably good humour: 'You call me mad,' he replied,[55] 'but it is a madness in which I glory.' Furthermore, Deleyre said he did not agree that an honest and violent passion was incompatible with philosophy; and he added pointedly: 'It seems to me that you thought the same when you wrote your *Julie*.' Deleyre assured Rousseau that he was happy to be in love, and he hoped that one day he might be able to reconcile Rousseau to his fiancée: 'Without being my friend, accept my friendship, and give me the time to deserve yours.'

During the summer weeks that the Luxembourgs spent at Montmorency, they not only received Rousseau daily at the château, they also allowed him once or twice to entertain them at the Petit Château. As the Maréchal did not eat dinner, Thérèse was not called upon to cook, nor had staff to be sent down from the château to officiate. There were no formalities. Like others of their kind, the Luxembourgs were developing a taste for rustic simplicity as a change from the pomp and splendour of Versailles; Mme de Pompadour might dress up as a shepherdess, but Mme de Luxembourg had at Montmorency the philosopher of rusticity himself.

In the *Confessions*, Rousseau explains that as a result of his own habit of not taking supper at the château, and the Maréchal's of not dining, 'I was for several months very familiar in the family without ever having eaten with him.'[56] When the Maréchal expressed regret at this, Rousseau decided to go in for supper 'from time to time when the company was not numerous',[57] having enjoyed a long walk with his host beforehand. Rousseau noticed that the Maréchal enjoyed good food, and that 'the honours of the table were done in a charming way by Madame la Maréchale'. Being always given privileged place at her side, Rousseau had every reason to think it charming.

Among the furnishings that Rousseau took to the Petit Château from Montlouis was a pastel portrait that Maurice Quentin de La Tour had made of him. He had commissioned the picture from the artist when he was still at the Hermitage, with the intention of giving it to Mme d'Épinay in exchange for her portrait. The artist had, however, taken so long to finish working on it, that by the time it reached Rousseau he had quarrelled with Mme d'Épinay. 'I gave her back her portrait,' he recalls,[58] 'and there was no longer any question of my giving her mine. I put it in my bedroom at the Petit Château. M. de Luxembourg saw it and liked it. I offered it to him. He accepted, and I sent it to him in Paris.'

The picture had to go to Paris because at the beginning of August the Luxembourgs had to abridge their summer stay at Montmorency. The defeat of French armies in the battle of Minden had provoked a crisis, and M. de Luxembourg was recalled to duty by the government. Nevertheless the Maréchal found time to write[59] with his own hand to thank Rousseau for the portrait: 'It has given me infinite pleasure, and provides much distraction while I read in the morning in my study ... a prospect all the more agreeable because it bears the lineaments of a friend I count on so much.'

In return for the La Tour pastel the Luxembourgs gave Rousseau a double portrait:

They had themselves painted in miniature by a very able artist and set in a sweet-box of rock crystal, mounted in gold, which they presented to me in a most handsome manner and which gave me great pleasure. Mme de Luxembourg would not allow her portrait to be placed on the upper part of the box. She had several times reproached me for being fonder of her husband than of her, and I had not denied it, because it was true. She made me aware of this politely, but very clearly, by the way she arranged their portraits; and she did not forget my preference.[60]

When the Luxembourgs had left the château, Rousseau turned his mind to practical matters. Having received no news – or money – from Rey since his letter of 11 June with the first modest instalment of the royalties for *Julie*, he wrote to the publisher on 6 August[61] pointing out that it was the fourth time that Rey had broken his word. Rousseau suggested tearing up the contract, returning the 400 livres he had received, and taking back the two parts of the novel that Rey had in his possession. However,

Rousseau said he was still willing to stick to the agreement if Rey would keep to his part of it: 'Give me a swift answer, or your silence will speak for you.'

Rousseau also made preparations for his return to the renovated cottage at Montlouis. He would need new furnishings, and again he recruited the help of Coindet to order materials from Paris that would serve to make the inside as pleasing as M. Mathas proposed to make the outside. The Luxembourgs had urged him to stay on as long as he liked at the Petit Château, and expressed the hope that he would also visit them in Paris. They had a palatial residence there, near the boulevard of Montmartre, not especially beautiful, but noted for its fine interior and many rooms. In one of her letters[62] Mme de Luxembourg urged Rousseau to come on one of the days when her husband would be there because, as she put it, 'You tell me you have less reserve with M. de Luxembourg than with me.' She added: 'At my age one no longer has a sex. What I do have left is a heart that will never grow weary of you and which you will always find tender towards you.'

Rousseau put up some show of resistance; 'How cruel is your kindness,' he wrote.[63]

Why do you disturb the peace of a hermit who has renounced the pleasures of life in order to be spared its fatigues? I have spent my days in a vain search for lasting attachments and failed to form them in the social milieu to which I belong. Should I then look for them in yours? . . . I have never been able to resist caresses. Why do you and the Maréchal pick on a weak spot that I ought to master? Oh how I detest titles, and how I pity you for having them. You seem to me to deserve the sweetness of private life. If only you dwelt at Clarens [the home of Julie and Wolmar in the novel], for then I would come in search of the greatest happiness of my life. But the Château de Montmorency, the Hôtel de Luxembourg! Is it there that Jean-Jacques ought to be seen?

Jean-Jacques's critics would undoubtedly answer no; but the fact was that he was writing these words from the Château de Montmorency and would soon be seen at the Hôtel de Luxembourg, for despite his resolution never to set foot in Paris again, he paid several short visits to the mansion near Montmartre. He would usually go in time for dinner and return to Montmorency next morning. He was able to persuade himself that he had not betrayed his principles by doing so, since the carriage from Montmorency was able to enter the garden of the Hôtel de Luxembourg without depositing him on the boulevard outside, 'so that I could say with the most exact truth that I never set foot on the streets of Paris'.[64]

Rousseau's reference to Clarens was not lost on Mme de Luxembourg, who wrote to him in reply to his letter, 'I would need to be Julie to live there – and I know very well that the Hôtel de Luxembourg does not resemble that place.' She simply explained that there was a small apartment in the house which would always be at Rousseau's disposal whenever he came to Paris. Her terms of endearment can hardly have failed to move a man who yearned for affection: 'There is not a moment in my life,' she wrote, 'when I do not miss you, want you and love you.'

Rousseau was soon to think of the small apartment in Paris as his own. Already at Montmorency, with free access to the Petit Château, and the cottage at Montlouis successfully restored and refurbished, he could boast to Daniel Roguin[65]* of having 'two of the prettiest apartments I have known'. The rooms at the Hôtel de Luxembourg made three. But he did not find much opportunity to go to Paris as he was devoting most of his time to writing *Émile*.

*Daniel Roguin (1691–1771), a Swiss who had served in the Dutch army, had been a loyal friend of Rousseau since Rousseau's first arrival in Paris.

ÉMILE

When Rousseau said of *Émile, ou de l'éducation* that it was not a treatise of education, he probably meant it was something more than that, an essay in philosophy, and we may read the same claim into his remark about its being addressed not to fathers and mothers, but to '*les sages*'.[1] Parents come into the book at the very beginning, but soon the education of Émile becomes an adventure with only two participants – the pupil and his tutor – and they stay isolated together until Émile is allowed, on reaching manhood, to meet a girl. By that time the book has turned into a novel, without, however, losing its right to be considered 'philosophical'.

Two theses of a philosophical kind inform the whole work. The first is that all knowledge reaches the mind through the senses, that there are no innate ideas. This is the epistemology which Rousseau may have learned from reading Pierre Coste's translation of Locke's *Essay concerning Human Understanding* or more probably from conversation with Locke's disciple Condillac,[2] who had been his friend since he worked as a private tutor in Lyons for Condillac's brother Mably. Rousseau built on this theory of knowledge a far more radical programme of education than did Locke himself. For the child to acquire knowledge, Rousseau argued, he must be educated through his senses, and not have instruction imparted to his mind by words and symbols; the only path to understanding was for the child to learn from his own experience.

The second thesis, and the one to which Rousseau attached even more importance, was that every child is born innocent. *Émile* begins with the words 'Everything is good as it comes from the hands of the Author of nature, but everything degenerates in the hands of man.'[3] If men we see around us are corrupt, society is responsible for their corruption. Translated into a method of education, this principle prompted Rousseau to re-commend keeping his pupil as far away as possible from society and its corrupting influences, and to 'follow nature' in designing a plan for his

upbringing. In the earlier stages, this takes the form of what Rousseau called 'negative education', preventing the pupil receiving the effects of a bad culture, before arranging for him to receive the imprint of a good one.

Although Rousseau read Locke's *Thoughts on Education*,[4] and acknowledged his debt to it, he owed rather less to that book than to Locke's epistemology. Locke's plainly stated purpose as an educationist was to design the upbringing of a young English gentleman with a predictable role in society – neither a scholar nor a landless commoner. Rousseau's aim was to outline what he called 'the education of a man'. He also drew a distinction between that education and 'the education of a citizen', which was something that could only be accomplished in a republic where there were citizens to be educated; a citizen's education would be public, while the education described in *Émile* is private, indeed domestic. Although Rousseau had never been, as Locke had, to a boarding-school, he disapproved of such institutions for much the same reasons, that they fostered vices and taught the young 'everything except their duties'.[5]

Rousseau envisaged the life of the pupil being divided into distinct periods, which corresponded to the stages of the evolution of the human race as he had traced them in his *Discourse on Inequality*. The age of infancy was 'the age of nature'. The infant child, like the savage in the state of nature, is good; but so far there is no morality in his actions; he is governed by *amour de soi* which has not yet turned into *amour propre*. Unlike the savage, however, the infant is dependent on others.

The new-born child is naturally dependent, first and foremost, on its mother; and Rousseau calls on all mothers to follow nature's promptings and breast-feed their children themselves. This was not at all the rule among the property-owning classes of the *ancien régime*. Half the babies born in France died before the age of three, and those born in richer families were promptly dispatched to wet-nurses, who wrapped them in swaddling clothes to prevent them doing harm to themselves, and doubtless also to make them less of a nuisance. Rousseau criticized the use of tight clothing no less than the employment of wet-nurses. He implored French mothers to give their children natural freedom as well as natural nourishment, and altogether to take both more pleasure and more interest in their offspring. It seems that his readers were moved by his words. Other authors had pleaded for breast-feeding, but only after the publication of *Émile* did it become fashionable in France; a somewhat envious Buffon observed: 'Monsieur Rousseau alone commands and gets himself obeyed.'[6]

Rousseau's message to parents to love their offspring was accompanied by a warning to them not to allow them to become their masters: 'The first tears of children are prayers, and unless we are on our guard, they soon become orders. Children begin by being helped, but end by being served. Thus from their very weakness, which produces at first their feelings of dependence, there soon springs the idea of empire or domination.'[7]

While Rousseau admits that such tendencies develop at an early age, he also insists that they come from the outside and are in no way innate. In defending the argument of *Émile* against the criticisms of Archbishop de Beaumont, he wrote: 'I showed that all the vices which are imparted to the human heart are not natural to it; I showed how they come to be acquired; I followed, so to speak, their genealogy, and revealed how by the successive corruption of men's original goodness, they became what they are now.'[8]

Rousseau suggests that many vices attributed to children are not vices at all. For example, their so-called 'destructiveness' he attributes to superabundant energy, which leads a child not deliberately to destroy, but accidentally to damage things as he thrashes about in an environment he does not yet understand: 'a child seizes a bird as he would a stone, and strangles it without knowing what he is doing'.[9]

Rousseau urges parents to understand their children, but not to spoil them. Indeed he recommends an extremely spartan training. Children, he says, should be hardened against the rigours of the seasons, the climate, the elements. Since nature itself disciplines infants by subjecting them to pains, colics, fevers and so forth, parents should not shrink from doing the same. They should feed their children at irregular intervals; let them go barefoot;★ make them used to being alone in the dark; let them become familiar with spiders, snakes and other ugly creatures; make their cold baths progressively colder until they are really icy. 'Inure your children to hunger, thirst and fatigue. Dip them in the waters of the Styx.'[11] The one form of discipline that Rousseau forbids is corporal punishment, and the reason he gives for this is that the child must not feel itself being opposed by another person's will. This is part of Rousseau's formula for training a boy to be a free man. He argues that the child should meet only the resistance of things, never that of human beings.

Experience will teach the child that he cannot, of necessity, do everything he would like. Parents should not forbid a boy to do certain things to prevent him learning painful lessons. Rousseau admits that a boy who is allowed to play freely in the fields will fall and hurt himself a hundred times, but 'the blessedness of freedom', he declares, will make up for many bruises: 'Prepare from afar the reign of the child's freedom and the use of

★'If the Genevese militia had not known how to march barefoot, who knows that the city might not have been taken in 1602?'[10]

his strength by letting his body follow its natural tendency and by putting him into a condition to be always master of himself and to exercise his will, as soon as he has a will, in all things.'[12]

The second book of *Émile* deals with the education of the boy from the age of five to twelve. It is at this stage that the tutor takes over from the parents; and Rousseau ceases to talk of children in general, and introduces one particular pupil, Émile, and one particular tutor, an ideal one, with whom he comes in time to identify himself. To simplify the tutor's monopoly, Émile is declared to be an orphan,[13] although he is clearly a rich one,* since he lives in a moated château with a retinue of servants besides his superhuman tutor, and has in time, like Locke's imaginary pupil, to learn how as a squire to extend charity to his cottagers.[15]

Although he puts Émile entirely into his tutor's hands, Rousseau insists that the tutor must respect the pupil's freedom: 'The happiness of children, like that of men, consists in the use of their liberty.'[16] This is not to say that Émile will be allowed to do what he wants to do. Émile must not know he is being commanded by his tutor. In fact he will be,† but he will not realize it; for the tutor's art will be to guide him without seeming to do so. Dissimulation and devious stratagems play a large part in Rousseau's pedagogical method.

He rejects Locke's proposal that a tutor should reason with his pupil, on the grounds that a child under twelve has not yet reached the age of reason.‡ A reasonable man is the product of a good education, and education cannot begin with a faculty which is not yet there. Instead, the tutor must arrange his pupil's life so that he learns through the medium of his own sense perceptions. Following Locke's theory of knowledge, Rousseau maintains that the child's lack of innate principles means he has no ability to compare and relate facts. His thinking remains at the level of the senses. The senses provide him with images of the external world and all his mind can do is to check the evidence of one sense against that provided by another.[19]

Émile learns science by the systematic observation of natural phenomena and making simple experiments§ as his tutor takes him for walks in the countryside, which is the only laboratory he enters. For example, he is shown what looks like a bent stick in a pool of water; the tutor helps him to discover that the stick is in fact straight and the image distorted, and so

---

*'There is no need to educate villagers; but in corrupt societies, talents must make up for the lack of virtue, and the wicked must be forced to be useful in spite of themselves.'[14]

†The tutor says: 'Émile must obey no one but me; that is my first or rather my only stipulation.'[17]

‡The earlier manuscript of *Émile* dates the 'age of nature' from birth to twelve, and the 'age of reason' from twelve to fifteen.[18]

§These experiments do not include dissection, which Rousseau considers disgusting.[20]

1. Rousseau in Armenian costume
a pastel copy after Gérard

2. Madame d'Épinay
by Liotard

3. L'Hermitage near Montmorency
an engraving by Désiré after Gautier

4. Rousseau
by Angélique Briceau

5. Diderot and Grimm
by Carmontelle

6. The Comtesse d'Houdetot
an engraving by Corot

7. The acacia at Eaubonne
an engraving by Choffard after Monsian

8. The Petit Montlouis at Montmorency
a drawing by Lameau

9. The Marquis de St-Lambert
a pastel by an unknown artist

10. The Maréchale de Luxembourg
an oil-painting by an unknown artist

11. Madame de Verdelin
a pastel by Lefèvre

12. Paul Moultou
an oil-painting by an unknown artist

13. Dr Théodore Tronchin
a pastel by Liotard

14. Chrétien-Guillaume Lamoignan
de Malesherbes, *an engraving by Bonnieu
after a pastel by Valade*

15. Voltaire in Russian costume
a watercolour by Schellenberg

16. Rousseau with his dog Turc and his cat
La Doyenne at the Petit Château, Montmorency
a sketch by Houel

to learn the principle of refraction. The tutor does not expound such principles; he always seeks to stimulate the curiosity of his pupil, so that he will learn for himself. Instead of mounting the usher's stool to give verbal lessons,* the tutor joins Émile in homely empirical research:

There are many ways of interesting pupils in the measurement and estimation of distances. There is a very high cherry tree. How shall we gather the fruit? Will the ladder in the barn be long enough? How are we to get across this wide stream? Will one of the planks in the yard reach from bank to bank? We want to fish in the moat from our windows. How many feet of line will we need? I want to fix a swing between these two trees. Will a rope of two yards be enough? ... We are hungry. Which of two nearby villages can we reach more quickly for our dinner? To determine the length of the road, the pupil can count the time taken to walk along it. But let nobody do this for him. He must do it himself.[22]

Together with such efforts to enlarge the boy's mind with experiments, Rousseau continues to practise 'negative education'. Believing that all evil comes from outside, he takes care to keep Émile in as much solitude as possible, avoiding not only other children but also domestic servants, who have a notoriously bad influence on children.[23] More surprisingly, Rousseau proposes to keep his pupil away from all books except one – *Robinson Crusoe*, which teaches a salutary lesson in living without dependence on other men. The conventional school studies of Latin, history, geography and so forth are postponed to a later stage, delayed, that is, until Émile's mind is mature enough to understand fully what he is studying. There must be no learning by rote, no stuffing of the pupil's memory with words. Even religion, Rousseau insisted – to the horror of many readers – should be given no place in the education of a boy under twelve.†

Nevertheless Rousseau's scheme for education is intended to be above all a scheme for moral education; and he claims that the methods used for this purpose in conventional pedagogy fail to achieve their end. For example, he suggests that the teaching of fables, such as those of La Fontaine, do not impress on children's minds the lessons that teachers assume. As a child reads the fable of the crow and the fox, it is the cunning of the fox in getting the crow to drop the cheese that comes to be admired; the child does not grasp the adult lesson about the folly of vanity: 'Fables

---

*Rousseau warns the tutor never to teach the boy what he cannot understand, otherwise he will fill his mind with empty words.[21]

†In *Julie*, Rousseau's heroine determines to bring up her children as Christians despite the opposition of her husband.[24]

may instruct grown men; but it is necessary to speak the naked truth to children.'[25]

So Rousseau asserts, and yet at the same time he proposes methods of moral education which depend on the concealment of truth and which are plainly designed to deceive the child. A remarkable instance of this is the stratagem used to teach Émile about the right to property.* The tutor encourages Émile to plant a row of broad beans in the garden. The boy becomes fond of his patch as he goes with his tutor every day to water the beans and observe their growth. The tutor increases his delight by telling him 'This belongs to you', and even confirms Émile's title to possession by recalling the Lockean doctrine about a right to property being earned by labour. Then Rousseau has the gardener tear up the beans, and inform a dismayed Émile that the land is his, the gardener's, who has it reserved for growing melons. Émile is thus made to understand that he had no right to plant beans without the permission of the lawful owner of the land.

Neither the cruelty nor the deceitfulness of the tutor's behaviour in this episode troubles Rousseau, who seems confident that his methods will serve not only to impart moral understanding, but to forestall the development of vices. He goes on to tell us how the tutor thwarts the burgeoning vanity of his pupil by making him endure a public humiliation. This time the tutor conspires with a conjurer at a fairground. Émile and his tutor watch the conjurer make a mechanical duck follow a piece of bread held in his hand. Émile guesses that the trick is done with the aid of a magnet, and he offers to perform the same trick at the fair himself. His challenge is accepted and he attempts to do the trick, before an audience, with a small magnet hidden in the bread he proffers to the duck. The trick does not work. The audience roars with derisive laughter, and the conjurer completes Émile's humiliation by taking the bread from his hand and successfully luring the duck to come towards him. The secret, which the tutor knows, is that the conjurer has an accomplice under the table with a stronger magnet. When the fair is over, the conjurer visits Émile, reveals the secret, and reproaches the boy for trying to interfere with the livelihood of a poor showman: 'What mortification,' exclaims Rousseau, 'attends this first movement towards vanity! Young tutor, if you know to make vanity result in humiliation and disgrace, you may be sure it will not recur for a long time.'[27]

Further stratagems are used by Émile's tutor when the time comes to motivate the boy to study. Émile is made to want to learn to read by being sent written invitations to parties which he cannot read or find anyone to

---

*'This first idea the boy should be given is not that of liberty, but of property.'[26]

read to him until the parties are over. If corporal punishment is banished from Rousseau's educational methods, his alternatives sometimes seem no less sadistic.[28] This does not hinder the tutor saying to his pupil: 'One must be happy, dear Émile; that is the end of every being that feels.'[29]

Émile develops a healthy body by vigorous open-air exercise and a wholesome diet. Doctors, Rousseau urges, are best avoided, together with inoculations and vaccinations − 'cleanliness is the best medicine'[30] − and Émile's occasional illnesses have to be endured as part of nature's training in suffering. Rousseau is especially insistent that his pupil is kept away from the dirty air of the city and its crowds: 'Man is not made to live in such ant hills, but in sparsely populated places. The closer people are packed together, they more they become corrupt. The breath of man is deadly to his fellows.'[31]

Émile also has plenty of rest.* Unlike most educational theorists, Rousseau does not expect his pupil to work hard, partly on the grounds that it is no use imparting knowledge until the instruments of knowledge have been fully prepared by the 'exercise of the senses'.† One of the reasons why books have no place in Émile's early education is that they are of no use for this purpose.

'The senses,' Rousseau writes, 'are the first faculties to form and mature in us. They should therefore be the first to be cultivated. They are generally the ones most neglected. To train them calls for more than the use of them. It means learning to judge properly by them; learning, one might say, to feel. We do not know how to touch, see or hear, until we have learned to feel.'[34]

At the age of twelve Émile enters what Rousseau calls the third stage of childhood. He is now able to go beyond the observation of facts to compare and reason about them. He can appreciate the use of the things, and he can understand why he himself must work. It is an age when the child does not lack physical strength and has both enough mental energy to undertake academic studies and enough maturity to take pleasure in study. Although he has as yet only a primitive understanding of social relations, and no true aesthetic or moral insight, he can appreciate the principle of utility and the value of useful activity. He learns because he wants to learn. Robinson Crusoe, the practical man who solves on his own all the problems of living, is Émile's hero and model.

*Even so, the tutor wakes him up from time to time 'less to prevent him sleeping too much than to accustom him to being woken, even brusquely'.[32]

†In his letter defending *Émile* to Archbishop de Beaumont Rousseau wrote: 'I call "negative education" that which seeks to improve the organs, instruments of our knowledge, before imparting knowledge to us, and which prepares for the use of reason by the exercise of the senses.'[33]

Among other things, Émile learns a trade, partly to have a means of earning a living should ill fortune ever force him to need to do so, and partly to exercise his newly developing faculties. Rousseau insists that it shall be a useful trade – not that of an artist, musician, actor or writer, nor a menial trade that requires little skill, but rather the trade of an artisan. The one he chooses for Émile is that of a cabinet-maker, something that the tutor and the pupil will learn together: 'Émile must work like a peasant and think like a philosopher in order not to be as lazy as a savage. The great secret of education is to make the exercises of the body and those of the mind each serve as a recreation for the other.'[35]

At the age of fifteen, Émile is 'born anew' as he passes from boyhood towards manhood. Up to this point he has been absorbed in himself and the physical world. Now he really begins to live, and other people are important to him:

The proper study of man is that of his social relations. While he knows himself only through his physical being, he ought to study himself through his relations with things, and this is the occupation of his childhood; but when he begins to be aware of his moral nature he ought to study himself through his relations with men, and this – the occupation of his entire future life – begins at the point that he has now reached.[36]

This is also a critical point in the development of Émile's own personality, the moment when *amour de soi* changes into *amour propre*: 'As a tempest is announced from afar by the roaring of the sea, so the stormy revolution of adolescence is foretold by the murmuring of the rising passions, and the rumbling agitation warns us of the approach of danger.'[37]

Rousseau suggests that it is more than ever necessary to slow down as much as possible the development of the pupil towards manhood. On such matters as 'sex education', he advises the tutor neither to stimulate the curiosity of his pupil nor to satisfy it. Lies should not be told, but neither need all questions be answered: 'If we do decide to answer them, let it be done with the greatest simplicity, without embarrassment and without a smile.'[38] Rousseau quotes with approval a mother who says to her son when he asks how babies are born: '*Les femmes les pissent avec des douleurs qui leur coûtent quelquefois leur vie.*'[39]

Rousseau was probably thinking of his own birth when he cited these words and extrapolating from his own experience when he added that children would understand such an answer because they would remember having painfully passed stones in their own urine – something which, in fact, few children ever do. We should in fairness note that he ascribes this whimsical description of birth to a mother and not to his ideal tutor.

Émile in adolescence is encouraged to experience friendship before he experiences love. The tutor himself has always tried to be the friend, as distinct from the governor, of his charge, and the time has now come for him to implant in the boy's heart the seeds of affection for others. Rousseau does not expect this to be difficult, for if Émile has been brought up in happy simplicity, he will be delighted to meet companions and his heart will be stirred by the sufferings of others. Rousseau connects man's need for friendship with his weaknesses: 'It is our common sufferings that incline our hearts to humanity,'[40] he writes, and he goes on to suggest that pity, the first social sentiment to affect the human race in its evolution from the savage stage to civilization, enters the experience of the individual in his adolescence. Émile will be able to sympathize with the sufferings of others because he has suffered himself. But Rousseau urges his tutor to exercise care in allowing Émile to witness the sufferings of others: if he sees too much he will be hardened by it.

In general, Rousseau urges the tutor to let the adolescent see only those things that will restrain rather than excite the imagination. If country life is boring and monotonous, that is all to the good. It will prevent passions from developing too rapidly. Companions, too, must be chosen carefully so that they do not exert a harmful influence. Friendship will come naturally to Émile. 'But do not imagine,' Rousseau adds, 'that Émile's new-born affections will embrace all mankind. At first they will be confined to his companions ... whose obvious identity of nature to himself will increase his *amour de soi*. It is only after he has developed his feelings in a thousand ways that he will understand the abstract idea of humanity.'[41]

At the age of eighteen, Émile begins his education in moral science. Only at this stage is he allowed to study history, a dangerous subject at the best of times, Rousseau suggests, because it portrays what is bad in man rather than what is good: 'Only the wicked achieve fame; the good are either forgotten or held up to ridicule ... History, like philosophy, slanders the human race.'[42] Moreover, Rousseau protests, most historians are not content to relate the facts of the past; they pretend to have knowledge of causes, and they give their work the colour of their own prejudices. 'The worst historians for a young man to read are those who pass judgement.'[43]

Ancient history, he continues, is more instructive than modern, and the historians of classical antiquity preferable to those of the contemporary world. The best introduction to history, he suggests, is biography, and the best of biographers is Plutarch. Even fables, which are excluded from the education of children, can, he feels, be recommended for a student of eighteen, on the grounds that they enable a reader who is ready to acquire moral knowledge to learn by observing the behaviour of other men. At

the same time Rousseau insists that Émile must acquire his moral knowledge from his own experience; he says he would not wish to protect him
against every temptation. He will let him run the risk, for example, of
being cheated by card-sharpers: 'The only snares from which I would
guard him with special care would be those of prostitutes.'[44]

One of Rousseau's chief objections to conventional education is that it
confines the studies of young men to speculative disciplines at the most
active time of their lives, and throws them into the world with no practical
knowledge of how to behave in it, 'trained for society as if they are going
to live in a monastery'.[45] By contrast, Rousseau claims that his own method
teaches Émile how to conduct himself in the world, to live a successful
life, to earn his bread, and to get on with other people.

In the fullness of time, Émile is led from the study of nature and man
to the search for the author of all things; in a word, he is introduced
at last to religion. Rousseau reiterates his objection to giving religious
instruction to children: 'At an age when all is mystery, there can be no
mysteries, properly speaking.'[46] To make a child learn a catechism he
cannot possibly understand is to put distorted images of God into a child's
imagination, and Rousseau holds that it is better to have no idea of the
Divine Being than to have one which is unworthy of him. So Émile will
not start to learn about God until his natural intelligence has led him to
ask questions about the unseen world. Until then the tutor will not teach
him anything that Émile could not learn for himself. Émile will not be
made to join any church or sect, but will be put in a position to choose
his own.

It is at this stage in the book that Rousseau inserts the 'Profession of
Faith of the Savoyard Priest' – a credo he puts not in the mouth of the
tutor, since Rousseau has never made the tutor a teacher of religion, but
in the mouth of an unusual Catholic curate. Émile is simply invited to
study it; the tutor does not comment on it. All the tutor is allowed to do
is to draw Émile as far towards the love of God as reason itself will carry
him.

At the age of twenty Émile enters 'the age of love', or 'the age of
wisdom', as Rousseau called it in an earlier version of the book.[47] 'Up to
this point,' Rousseau explains – and by this time he has himself assumed
the role of tutor and writes in the first person – 'I have controlled him by
his ignorance; now the control must come from knowledge.'[48] This does
not mean that the tutor is any less active. Because he thinks that reading,
solitude, idleness, a sedentary life and the company of women are all bad
for a young man, Rousseau seeks to educate Émile's senses by providing
other objects of sensory satisfaction. He makes Émile take strenuous
exercise, for 'when the limbs are busy, the imagination is quiet'.[49] The

exercise he most favours is hunting; not so that the whole of Émile's youth should be spent in the slaughter of animals, but because hunting 'serves to hold him back for a time from more dangerous inclinations'.[50]

Those more dangerous inclinations are, of course, sexual. While Rousseau admits that Émile is destined by nature to need a mate, he does not allow him to find one for himself. The tutor sets about arranging things, and again he employs the sort of deceitful stratagems which characterized his pedagogical method when he was 'controlling Émile by ignorance'. This time his technique is to build up in Émile's imagination a picture of the ideal woman – not one so perfect that she could not exist, but one possessing the sort of defects that will match Émile's own. Having developed this image in his pupil's mind, the tutor suggests to him: 'let us call your mistress Sophie – Sophie is a name of good omen. Even if the girl you choose does not bear it, she will still be worthy of the name.'[51]*

Émile is not allowed to meet 'Sophie' immediately. First he has to finish his *dressage* for polite society. He will go to spend a year in Paris, where, thanks to his upbringing, he will prove himself to be cultured and urbane while remaining simple and unpretentious. In Paris he will meet authors, and, at last, read their books. He will be taken to the theatre – 'not for the study of morals, but for the cultivation of taste'.[52] He will be entertained in the *salons* and find favour with the hostesses. The one person he will not meet in Paris is his ideal woman.

Although Émile does not yet know it, 'Sophie' actually exists and she lives in the country. His tutor has already found her; and the reason why he suggested to Émile that he should call his ideal woman 'Sophie' is that Sophie is the name of the girl he has chosen for Émile to choose. When the moment is ripe, a series of contrivances and coincidences bring Émile and Sophie together, and as Rousseau describes this meeting the book becomes more than ever like a novel.

Sophie is 'well-born';[53] that is to say born into a family of landed gentry. She is a girl with a sensitive heart, so much so that her imagination is difficult to control. She is not especially striking in appearance, but she is attractive and charming. She dresses well, with simple elegance. She does not vaunt her charms, but hides them to advantage. She has natural talents; she can sew, cook, make lace, and is a capable housekeeper with almost too much zeal for cleanliness. She is well-read and intelligent, not brilliant, and while she is religious she has few dogmas and fewer observances and her ruling passion – like that of Rousseau's Julie – is her love of virtue. Unlike Julie – and indeed unlike most girls of her class – Sophie is told by

---

*Until Rousseau's *Confessions* were published, readers would not have known why he thought the name Sophie so felicitous.

her father that she may choose her own husband. She is sent into society, but meets no one who pleases her. In her reading she has encountered Telemachus, the hero of Fénelon's novel, and he has become her ideal man – the man she is waiting to meet.

With the stage thus set, the tutor takes Émile on a journey to the country, travelling on foot. By chance, it would seem, they lose their way and are offered shelter one evening at a gentleman's house. As dinner is about to be served, the host's daughter is introduced and the name of Telemachus is uttered. The girl blushes and the father exclaims 'Sophie, control yourself.' Hearing the name 'Sophie', Emile looks up at the girl and immediately recognizes her as the idol of his dreams; and she, returning his gaze, realizes that she has found her Telemachus. However, Rousseau will not allow his love-birds to be united too swiftly. Émile's education is not yet complete.

As for Sophie's education, it has to be understood in the context of Rousseau's whole theory of the relations between the sexes. In the *Discourse on Inequality*, he depicts a world where men and women are not only equal but alike – alike in the state of nature as it 'must have existed' before human societies were formed and natural man roamed the primeval forests as a solitary being, occasionally meeting, copulating with, and promptly separating from a female, who, being equally solitary, brings up her young unaided. The family, Rousseau insists in that *Discourse*, is not natural, as Locke and most philosophers of the Enlightenment said; it came into being only after the introduction of society. Women in the original savage state were as independent as men. It was only when human beings started to live in huts and caves with companions that the same individuals were in each other's company for long enough to become aware of each other's identities; only then did a man discover what it meant to be a father, and only then could sentiments of affection arise between him and his mate. 'The habit of living together gave rise to the sweetest sentiments known to men: conjugal love and paternal love.'[54] This emergence of conjugal love is seen by Rousseau as a felicitous development, if also as the development that marked the end of sexual freedom.[55]

Women grow weaker in the context of the family, while men become less independent; domesticity softens both. And yet Rousseau considers this stage of nascent society and conjugal love to be the 'golden age' of human experience before subsequent developments spoil it. Sex is central here. Rousseau claims that sexual desires are weak in the state of nature because they are like those of animals, directed to any available object; in the social state sexual desires become strong as they come to be concentrated on a chosen person. As a result, there emerges not only conjugal love, but romantic love, a violent passion which breeds as much jealousy as joy.

Sex, a trivial thing in the state of nature, serves from the earliest stages of civilization both to bind human beings together in affection and to divide them in bitter rivalry.

Love is promoted by women; it is an instrument of their purpose: 'Love is extolled by women in order to establish their ascendancy and make dominant the sex that ought to obey.'[56] How does this come about? Rousseau's argument is that women, weakened as they become domesticated, and dependent on men to an extent that men are not dependent on women, have to use cunning to make men stay attached to them. Each must make some man or men love her enough to shelter and protect her, choose her as a cherished mate. For women to make men as dependent on them as they are dependent on men, they must dominate men, and dominate them by devious manoeuvres and manipulations, since they cannot dominate them by force. Thus sexual relationships in human society are from the beginning 'political' – that is to say, relationships of power.[57]

Rousseau maintains that in order to understand sexual relationships in human society it is necessary to bring to the forefront the differences between male and female, and not to imagine, as feminists such as Mme Dupin believed, that those differences can be safely brushed aside as products of culture and conditioning; even though these differences are minimal in the state of nature, they must be understood as part of the very constitution of society.

Rousseau therefore wastes no time lamenting the absence of natural equality between the sexes in the socialized world, but instead deplores what he calls the unnatural predominance of women in civilization. How have women achieved this? In his *Discourse on Inequality* he does not tell us. But in *Émile* he unveils their strategy. Since sexual desire in the male is less intense than in the female, females have to stimulate it, and they do so by hiding their sexual charms, making themselves mysterious, and playing hard to get.

This strategy is advantageous for everyone. When women become modest, men are not only spared the ordeal of being devoured by the female's voracious sexual appetite ('dragged to death'[58] in Rousseau's lurid language), they are also 'civilized', that is, trained in the art of pleasing women. Once his sexual desire has been elevated to a ruling passion, and once the females refuse to satisfy that passion unless the male does a great many tricks to earn his reward, it becomes as important for men to study to please women as it is for women to study to please men: 'A law of nature causes man to depend on woman's wish, and makes him seek to please her in turn, so that she will consent to let him be the stronger.'[59]

One of the reasons why male sexual desire is weak in the state of nature is that there are plenty of females in the forest and no limits to the mating

season. This situation is reversed in society by the introduction of female
modesty, a somewhat bogus virtue as Rousseau describes it, but one very
necessary to the female if she is to transform the male's weak lust into a
strong abiding love. Although modesty is not natural (in a way, it goes
against the female nature), Rousseau claims that it is suggested together
with shame to women by nature, 'to arm the weak in order that they shall
enslave the strong'.[60] Rousseau's 'nature' does not always operate in the
same way. By original nature, women are immodest and shameless; in the
social context, nature propels them towards modesty and shame. The
ambiguity of the natural impulse is reflected in women's actual behaviour.

Torn two ways at once, women find it hard to be chaste. Religion tries
to help them – but Rousseau is sceptical about its efficacy. Religion, he
says, cannot be expected to make women chaste: 'a young and beautiful
girl will never ... shed tears before God for being a coveted object'.[61]
Pride is the effective agent: when a woman 'sees the whole earth at her
feet, she triumphs over all and over herself'.[62] Rousseau sees women's
modesty and chastity being motivated and secured by women's desire to
rule – to rule men and rule the world. He deplores the fact that in modern
times women have been able to satisfy their extravagant desire. He does
so from the ideological standpoint which informs all his political writings:
that of a convinced republican, an adherent of the doctrine that the model
of the ancient state, Rome or Sparta, can be reproduced in the modern
world. It is as a republican that he attacks the sexual relationships which
prevail in the decadent kingdom of France, where he discerns a deplorable
form of sexual uniformity in which the men are as effeminate as the
women.

In this most advanced form of modern culture, boys, he protests, are
simply brought up to be young ladies in jerkins; and men, being unable
to make themselves men, are turned by women into women. Rousseau
advances more than one explanation for this. First he suggests that the
barbarian invaders destroyed the Roman tradition of separating the sexes,
and introduced both licentiousness and fantasies of chivalry into sexual
relationships. Secondly, he argues that Christianity has undermined virility
by making virtues of submissiveness and other-worldliness; Christianity
has subordinated conjugal love to love of divine beings; and then made
matters worse by imposing duties of marriage so excessive as to be imprac-
ticable and vain, even ridiculous. Christianity, by denigrating both the
love of country and love of spouses in the name of love of God, has only
served to promote the love of mistresses.[63] Thus, in France, men have
become foppish slaves of women in society and of a despot in the state.

From the same republican standpoint, Rousseau praises the sexual
relations which prevail in his own puritan city-state of Geneva. In dedi-

cating his *Discourse on Inequality* to the republic of Geneva, he wrote: 'Lovable and virtuous women of Geneva – the duty of your sex will always be to govern ours. Happy are we that your chaste power, exercised solely within the marriage bond, makes itself felt only for the glory of the state and the happiness of the public. It was thus that the women commanded at Sparta.'[64]

Rousseau sees no place for women in public politics because his conception of a citizen is that of a citizen-soldier, and women cannot be asked to bear arms (they are too frail and too precious as bearers and breeders of future soldiers), nor can a good mother be relied upon to alienate her will (as a citizen must) from the interests of the family to those of the state. Women's political skill is skill in the use of hidden, personal, devious power. Public politics requires impersonal, rational legislation and open forthright utterance; it is a man's job. The abilities of each sex, as Rousseau sees them, are distinct: man is the arm, woman the eye in the partnership. If everything is in its place there will be no confusion of roles; in the family and society women will rule men, but in the state men must govern. This, at any rate, is what he says in the *Discourse on Inequality*. It is not what he says in *Émile*.

Rousseau has, in effect, two doctrines about the relationship of women to men: the first, that women should dominate in the home while men are dominant in the state, the second, that women should be subordinate in the home as well as in the state. Clearly these two doctrines are incompatible, and so far as the education of Sophie is concerned, Rousseau's first doctrine is given no consideration at all. Sophie is simply brought up to obey. Since this is his purpose, it is not surprising that the education of Sophie, as prescribed in Book V of *Émile*, is almost wholly in accord with the prevailing practice of the *ancien régime;* the programme of her education is as conservative as Émile's is revolutionary.

While Rousseau recommends the same regime of wholesome food and exercise for children of both sexes, he claims that different inclinations will exhibit themselves at an early stage, so that an educational method that 'works with nature' will soon ordain different curricula for boys and girls.

On the good constitution of mothers depends in the first place that of the children; on the care of women depends the early education of men; and on women, again, depend men's manners, their passions, their tastes, their pleasures, even their happiness. Thus the whole education of women ought to be relative to men. To please men; to be useful to them, to make themselves loved and honoured by them; to educate them when young; to care for them when grown; to counsel them; to console them and to make life agreeable and sweet to them – these are the duties of women at all times, and what should be taught them from their infancy.[65]

Rousseau notes that little girls have a taste for dress, which boys do not; and that they like to play with dolls. This, he says, should be encouraged and exploited in order to teach girls needlework, embroidery and other such skills. He also suggests that girls should learn arithmetic at an early age 'because it offers more utility at all times than any other subject, and takes rather longer practice to master'.[66] The importance of this lies in the fact that a girl 'will one day have a household to manage'.[67]

While Rousseau wants a girl to learn to be sweet and docile, he suggests that she should be allowed to develop her natural cunning: 'Cunning is a natural gift of her sex, and since all natural gifts are good, this one should be cultivated with the rest.'[68] He also claims that girls are naturally more artistic than boys, and that the aesthetic element in their education should therefore be more prominent than the academic. Even so, he insists that the girl's studies must be restricted to those of a practical use – the designing of clothes, for example, and the decoration of the home, and not the painting of landscapes, still less that of portraits. Girls should learn music, dancing, singing and the art of speech because these are social accomplishments; and above all girls should acquire the moral qualities appropriate to their sex: gentleness, submissiveness, modesty: 'Do not deny them gaiety, laughter, noise and games, but prevent them being either satiated with one or obsessed with another, and never allow them for a single moment of their lives to know themselves free from constraint.'[69]

This last interdiction marks perhaps the most fundamental difference between the education of Sophie and that of Émile – it being a cardinal principle in Émile's case that he shall never for a single moment know that he is under constraint. Another notable difference between the two educations is that religion is taught at an early age to the girl for the reason – decidedly unflattering to the female sex – that a true conception of religion is something she is unlikely ever to attain. Her faith must be subject to authority: 'Every girl should have her mother's religion, and every woman her husband's.'[70] However, Rousseau argues that a girl cannot be left with social prejudices as the only guide to living. She must also follow the rule of conscience, and in order to be able to judge between the promptings of conscience and the exigences of convention, she will need to cultivate the faculty of reason.

Reason, he claims, will serve a girl or woman both in keeping conscience from going astray and in correcting the errors of prejudice. And yet he does not offer much opportunity in his programme of education for her to develop that faculty. He insists that the search for abstract truths and general ideas lies outside a woman's compass; she must leave philosophy to men. A woman's talent is to read into the hearts of humankind; 'it is for her to discover experimental ethics, and for men to reduce it to a system ... Woman observes; man reasons.'[71]

The Sophie who has been introduced to Émile has had the greater part of the ideal education that Rousseau would like every girl to have, which is why she is so fitted to be Émile's mate. There remain, however, a few things for her to learn, and Émile himself is able to teach them to her. Being allowed to spend a day or two every week with her in chaste association, Émile instructs Sophie in music and dancing; he teaches her natural science as they go for walks in the countryside, and they cultivate together the virtue of benevolence as they dispense sympathy and relief and benefactions to the poor of the neighbourhood.

Émile does not neglect his artisan's trade, and on one occasion Sophie finds him in his workshop, sweating over the joinery; she is both touched and impressed to see a gentleman at work with his hands, and loves him all the more. But Rousseau will still not allow his young people to be married. The tutor has more torments in store for Émile. One day he says to his pupil: 'What would you do if you were told that Sophie was dead?'[72] Émile gives a low cry, springs up and gazes at the tutor with haggard eyes – the style of *Émile* becomes at this stage almost that of a novelette. 'Reassure yourself,' the tutor continues; 'Sophie is alive and well. But we must talk things over.' The tutor then tells Émile that he is too young at the age of twenty-two to marry Sophie and needs to study more before he assumes the duties of a husband and father. He promises Émile that he may marry Sophie in two years' time; in the interim he must undertake a tour of Europe and learn the ways of the world.

'Up to now you have not been your own master, but have lived under my direction,' says the tutor, revealing at last the secret that has hitherto been concealed from Émile. 'Now you must decide for yourself what life you want to lead.'[73]

After two years of travelling through the great cities of Europe, Émile returns to marry Sophie. The tutor gives them his blessing, together with the warning that romantic love is bound to cool and that they must look to a sweet habit of companionship to take the place of their early transports of passion. To Émile he says: 'Today I abdicate the authority you have allowed me. From this time on, Sophie is your tutor.'[74]

This sounds very like a return to the doctrine of the *Discourse on Inequality* that the woman should rule in the home, but Émile's reply suggests that he is still in thrall to his tutor: 'Advise and direct us,' he begs. 'We shall be willing to learn. I shall have need of you as long as I live. I have more need of you than ever now that my duties as a man begin.'[75]

The end of *Émile* is not, however, the end of the story. Some time after he had finished the book Rousseau wrote a sequel called *Les Solitaires*, relating what happened to Émile and Sophie after the tutor had withdrawn from the scene. This is one of Rousseau's most paradoxical productions. It might have been expected that the story would offer some confirmation of the success of the educational method, showing the two young people who had been so well trained for happiness being happy. Instead Rousseau has both Émile and Sophie err. Émile takes his bride to 'the capital' – presumably Paris – where both succumb to the corrupting influence of the city. Émile is so taken up with the business and the pleasures of metropolitan life that he neglects Sophie and their two little children. Sophie falls under the spell of a *femme du monde* who teaches her that in polite society the duty of husbands and wives is to behave decorously and amiably to one another, but not to deny themselves sexual gratification with other partners. When misfortune afflicts them in the death of their little daughter, Émile attempts to resume his loving attentions to his wife. Sophie resists, and eventually confesses to him that she is pregnant by another man. Émile is convulsed with jealousy – a passion he describes in vivid detail in letters to his former tutor, for *Les Solitaires*, like *Julie*, is a *roman épistolaire*. It is only in the depths of his despair that the education he has received begins to guide his conduct. He leaves his family, gives up his fortune, and starts a new life as a cabinet-maker in the country. Sophie discovers him there, but dreading that he may take his own son from her, she disappears, and Émile, who cannot face acting as father of the other man's child, does not pursue her, but goes even farther away. On a voyage across the Mediterranean he is captured by pirates. As a slave in Algeria, his early education serves him again: he is physically fit enough to endure hard labour easily, and stoical enough to be happy in spite of his chains; he even claims to have kept his freedom, saying 'he who knows how to will what necessity ordains is the most free, since he is never forced to do what he does not want'.[76] He proves so efficient a worker that he is promoted to be a slave of the Bey of Algiers himself.

Rousseau left *Les Solitaires* unfinished, but according to the testimony of friends, he envisaged giving the novel a happy ending, with Émile and Sophie reunited by some extraordinary coincidence, but even such an ending could hardly prevent *Les Solitaires* conferring on the educational methods of *Émile* a certificate of failure, in the sense that Émile, so elaborately trained to be a man, has his only success in the role of a slave, and Sophie, brought up to be the ideal wife, is easily seduced into adultery.

Rousseau's fullest statement of his religious beliefs, the 'Profession of Faith of the Savoyard Priest'[77] is inserted in Book IV of *Émile*, as part of the pupil's delayed introduction to religion. To judge from what happens to Émile in later years, its message seems to have been lost on him. Faith in God plays no part in Émile's later life; he proves to be Stoic rather than a deist; in his adversity his consolations come from philosophy and not from religion. For Rousseau himself, on the other hand, religious faith, as the Savoyard priest explains it, provided the one consolation in all his sorrows. Therein lies the importance of the credo.

Towards the end of the 'Profession', the priest says, 'Dare to confess God among the philosophers, and preach humanity to the intolerant. You will perhaps be alone in your party, but you will carry in yourself a testimony which will make that of others unnecessary.'[78] This is what Rousseau had attempted to do in *Julie* and he attempted to do it again in *Émile*. In the event, instead of moderating the mutual hatred of the pious believers and the atheists, he brought on his own head the aggression of both.

His own attitude towards both parties was undoubtedly hostile. In an unpublished note[79] to Book IV of *Émile* he wrote:

Have compassion, my child; love those who have it, but fly from the pious believers. Nothing is more dangerous than their company, their humble pride. They must either dominate or destroy; they are inquisitorial, jealous, vindictive, mysterious in all their doings ... The best policy is keep your distance from them; those who avoid them they only despise, but those who desert them have everything to fear.

His comments on the philosophers were no more kindly: they are 'angry wolves':[80] they are 'ardent missionaries of atheism and very imperious dogmatics who will not endure without fury that one might think differently from them'.[81]

The whole tone of the Savoyard priest, by contrast, is one of sweet reasonableness. The first part of the 'Profession' is his statement of the case against the materialist metaphysics on which fashionable atheist philosophy is based. Rousseau takes particular care in the presentation of this argument since the author against whom it is mainly directed is Helvétius, and Rousseau did not wish to add to the sufferings of a philosopher who was already subject to more persecution than most, and for whom he had a particular esteem. The Savoyard argues, against the teaching of materialist metaphysics, that the universe is not a self-moving entity, but must receive its motion from some external cause: 'It is impossible for me to observe the rising and setting of the sun without conceiving that some force must urge it forward; or if it is the earth itself that turns, I cannot but believe that some hand must turn it.'[82]

He goes on to claim that every motion which is not produced by some other motion, must be produced by a will: 'In what manner volition produces physical and corporeal action I do not know, but I know from experience within myself that it does so. I will to act, and the action immediately follows.'[83] He concludes that the universe would be unmoving unless some *cause motrice* acted on matter.[84] 'I believe therefore that the world is governed by a wise and powerful will. I see it; or rather I feel it; and this is important for me to know ... That Being whose will is his deed, whose principle of action is in himself, that Being ... who gives motion to all the parts of the universe, and governs all things, I call God.'[85]

The Savoyard goes on to maintain that the design of the universe also reveals the benevolence of the creator. Rousseau, in his *Letter on Providence*, had rejected Voltaire's claim that the disaster at Lisbon in 1755 was evidence of God's indifference to human misery. Here rational arguments are less important than an existentialist affirmation. The Savoyard believes in God's love because he has to. Rousseau had told Voltaire: 'I have suffered too much to live without faith.'[86] The Savoyard declares:

Whatever we call infinite is beyond my understanding. What can I deny, or assert, what arguments can I employ on a subject I cannot conceive? I believe that the soul survives the body so long as is necessary to justify Providence in the good ordering of things, but who knows that this will be for ever? I can readily conceive how material bodies wear away, and are destroyed by the separation of their parts, but I cannot conceive a similar dissolution of a thinking being, and since I cannot imagine how it can die, I assume it does not die at all. This assumption consoles me and as it is not unreasonable, why should I be afraid to entertain it?[87]

Having given rational grounds for belief in the existence and benevolence of God, the Savoyard next invokes the testimony of feeling; in seeking to lead a virtuous life, he says that he feels himself to be an instrument of the Supreme Being 'who wills the good, who does it, and who will bring about my own good through the cooperation of my will with his and by the right use of my freedom. I yield to the order he establishes, confident that I shall one day fully enjoy that order myself and find happiness in it.'[88]

To the testimony of feeling is added that of conscience, 'a faculty which resides in the soul just as instinct resides in the body'.[89] Conscience is the voice of God within each individual and 'whoever obeys conscience walks in the true path of nature and need not be afraid of being misled'.[90]

This is not to say that reason is sacrificed. At one point the Savoyard declares to God: 'The most worthy use of my reason is to annihilate it before Thee',[91] but he also asserts that since reason is God-given, he is fully entitled to use it to discover God's will and learn his duties.[92] He will not bend his reason to the authority of any church, prophet, priest or even that of Holy Scripture. And although he loves God, he does not believe in prayer. His worship is confined to sublime contemplation:

I immerse all my faculties in God's divine essence. I am overwhelmed by his goodness. I bless him for his gifts, but I do not pray to him. What should I ask of him? To alter the course of nature and do miracles for my sake? Should I who am bound to love the order his providence has established in the universe ... wish it to be disturbed for my private advantage? Neither do I pray to God for the power to do right, for why should I ask for what he has given me already?[93]

How far can this 'Profession of Faith' be considered a profession of Christianity? It claims to be one. And Jesus is at least favourably compared to Socrates: 'The life and death of Socrates are those of a sage; the life and death of Jesus are those of a God.'[94] But this is as near as we come in Rousseau to an affirmation of the divinity of Christ. The Savoyard does not speak of Jesus as the Redeemer, nor does Rousseau ever think of him in this way. Having rejected the doctrine of original sin, he sees no need for the atonement. On another occasion[95] Rousseau described Jesus as the wisest and most lovable of mortals, and 'mortals' is not the least important word in that sentence. Jesus is seen as an exemplary man and a sublime teacher whose central message of love has been distorted by St Paul and the Church.

Thus although the Savoyard is a priest, he attacks priestcraft, saying he has no need of intermediaries to reach God. 'Always human testimony!' he protests. 'How many men between God and me!'[96] Theologians, he suggests, are not less corrupted in their thinking by *amour propre* than other men, indeed are rather more so, so why should their opinions be authoritative? Priests are useful not because they know more about God, but because they discharge valuable pastoral duties and teach their flocks to lead good lives: the function of the priest, in an expression Rousseau took from the Abbé de St-Pierre, is that of an *officier de morale*.[97]

As for the doctrine of revelation, to which all churches attach so much importance, the Savoyard declares his attitude to be one of *doute respectueux*.[98] But what he has to say on the subject is more like outright rejection: 'Men's revelations only degrade God by giving him human passions. Far from clarifying our notions of the Supreme Being, their particular dogmas only confuse them, and instead of ennobling, they sully them. To the inconceivable mysteries which surround God, they add absurd contradictions, and instead of bringing peace on earth, they make men proud, intolerant and cruel.'[99]

Miracles are rejected no less emphatically. God, says the Savoyard, proves his goodness by providing a universe which moves in an orderly way so that men may feel at home in it. So how could God be said to prove his existence by violating the laws of his own creation? If there are inexplicable events in nature, that is evidence of the limitations of human science rather than of heavenly intervention. Far from considering the doctrine of miracles an aid to Christian faith, Rousseau always regarded it as an impediment. 'Remove the miracles from the Gospel,' he wrote in another text, 'and all the world would be at the feet of Jesus Christ.'[100]

The Savoyard respects the Gospel. He describes it as 'holy' and in a marginal note to a draft of the 'Profession' Rousseau wrote 'NB: to speak of the beauty of the Gospel'.[101] He had come to be a regular and devout reader of the Bible since living at Montmorency. Even so, he has the Savoyard assert that the Gospel is 'full of incredible things, things repugnant to reason and impossible for any sensible man to conceive or admit'.[102]

Furthermore he goes on to observe that the Holy Scriptures are only books and that their authority is no more certain than that of priests. Most such books, he adds, are written in languages the faithful do not speak. Christians do not understand the Hebrew and Greek of the Bible any more than Turks understand the Arabic of Muhammad. Believers must rely on translations, without anyone to certify the accuracy of the translations. In any case, all sacred books are written by men. 'Why then,' the Savoyard asks, 'should people need books to teach them their duty, and did people not know their duty before these books existed?'[103]

When the Savoyard has thus disposed of sacred books, together with revelation, miracles, churches and priests, all that remains is what he calls natural religion: 'In my exposition,' he declares,

you will find nothing but natural religion. It is not strange that more should be needed for salvation. How should we know of any such necessity? Of what am I guilty if I serve God according to the light he has given to my reason and the feelings he has inspired in my heart? What purity of morals, what dogma useful to mankind and worthy of its Author can I derive from a theological doctrine that cannot be learned without it by the right use of my own faculties? Show me what you can add for the glory of God, for the good of society, and for my own advantage to the duties already prescribed by natural law ... The noblest ideas of the divine come from the reason alone. Behold the spectacle of nature. Listen to the inner voice. Has God not addressed everything to our eyes, to our conscience, to our judgement? What more can men tell us?[104]

These then are the central imperatives of Rousseau's religion: look inward to reason and conscience; look outward to nature. It was because nature revealed God to him that he chose to worship God in nature. And worship Rousseau undoubtedly did. He looked on the external world with different eyes from his contemporaries, although he persuaded many to learn to see it as he did. He saw God's majesty most clearly in high mountains and dense forests; the peaks and summits of the Alps spoke more directly to him than the Gothic spires and baroque domes of Christian cathedrals. He needed no church, although he was content from time to time to worship in one.

At the end of his exposition the Savoyard claims not only that natural religion is true religion, but that it is true Christianity, and Rousseau made the same claim in his defence of *Émile* against the criticisms of Archbishop de Beaumont: 'I am a Christian, not as a disciple of priests, but as a disciple of Jesus Christ.'[105]

Rousseau's Savoyard priest was based in part on the Abbé Gaime,[106]★ who had befriended him when he was a Catholic convert in Turin at the age of sixteen, and his 'Profession of Faith' is presented as the exposition of such a curate to a young man who has wandered from home and changed his religion. The curate's parting advice to the boy is to go home and return to the Protestant Church of his fathers, even as he himself, for all his doubts and heterodox opinions, intends to resume saying Mass.

This ending of the 'Profession of Faith' has surprised those readers who expected someone as much at odds with established religion to be a dissenter. But although Rousseau's religious ideas were close to those of Unitarians, Quakers and other such nonconformists, he did not approve of people seceding from the established church of their country simply because they disagreed with its teachings. Organized dissent he saw as a danger to public order, and, like Henri IV, he put public order before religious scruples. If Émile is not baptized and confirmed in a conventional way, it is because Émile grows up in a kind of limbo. As a general rule, Rousseau lays down that people should conform to the religious institutions of their homes and countries. No individual, he insists, has the right to introduce a new *culte*. He upholds the principle: *cuius regio eius religio*.[108]

In *The Social Contract* he carries to even greater lengths this policy of putting the demands of politics before the claims of religion. While repeating his belief that Christianity of the Gospel is the true religion, he asserts that it does not serve to form good republican citizens, and thus,

---

★Although Rousseau does not name the Abbé Gaime, he has his Savoyard refer to 'M. Mellarède' helping him secure reinstatement to his clerical functions.[107] The Abbé Gaime was tutor in the family of Mellarède. But whatever Rousseau's curate owed to the Abbé Gaime, the 'Profession of Faith' was very much a profession of his own faith.

no less squarely than Machiavelli, he banishes the religion of the Gospel in favour of the religion of the state. But that is the argument of another book, and will be considered in a later chapter.

MONTLOUIS RESTORED

By the end of the summer of 1759 Rousseau was re-established once more in his cottage at Montlouis. M. Mathas had allowed him to direct the restoration of the building according to his own taste and Rousseau was pleased with the result. Not only had it become 'one of the prettiest cottages in the world',[1] it had also been made more commodious. He had converted the one room on the first floor into a suite of bedroom, dressing-room and *garde-robes* for himself, arranged a bedroom for Thérèse on the ground floor, next to the new kitchen, and made the *donjon* into a comfortable study, complete with windows and a fireplace, the fireplace being a gift from M. de Luxembourg. He took particular pleasure and pride in the garden, which was sheltered by a double row of lime trees. He planted more trees around a stone table and benches to make an open-air salon, surrounded it with lilacs and honeysuckle and put a border of flowers under the trees. This terrace, he recalled, was even higher than that of the château, and commanded a view at least as fine: 'It was there that I tamed a great number of birds, and there that I entertained M. et Mme de Luxembourg, M. le Duc de Villeroy, M. le Prince de Tingry, Mme la Duchesse de Montmorency, Mme la Duchesse de Boufflers, Mme la Comtesse de Valentinois, Mme la Comtesse de Boufflers and other persons of rank who did not disdain to make the very tiring pilgrimage up the hill to Montlouis.'[2]

Mme de Luxembourg restrained herself from offering Rousseau a house-warming present, but she took the risk[3] of sending to Montlouis a modest gift for Thérèse. Rousseau responded with a reproachful note,* short and barely polite. The Maréchale protested gently:[6] 'Is it possible that you

---

*At the same time Rousseau wrote a very polite letter to M. de Luxembourg, congratulating him on the appointment of his son, the Duc de Montmorency, as Capitaine des Gardes in the royal household.[4] The Maréchal, in thanking him, expressed the hope of seeing Rousseau in September.[5]

could be so unjust to me as to forbid me to give Mlle Levasseur a cotton frock? ... You scold me, Monsieur, and you have written me the most wounding letter, and you threaten to stop loving me. Ah well, Monsieur, in spite of your threats I love you with all my heart and I shall never change.'

On 5 September[7] Rousseau sent Rey the third part of *Julie*, having by that time received[8] further instalments of his royalties with profuse apologies for the delay. In a later letter Rousseau told Rey,[9] somewhat artfully, that while he himself was in no hurry to see *Julie* in print, it would be wise to get the book published before all the other novels which were coming on to the French market had exhausted the public's appetite for such literature. Rey[10] wanted Rousseau to divide the novel into six equal parts, since the existing disparities of length would produce a series of volumes of uneven thickness. Rousseau was unwilling to comply; however inconvenient, the unevenness of length was inevitable, 'one cannot measure this kind of work', he protested,[11] 'by the yard'.

Before the end of October,[12] Rey was able to acknowledge receiving the fourth part of *Julie*, and he offered to send print samples to the author to enable him to make a choice of the type-face. Rey declared that no part of his trade was more important to him than publishing Rousseau's writings, and said he hoped to begin the printing of *Julie* within two or three months.

Rey was not the only person for whom Rousseau had to prepare a manuscript of *Julie*. He had also undertaken to make one for Mme de Luxembourg, although by the end of October[13] he had to admit to her he had not yet started work on it: 'Someone is ahead of you in the queue and that someone is pressing me,' he added, referring to Sophie d'Houdetot.[14] He said he felt badly about taking money from the Maréchale for the copy: 'Properly I should be paying you for the pleasure of working for you.'

Mme de Luxembourg, who was with her husband at Versailles, assured[15] Rousseau that she was thrilled to have his news. She quoted without comment his gallant suggestion that he ought to pay her for the pleasure of working for her, and only complained that he had given her no news of his health. She sent him loving wishes from both her husband and herself.

Rousseau, in his reply,[16] lamented that his health was less good than it had been: 'The approach of winter is always bad for me, and the first frosts this year were so sharp that I believed I would be immobilized. However, the milder air has brought relief in the past day or two, and I hope I shall not have to complain again about my health.'

The next day[17] Rousseau sent a note to Mme de Luxembourg saying he had been rereading his sentence about being paid for the pleasure of working for her and declared himself to be puzzled as to why she had quoted it: 'I do not know whether I owe you an apology or whether you owe me one.'

A week later, having not heard from her, Rousseau wrote[18] again to the Maréchale, troubled by the thought that he had done something wrong: 'I do not know what to blame myself for ... If you were less the great lady, I should fly to you. I should come and throw myself at your feet and spare neither supplications nor prayers to end your displeasure, whether well- or ill-founded. But in view of your rank, you will not expect me to do everything that my heart desires.'

Writing from Versailles,[19] Mme de Luxembourg hastened to assure Rousseau that he had done nothing wrong: she was only alarmed that he had taken seriously something meant as a joke. She was dying to see him, she said. Her husband's tour of duty as captain of the King's bodyguard would end in a month's time, and if Rousseau did not come to visit them in Paris, they would come to seek him out at Montmorency.

A few days later,[20] Mme de Luxembourg sent Rousseau further words of reassurance: 'It is not for you to throw yourself at my feet, but for me to throw myself at yours to ask for clemency and friendship.' She realized she had upset him, and she was very sorry; she wanted him to believe that 'M. de Luxembourg and I love you tenderly.' She ended by begging 'on my knees for a little word to tranquillize me'.

Although he was now giving most of his time to literary work, Rousseau still insisted that his trade was that of music copyist. Even so, when Coindet asked if he was willing to accept commissions, Rousseau implored[21] him not to send any French harpsichord music: 'it bristles hideously with notes and it is as painful to the eyes as it is to the ears'. When Vernes wrote from Geneva to ask Rousseau for one of his musical compositions, Rousseau answered:[22] 'My God, dear Vernes, what are you talking about? I have no music here beside that of the nightingales, and the owls of the forest are my compensation for the Opera of Paris. Having a taste now only for the pleasures of nature, I have come to despise the amusements of the town.' In the same letter, Rousseau told Vernes: 'there is nothing of mine in the press'. This was, of course, untrue, since Rousseau had sent *Julie* to his publisher, but he did not feel himself to be on oath in writing to Vernes, if only because he knew full well that Vernes was meeting Voltaire socially in Geneva; about Geneva Rousseau added: 'I sing the old Genevese songs with a faint voice, and end by weeping for my homeland.'

A new friendship that developed after Rousseau's return to Montlouis was with the Marquise de Verdelin.* A close friend of Sophie d'Houdetot, and rather better looking, she was the daughter of an impoverished nobleman, Charles de Brémond, Comte d'Ars, who had married her off at the age of twenty-two to a marquis aged sixty-four and described by Rousseau as 'old, ugly, deaf, harsh, brutal, jealous, grumbling, irascible, covered with sores, and one-eyed'.[23]

Even so, Rousseau says, Mme de Verdelin always got her own way with her husband, and forced him to accept on her terms her liaison with the Seigneur de Margency. Rousseau had not always been much drawn to her, despite her beauty and her blue blood. She had first come into his life at the time of his romance with Sophie, when she was living in her lover's house at Margency and had lent the key of the garden to Mme d'Houdetot, so that Rousseau could cross the garden with her towards their favourite walk, that near Mont Olympe. At this time Rousseau discouraged any acquaintances that might intrude upon his meetings *tête-à-tête* with Sophie, and Mme de Verdelin was quickly brushed aside. However, when Rousseau moved from the Hermitage to Montlouis, Mme de Vendelin moved from Margency to Soisy, which was even nearer to Montmorency, and she renewed her efforts to get to know Rousseau better.

'She came to see me several times at Montlouis without finding me at home', Rousseau writes in the *Confessions*,[24]

and as I did not return her visits, she had the idea of sending me some pots of flowers for my terrace to force me to do so. I was obliged to go and thank her. That was enough. The aquaintance was made. Our association was stormy at first, like all those I have made in spite of myself. Her mind was altogether antipathetic to my own. I rarely heard her say anything good of her absent friends without slipping in something nasty. What she did not put a bad construction on, she turned to ridicule, her friend Margency not excepted. Another thing which I found unendurable was the continual nuisance of her letters, messages, presents and notes which I was at a loss to know how to answer.

It must be understood that when Rousseau wrote his *Confessions* he had quarrelled with Mme de Verdelin, and looked back with a somewhat jaundiced eye on their friendship. Everything he wrote at the time, on the other hand, indicates that he enjoyed her company and appreciated her attentions. Even in the *Confessions* he admits that as a result of seeing her often, he became attached to her: 'Like myself she had had her sorrows,

---

*Marie-Madeleine de Brémond d'Ars, Marquise de Verdelin (1728–1810), descended from a family which traced its ancestry to the knights of the crusades.

and mutual confidences made our conversations interesting. Nothing unites hearts so much as the pleasure of shedding tears together.'[25]

Portraits of Mme de Verdelin depict a melancholy beauty,[26] with a pale face and long neck. She was still only thirty-one years old when she came knocking on Rousseau's door at Montlouis; she had fine delicate features and all the graces of the *noblesse de race* that Rousseau seldom failed to notice and admire. The sorrow he speaks of was almost certainly provoked by the cooling of Margency's love for her. It was not a case of her lover's having found another mistress; altogether more unexpectedly, in an *habitué* of Holbach's salon and an aspirant Encyclopédiste, Margency was turning to religion, and the more devout he became, the less attentive he was to his mistress.

The earliest known letter from Rousseau to Mme de Verdelin is dated 18 November 1759[27] and is wholly affectionate in its tone and style. She had returned to Paris for the winter and Rousseau tells her that he is not surprised to learn from her that Paris is sad: 'The country has become sad, too, since your departure. That would be another grievance against you, if I come to feel lonely in my solitude and you are the cause.' In the same letter he speaks of commissions she has undertaken for him, and he reproaches her – gently this time – for paying the postage on a packet she has sent him, and for not telling him the price of a box of tea. He speaks with approval of the forthcoming marriage of Margency's great friend Desmahis, and suggests – hardly sincerely in view of his contempt for the aged and irascible Marquis de Verdelin – that her own marriage might afford the bridal pair a model of domestic happiness.

It was about this time that Margency himself offered Rousseau a part-time job in literary journalism as a regular contributor to the *Journal des savans*. He explained[28] that it would entail very few duties, simply that of writing abstracts of new books of history, philosophy and literature which would be delivered to him; the salary would be eight hundred livres a month for eight days' work. Margency said he felt sure he could persuade M. de Malesherbes to offer him the job, but Rousseau guessed, correctly, that Malesherbes was already behind the offer, and he speaks of it in the *Confessions* as 'another mark of M. de Malesherbes's kindness'.[29]

He says there that he deliberated a few hours before deciding, and adds: 'I can swear that the only reason for any hesitation was fear of annoying Margency and displeasing M. de Malesherbes. But at length the thought of the intolerable constraint of not being able to work when I pleased, of being a slave to time, and, even more, the certainty of doing the duties badly, prevailed over every other consideration and made me refuse a job for which I was not suited.'

Rousseau goes on to say in the *Confessions*[30] that he explained the reasons

for his refusal in a very polite letter to Margency. The text of the letter
has not been traced, but there is no reason to doubt Rousseau's claim that
his refusal gave no offence to Margency or to Malesherbes. Neither blamed
him, and years later Malesherbes said that if he had known Rousseau as
well then as he did afterwards, 'I would have taken care not to offer him
the job.'[31]

In one[32] of many friendly letters from Paris, Mme de Verdelin sent
Rousseau the news that Grimm had been appointed minister to the Court
of Versailles in the diplomatic service of Ratisbon,* which prompted
Rousseau to say[33] that he was not at all surprised that 'the man you
mention' – 'Grimm' being a name he could no longer bring himself either
to speak or write – was a diplomatic minister: 'I should not even be
surprised if he became a minister of state.'

Rousseau soon began to find his correspondence with Mme de Verdelin
too time-consuming, especially when the Marquise started writing letters
to Thérèse as well. 'Madame,' he protested,[34] 'we must end this commerce;
it is too agreeable and therefore too onerous. It means I must either be too
precise or too ungrateful. Precision is beyond my powers, and ingratitude
hurts my heart. What can you do to put my mind at rest? The more often
you tell me that I am not obliged to answer your letters, the more you
oblige me to do so. The less you reproach me, the more I reproach myself.'

He went on to say that he was sorry to hear that she was unwell, but
hoped that that might prompt her to leave the unhealthy air of Paris and
return to Soisy, so that he could answer her letters by walking over to
visit her. He warned her not to expect any reply to the letter she had just
sent to Mlle Levasseur: 'She is too sensible a girl to enter into a correspondence with you or ask you to undertake any commissions on her
behalf.' Again Rousseau sent a kind message to her husband, M. de
Verdelin, and expressed the hope of getting to know him better on their
return to Soisy. Either Rousseau had not yet formed the low opinion of
the old marquis which he expresses in the Confessions, or he was sufficiently
courteous to dissimulate it in writing to his wife.

A few days later Rousseau wrote a decidedly maladroit letter of condolence to M. de Luxembourg on the death of his sister the Duchesse de
Villeroy. He spoke only of the hardness of life, especially his own; saying
he was better able to suffer with his friends than to console them and that
his own afflictions became more bitter as he wept over others. The
Maréchal, however, took these self-centred lamentations very well; and in
his reply[35] he assured Rousseau: 'I know your heart too well, and I am

---

*It was actually Frankfurt. Subsequently Grimm rose to be Minister-Plenipotentiary for
the Duke of Saxe-Coburg in Paris. A fervent reactionary in later years, he tried to persuade
Catherine of Russia to intervene against the French Revolutionary regimes after 1789.

too sure of your friendship not to be convinced that you share my sorrow.' He only regretted that his duties at Versailles deprived him of the consolation of Rousseau's presence.

Another friend of Rousseau's who was bereaved just then was Lenieps, whose grandson, Jean Lambert, died at the age of four on the Genevese National Day, 12 December, which Rousseau had hoped to spend with Lenieps. At the beginning of December,[36] Rousseau had invited Lenieps to celebrate the occasion with him and two other Genevese friends, Coindet and Roguin – 'who will have to give up his diet for the day, since we shall not celebrate with milk, but with wine' and 'not in a café, but in my house'. In the event, only Coindet went to drink the wine at Montlouis. As soon as Rousseau learned of the infant's death he forgot his own afflictions for once, and sent both to Lenieps and his daughter Mme Lambert very decently worded letters of condolence. To Lenieps himself Rousseau wrote:[37]

I have never regretted as much as I do now living so far away from you. If it were not for your daughter I should like you to come and spend some days here, but I realize how much you and she need one another at present. Even so, one must say that your daughter is so young that I cannot regard the loss as irreparable, although, in truth, there are very few children as lovable as that boy was. Let us only hope for another child! ... Dear Lenieps, I would like my friendship for you to mean something. I never feel so much attachment to my friends as when they are distressed, and you were never so dear to me as you are in this moment.

To the bereaved mother, Rousseau wrote,[38]

In learning of your loss, Madame, I felt how much I was your father's friend and yours. I would have mourned that lovable child even if he had not been yours. No one can expect from me the formal condolences that hard hearts are always ready to express for sorrows they do not feel. Friendship knows only one sort of consolation, which is the sharing of suffering, and I am sure that no one outside your family does that sad duty more sincerely than I do. ... Think of what you still have, and you will mourn less for what you have lost.

Disappointed of a visit from Lenieps, Rousseau received at Montlouis two other Genevese visitors, François Fayre* and one of the brothers De Tournes. Favre sent an account[39] of the visit to Moultou, who had given

*François Favre (1736–1813), a merchant in business in Marseilles.

him a letter of introduction. He reported that they had found Rousseau working at his kitchen table, from which place the great man leaped up on hearing two Genevese names. De Tournes had tried to flatter Rousseau by calling him a philosopher, whereupon Rousseau declared that he was not a philosopher but aspired only to be a good man. After that Rousseau took his visitors to see his study, which Favre described as very pretty and decorated with prints engraved by Sophie's brother, Lalive de Jully, and another amateur artist-engraver, Blondel d'Azaincourt.* Favre reported Rousseau saying 'They are in good taste – not that I have any myself. I don't know anything about art.' Then, Favre noticed, Rousseau went on to prove that he knew a great deal about art by offering a commentary on Poussin's painting of the Deluge:† 'He made us perceive all the beauties of that masterpiece.'‡ Next Rousseau took the young men to his bedroom, where Favre noticed that the ceiling was decorated with frescoes of garlands of fruits and that all the furnishing proclaimed the *philosophe campagnard*; he was only surprised to see on the table a large album of gastronomic recipes and menus. Rousseau explained that a butler had sent them to him, so that he could learn the names of 'all the fine dishes that poison us so agreeably'. Having been impressed by the order and neatness of Rousseau's rooms, Favre and his companion were shown the garden with 'the most beautiful view in the world, and a border of trees – which, fortunately for Rousseau – hides Paris'. In the garden, they all talked of friendship, which Rousseau said he found in his dog more than in human beings, but added that among men his best friends were the Maréchal de Luxembourg and his mason, Pilleu. Favre was struck by the force of Rousseau's grievances against Diderot and Grimm, especially Grimm, about whom Rousseau had exclaimed, 'He's an evil man, a heartless man; let's go in, Messieurs, and not talk about that monster; I do not want his name to soil this house.'

'We returned to the kitchen,' Favre continues.

And we sat down to table with his servant§ and dog as in the time of the Patriarchs. The dinner owed nothing to the butler's album. 'How do you find the wine?' Rousseau asked me, 'Eh! but rather bad.' 'You are right. The Comte de Lauraguais found it so detestable that he said he did not

---

*Barthélémy-Augustin Blondel d'Azaincourt (b. 1719), a former soldier, wounded at Fontenoy, took up drawing and engraving in his retirement.

†The famous painting that now hangs in the Louvre, Rousseau had seen in the Hôtel de Luxembourg.[40]

‡Rousseau once said 'If I do not much care for paintings, I am extremely fond of prints, because they leave something to the imagination. One's fantasy colours them, and I seem to see in them objects as they are in nature.'[41]

§It tells us something about Rousseau's behaviour towards Thérèse and her own bearing, that all strangers entertained at Montlouis took her to be his servant.

drink wine that had gone to the dogs.' Saying this, our dear Jean-Jacques swallowed down two well-filled glasses with such appreciation that it might have been nectar. For myself I drank ... water. Our warmed-up soup was followed immediately by the dessert; the fruit and the cheese with a pot of preserves made the prize dish of the meal.

Talking of literature after dinner, Rousseau had expressed his criticisms of Voltaire with considerable moderation, saying it was a pity he had chosen to be the jester of Geneva instead of its Plato. Later on, taking his visitors for a walk, Rousseau prophesied to them that they 'would soon see a revolution', in which the Jesuits would become masters of France, and that elsewhere they would see the English build up a great empire, destroy the Spanish fleet and dominate the commerce of the southern seas.

'As we went on walking,' Favre continued, 'we came to speak of liberty. Rousseau is singular on the subject. He not only wants to be free himself; he wants everyone to be, even his dog, which he never calls to his side but only has it come to him from affection and goodness of heart.' Favre ended his account of the visit by saying that his companion and he had left Rousseau enchanted by his conversation and by a 'politeness of the heart which is worth much more than that of formal manners'. He added that despite being in constant pain from the retention of urine, Rousseau was cheerful and good-humoured: 'What a great man is Rousseau! There is neither affectation nor falseness in him; I suspect there is a little pride in his way of acting and thinking, perhaps without his realizing it – since our pride is so adroit that it knows how to disguise itself under the name of elevated feelings.'

François Favre promised to pay Rousseau a second visit, but when he had failed to appear in six weeks, Rousseau assumed he would not come, and suspected he had been put off by the frugal hospitality he had been offered. At all events, in reporting[42] Favre's non-appearance to Moultou, he wrote: 'I received him with simplicity, but with joy, and I cannot imagine such a reception could put off a Genevan and a friend of Monsieur Moultou.' Rousseau mentioned that Favre had read him extracts from Moultou's sermon on luxury, and he congratulated the pastor on its argument, especially the part where he demonstrated that so-called charity was just another luxury for the rich, who fed the poor as they fed their horses; but he reminded Moultou that horses added to the pleasures of the rich whereas the poor only bored them. He warned Moultou that it was no good arguing that luxury increased inequality, because the partisans of luxury wanted inequality, and 'by saying it diminishes equality you make them love luxury more'. The point to make, Rousseau suggested, was that luxury increased the power of the rich in the state at the expense of that of the civil rulers: 'There might be a sermon to make on that theme.'

Moultou, in his letter introducing François Favre, had mentioned the popularity of Voltaire in Geneva, and this prompted an angry outburst from Rousseau:

You speak to me of Voltaire! Why do you let the name of that buffoon soil your letters? The wretch has ruined my country. I would hate him more if I despised him less. I can only see in his great talents something which dishonours him in the unworthy use he makes of them. His talents only serve, like his wealth, to nourish the depravity of his heart. O citizens of Geneva, he makes you pay dearly for the refuge you offer him! He knew of nowhere else to go to do his mischief; you will be his last victims.

Rousseau went on to assert that the corruption of Geneva was now so complete that he would have to withdraw the argument he had put forward in the *Letter to M. d'Alembert*: 'I was mistaken. I did not believe that our progress had been so great or our morals so advanced. Our ills are henceforth incurable. Only palliatives are called for, and the theatre is one of them.'

Rousseau had hardly finished writing this letter when Favre made a second appearance on his threshold, and Rousseau was able to add a postscript: 'I have been charmed to see that he was not disappointed with me. I have spent a pleasant half-day with him.' Moultou, for his part, was delighted with the account Favre sent him of his visit to Montlouis: 'I felt I was making the journey with you,' he told him.[43]

Meanwhile, in Paris, Mme de Luxembourg was impatiently awaiting the copy of *Julie* that Rousseau had promised to make for her. She seems to have asked him if he had forgotten her, for we find him writing to her in mid-January 1760[44] protesting that he would never forget her and begging her to accuse him only of tardiness, not negligence. He explained that he had been working for three years on the copy of *Julie* destined for Mme d'Houdetot whereas he had been working only two months on hers, and yet 'in eight days you shall have the first part.'

He was as good as his word, and before the end of the month Mme de Luxembourg was able to thank[45] him for 'the most charming object in the world'. She added: 'Never has anything been so well written, so touching. I am dying with the desire to see you.' The Maréchale believed the novel would become a universal success, and she was right. The printing of *Julie* took up most of the year 1760, and in the months leading up to its appearance there was a constant exchange of letters between Rousseau and Rey. Rousseau was in two minds about the book. On the one hand, he was half-ashamed of it, because it was novel, and he was worried about what might be said about it, especially in Geneva.* On the other hand, he was anxious to make it as perfect a work of art as possible.

On 18 January 1760 he sent his publisher a long list[47] of alterations to be made to *Julie*. The most substantial change was the introduction of an eloquent assertion of the belief that love purifies sex. This romantic opinion, so pleasing to many of Rousseau's readers, and shocking to others, was put into the mouth of Julie:[48]

What do I say? A lover, is he not only a man! Ah, but he is a much more sublime being. He is not just a man in the eyes of the one who loves him. Her lover is more than a man and all others are less; she and he are above their kind. They do not desire; they love. The heart does not follow the senses, it guides them. It covers their frenzies† with a delicious veil. No, there is nothing obscene except debauchery and its crude language. True love is always bashful and does not wrest its favours audaciously; it steals them shyly. Mystery, silence and trembling timidity heighten and conceal its delicious raptures: love's flame exalts and purifies all the pleasures it makes us taste and all its caresses; decency and honesty are not lost even in the midst of its sensuality; love alone knows how to yield everything to desire without taking anything away from modesty.

Rousseau was well-enough aware that this kind of utterance was at odds with everything he had said elsewhere; and he sometimes spoke of *Julie* shame-facedly, especially to his Calvinist friends from Geneva, calling the novel 'the chatter of a fevered brain', in which 'I contradict myself so flatly and so clearly'. But he did not take advantage of the opportunity he had, in sending corrections to Rey, to modify the contradictions. On the contrary, the amendments he made in his memorandum of 18 January only increased the erotic temperature of the novel, and subsequent corrections were purely stylistic.

Rousseau's threat to end his epistolary commerce with Mme de Verdelin was never seriously intended, although he seems to have been less attentive to her in midwinter than he had previously been and was reproached on that score by Margency, ironically in view of the fact that Margency's own neglect of his mistress was the chief cause of her sorrows. On 15 January[49] Rousseau wrote to apologize for his silence; he urged Mme de

---

*Rey wrote to Rousseau on 24 December 1759 to say that the Genevese authorities had asked him what the book contained: 'I refused to tell them out of deference to you.'[46]

†Rousseau writes first '*erreurs*', and then changes it to '*égarements*', which could perhaps also be translated as 'deviations'.

Verdelin to go on writing to him and scolding him. He asked for news of her health, and again tried to persuade her that she would feel better if she came back to live at Soisy.

In her reply[50] Mme de Verdelin explained that she had a bad cold, which she was nursing at her fireside; she said she only wished that Rousseau took as good care of his health as she took of hers. She had heard – doubtless from Margency – that he had nose-bleeds, for which she recommended *orgeat*, a herbal remedy; she had also been told that he never slept but was working without respite on his books – making his friends distressed about his health – in order to instruct people who would not listen: 'My dear friend, your excellent books will never do as much good as the virtuous example of your life.'

Rousseau assured[51] Mme de Verdelin that the sweetness of her lessons did not mean they would go unheeded, but he continued to work long hours at his writing, and although he had now a more comfortable place to work in, he made himself almost as ill as during the previous winter. He declared to M. de Luxembourg at the beginning of February[52] that the winter seemed to him to be even longer than others, because he was counting the days of their separation: 'I await with patience your Easter journey to celebrate an anniversary that will always be dear to me' – the anniversary of the Maréchal's first visit to Montlouis. Rousseau said he would like to visit the Maréchal in Paris, only his health and the weather forbade it. Replying,[53] M. de Luxembourg assured Rousseau that he shared his impatience for their reunion; he mentioned that his compensation, in the meantime, had been reading 'the papers you sent to Mme de Luxembourg', the manuscript of *Julie*.

Once again Rousseau had to write a letter of condolence: this time to Jacob Vernes, whose wife, still only seventeen, had died in childbirth. Hearing the news in the middle of January, Rousseau put off for a fortnight the difficult duty of writing to Vernes. When he did so he invoked[54] illness as an excuse for his delay, although he had in fact been fit enough to write many other things in those days:

I do not want to compare my condition to yours, for my present sufferings are physical, and as one whose life is an alternation of physical and moral pain, I know that the former is not the worst. My heart can share your grief but not console you for it. I know too well from experience that nothing consoles but time, and then it is often only a further affliction to think that time will console us ... Oh believe me, you do not know the most cruel way to lose the one you love, and that is to weep while the loved one still lives. My good friend, your troubles make me think of my own; it is a natural reaction of an unhappy man. Others will be able to show a more disinterested feeling for your grief, but no one, I am sure, can show it more sincerely.

Once again, we see Rousseau incapable of directing his attention from his own misfortunes to those of others; incapable of getting over his disappointment with Diderot; incapable, perhaps, of imagining how bitter Vernes's grief must be. In his own life, Rousseau had reached the age of forty-eight without experiencing anything that could properly be called a bereavement; his mother died soon after giving birth to him, his brother and his father had passed out of his life before they died. Thérèse and Mme de Warens and others he had loved, in one way or another, were still alive. But at least he was sufficiently moved by the death of the young Mme Vernes to write some verses about it and set them to music. Vernes himself told[55] Rousseau that he needed no consolation beyond that which he found in the Gospel: 'I shall join her one day, that beloved wife, never again to be separated. She awaits me in the sky.' Faith in the immortality of the soul if not the resurrection of the flesh, was, as we have seen, one of the few things that comforted Rousseau in his own sufferings.

Madame de Verdelin's 'bad cold' developed into 'fluxions', but it did not prevent her writing regularly, and fairly cheerfully, to Rousseau at Montlouis, and he always answered her letters promptly, if sometimes only to scold her. 'O Frenchmen, O Frenchwomen, you nation of talkers – how much importance you give to words, and how little to things!' he protested in one of his letters,[56] forgetting perhaps that he had once urged Mme d'Épinay to pay more attention to words – 'study my dictionary if you want to understand me.' His letters brought Rousseau news and gossip from Paris that he would not receive from any other source, even though Coindet continued to visit him on most Saturdays or Sundays, and acted as his emissary, if mainly on business matters, and must have brought him some news from the literary and social worlds he had contrived to penetrate.

It was from Mme de Verdelin that Rousseau learnt of Marmontel being sent to the Bastille on suspicion of writing a parody of *Cinna* mocking the Duc d'Aumont. Imprisonment for something that had only been read in private was in this case an exercise of noble privilege, not of government action of the kind which was in time to threaten Rousseau himself. Mme de Verdelin also gave Rousseau reports of the progress of the war, which she followed anxiously because her beloved brother, the Marquis d'Ars, was a naval officer on active service. Other members of her family added to her worries in the early months of 1760; her husband had an accident, her daughter had an illness which she thought was smallpox, so that in spite of her own 'fluxions', she had to be a nurse as well as a patient. There was also her continued dismay about Margency's changed attitude towards her: 'Imagine the state of a soul affected beyond all words, a soul that for seven years has lived and breathed only for a being who is ready now to sacrifice her to the fanaticism of religious devotion.'[57]

For the most part, however, Mme de Verdelin tried to keep her letters entertaining, and she sent Rousseau more titbits about other people than reports of her own health and welfare. Not all her letters to him have been traced, but in one of his[58] to her we find him reproaching her: 'You are falling back, Madame, into your old habits. You are malicious enough to write me such amusing things as to make me overlook the fact that you do not tell me anything about yourself.'

When she assured him that her health was so good that she was almost ashamed of it, Rousseau asked Mme de Verdelin, in mid-March[59] whether he ought not to say the same of himself: 'Since I have hardened my heart, and no longer love anyone, and call the whole human race my friend, I have grown fat like a pig. I do not know a better recipe for good health than insensitivity. If it is your recipe, I congratulate you.'

Mme de Verdelin would not accept this uncharacteristically cynical advice from Rousseau. She told him that suppressing her feelings had brought neither joy nor *embonpoint*, and she implored him to quit the error of cultivating any such insensitivity in himself.

It was about this time that Rousseau received a visit at Montlouis from Margency, accompanied not by his mistress, but his great friend Desmahis. In advising[60] Rousseau of the visit, Margency spoke of 'begging a slice of mutton', evidently counting on more liberal hospitality than François Favre had received, and promised to bring Rousseau the five volumes of Buffon's *Histoire naturelle*. In the same letter, Margency mentioned Malesherbes's goodwill towards him: 'He asked for news of you with very great interest and seemed filled with respect and consideration for you.' Margency also informed Rousseau that Mme de Verdelin – 'who still loves you in spite of all your scolding' – would be installing herself at Soisy in mid-April.

From Vienna Deleyre sent[61] Rousseau the news that the director of court entertainments, Giacomo Durazzo, an admirer of *Le Devin du village*, wanted to put on his early ballet *Les Muses galantes* at the imperial theatre – giving it in effect its first public performance. Deleyre also asked Rousseau to send him a copy of another early work, the poem *L'Allée de Sylvie*, which he wanted to show to the imperial Poet Laureate, Metastasio, another admirer of his writings. Rousseau sent[62] Deleyre a signed copy of his poem, but warned him that *Les Muses galantes** was an inferior work,

---

*A revised version of this ballet was performed under the patronage of the Prince de Conti in 1761.[63]

with music in an 'arch-French' taste. This warning put Durazzo off, and we find Deleyre writing in his next letter,[64] 'What you say about its being "arch-French" made him hesitate. He finds he could not make use of it where they are mad (as you are) about Italian music.' Rousseau thus spoiled an opportunity of having something staged in Vienna. On the other hand, Deleyre was able to inform Rousseau that he had read *L'Allée de Sylvie* to the Abbé Metastasio, 'who was truly enchanted by it'. The theme of this poem is summed up in the lines about man being happy only *'quand son coeur est sans passion'*.[65] Deleyre asked Rousseau if he still thought this true. As for himself, he said he had become disgusted in Vienna with both men and politics, and hoped to find happiness in 'entire solitude', adding that Rousseau would understand that his 'solitude' would be spent with the young woman Rousseau had advised him not to marry: 'You will envy me one day the fate you have scorned.' Deleyre went on to congratulate Rousseau on his decision to abjure philosophy: 'Paris is absurd and you are an honourable man, a free, independent, courageous being armed against both misery and flattery. Because of all this you will always have my respect and my friendship.'

Another friend – possibly Mme de Verdelin – sent to Montlouis a present of a capon, truffles and an almond cake at the beginning of March. Rousseau suspected that they had come from Mme de Luxembourg, and scolded her for doing so. She denied[66] that she had sent the presents, saying that the only thing she had ever given him was game from her husband's hunt. At the same time she thanked Rousseau for the second part of *Julie*, and added, 'I have a great desire to come to Montmorency; truly, it is cruel never to see you.' Later that month,[67] M. de Luxembourg informed Rousseau that his wife had been ill with a fever, having neglected a cold, but he was pleased to say that she was recovering, and that they both hoped to see Rousseau at Montmorency at Easter. The Maréchal had less good news about his 'poor daughter' – the Princesse de Robecq* – whose strength was fading: 'I fear she has not long to live.'

Immediately Rousseau wrote[68] to express his concern and his dismay at not having known sooner of the illnesses of the two women, and went on, with inconsiderate precipitation, to speak of the daughter's death; after having wept over her suffering, he suggested to the Maréchal that he would 'view as a sort of consolation the moment which ends her pain'.

A few days later[69] the Maréchal sent a note to say that his daughter was rather less ill and that his wife, after a series of purges, was getting over her fever. He said he looked forward to seeing Rousseau in person the following week, when the Easter holiday would bring him with his wife

*Anne-Marie de Montmorency, the Maréchal's daughter by his first wife.

to Montmorency. That visit was to prove a short one, and less joyful than the previous summer's stay. The Maréchal was tired from arduous work at Court; he was still worried about his daughter's sickness. The Maréchale felt poorly. Rousseau began badly with her by showing her a letter[70] he had written to the former Controleur-Général, M. de Silhouette, congratulating him on his efforts to curb the profiteering of private investors in the tax-farms, efforts which had led to his losing his job as a result of the intrigues of the offended investors. 'The curses of scoundrels are the glory of the just man,' Rousseau declared in his letter to Silhouette. Mme de Luxembourg's only comment was 'I think your letter is very fine, but he does not deserve it.'[71] Only later did Rousseau learn that the Maréchale was one of the private investors that Silhouette had antagonized.

'It looked,' he writes in the *Confessions*,[72] 'as if I wanted deliberately to arouse the hostility of a friendly and influential woman to whom I was becoming more sincerely attached every day, and whose displeasure I was far from wishing to bring down upon myself.'

During the Luxembourgs' stay at their château, Rousseau resumed his readings aloud at the Maréchale's bedside. When he reached the end of *Julie*, he started to read from *Émile*, on which he was still working. In the *Confessions*, he says this did not succeed so well: 'either the subject was less to her taste, or she was fatigued at listening to so much reading'.[73] The Maréchal, however, seems to have appreciated the book keenly enough, for he wrote[74] to Rousseau from Rouen that summer to tell him how much he missed *Émile* – 'and I miss the tutor, whom I know, and I miss the little Sophie, whom I do not yet know, because it is you who have created her'. From this remark we may infer that Rousseau had not yet read to them, and perhaps not yet written, Book V in which 'the little Sophie' is introduced to Émile and to the reader.

If Madame de Luxembourg enjoyed the readings from *Émile* less than those from *Julie*, she nevertheless took an active interest in the publication of the book. Rousseau had grumbled so much in the presence of Mme de Luxembourg about Rey that she had been led to think that a better publisher should be found for his next book, *Émile*, and from this excellent motive she set in motion a train of events which was to have disastrous consequences for the author. She had come to believe that Rey was inefficient, unreliable and slow, and above all, that he did not pay a fair price for Rousseau's copyrights. Rey hardly deserved all these criticisms, but Rousseau, when he complained about him to Mme de Luxembourg and others, showed little understanding of the difficulties under which Rey laboured, despite all Rey's efforts to explain them.

Rey could not make an immediate start on the printing of *Julie* when he received the sixth part at the end of January because, as he informed the author, the canals of Amsterdam were frozen and the paper could not be delivered to the printers,[75] and even when the canals had thawed by the end of February, Rey had difficulty finding workers because as he explained,[76] 'the war has taken them away'. When Rey sent him preliminary proofs for approval, Rousseau protested[77] that the layout was inelegant and the quality of the paper poor. 'For the rest,' he said, 'do what you can; I leave you master of everything.' Despite this promise, Rousseau continued to harass Rey with objections on the smallest points of detail – such as the abridgement of 'Monsieur' to 'Mr.' instead of 'M.'. He held up work on the book with numerous corrections and emendations to the proofs, polishing the style as each opportunity arose. On the other hand, he did not take kindly to corrections suggested by the publisher. Once when Rey proposed a change in the interests of historical accuracy, Rousseau refused to alter the wording: 'the phrase is cadenced in such a way that a single added syllable would spoil its euphony'.

Rousseau also took steps to ensure that Rey's edition of the book would be admitted to the French market. He asked[78] Malesherbes if he would be willing to read the proofs of what he called an 'insipid volume' and to do so in person; 'I shall try to justify that favour, Monsieur, by a future production more worthy of the attention with which you have honoured my previous efforts.' Malesherbes's reply[79] was cordial but equivocal. He said he would be delighted to receive the proofs of *Julie* from Holland and forward them to Rousseau, but added: 'Eager as I am to read your book, I will not hold up the proofs by taking advantage of your invitation to read them.'

Rousseau duly instructed[80] Rey to send him the proofs through Malesherbes's office, imploring him at the same time to pay the closest attention to the corrections he would have to make. Rey in the meantime had asked[81] Rousseau to suggest vignettes to serve as ornaments to the novel. Rousseau did not like the idea of vignettes. 'It is plates that are needed,' he insisted,[82] recalling his proposal to commission Boucher to provide the drawings. 'Their subjects would have been stimulating; they would have been charming; they would perhaps have been the most pleasing collection of prints of the century; I am certain they would have made the book's fortune.' However, he added that if Rey was determined to have vignettes, he must at least be allowed to see proofs of them.

One thing he forbade Rey to use was his device – *Vitam impendere vero.*★ He told[83] Rey it would be very bad taste to clutter up the title-page with words in Latin as well as in French and Italian.† He also wanted his name

---

★'To stake one's life for the truth.'

†Rousseau had chosen a quotation from Petrarch for the title-page: '*Non la conobbe il mondo, mentre l'ebbe; Conobill'io ch'a pianger qui rimasi*' ('The world did not recognize her while she was here: I who did so am left to weep').

to appear on the title-page as 'editor' not 'author' and as plain 'Jean-Jacques Rousseau' not 'Jean-Jacques Rousseau, Citizen of Geneva' as he chose to be styled on all his other books. He suggested to Rey that he should send M. de Malesherbes page proofs as well as galleys, since they would be easier to handle; Rousseau was still hoping that Malesherbes would read them personally so as to forestall any trouble from other French authorities. And indeed Malesherbes promised to do so in his next letter[84] to Rousseau: 'I shall read the proofs with the utmost alacrity.'

When Rey sent[85] Rousseau the next instalment of proofs he told him squarely that the cost of producing plates would have been too great. As for vignettes, he explained that since no one in Amsterdam had read the text of *Julie*, Rousseau would have to send him subjects and he would have them executed as best he could. While the book was in the press, publisher and author each urged the other to speed up the work. On 3 May[86] Rey begged Rousseau to be on time in returning corrected proofs because he did not have enough metal type to set more than six or seven sheets at at a time, which meant that he was obliged to complete a print-run and redistribute the type before setting the next. As he was producing 6,000 copies of each sheet, he could produce only three sheets a week.

Rousseau protested[87] that he could not be more punctilious than he had always been in keeping to the schedule. He expressed his satisfaction with the appearance of the first sheets, but added, with some bitterness, 'It is a pity I do not have that pleasure more often.' He also said he had more corrections to insert, but had difficulty in making his instructions clear since he did not know the conventional proof-readers' signs.

This letter crossed one[88] from Rey in which the publisher warned Rousseau that if he did not hurry up with the corrections the book would not be ready 'this year'; Rey reminded him that he wanted to bring it out in October. Rousseau refused[89] to be bullied: 'You send me proofs full of appalling faults and they are printed on paper that soaks up so much ink that one cannot write on it. Is that not depressing?' Again, he begged Rey to ensure that his instructions were followed with exactitude. Rey once more pressed Rousseau to speed up the work, and even took it upon himself to write personally to M. de Malesherbes asking him to make sure that the proofs which passed through his office were forwarded without delay. Rousseau had another reason for being worried about his proofs being held up in Malesherbes's office; as he informed[90] that magistrate, he was afraid that they might be read, without his knowledge, by other eyes than his. On the same day[91] Rousseau wrote to Rey to express his indignation at being blamed for the delays, when he was having to wait fourteen months for the publication of the novel. 'I do not understand your procedures,' he declared, and he went on to suggest that since Rey did not seem to attach much value to the book, he should hand its production over to a French publisher, Jean-François Bastide, who had offered him 200 louis for the copyright.

In better health at this season, Rousseau paid more visits to the Luxembourgs in Paris, always taking care to step off the carriage inside the gate and always using the rooms that were kept in reserve for him. Some time in May, he thought of offering Mme de Luxembourg a present – an appendix to *Julie* in manuscript form 'which will not be in the printed text'.[92] This was the story he entitled *Les Aventures de Milord Édouard*,* describing what happened to one of the main protagonists of the work after he had left Switzerland for Rome.

It is a curious story, and one can more easily understand why Rousseau left it out of his novel than why he wrote it in the first place, for it is a breathless tale of sexual desire and frustration with an equivocal ethical content. It tells how Lord Édouard Bomston falls in love in Rome with a passionate and unscrupulous Neapolitan *marchesa*, who traps him into bed by pretending to be a widow. When Lord Édouard finds out that she has a husband, he ends their liaison, because the virtue to which his life is dedicated forbids adultery. However, he remains friends with the *marchesa*, and she, realizing that she will never again have him as a lover, procures a young courtesan named Laure, and introduces her to Lord Edouard in the hope of having the vicarious satisfaction of seeing her own nominee become his only mistress in her place. But things work out unexpectedly. Laure falls sincerely in love with the English nobleman, but when he tries to make love to her, she refuses to let him touch her. Her argument is that having slept with innumerable men without loving them, she will not sleep with the one man she does love. Lord Édouard tries to win her round with presents of jewels which she, while disclaiming any right to reject them, rejects, and which he then makes the mistake of offering to the *marchesa*, who, learning that they have already been offered to, and refused by Laure, promptly throws them out of the window. Lord Édouard then gives lessons in virtue to Laure until she is ready to abandon her sinful life and enter a convent, where he continues to visit her regularly. The *marchesa*, horrified by these proceedings, pursues Lord Édouard with redoubled efforts until she regains some part of her empire over him, finishing '*par donner à son amour sans espoir les suppléments que n'avait pu supporter celui de Laure*'.[94] Her husband has, in the meantime, died following a duel with Lord Édouard. It is only after passing several years dividing his life between

---

*This is the title Rousseau gives the story in the *Confessions*. The manuscript (now at Neuchâtel) is entitled '*Les Amours de Milord Bomston*', but that manuscript is not in Rousseau's hand.[93]

two women in Rome, the purified Laure and the depraved *marchesa*, that Lord Édouard comes under the noble influence of Rousseau's heroine Julie and finds redemption.

When Mme de Luxembourg read this story she made no comment on it to the author. He realized he had made a mistake in giving it to her. In the *Confessions*[95] he suggests that she disliked it because some of the characteristics of the 'odious *marchesa*', without actually being applicable to her, 'might perhaps have been applied to her by those who knew her only by reputation, so that what had been intended to be the most beautiful thing in the world was something at which she could be easily offended'.[96] It is by no means obvious that Rousseau judged her reaction correctly. Mme de Luxembourg had never been accused of anything worse than sexual promiscuity in a society where that was the order of the day; she had never had the reputation of intriguing or deceiving or doing any of the other 'odious' deeds of Rousseau's *marchesa*. She is most unlikely to have seen herself in the character. After Rousseau's death she did not hesitate to give the manuscript to Rousseau's friend the Marquis de Girardin, and did nothing to stop him passing it on to Pierre-Alexandre du Peyrou for its first publication in Geneva in 1780. Her silence on the subject in Rousseau's presence may have had another motive. 'She did not compliment me on the piece as I expected,' Rousseau writes.[97] 'To my surprise she never spoke to me about it.' She could easily have felt that the author deserved no congratulations and was too tactful to tell him what she thought of his story.

There is no sign of any cooling of her affection for him in the letters she wrote at this time, although it was the Maréchal, and not the Maréchale, who wrote to him on 26 May[98] urging him to spend some days with them in Paris. Rousseau evidently accepted with alacrity, because we find Mme de Luxembourg's steward writing to Coindet on 28 May[99] inviting him to supper that same evening saying 'M. Rousseau has just arrived.' The extending of such invitations to Coindet came to annoy Rousseau as he saw his young compatriot worm his way into the Luxembourg's inner circle. As he puts it in the *Confessions*:[100] 'It was thanks to the extreme goodness that M. and Mme de Luxembourg had shown me that a clerk to the banker Thélusson, who was sometimes pleased to have him at his table when he had no one else to dine with him, was suddenly placed at that of a Maréchal de France with princes, duchesses and other persons of the highest rank at Court.' The friendliness of the Maréchal to Coindet, Rousseau claims, went to Coindet's head.[101] It was during this particular visit to Paris that Rousseau sent a message[102] to his old Spanish friend François-Xavier de Carrión,* now risen to be chargé d'affaires at his

---

*In Venice he had been known by the Italian form of his name: 'Carrio'.[103]

embassy, saying he would not be seeing him because he had changed too much, 'Checco' having turned into '*le magnifique Chevalier de Carrión*'.

Carrión, in his reply,[104] protested that this was not true; 'Checco and Carrión will always be the same for my very dear Jean-Jacques Rousseau.' He assured his old friend of his love and embraced him wholeheartedly. He ended his letter in Italian: '*Addio Caro, Caro*'. Then he, too, had a friendly word for Coindet: 'Give my apologies to our dear and amiable Coindet for not writing to him.' The letter seems to have succeeded in patching up the friendship; Rousseau continued to send Carrión presentation copies of his books as they were published, but even so their correspondence languished. Again, Rousseau in the *Confessions*[105] puts the blame on Coindet: 'Carrión and I would have renewed our former intimacy had not Coindet interposed himself in his usual way and taken advantage of the distance I was from Paris to insinuate himself into my place and supplant me.'

Just before he left Montlouis to visit the Luxembourgs in Paris, Rousseau had received a copy of a comedy by Palissot called *Les Philosophes*, which satirized the Encyclopédistes and represented Diderot in particular as a scoundrel. Despite the fact that he had quarrelled with Diderot, Rousseau was not amused. He sent[106] the book back to the publisher, Duchesne: 'On looking through the play you sent me, Monsieur, I shuddered to see myself praised in it. I cannot accept such a horrible present. I am willing to believe that you had no intention of offending me in sending it, but doubtless you do not know, or have forgotten that I was once the friend of the worthy man who is shamefully blackened and calumnied in this libel.'

When Duchesne apologized for the unintended offence, Rousseau accepted[107] his explanation, but added, 'I detest personal satire and cannot see merit outraged without feeling indignation.' Rousseau seems to have written as he did to Duchesne in the expectation that Duchesne would show the letter to Diderot as evidence of the solidarity of a former friend. According to the *Confessions*,[108] Duchesne did so and Diderot was unimpressed: 'His pride', said Rousseau,' could not forgive me the superiority of a generous gesture.'

Diderot then found a champion more to his liking in Morellet, who wrote against Palissot a satire in prose called *La Vision*.[109] Morellet was, however, unwise enough to make a cruel reference in this piece to M. de Luxembourg's dying daughter, the Princesse de Robecq, who had been the protectress, in happier days, of the Christian adversaries of the Encyclopédistes. This led to Morellet being imprisoned in the Bastille. Malesherbes,[110] who was tolerant enough of authors abusing each other in print, was outraged by this attack on a private person, and stipulated a '*sanction impitoyable'*, even the Bicêtre madhouse, for an offence which was all the more *'odieux'* in view of the circumstances.★

The task of correcting proofs of *Julie* proved increasingly irksome for Rousseau. At one point he protested[112] to Rey of a 'terrible migraine' which meant that he could 'hardly open' his eyes to read the proofs; then he complained[113] that he had no time to read through one set before another set appeared. Rey, on his side, grumbled[114] about delays in the transmission of the proofs, and he begged Rousseau to make M. de Malesherbes understand how harmful these delays were commercially. If the work was not printed in October, its distribution would be held up for the whole winter by the closing of the Dutch canals, and as Rey sold his stock on credit, this would mean his having to wait for twelve months after the spring of 1761 for any return on his investment.

Rousseau would not accept that either he himself or Malesherbes was to blame for the delays. He told[115] Rey that if Rey was so eager to print the book in October he should have started sooner: 'I have refrained from reproaching you for your negligence and tardiness but you have abused my patience and ended up by reproaching me. I will not refuse to accept the reproaches I deserve provided you tell me what I have done wrong.'

Rey had in the meantime apologized[116] for blaming Rousseau for delays which were not his fault, and explained that delays on his side were due to the lack of metal type and to public holidays which kept the printers away from work. In another letter[117] Rey mentioned that Duchesne had sent him a copy of Palissot's comedy *Les Philosophes* with the proposal that he should publish it in Amsterdam. Rey declared himself scandalized – the play was 'a disgrace to France' – and he said he was willing 'to bet a hundred to one' that Duchesne had made the proposal at the instigation of Palissot himself 'to promote a breach between you and me'.

In June 1760 Rousseau learned that his letter to Voltaire on Providence had been published and was on sale in Berlin. The report came from M. Formey†, a protégé of Frederick II. Rousseau asked[118] Rey to investigate the matter, to find out how 'this letter which was not at all designed to be printed' had come to be published. He also asked[119] Malesherbes for information, and begged that magistrate not to allow the letter to be reprinted in France. If Rousseau was being disingenuous in saying that the letter had not been designed for publication, he did not at this stage wish to have it published without the consent of Voltaire; and indeed he wrote[120]

★Rousseau claims that the Princesse de Robecq herself had no hand in this: 'She was not vindictive by nature; and in any case, she was dying.'[111]

†Jean-Henri-Samuel Formey (1711–97) was permanent secretary of the Royal Academy of Berlin and editor of the *Nouvelle Bibliothèque Germanique*.

to Voltaire to deny that he had authorized the printing of the letter or even shown it to more than three persons, 'Mme de Chenonceaux, Mme d'Houdetot and a German named Grimm'.

Rousseau had taken up his pen with some reluctance to write to Voltaire. He began by saying: 'I did not think I would ever again find myself in correspondence with you', but since the publication in Berlin of his *Letter on Providence* had made it his duty to do so, he intended to 'discharge that duty with truth and simplicity'. Rousseau was uncomfortably aware that Voltaire was now exercising a kind of cultural empire over the republic of Geneva, for although he had acquired two châteaux in the neighbouring countryside, at Tournay and Ferney, the poet (or jester, as Rousseau thought of him) was still installed at Les Délices within the city, and had indeed enlarged the villa and its gardens as if it were his own. Moreover, in spite of the interdiction on drama on Genevese territory. Voltaire was putting on plays at Tournay, notably that summer his own *Tancrède* and *Mahomet*, and persuading the citizens of Geneva to act in them; he was also giving huge house-parties at his three homes where the solid Genevese burghers were thrown together with the smart corrupt society of Burgundy and France. All this Rousseau considered scandalous.

In his letter to Voltaire, he mentioned that Mme de Chenonceaux was eager to see his thoughts on Providence in print, but he did not believe that she could have let her copy of the *Letter* out of her hands.

Rousseau also became convinced that Formey, who reported finding the letter printed in a magazine, had in fact printed it himself, and in the *Confessions*[121] Rousseau repeats the charge; but he was mistaken. Voltaire's friends, the brothers Cramer, were the original publishers, and the publication that Formey had found in Berlin came from Geneva.[122]

Rousseau did not, however, accuse Formey in writing to Voltaire about the publication. He said he had heard about it only through the Abbé Trublet, and added that he would do his best to prevent its being published in France. Up to this point, he addressed Voltaire very politely; then abruptly his tone changed, and the letter ended with a paragraph of singular rudeness such as is not to be found elsewhere in Rousseau's correspondence:

I do not like you, Monsieur; you have done me injuries of the most harmful kind; done them to me, your disciple and your enthusiastic admirer. You have ruined Geneva, in return for the asylum you have been given there. You have turned my fellow citizens against me as a reward for the praise which I have secured for you among them. It is you who have made living in my own city impossible for me; it is you who force me to perish on foreign soil, deprived of all the consolations of the dying, cast unceremoniously like a dog on the wayside, while you, alive or dead, enjoy in my homeland all the honours to which a man could aspire. I despise you. You wanted me to. But my hatred is that of a heart fitted to have loved you if you had wanted it. Of all the feelings of which my heart was once filled for you there remains only the respect which cannot be denied to your genius. If I cannot honour your talents it is not my fault. I shall never fail to show the respect that I owe them, or fail to observe the conduct that such respect demands. Farewell, Monsieur.

Rousseau could hardly have written a more aggressive declaration of war. Voltaire did not answer it. Instead he wrote[123] to Mme d'Épinay saying: 'Jean-Jacques has gone off his head ... He has just written me a letter in which he says I have ruined Geneva. He speaks of M. Grimm, calling him "a German named Grimm". He says that because of me he will be cast on the wayside when he dies, while I shall be buried with honour. What can I say?'

Malesherbes, on the other hand, did write[124] to Rousseau. He said he had no knowledge of the *Letter on Providence* being published abroad, but suggested that since it would be useless to try to stop its being reprinted in France, Rousseau would be well advised to publish it there himself immediately. It appears that Rousseau had once again declared his intention of giving up writing, because Malesherbes urged him not to: 'Neither your health nor your philosophy seems to me an adequate motive for renouncing an author's life.'

Rousseau acted on Malesherbes's advice.[125] He invited two publishers who had houses near his at Montmorency, Guérin* and La Tour,† to bring it out as soon as they had Malesherbes's permission.[126] Malesherbes, pleading he was leaving for a holiday, but perhaps afraid of committing himself, referred the matter to one of the censors, Salley‡ instructing him at the same time to report directly to a higher authority than himself, the Chancellor, M. de Lamoignon (Malesherbes's father). But even when he received an authorization,[127]§ Guérin did not want to publish the letter. He warned[128] Rousseau that 'the consequences of printing such a work would be too serious in a country such as this. Our theologians are terrible people.' Rousseau did not press the idea and it was four years before the *Letter on Providence* came out in France, and then the publisher was the same man who had published Palissot's *Les Philosophes*, Duchesne.

Having been forced to recall the odious name of Grimm in writing to

---

*Guérin had already published the French edition of the *Discourse on Inequality*.

†Louis-François de La Tour, Guérin's son-in-law and partner.

‡Charles-Alexandre Salley, Inspecteur de la Librairie since 1757.

§Malesherbes notes, 'This authorization was not acted upon. M. Guérin and M. Rousseau agreed that the letter could not be published in France.'

Voltaire, Rousseau was dismayed to read it again in a letter[129] he received from his Oratorian neighbour, Father Berthier, informing him that his erstwhile housekeeper, Mme Levasseur, supposedly living with relations in Paris, had received 'a kind offer from M. Grimm' to house and maintain her at Deuil, a village between La Chevrette and Montmorency. Father Berthier said he had advised the old woman to accept the offer, but that she had 'refused to do so without M. Rousseau's consent'.[130] Rousseau never forgave Father Berthier for encouraging Mme Levasseur to come back to live near him, but he could see no way of thwarting the scheme:

I learned that it involved Grimm giving Mme Levasseur an annuity of three hundred livres, which would have been less amazing if Grimm commanded ten thousand livres of income or had some easily understood relationship with that woman, and if I had not been made out to be such a great criminal for taking her to the very country where it now pleased Grimm to send her, as if she had grown younger in the meantime.[131]

Rousseau suspected that Mme Levasseur had talked of having his consent only in order to force him to match Grimm's offer if he did not like her accepting it. As he had no intention of bidding against Grimm, he consented.

Early in the summer of 1760, Rousseau received a visit at Montlouis from the Comtesse de Boufflers which marked the beginning of another of his flirtatious friendships. She brought with her her usual companion, Lorenzy. Rousseau had already met her several times in the entourage of Mme de Luxembourg without, apparently, paying much attention to her. It was when she began to pay special attention to him that he became aware of her sexual charms. She was now aged thirty-five, and had been for eight years the mistress of the Prince de Conti, and although she had not given up hope of marrying that royal personage, she allowed her eyes to wander from time to time to other interesting men.

In the *Confessions*,[132] Rousseau admits that he only narrowly escaped becoming 'a rival of the Prince de Conti' for the favours of the Comtesse.

She was beautiful and still young; she cultivated a Roman spirit, and I was always romantic, and that brought us rather close. I was almost caught. I believe she saw it, and Lorenzy saw it too. At least he spoke of it, and not in a manner to discourage me. But for once I was wise, and at fifty it was high time that I should be ... And perhaps not being fully cured yet of my passion for Sophie d'Houdetot, I felt that no one could take her place in my heart. I bade adieu to love for the rest of my life.

The Comtesse de Boufflers had much to recommend her to Rousseau. She liked to talk about morality, as well as literature and philosophy, she detested licentious conversation and never tired of declaring her devotion to the ideal of virtue, even though her critics, such as Mme Du Deffand,[133] claimed that she never allowed her principles to interfere with her pleasures. Loyal as she was to the Prince de Conti, she was no more faithful to him in the strictest sense than he to her. She liked the idea of sexual intimacy with a famous philosopher, and even succeeded, some years later, in breaking down the inhibitions of David Hume. She had perhaps more in common with Rousseau's first love, Mme de Warens, than with Mme d'Houdetot. It would have been an imprudent liaison; Mme de Luxembourg might even have become as jealous as Mme d'Épinay, and withdrawn her protection. The domestic peace with Thérèse in Montlouis would have been jeopardized. But it was probably the wounds inflicted by Sophie that did most to hold him back from an easy conquest.

At Versailles, in a year when the government was facing more problems than usual, with the war going badly for France abroad and the *parlements* growing increasingly restive at home, M. de Luxembourg's duties became so demanding that he could not take his family to Montmorency for the usual summer stay. Rousseau had to visit them in Paris in order to see them, and soon it became generally known that he was wholly *chez soi* at the Hôtel de Luxembourg. D'Alembert, who was distressed over Morellet's imprisonment in the Bastille, asked Rousseau to use his influence with the Maréchale to secure the release of a fellow writer. Rousseau cannot have had much sympathy with Morellet. Knowing how anxious M. de Luxembourg was lest his daughter's illness proved fatal, he was naturally shocked by Morellet's heartless remark about 'a great lady who is making a pious bequest in her will to provide tickets in perpetuity for Palissot's claque to attend his play'. D'Alembert wrote to Rousseau promising to publish a tribute in the *Encyclopédie* to Mme de Luxembourg if only she could secure Morellet's release.[134] In his reply,[135] Rousseau assured d'Alembert that if Mme de Luxembourg did prove to be willing to press for his friend's release, it would be only from a motive of generosity, without any wish for public acknowledgement.

Clearly Rousseau did his utmost to persuade the Maréchale to help Morellet, and we find her writing to him from Versailles on 23 July,[136] saying 'I will not leave M. de St-Florentin in peace until the affair is ended as you desire.' Five days later,[137] she was able to inform Rousseau: 'The Abbé Morellet left the Bastille today.'

D'Alembert was quick to thank[138] Rousseau for his intervention on Morellet's behalf, but Morellet's own letter[139] of thanks brought him less pleasure. Morellet reported that he had already visited Mme de Luxembourg to express his gratitude, and having made her acquaintance, he said he could well understand that Rousseau 'had made an exception in her case' to his rule of 'renouncing the world and its splendour'. Annoyed by this remark, Rousseau suggested[140] to Mme de Luxembourg that Morellet's words implied that 'if I am ever accused of conducting myself in contradiction with my principles, I shall have my answer ready when it pleases you to provide it'.

Morellet had mentioned that he was staying in the country not far from Montmorency and offered to come to see Rousseau at his cottage. Rousseau did not encourage the visit. Morellet went instead once more to see Mme de Luxembourg, who described[141] him to Rousseau as 'amiable'; Rousseau considered him no more than estimable.[142] Among the Encyclopédistes, Morellet was known for his biting tongue – '*Mords-les*' was the nickname d'Alembert used in writing to Voltaire[143] – and that was not a quality Rousseau cared for. In his published memoirs,[144] Morellet ungratefully and untruthfully, states that d'Alembert and Malesherbes, rather than Rousseau, were the persons who persuaded Mme de Luxembourg to secure his release from the Bastille.

Mme de Luxembourg had taken up the case of Morellet at a time when she had many other worries on her mind. Her husband, who held the office of Governor of Normandy, was sent to Rouen by the King on an important mission to discipline the rebellious *parlement* of that province, which not only refused to ratify the war tax that the King had imposed, but had even demanded the convocation of the Estates-General. M. de Luxembourg was instructed to make a show of force to impose the royal will.

He found the situation less serious than was feared, and Mme de Luxembourg felt able to tell Rousseau in a letter of 25 July[145] that the Maréchal had been 'very well received in Rouen' and that a deputation of magistrates from the *parlement* of Normandy was going to wait on the King the following week. Rousseau thanked[146] her for keeping him informed, explaining that while he usually took little interest in political news, and would not have troubled much about the fate of Normandy, the fact that the Maréchal was there made all the difference: 'Nothing concerning him could leave me indifferent.'

Mme de Luxembourg's next letter[147] was less reassuring. She reported that her husband had been taken ill in Rouen, and that she was concerned about him. However, the illness proved transitory, and a few days later, the Maréchal wrote[148] in his own hand to inform Rousseau that everything was much more peaceful in Normandy than the Court at Versailles believed, and that he was being kept there unnecessarily. The next day, Mme de Luxembourg wrote[149] to tell Rousseau that her husband was well

again, but would have to stay in Rouen until the delegates from the
Norman *parlement* had returned from their visit to Versailles.

Proofs of *Julie* continued to pass at intervals for several months between
the author and publisher. Their system of sending them through Malesherbes's office served only to add further delays to those of the postal
services. At one point[150] Rey tried to sweeten Malesherbes with the gift
of a book, the *Bibliotheca regni animalis* of Gronovius the Younger which
had just been published in Leyden; but at the same time he complained to
him about proofs being held up in his office. Rousseau scolded[151] Rey for
pestering Malesherbes, and suggested that the best way to accelerate their
correspondence would be to mail the proofs directly from Amsterdam to
Montmorency.

Rey was reluctant to adopt this procedure. Instead, he continued to
complain of delays, and Rousseau to grumble about the 'gross carelessness'
of Rey's compositors. At the end of June, Rousseau had also to express
his displeasure that the latest packet of proofs had been so badly wrapped
that they reached him 'soaked with rain'. Next,[153] he protested that Rey
had ignored his instructions, in printing vignettes together with his Latin
motto on the title page. Rey thereupon sent[154] Rousseau a revised set of
preliminary pages, in which the first title of the novel was printed as *Lettres
de deux amans. Habitants d'une petite ville au pied des Alpes* and the second
title printed as *Julie, ou la nouvelle Héloïse*. Although Rousseau continued
to refer to the book in conversation and correspondence as *Julie*, he
approved of the principal title – which was that under which the earliest
editions were sold – being *Lettres de deux amans*, with his own name
figuring underneath as 'J.-J. Rousseau, editor'. In response to Rousseau's
insistence[155] Rey agreed[156] to omit both the 'Citizen of Geneva' and the
Latin motto. At the same time Rey explained that he was using a different
format for Volume II of the novel, and this meant that the later volumes
would be printed before the earlier ones. In August, having first complained[157] that he could not hold a pen because he had rheumatism in his
left arm, Rey wrote[158] at some length to report that proofs were not
coming back to him on the appointed dates. He added: 'All the delays are
the fault of M. de Malesherbes's office. If they continue, I shall send the
proofs directly to you, although the postage will be much more costly.'
Rousseau expressed[159] sympathy over Rey's rheumatism and suggested
that it was unnecessary for him to go to the trouble of writing a letter to
accompany every batch of proofs. At the same time he pointed out that
the proofs were still full of misprints, and he raised queries about points
of detail which he clearly expected Rey to answer.

Although the Luxembourgs were unable to go to Montmorency in the
summer of 1760, Rousseau made use from time to time of the Petit

Château. It is there that he received the first visit from the Prince de Conti,* and was thus able to entertain a royal guest in an environment suited to his rank. In the *Confessions*, Rousseau mentions the visit, but does not describe it, as he does the Prince's second visit in the autumn to Montlouis. The Comtesse de Boufflers, as part of her campaign to capture Rousseau's friendship, brought the Prince to Montmorency and presented Rousseau to him. It is not altogether clear when that introduction took place. The Comtesse is known to have visited Rousseau on Sunday 8 June†, Monday 30 June‡ and Friday, 18 July. After this last visit the Comtesse wrote[162] to say that she realized her visit had been 'very indiscreet' – evidently because Rousseau had been unwell. She told Mme de Luxembourg next day that Rousseau had been suffering from a bleeding nose, information which prompted the Maréchale to write[168] at once to urge 'the most tenderly loved man in the world' to take more care of himself and to send her news of his health. It is probable that the visit of the Prince de Conti to the Petit Château took place in August, when Rousseau was, as he put it to Mme Dupin,[164] 'nailed to Montmorency'.

Mme Dupin had invited Rousseau to her château at Clichy but, pleading bad weather and other engagements, he postponed the journey until the end of the month, when he paid her only a lightning visit. In Paris, however, it was reported in mid-August that Rousseau had already gone to Clichy, and Deleyre, who had returned from his diplomatic mission in Vienna, gave that as his reason, when writing[165] to Rousseau, for not coming to visit him at Montmorency, adding in his teasing way: 'If you had really wanted me to visit you, you would have reproached me for not coming.'

A friend Rousseau did press to come to Montmorency that month was Lenieps, who had been seriously ill. Rousseau suggested that the air of Montmorency would do him good in his convalescence. He was less eager to receive Coindet, who had planned to come for dinner with Blondel d'Azaincourt. Rousseau first invited the pair of them, then cancelled[166] the invitation. But Coindet was not to be rebuffed. He arranged for Rousseau to be invited instead to the house of his friend. Rousseau refused§ the proposal, but finally agreed[167] to receive Coindet and d'Azaincourt – 'at the Petit Château if it is fine, and at Montlouis if it is raining'.

In September,[168] Rousseau again asked Coindet to postpone a projected

*Louis-François de Bourbon (1717–76).

†Lorenzy wrote to Rousseau on 7 June 1760 to say how much the Comtesse had been pleased to see him again.

‡Lorenzy informed Rousseau on 29 June 1760 that he would be bringing the Comtesse to visit him the following afternoon.

§'I do not like those visits to the country where one does not drink together.'

visit, because, as he put it, 'I expect a carriage-load of people next Sunday, and again the following Sunday ... this is the holiday season, when the whole world comes to the country.' Among his visitors was Lalive de Jully,* who offered to give Rousseau portraits he had engraved of Fontenelle and of the Italian composer Jomelli, two men 'whose talents,' Lalive suggested,[170] 'you combine'. Rousseau already had some of Lalive's engravings decorating his study, and he accepted[171] the two portraits with gratitude: 'Come, Monsieur, whenever you please, to see my retreat ornamented with your benefactions; your presence will add to them, and the moments you lose will not be lost to me.'

Such gracious words were seldom extended to people who gave him things, least of all to Mme de Verdelin, with whom he was spending more time than usual that summer since he was not expected to keep company with the Luxembourgs. Even the Comtesse de Boufflers became the victim of Rousseau's tendency to bite the hand that fed him, although she was less disposed than Mme de Verdelin to reward his ingratitude with increasing devotion.

Nevertheless, when the Comtesse took the Prince de Conti on a second visit to Montmorency within a space of two months, Rousseau was suitably pleased and flattered, especially because the Prince did not simply come up from the château, but made the entire journey from Paris to Montmorency with the Comtesse de Boufflers, Lorenzy and some other courtiers, simply to see him. This time he received the Prince at Montlouis, and he describes the visit in the *Confessions*:[172]

As my cottage was very small, and the situation of the *donjon* charming, I took the Prince there, and he, to crown his favours, asked if I would do him the honour of playing a game of chess with him. I knew he could beat Lorenzy, who was a better player than I. However, in spite of the signs and grimaces, which I pretended not to see, of Lorenzy and the courtiers wanting me to let the Prince win, I won the two games we played. At the end I said to the Prince in a respectful, but serious voice: 'Monseigneur, I honour your Serene Highness too much not to beat you at chess.' This great prince, so intelligent and so enlightened, and so deserving to be spared flattery, felt, or so I believe, that I was the only person who treated him as a man, and he liked me for it.

Rousseau was probably correct in thinking this. The Prince de Conti was noted for his liberal opinions, his informality and his appreciation of

*In the *Confessions* Rousseau mentions Lalive among the people he saw from time to time at Montlouis. Others were Condillac, Mably, Mairan, Boisgelou, Watelet and Ancelet.[169]

sincerity. Unfortunately Rousseau went on to behave in what he himself admitted was a boorish way towards him. After the visit to Montlouis the Prince sent Rousseau first one, then other presents of game. Instead of expressing thanks, Rousseau wrote an angry letter[173] to the Comtesse de Boufflers about it:

Accept my just complaints, Madame. I have received on behalf of M. the Prince de Conti a second present of game for which you are surely responsible even though you know very well that after receiving the first I was resolved not to accept any more. As his Serene Highness pointed out in his letter that the game had been killed by his own hand, I felt I could not refuse his second gesture out of respect for such flattering attention. But having thought twice only of my duty to the Prince, it is only just if, a third time, I think of my duty to myself.

I am very touched by the marks of esteem and kindness with which his Serene Highness has honoured me, and which I had the least reason to expect ... But with all that, Madame, I will not act against my principles any longer, even for him.

These presents are merely game, I grant, but what difference does that make? They are all the more valuable on that account, and I see all the more clearly how I am being forced to accept them. Nothing one receives is without its effects. If one begins by accepting anything, one ends by accepting everything. As soon as one accepts everything, one demands everything, and whoever reaches the stage of demanding everything will stop at nothing to get it. This evolution seems to me inevitable. But, Madame, whatever happens, I do not want to reach that stage.

Looking back on the episode, Rousseau came to reproach himself for his ill grace towards the Prince. In the *Confessions*,[174] he notes that his letter to the Comtesse de Boufflers 'was generally blamed and deserved to be ... To refuse presents of game from a prince of the blood who had put so much tact into sending them is less the delicacy of a proud man wishing to preserve his independence, than the bad manners of an oaf who does not know how to behave. I have never reread my copy of that letter to Mme de Boufflers without reproaching myself for having written it.'

At the time, Rousseau reacted altogether differently to a present of partridges from M. de Luxembourg. In a letter[175] of thanks to the Maréchale, he said the gift gave him all the more pleasure because it confirmed that her husband was in good health: 'You and Monsieur le Maréchal have given me back my love of life; and my life will always be dear to me while you take an interest in it.' For this reason, he added, she had no need to worry about his taking too little care of his health: 'Never an hour passes in the day when your name is not spoken in my retreat with tenderness and gratitude.'*

Although Rousseau assumed that the Comtesse de Boufflers had shown his letter refusing the Prince's game to all and sundry, she did not answer it immediately. Instead, she asked Lorenzy to send him a message on her behalf. Lorenzy wrote: [177] 'I hope that on my return from L'Isle-Adam in a week's time, Mme de Boufflers and I will be able to pay you a visit. She asks me to send you a thousand greetings and say a thousand kind words on her behalf; she has not yet answered your last letter because M. the Prince de Conti has said he wants her to tell you something, but has not yet said what.' Lorenzy's letter ended with the suggestion that Rousseau should join him on a visit to M. de Luxembourg at Versailles, 'if the thought of the Court does not alarm you'.

One can believe that the thought of Versailles did alarm the man who had run away from Fontainebleau rather than meet the King after the success of *Le Devin du village*. As it was, Rousseau simply made an effort† to go to Saint-Brice, the house of the Comtesse de Boufflers in the valley of Montmorency, when he heard that Mme de Luxembourg would be spending the day there. The effort was abortive. As he explained to the Maréchale afterwards[178] he had risen early, dined at 11.30 a.m. and set out on foot for Saint-Brice. Just as he was within sight of this destination, it started to rain heavily, so that he had to retrace his steps; he arrived home 'soaked to the skin', and immediately caught a cold.

The same bad weather prevented Lorenzy from keeping his promise to bring the Comtesse de Boufflers from Saint-Brice to Montlouis the following week. Writing from Paris,[179] Lorenzy explained that the Comtesse had much regretted being so near Rousseau and not seeing him. In his less than perfect French, he tried to explain how sincerely the Comtesse was attached to him. 'Beauty and other charms which are the principal attractions possessed by other women are in her case but the ornaments of a solid intelligence and an excellent character.'

Rousseau had already written[180] to Lorenzy to say he had been more upset than alarmed when he failed to appear on his projected visit: 'I should have only half enjoyed the pleasure of spending an hour or two with you because I was ill and unsociable. I am more or less better now, but I doubt whether the winter, which approaches bearing a coat of snow, will allow me to recover the lost pleasure as quickly as my health does.' He did not

---

*Knowing that the Comtesse de Boufflers was an intimate friend of the Luxembourgs, Rousseau did not deny that he accepted from them what he refused from the Prince de Conti; but that, he told her, was because 'M. le Maréchal de Luxembourg is a unique case for me.'[176]

†On 25 October 1760.

mention the Comtesse de Boufflers in this letter, but Lorenzy in his reply[181] said that the Comtesse was extremely sorry to hear that he had been ill and she sent him a thousand good wishes. 'Write her a line,' Lorenzy suggested, 'about her disappointment in not being able to come to see you.'

Rousseau, feeling he was being bullied by Lorenzy, resisted. 'I hope that you will not suspect me,' he wrote,[182] 'of being unresponsive to the good wishes of the Comtesse. If I am not mistaken, you can be very sure that I will never err in that respect. But when you tell me to write to her, you and I are very far from understanding one another, for I have a hard enough time replying to those who write to me, without writing to people who do not write to me in return.'

The Comtesse had, in fact, written to him only the day before,[183] saying that she could see from his letter to Lorenzy that the Chevalier had failed in the commission she had given him, and hence that she must have appeared to Rousseau to be negligent. The fact was that she was still waiting for a message for him from the Prince de Conti, who had been caught up in the other business, and she had asked Lorenzy to explain that to Rousseau. Lorenzy had assured her that he had written to Rousseau with her explanation, but she could tell from Rousseau's letter to Lorenzy that Lorenzy had lied to her.

Lorenzy had not lied: Rousseau had simply not commented on the message; and he wrote to the Comtesse to defend her friend against the charges. Rousseau's letter to her on the subject has not been traced, but it is evident from her reply[184] to it that he had both exculpated Lorenzy and admitted to being rather cross with her. 'I do not think it a bad thing that you should be cross with me,' she wrote; 'I thank you for it and I only regret having caused you unwittingly some pain.' She then gave him the message from the Prince de Conti. He wanted Rousseau to understand that he respected him and liked him and that the few bits of game he had shot and sent him were not to be regarded as a present. They were simple marks of esteem, honourable for that reason, and not commercial: 'Fabius, Quintius and Regulus would have accepted them without feeling wounded in their disinterestedness and their frugality.'

The Comtesse went on to say that she realized she had been unjust to the Chevalier de Lorenzy. As for Rousseau's letter which blamed her for encouraging the Prince to send him presents of game, 'I was moved and charmed by it, but I was also hurt, without however being shocked, that you should think me capable of frivolity, inconsequence and blindness. You do not know me well enough to do me justice on these matters, but time will prove that I have a heart made for friendship.'

Throughout the autumn months Rousseau and Rey continued to

exchange letters about the publication of *Julie*, letters punctuated on both sides with lamentations and recriminations. Rey went on complaining about the unreliability of the people he dealt with. He tried to make Rousseau understand that while his business was not very extensive, it was one which demanded detailed attention and caused him great anxiety. He told[185] Rousseau he would like to retire 'like your M. de Wolmar and Julie' and devote himself to good works. Rheumatism still afflicted him, although he hoped that time and patience would bring relief.

Rousseau, for his part, grumbled[186] about the delays and the 'gross misprints' that continued to figure in the proofs that reached him. He also accused[187] Rey of disclosing the contents of the novel to certain persons, and of breaking his promises in the matter of the author's royalties that were owed to him. Rey in his reply[188] to these accusations said he had nothing on his conscience about the delays or the royalties. As for the charge of disclosing the contents of *Julie*, he swore that despite his being questioned about it almost every day, he had not even revealed the title. He suggested that Rousseau would never have any peace if he went on listening to rumours, and he said he hoped to be able to clear up all the misunderstandings between them when he came to Paris in November.

When Rousseau renewed his complaints about delays, Rey assured[189] him that he was doing all that was humanly possible to speed up publication. Rousseau agreed[190] that Rey was not to blame; 'I am convinced there is a packet of proofs in M. de Malesherbes's office. I have already lodged a complaint. I cannot repeat it.' A letter from Rey dated 6 October[191] returned to the subject of royalties. Since Rousseau seemed to need money, Rey offered him an advance of a hundred livres, which he could accept without committing himself to anything. At the same time, Rey asked Rousseau's advice: 'Should I send M. de Malesherbes a copy of your book as soon as it is ready? I asked him for an import licence six weeks ago and I have not yet had an answer. I have a contract to supply a publisher in Paris with two thousand copies. If this succeeds, my outlay will be recovered (this between you and me, please). I have still not revealed the title of the book to anyone to whom I sell it on order.'

Rousseau advised Rey to go ahead and send an advance copy to Malesherbes as soon as possible, but to do so in the author's name. He himself wrote[192] to Malesherbes to ask if he would do him the honour of accepting it: 'Although a book of this kind hardly deserves a place in your library, some of the numerous letters in it may amuse Mme de Malesherbes – I hope she will not look a gift horse in the mouth. I only beg you, Monsieur, not to let the book out of your hands before the date of publication. Then I shall be sure that its success will not tempt anyone to counterfeit it, and even more sure that you would not allow that to happen.'

Within a week Malesherbes wrote[193] to thank Rousseau for 'the confidence you have shown in sending me your book before it is published', and he promised him to exercise the discretion he had pleaded for. Malesherbes knew that Rousseau wanted such discretion because of his fear of a pirated edition being printed in France, and he took the opportunity of stating the principles which governed his thinking on the subject of pirated editions:

No country prohibits the counterfeiting of foreign books. One must consider two altogether different interests, that of the publisher and that of the author. The interest of the publisher cannot be a motive for prohibiting the reprinting in France of a book published in Holland unless one also prohibited the reprinting in Holland of books published in France. For this to happen there would have to be a treaty between the two governments. Far from such a treaty being in existence at present, foreigners, and especially the Dutch, reprint everything that is published in France. It would therefore be absurd if the French government had scruples over reprisals.

As for the interest of the author, it is only just that in every country in the world, an author should derive from his work every possible advantage, and it is for that reason that we give an author the privilege of publication, or, which comes to the same thing, we give the privilege to the publisher he has chosen and nominated.

Following these principles, we cannot forbid French publishers to reprint a work which Rey has printed in Holland, but it will be right to give preference to the French publisher you name – it being understood that the French publisher really does produce an edition, and does not use the permission he is given simply to prevent another French publisher competing with Rey.

Malesherbes went on to suggest that Rousseau ought not to feel bound by his engagements to Rey to refuse to make an agreement with a French publisher for a reprint of his novel. The book would in any case be reprinted in France, and the French government wished Rousseau to have, as author, the same rights over a French as over the Dutch edition: 'There is a profit that belongs to you; it is the price of your work, and it does no injury to Rey since a French reprint, which he calls "pirated", is bound to appear, with or without your consent.' The only way Rey could forestall the French counterfeiters, Malesherbes concluded, would be to send a large number of copies promptly to the French market.

Rousseau was not unappreciative of the consideration Malesherbes had shown him in thus explaining the situation to him, and giving him such friendly advice, but he made it clear to the magistrate in his reply[194] that he would not agree to any arrangement which would violate the rights of Rey, and he therefore rejected Malesherbes's proposal for a French reprint of *Julie*. He also expressed his disagreement with Malesherbes's statement of the principles which should govern copyright in books. Malesherbes had invoked the law, but Rousseau reminded him that there was a great difference between positive law, 'which varies from nation to nation', and natural law 'which is the same for all men'. As between states, positive law was what the great could impose on the small, keeping their own advantages to themselves and sharing those of the small. Since Holland had a free press and France neither had nor could have one, a copyright treaty between those two nations would soon be ineffective. As it was, books were printed in Holland, where they sold hardly any, to be exported to France, where the market was prodigious. In effect, the manufacture of books took place in Holland, the consumption in France. The French government might well wish that books were produced in France, but that was prevented by the rigour of its own censorship. The censorship would not be relaxed 'because a government that can do everything cannot rid itself of the chains it is forced to give itself in order to be able to do everything'.

According to the principles of the French government, there are many things that cannot be formally permitted, but may conveniently be tolerated. From this it follows that France can put up with the importation of a book it cannot allow to be printed on its territory. Indeed, without such toleration, France, reduced to its own output of books and cut off from the republic of letters, would soon relapse into barbarism. However, when a book which has been printed in Holland because it cannot be printed in France, is then allowed to be reprinted in France, the French government sins against its own principles, and puts itself into contradiction with itself.

Moreover, Rousseau continued, the so-called parity which resulted from this policy was illusory, since the reprinting in Holland of a book published in France did no harm to French publishers, while the reprinting in France of a book published in Holland ruined a Dutch publisher. Rousseau apologized for spelling all this out to a magistrate and statesman who was an expert in the field, but he wanted to draw attention to the peculiar case of his own publisher, Rey, who had arranged a deal with the French publisher under which he would exchange books for books, sending half the print-run of *Julie* to Paris and receiving French books in return:

'Hence a counterfeit edition of that novel would not hurt the publisher in Amsterdam but the publisher in Paris with whom he deals. It would be one French publisher ruining another.'

On these grounds, Rousseau renewed his plea to Malesherbes to prohibit a French reprint of *Julie*. As for the money offered to himself as part of such an undertaking, he protested: 'If I took from Paris the profit I have already taken from Amsterdam, I should be selling the same manuscript twice over.' He agreed that he had not alienated all his rights in the book, but he refused to acquiesce in any action that was inimical to the interests of his Dutch publisher. Whatever M. de Malesherbes might decide about a French reprint, Rousseau stated categorically that he would neither nominate a French publisher nor accept any money from one.

Malesherbes was so impressed by such an upright attitude that he arranged to have the letter made public 'as an example of M. Rousseau's scruples over accepting a payment he felt he was not entitled to'.[195] Malesherbes also gave permission to Rousseau and the publisher Guérin, to bring out, separately from *Julie*, a *Second Preface* to the novel, in dialogue form, which Rousseau had written in an effort to explain why he, who had come before the public as a serious moralist, should put his name to a work of epistolary fiction. Rousseau offered this to Guérin because he had completed it too late* to send to Rey to include in the first edition of the novel. Since the illustrations to *Julie* which, after the collapse of the proposed deal with Boucher, Coindet had organized with Gravelot in Paris were also too late for Rey to use, Rousseau proposed that Guérin might bring them out as a separate publication together with the second preface. Rousseau explained this plan in a letter to Lorenzy dated 31 October 1760:[197] 'It is not my Dutch publisher who is in charge of the enterprise. It is M. Coindet, my compatriot, a man of taste, who loves the arts, and knows about them. He has chosen excellent artists, and the publication will be executed with the utmost care. I think it will be one of the most pleasing collections of prints that has been seen for a long time, and I do not doubt that if there is any success to be hoped for for the book the prints will contribute much to it. The trouble is that they will have to be sold separately.' Rousseau showed rather less appreciation of Coindet's connoisseurship and of Gravelot's talents in other letters.† Having served as a boy an apprenticeship in an engraver's workshop, Rousseau could claim to look with a trained eye at the drawings and proofs that Coindet sent him. He impressed[198] on him the need for the figures depicted in the

---

*In a letter to Guérin written in late October or early November, Rousseau explained that the manuscript of the second preface was not yet finished.[196]

†He never ceased to regret that money could not be found to commission François Boucher.

illustrations to have the lineaments and bearing of characters described in the text: Wolmar should be 'cold and distinguished', St-Preux 'upright'; Julie should have 'grace and a touching, penetrating air' and the prostitute should appear 'immodest without being naked'. He complained that Gravelot's drawings depicted both Julie and Claire with too small breasts: 'Swiss women are not like this. Probably Monsieur Coindet does not know that the women of our country have bigger tits than Parisiennes.' In another letter[199] to Coindet, Rousseau protested that his messenger was driving him to despair by forcing him to examine Gravelot's drawings in a hurry, and four weeks later[200] he was still finding faults with the illustrations: 'It is not the left eye of Julie that is too big, but the right eye that is too small.' By this time, however, Rousseau advised that there should be no more changes for fear of spoiling everything.

As soon as the engraving was complete Rousseau asked Coindet for the originals. 'I had the idea,' he writes in the *Confessions*,[201]

of embellishing the manuscript of *Julie* that I had copied out for Mme de Luxembourg ... with the drawings which were the same size as the manuscript paper. I asked Coindet for them, since I had every right to them, having let him take the profit on the plates ... But Coindet had as much cunning as I had little. From my request for the drawings he came to know the use I intended for them. Under the pretext of adding some ornaments to the drawings he got me to leave them with him, and he ended by presenting them to Mme de Luxembourg himself.

Ego versiculos feci, tulit alter honores.

At about the same time Rousseau accused Coindet of contriving to ingratiate himself with Mme de Verdelin. The bad weather which descended on the Île de France at the end of autumn brought an end to the exchange of visits between Soisy and Montmorency. In November, when both Rousseau and Mme de Verdelin had nasty colds, she arranged for Coindet to take gifts of victuals and wine up the hill to him. These included a ragout, a bottle of wine from her father's vineyard of the 1750 vintage, and a cake.[202] Although Rousseau's letter of acknowledgement has not been traced, it must have expressed more displeasure than gratitude, for we find her writing to him two days later[203] apologizing for offering him 'what you call presents' and explaining that it was simply pride in her Saintonge cake and her father's wine that had prompted her to give them to M. Coindet when she heard he was on his way to dine at Montlouis.

Rousseau replied[204] to this apology with a cruel rebuff: 'You offer me an apology to teach me that I owe you an apology.' He agreed that in the past he had accepted her 'presents or offerings or gifts or whatever you please to call them', but he said he had accepted them only as signs of friendship; and when they had become less acceptable, he had told her so. Then, he continued, she had started to use Mlle Levasseur as a pretext for giving him things, and now she was using M. Coindet 'as if what was sent to be eaten in my house could appear on some other table'. He warned her that such little games bored him and that he did not intend to put up with any more of them.

Again Mme de Verdelin replied[205] to his anger with soft words, assuring him that she was far from taking pleasure in causing him displeasure. She tried to explain that it was not his intellectual accomplishments, which she was unworthy to appreciate, that made her desire his friendship; it was the qualities of his soul that had attached her to him in a way that would never change. 'Your letter has hurt me deeply. I hope you will allow me to come to say goodbye to you. I beg you not to leave your fireside.'

In the *Confessions* [206] Rousseau prints part of his cruel letter to Mme de Verdelin, and comments on the 'incredible moderation' she showed in her reply and in her subsequent behaviour towards him. But he expresses no more remorse for his harshness towards her than he does for that towards the Comtesse de Boufflers. Indeed he even calls into question the sincerity of Mme de Verdelin's forgiveness of him.

At the time, however, she succeeded, by turning the other cheek, in regaining his friendship. She visited him as arranged on Friday, 6 November, and although she could not keep her promise to come again the following Friday, she told[207] him she was determined to do so before she left Soisy to spend the rest of the winter in Paris. In the event Rousseau stirred from his fireside to visit her instead; although it appears from her next letter to him[208] that he was punished for his good deed by catching another cold on the road home from Soisy to Montmorency.

Even when he had come to mistrust Mme de Verdelin, Rousseau had to admit he had once been fond of her and he seems never to have ceased to feel jealous of the friendship that Coindet acquired as a result of meeting her through him. In the *Confessions*[209] he comments on Coindet's success in worming his way into Mme de Verdelin's house and becoming 'unknown to me, more familiar there than I was'. Without shame for being jealous, he put Coindet down from time to time. For example we find him writing[210] to Coindet towards the end of 1760 saying

Dear Coindet:
I try to love you. Dear God, do not spoil that fantasy. I tell myself a hundred times a day that it is folly to seek perfect affinities, and I am far from finding them between you and me. But let us try to accommodate

ourselves to each other as we are, for if we change, we risk changing for the worse. It is for you as the younger to put up with me, and not to upset my fantasies. At times, perhaps, I shall tell you harsh truths and there are indeed some harsh truths to be told, but you can justly answer me with even harsher ones, and I shall never be angry. For the rest, preserve your liberty and leave me mine.

One curious feature of this letter is that it gives no hint of Rousseau's main grievance against Coindet – that he was taking over all his friends. On the contrary, he suggests at one point, 'it seems to me that we could form together, with dear Carrión, you and I, a little exclusive society to which no other mortal being would be admitted. That would be delicious.' In the *Confessions*, Rousseau says 'Coindet interposed himself between us – and supplanted me as Carrión's friend',[211] just as he complains about Coindet's supplanting him *chez* Mme de Verdelin. The one accusation that Rousseau addresses squarely to Coindet in the letter, and repeats in the *Confessions*, is of secretiveness.

Malesherbes not only arranged for Rousseau's letter to him about the international trade in books to be published, he also wrote him a considered reply.[212] He said he was willing to accept almost all the principles Rousseau had laid down, but did not agree with him about the effects they would have in practice. While it was true, he suggested, that republics or states with mixed governments had advantages over an absolute government in the trade in books, it did not follow that one ought not to try to minimize the disadvantages that a great monarchy suffered. If Versailles could not prevent the Dutch having the advantage over the French, it should not add to that advantage by forbidding the reprinting in France of works that had been printed in Holland.

Malesherbes went on to express the hope that he might discuss the question in conversation with Rousseau, since it was not a matter to be dealt with in letters. As for granting an import licence for *Julie*, Malesherbes explained that he never issued a written permit without an official scrutiny of a book, but in Rousseau's case, he was willing, even without seeing the entire text, to authorize him to inform M. Rey that he could send his edition to Paris.

Rousseau was not altogether satisfied with this informal permission, as is evident from his next letter[213] to Malesherbes:

I have never thought nor wished that you should have patience to read the entire compilation. But I do wish exceedingly, Monsieur, that you would find time to run through it and judge what it contains. I do not have the temerity to offer you my own judgement of a book I publish; I could only appeal to yours on the assumption that you had read it. Otherwise, I retract and beg you to deal with the book as if I had said nothing about it. My young letter-writers* are Protestants and republicans; it is very natural that they speak according to the principles they ought to have; it is very certain that they speak as honourable people, although that is not always enough. For the rest, I think that everything that might be subject to scrutiny in the novel is all in the last two or three volumes, and I must say that I do not consider them unworthy of being read.

As for the questions about the book trade raised in their previous letters, Rousseau added politely that it would be improper for him to argue with M. de Malesherbes until he had had the opportunity of learning more from him.

In November 1760 Rousseau's opera *Le Devin du village* was performed at the Paris Opera once again against his will. There is no mention of the performance in his correspondence of the time, but he had not forgotten his grievance and he even recorded his displeasure in one of the letters in *Julie*,[214] where St-Preux describes the Paris Opera as 'a kind of sovereign court which acts as judge in its own cause and has no other idea of justice or fidelity'. The 'Editor' adds in a footnote: 'If one is less subject to laws than to men, one must know how to endure injustice.' When Mme de Chenonceaux read these words in manuscript, she reproached[215] him sharply: 'Those attacks on Rebel and Francoeur of the Opera make me despair; do you not see that such accusations are indecorous? Your books should be above such things.' But Rousseau did not delete the words and Mme de Chenonceaux was lucky, after administering her rebuke, to receive a presentation copy of the printed book.[216]

Another friend who commented on *Julie* was Charles Duclos,[217] the one man in the whole literary establishment of Paris with whom Rousseau remained on terms of intimacy, trust and mutual esteem. Duclos, who had risen from humble origins to be permanent secretary of the Academie Française, with rooms in the Louvre, was as circumspect as he was ambitious, and he felt impelled by friendship to urge Rousseau from time to time to be more prudent and worldly-wise than it was Rousseau's nature to be. Since Rousseau sent him *Julie* in proof form, Duclos was one of the first persons to read it in anything other than manuscript. The first question[218] he asked was whether Rousseau was really the 'editor' of the letters in *Julie* or the author. While this was plainly a question to which Duclos knew the answer, Rousseau was slow to give him the satisfaction of telling him. When invited to offer criticisms of the book, Duclos

---

*The protagonists of his novel *Julie*.

suggested[219] that there was a certain obscurity concerning the period of Julie's first *faiblesse*, and he suggested that several more letters were needed to provide a bridge between the various episodes. He also urged Rousseau to cut several footnotes. But for the most part Duclos congratulated the author – 'if you are the author' – on an enjoyable novel. He only allowed himself to wonder 'how the champion of savages can have cultivated such delicate ideas of love and virtue, of which the seed is undoubtedly in the heart, but which society alone – however corrupt – can develop'.

When Duclos had read further instalments of the novel, he again congratulated[220] Rousseau without pressing him to admit that he was the author: 'It is not only a pleasing book to read, it is a good book.' He said he had been so absorbed by it that he had neglected his work on the new *Dictionary* of the Académie Française. One thing he did urge Rousseau to, was to give up the idea of printing a preface to the novel declaring it to be unsuitable reading for very young women.

Rousseau weighed this last advice. 'Despite what you feel,' he wrote[221] to Duclos, 'I persist in believing that the book is dangerous for girls. I even think Richardson is gravely mistaken in wanting to instruct girls through novels. It is a case of setting fire to the house in order to give work to the pumps.'

So Rousseau kept his first preface:[222]

Theatres are needed in great cities, and novels for corrupt peoples. I have witnessed the morals of my time, and I have published these letters. If only I could have lived in an age when I could have thrown them in the fire! ... This book is not meant for universal circulation, and will suit very few readers ... its Gothic tone makes it more suited than books of philosophy to women. It may even suit women who have kept, in a dissipated life, some love of honesty. As for girls, that is another matter. No chaste maiden has ever read novels ... She who, despite the title,* dares to read a single page of this book is a lost girl.

It is a measure of Rousseau's unworldliness that he imagined a warning so worded would deter any girl from reading his novel. In his obstinate way, he not only rejected Duclos's advice in the matter, but went on to publish his *Second Preface*, the *Préface dialoguée*, saying the same sort of thing at greater length.

In his letter[223] to Duclos, Rousseau mentioned one of his aims in publishing *Julie* that he had not set out in his first preface, namely to teach toleration: 'If Wolmar, the virtuous atheist, does not displease the pious,

*The original title was *Lettres de deux amans*.

and his wife, the virtuous believer, pleases the philosophers, I shall have published the most salutary book of these times.' He repeats this in the *Confessions*,[224] where he says he designed his two characters with this purpose in mind. Although he had broken with the atheists of the *Encyclopédie*, he did not wish to see them go on being persecuted as they had been in the years when he was working on his novel; and he also hoped to induce the atheists to feel less contempt and bitterness towards the Christians: 'I wanted to show each party merits and virtues in the other.'

By the time Duclos had received and read the last proofs of *Julie* he declared[225] that he was only unhappy that it was the last. Indeed he urged the editor (having ceased to question the pretence that Rousseau was only the editor) to add a further volume to tie the loose ends of the narrative together. A novelist himself, Duclos believed a dénouement was necessary, and also that readers should know what happened to Lord Édouard Bomston. He expressed some concern about Rousseau's idea of giving a lesson in toleration. Julie, he agreed, presented no problem; any philosopher who did not appreciate her would be very lacking in enlightenment, but the character of Wolmar, he said, 'alarms me on behalf of the editor'. Depicting a man who was both an atheist and virtuous was asking for trouble from the Church.

Rousseau had perhaps already had the possibility of such trouble in mind when he pressed Malesherbes to read the whole book, but he assured[226] Duclos that he had no fear of persecution: 'They will never have just grounds for attacking me, and it is folly to take precautions against injustice.' As for Duclos's other suggestions, Rousseau explained that the book had now been sewn and could not be rearranged. The adventures of Lord Édouard had been written, but, Rousseau explained, 'fearing to succumb to the temptation of publishing them, I have already thrown them in the fire, except for a short extract I made for Mme de Luxembourg, which is in her hands'. If Duclos had read that extract, he would probably have suggested that Rousseau should discard it with the rest.

By this time the novel had got well beyond the stage of being sewn. The whole first edition had been packed and dispatched from Amsterdam. The six bales destined for the French market left Rey's warehouse on 22 November for Brussels.[227] Rey himself was planning to go to Brussels to supervise the transport to Paris, and he intended to be in Paris by the middle of December to do business with his French concessionaire and to discuss future projects with Rousseau in person. Rey's French concessionaire was Étienne-Vincent Robin, who traded at the Palais Royal; Robin wrote on 30 November[228] to thank Rousseau for securing from

M. de Malesherbes consent to import *Julie*,* and to say that he was expecting a consignment of bales from Brussels, together with a parcel of sixty author's presentation copies. He asked the author for a list of persons to whom these should be sent. He only warned Rousseau that he had no knowledge of how long the delivery would take. In the event it took longer than usual. The consignment for Paris was held up *en route*, with the result that *Julie* was on sale in the London bookshops several weeks before Robin had any copies to distribute in France.

It was the talk of Paris well before it was published. Lorenzy wrote to Rousseau on 4 December[229] telling him that Robin was as 'impatient as a Sienese racehorse at the Palio' to have the book. He also asked Rousseau on behalf of the Comtesse de Boufflers and himself what they should say to people who inquired whether he was, or was not, the actual author of the book. At a session of the Académie Française, Duclos, as permanent secretary, made a speech in praise of the novel, as Rousseau reported,[230] with evident gratification, to Mme de Luxembourg: 'It is not his courage in doing it that amazes me, but can you imagine M. Duclos really liking that slow procession of honeyed words and dull nonsense?' In the same letter Rousseau brought up the matter of the publication of his 'treatise on education' [*Émile*] in which the Maréchale was taking a lively interest; he told her that he would make no decision without her consent. He explained that his present publisher, Rey, was coming to Paris, and would be asking for an option on the book, which he, Rousseau, would like him to have. He asked the Maréchale whether she would receive Rey if he came to her to seek her approval of their agreement.

He knew that she had a poor opinion of Rey, largely on the strength of all the criticisms that he himself had made of Rey's procedures; she had probably heard from Malesherbes how much money Rousseau's books could earn from the right French publisher. Duclos expressed the same opinions; he had already communicated[231] to Rousseau an offer from Jean-François Bastide to publish *Émile* at four louis a sheet. Knowing that Rousseau did not believe the authorities would allow *Émile* to be published *in extenso* in France, Duclos suggested that the controversial passages could be cut out for publication elsewhere. In another letter[232] Duclos wrote: 'If you do not treat Rey as a fool you are doing him too much kindness. Do not let that crude thickhead imagine that you had no reason for having your novel printed in Holland, or forget that you have given him for a hundred louis what you could sell here for five hundred.' The only advantage, as Duclos saw it, of printing the book in Holland had been to

---

*Robin referred to the book as *La Nouvelle Héloïse*, perhaps the first use of what became the familiar title of the novel. The principal title printed in the book was still *Lettres de deux amans*.

avoid trouble with the censorship, but Rey's inefficiency in getting the novel into the French bookshops meant that the censors would have time to intervene and the pirate publishers time to copy it. Duclos had less confidence than Rousseau in Malesherbes's power (or willingness) to protect a book that could 'lend itself to a wrong interpretation'. In the event, Duclos's fears for *Julie* proved unfounded: on the other hand, it is difficult to understand why, given what he felt about French censorship, he encouraged Rousseau, against Rousseau's own judgement, to offer *Émile* to a French publisher.

Rousseau did not offer it to Duclos's friend, Bastide; instead he offered him another work he had had on the stocks for a long time, his abridgement of the Abbé de Saint-Pierre's *Project for Perpetual Peace*. Bastide accepted it,* but even this innocuous work made Duclos nervous. He approved of Rousseau's abridgement in general, but advised him against using offensive words such as '*secte*' in speaking of Christian congregations; '*culte*', he suggested, would be more decent.

As the Genevese National Day, 12 December, approached, Rousseau who always observed it most faithfully, thought again of his compatriot Lenieps, and proposed joining him to celebrate the occasion in Paris. When the time came he was not well enough to go: 'Winter is a season when it is impossible for me to leave this place,' he wrote on 11 December to Lenieps,[233]† and much more so this year, because although it has been mild so far, it has been no kinder to me than last year.'

The Luxembourgs, having been robbed of their usual summer holiday at Montmorency, planned to go to their château at Christmas. Rousseau was delighted. 'I look forward to those mornings when I shall spend an hour chatting with M. le Maréchal at your bedside,' he wrote[234] to Mme de Luxembourg, 'and so long as my tongue speaks for my heart, I shall not be afraid that its prattling will dry up in your company. But as for your suppers, I do not aspire to the honour of being there, unless you are charitable enough to receive me *gratis*, for I feel less fit than ever to sing for them.'

In the event, Rousseau was not well enough to make the most of their presence at Montmorency. He told the publisher Guérin, on 21 December,[235] that he had been confined to his bedroom for the previous six weeks; and it was while he was laid up in this way that Rey paid his promised visit to him. There is no record of what they discussed together,

---

*He proposed to pay 12 louis for it, and to pay promptly through Duclos. Twelve louis was equal to 288 livres in *monnaie de compte* or approximately 300 francs in *monnaie réelle*.

†In the same letter Rousseau expressed dismay that their compatriot Gauffecourt had 'forgotten his old friends to pursue the star that shines and burns' – in other words, had gone to Geneva to seek out Voltaire.

but Rousseau probably told Rey that he was thinking of placing *Émile* with a French publisher. He appears to have promised Rey another book instead, namely *The Social Contract*, which was all that remained of a larger book he had originally intended to write on the subject of political institutions.

Guérin had urged[236] Rousseau to allow his works to be brought out in France, and advised him to forget about Rey, who had already made a deal for the sale of his edition of *Julie* which was profitable to himself but disadvantageous to the author: 'Besides', Guérin added, 'Rey's situation as a foreigner gives him no right to any grace and favour of our Minister [M. de Malesherbes] which would be prejudicial to French citizens.' Rousseau answered[237] all this by saying that while he was grateful for the friendly efforts that Guérin was making in collaboration with M. de Malesherbes to help him as an author, he would not agree to any arrangement that did not have Rey's approval. If Rey consented to there being a second or French edition of *Julie*, as M. de Malesherbes had suggested, then he, as author, would willingly provide the corrections of which the first edition was much in need; and he suggested that Coindet should be consulted about the illustrations. In the case of *Émile*, however, Rousseau reasserted his belief that it would never receive authorization for printing in France, 'except with mutilations that I would not agree to'. The best he could hope for in France would be the toleration of a re-impression of a foreign publication of *Émile*.

Guérin sent Malesherbes an abridged account[238] of his dealings with Rousseau: 'It seems that his delicacy of feeling attaches him to Rey's interests, but I know for certain that he has good reason to be discontented with Rey. Rey knows Rousseau's tendency to sacrifice his own interests, and he shamelessly takes advantage of the austerity of Rousseau's principles to get the better of him in their dealings.' Rey himself, waiting in Paris for the consignment of books that was still held up in transit, informed[239] Rousseau that while he agreed to a French edition, he was asking Malesherbes to delay it for six months, and to authorize no publication other than that of Robin and his partner Grangé, who were willing to pay Rousseau thirty new louis for the rights. Rey also mentioned that he had sold the 2,000 copies which were 'still in Brussels' to Robin, and he enclosed a credit note for 1,000 livres for the author.

Five days later,[240]* Rey had to tell Rousseau that the 2,000 copies of *Julie* destined for the French market had not even reached Brussels. They were still in the hold of a vessel that could not dock because of high water. Rey admitted to being in a state of great anxiety, lest the delay enabled

*In the same letter Rey reported that *Julie* had been on sale in England and Germany since 20 December.

the French pirate publishers to flood the market before his edition reached Paris. He faced a loss of 16,000 livres: 'When all this comes to my mind and I think of the wife and children whose fate is attached to my fortune, I cannot help weeping and falling into a state of total despair.'

Rousseau's sympathy for Rey in his distress was not unqualified, or so we may judge from what he said in a letter[241] to Mme de Verdelin: 'My publisher, who is in Paris at present, still has no news from Brussels about the arrival of *Julie*. Personally I suspect that in order to economize on the freight, he sent the books by sea, and that the ship was seized by the English, so that instead of boring the ladies of Paris, *Julie* is at the moment boring the ladies of London.'

The advance copies which Rey had promised Rousseau for presentation to his friends had also not arrived. Rey was even unable to give Rousseau the single copy he had promised him on his visit to Montlouis; he explained that he had lent the only one he had to Coindet, and Coindet had 'pleaded a foolish excuse'[242] for not returning it. Lorenzy reported to Rousseau on 22 December[243] that there were only two copies of *Julie* in Paris and 'these pass from hand to hand, to be successively devoured by those who get hold of them; sleepless nights are spent reading them'.

Having no copies of *Julie* to give to his friends, Rousseau sent cards to several of them saying he had instructed the Paris publisher Robin to send them the books in his name when they arrived. One of the first on the list went to Sophie d'Houdetot. Her manner of thanking him for the card bespeaks the distance that had by this time grown up between them; she wrote[244] in her own hand and in the third person, and in the coldest of formal French: '*Madame d'Houdetot accepte avec reconnaissance et sensibilité l'exemplaire de la Julie que Monsieur Rousseau a bien voulu luy destiner.*' She reminded him that she was still awaiting the remaining parts of the manuscript of the novel which he was copying for her. Earlier in the month she had written,[245] also in the third person, to ask him to make a copy of *Émile* for her, and to allow M. de St-Lambert to read it to the King of Poland. Rousseau did in the end complete her manuscript of *Julie*, but there is no evidence that he made a copy of *Émile* for Sophie d'Houdetot; and after December 1760 there is no trace of further correspondence of any kind between them.

In the case of Mme de Verdelin, Rousseau sent her a note which would, he explained,[246] enable her to procure her copy of his 'dull rag' from the booksellers – publishers being at that time in Paris, as in London, book-sellers as well. He also asked her to collect at the same time the copy reserved for M. de Margency.* Rousseau mentioned Margency again in

*Margency.

a later letter[247] to her: 'What do you say about him? He is cold, I think, but is he constant in his friendships? I see he forgets me, and he does not remember you too often. It seems he is cold and changeable. If that is the case, one must regret not seeing him, but not regret too much the loss of his friendship.'

Rousseau realized that Margency was distressed about the serious illness of Desmahis;* indeed hearing that Desmahis was being attended by three doctors, Rousseau considered he was as good as dead. Mme de Verdelin already feared that Margency loved Desmahis more than he loved her, and that the death of Desmahis, who had himself become extremely pious, would plunge him into such grief and religious devotion as to leave no place at all for her in his life. Desmahis did indeed die two months later with the consequences that Mme de Verdelin dreaded.

Another friend to whom Rousseau wrote[248] promising a presentation copy of *Julie* – 'my dull and wretched novel' – was Lenieps. He told Lenieps that he would receive only one copy, which he would have to share with his married daughter, Mme Lambert. Rousseau said he knew full well that Lenieps would hate the book, and, as it was written for women, he advised him to pass it on to Mme Lambert at once, without reading it. Rousseau only warned him to keep it out of the hands of Mlle Barton, their young English friend, 'for reasons which the preface will explain'.

Again Rousseau told Lenieps that he was giving up writing for good. 'There remains an old sin to expiate in print; after that the public will never hear of me again.' The 'old sin' (about which Lenieps is unlikely to have known) was Rousseau's placing of his infant children in the Paris orphanage. The expiation was writing *Émile*, a treatise originally designed for the instruction of parents who kept and reared their offspring as he himself had not. The book itself contains a veiled confession:[249] 'A man who cannot fulfil the duties of a father has no right to become one. Poverty, work and other people's attitudes are no excuse for not feeding his children and raising them himself. Readers, you can believe me. I predict that whoever has entrails and neglects such sacred duties will shed bitter tears for his fault and will never be consoled for it.'

---

*Joseph-François-Édouard de Corsembleu de Desmahis (1722–61), fashionable poet and Encyclopédiste, who turned devout.

9

THE YEAR OF *JULIE*

The year 1761 witnessed the publication of *Julie* – or *Lettres de deux amans* as it was then entitled, *La Nouvelle Héloïse* as it was afterwards known. Its appearance transformed Rousseau from a celebrated author into the object of a cult. Already, in his controversy about music with Rameau, Rousseau had propelled French taste from rationalism and classicism towards romanticism. *Julie* did even more to establish him as a dominant figure in European culture. It changed the ways in which people thought and felt and acted. It was also one of the great commercial successes of the century in the bookshops, even though it did not bring the author more than a modest return. Had publishers been more honest, or Rousseau himself less scrupulous, less unbending towards the censors, the book could have made his fortune.

The delay of the appearance of *Julie* in the Paris bookshops caused him intense irritation. He repeated to several friends the story that Rey had sent the books by sea in order to save money. 'I shall be furious with your publisher,' M. de Luxembourg wrote him on 4 January 1761,[1]* 'if your suspicions are well founded and Rey's meanness made him send poor Julie by sea.' The one consolation, the Maréchal added, was knowing that Rousseau had decided to break with Rey and allow his wife to arrange for the publication of *Émile* in France.

Rousseau was, in fact, being unfair to Rey, who was about to be cheated, together with Rousseau himself, by the French publishers of *Julie*. While Rey's copies of *Julie* were languishing somewhere in the Austrian Netherlands, the so-called 'second edition' which Malesherbes had allowed Robin to produce was being rapidly printed and manufactured in Paris, and far from being held up, as promised, for six months to allow Rey's

---

*In this letter M. de Luxembourg also expressed his hope of being able to visit Rousseau with the Maréchale during the following week.

edition to be sold first, the 'second edition' reached Robin's warehouse in
time to be marketed in advance of Rey's. The pirate publishers in the
provinces were not far behind.

On Saturday, 17 January,[2] Rey wrote from Paris to inform Rousseau
that the bales of books had at last arrived, and would be opened at the
customs by Robin, to whom they now belonged. Rey said that he
proposed to return to Amsterdam early on the following Monday morning
and that he had entrusted the distribution of the author's presentation
copies to François Coindet. The list[3] stipulated five copies to be sent to the
household of M. de Luxembourg, three to Lorenzy (of which one was for
the Comtesse de Boufflers and one for the Prince de Conti), two to Mme
de Verdelin (one being for Margency); one each to Mme d'Houdetot,
Mme de Créqui, Mme Dupin, Mme Sellon, Mme de Chenonceaux, and
one each also for Duclos, Lenieps, Lalive, d'Épinay, Gauffecourt, Roguin,
Carrión, Guérin, Watelet, Blondel d'Azaincourt, Sevelinge, La Tour,
d'Alembert, Loyseau de Mauléon, Francueil, Coindet. He left Coindet to
decide whether to offer a copy to the artist Gravelot and instructed him
to take care that 'the copy addressed to M. d'Épinay has the name of
"Monsieur" written legibly and not "Madame"'. Rousseau's alienated
benefactress had by this time returned from Geneva to La Chevrette,
although financial embarrassment soon forced her to leave that splendid
château for ever and cultivate her talents as a novelist in more modest
quarters at La Briche.

This list gives us a good idea of the people Rousseau regarded as friends
at this period of his life. Only two of them – d'Alembert and Duclos –
remained from the circle of Encyclopédistes among whom he had lived
in Paris, although the painter Maurice-Quentin de La Tour had a place in
that milieu. Francueil and Carrión were on the list as old friends and
Loyseau de Mauléon as a new friend; Guérin was the one publisher to be
honoured. Two others of those named to receive *Julie* were, together with
Lalive de Jully, amateur artists. Watelet,* who had inherited the lucrative
sinecure of Receveur-général des Finances in Orléans, was not only a
painter and engraver, he was a successful writer, having been elected in
1760 to the Académie Française on the strength of a poem, *L'Art de peindre*,
of which he had sent Rousseau a copy.† Watelet continued in future years
to correspond with Rousseau, and his writings on art and aesthetics,

---

*Claude-Henri Watelet (1718–86) is perhaps best remembered for a book which did
much to make the English garden popular in France, *Le Jardin anglais*, and for his five-
volume *Dictionnaire de peinture et sculpture*.

†It was in February 1760 that Watelet sent Rousseau the presentation copy, saying he
hoped it might earn him 'the esteem and friendship of a virtuous man'.[4] It appears from
this letter that Watelet had heard from Loyseau de Mauléon that Rousseau might be
interested to receive the poem, which Watelet had had published with his own illustrations.

published in the *Encyclopédie* and elsewhere, expound ideas on art and aesthetics akin to those of Rousseau on music and literature. The Blondel d'Azaincourt, who had only taken up art on his retirement from the army, became an honorary member of the Academy of Painting at the same time as Watelet, and engraved among other things several works by the painter that Rousseau admired and Diderot detested – Boucher; some of his works adorned the walls of Rousseau's *donjon* at Montlouis. The only Genevese names on the list are those of Gauffecourt, Roguin and Lenieps, although the copy assigned to Mme Sellon was doubtless intended for her to share with her husband, Jean-François Sellon, Minister-Plenipotentiary of Geneva at Versailles. The identity of 'M. de Sevelinge' is uncertain.*

A conspicuous absentee among those designated to receive a presentation copy of *Julie* was Alexandre Deleyre. It does not seem that he had done anything – apart from becoming attached to a girl Rousseau disliked – to lose the favour of a friend to whom he had always been loyal. Deleyre had left his diplomatic job in Vienna and returned to Paris in July 1760, and appears to have visited Rousseau at Montmorency that summer. He married the girl – Caroline-Alexandrine Loiseau – at the church of St-Sulpice on 27 October 1760. There is no sign of Rousseau sending any message of congratulation, and when Deleyre wrote to Rousseau on 13 February 1761,[6] he had to apologize for four months of silence. That letter came from Parma, where Deleyre, having failed to find a job in Paris, had accepted the post of librarian to the Duke.† Rousseau may have known of his absence abroad in January 1761, and omitted Deleyre's name from the list of friends for that simple reason; or he may have suspected Deleyre of renewing in Paris his links with Diderot. In the *Confessions*[7] Rousseau speaks of Diderot 'detaching from me a friend [Deleyre] he had procured from me', but that refers to an earlier period, and there is no sign of any dealings between Deleyre and Diderot in the 1760s. In his letter to Rousseau of February 1761 Deleyre was mainly concerned to explain and justify his marriage. He spoke of the love and the sensibilities of his bride, of the hostility to their marriage of their two families, and the bitterness of separation while he was in Vienna; he explained how his wife had now left her beloved mother in Paris to join him in Parma. But for all the happiness he had found in 'the sweetest of reciprocal love', Deleyre assured Rousseau that he was still the man *'le plus proche de ma conscience'*: 'If your friendship for me has cooled … but no! I need it even in the bosom of love, and I count on it although you have not

*Leigh suggests that it was Nicolas-Louis Sevelinge, tax-farmer, who lived at the quai de l'École in Paris.[5]

†Deleyre was however no royalist. As a member of the Convention during the French Revolution he voted for the execution of Louis XVI.

assured me of it again!' Rousseau's reply to this letter has not been traced.

Before the end of February Malesherbes authorized the clearance of Rey's edition of *Julie* from the customs, but he allowed Robin to keep them in his warehouse until his own edition of the book was sold out. Coindet, unaware of this arrangement, warned[8] Rousseau that Robin was distributing advance copies of his own edition pretending it was the first edition. He said that although Robin and his partner Grangé were making a mystery of their activities, he believed that the French edition would be on sale 'by Monday or Tuesday' – he was writing on a Sunday. Coindet's suspicions were well founded. When Robin made a journey to Montmorency to pay his respects to the author and deliver in person the copies of *Julie* that Rousseau had asked for, it was copies of the French edition that he took with him.

In the meantime Rousseau had been corresponding further with Coindet about the publication of the *Second Preface*, or *Préface dialoguée*, to *Julie* and the illustrations based on Gravelot's drawings. Despite his promise to ask for no more modification in the engravings, Rousseau continued to express dissatisfaction. Having received another set of proofs of the prints, he wrote[9] to Coindet saying that changes would have to be made. The engraving which represented 'The Death of Julie' he described as 'ignoble'; the figures of Claire and Wolmar, he insisted, needed to be given a certain aristocratic bearing to distinguish them from the common people shown with them in the same scene. As it was, 'Wolmar looks like an old apothecary and Claire has the fat cheeks of a servant with a duster.' Rousseau complained that the richness of the furnishings clashed absurdly with the vulgarity of the characters and that the dead Julie looked like a rag-picker. He added some detailed suggestions as to how the engraver could give Claire the appearance of a decent *déshabillé* and make Wolmar look more elegantly dressed. Once again, in matters of class distinctions, Rousseau proved himself to be exceedingly fastidious.

Coindet promised[10] to have the corrections that Rousseau wanted made to the engravings, even though they had come very late. He hoped Rousseau would find Julie's face pretty enough in the plate entitled 'The Monument of Past Loves'. Rousseau had already written[11] – the first of two letters on the same day to Coindet – to say that the face of Julie was good in 'The Monument of Past Loves' but very bad in 'The Morning *à l'anglaise*' – but he added: 'Let us say no more about all this. Leave the plates as they are – they will be out of your hands.'

It was just after Rousseau had finished this letter to Coindet that Robin appeared at Montlouis armed with copies of the French edition of *Julie*. Forewarned, Rousseau refused to accept more than a single copy of this printing, demanding instead those from Rey's edition. Robin seems to have yielded promptly, since we find Rousseau writing[12] to Coindet immediately after the publisher's departure saying, 'Robin came ... I do not want his copies; and as for the money, I will have it sent back. He has promised that he will give you either this evening or tomorrow morning eighteen copies of the Dutch edition.' Rousseau asked Coindet to send him six copies to Montlouis by the carrier l'Épine, and to distribute the other twelve to the most urgent on the list of friends he had prepared – Lorenzy, Duclos, Carrión, etc. – with the request that they should not lend their copies to anyone for a fortnight, 'without, however, explaining the difference between the Dutch and the French editions, so that there will be the least possible discussion of cuts'.

There were substantial cuts in the French edition. When Rousseau came to examine more closely the copy that Robin had given him, he declared to Coindet[13] that the book was 'so much disfigured and so full of misprints' that he did not recognize it as his own; the 'terrible cuts', he added 'make the book ridiculous to read because there is nothing to fill the gaps they leave'. He told Coindet that he intended to disavow the book publicly, and he instructed him not only to return the money that Robin had offered for the French edition, but to explain his reasons for doing so to M. de Malesherbes.

However, Malesherbes himself had just written[14] to Rousseau explaining that he had authorized the sale of the Dutch edition of *Julie* to be held up until the French edition was sold out in order to avoid 'an irreparable injury to the French publisher'. Malesherbes further stated that he had been assured by Robin that Rousseau had promised to keep at home the copies of the Dutch edition that were being sent to him until such time as it was convenient for him to release them; and on this understanding, he had allowed Robin to send Rousseau the number of copies he wanted. Malesherbes went on to say that he was retaining the fifth and sixth volumes of *Julie* until he had seen what cuts would have to be made. Finally, Malesherbes made some attempt to placate Rousseau by telling him that any further cuts would be simply cuts and that nothing would be substituted without the author's consent.

In view of the enormous demand which had already built up for Rousseau's novel, Malesherbes's claim that the sale of Rey's edition threatened 'irreparable injury' to the French publisher looks absurd. Admittedly, if word spread abroad that the French edition was expurgated and the Dutch unexpurgated, and if there was a choice between them, French readers would insist on the latter; but as there were only 2,000 copies in the Dutch edition, that option would not last long. Even so, it is unlikely that Malesherbes was really worried about Robin's potential losses, especially as Robin was only a minor publisher, and not one of the chartered *libraires* with whom he was accustomed to dealing; his chief motive for holding up the sale of Rey's edition was probably to keep a controversial text out of sight for as long as possible and then to overlook its existence when it finally appeared.

Rousseau, in writing[15] to Malesherbes, pointed out that Robin's so-called 'second edition' had been produced without his knowledge or consent and that the publisher had added to the misprints of the Dutch edition a multitude of absurdities which could have been avoided if he, as author, had seen the proofs; he could even have sewn up the gaps left by the cuts and made the *lacunae* less shocking.

'Robin has done a great wrong,' he continued, 'in telling you that I promised to keep at home the copies of the Dutch edition that he must provide for me. Such a promise would be ridiculous, for what would be the point of having them if only to make no use of them? I promised to distribute them as sparingly as possible and in a way to do him the least harm.' However, since Rousseau did not wish to alienate Malesherbes, he undertook to recover the six copies that Coindet had already distributed, and to send out no more until he had the magistrate's permission.

Malesherbes would not accept Rousseau's claim that the French edition of *Julie* was produced without his consent: 'It is not true,' he told him squarely in his next letter.[16] He suggested, at the same time, that Rousseau could justly disavow the French edition on the grounds that he had not corrected it and that it contained errors which disfigured it 'because that is true'. On the other hand, Malesherbes suggested that such a public declaration would be worthless, because by the time it was printed, the French edition would be sold out, and the Dutch edition would have come on the market, so that readers would be able to make the comparison for themselves. For this reason, Malesherbes suggested that despite his disavowal, Rousseau might with a clear conscience accept the payment which the publishers of the French edition owed him. Indeed Malesherbes hinted that Rousseau's disavowal might open the way to the publication 'somewhere' of a third edition 'without cuts'.

Whatever he meant by 'somewhere', he did not mean Paris. It is clear from his subsequent letter that Malesherbes had not the slightest intention of authorizing the publication of an edition of *Julie* 'without cuts'. What Malesherbes did authorize, in another letter[17] to Rousseau, was the free use of the eighteen advance copies of the Dutch edition that Robin had provided: 'You may dispose of them as you please.' Malesherbes was willing to admit that Rousseau had a grievance, but said he could not go into the details of the case in writing. He promised to explain everything *viva voce* to Guérin and Coindet, from whom Rousseau would hear what he had to say.

For a while Rousseau was appeased. He told[18] Coindet: 'I am already so calmed down over all this that I shall not bother to make a public disavowal unless the publishers themselves want it.' To Malesherbes himself Rousseau wrote[19] saying he would make the disavowal only if the publishers desired it and Malesherbes himself drafted it. As for the idea of a 'third edition', Rousseau said he would willingly agree to one 'provided it is well printed and on good paper'.

There is no record of Malesherbes's conversation with Guérin and Coindet, but it is apparent from what Rousseau wrote to Malesherbes that they communicated Malesherbes's views on the cuts that had been ordered in the French edition and which he insisted on. Rousseau told Malesherbes that he would 'sacrifice without repugnance' all the footnotes that the censor wished to suppress, but would sacrifice most unwillingly the cuts stipulated to the text of the novel, 'because they are precisely the places where it can be a good and useful book'. He suggested that both his *Letter to M. d'Alembert* and his *Discourse on Inequality* contained passages more daring and more boldly developed than anything in *Julie*: 'Neither the public nor any individual can think it wrong that a Protestant should speak like a Protestant,' he wrote in response to the charge that the Swiss characters in his novel expressed opinions at variance with Catholic orthodoxy.

Malesherbes was as good as his word in encouraging the production of a third edition of *Julie*, but his solicitude for Catholic sensibilities was such that he chose one of his censors who was close to the Jesuits, the Abbé de Graves, to negotiate in secret for Duchesne to publish and Guérin to print the proposed third edition. Robin, not being a chartered bookseller* was left out of the negotiations. The Abbé de Graves reported to Malesherbes that Duchesne and Guérin were willing to produce the novel in four volumes with the preface and plates on good paper, and would pay the author fifty louis if he would knit together the loose ends that would be left by the cuts that would have to be made. This had not been revealed to Rousseau, when, on 10 February 1761 he wrote[20] to thank Malesherbes for the interest he was taking in his welfare as an author, and to tell him that, having heard that Rey had no objection to his being paid 1,000 livres for the 'second edition' of *Julie*, he was willing to accept it. 'I find myself rich as a result of your kindness,' he told Malesherbes, adding that he hoped to meet him in person when he visited the Luxembourgs at the château of Montmorency.

---

*According to Guérin, a mere 'book trader at the Palais Royal', a considerably less respectable location at that time than the name might suggest. The truth of the matter was that Robin was in partnership with a more important figure in publishing and printing, Jean-Auguste Grangé, who remained, for some reason, in the background.

Less pleasing to Rousseau was the news that his *Letter on Providence* was going to be published in Geneva, published by – of all people – his friend Jacob Vernes. He sent Vernes a stern rebuke:[21]

I was angry when the *Letter* was printed in Berlin without my knowledge. I have prevented its publication in Paris, and even in Amsterdam. It is a courtesy I owe M. de Voltaire not to print anything addressed to him without his approval. But since you do not consult me here about it, I have nothing to say to you. I appreciate that the interests of an editor have made you forget those of an author, and although I note that you speak of friendship, I do not observe you respecting its laws.

His anger had evidently made Rousseau forget that he himself had planned with Guérin and La Tour to publish the *Letter on Providence* in Paris and had only abandoned the project when the publishers decided against it. It was not long, however, before Rousseau was relieved to hear that Moultou[22] had intervened with Vernes to persuade him against publishing the *Letter*. Moultou also reported with pleasure that the authorities of Geneva had passed an order prohibiting the Genevese to engage in theatricals, but since Rousseau had decided that Geneva was now so corrupt a city as positively to benefit from the drama, he had no reason to rejoice in this news. Nor can he have been altogether happy to supply Moultou's request for a copy of *Julie*, since the Geneva clergy were not among the readers for whom that book was written.

One of the first friends who wrote to thank[23] Rousseau for his presentation copy of *Julie* was Margency. He said he found Rousseau's writings a source of comfort in a time of spiritual travail:

I must tell you that I have more peace of mind than I had before, and it is to you that I owe that happier state ... in rereading your books I have formed a taste for the retreat in which I am now obliged to live and I have found in you the consolation I needed ... I have seen that solitude calms the soul and stills the passions to which the disorder of the world gives birth.

Margency also gave Rousseau the sad news that Mme de Verdelin's brother, the Marquis d'Ars, who had done heroic deeds in the war as the captain of a frigate, had just been killed in action at sea.

Rousseau must have read this letter with mixed emotions, for he knew that Mme de Verdelin regarded Margency's withdrawal into spiritual meditations as a reason for his diminishing attentions to her; and realizing also that the death of her brother would only increase her need for the warmth of a lover, he cannot have been entirely gratified at being thanked for having inspired the lover's retreat into solitude. Rousseau wrote at once to Mme de Verdelin, a short but sincere and moving letter[24] of condolence in her bereavement, although as usual he brought in his own sorrows: 'I am not without sufferings of every sort, but I forget them in sharing yours, or at least I shall be delivered from the saddest of all, which is to weep alone.' To Mme de Créqui, who was mourning the death of her best friend, the Chevalier Antoine d'Aydie, he wrote:[25] 'You weep for the death of a friend: I pity you: but I know those more unfortunate than you. Ah, Madame, it is a very cruel loss to weep for a friend who still lives.' Diderot, it would seem, was never far from Rousseau's thoughts.

When Mme de Luxembourg heard that Rousseau would be sending her a copy of Rey's edition of *Julie*, she urged[26] him to offer one also to the Comtesse de Boufflers. She brought up the matter of the Comtesse de Boufflers and the Prince de Conti being offended at Rousseau's refusal of a present of game which was meant as a sign of friendship, but she assured Rousseau that the Comtesse would have come to visit him at Montlouis if the severe winter had not prevented her: 'She always speaks of you in the same affectionate terms that I have heard since she first knew you.' Rousseau had in fact included a copy of *Julie* for the Comtesse de Boufflers in the three he had noted to go to Lorenzy, the second name on his list. Lorenzy accepted it on her behalf on 28 January,[27] and a few days later the Comtesse herself went to visit Rousseau, bearing a pot of honey, a gift modest enough for him to accept.

The mails brought Rousseau letters of praise for his novel from friends and strangers alike. La Condamine told[28] him he wanted to finish the book only in order to start reading it again: 'You speak to the heart, and no one speaks to it as eloquently as you do.' Margency, when he had finished it, wrote[29] to express his admiration:

I believe that your charming Julie actually exists and I believe it for the honour of the humanity which I love. I believe that such a perfect character is not often found in society, but it is enough that there is one in nature. I do not know if I am acquainted with a Julie who has some of the traits of yours. Mme de Verdelin maintains that Julie is an incomparable woman and that you are a divine man. I am much of her opinion on the latter point. Ah, Monsieur, what a book! What a prodigious number of beauties. Feeling is everywhere depicted with a candour that reveals and a warmth that expresses it. From the happy contrast of savage nature and nature embellished you have drawn sublime and delightful pictures. As for Julie, one can never tire of returning to her ... one must love her.

The Comtesse de Boufflers told[30] the author that what impressed her most about the book was its 'admirable foundation of virtue, the energy and interest and feeling'. The other Mme de Boufflers – the Duchesse, daughter-in-law of Mme de Luxembourg – suggested[31] that the book ought to be inscribed in letters of gold: 'I do not look on it as a novel: it is the most perfect book I know.' Even the Dauphine sent word through Mme de Luxembourg to say she considered *Julie* to be an altogether ravishing book.[32] As for Mme de Luxembourg – one of the few people who knew the novel already as a result of hearing Rousseau read it aloud – she declared:[33] 'Your *Julie* is the most beautiful book in the world: there is not another soul like yours that could have produced it.'

Even the sober and self-controlled d'Alembert admitted[34] he was thrilled by *Julie*: 'I have read, or rather devoured, the new book you very kindly sent me. The eloquence of the heart, the warmth, the life, which is characteristic of all your books, shines above all in this one, which must, I think, set the seal on your reputation.' D'Alembert did, however, add a few criticisms. He wished Rousseau had omitted the footnotes, which he thought unworthy of the book, and had cut out a dozen pages of which the tone was not noble enough; he also said he would have liked to see 'perhaps the softening of some phrases in the preface'.

Rousseau welcomed d'Alembert's praises all the more warmly, he told[35] him, because of the 'frank and judicious criticisms' he had added. He said he recognized the language of friendship in everything d'Alembert had written: 'Your letter pleased me greatly.' It is not at all clear, however, that Rousseau really appreciated criticisms, especially when Duclos and others qualified to judge made the same points as d'Alembert. He confessed[36] to Mme de Luxembourg: 'The publication of *Julie* has caused me more worry than any of my other writings. I receive letters about it which are so different that I would not be able to believe in its success if M. le Maréchal had not had the goodness to reassure me. The preface is unanimously decried, and yet such is my own preference for it that the more often I reread it, the more it pleases me.' Rousseau cannot seriously have doubted the popularity of his novel, which was confirmed, if in no other way, by the number of visitors and letters he received. 'They plague me terribly,' he complained to Lenieps;[37] 'they do not let me eat or sleep – and that is not the worst of it; they rob me of the time to write to you.'

News of the difference between the expurgated French and the unexpurgated Dutch editions of *Julie* spread, as one might imagine, quickly. Already by 28 January[38] Lorenzy informed Rousseau that Robin was refusing to sell 'at any price' any edition of the book except his own, which was known to have 'suppressed passages', but the public was so eager to read the book in any form that they were seizing what Robin offered them.

The publication of *Julie* coincided with the appearance of another novel in Paris, one entitled *Daria*, by M. de La Poplinière, the immensely rich patron of the arts at whose house Rousseau had made his Paris *début* as a musician. The proud author sent[39] Rousseau a complimentary copy with a message: 'Your charming Héloïse deserves every kind of homage. Accept this from an unfortunate child of whom I have narrated the adventures.' If not the worst novel ever written, *Daria* was very much the work of an amateur. Apart from La Poplinière himself, the only man to bracket it with *Julie* was the malicious Voltaire, who remarked, 'Both authors depict themselves in their novels. La Poplinière's hero is a man who needs a seraglio; Jean-Jacques's is a tutor who takes his pupil's virginity for his wages.'[40]

Rousseau avoided embarrassment by thanking[41] La Poplinière promptly for his novel before he had time to read it. He expressed the hope that he would one day be well enough to leave his retreat and visit his old friend and 'witness the spectacle of a happiness which you deserve'. These last words are a reference to the fact that La Poplinière had just remarried, late in life, after divorcing his colourful and notoriously unfaithful first wife.[42] Neither his new-found happiness nor his career as a novelist was destined to last; in less than two years La Poplinière was dead.

The *Second Preface* – or *Préface dialoguée* – to *Julie* was published by Guérin in pamphlet form[43] on Monday, 16 February. It ran to some ten thousand words, and presented the author – or 'editor' – of the novel in conversation with an imaginary critic, who accuses him – as Rousseau realized that he would in fact be accused in the press – with inconsistency in publishing a work of romantic fiction after attacking dramatic literature so radically in the *Letter to M. d'Alembert*. Rousseau presents the case against him as forcefully as anyone might put it, but he has his answer to every charge. His central argument is that he is writing for a sophisticated public, not an innocent one. People who have been corrupted by art can be healed by art; people accustomed to immoral literature may be led towards virtue by moral literature. By moral literature he does not mean the preachings of conventional moralists, to which no one listens. His defence of *Julie* is that it offers the vision of a better world than that of contemporary Paris – the little community of Clarens, where his heroine and her family and friends, young people with pure hearts, live according to their ideals of virtue, tolerance and love.

A week before the *Second Preface* was published Rousseau sent[44] Coindet instructions for the distribution of complimentary copies. He stipulated that fifteen should be sent at once to Pastor Vernes for his friends in

Geneva, but emphasized that he did not want copies given to M. de Bettier, private secretary to the Maréchal de Luxembourg to whom Rousseau had sent six copies of *Julie* – or to 'those ladies' – because 'this pamphlet is for men of letters. It is not a novel.' It is not clear which 'ladies' Rousseau had in mind; the only lady notably absent from the list is Mme d'Houdetot. He included Mme de Luxembourg, Mme de Verdelin, Mme Dupin, Mme de Chenonceaux and Mme de Créqui, and the three copies for Lorenzy must have included one for the Comtesse de Boufflers as well as one for the Prince de Conti. The men on the list were M. de Luxembourg, Cahagne, Duclos, d'Alembert, Mairan, La Condamine, Margency, Clairaut, Le Mière, Carrión, Lalive, Watelet, Lenieps, Roguin, Blondel d'Azaincourt, Sellon, Bastide, Francueil, Loyseau de Mauléon, Maurice-Quentin de La Tour, Gauffecourt and Trublet.*

This list prompts a question: who among those named, other than those who had been presented with a copy of the novel itself, is to count as a man of letters? La Condamine, Mairan, Le Mière† and Clairaut‡ were men of science rather than of letters. Bastide was a publisher, Crevier§ a scholar and Trublet‖ a literary journalist rather than a man of letters. Cahagne,* however, whose job was that of secretary to the Maréchal de Luxembourg, proved himself an acute literary critic in his correspondence with Rousseau about *Julie*.

Publication of Gravelot's illustrations for *Julie* continued to be held up by Rousseau's exigencies. Although he had promised to say no more about the engravings, he brought the subject up again in another letter[45] to Coindet. He said he had heard doubts expressed about the propriety of the caption 'The Inoculation of Love' being applied to the scene depicting St-Preux kissing the hand of Julie while she was infected with smallpox. Rousseau protested that his own ideas were all pure, and that he was not to blame if a reader chose to soil them. However, he instructed Coindet to find out from Mme de Luxembourg if she thought the words should be suppressed, and if so, to do as she advised. But two days later,[46] he told Coindet that the caption could not be changed because the same words appeared in the text of the novel – so that either the words must stay or the plate must go. In the same letter, Rousseau introduced further criticisms of some of the other plates in the collection. He suggested that the

---

*Added later were Duvoisin, Chaplain at the Dutch Embassy, Crevier, historian of the Roman Empire, and La Poplinière.

†Antoine-Marin Le Mière (or Lemierre), elected a member of the Académie Française in 1780.

‡Alexis-Claude Clairaut (1713–65), geometer.

§Jean-Baptiste-Louis Crevier, professor at the (Jansenist) Collège de Beauvais.

‖L'Abbé Nicolas-Charles-Joseph Trublet (1697–1770).

*L'Abbé Cahagne (1700?–1767) a member of the Académie de Rouen.

engraving captioned 'The Ghost is in Your Heart' would have been admirable if only the face of St-Preux had been given more character and a younger look; the next plate 'Claire, Claire, the Children Sing' was very pretty, but there was still something unsatisfactory about Claire's face and throat and the way the figures were dressed. Besides, he pointed out that the hands of the clock in the illustration 'The Game of Chess' pointed to the wrong time. However, he brought himself to admit that Coindet had put together a charming collection of prints, and he was really displeased only with the last, 'The Death of Julie', and there he was cruelly displeased.

In the same letter Rousseau scolded Coindet for having arranged to bring Bastide with him to Montlouis the following Sunday, since he thought Coindet understood he was not to bring visitors when he came. However, Rousseau could not deny that he would be pleased to see Bastide since he had matters to discuss with him concerning the publication of his abridgement of the Abbé de St-Pierre's *Project for Perpetual Peace*.

In the *Confessions*[47] Rousseau says that he originally gave the text to Bastide to print in his journal *Le Monde* for a fee of twelve louis; then 'as soon as he had possessed himself of the manuscript, he had it printed as a separate pamphlet with some cuts demanded by the censors'. In fact, Bastide kept Rousseau fully informed of what he was doing. On 12 February[48] he told him that a 'cabal' had written against his *Le Monde*, and that St-Pierre's work could not be used there. Instead he proposed to have it printed in pamphlet form in larger type on good paper, with a frontispiece engraved by Cochin of the monument by Pigalle in Reims which represented the 'Fruits of Peace'. Bastide also explained that he had persuaded M. de Malesherbes to censor the abridgement in person, and that it had come back with nothing more than trivial cuts.

Rousseau replied on 13 February[49] protesting that the cuts did not seem to him to be trivial: 'Did you believe that you could make me think that they were? I have never encountered such severity in all I have had printed in France.' Rousseau flatly refused to accept the introduction of the phrase 'without forgetting the virtues of princes,' although he would tolerate the words 'whatever the virtues of princes, let us speak of their interests'. In general, however, he told Bastide that he should consult Duclos about the cuts and do whatever he advised. Rousseau said he was resigned to putting up with mutilations of the pamphlet *'pour l'amour de vous'*.

In any case, the abstract presented St-Pierre's proposals for peace, not Rousseau's own, even though it was something other than a straightforward abridgement. Bastide suggested to Rousseau that 'as the piece is almost entirely yours', it should have a different title. But Rousseau refused to have any title which would make the pamphlet seem more his work than it was: 'I am too proud to have a usurped glory', he wrote.[50] He did not let Bastide see the commentary on St-Pierre's project where he set down his own ideas on peace. 'What would have happened,' Rousseau asks in the *Confessions*,[51] 'if I had added my *Judgement*? Very fortunately I did not speak of it to M. de Bastide, and it was not part of our bargain. It is still in manuscript form[52] among my papers.'

What Bastide did publish, as an introduction to the pamphlet, was Rousseau's letter to him of 5 December 1760 in which he said he had abandoned his original design to produce an abridgement of all St-Pierre's political writings together with a commentary on them, and simply offered the public an abstract of the Abbé's thoughts on peace. Together with this letter from Rousseau, Bastide published a foreword[53] of his own, in which he wrote, 'the analyst is here the creator in many regards'. He cited the '*noble refus*' of Rousseau to be named as even part-author of the work in a manner which could only suggest to the reader that Rousseau was exactly what he denied being. Bastide gave the world the entirely false impression that Rousseau was in substantial agreement with St-Pierre's proposals.

As Rousseau's relations developed with French publishers,* they worsened with Rey. The Luxembourgs and other friends continued to urge him to have no more dealings with the Amsterdam publisher, and Duclos declared[54] that he could not conceive how after Rey's careless blunders, Rousseau could have given him another book. Finally, on 18 February 1761,[55] Rousseau sent Rey a *lettre de rupture*. In it he alleged that Rey had told all the world that he was taking back to Holland the manuscript of *The Social Contract* which Rousseau had entrusted to him 'in the greatest secrecy', a falsehood which Rousseau considered all the worse since he had sold him for 1,000 francs a book for which he could have got 2,000 francs in Paris or even 2,500 francs. 'I am distressed, Monsieur,' the letter ended, 'that we cannot continue to understand one another, but after six years of patience, one gets tired, and as for me, I have reached the end.'

Rey responded[56] vigorously to this attack. He said the allegations against him were false, and could only be the result of the devious behaviour of Coindet, who was always trying to drag information out of him about Rousseau's affairs. Rey insisted that whatever else Rousseau might reproach him for, he could not accuse him of bad faith: 'I do not know how you can carry your charges to the point of having me say I had taken one of your manuscripts away with me. Your portrait was the only thing I brought away, and that was with your consent.'

---

*Rousseau was dealing, through Coindet, with Hippolyte-Lucas Guérin and Pierre-Alexandre de La Tour, for the *Second Preface*, with Nicolas-Bonaventure Duchesne for the *Album of Engravings* for *Julie*; with Étienne-Vincent Robin and Jean-Auguste Grangé for *Julie*; and with Jean-François Bastide for the abridgement of the *Project for Perpetual Peace*.

Rey recalled the agreement he had reached with Rousseau at Mont-morency – that Rousseau should provide a new manuscript; and that he, Rey, would pay 1,000 francs for it, speak of it to no one, and publish it without disclosing that Rousseau was the author: 'I swear to you on everything that is sacred that I have kept my word.' Rey added that there were fifty booksellers in Paris with whom he had had dealings for many years who would testify that he had never done wrong to anyone. Rey did not omit to mention that his wife had read Rousseau's letter – and been 'petrified' by it. He also sent cordial greetings to 'Mlle Levasseur and her mother' – evidence that Mme Levasseur, installed by Grimm at Deuil, was again a presence in Rousseau's household, and surely an unwelcome one.

One of the most emotional letters[57] that Rousseau received about *Julie* came from Charles-Joseph Panckoucke, yet another publisher. Panckoucke did not simply praise the novel, he said it had profoundly influenced him morally, even producing a sort of conversion. In the past, he confessed, he had sought happiness in pleasure, but after reading *Julie*, he had started to 'burn with the love of virtue'. It had needed a divine being to pull him back from the precipice, 'and you, Monsieur, are the god that has wrought the miracle'. Rousseau's reply to this effusion has not been traced; he certainly wanted the moral qualities of *Julie* to be recognized, but he may have suspected that Panckoucke was simply spreading the sort of bird lime with which an aspiring publisher might hope to catch a celebrated author. But there can be no doubt that the book excited genuine emotions.

One *femme du monde* swept off her feet by reading *Julie* was Mme de Polignac, who informed Mme de Verdelin,[58] that while she had never wanted to make the acquaintance of Rousseau as a philosopher, 'Rousseau as the lover of Julie is altogether different ... In my first impulse I was on the point of getting out the horses and going to Montmorency to see him at all costs and telling him how much his tenderness seems to me to elevate him above all other men; to make him show me the portrait of Julie and to kneel before the image of that divine woman.'

Mme de Polignac thought better of her impulse, but Mme de Verdelin passed her letter on to Rousseau, who kept it, making a little collection of the *courrier des admiratrices* he received from the ladies of Paris. Their enthusiasm for the novel seems even to have made him revise his adverse moral judgement of their character. In the *Confessions*,[59] having recalled their praise for a book in which both Frenchmen and Frenchwomen were harshly criticized, he goes on to say that while virtue and morality no longer exist anywhere in Europe, at least some love of virtue and morality can be found in Paris and in Paris alone: 'There exists in Paris an exquisite sensibility which carries the heart towards the image of friendship, love and virtue and makes us cherish in others the pure, tender and noble feelings we no longer have ourselves.'[60]

One of the friends to whom Rousseau sent copies of *Julie* admitted she was hesitant about reading it. This was Mme de Créqui, and he cannot have been surprised by her reaction, since he had written in the first preface, 'novels are necessary for corrupt people' and he knew that the Marquise took pride in her adherence to a Christian life. In thanking the author for the presentation copy, she congratulated[61] him on the preface and expressed the hope that the book contained something more than the science of sex.* She said she knew his writings well enough to be sure there would be good things in it, morality and character – and she asked him to tell her what parts of the book she could allow herself to read. However, in a postscript she reported at midnight that the book had been taken from her – presumably by the priest who acted as her director of conscience.

In his reply[62] Rousseau admitted that *Julie* was a 'dangerous' book: 'I believe, in fact, that it is dangerous for the wicked because it makes one love honest things.' He said he would rather have the blame than the approval of the kind of people who attacked his novel; and he urged Mme de Créqui to form her own opinion of it by reading, or at least running through, the last three volumes, these being the ones where he described Julie's religious experience. He maintained that the worst thing would be for Mme de Créqui to suspend her reading the moment she was scandalized: 'You do not realize, Madame, that I have never made a great thing of philosophy, and I have absolutely detached myself from the party of the Philosophes. I dislike the parade of impiety, and that is a crime they will not forgive. On the other hand, I condemn intolerance, and I wish the unbelievers could be left in peace, since the party of the pious is no more forbearing than the other. Judge into what hands I have fallen!'

Mme de Créqui had evidently sent Rousseau a present in return for the gift of *Julie*, because we find him refusing to accept it: 'I do not sell my books, and if I did I would not sell them so dearly.' As for his health, he told the Marquise that his solitude not only cured his pains, it cured his cares: 'and that means I am getting fat'.

Mme de Créqui protested[63] that she had not attempted to 'pay for the book' and failed to understand how friendship could refuse to accept the trifling bagetelles she had offered him. She explained that she did not know how much of his novel she would read, although she had evidently got it back into her hands once more. She told Rousseau that she had already read the letter in the first volume where duelling was condemned. She

---

*The expression she used was '*l'érudition du coucher*'.

doubted whether reason could abolish such customs; for it was not that men wanted to fight duels, but that they were afraid of other men's contempt if they refused: 'it is a ridiculous weakness, but everything is sacrificed to that folly'.

In Geneva, as in Paris, *Julie* was devoured by readers, and attacked, as Rousseau expected it to be, by the magistrates, the clergy and most, but not all,* of the critics. The first letter[64] of appreciation the author received from his native city was written by Mme Cramer, the wife of the bookseller who imported the novel, Gabriel Cramer. She reported that the first volume had upset the pious, but she suggested that that was only because the author had made his heroine err at the beginning of the story, whereas the pious readers were accustomed to forgiving a sin only when it occurred in the last chapter of a novel. She told the author that while she could not offer him a dissertation on the beauties of his book, she was able to feel them; and as for the author's remark about corrupt people reading novels, she declared, with the gentle cynicism for which she was well known in Geneva, that she rejoiced in such 'felicitous corruption'.

Predictably Rousseau's most hostile critic in that city was Voltaire. 'Stupid, bourgeois, impudent, boring' were his words† for *Julie*; and, guessing that the novel would be a success 'to the shame of this country',[66] he wrote an attack on it entitled *Quatre Lettres sur La Nouvelle Héloïse*, to be published under the name of the Marquis de Ximénès.

The Consistoire of Geneva pronounced the novel 'very dangerous for morals' as soon as it was published, and the Petit Conseil passed a resolution[67] forbidding the Genevese circulating libraries to lend it to their subscribers. Rousseau believed that the actual sale of *Julie* had, at Dr Tronchin's instigation, been banned in Geneva, but in this he was mistaken. The Petit Conseil decided that it would be 'useless' to close the market to a book that was on sale everywhere.[68]

One correspondent[69] wrote from Geneva to assure the author of *Julie* that the applause was universal: 'Everyone here prides himself on having the same *patrie* as you.'[70] Antoine-Jacques Roustan,‡ a young Genevese minister who described himself as Rousseau's 'disciple', was more qualified in his praise. He told[72] the author that while he had read the novel with delight, he was worried about the moral aspects of it. Why, he asked, were

---

*The *Journal Helvétique*, February 1761, could hardly have been more favourable: 'This book will be ranked among the finest that have honoured this century.'

†Another reader who made a joke of Rousseau's remark about novels being for the corrupt was Francueil: 'I must admit I am rather corrupt ... and I read novels with great pleasure and above all yours.'[65]

‡Antoine-Jacques Roustan (1734–1808) was a poet as well as a minister. He had sent some verses to Rousseau in 1757 while still a theology student, and received measured praise for them together with a warning against seeking a career as a man of letters.[71]

there such inflamed descriptions of adulterous love? If the virtue of the lovers was the justification, did not that make it all the more dangerous? Had not Rousseau himself pointed out that representations of love on the stage made a greater impression than the precepts of wisdom? Had he forgotten that the cold exterior of the Genevese people hid a passionate soul? Did he really believe that the youth of Geneva could be prevented from reading his book? Moreover, Roustan said he was dismayed to see that the author had given equal weight to the reasons in favour of atheism and to those against it, and indeed offered hope alone as a basis for belief in God. Roustan suggested that his '*cher Maître*' was well advised to stay in Montmorency since he himself, in Geneva, had been admonished by the magistrates for saying 'in the pulpit much the same things as you'* about the unsuitability of novels as reading for the young.

Another Genevese friend, albeit an exiled one living in Paris, who wrote to Rousseau about *Julie*, was Daniel Roguin, who declared[74] that he met no one who was not enchanted with the book. All the women he knew were persuaded that it was a true story and not a novel, 'on the grounds that no one could speak with such truth of love without feeling it'. Rousseau himself suggests in the *Confessions*[75] that it was just this belief in *Julie* being autobiographical which made it so successful with women:

Everyone believed that an author could only depict the raptures of love if he looked to his own heart as a model; and they were right. I wrote the novel in a state of burning ecstasy. But they were mistaken in thinking that I needed a real object to produce it. They could not understand how intensely I could be excited by imaginary beings. And yet without memories of my youth and of Mme d'Houdetot, what I felt and described would have been no more than the love of Sylphides.

He admits that he deliberately left the public in suspense as to whether the story was fact or fiction: 'Strict moralists may say I should have declared the truth openly, but I think that if I had done so I would have shown more stupidity than candour.'[76]

In the same chapter of the *Confessions*, Rousseau compares his *Julie* with the novels of Richardson, something several critics at the time were doing to his disadvantage. He makes the point that Richardson was admired for the prodigious variety of his scenes and the number of his characters; and he suggests that the merit of his own novel lies precisely in the fact that it has a simple plot, very few characters, and no colourful adventures. He

---

*Roustan had been reprimanded for accusing the authorities of Geneva for allowing the youth of the city to read 'bad books'.[73]

suggests that his critics in looking for another Richardson were bound to be disappointed, since he had different aims from Richardson's.

Ordinary readers, Rousseau is pleased to recall, were not disappointed and he reports in the *Confessions*[77] one anecdote which he found 'more flattering than all the compliments' he received: 'A certain *grande dame* was dressing for a carnival ball after supper, when she began reading *Julie*. When the servants told her her carriage was ready she instructed them to wait. At 2 a.m. she was still too engrossed in reading to go to the carriage. At 4 a.m. she told her staff to take out the horses, and she went to bed to spend the rest of the night reading.'

One of the most carefully considered criticisms[78] of *Julie* that Rousseau received came from a private secretary attached to M. de Luxembourg, the Abbé Cahagne, who in commenting on Julie's rejection of St-Preux in the novel, referred to Rousseau's heroine as being 'unfaithful to love'. Rousseau tried[79] to refute this accusation. 'To what is she unfaithful?' he demanded.

To her word? She made no promise that she did not keep. To her love? It is all too clear that that remained in her heart intact. To her duty? There you raise, Monsieur, a big question. By nature, she must be more faithful to her character than to her lover. She felt remorse over the death of her mother. Her father dared show her that the same danger faced him. What shall she do in such a situation? Does she want to run that terrible risk? Could she bear the thought of having brought death to her father and her mother? ... Always in a novel when one depicts a particular action, it is not a matter of the moral question but the imitation of nature. It is not a matter of knowing whether Julie did well or ill in marrying Wolmar, but whether ... in accordance with her character, she would choose to obey her father, or having seen him on his knees shedding torrents of tears, she could bear to witness his despair without flinching.

The Abbé Cahagne was perhaps the first to question an element of Rousseau's novel which has continued to puzzle many readers and critics: its patriarchalism. The novelist neither expresses nor implies any disapproval of the tyranny – the moral blackmail, indeed – exercised by Julie's father over her: and he treats as normal and virtuous the preference Julie gives to her filial love for a despotic father over her romantic love for her tutor, having her agree not simply to obey a paternal injunction to marry within her class but to marry the one man her father chooses. As Rousseau makes clear in his letter to Cahagne, his novel does not depict a conflict between love and duty, but between one form of love and another.

The one place in which Rousseau does seem, indirectly, to condemn the patriarchalism of his story is in a footnote where he recalls the lawsuit of the Comte de La Bedoyère, who secured the annulment of his son's marriage on the grounds that the bride was an actress. Rousseau cites this as an example of parental tyranny, 'where the honour of rank insolently and publicly attacked decency, duty and conjugal trust, and where the unworthy father, having won the suit, dared to disinherit his son for refusing to be an unscrupulous man'.[80]

Ironically, this was the first cut demanded by the censors of his novel in Paris and the one Rousseau most readily agreed to, if only on the grounds that he had been misinformed about the details of the case. In accepting the cut, Rousseau told[81] Malesherbes he did not know that the Comte de La Bedoyère had been reconciled with his son and died; 'we must leave the ashes of the dead in peace'.

Rousseau's accommodating attitude in the matter of this cut encouraged Malesherbes to press forward with his efforts to have a third edition of *Julie* published in Paris on terms that would be advantageous to the author. On 16 February,[82] Malesherbes was able to inform Rousseau that all was arranged. He told Rousseau not to feel indebted to him for his intervention, since 'I have only done what I thought just.' One cannot doubt that Malesherbes was well disposed to Rousseau, quite apart from responding to pressure from Mme de Luxembourg to help him. On the other hand, Malesherbes was operating in an atmosphere of mounting intolerance in matters of religion; and he made it clear to Rousseau that there would have to be many more cuts in addition to the footnote about the Comte de La Bedoyère. To his letter of 16 February Malesherbes attached a list of nearly fifty excisions and amendments that would be required for the 'third edition'. All occurred in the last two volumes of the novel, and all concerned utterances offensive to Catholic orthodoxy, although the censor suggested that some of the opinions went beyond Protestant heresy and called into question any religious belief.

In his reply[83] to Malesherbes's letter, Rousseau expressed his gratitude for the magistrate's efforts on his behalf, and explained, with a certain lightness of touch, his difficulty in accepting the cuts which 'the theologians' had demanded. He observed that they were trying to convert his Julie into a very orthodox person, and were doing so without much subtlety: 'I confess I like her better, lovable if heretical, than bigoted and narrow as they make her.'

Rousseau realized that it was not Malesherbes himself who had drawn up the list of cuts – he suspected the Abbé de Graves, although it was, in fact, the new Chief Censor, Christophe Picquet* – and Rousseau attached

---

*Appointed on the death of Charles-Alexandre Salley in January 1761. Salley was an enlightened man and a close friend of Deleyre's. Picquet was more rigid and severe.

to his letter to Malesherbes a memorandum,[84] written with more severity and designed to be read by the censor, in which he said what he thought of the various cuts proposed. Some he considered tolerable enough, but others, and the most important, he would not accept because they would undermine the whole purpose of the book. He said he did not wish to be read in France if that meant using six volumes of tedium simply to provide a handbook of love for youth and instruct his readers in the science of sex.* He complained that the Catholics who censored the book wanted a Protestant to be a Protestant in their way and not in his own. As for Julie's 'profession of faith' Rousseau refused categorically to suppress it, since such a suppression would be taken as a repudiation by him of his own Protestant beliefs. He ended the memorandum by declaring that he could not see how the novel could possibly be put into a form that would be acceptable for printing in France.

Nevertheless, Rousseau seems to have had some hope of persuading Malesherbes to overrule the censor, since he wrote[85] to Coindet, after he had received Malesherbes's letter and memorandum, to say that the proposed 'third edition' which Duchesne and Guérin had been offered could not be published immediately since time must be allowed for Robin to sell out the two earlier editions – the Dutch edition and his own. Otherwise Robin might use that as a pretext for not paying Rey what he owed him.

In spite of Malesherbes's efforts to keep secret his plans to have a 'third edition' of *Julie* brought out by Duchesne and Guérin, rumours reached the ears of Robin, who wrote[86] frantically to Rousseau saying that such a publication would be ruinous for him and a violation of his agreement with Rey. He said he still had 300 unsold copies of his own edition in his warehouse and the whole stock of the Dutch edition: 'You owe it to yourself and your reputation to oppose with all your strength the promotion of this third edition.' For some reason this letter did not reach Rousseau, and Robin also approached him through the intermediary of a friend of Rey's, a Protestant banker named Dangirard, who asked[87] Rousseau to intervene in the interests of Rey, whose edition of *Julie* had yet to be sold, and of Robin, who still had two thousand copies of the novel he had difficulty in selling. Once Robin had sold out his stock, Dangirard explained, he would be able to meet his commitments to Rey and pay him.

Rousseau smelt a rat in all this, and he said so. Knowing the enormous demand for *Julie*, he did not believe that Robin had sold only the few copies he claimed to have sold. So he replied[88] to Dangirard saying first that he doubted whether a third edition of *Julie* was in preparation, and

---

*Rousseau repeated Mme de Créqui's phrase '*l'érudition du coucher*'.

secondly that if there was, he had no part in it. He suggested that Robin had himself circulated the rumours of a third edition as a means of evading his obligations to Rey. He added: 'I have received no letter from Robin, and if I had, I am sure I would not have found a single word of truth in it.'

Dangirard attempted[89] to persuade Rousseau that Robin was honest, saying that he himself had received from him, on behalf of Rey, 8,000 livres six weeks before it was due, and declaring that Rousseau had no reason to be suspicious of him. Rousseau, in reply,[90] said he did not suspect, he judged and would willingly testify to Robin's inexactitude: 'The calculation of Robin's profits is easy, because it is obvious ... and I will say to you that it is even more uncommon for a liar to declare his true profits than it is for people in the trade to know them.' Rousseau made no attempt to soften his rebuff to Dangirard – 'if friends of Robin want to give me advice they should wait for me to consult them' – and he made it clear that nothing said on behalf of Robin would influence his attitude. The anchorite of Montmorency was wiser to the tricks of the book trade than the banker of the rue Coquillière.

Rey himself wrote an agitated letter[91] at the beginning of March, having heard from Robin about the rumoured 'third edition' of *Julie*. He said he did not believe the rumour, but if it was true, he suspected Coindet was involved. He said he assumed Rousseau was too honest not to have written to M. de Malesherbes to protest against something which would be inimical to Robin's interests and his own. The same letter mentioned that *Julie* had gone into a second edition in London, and would soon be available there in an English translation.

Rousseau had indeed been thinking about writing to Malesherbes, not to support Robin's protest against a third edition, but to explain his own position on the cuts that Malesherbes wished to have made in order to allow a third edition to be authorized. Rousseau took his time over this, as he informed Coindet on 4 March,[92] because he was kept so busy by visitors and correspondence.

Coindet, having seen Malesherbes in Paris, advised[93] Rousseau that it would be useless for him to go to the trouble of replying in detail to the magistrate's observations. Evidently Coindet had the impression that Malesherbes would not insist on the cuts. 'He is persuaded that you are not without good reasons for wishing to leave *Julie* as it is in preparing a new edition.' Coindet was mistaken. Malesherbes was determined not to allow a third edition of *Julie* unless the cuts were made; and Rousseau, who did not share Coindet's optimism on the subject, wrote again at some length[94] about the various cuts that were called for in Malesherbes's memorandum. Again, he said he would allow some minor excisions, but for the most part, he insisted the pages must stay exactly as they are. If St-Preux chooses to be a heretic on the subject of divine grace, that is his affair. Besides, it is necessary that he should defend the freedom of the will, since he speaks elsewhere of the abuse of that freedom as the cause of moral evil. It is absolutely essential that he should be a Molinist so as not to be a Manichean, and it ought to be better for him to be seen joining the Catholics in rejecting the doctrines of Calvin than to be seen rejecting those of the Pope. As for what M. de Malesherbes calls a revolt against the Scriptures, I myself call it a submission to the authority of God and Reason, which ought to have priority over that of the Bible, and serve as its basis.

Rousseau claimed that Protestants – unlike Catholics, who 'did not want to yield on a single point of dogma' – were willing to 'shed a few branches in order to save the trunk of the tree of their religion.' The protagonists of his novel were Protestants, 'and what right,' he demanded, 'and what inspection can the Catholic Church claim over anyone who does not acknowledge its authority?'

After Rousseau's death, Malesherbes recorded his own account[95] of the episode:

It was Mme de Luxembourg and Mme de Boufflers who told me that Rousseau had sold his works at a miserable price to a Dutch publisher, and they thought it scandalous that he was reduced to copying music for a living. So I tried to help him by arranging for a French publisher to pay him well for a new edition of *Julie* to be printed in France. The trouble was that in passing it to the censor, some small points offensive to Catholics were found. These called for only trivial cuts, but I knew that Rousseau would be incensed if the cuts were made without his consent, so he was told about them. He protested that we wanted to make his Julie a Catholic. He refused to make the cuts, so I could not grant the *privilège*. As a result, all he received was a sixth of what he would have had if the book had been authorized by my office. I do not know if the publishers provided such royalties as Rousseau did receive, or whether Mme de Luxembourg contributed the larger part. The book was pirated in several places. Rousseau wanted to be unhappy; he wanted to be poor.

Malesherbes was mistaken in suspecting that Mme de Luxembourg contributed to the moneys Rousseau received for *Julie*. It was the publication of *Émile* in which she interested herself from the start; and indeed no sooner was the idea of an authorized third edition of *Julie* abandoned, than Malesherbes was pressed by Mme de Luxembourg to give *Émile* his blessing and encouragement. In connection with *Émile*, it was not fanciful to believe that Mme de Luxembourg, as Rousseau's honorary literary agent, might have found a way of subsidizing him without his knowledge. But Malesherbes is manifestly unfair in claiming that his office had asked only for 'trivial cuts', and that Rousseau was motivated by a perverse desire to be unhappy and poor. Whatever Rousseau's motives in other cases, he can clearly be seen, in resisting the distortion of things said in his novel and its mutilation, to be taking a stand on a matter of principle and accepting the financial loss not joyfully but stoically, as the price of his integrity.

Mme de Créqui was one devout Catholic who found nothing offensive in *Julie*, once she had allowed herself to read it from cover to cover. She remarked in a letter[96]* of praise to the author that many people imitated his heroine in her sin, but very few devoted themselves, as she did, to educating their children with care, and living in domestic peace and honouring their husbands. Rousseau was especially pleased to have his friend's approval and promised[97] to visit her when he was less harassed than he was at that moment; he added that even if she acted on her plan to leave Paris for a distant corner of the kingdom, 'I will come on foot to make a pilgrimage to you.'

Rousseau's abridgement of St-Pierre's *Project for Perpetual Peace* was published with 'tacit permission' at the beginning of March and again Rousseau sent Coindet a list[98] of people to whom presentation copies should be sent, a list that was short, he explained, because he was the editor and not the author of the work. He allocated one each to M. and Mme de Luxembourg, two for the Comtesse de Boufflers (the second presumably for the Prince de Conti), and one each for Lorenzy, d'Alembert, Carrión, Lenieps and Roguin. Rousseau also proposed to send several copies to Geneva. He explained to Coindet that he was extremely busy 'keeping open house despite myself and running a bureau of correspondence'.

One of the people who took advantage of that 'open house' made a record[99] of his visit in his journal – a Hungarian count named Joseph Teleki de Szek, who had achieved some success with a book entitled *Essai sur la faiblesse des esprits-forts*, first published in Leyden in 1760. Teleki recalls that Rousseau had walked five miles from Montmorency to Saint-Denis to meet him and his companion, Duvoisin, Swiss chaplain at the Dutch Embassy, only to be disappointed because they had to postpone their visit to the following day. They were nevertheless warmly welcomed when they finally arrived at Montlouis, although Teleki was startled to see their host dressed in a shabby old dressing-gown, covered with stains: 'If we

---

*In the same letter she mentioned that she was buying her difficult son a colonel's commission for 50,000 livres. In the end it cost her 80,000.

had not known it was Rousseau, we should have taken him for a scruffy
cobbler, seeing him in a room without any elegance whatever where he
eats and where his meals are cooked.'

Even so, the rustic charm of the cottage in which Rousseau himself
delighted was not entirely lost on the Hungarian count. If he was unimpressed by the ground-floor room which served as the dining-room and
kitchen, he noted on the floor above 'a room which is prettier – indeed
one could describe it as really pretty'. Teleki was even more pleased with
the *donjon*:

In this *donjon* there are some pretty things, very simply displayed. I
observed a printed – or engraved – portrait of Frederick II of Prussia. At
the foot of the frame there was stuck a piece of paper bearing two French
verses violently attacking the Prussian king, although I do not remember
exactly how they were worded. We started to chat in the *donjon*; Rousseau
spoke about my book *Essai sur la faiblesse des esprits-forts* and praised it
more than it deserved. Afterwards we repaired to a table in the kitchen-
cum-dining-room. We ate little, but well. There was soup, veal and rabbit
in a sauce. Also a *pâté*, well cut into, good butter, ripe grapes; in a word,
an excellent dinner, but utterly simple, without any kind of ceremony,
and it did not please me any the less for being so simple.

A girl, or rather a woman, dined with us. She was, as I saw, M.
Rousseau's servant, housekeeper, cook, etc. She was not beautiful, so no
one would suspect that she was anything else.

Count Teleki's judgement of Thérèse's looks was generally shared; but
time was to prove that if she had lost her sex-appeal for Rousseau, she had
not lost it for others. After the dinner at Montlouis, Rousseau accompanied
Teleki and Duvoisin on foot to La Barre to meet their carriage for Paris.
On the way he showed them the château and gardens of the Maréchal de
Luxembourg, and the Petit Château. Nearby, Teleki noted seeing 'some
Indian arrows which Rousseau sometimes amuses himself by shooting'.

The entry in Teleki's journal ends with a description of Rousseau
himself.

He is forty-five years old★, thin, small rather than large of stature, stooping
a little, quick and vivacious in his speech. Endowed with an extraordinary
intelligence, he has much of what the French call *esprit*. His judgement is
sure, his thought penetrating and he expresses himself easily. I do not
believe that at this time any author knows how to put more substance into

★In 1761 Rousseau was actually forty-nine, so he must have looked younger than his
years.

his writings than he. His conversation does not languish. He talks a lot –
on this occasion, at any rate, he was talkative; and yet one cannot think
of him as a good-humoured man. In his style and his utterances, he is
bizarre, or so it seemed to me, and he tries to appear more bizarre than he
really is.'

Teleki also suspected that Rousseau dressed in the odd way he did just
to be original: 'Probably because of his hammer toes, or for some other
reason, he has a hole like a star cut at the tip of his slippers, and the sole
of the slipper is made of wood – this, he says, is in order to have something
dry to walk on, not to make the slippers last longer.' Rousseau told Teleki
he slept only one hour a night, but Teleki, like others to whom Rousseau
complained of insomnia, seems to have considered the claim exaggerated,
especially as Rousseau looked fit and fresh with 'bright, clear eyes'. Teleki
also repeats the widespread opinion that Rousseau was poor 'because he
liked to be poor'. His journal entry ends with the note: 'I had returned to
Paris by eight o'clock in the evening.'

Another admirer who descended on the author of *Julie* was Jacques
Necker, the future Finance Minister of Louis XVI, who took with him to
sup at Montlouis the Abbé Morellet. Although Rousseau may have been
less than wholly delighted to entertain Morellet, Necker would have been
assured of the special welcome Rousseau reserved for compatriots from
Geneva; the more so after Necker had written[100] to Rousseau about the
moral qualities of his novel *Julie*: 'What subtlety in those six volumes –
not the subtlety of metaphysical floating in the clouds, but that which
pushes everyday virtues to their highest level without discouraging those
who want to reach it.'

Rousseau was less impressed by an admiring letter[101] about *Julie*, written
the same day by Bastide, who declared himself, in similar terms to those
of his fellow-publisher Panckoucke, to be eager to have Rousseau as his
moral guide in life. 'I am inflamed with the desire to find a master to teach
me and put me on the path of truth,' he declared, only to go on to make
it obvious that what he really wanted was to interview Rousseau on the
subject of *Julie* and then to publish 'my reflections and your replies' in
book form.

Rousseau was horrified by the project. He wrote[102]* at once to Coindet
instructing him to tell Bastide that he could publish what he liked about
Julie, but 'as for me, I want no interviews or conferences about it, and I
absolutely do not wish to hear it talked about'. He added that he was far

---

*Bastide's letter may have reached Montlouis with Coindet's courier, as Rousseau was
able to reply on the same day, a Monday, on which Bastide wrote.

too busy to see Bastide until the following Sunday,[103] when Coindet might bring him with him to Montlouis on condition that the subject of *Julie* was not introduced into their conversation.

The success of *Julie* left little room for the author to think about that of his abridgement of St-Pierre's *Project for Perpetual Peace*, but its appearance was nevertheless welcomed. The Seven Years War was going badly for France, despite the victories at Minorca, Fort St David and elsewhere, and the public was increasingly impatient for the conflict to end. In the early months of 1760 there were diplomatic overtures at The Hague towards an armistice, but they had been suspended without accomplishing anything. Rousseau's note to Bastide, dated 5 December 1759, and printed[104] at the beginning of the abridgement, speaks of seeing 'peace soon re-established between the powers'; but that peace did not come until 1763, by which time France had suffered even more reverses in battle. And yet however earnest Rousseau's own desire as a neutral but deeply francophile observer to see the war end, he had not, as we have seen, any faith in St-Pierre's project for future peace. More than most people, Rousseau realized that the Seven Years War was a new kind of war, different from the dynastic wars which had exercised the mind of St-Pierre, and for which his formula of federating monarchies might seem an appropriate remedy. In the course of his duties at the Embassy in Venice in 1744 Rousseau had monitored the progress of one such dynastic war; and he could see that the Seven Years War was not a similar quarrel over thrones in Europe, but a struggle for colonial territory overseas. When he had received his two compatriots, Favre and De Tournes, at Montlouis in December 1759, he had outlined[105] to them his understanding of the war as an imperial conflict; the English were out to take the place of the Spanish in building the greatest colonial and commercial empire in the world, and were fighting to prevent the French from doing likewise. Thus Rousseau saw as the significant events of the war, not the battles of Westphalia, Minden or Marburg, but the defeat of French armies in India and Canada and the Caribbean.

His own formula for peace, which he kept unpublished – and congratulated himself in the *Confessions*[106]* for his prudence in doing so – was to forbid territorial expansions; peace, he argues in that text, depends on states being content with their existing frontiers. Unlike most liberals of the French Enlightenment, Rousseau had never looked on England as the 'mirror of liberty', for no form of kingdom could be that for him. Only in a republic, he believed, could true liberty be achieved; and only republics

---

*Rousseau suggests that St-Pierre was able to publish dissident opinions with impunity because he was regarded 'rather a religious preacher than a political writer'; he himself, as a layman who was not even French, could not expect the same tolerance.

could be expected to live side by side in orderly tranquillity. And while Rousseau kept his criticisms of St-Pierre under wraps, he made no secret of his republicanism. The manuscript he had promised Rey for publication – the book that was to be known as *The Social Contract* – had nothing to say about international relations; but it put a case for republican government which was soon to rival the claims of the constitutional liberalism of Montesquieu and the enlightened absolutism of Voltaire, for the support of French political opinion. As the experience of the Seven Years War changed the popular French image of England from a 'mirror of liberty' into that of a nation of rapacious *conquistadores*, Rousseau's version of a *thèse républicaine* was to become increasingly influential. But when he said to Favre and De Tournes, 'You will soon see a revolution,'[107] he cannot have imagined what was to happen in 1789, still less that he would be accused of provoking it.

The visit of the publisher Bastide to Montlouis seems to have passed off without embarrassment, and although Rousseau had nothing further published by him, he did send Bastide presentation copies of his next few books. One visitor Rousseau was most reluctant to receive was the Abbé de Graves, the priest with Jesuit affiliations whom Malesherbes had used as the intermediary in organizing the projected third edition of *Julie*. Rousseau was not fully informed about these negotiations, but he suspected that 'Jesuits', and the Abbé de Graves with them, were responsible for designating the cuts that Malesherbes had demanded in the text of *Julie*. To Coindet's suggestion of bringing the Abbé with him to Montlouis at the end of February, Rousseau replied coolly:[108] 'However amiable the Abbé de Graves may be, since I do not know him, and since everyone in France is amiable, it seems to me that nothing is less pressing than exploiting his goodness to bring him to Montmorency without knowing whether or not you will make him spend a disagreeable day here, and me too. You are always so little sensitive to such dangers that I must be wary on behalf of us both.'

It was at about this time that there appeared in Paris the *Quatre lettres* of the Marquis de Ximénès on the subject of *Julie*, a pamphlet which was actually written by Voltaire. Among Rousseau's remarks in the novel which are singled out to undermine the author's standing with his aristocratic friends is one to the effect that 'any nobleman is descended from a knave'. To drive the point home more heavily, a question is added: 'Do you not know that a certain Montmorency who has the honour of providing your lodging is a rather fine nobleman?' Fortunately for Rousseau, neither the nobleman concerned nor his wife was swayed by such cheap polemics. Mme de Luxembourg wrote[109] to Rousseau as soon as she had read it:

There is a lackey of a Marquis de Ximénès who is staying with M. de Voltaire at Les Délices, and who has written *Quatre lettres* against *Julie* which are stupid, malicious, impertinent. Is it possible that a man as intelligent as Voltaire should allow such base jealousy to enter his soul? However, one can only believe that he knows he could never write a book like yours. We see nowhere in his writings the elevation and force of genius which is everywhere in the charming *Julie*. Farewell, most lovable of men – and most loved.

Rousseau, profoundly relieved by the generosity of this reaction to Voltaire's malice, wrote[110]: 'One must throw oneself on one's knees in reading the words at the end of your letter, kiss them, sigh and say "Why is she not here?"' Ximénès and Voltaire, he declared, could attack *Julie* as they liked; his book did not aim to please them. He added that he was counting the hours to see the Maréchale and her husband once more at Montmorency. In the event, Rousseau did not have to wait long. They were installed in their château for their Easter visit by 12 March, rather earlier in the spring than usual.

However, the Luxembourgs' Easter visit to Montmorency in 1761 afforded Rousseau less pleasure than other times he had spent in their company at the château. In the *Confessions* he speaks of a feeling that he was losing favour with Mme de Luxembourg if not with the Maréchal, 'who seemed to redouble in every day his kindnesses and friendship towards me'.[111] Since Rousseau had no more books that he wanted to read aloud to them, he was no longer invited to Mme de Luxembourg's bedroom, and he hardly saw her except at table, and even there, he says, 'the place next to her was no longer reserved for me'.[112]

He was perhaps being less than reasonable in expecting this privilege to continue indefinitely, for the fact that the place next to his hostess had been reserved for him for so long is itself remarkable, considering that the Maréchale was accustomed to entertaining guests of the highest rank. Rousseau mentions several dukes and marquises being regular guests and the Duc de Choiseul, the most important minister* of the kingdom as an occasional one. It is a measure of Rousseau's personal charm as well as of the esteem in which literary men were held in the France of the Enlightenment that he could have been given precedence over such persons at anyone's table.

The Duc de Choiseul, Rousseau recalls,[113] was well disposed towards him and even offered him a job if he wished to return to the diplomatic

---

*Nominally Foreign Secretary, Étienne-François, Duc de Choiseul (1719–85) dominated the government of Louis XV from 1758 to 1770.

service; Rousseau did not take advantage of the offer, but he says he conceived the highest admiration for Choiseul as a politician. At the time of the struggle for power at Versailles between Choiseul and Mme de Pompadour, Rousseau says[114] he 'prayed' for the success of M. de Choiseul, if in part, as he admits, because he had always disliked Mme de Pompadour 'who on no occasion was ever disposed to be of service to me'. In saying this, Rousseau seems to have forgotten that he had himself rebuffed the gestures of interest she had once extended to the author of *Le Devin du village*. Choiseul, too, was destined to be regarded a year or two later as an enemy.

In the *Confessions* Rousseau speaks of several friends of Mme de Luxembourg who showed themselves reluctant to be friends of his. Among the 'literary set' there was the President Charles Hénault, who had some renown as an author, although Rousseau noted chiefly his vanity; there was Mme Du Deffand, who had the kind of malicious wit that made Rousseau feel particularly uncomfortable, and there was also her *protégée* and d'Alembert's platonic mistress, Mlle de L'Espinasse, whose superior moral and intellectual qualities might have recommended her to Rousseau, but whom he mistrusted because he thought of her as 'a great friend of Voltaire's'.

Rousseau sought consolation for the coolness of such people in further intimacy with the Maréchal, whose friendliness was unfailing. Banished from the seat next to his hostess, he took to sitting next to his host, and in order to do so, he stopped going to the château for dinner – an afternoon meal which the Maréchal seldom took – and went there for supper instead. They would go for walks together in the grounds of the château. Rousseau noticed that the Maréchal was ageing, losing his old vigour, and eager in the evening to retire, but since Rousseau also went early to his insomniac's bed, he was happy to leave the table at the same time as his host.

Letters about *Julie* continued to reach the author from correspondents all over Europe. One persistent admirer was Charlotte Bourette,★ the *patronne* of a Paris hostelry named the Café Allemand, who made a habit of addressing celebrated authors in verse. Well known in literary circles as '*la Muse limonadière*,† she had started sending poems to Rousseau as early as 1754, and in February 1761[116] she burst once again into rhyme: *Avec quel art vous nous peignez, Rousseau ... C'est votre coeur qu'en forme le tableau.* However, Mme Bourette made the mistake of begging in exchange for this encomium a cut-price extra copy of *Julie*, having already put her foot

★Born Charlotte Reynier, 1714.

†This was also the title of a collection of verses she published in Paris in 1755, in which she printed[115] a guarded letter to her from Rousseau, dated 13 September 1754, acknowledging some verses addressed to him.

in it by inviting[117] Rousseau to visit her and drink coffee out of a gold-encrusted cup that Voltaire had presented to her.

Rousseau in his reply, informed her briskly that he had no spare copies of his novel to dispose of; he also expressed the hope, if he was ever able to accept her kind invitation to take coffee with her, that she would not offer him the gilded cup of M. de Voltaire: 'for I would not drink from the cup of that man'.[118]

A rather more serious letter[119] about *Julie* reached Rousseau about this time from Moultou in Geneva. The letter began with words of praise for a book which made a reader feel the 'dignity of man' and which defended nature against those who would impute men's crimes and follies to her. Moultou then went on to explain why the book had met with so much disapproval in Geneva, and did so in a way which made it clear that he himself was among those who disapproved.

'A seducer is shown as a philosopher, and a girl who throws herself at his head is shown as a model of virtue,' Moultou observed laconically. He was ready to admit that the noble conduct of St-Preux almost compensated for the faults of Julie, but he agreed, he said, with Rousseau's critics on the subject of Julie's marriage: 'How can one understand Julie's breaking a sacred union, one sworn to heaven, and then contracting a marriage that is almost adulterous, thus betraying two men at the same time? I confess that my mind has no answer to that question, although my heart feels that Julie would not be Julie if she did not have the same tenderness for her father as for her lover.'

Moultou went on to implore Rousseau to use his great gifts to write something that would speak to the condition of Geneva, since *Julie*, as he realized, had been written chiefly for Paris. He pointed out that in Geneva there were neither atheists to be taught respect for faith nor pious persecutors to be taught toleration. The problem of Geneva was that its citizens were falling short of that civic virtue which Montesquieu among others had said was necessary to the health of any republic. 'How is it that the principles of a republic become corrupt? What means can be found to retard that process? There, Monsieur, is a subject for you; one which is worthy of you; and now is the moment for you to address yourself to it.'

This was, in fact, something Rousseau had already done in the book he had offered to Rey, *The Social Contract*.[120]

CENSORSHIP

The *Four Letters*[1] against Rousseau's *Julie* which Voltaire had published in the name of the Marquis de Ximénès put an end to any pretence of friendship between the two philosophers. The pamphlet contained more abuse of the novelist than criticism of the novel, and seems to have done more harm to Voltaire than to Rousseau.[2] Several of Voltaire's closest friends were shocked by it, among them d'Alembert, who wrote[3] to Voltaire saying he had a 'serious quarrel' to pick with him 'about that letter you had addressed to you, full of injuries and personal abuse of Rousseau. You will not believe how much it is condemned, even by those who are most critical of Rousseau's novel and his conduct.'

In his reply[4] to d'Alembert, Voltaire blamed 'your Jean-Jacques' as he called him, for the disunity which prevailed among the *philosophes*:

That arch-fool, if he had let himself be guided by you, might have amounted to something, but he prefers to stand alone; he writes against the theatre after producing a bad play; he writes against France, which nourishes him: he finds four or five rotten planks of the barrel of Diogenes and climbs inside to bark; he forsakes his friends, and he sends me the most impertinent letter a fanatic ever scribbled. He accuses me, in these very words, of having corrupted Geneva in return for the refuge the city has given me.

D'Alembert stuck to his view that Voltaire had done wrong to attack Rousseau publicly at a time when, more than ever, philosophers should present a united front to the world. He repeated[5] his reproaches to Voltaire: 'Jean-Jacques is a sick man of great intellectual powers, but he has those powers only when his mind is inflamed; he must neither be cured nor abused.'

Besides d'Alembert, Rousseau had an even more useful champion in

Malesherbes. Voltaire's attacks on *Julie* did nothing to diminish that magistrate's eagerness to have a third edition published on terms which would be advantageous to the author, but he did find Rousseau an extremely difficult author to help. After Malesherbes had explained once more that certain cuts would be necessary before the book could be published in France, Rousseau dug in his heels and refused.

While this uncompromising attitude put a brake on the project for an official 'third edition' of *Julie*, it did not prevent the proliferation of pirate editions, from which the author received no fees or royalties. As his fame grew the public assumed that he must be doing well financially, and his postbag brought regular appeals for charity. One such correspondent was Francis-Joseph Marteau, who wrote[6] to ask Rousseau's help for a young girl he described as 'another Julie'. Her name was Louison and her story was that she had been sold by her mother at the age of fifteen to a lascivious nobleman from whose house she had recently fled after giving birth to his child; she now sought work as a domestic servant to avoid being sold by her mother to another libertine. M. Marteau begged Rousseau to find a decent place for the girl; 'her fate,' he wrote dramatically, 'is in your hands'.

Rousseau showed the letter to the Luxembourgs, and arranged for the girl to be taken to be interviewed by Mme de Luxembourg on her return to Paris. M. Marteau's 'Julie' appears, however, to have been lacking the somewhat stringent qualifications needed for a place on Mme de Luxembourg's domestic staff, and she had to be content with a gift of money.

Another unknown correspondent had a curious grievance to voice to the author of *Julie*. He complained[7] that his mistress had been so inspired by the virtuous conduct of Rousseau's heroine that she had refused to go on sleeping with him, despite the fact that she had borne his child. 'I have sworn eternal hatred for you,' the writer declared. 'Only death can end the agony you have caused me.'

In the same month of April Rousseau received the first of a series of letters[8] from Dom Deschamps, a Benedictine monk with the incongruous aim in life of providing for atheistical materialism a better metaphysical basis than he thought it had been given by its adherents, and he tried to capture the interest of Rousseau as well as that of more likely sympathizers such as Helvétius, d'Alembert and Diderot. Writing under the pseudonym of Du Parc, he sent Rousseau the preface of his projected book and offered to send more. Rousseau's immediate response[9] was predictably negative: 'I was ill, Monsieur, when I received your preface, and now I return it for you to burn.'

Why, he demanded, did M. Du Parc wish to disturb the tranquillity of a solitary man whose one consolation amidst every kind of suffering was the simplicity of his faith and his hope for another life?

Rousseau observed that his correspondent based his system on the purest abstractions, and that, he said, was 'a method which is very suspect to me, as too little within the range of my faculties ... The method of analysis is good in geometry, but in philosophy it seems to me to be worthless.' He summed up Du Parc's whole system as a *rêverie*.

The metaphysician was not to be put off. 'If my system is a *rêverie*,' he demanded in a second letter,[10] 'how can my preface have disturbed your tranquillity?'

During the Luxembourgs' Easter visit, Rousseau told them he was thinking of leaving Montmorency. The reason he gave them was that he had discovered that the local water was bad for his condition. But it seems from the *Confessions*[11] that he was also contemplating retirement to a more isolated area for the sake of greater repose. As soon as he had accumulated a capital of eight or ten thousand francs, he says, he hoped to move to some provincial place where he would 'cease to trouble the public with my affairs and end my days in peace'. He told the Luxembourgs that he had heard of something in the region of Touraine where the water was better. The Maréchal, dismayed at the thought of his going so far away, offered him a house at Merlou in the valley of the Oise. Mme de Luxembourg, after her return to Paris, reminded[12] him to visit Merlou to see if he liked the house. In the *Confessions*,[13] Rousseau says he was attracted by the idea, but on the day appointed for him to make the trip in one of the Maréchal's carriages he was too ill to travel, and the project came to nothing, which he afterwards thought was all to the good since he discovered that Merlou belonged to Mme de Luxembourg and not to her husband, and he did not want to be bound to her by the sort of obligations which had bound him to Mme d'Épinay.

An embarrassing situation arose at about this time between Rousseau and the Comtesse de Boufflers. 'It has always been my misfortune,' he writes in the *Confessions*,[14] 'to have had to deal with women writers.' He says he might have expected in the company of the highest nobility at Montmorency to escape them, but, to his dismay, the Comtesse de Boufflers wrote a tragedy in prose which was read – and applauded – in the Prince de Conti's circles, and then thrust upon him in the expectation of further praise. 'This,' Rousseau continues, 'I gave her, albeit in moderation, as the play deserved.' He says he then made matters worse by pointing out to the author that her play was very like *L'Esclave généreux*, which was based on the play *Oroonoko* by the English writer Aphra Behn. When he wrote his *Confessions* Rousseau had grown to dislike the Comtesse intensely, and he goes so far as to describe her play as a 'plagiarism', which it was not.

Nevertheless, he must have made some such accusation when he wrote* to her about it, for we find the Comtesse protesting[15] to him: 'I am very touched by your generosity, your frankness and your friendship for me, Monsieur, and I thank you for it, but I see very well that you do not know me yet. I am incapable of appropriating what does not belong to me – not only because of honesty, but also partly from pride.' The Comtesse sent him the complete manuscript of her play so that he could judge for himself how original it was. She also sent him a cutting from the English *Spectator* which recorded the incident in the Caribbean which had inspired her play.

A few days later,[16] the Comtesse wrote again to inform him that she would obtain from England the play by Aphra Behn which he had mentioned to her, and which she had previously not read. If it proved to be so like hers as to provoke suspicions of plagiarism, she said she would suppress her own play. In the meantime, she would revise her play as Rousseau had advised. She invited him to dine with her the following Saturday in the company of Lorenzy, at the Trois Pavillons inn at Saint-Denis. Rousseau accepted the invitation to dinner, but questioned whether the presence of Lorenzy might not hinder a frank discussion of the problem of her play. The Comtesse then assured[17] him that she had nothing to hide from Lorenzy or anyone else: 'The opinion you have expressed is a service you have done me, worthy of your honesty and your heart ... There is no need for any mystery. It does not go with my candour or my gratitude to hide things.'

Rousseau must have sent a somewhat brusque reply to her earlier letter, for we find her ending hers by assuring him: 'You do me great pleasure by banishing compliments. You will notice that I address none to you, but I shall always be very appreciative of marks of your friendship for me.'

The dinner at Saint-Denis seems to have been a success, because the next surviving letter[18] from the Comtesse to Rousseau is unclouded by any hint of reproach or tension; it is indeed full of endearments. She even promises to come to Montmorency on horseback† – 'although I am not a very brave rider' – to visit him. Rousseau says in the *Confessions*[19] that he had offended her 'in a way that no woman or author ever forgives', but there is no evidence in what she wrote at the time to suggest that this was the case.

---

*His letter has disappeared, but its contents may be deduced from her reply.
†Did this promise conjure up memories of Sophie's arrival on horseback in 1757?

The publication of Rousseau's abridgement of St-Pierre's *Project for Perpetual Peace* brought messages of congratulation from several friends. Charles Duclos[20] reported on its success in Paris and he urged Rousseau to publish more on the same subject: 'You owe it to the public and yourself.' From Parma, Deleyre wrote[21] praising both the pamphlet and the timeliness of its publication, when moves were on foot for a negotiated settlement of the European war.* Deleyre said that if he were still in the diplomatic service he would have copies of it sent to all the plenipotentiaries taking part. Like Duclos, he urged Rousseau to publish his own ideas on peace, clearly unaware how much they were at variance with those of St-Pierre. He even asked Rousseau whether it would be useful for him to join him in preparing further writings of St-Pierre for publication. Deleyre explained that Rousseau's old friend Condillac, who was now in Parma, working, as he was, in the ducal household, had suggested that he, Deleyre, should edit a series of works by philanthropic writers for publication in an abridged form, and he thought that St-Pierre might be one of them. There is no sign that Rousseau gave any encouragement to this project.

Rumours of a sequel to *Julie* seem to have reached Lenieps's ears, for we find Rousseau writing to him in April[22] to deny that he had 'even dreamed of publishing a sequel'. He admitted he had written about the subsequent adventures of Lord Édouard in Rome, 'but for a good reason, I threw that manuscript in the fire after I had made a short extract for Mme de Luxembourg; that was the only manuscript there was and now there is no copy in existence.' He assured Lenieps he would add nothing to the novel, and only wished there were a less defective edition of it in print, explaining that he had declined to prepare one for the French publishers out of consideration for his Dutch publisher, Rey, 'who has rewarded me with extravagant letters', while 'furtive and faulty editions multiply'. He advised Lenieps to hold on to the edition he had since it was no use his expecting to see a better one.

The warmer weather did nothing to improve Rousseau's health, which seems to have taken a turn for the worse after the departure of the Luxembourgs from their château. The Maréchal, writing in his own hand from Paris on 9 May,[23] expressed his concern, which he said was all the greater because Rousseau had refused to see a doctor. He feared he had himself offered bad advice in urging Rousseau to drink milk, which was doing him no good. He explained that his court duties would keep him at Versailles until June, but he hoped to see Rousseau at Montmorency towards the fifteenth of that month: 'Farewell, Monsieur, try to get well, work less hard, and look after yourself for the sake of your friends ... you

*The war afterwards known as the Seven Years War.

have no friends more tender than Mme de Luxembourg and myself.' Mme de Luxembourg wrote[24] in equally solicitous terms about Rousseau's illness, urging him to come to stay at the house in Paris, 'not to see doctors, but to be cared for by people who will do so without irritating you ... I love you with the most sincere attachment and I hope you are persuaded of it.'

Rousseau did not accept the invitation, and – whether or not because he stopped drinking milk – he soon began to feel better. On 17 May, when Mme de Luxembourg was visiting the Comtesse de Boufflers at Saint-Brice, Rousseau had even contemplated going on foot to greet her there, but, as he told her afterwards,[25] being unsure of the time she would arrive, and afraid it would rain, he had given up the idea. He begged her not to worry too much about his health: 'I suffer more,' he told her, 'from anxiety than from pain.'

He said more about his health in a letter[26] to Coindet, to whom he admitted he was better but by no means recovered: 'A hernia is not the worst part of it; indeed one of my afflictions seems to relieve the other.' At the same time he scolded Coindet for communicating reports of his ill health to the Luxembourgs. Coindet was probably the informant M. de Luxembourg quoted when he wrote to Rousseau on 22 May[27] saying that 'someone' had told him that 'your health is not too good and I am afraid you do not speak too frankly to me on that subject.'

M. de Luxembourg exhibited this great concern about Rousseau's health at a time when he was himself afflicted with grievous sorrows. His sister the Duchesse de Villeroy died in December 1759; his daughter, the Princesse de Robecq, in July 1760; now, within two months in the year 1761 he lost first, in May, his only son, the Duc de Montmorency, and in June his grandson, the Comte de Luxembourg.

In the *Confessions*[28] Rousseau writes: 'The Maréchal endured all these losses with manifest courage, but his heart did not cease to grieve for the rest of his life, and his health slowly declined. The deaths of his son and grandson must have been all the more painful in taking place just when the King had granted him for his son, and promised him for his grandson, the appointment of Captain of the Royal Guard.'

The Maréchal's son, a brigadier, died on active service with the Army of the Rhine. The death of the little grandson Rousseau ascribed to the incompetence of the doctors who had been engaged to look after him. In the *Confessions*[29] he says that those doctors killed the child by starving him of everything but drugs: 'If the family had listened to what I said,' Rousseau claims, 'he would still be alive.' As it was, the boy's mother, the Duchesse de Montmorency, put all her trust in Dr Bordeu, and her son, according to Rousseau, became his victim: 'How happy the poor child was when he could get permission to come to Montlouis with Mme de Boufflers and take a snack from Thérèse to put some nourishment in his stomach. How I deplored the miseries of the great when I saw the sole heir to that vast estate devour a piece of bread like a starving beggar.'

According to Rousseau, the same charlatans who killed the grandson next set about killing the grandfather. When the Maréchal complained of a pain in his big toe Rousseau suggested he had gout, but the surgeons would not hear of it and gave their patient some exotic treatment which made the condition worse instead of better. Rousseau believed that the Maréchal was being overworked at Versailles, and thought that he would do well to retire. He even told him to his face on one occasion that he ought to do so.

'He sighed,' Rousseau recalls.[30] 'But he said nothing definite. Then Mme de Luxembourg, at the first opportunity of speaking to me alone, reproached me for giving him that advice. It seemed to alarm her. She said that the long habit of living at Court had made it a real need for the Maréchal, a distraction for him; and that the retirement I had advised would be less a rest for him than a form of exile.'

One friend who had resigned himself to a life of retirement, and shown few signs of recovering from his stroke, was Gauffecourt, of whom Lorenzy sent[31] news in May from Lyons, saying that, despite the old man's physical condition, he was very sound in mind and talked endlessly about Rousseau. Gauffecourt himself managed to scribble a message[32] to say he wished he were well enough to come to Montmorency: 'But old age! Old age!'

From Geneva, Pastor Vernes wrote[33] to tell Rousseau that he had been reading his abridgement of St-Pierre's *Project for Peace*, but was rather less than enthusiastic about it: 'I fear, my dear friend, that French music will continue despite your *Letter* against it, that the sciences will continue despite your *Discourse* against them, and that war will do its destructive work despite your *Project for Perpetual Peace*.' In the same letter Vernes resumed his criticisms of *Julie*, saying of the character Wolmar that he could not understand how Rousseau could make such a good man not believe in God. Somewhat impatiently, Rousseau pointed out to Vernes in his reply[34] that he had evidently failed to achieve his purpose, which was to teach the philosophers that one can believe in God without being a hypocrite and to teach the Christians that one can be an atheist without being a scoundrel.

Rousseau was still eager at this period to have his collected works edited for publication and, believing that his health would not allow him to complete the task himself, he thought of asking someone else to take on the job. Very pointedly, he did not choose Vernes, although he wanted it done by one of his friends who was a pastor at Geneva. His first choice was Moultou – with Roustan as the only possible alternative.

He asked[35] Moultou whether, in the event of his incapacity or death, he, Moultou, would be willing to travel to Paris to sort out his papers and determine which were worth including in the proposed collected works.* He warned Moultou that he would find opinions he would not agree with on religious questions, but he wished nothing to be changed on that score, and he asked whether Moultou would accept the commission on the understanding that there were to be no alterations or excisions. If Moultou's answer was negative, Rousseau said he would have to approach Pastor Roustan, since he was determined not to let any Frenchman handle his manuscripts. He begged Moultou to keep the matter a secret and on no account to communicate with him on the subject through Coindet.

Moultou accepted,[36] in principle, Rousseau's invitation to collaborate in editing the collected works, saying he was both moved by the honour and troubled by the thought of Rousseau's failing health. He saw no difficulty in the religious aspect, but felt it his duty to point out that he had many obligations, including family ties; he could not leave a pregnant wife to come to France. He also reminded Rousseau that his name was unknown to publishers, and he feared that 'the lack of celebrity on the part of the editor might be injurious to the interests of the author'. However, if he did do the job, he promised to look after Rousseau's heirs and to ensure that they were not deprived of the proceeds of his works.

Another Genevese correspondent, an unknown admirer named Jean-Louis Mollet, wrote on 10 June[37] to tell Rousseau that he was being fêted in his native city. Various public manifestations – parades, games, and so forth, as advocated in the *Letter to M. d'Alembert* – had been organized on 5 June, and, as Mollet recounted: 'Your name was the signal for us all to dance around the fountain of St-Gervais.' Rousseau was pleased enough by the news to show the letter to Mme de Luxembourg, who congratulated[38] him on all he had done to 'fortify the patriotism' of his countrymen; and he wrote[39] to Mollet to express his pleasure in the success of the public festivities, 'where joy was allied to morality and virtue'. The thought of it all, he said, had been a consolation to him at a time when he was extremely ill.

Rousseau was indeed more than ever convinced that he was about to die, and in his troubled state he decided to write[40] to Mme de Luxembourg about a subject which had been on his conscience for many years – the fate of his illegitimate children. He began by confessing something that

*In a postscript to this letter Rousseau wrote: 'You understand, of course, that *Julie* is not to be included in the collected works.'

the Maréchale must surely have already known, that Thérèse had been his mistress for sixteen years, although 'since my retirement to Montmorency, my state of health has forced me to live with her as brother and sister'. He went on to say that there had been five children of their union, all of whom were sent to the Foundling Hospital without his keeping any record of their identity or even of their dates of birth:

For many years remorse for that negligence has disturbed my repose, and now I shall die without being able to rectify it, to the great regret of the mother and myself. All I did was to put on the clothes of the first-born a mark of which I kept the duplicate; it must have been born, it seems to me, in the winter of 1746 or thereabouts. And that is all I can remember. If there were means of recovering that child, that would make for the happiness of his loving mother; but I have no hope of success, and I do not promise myself that consolation as I die.

Rousseau then explained why he had not married the mother of his children. He said he had always told her squarely that he would never marry her, and also that a public marriage would have been impossible 'because of the difference of religion'. Mme de Luxembourg can hardly have been impressed by these excuses, especially as Rousseau and Thérèse had been of the same religion until Rousseau's re-conversion to a Protestant Church ten years after his liaison with Thérèse began. Nevertheless Rousseau declared that he had always treated Thérèse as a wife, and was as anxious as a husband would be about her future welfare. He hoped that the Maréchale would be willing to take care of her after his death; not to take her into her own household or to set her up in Paris or to send her to her mother; but ideally to enable her to go on living at Montlouis or otherwise to install her in some community in the provinces where she could earn her keep. He ended his letter by assuring Mme de Luxembourg that his heart was now beating only for her 'and Monsieur le Maréchal and that poor girl [Thérèse]', and 'that at whatever hour death overtakes me, it will find me thinking of you'.

In the *Confessions*[41] Rousseau says that Mme de Luxembourg received his disclosures about the illegitimate children very well, even too well, sparing him the reproaches he felt he deserved. He also recalls that she responded generously to his appeal on behalf of Thérèse, upon whom she proceeded to shower presents and kindnesses, even indeed 'embracing her often in front of the whole world'.

Mme de Luxembourg also undertook to mount a search for Rousseau's lost child. She instructed her steward La Roche to go through the records of the Foundling Hospital in an effort to trace any clues, but he was unable to make much progress on the basis of the scanty information Rousseau had provided. Several weeks later, Mme de Luxembourg reported[42] to Rousseau that tracing the mark he had put on the child's linen was proving most difficult. She also explained that she was having some problems with the man engaged on the search: 'He refuses to be paid for the work, so I cannot very well press him.' She did not name the man, but Rousseau knew it was La Roche.

'He wants to spend months on the task,' the Maréchale continued, 'because he has so little evidence to work on, and he needs to go through at least six months of registers. I do not give up hope of tracing the girl who was the first born.'

This letter from Mme de Luxembourg reveals one detail on which Rousseau's *Confessions* are silent: the sex of his first child. His immediate reaction to her letter was to implore her to abandon the search. His health had at that point deteriorated to a point, he said, where he did not expect to live long enough to learn the outcome of La Roche's prolonged researches.

'Do not do anything to counter your first efforts,' he wrote[43] to the Maréchale,

but I beg you to take no further steps. You have already given me the most moving proof of your friendship for me in this matter, and that sweet memory will take the place of everything; my heart is too full of you for it to feel the void of what is lacking. In my present state, the search for the child is of interest rather to another than to myself, but as that person [Thérèse] has a character that is easily dominated, it is by no means sure that the recovery of her child, now fully grown for good or ill, might not prove to be disastrous; it would be a cruel bequest for me to leave her to be the victim of a tyrant.

In the *Confessions* Rousseau tells a different story from what is revealed in this letter; for there[44] he says not that he asked Mme de Luxembourg to call off the search, but that La Roche's inquiries were fruitless: 'He found nothing, although at a distance of twelve or fourteen years, the mark should not have been untraceable if the registers of orphanages were in order and the search were made systematically.'

Again, whereas in his letter to Mme de Luxembourg Rousseau says that it might be just as well for Thérèse's sake that the child remained untraced, in the *Confessions*[45] he suggests that La Roche's 'failure' was probably a blessing for himself:

Doubt as to whether the child was really mine would have torn my heart with uncertainty, and I should not have experienced the true feelings of nature in their full charm, since such feelings need to be nourished by habit, at least in one's child's infancy. A long separation from a child one does not know weakens, and finally extinguishes paternal and maternal feelings, and one never learns to love a child one has failed to nurse as much as one who is suckled under one's own eyes.

Rousseau may well have put the whole subject out of his mind at this time; he was to be forcefully reminded of it three years later when Voltaire, with malicious glee, told the whole world the story of Rousseau's abandoning his children in a pamphlet called Le Sentiment des citoyens;[46] Voltaire had apparently by that time learned Rousseau's secret from Grimm.

When the Luxembourgs returned to Montmorency in mid-June 1761, Rousseau moved once more to the Petit Château, where his hosts were able to watch over him in what proved to be one of the most painful illnesses of his life. The attentions of Mme de Luxembourg were exceeded only by those of her husband, who visited Rousseau every day, and finally prevailed on him to consult the celebrated surgeon Frère Come. When Frère Come decided that surgery would be necessary, the Maréchal remained in the room throughout the operation, which Rousseau remembered as 'long and painful'.[47] The presence of the Maréchal, he recollects, 'meant that I had to put a brave face on the ordeal and to smother my groans so as to spare the feelings of my tender-hearted friend'. Frère Come at least found out what was wrong. He succeeded in introducing a small probe into the urethra, and pronounced after the examination that there was no stone in the bladder. He diagnosed instead a swollen and scirrhous prostate gland.

It seems that Rousseau put up some resistance to the remedy prescribed by Frère Come, for we find Mme de Luxembourg writing[48] to him after the operation, pressing him to obey the orders 'on which your recovery depends', if only for the sake of others who cared for him. Suffering did not improve Rousseau's temper. When La Condamine went in the company of a friend to visit him at Montmorency, his reward was to be roundly castigated[49] for disturbing the peace of an invalid and making matters worse by bringing with him an affected young man whom Rousseau had no desire to meet. La Condamine[50] defended himself by assuring Rousseau that he had simply come as a visitor to a sick friend, and that his companion was not 'an affected young man', but a distinguished Dutch philosopher and writer named Isaac de Pinto,* who knew and greatly admired Rousseau's work.

*Pinto was hardly even young – he was forty-six at the time.

Lenieps, too, received a rather curt letter[51] from Rousseau at a time when he was receiving treatment from Frère Come, with the explanation that he was too tired to write more. However, a few days later[52] Rousseau found the strength to write at some length to Dom Deschamps, who still communicated with him as 'Monsieur Du Parc'. The letter provides a good summary of Rousseau's general philosophical position:

The truth I love is not so much metaphysical as moral. I love the true because I hate the false, and I could only be in bad faith if I were inconsistent in this. I would love metaphysical truth just as much if I believed it could be reached, but I have never found it in books, and in despair of finding it there, I have no interest in what books teach. I am persuaded that the truth which is useful to us is much closer to us, and that it is not necessary to have such a great apparatus of science to acquire it. Your work, Monsieur, may provide that demonstration which all philosophers promise and no philosopher succeeds in giving, but I cannot change my principles for reasons I do not know. And yet, your confidence impresses me. You promise so much and with such assurance, and I find so much judgement and good reasoning in your style of writing that I should be surprised if there were not much of the same in your philosophy, and, considering my short sight, I ought not to be surprised that you should see where I never thought it possible to see. But doubt makes me uneasy, because the truth, or rather what I take to be the truth, is very pleasing, and produces a sweet state of mind, and I do not see how I could change the one without losing the other. If my own views were based on demonstrative proof I should not be disturbed by yours, but, to speak frankly, I am persuaded rather than convinced; I have belief, not certain knowledge. I do not know whether the knowledge I lack would be good or bad for me to have, or whether, after acquiring it, I would not have to say, 'I have searched the heavens for light and lamented what I have found.'*

Rousseau ended his letter by replying to 'M. Du Parc's' request for advice on the publication of his book. He simply warned him of the dangers:

I have often heard that it was said by Fontenelle that no book ever gave its author as much pleasure as trouble, and it was the fortunate M. de Fontenelle who said that. Until I was forty I was wise. I took up the pen at that age and now I am putting it down before I am fifty, cursing every

*The quotation, which Rousseau gives in Latin, is from Virgil, *Aeneid*, IV, 691–2: 'alto/quaesivit caelo lucem ingemuitque reperta'.

day I live the moment my foolish pride made me take it up in the first place, only to see my happiness, my repose, my health all go up in smoke without any hope of ever recovering them again. And this is the man to whom you turn for advice about the publishing of your book! I greet you Monsieur, with all my heart.

Dom Deschamps attempted in his reply[53] to refute Rousseau's suggestion that it is possible to have morals without metaphysics, arguing that only an exact knowledge of metaphysical truth can provide a logical basis for knowledge of moral truth. 'Sound metaphysics,' he claimed, 'is true religion, and the only true and solid sanction of morality.' However, he was ready to admit that enlightenment could only profit a man if he lived in an enlightened society.

Rousseau was not easily persuaded. 'You tell me,' he replied,[54]

that I would gain from adopting your principles if I lived in an enlightened society where others did the same. That I can well believe. But on those conditions every moral system would be proved. If people repaid good with good, it is obvious that virtue would make the human race happy, but can one find any concrete and worldly advantage in being good among the wicked? There you have the philosopher's stone, which remains to be discovered.

Rousseau told Dom Deschamps that he had a passionate desire to read his book, but warned him again of the perils of authorship: 'When I was obscure and loved I was happy; now with a well-known name I live and I shall die the most wretched of creatures.' He explained that as a result of literary fame his friends had become first his rivals, then his enemies; and the bonds of friendship had been transformed into the snares of perfidy.

Once Rousseau had thus bared his wounded soul to him, Dom Deschamps clearly felt he could no longer go on concealing his own identity. So he wrote[55] to tell Rousseau who he was. At the same time, he made it clear that, despite Rousseau's warnings, he proposed to publish his philosophical writings, and even suggested that he should print the letters he had exchanged with Rousseau as a sort of introduction to his book.

Rousseau was startled to learn that his correspondent was a monk and appalled at his proposal: 'What you tell me, Monsieur,' he wrote,[56] 'makes me tremble at the idea of your publishing your book. I had ten reasons for discouraging you before. I have ten thousand now.' He pointed out to him that publication could only have disastrous consequences for someone in Dom Deschamps's position. As for the suggestion that the private letters that had passed between them should be printed as an introduction, Rousseau reproached Dom Deschamps for failing to understand that such letters were not written to be printed, or even reread, much less to be copied: 'I want to be as free, inaccurate, and inconsequential in my correspondence as in my conversation.'

Dom Deschamps evidently responded to this letter by inviting Rousseau to visit him at his religious community in Saumur, but although Rousseau retained for that part of France an affection which dated from his summers with the Dupins in their château at Chenonceaux, he declined[57] the Benedictine's offer. There were, he pointed out, too many obstacles: he could not expect to travel *incognito*; his 'housekeeper of fourteen years' service' would feel abandoned if he left her behind, and he had no wish to attend mass. The greatest obstacle of all was his deplorable state of health: 'Do you realize that as I write to you I am fitted with a very painful catheter that hardly allows me to walk four steps in my bedroom, and which I cannot remove for more than eight hours without the bladder sealing up entirely. Is that a practical device for travelling? What do you say?'

As for his differences with Dom Deschamps on philosophical ideas, he said that in his love of truth he was not so blessed as to be sure that he possessed it, and he suggested that both of them, in the absence of certainty, should ask themselves what was most useful to the human race and be guided by that.

The *Journal encyclopédique* in its edition of June 1761 carried an editorial note defending Rousseau's *Julie* against an attack it had published in its previous number, an attack Rousseau believed to have come from Voltaire, but which was actually written by Charles Borde. The note was followed by an even more spirited defence of *Julie* by Charles Panckoucke, the publisher, who also followed up the letter[58] of lavish praise, already quoted, with an offer to enrol Rousseau as an author with his publishing house in Antwerp, where he had set up after leaving France to avoid prosecution over the publication of *erotica*. Panckoucke proposed to bring out all Rousseau's works in a definitive edition, which would be 'a masterpiece of typography, embellished with your portrait, illustrations and vignettes'. Rousseau did not take up Panckoucke's proposal, but Panckoucke did have the satisfaction, after Rousseau's death, of publishing the first six books of the *Confessions*.

In Paris, publishers continued to quarrel over *Julie*. Jean-Augustin Grangé surfaced as Robin's partner and complained[59] that Duchesne had been given permission to reprint the novel, despite the fact that he, Grangé, still had a thousand unsold copies of the Dutch edition in his warehouse,* as Duchesne well knew. Grangé protested that when he had offered to

---

*It is hard to believe that this statement is true, and Rousseau did not believe it.

collaborate with Duchesne in bringing out a joint publication, Duchesne had asked for time to consider the proposal and then used that time to reprint the novel on his own. Grangé said he believed all this was done without the author's knowledge, since he knew him to be too honest a man to lend himself to Duchesne's unworthy manoeuvres.

From Amsterdam Rey wrote at the beginning of June[60] to say that despite all the pirating of *Julie* in France, he proposed to bring out a new edition in three volumes, and he invited the author to provide corrections for the new impression. He also told Rousseau that he intended to reprint all his other works, having obtained a privilege from the Dutch authorities to do so. He explained that if he did not reprint the works, 'others will'.

This letter from Rey made Rousseau very angry, but he took over two months to reply,[61] feeling too ill to do so sooner. Finally Rousseau wrote:

Since you have prepared, Monsieur, without my participation a collected edition of my works, including those that do not belong to you,* and since you have obtained a privilege, robbing me of the right to have my books published where I choose, you must care very little to have my approval of the execution of the project, and whether the edition appears to me to be well or badly produced is all the same to you. Besides, the fact that you are my publisher means that if I keep silent, everybody will assume that the edition has been produced under my supervision and I shall be held responsible for its defects. People will think that I have deliberately chosen not to correct the passages that needed correction. Hence, you must have assumed that your edition, whether good or bad, would not be disavowed by me ...

Rousseau went on to say that he could not help Rey secure a share in the publication of *Émile*: 'It is not I who am involved in that enterprise, and I am not sure that those who are think well enough of your methods to wish to give you a share.' As for *The Social Contract*, Rousseau assured Rey that he would not go back on his promise to let him publish it; he only insisted that it should be published before *Émile* appeared, and be well printed on good paper, because 'it is the last book I shall write'.

Rey, in his reply[62] to this ungracious letter recalled that his decision to reprint those works to which he was entitled under Dutch copyright law dated from the time when Rousseau had announced his intention to end relations with him. He agreed that the privilege he had obtained prevented Rousseau reprinting those same works in Holland, but he asked why

---

*Rey had no rights to Rousseau's two *Discourses*, *Narcisse*, the *Lettre sur la musique française*, *Le Devin du village*, the *Économie politique* or the *Extrait* of St-Pierre's *Projet de paix perpetuelle*.

Rousseau should want to see something that was legally his – Rey's – property, pirated by others. He declared that he always tried to deal fairly and squarely with Rousseau, but, he added: 'You are very suspicious and you take totally false reports for the truth. My great fault is to be too open; but as to my probity, I have an utterly clear conscience.' On the subject of *The Social Contract*, Rey promised to produce it with every possible care, but he could not undertake to publish it as soon as Rousseau wished. The earliest possible date was March 1762.

To add to Rousseau's sorrows at this stage an accident befell his dog Turc and it had to be put down. Once again M. de Luxembourg found time to write[63] to express his sympathy, knowing how keenly Rousseau was attached to his pet. He also knew that the dog had once been called Duke and that Rousseau had changed its name to avoid giving offence to the Maréchal, who was a duke. The change had, in the event, only caused Rousseau embarrassment, because Mme de Luxembourg's nephew, the Marquis de Villeroy, had maliciously brought up the subject at dinner one day, and Rousseau was obliged to explain in the presence of the whole table what he had done, and why. This made him regret 'the stupid pusillanimity which had prompted me to change the name, as if there were not thousands of dogs called "Marquis" without any Marquis being upset'.[64]

In Houel's sketch of Rousseau with his pets, Turc bears the aspect of a mongrel, but Rousseau speaks of it as being celebrated at the château for its friendly nature and for its devotion to its owner; it had been with him since he first arrived at the Hermitage, and quickly became his 'companion and friend'.[65]

Knowing of his attachment to the dog, several of his friends wrote to express their sympathy on hearing of its death – not only the Maréchal but also the Maréchale, and their daughter-in-law, the Duchesse de Montmorency, together with Lorenzy and the Comtesse de Boufflers, who sent a message from the Prince de Conti, saying he would like to give Rousseau another dog if he would agree to accept it.

Rousseau said in his reply[66] to the Maréchale's letter:[67] 'My poor Turc was only a dog, but he loved me; he was sensitive, disinterested and good-natured ... there are many so-called friends who are not worth as much.'

The Duchesse de Montmorency's letter[68] of sympathy over the dog's death was rather more warm-hearted than the letter[69] Rousseau wrote her about the death in battle of her favourite uncle, the Duc d'Havrec, so soon after the loss of her husband and son: 'It is true, Madame la Duchesse,' he wrote,

that a harsh fate continues cruelly to afflict you and yours, but the losses you have already suffered should make you less sensitive to the latest; even though a fresh sorrow is a sad diversion, it takes one's mind away from those which affect one more; and one feels one's affliction with less bitterness in giving one's heart to others who are dear to us; and it is natural to keep a little for oneself of the consolation one tries to offer to others.

The fact is that Rousseau did not like Mme de Montmorency. He describes her in the *Confessions*[70] as 'a foolish young woman, rather spiteful, and, I believe, a bit of a mischief-maker'. In her letter expressing sympathy over the death of the dog she asked Rousseau whether he would approve of her appointing M. Girard, a schoolmaster at the Port-Royal, as tutor to her daughter. Rousseau recommended the candidate eagerly: 'He lacks neither wit nor knowledge, and I believe him well qualified to teach.' Rousseau did not mention that Girard had written him a few weeks earlier an enthusiastic letter in praise of *Julie*.[71]

In his letter of 20 July[72] to Mme de Luxembourg he told her he had been very sick, with frequent vomiting, since she had left Montmorency, but he was now rather better, more depressed and bored than actually ill, and not able to concentrate, even on reading novels. Nevertheless, he informed Moultou, a few days later,[73] that he was using the strength he had to prepare the papers Moultou would need when he edited his collected works. He explained that the editorial assignment would entail Moultou's making a journey to Paris, but assured him that he would be able to choose when to go. In the same letter Rousseau mentioned that he had learned with dismay that Jean-Louis Mollet, who had corresponded with him about the public festivities at Geneva on 5 June when he, Rousseau, had been honoured, was planning to publish the letters they had exchanged. Moultou evidently told Mollet of Rousseau's displeasure, for we find Mollet writing[74] to Rousseau in August to say his project was intended 'as an act of homage to you' and an opportunity also to give publicity to Rousseau's thoughts on the evils of the stage at a time when a theatrical season was being opened at the gates of Geneva at Châtelaine in the French province of Gex. Mollet was tactful enough to omit to mention the fact that the repertory there included Rousseau's own opera, *Le Devin du village*. What he did tell Rousseau was that he often saw his old nurse, Jacqueline Danel, and found her in excellent health.

Rousseau had himself heard from Mme Danel a few days earlier, and in his reply[75] he assured her, 'I have never stopped thinking of you and loving you. Often I have said to myself in my sufferings that if my good Jacqueline had not taken so much care to keep me alive when I was a child, I should not have lived to endure so much pain as a man ... May

God keep you in good health and cover you with all the blessings you desire.'

In August the Luxembourgs were able to return once more to their château;* but this time it seems that Rousseau did not feel up to the social life that was expected of him. As he puts it in the *Confessions*,[77] it was only his affection for Mme de Luxembourg and her husband that made him tolerate the people who surrounded them at Montmorency: 'My problem was to reconcile my attachment to them with a way of life more agreeable to my own inclinations and less injurious to my health.' In these circumstances, he was probably rather relieved when the Luxembourgs went back to Paris after a very short stay. He continued to invite only carefully selected persons to visit him at Montlouis. One thus chosen was a Swiss pastor, Leonhard Usteri,† whom Rousseau invited[78] to come in the company of a traveller from London named Le Roux, who had promised to bring a copy of the English translation of *Julie*.[79] He warned Usteri, however, that he might prove to be too ill to receive them.

Rousseau spoke of his illness again in a letter[80] to Lenieps, who had apologized for putting off a visit to Montmorency: 'I am not too upset by your postponement; my health is in too sorry a state to be quickly restored, but when it does improve it means I shall be able to enjoy your visit more.' In the same letter Rousseau mentioned that he had taken a firm line with Coindet: 'I told him to suspend his visits, and when he did not take my instructions seriously, I was obliged to repeat them more harshly.' The irrepressible Coindet seems to have tried to restore himself to favour by sending Rousseau a present of a pair of spectacles, but Rousseau found them useless and sent them back at once.

The visit of Usteri and Le Roux took place as planned, after which Rousseau sent[81] the English version of *Julie* they brought him to Mme de Luxembourg, saying that he did not know the language well enough to judge the translation himself and expressing the hope that the Comtesse de Boufflers would be willing to read it through and send him any comments which he might forward to the English publisher. The Comtesse had not yet received the book when she wrote[82] to him the following day offering to pay him a visit on her way to L'Isle-Adam early in September. She assured him that her friendship for him was unchangeable, evidently replying to a letter from him, which has disappeared, expressing the hope that she was still his friend. His doubts on the subject were probably due to misgivings over his error in accusing her of plagiarizing *Oroonoko*

*Mme de Luxembourg informed Rousseau in a letter dated 'Tuesday' that they were coming 'tomorrow after dinner ... I have the greatest impatience to embrace you'.[76]

†Leonhard Usteri (1741–89) from Zurich had made friends with Moultou in Geneva and secured from him an introduction to Rousseau.

(although he repeats the charge in the *Confessions*). She may have discussed the English translation of *Julie* in conversation with him, but no written comment of hers can be traced.

At the end of August 1761 the contract[83] for the publication of *Émile* by Duchesne was finally presented to the author for his signature, approved[84] by him and then sent to Malesherbes, who made some alterations in the wording to give more protection to the author. Although Rousseau had reservations about publishing *Émile* in France, he was too angry with Rey to wish he had given it to him for publication in Holland. In a letter[85] to Rey he told him he could not accept Rey's excuse that he was making his own edition of Rousseau's collected works to prevent others from pirating them: 'You claim that because others pirate, you must pirate; and you make yourself the sole owner of all my copyrights in Holland. Is this your way of repaying the honesty with which I have always dealt with you?'

Rousseau insisted that the right to publish his collected works belonged to him alone. Moreover, it was a right to which he attached particular value because his future reputation depended on those collected works, and also because it was his last material resource 'to provide my bread when my afflictions end my capacity to earn it'. Rousseau did not mention that he had asked Moultou to help edit the collected works or that he was negotiating with Duchesne to have them published in France. The contract he had just made with Duchesne for the publication of *Émile* gave that publisher the first option on what is there named as an *édition générale* of his writings ('if, when we discuss terms, we can agree on the conditions').[86] Rousseau ended his letter to Rey on a more friendly note, accepting March 1762 as the publication date for *The Social Contract* and expressing the hope that Rey and he would understand each other better in the future than they had in the past.

Leonhard Usteri, the pastor from Zurich, had taken away from Montmorency on the occasion of his visit to Rousseau a manuscript copy of *Émile*, and he sent[87] him after reading it some pertinent criticisms of the method of education recommended in that book. He suggested that the employment of ruses and strategems by the tutor would not be morally sound; it could only teach the pupil to answer cunning with cunning. Indeed Usteri suggested that the method used by the tutor to teach Émile the meaning of property by having his beans destroyed and teaching him good behaviour by locking him up all night for no reason at all would simply inspire in the boy a desire for vengeance against the tutor, and the belief that both property and discipline were based on fraud or violence.

Against these criticisms, Rousseau protested[88] that his tutor did not use cunning, but skill; he also maintained that since neither force nor reasoning was effective in dealing with children, such skill was necessary. The main problem in education, he argued, was to overcome the spirit of domination in a child already spoiled by a poor upbringing, and for this purpose verbal lessons were useless talk; to be effective, lessons must take the form of action.

To another Swiss friend, Daniel Roguin, who was just about to leave Paris to return to Switzerland, Rousseau wrote in mid-September[89] expressing the hope that he would be well enough both to come to Paris in a few days' time to bid him farewell and to visit him in Switzerland in the following year. It appears that Rousseau did indeed pay a short visit to Paris that month, mainly in the hope of seeing Malesherbes, who proved to be at his country house. On his return to Montmorency, Rousseau wrote[90] to Malesherbes, asking if he would be willing to read and advise on the publication of a 'little essay' he was thinking of including in his collected works. This was almost certainly his *Essai sur l'origine des langues.*[91] Rousseau had doubts about publishing such a fragmentary work, but Malesherbes reassured[92] him: 'The entire essay gives me the same pleasure as everything else that comes from your pen. I believe you would do the public a great disservice if you held it back to publish it in your collected works.' Despite this advice, Rousseau did not feel the essay was worthy of immediate publication, and it was not to appear in print until after his death,[93] and in that edition he says he is including it 'only because an illustrious magistrate who cultivates and protects letters, has thought better of it than I'.[94]

In the autumn of 1761 Rousseau's health improved, even to the point where he could declare with some sincerity that he was more worried about the health of M. de Luxembourg than about his own. He then persuaded the Maréchal to adopt a method of signalling that he was well without going to the trouble of writing a letter, and that was to send Rousseau a blank sheet through the mail. When M. de Luxembourg actually adopted this method, however, Rousseau made[95] something of a mockery of it: 'I never tire, Monsieur, of reading your last letter again and again. What richness! What eloquence! ... No, Monsieur le Maréchal, never has a Montesquieu, a Pascal, a Tacitus said so many things in so few words.' In the same letter, Rousseau reminded M. de Luxembourg that he was expecting to receive from the Maréchale a reply to a letter he had written her. To the Maréchale herself he wrote[96] suggesting that she should use the same system of sending blank sheets to signal her news: 'you will have less trouble in writing and I shall have the pleasure of reading messages less agreeable perhaps than those you would have written, but as tender as I choose to make them'. As days went by, neither blank sheets from M. de Luxembourg nor letters from his wife appeared often enough to satisfy

Rousseau. At the beginning of November he wrote[97] to the Maréchal declaring that 'the invincible silence of Mme la Maréchale alarms me and makes me fear I have been too confident . . . For mercy's sake, put an end to this cruel silence.'

Mme de Luxembourg seems to have been somewhat impatient when she wrote[98] next to Rousseau: 'Will you never understand the feelings I have for you? Then I must tell you for the hundredth time that I love you with all my heart and that I shall never change – as long as I live you will be loved with the same tenderness and the same fidelity.' She told him that she would not venture to send him letters as brilliant as her husband's blank sheets: 'You will have to make do with my heart, which is not as witty as yours, but more loving.'

Rousseau continued to reproach her for her delays in answering his letters. The more he cared for her and her husband, he protested, the more he needed to have news of their welfare. 'Please God,' he wrote,[99] 'that I do not cause you a quarter of the worry and anguish you have made me suffer these past two months.' He clearly failed to understand that the Court duties of the Luxembourgs, which kept them constantly on the move between Paris, Versailles and L'Isle-Adam, inevitably delayed both the delivery and the dispatch of their letters, even without considering the fact that they had so many other claims on their time.

Rousseau himself, despite the demands of literary work and the copying of music, seems never to have failed to find time for writing letters. While correspondence with the Luxembourgs languished, he began to receive a whole series of letters from two admirers of his novel who introduced themselves as 'Julie' and 'Claire', and whose real names were Marie-Anne Alissan de La Tour and Marie-Madeleine Bernadoni. Although both these correspondents concealed their identity from Rousseau for several months, and wrote him letters made up for the most part of foolish chatter and badinage, he obviously enjoyed the game they played, and found time to keep up the correspondence with one of them for fifteen years; it was a kind of flirtation which evidently satisfied some of his emotional needs.

It was the 'Claire' of the partnership, Mme Bernadoni, who began the correspondence[100] by telling Rousseau that his 'Julie' was not dead, but lived so as to love him. In order to guard her incognito she invited Rousseau to reply to her care of the Marquise de Solar★ at Versailles. He replied[101] to her advances in a decidedly encouraging way by saying that while he had decided to cease writing for publication, that resolution did not extend to private letters: 'In any case, I cannot hide from you the fact

---

★This lady was a member of the family of Solaro for whom Rousseau had worked as a footman in Turin in 1729.

that your letter has given me a secret desire to make the acquaintance of you both.' More serious correspondents did not receive the same encouragement. To one importunate person Rousseau protested[102] that it was an unjust and cruel tyranny to expect a sick man to reply 'to a crowd of idle people who are all the more eager to take up his time because they do not know what to do with their own'.[103]

News of an ominous kind reached Rousseau in October from a fellow Protestant named Jean Ribotte, who informed[104] him that their co-religionists were being cruelly persecuted in the south-west of France. This was the beginning of a tidal wave of religious fanaticism by which Rousseau was himself to be swept away within less than a year. Ribotte explained that a Protestant pastor named François Rochette had been arrested and taken to Toulouse on a capital charge of holding a religious assembly and that three Protestant laymen, the brothers Grenin, who belonged to the petty nobility, had been arrested, together with seven peasants, for attempting to liberate the pastor. Their lives, Ribotte believed, were in danger, and he implored Rousseau, who had 'written so eloquently about peace', to come to their aid by publishing a manifesto in favour of toleration and writing to the provincial Governor, the Duc de Richelieu. Ribotte added that he was making the same appeal to Voltaire.

Rousseau's reaction to this plea was guarded. He assured[105] Ribotte that he had read with mingled grief and indignation about the sufferings of 'our unfortunate brothers in your part of the country'. Nevertheless, he said he doubted that the authorities would carry their cruelty to such extremes if 'the conduct of our brothers were not giving them some reason for doing so'. He reminded Ribotte that Holy Scripture 'is explicit about the duty of obeying the laws of princes', and he suggested that the prohibiting of religious assemblies was undoubtedly within the rights of a government. 'After all,' he added, 'such assemblies are not an essential part of Christianity and one can dispense with them without renouncing one's faith.' Moreover, Rousseau pointed out that the attempt to liberate a prisoner, even if unjustly arrested, was rebellion, which could not be justified and which the government had a clear right to punish. 'These objections may be poor ones, but if anyone made them to me, I do not know what I could say in reply.'

For these reasons, Rousseau told Ribotte that he could not run the risk of saying anything. He could not intervene with the Duc de Richelieu, because that nobleman had wronged him in the past, and would surely be ill-disposed towards him still, since 'he who is offended against sometimes forgives, but the offender never'. As for publishing something, Rousseau declared that he had already preached humanity and toleration in his writings to the best of his ability, though never attacking any particular act, but only the vice itself: 'You did better to write to M. de Voltaire. He is a great friend of the Duc de Richelieu and could certainly make himself heard if he pleads for our brothers, but I doubt if he will put much urgency into his plea. He lacks the will, my dear Monsieur, and I lack the power to act; and in the meantime the just man suffers.'

Rousseau was less than fair to Voltaire, who soon proved abundantly that he had the will to act; the persecutions of the Protestants of Toulouse spurred him to the most vigorous activities of his life, earning him fame as a champion of liberty which even exceeded his fame as a writer. But he did not do much for Rochette. He wrote[106] to the Duc de Richelieu, pleading for clemency, but that was all.* A few weeks later, the pastor was hanged, and the three brothers who tried to deliver him were executed with him, although out of respect for their noble birth they were allowed to die by the axe instead of the rope. Voltaire's comment was entirely flippant: 'All that for singing the psalms of David: evidently the *parlement* of Toulouse does not like bad verse.'[108] Nevertheless, the Rochette case served as what his biographer calls a 'curtain raiser'[109] to Voltaire's campaigns on behalf of other Protestants, beginning with Jean Calas. Compared to Voltaire's endeavours, Rousseau's reaction to the case of Rochette seems pusillanimous, even heartless; yet he was undoubtedly correct in saying that he was powerless to help. He was himself a Protestant and a foreigner, living in France as a privilege, not by right; he was already stretching the tolerance of the French authorities with his own writings; he was at great risk himself, whereas Voltaire had both the status of a Frenchman and a Catholic and the security of his Genevese refuge. Rousseau was in no position to do the things that Voltaire did. On the other hand, he had just finished a work that was to prove far more explosive, far more subversive of the *ancien régime* than anything Voltaire wrote, namely *The Social Contract*.

That book was now ready for the press. Having heard from Rey[110] that he was sending Duvoisin, the Swiss chaplain at the Dutch Embassy in Paris, to collect the manuscript and to pay him the agreed sum of a thousand livres in French money for the author's rights, Rousseau put the finishing touches to the text. He had by this time warmed once more to Rey, partly perhaps because he was beginning to lose patience with the French publisher Duchesne. Originally he had been satisfied with the deal whereby Duchesne was to print *Émile* for a fee of 6,000 francs,[111] even though only half was to be in cash, and only half of that cash paid on

*Voltaire was much taken up in October 1761, organizing the new theatre he had set up in his château at Ferney, at the gates of Geneva.[107]

signature; but by the end of October, Rousseau was complaining bitterly about the delay* in setting up the book in type.

'You promised to come and see me,' he reminded[112] Duchesne, 'and you have not appeared. You promised me proofs and drawings for the plates, and I have heard no more about it.' He warned Duchesne that pirate publishers would have heard about the book and 'your delays will give them all the time to load their guns to surprise you'. Although he did not claim to know much about publishing, Rousseau suggested there were only two ways to thwart the pirates, secrecy and diligence; and since there was no longer any secrecy about *Émile*, diligence was all the more necessary.

Growing ever more disturbed by Duchesne's delays, Rousseau wrote to him on 8 November:[113] 'It is manifestly clear, Monsieur, that my book is being held up without my being able to imagine the reason; and it is no less obvious that I shall never learn the truth from you. So please do not trouble to offer me lame excuses or invent pretexts which would be pointless.'

Two days previously, Rousseau had handed the manuscript of *The Social Contract* to Duvoisin, who went to Montmorency to collect it and pay the author's advance on behalf of Rey. Rousseau handed him the sealed packet without satisfying his obvious curiosity about the contents. Afterwards[114] Rousseau reported to Rey that all he had said in answer to Duvoisin's inquiries was that the book was on a political subject, 'and there we let the matter rest'.

---

*In fact it was only eight weeks since he had signed the contract.

TWO SOCIAL CONTRACTS

Rousseau's name is always associated with the idea of a social contract – that is, of civil societies coming into being as a result of individuals pledging themselves to live together as members of one political community. Not many such pacts are actually recorded in history.[1] There is a notable one in the Old Testament: the covenant that was given by God to the people of Israel through Moses on Mount Sinai; there was also the covenant of 1620 which united the original colonists of New England in a body politic. Rousseau's social contracts are less specifically historical events. Two quite distinct types are in fact depicted in his writings: the first is the social contract which 'must have happened', generally at an early stage of human evolution; and the second is one which would need to take place if men are to live together in freedom.

The idea of societies being contractual in origin springs from the observation that men are not social beings in the ways that ants and bees, for example, are social; our instincts do not impel each of us to do automatically what is advantageous for the group or tribe. We may have, some of us more than others, altruistic feelings which drive us to do for the community as much as, or more than, we do for ourselves; but even that entails a process of reasoning, thinking out what course of action would be best for society. There is no instinct impelling every individual to fill an allotted social role, as there is in the social insects. Each human being has to decide what part he is to play, and where there is this freedom there is controversy. People do not all agree as to what is to be done for the good of all, even if all agree that the good of all should be promoted. Every human has a mind of his own, and every person's instincts are self-protective.

Rousseau believes more than most philosophers in the radical individualism of human beings. He does not think that society is natural, and he does not think that society introduces peace. Although he suggests that men have a natural feeling of pity or compassion in the presence of a fellow creature's suffering, Rousseau's thinking about man's nature is closer to that of Thomas Hobbes than to Aristotle's. And indeed while Rousseau rejects Hobbes's claim that the state of nature is a state of war between all men, he gives a Hobbesian picture of primitive society as it was before the introduction, by a 'social contract', of the institutions of government and law. The great difference between Rousseau and Hobbes is that Rousseau argues in the *Discourse on Inequality* that a social condition, and not a state of nature, immediately preceded the introduction of government. Rousseau claims that the state of nature was peaceful and innocent, and that it was only after the experience of living in society that men were led to introduce government – led to do so because conflicts over possessions arose with the division of labour. It was because of such quarrels that primitive society, originally idyllic, eventually gave place to 'the most horrible state of war'.[2]

This state of war in pre-political society is seen by Rousseau as having different causes from the state of war depicted by Hobbes. Hobbes speaks of a war between equals; Rousseau sees a war provoked by inequality, by what he calls 'the usurpations of the rich and the brigandage of the poor'.[3] War begins when the idea of property is born and one man claims as his own what another man's hunger prompts him to seize, when one man has to fight to get what he needs while another man must fight to keep what he has.

Both Hobbes and Rousseau envisage men finding the same remedy for this state of war between each and all; namely, by the institution, through common agreement, of a system of positive law which all must obey. But whereas Hobbes's social contract is a rational and just solution equally advantageous to all, Rousseau's social contract, as it is described in the *Discourse on Inequality*, is a fraudulent contract imposed on the poor by the rich. In *The Social Contract* Rousseau describes an altogether different sort of social contract – a just covenant which can ensure liberty under the law for everyone. But that is something men must enter into with knowledge of what they are doing. In the *Discourse on Inequality*, Rousseau describes a contract which took place in the remote past, where men first emerged, most of them without much intelligence, from anarchic communities to political society.

There Rousseau imagines the first founder of civil government as a wily rich man saying to the poor: 'let us unite ... let us institute rules of justice and peace ... instead of directing our forces against each other, let us unite them together in one supreme power which shall govern us all according to wise laws'.[4] The poor, who can see that peace is better than war for everybody, agree; they do not see that in setting up a system of positive law they are transforming existing possessions into permanent legal property and so perpetuating their own poverty as well as the wealth of the rich. And so, Rousseau puts it, 'all ran towards their chains, believing that they were securing their liberty'.[5]

Man's history of servitude begins as soon as he enters nascent society, even though Rousseau speaks of nascent society as an ideal moment in man's life on earth: 'the golden mean' between the 'indolence of the original state of nature and the petulant activity of modern pride, the best period the human race has ever known' and 'the true youth of the world'.[6]

An early form of servitude which man experiences in society is servitude to others, or social servitude. This again originates in nascent society when men begin to make frequent contacts with their neighbours, and each to compare himself with the others. Individuals look at one another, and each knows that others look at him or her. Each wants to excel in his neighbours' eyes: 'He who sings or dances the best, he who is the most handsome, the strongest, and most adroit or the most eloquent becomes the most highly regarded; and this is the first step towards inequality, and at the same time towards vice.'[7]

Men come to base their conception of themselves on what other people think of them. The idea of 'consideration' enters their minds; each wants respect, and soon demands respect as a right. The duties of civility emerge even among savages; a man who is wounded in his pride is even more offended than a man who is wounded in his body, and each 'punishes the contempt another shows him in proportion to the esteem he accorded himself'.[8]

In society, says Rousseau, man becomes 'denatured'. His *amour de soi-même*, or self-love, an instinctive, self-protective, self-regarding disposition derived from nature, is transformed in society into *amour-propre*, the desire to be superior to others and to be esteemed by them. In this way, every man loses an important part of his autonomy: he becomes enslaved to the opinion of others, almost owing his identity to his character in the judgement of others.

Another type of servitude which men experience in society is moral servitude: this takes two forms, the first, servitude to passions. In the state of nature, Rousseau argues, men's passions are weak. Having no prolonged contact with other human beings, and no experience of shortage, men's lives are calm. Nothing happens to inflame their passions. Even in their sexual relations, 'everyone waits peaceably for the impulse of nature, yields to it involuntarily with more pleasure than frenzy'.[9] But once they acquire mates, human beings develop the passion of love and this in turn leads to the destructive passion of jealousy. And once they associate with neighbours, individuals all develop vanity, pride, egoism, envy and greed. As society progresses these passions become so strong that people's conduct is dominated by them, instead of being governed, as social man's conduct ought to be, by reason and conscience, together with compassion.

This enslavement by the passions goes together with enslavement to desires. In the state of nature man only desires what he can easily acquire:

savage man, when he has eaten, is at peace with the whole of nature ... But for man in society, it is a question of providing first what is necessary, next what is superfluous, then afterwards come luxuries, then immense riches, then subjects, then slaves; man in society does not have a moment of respite. What is more singular is that the less natural the desire and the less urgent the needs, the more the desires increase.[10]

Once agriculture and metallurgy have been invented, social man also experiences economic servitude – but this is rather less evenly distributed than the other forms of servitude. As a result of the division of labour, which has produced the two categories of rich and poor, the poor become slaves of the rich. The rich, however, are not free – since they are more enslaved than are the poor to desires, passion and the opinion of others; but the establishment of property separates those who have from those who have not, and forces the latter to become dependent on the former. As Rousseau wrote to Mme de Francueil, in the famous letter explaining why he had put his children in an orphanage: 'The earth produces enough to feed everybody; it is the life-style of the rich, it is your life-style which robs my children of bread.'[11] In robbing the poor of a fair share of the earth's wealth, the rich also enslave them, for without servitude to the rich, the poor cannot even acquire an unfair share.

Next, there is political servitude. From the historical perspective, Rousseau argues that the establishment of law and the right of property was the first step in the evolution of political institutions; then came the introduction of magistrates, and then the transformation of legitimate into arbitrary power. In the first stage there are rich and poor; in the second, strong and weak; in the third, masters and slaves. At the end of this process of evolution, as Rousseau puts it, 'the circle is closed'; and we 'return to the point from which we started'. These words end the *Discourse on Inequality*.

In *The Social Contract* he develops the idea of a new beginning. Men, reduced at the end of the *Discourse on Inequality* to a condition of brutalized, rough creatures of limited intelligence, can be visualized as negotiating a genuine social contract and establishing institutions which will enable them to recover freedom, or rather to discover a new kind of freedom, since the anarchic freedom for the state of nature has been lost for ever. Together with this new freedom, he suggests, men attain a new form of equality –

not the equality of condition which prevailed in the state of nature, but an equality of rights, even indeed a moral equality.*

The first chapter of *The Social Contract* begins with a sensational assertion 'Man was born free, but he is everywhere in chains.'[13] But the argument of the book is that men need not be in chains. In a state based on a genuine social contract, men would receive in exchange for their independence a better kind of freedom, true political freedom or republican freedom. In making this kind of social contract, man loses his 'natural liberty and his unqualified right to anything that tempts him', but he gains 'civil liberty and the rightful ownership of what belongs to him';[14] to this is added the moral liberty which makes a man master of himself 'for to be governed by appetite alone is slavery, while obedience to a law one prescribes for oneself is freedom'.[15]

Thomas Hobbes was in Rousseau's mind as he developed his theory of political freedom. Hobbes, as Rousseau understood him, argued that men had to choose between liberty and law, between being governed and being free. For Hobbes, freedom meant the absence of constraint; law entailed the rule of an absolute sovereign. Rousseau did not agree that liberty stood thus opposed to law. Freedom was not the absence of constraint, but the activity of ruling oneself. He believed it was possible to combine liberty with law by instituting a state in which men could make the laws they lived under. It would entail, as did Hobbes's system, a covenant being made whereby individuals yielded their natural rights to a sovereign, but that sovereign would be none other than the people themselves united in one legislative body.

In this formulation of Rousseau's argument we confront a serious problem. It is easy to understand that an individual can be said to be free if he prescribes to himself the rules he obeys in his life; but how can a group of people be said to be free in prescribing for themselves the rules they obey? An individual is a person with a single will; but a group of people is a number of persons each with his own will. How can a group of persons have *a* will, in obedience to which all its members will be free? For it clearly must have such a single will, if any sense is to be made of Rousseau's proposition.

Rousseau's solution to the problem is to suggest that the civil society men bring into being is itself an 'artificial person' possessed of a single

*Wokler writes: 'In the *Discours sur l'inégalité*, Rousseau claimed that the political associations which men must have formed were responsible for the maintenance of those moral differences which set them apart from one another. In *The Social Contract*, on the other hand, he was later to argue that the associations which they ought to form should take no account at all of those differences and should instead substitute a principle of moral equality that would render their natural variations irrelevant and insignificant in social life.'[12]

'general will' or *volonté générale*. Civil society comes into existence through a pledge, and it remains in existence as a pledged group.

By the pledge which constitutes the social contract, the adherents are converted from a series into a group, from people into *a people*, from a multitude into a single whole, a nation. Ernest Renan defined the nation as a 'plebiscite renewed every day' and this is exactly Rousseau's conception: the republic is the creation of will and the same will animates its continued action. As men transform themselves into citizens, they acquire this will to further the public good or common interest, even if it may sometimes conflict with the personal interest which their private will may seek. As a citizen, the individual identifies his own highest good with the common good.

Rousseau sounds very much like Hobbes when he says that under the pact by which men enter into civil society, everyone makes a 'total alienation of himself and all his rights to the whole community'.[16] However, Rousseau represents this alienation as a form of exchange – men give up natural rights in return for civil rights; the total alienation is followed by a total restitution, and the bargain is a good one because what men surrender are rights of dubious value, secured by nothing but an individual's own powers, rights which are precarious and without a moral basis, while what men receive in return are rights that are legitimate and enforced. The rights they alienate are rights based on might; the rights they acquire are rights based on law.

Rousseau's solution to the problem of how to be at the same time free and ruled might plausibly be expressed as democracy. But this is a word he seldom uses, and then only in a particular fashion. This is because of the distinction he is careful to draw between the two forms of political authority. Legislation, in the strict sense of making the laws which everyone must obey, is a function which people must keep in their own hands and exercise in person. This is what he calls sovereignty, and he distinguishes it from government, or the execution, administration and interpretation of the laws, which he proposes to entrust to magistrates or ministers, even to a chief executive which he sometimes calls the 'prince', although when he uses this word he is thinking of the Roman republican *princeps* – not a royal prince of the kind favoured by such constitutional monarchists as Montesquieu or Locke.

Rousseau sometimes spoke of his political thinking being indebted to Locke, but he is plainly contradicting Locke when he says that men alienate all their natural rights when they make the social contract, Locke having said that men make the social contract precisely in order to preserve their rights. However, Rousseau is really thinking in different terms from Locke. He does not claim that men have in the state of nature the kind of God-given natural rights that Locke describes − the right, for example, to property. For Rousseau there is only possession in the state of nature − property, which is by definition lawful possession, can only come into existence, he argues, when a social contract institutes positive law.

Where Locke says that men carry their natural rights from the state of nature into civil society, and thereupon invest a sovereign with the powers needed to protect them and their rights, Rousseau envisages men converting natural rights into civil rights and keeping sovereignty in their own hands. Locke looks to representative government to ensure the continued fusion of liberty and law, but Rousseau rejects the principle of representation categorically. He writes scornfully of the parliamentary system of legislation by elected deputies: 'The English people believes itself to be free. It is gravely mistaken. It is free only during the election of Members of Parliament. As soon as the Members are elected, the people is enslaved; it is nothing.'[17] Rousseau argues that sovereignty cannot be delegated; it can only be exercised in person; and since his formula requires the people to be sovereign over itself in order to be free, the citizens must legislate in person in assemblies at which all are present and all vote. Even so, Rousseau followed tradition in limiting citizenship to adult males; so that there is at least one kind of representation in his system: the head of the family represents the woman and children.

Lord Acton, in his *Lectures on the French Revolution*,[18] says of Jean-Jacques Rousseau that by introducing 'the idea of pure democracy to the government of nations' he gave 'the first signal of universal subversion'. Others have said much the same thing.[19] Any attentive reader of Rousseau's writings must, however, observe that Rousseau did *not* advocate 'pure democracy'; indeed he explicitly rejected it. In *The Social Contract* he writes: 'If there were a nation of gods, it would govern itself democratically. A government so perfect is not suited to men.'[20] In the *Discourse on Inequality* he writes: 'I would have wished to be born under a wisely tempered democracy',[21] adding that his ideal country would be one 'where the right to legislate was common to all the citizens' but where the citizens had no right to initiate legislation, or to have plebiscites, and where the magistrates had the right to exercise the executive function; it would not be democratic on the model of Athens.

Rousseau wishes to have democracy only in the legislative organ, the sovereign body whose every act is the promulgation of a law; but since he rejected democratic government, it would be better to speak of him as a republican, or champion of popular sovereignty rather than a democrat. Besides, Rousseau did not have the temperament of a democrat; he did not have much confidence in the wisdom of the common people. At the very founding of the republic which his ideal social contract brings into being, a Lawgiver is called up to draw up for the people the table of laws they must adopt. Because the people do not understand what has to be done, a superior intellect like Lycurgus or Solon or Moses – or Calvin – is needed to design for them the constitution of their republic. Rousseau even suggests that this Lawgiver must pretend that the laws he proposes have been suggested to him by heaven, 'thus compelling by divine authority persons who cannot be moved by human prudence'.[22] He even offers for this proposal the authority of Machiavelli, printing, admittedly in Italian, a passage from the Discorsi,[23] where Numa is praised for invoking religious sanctions to tame a ferocious people. However, it is necessary to notice that Rousseau limits the intervention of the Lawgiver to the founding phase of the republic: once it is set up the Lawgiver will disappear, and the people will rule themselves – or, more precisely, since 'the people' have now become 'a people', we must say that the people will rule itself. And although the people does not govern itself in Rousseau's sense of 'govern', it will elect the magistrates who do govern.

The point Rousseau dwells on is that superiority in public office must correspond to superiority of capability and rectitude, or 'virtue'. Such a system he can call 'aristocratic' in the true classical sense of that word: government by the best. This is clearly the sense he has in mind when he speaks in The Social Contract of an elective aristocracy as 'the best form of government'.[24] He contrasts this with hereditary aristocracy, 'the worst form of government'.[25]

There is no more haunting paragraph in The Social Contract than that in which Rousseau speaks of forcing a man to be free.[26] But it would be wrong to put too much weight on these words, in the manner of those who consider Rousseau a forerunner of modern totalitarianism. If he is 'authoritarian' in the sense that he favours authority, his authority is carefully distinguished from mere power, and is offered as something wholly consistent with liberty – being based on the expressed will and assent of those who follow it. Rousseau does not say that men may be forced to be free, in the sense of a whole community being forced to be free; he says that a man may be forced to be free, and he is thinking here of the occasional individual who, as a result of being enslaved by his passions, disobeys the voice of law, or of the general will, within himself. The general will is something inside each man as well as in society generally, so that the man who is coerced by the community for a breach of that law is, in Rousseau's view of things, being brought back to an awareness of his own true will. Thus in penalizing a law-breaker, society is literally correcting him, furthering his real interests. Legal penalties are a device for helping the individual in his struggle against his own passions, as well as a device for protecting society against the antisocial depredations of law-breakers. This explains the curious footnote where Rousseau writes: 'In Genoa the word *Libertas* may be seen on the doors of all the prisons and on the fetters of her galleys. This use of the motto is excellent and just.'[27]

For Rousseau there is a radical dichotomy between true law and actual law. Actual law is what he describes in the *Discourse on Inequality* and again in *Émile*, where he writes: 'The universal spirit of laws in all countries is to favour the stronger against the weaker, and those who have against those who have nothing.'[28] True law, which is what he describes in *The Social Contract*, is different. It is just law, and what assures its being just is that its rules are made by a people in its capacity as sovereign and obeyed by the same people in their capacity as subjects. Rousseau is confident that such laws cannot be oppressive on the grounds that no people would forge fetters for itself.

The distinction between true law and actual law corresponds to the distinction Rousseau draws between the general will and the will of all. The general will is a normative concept, its rightness is part of its definition. The will of all is an empirical will: the only test of the will of all is to ascertain what all actually do will. Rousseau takes care to note the logical distinction between 'right' and 'fact'.

Why should an individual abide by the decision of the majority? Because by the deed of the social contract itself, to which everyone must subscribe and pledge (there is no question of a majority decision here: you either pledge or you are out of civil society altogether), each contractant agrees to accept the decision of the majority in the formulation of the laws. It is also understood that the members of the majority, whose decision is accepted as binding, do not will as exponents of a majority interest but simply as interpreters of the general will – so that it is a majority interpretation of the general will which is binding, not the majority will.

Rousseau clearly subscribed to that philosophy which divides man into soul and body. When the soul rules the body, a man is free; when the body rules the soul, he is a slave. The metaphysical freedom – or free will – of man is not of real importance in the state of nature, but in the social state it is crucial. The soul has a voice, as Rousseau explains in the 'Profession of Faith', a divine instinct, an immortal celestial voice, which is conscience.[29] A man who acts in obedience to conscience acts in obedience to the voice of his own soul; if he acts in obedience to the passions and desires which have their seat in his body, he is acting in obedience to something which is alien to him.

In *The Social Contract*, however, where the general will guides all men, Rousseau does not allow the voice of private conscience to have the supremacy he assigns to it in the 'Profession of Faith'. Indeed, in what is perhaps the most astonishing chapter in the whole book, he banishes

Christianity in favour of a more manly church. He continues to say that Christianity is the true religion, but adds that it is worse than useless as a civil religion.

> Christianity is a wholly spiritual religion, concerned solely with the things of heaven. The Christian's homeland is not of this world. The Christian does his duty, it is true, but he does it with profound indifference towards the good or ill success of his deeds ... The essential thing is to go to paradise, and resignation is but one more means to that end ... [In war] all will do their duty, but they will do it without passion for victory; they know better how to die than to conquer.[30]

In this chapter Rousseau does not quote Machiavelli by name, but he repeats Machiavelli's arguments against Christianity, that it teaches monkish virtues of humility and submission instead of the civic virtues a republic needs – courage, virility, patriotism, love of glory, and dedication to the service of the state. Rousseau agrees with Machiavelli: there can be no such thing as a Christian republic, 'for each of these terms contradicts the other'.[31] What is needed as a civil religion is a patriotic cult. Rousseau does not go so far as Machiavelli in proposing a revival of bloodthirsty pagan rituals, but he does propose a civil religion with minimal theological content which will encourage tolerance but not impede (as Christianity impedes) the cultivation of republican virtue.

For Rousseau to proclaim such ideas was asking for trouble, not least in Geneva. Assuredly Calvin himself had banished what had been traditionally understood as Christianity by abolishing the Catholic Church in Geneva and setting up his own Protestant national Church in its place; but Calvin, of course, considered this reform as the institution of an authentic form of gospel Christianity. Rousseau in his private religion claimed to do something similar, to subscribe to the true teaching of Christ which all the churches, Protestant as well as Catholic, had betrayed. But Rousseau's public religion – the civil religion described in *The Social Contract* – is opposed to the religion of the Gospel, and he makes no attempt to disguise that fact.

Rousseau regarded *The Social Contract* as an essay in political science, and not as a contribution to the literature of Utopias. He complained after its publication that 'critics have been pleased to relegate it with the *Republic of Plato* ... to the land of chimeras'.[32] But he protested that it was solidly based on the model of the constitution of Geneva, and the political experience of the Genevese people. He refused to believe that civil freedom was an idle fantasy. Man had known it both in Geneva and in the republics of antiquity.

And yet, as an essay in political science, *The Social Contract* has a pessimistic conclusion. While Rousseau insists that government in the sense of the executive and administrative function must be conferred on a prince or magistrates, he also argues that that prince or those magistrates will naturally tend, with the passage of time, to 'encroach on the territory of legislation'[33] and make more and more of the decisions that ought rightly to be made by the sovereign body: 'since sovereignty tends always to slacken, the government tends always to increase its power. Thus the executive body must always in the long run prevail over the legislative body, and when the law is finally subordinate to men, there remains nothing but slaves and masters, and the republic is destroyed.'[34]* Readers in Geneva could hardly fail to see in these words a reference to the situation of their own city, where with the passage of time the magistrates had taken over the control of the republic from the legislative council, reducing that assembly, which had been the democratic element in the original constitution, to mute compliance with the decrees of the patriciate, in effect to nullity.

Between writing the dedication to the *Discourse on Inequality* and writing *The Social Contract* Rousseau had lost his illusions about his native city; no longer did he represent it as an ideal fusion of democratic sovereignty with elective aristocratic government; he saw it for what it really was (and had been for several generations), a hereditary patriciate veiled by the forms and ceremonies of Calvin's republic.

Here was another reason for *The Social Contract* being ill received by the ruling élite of his native city. However much he might protest that he was holding Geneva up to the world as a model, he was all too clearly showing how it had fallen short of its own image.

Even so Rousseau is not wholly correct in saying to the Genevese that in writing *The Social Contract*, 'I took your constitution as my model.'[36] He also used as models the republics of the ancient world, and especially Sparta. Like Machiavelli, once more, Rousseau was in love with the political systems of antiquity, as he admitted when he declared, 'I was a Roman at the age of twelve';[37] in time he came to have a certain preference for Sparta over Rome, because its republican austerity did not yield to imperial grandeur, but both ancient models were as much in his mind as was Calvin's Geneva, and in the later chapters of *The Social Contract*, when he sets out the duties, not only of the civil religion, but of the censorial tribunals, of the prince, of dictators and of councils – all of them very powerful institutions – his emphasis is more on the preservation of order

---

*Cf. 'The body politic, no less than the body of a man, begins to die as soon as it is born, and bears within itself the causes of its own destruction' (*The Social Contract*).[35]

than of liberty, and he takes his examples from the institutions of antiquity.

However, it must be remembered that for Rousseau there was no antinomy between liberty and authority. So long as the people made the rules they lived under, and elected the officers of the state, they were free – free because a citizen's obedience in the state he depicted was nothing other than obedience to himself. Moreover, Rousseau envisaged the officers of the state less as persons than institutions. In the *Letters from the Mountains*,[38] written two years after the publication of *The Social Contract*, Rousseau explained once more what he understood by liberty:

Liberty consists less in doing one's own will than in not being subject to that of another; it consists further in not subjecting the will of others to one's own ... In the common liberty no one has a right to do what the liberty of any other forbids him to; and true liberty is never destructive of itself. Thus liberty without justice is a veritable contradiction ... There is no liberty, then, without laws or where any man is above the laws ... A free people obeys, but it does not serve; it has magistrates but no masters; it obeys nothing but the laws, and thanks to the force of the laws it does not obey men.

A curious incident happened – or at any rate was said by Duvoisin[39] to have happened – on the chaplain's journey back to Paris bearing the manuscript of *The Social Contract* for Rey. At the municipal customs house an officer seeing that Duvoisin had something hidden under his cloak, demanded to know what it was. When Duvoisin told him it was a parcel of books, he promptly took it from him. At this point, as Duvoisin informed Rousseau, he thought of claiming the diplomatic privilege to which he was entitled as chaplain to the Dutch Embassy, but fearing it would be foolish to make a fuss, he simply 'watched the wretched officers leaf through your book and give themselves the air of reading it'. They told him that literary manuscripts could not be imported into Paris, but eventually he recovered it and returned to his carriage. Thereupon, he confessed to Rousseau, he decided that since the packet had been opened, he might as well read the manuscript before he put it on the mail coach for Brussels. He expressed the liveliest admiration for the work, without making any further comment on it.

Rousseau was none too pleased about all this, and he put his own interpretation on Duvoisin's failure to comment on what he had read. He assumed that the book must have shocked him since the chapter on 'The Civil Religion' was bound to shock any Protestant pastor. In the *Confessions*[40] Rousseau suggests that Duvoisin 'was saving up the role of the Christian avenger until the book appeared in print'.

After feeling tolerably well throughout the autumn of 1761, Rousseau was in bad shape again at the beginning of winter. This time it was not the onset of the cold weather, but an accident which ended his repose: 'A piece of the soft end of the catheter I have to wear', he reported[41] to Moultou, 'and without which I could not urinate, has stuck in the urethal canal, and makes it much more difficult for the urine to pass, and, as you know, foreign bodies in that part do not remain in a constant state, but go on developing and become the nuclei of so many stones.'

News of this accident circulated swiftly. The correspondent who claimed to be his 'Julie' heard of it and urged[42] him to consult a surgeon named Sarbourg, less famous than Frère Come, but in her opinion, more enterprising. It is some indication of Rousseau's wretched condition that he agreed[43] to see her surgeon, although he stipulated that it would only be for an examination, not for treatment. He told her that he had experienced in his childhood the first symptoms of his present malady: 'it has its origin in some deformity which dates from my birth, and the most credulous dupes of medicine would never imagine they could be cured of a thing like that'.

'Julie' had by this time revealed that her name was Marie-Anne Alissan de La Tour; he had demanded to be told, and at the same time warned her that he did not wish to have any acquaintances, but only friends. He made it clear that he would like Mme Alissan to be one such friend. He even encouraged her to continue writing to him by telling her not to frank her letters, since, he said, he could well afford the postage: 'I am very rich just now, and I hope I shall long continue to be for such a purpose. What I save from vanity in my spending, I give to real pleasure.' It was because he had received a thousand francs from Rey and fifteen hundred from Duchesne that Rousseau had, for once, this sensation of affluence.

The correspondent who styled herself his 'Claire' – Mme Bernardoni – reinforced[44] Mme Alissan's urgent plea to Rousseau to consult M. Sarbourg, who had, she declared, already effected miraculous cures and might be able to succeed with Rousseau where Frère Come had failed. She mentioned that Mme Alissan – 'your Julie', as still she called her – had been taken ill,* and she begged Rousseau to help her by helping himself, and allowing M. Sarbourg to treat him. Rousseau did not yield easily: 'These damned doctors are killing me with their blood-letting,' he declared.[46] 'I do myself more good with gargles and hot foot-baths.' In the case of 'Claire' he did not demand to know her identity as he did that

---

*A few days later Mme Bernardoni informed Rousseau that his 'Julie' was being purged and had completely recovered.[45]

of 'Julie'; on the contrary, he assured his correspondent that he approved of her continuing to remain incognito.

The use of incognito was recommended to Rousseau himself just then by Daniel Roguin, who, having settled down at Yverdon in Switzerland, was eager for Rousseau to visit him there, but considered it unwise for his celebrated friend to travel under his own name. He suggested[47] that Rousseau should assume the identity of 'Monsieur Galafrès, a lawyer from Nîmes'. Rousseau had evidently expressed some reluctance to visit such a cold place as Yverdon, for Roguin assured him that he was kept warm in body by excellent stoves in every room of the house and warm in soul by the affection of his three nieces, a great change, he remarked, from his situation in Paris, where he had not even had servants to look after him.

Roguin's invitation to Rousseau – which was soon to prove more opportune than he realized – prompted him to ask[48] whether a passport would be needed for him to cross the Swiss frontier; he envisaged travelling through Besançon and Pontarlier, since he had learned from experience that the journey by coach from Lyons was unbearable. He rejected Roguin's proposal that he should travel incognito. He detested the pseudonym 'Osaureus' which had been given him by certain critics. It was an anagram of 'Rousseau' but also meant 'a mouth of gold', and he felt it to be another piece of mockery 'since I have the most horrible teeth any human creature ever had'. He was determined, he said, to be Rousseau and stay Rousseau at whatever risk.

By mid-November the manuscript of *The Social Contract* had reached Rey, who acknowledged[49] it with expressions of pleasure at being once more Rousseau's publisher. He also mentioned his regret at not publishing *Émile*, suggesting that he could have done better with it than Duchesne was doing in Paris. This last claim Rousseau was in no mind to dispute. Indeed he had now come to believe that Duchesne's delays in printing *Émile* were not the result of his inefficiency, but of a deliberate conspiracy, organized by the Jesuits.

He wrote[50] to Duchesne on the subject in a tone of bitter irony: 'There is no need to accelerate the printing of my book. Since I know the reason for your delays, Monsieur, I forgive you. Indeed I am sorry for you. When the Reverend Fathers have done what they will with the book, you may print it, if they allow you. In the meantime, keep calm, as I do.'

He wrote[51] with more heat to Malesherbes: 'You will learn with surprise, Monsieur, the fate of my manuscript. It has fallen into the hands of the Jesuits.' He went on to say that he had originally thought the Jesuits wished only to delay the publication of the book in order to have time to prepare their refutations of it, but now he was convinced that they were trying to have it suppressed altogether – or at least to suppress it until after his death and then to release it in a falsified form. He begged Malesherbes to thwart this plot and do 'what justice and humanity inspires you to do'.

It is strange that Rousseau should have entertained these suspicions at a time when the Jesuits were subject to intense persecution in France, victims of the same wave of fanaticism as the Protestants. In his youth at Chambéry, Rousseau had been very attached to two Jesuit fathers,[52] as a result of which, according to the *Confessions*,[53] he had 'never been able to hate the Jesuits', although he considered their teachings dangerous. In spite of this he was influenced by a prejudice which united Protestants, free thinkers and Jansenist Catholics against what they all believed to be the furtive, devious and Machiavellian activities of that most worldly of religious orders. Rousseau was correct in believing he had enemies, but he was strangely inept in his assumptions and conjectures as to the identity of those enemies. Yet if he was too anxious and suspicious to see clearly, he was not alone in this in France in the years 1761 and 1762, years of war, of a war that the French were losing and which seemed to be eating away the social harmony, the toleration, the nervous equilibrium and *bon sens* of what was supposed to be an age of Enlightenment and Reason.

Moreover, Rousseau's suspicions were not entirely unfounded. The Jesuits had led the campaign for the suppression of the *Encyclopédie*. He says in the *Confessions*[54] that he had heard of passages from the as-yet-unpublished *Émile* being cited by a Jesuit father named Henri Griffet, who did indeed go into print, after the appearance of the book, with an attack on *Émile*, published by none other than Grangé. Rousseau had good grounds also for believing that the Abbé de Graves, who undertook various commissions for Malesherbes, was close to the Jesuits.[55] There was also evidence of Guérin having Jesuit friends and connections. And however little sympathy Malesherbes himself had for the Jesuits, his father, the Chancellor, was more than friendly towards them.[56]

Rousseau reported his suspicions of the Jesuits to Malesherbes on the very day – 18 November 1761 – when an order was signed banishing the Society of Jesus from France. This event seems to have stunned Rousseau, for he wrote[57] at once to Malesherbes to retract his accusations:

Ah Monsieur, I am guilty of an abomination. I fear, or rather I hope, I am wrong, for it is a hundred times better that I should be mad, a stupid idiot deserving disgrace and that there should remain one good man on earth. Nothing is changed since the day before yesterday, but everything has a different complexion in my eyes, and I now see only very ambiguous signs where I once fancied I saw the clearest proofs. Ah, it is cruel for a sad and solitary invalid to have an unhinged imagination and to know nothing about the things that concern him!

This is one of the very rare occasions where we find Rousseau asserting what he so often denied, that solitude was bad for him. While he was in this same contrite mood, he wrote[58] to Duchesne to try to persuade him to accelerate the publication of *Émile*: 'It is the last, and most useful and the most substantial of my writings, the one which is closer to my heart than all the others.' He went on to say that he had time on his hands just then, and would be pleased to have proofs to correct. In the same letter he warned Duchesne against 'discussing my affairs with Coindet', and yet, surprisingly, in view of the fact that he had suspected the publisher Guérin of being in league with the Jesuits, he said he did not mind Duchesne discussing his business with him or his partner La Tour; 'they are friends we have in common: they are mediators between us'.

As things turned out, Rousseau's anxieties eased only to return more intensely a few days later. Again Malesherbes tried to calm him, first by assuring[59] him that the manuscript of *Émile* would not be altered in any way, then by promising[60] him that he would preserve the confidentiality of their correspondence. Nevertheless Rousseau returned[61] to the charge that Duchesne was deliberately delaying the printing of *Émile*: 'For two months the same proofs keep coming back to me, and I have not received one corrected sheet.' He begged Malesherbes to advise him what to do in the situation. Without waiting for Malesherbes's advice, he wrote again the next day to ask[62] him to cancel the contract with Duchesne and have his manuscript returned to him. What Rousseau proposed was that he should repay the publisher's advance, and ask no indemnity for the delay in publication. He offered[63] Duchesne in place of *Émile* the manuscript of his *Dictionnaire de musique*. If Duchesne rejected this offer, and insisted on keeping *Émile*, then Rousseau demanded that Duchesne should be obliged to stipulate a publication date, and should furthermore retrieve from the Dutch publisher Jean Néaulme the authority he had assigned to him to print in Amsterdam any work by Rousseau he, Duchesne, acquired the rights to publish.

After he had received this proposal from Rousseau, Malesherbes interviewed Duchesne in person, and then wrote[64] to Rousseau to tell him that he was fully convinced of Duchesne's probity. He reminded Rousseau that publishers were habitually behind schedule, and that tardiness in printing was no evidence of bad faith. Duchesne had agreed to stipulate a date for the publication of *Émile*, which would be March 1762, if not February. Malesherbes urged Rousseau to have confidence in Duchesne. He also said he believed Duchesne would have the book printed outside France; 'but I do not want to go into details about that in writing'.

This dark reference to things that could not be put in writing did nothing to set Rousseau's mind at rest. His reply[65] to Malesherbes proved he was not at all convinced by the magistrate's assurances. He agreed that delays were usual in publishing, but insisted that Duchesne's behaviour and 'the impenetrable mysteries in which he wraps himself' were *not* usual. Duchesne, he pointed out, had first set the book in type, sent proofs to Rousseau, only to distribute the type again on a foolish pretext, and then start afresh, so that all the author's work correcting the proofs was wasted. As for Duchesne's promise to publish the book in February or March, Rousseau wanted to know how, if the correction proceeded at the agreed rate of three sheets a week, a work of sixty sheets, which was the length of *Émile*, could be set up, corrected and printed in two or three months.

Far from being persuaded of the good faith of Duchesne, Rousseau returned to his original theory of a Jesuit conspiracy. In a letter[66] to Moultou, dated 12 December, and carefully marked 'for your eyes only', Rousseau revealed his anxieties about *Émile*. He spoke of the curious behaviour of Duchesne in delaying the printing of the book by sending him the same proofs and drawings over and over again, at a time when any publisher, in his own interest, would wish to speed up the printing, especially as he had paid the author a cash advance. He believed he knew the explanation: 'This publisher, Duchesne, is answerable to another publisher named Guérin, who is much richer, far better established and even prints for the police; he sees Ministers, is inspector of the library at the Bastille, is involved in secret dealings, has the confidence of the government and is absolutely devoted to the Jesuits.'

Rousseau went on to suggest that the Jesuits had been alarmed at what they had learned about his ideas on education, even though there was no question of their Society or their schools in *Émile*. They must have found out that the book contained 'a Profession of Faith which is not favourable either to the intolerant or the unbelievers'. What he feared was that the Jesuits were trying to hold up the publication of his book until he died and then to manipulate the text according to their whims; 'the public will be astonished to see a Jesuit doctrine appear under the name of J.-J. Rousseau'. He implored Moultou, together with Roustan, to use their authority to see that this Jesuit plot would not succeed after his death. Again he suggested that Moultou should come to France to work on his manuscripts, and even hinted that he might afterwards travel back to Switzerland with him, having presumably in mind the projected visit to Yverdon rather than a return to Geneva.

The next day Rousseau wrote frantic letters[67] to Malesherbes lamenting the fact that the secret of *Émile* was out, and to Mme de Luxembourg repeating the charge that the Jesuits had seized his book with the aim of producing a doctored version after his death. 'Duchesne is deceiving M. de Malesherbes; he is deceiving you', Rousseau wrote to the Maréchale, 'and he mocks me with the impertinence of a scoundrel who has no fear because he knows he is well supported.' Rousseau begged her to intervene with Malesherbes to make Duchesne sell him back the manuscript: 'the 1,500 francs I have received should be no obstacle'.

Malesherbes tried once more to calm Rousseau. He informed[68] him that he had sent a confidential agent to investigate the situation at Duchesne's publishing house and watch over the printing of *Émile* until it had been completed. Mme de Luxembourg was no less energetic on Rousseau's behalf. She went in person to visit Duchesne, and satisfied herself that the publisher was not guilty of what Rousseau suspected. She reported[69] to Rousseau Duchesne's own explanation of the delays, which, as one might guess, was that the author himself had held things up by his corrections and alterations on the proofs. Both Duchesne himself and his partner, Pierre Guy, gave her their word that the book would be published by March, as M. de Malesherbes had been promised. As for the Jesuits, Duchesne had sworn to her that when the Abbé de Graves had asked to read the manuscript of *Émile*, he had been refused any sight of it. Mme de Luxembourg could not believe that Duchesne could have any interest in allowing the Jesuits to hold up a publication in which he had invested his capital: 'Adieu, Monsieur, calm your mind, and believe that no one loves you more tenderly than I do.'

The Comtesse de Boufflers also begged[70] Rousseau to stop fretting about his book, and Malesherbes made one final effort to persuade him that his suspicions were unfounded. In the course of a very long and detailed letter,[71] the magistrate told him – somewhat belatedly, it must be admitted – what he believed to be the true story behind the delays in the publication of *Émile*. He said that Duchesne had originally signed the contract for the book in the belief that he would have it printed in Holland:

Afterwards it was decided that it would facilitate matters for it to be printed in France. I knew this, but pretended not to know for reasons that are too lengthy to be set down in a letter . . . You will remember, Monsieur, that you yourself did not think that your book could be printed openly in France. You did not desire it, since that meant you would have to submit it to censorship, which is something you did not like the thought of. That is why it has been necessary to shroud in some darkness the edition which is being printed in France, and why all these misunderstandings have arisen. The cruel state of mind you are in has forced me to acknowledge much more awareness of this French edition than I would have wished, since it has been necessary for me to discuss it with Duchesne in order to be able to allay your fears. That is the sum total of the intrigue.

Malesherbes again insisted that Rousseau's suspicions of the Jesuits were unfounded. The Abbé de Graves may have told them of the book's existence, but Rousseau had no need to fear them; even if they disapproved of him as a Protestant and a philosopher, they had too many other people to hate to have any hatred for him. Although Malesherbes admitted that he did not trust the Abbé de Graves,* he did not believe that the abbé had the least intention of harming Rousseau. He repeated Duchesne's claim that Rousseau's own alterations to the proofs were responsible for the delays, and he suggested that Rousseau should come to Paris to oversee the printing of the book in person. A few days later,[72] Malesherbes was able to tell Rousseau that eight proof-sheets of *Émile* had been sent to him. He urged him to fret no longer over past delays: 'it is enough to know that your wishes will be respected – and the proofs will prove to you that there has been no tampering with the text'.

At last Rousseau allowed himself to be reassured. On 22 December he wrote[73] to Duchesne apologizing for the 'great wrongs' he had done him, adding that if only Duchesne had sent even one of the proof-sheets sooner, he would have 'spared much suffering to a poor invalid'. Rousseau ended his letter with the proposal that they should both forget past grievances and attempt to give each other cause for satisfaction in future. To Malesherbes, Rousseau sent[74] more fulsome apologies, blaming himself for six weeks of 'crimes, folly and impertinence' in his behaviour: 'I have compromised you, Monsieur, and I have compromised Mme de Luxembourg in the most reprehensible manner possible ... I do not ask for pardon because at my age I do not deserve it.' However, he asked Malesherbes to believe that he was no longer the same person who had acted so badly, and he begged him to respect 'a changed man'. To Mme de Luxembourg herself Rousseau declared[75] that he was acutely aware of his faults and was expiating them: 'Forget them, Madame la Maréchale, I implore you ... I do not ask this grace because I deserve it, but because it would be noble of you to accord it.'

He beat his breast less in writing[76] to Mme de Verdelin about the matter. While admitting that he had misjudged Duchesne in thinking he was conspiring with the Jesuits, he declared that Duchesne was a man who knew nothing about his trade, and was working so inefficiently on the printing of *Émile* that the book would take a year to appear, if it appeared at all.

Mme de Verdelin had asked Rousseau if she could have a copy made of Maurice-Quentin de La Tour's portrait of him, which she had seen in

---

*Rousseau may fairly have wondered why, if Malesherbes did not 'trust' the Abbé de Graves, he had employed him to work on *Julie*.

the house of a well-known collector, Jean de Julienne. Rousseau explained to her that La Tour had made two portraits of him, one of which the artist had presented to him, and which was now hanging in M. de Luxembourg's study. The other, he agreed, 'could well be in M. de Julienne's collection' and he said he would have no objection to its being copied. In the same letter, he urged Mme de Verdelin to return with her husband to Soisy, where the air of the valley of Montmorency would be good for the health of both of them.

Rousseau could not easily persuade people that the air of the valley was good for his own health. Malesherbes, in replying[77] to Rousseau's apology for misjudging Duchesne, commented on his 'extreme sensibility, depth of sadness and marked disposition to see things from the blackest angle', which he believed was made worse by solitude and 'the way of life you have chosen'.* Rousseau was indeed feeling so wretched at this time that he contemplated suicide. He confessed as much in a letter[79] he wrote, but did not send, to Moultou. Physical suffering coupled with remorse 'over an injustice I have done to two honest publishers' was tormenting him, while 'delirium and pain are making me lose my reason before I lose my life'.

He added some instructions concerning Moultou's duties as his literary executor after his death. He authorized him to deal with Rey as his publisher and expressed the hope that his 'disciple', Pastor Roustan, would write a preface for his collected works. He mentioned Thérèse, describing her as 'a housekeeper and nurse of seventeen years' service', and he begged Moultou to look after her. Rousseau also admitted to Moultou that the 'Profession of Faith of the Savoyard Priest', which would appear in *Émile*, was his own profession of faith: 'I desire too much that there should be a God to be able to doubt it, and I die with the firm conviction that I shall find in His bosom the happiness and the peace that I have not enjoyed in this world.'

Rey himself was as determined as ever to publish the collected works, and having restored friendly relations with the author, ventured to suggest to him he might make the edition all the more desirable by writing an autobiography to be printed in the first volume. By way of bait, Rey offered to provide Thérèse with an annuity of 300 French francs on Rousseau's death. He begged Rousseau to accept this offer as 'a recognition of the good you have done me'. Since Rousseau felt that Rey was heavily indebted to him as publisher to author, it is hard to see why he should choose to look on this offer as an act of grace, and yet he did so.

---

*Writing to Mme de Luxembourg, Malesherbes suggested that one could see in the agitation of the 'unfortunate Jean-Jacques' a mixture 'of honesty, nobility, melancholy and occasional ecstasy which is the torment of his life but also the source of his work'.

More, and worse, news of persecution in Toulouse reached Rousseau from his co-religionist, Jean Ribotte, who reported in December[80] that a Protestant named Calas had been arrested and charged with murdering his son to prevent that son from converting to Catholicism. Ribotte begged Rousseau to write a letter on the subject which could be published in support of the campaign to save Calas. Rousseau declined. He explained[81] that he was too ill to produce anything of the sort that Ribotte wanted. While he would support a petition on behalf of 'our brothers', the persecuted Protestants, 'it is absolutely impossible for me to write one'.

Unfortunately for Calas, others besides Rousseau failed to intervene. Even Voltaire, famous as '*l'homme de Calas*', acted only after it was too late to save the victim. Calas was found guilty of murdering his son, tortured and put to death by being broken on the wheel. His fate should have acted as a warning to the author of *Émile*, but Rousseau did not detect it. He did not even pay attention to signals given by his worldly-wise friend, Charles Duclos.

'Duclos came to see me while *Émile* was in the press and spoke to me about it,' Rousseau recalls in the *Confessions*.[82] 'I read him the *Profession de foi*, to which he listened attentively and, I thought, with pleasure. When I had finished he asked "Well, Citizen, is this a part of the book they are printing in Paris?" I answered: "Yes, and it ought to be printed at the Louvre by orders of the King." "I agree," he replied, "but please do not tell anybody that you have read it to me." This singular utterance surprised, but it did not alarm me.' It did not alarm Rousseau because he had at last been persuaded that his *Émile* was safe in the hands of Malesherbes.

BANISHMENT

Rey's suggestion to Rousseau that he should write his autobiography was not immediately brushed aside despite Rousseau's repeated assertions that he had given up writing for publication. Coupled with Malesherbes's attempt to provide an analysis of his personality, it prompted him to take a fresh look inwards, and he settled down in January 1762, to give Malesherbes an account of himself and his experience of life in a series of letters which later formed the nucleus of the *Confessions*.

In the first[1] of these letters, Rousseau tried to rebut the accusation that his withdrawal from the society of his friends in Paris was proof of misanthropy. He said he had been born with 'a natural love of solitude' and was happier among the creatures of his own imagination than among those he saw around him. He assured Malesherbes that he was not, as Malesherbes thought, consumed with melancholy: 'In Paris I was. It was in Paris that a black bile corroded my heart, and the bitterness of it is all too obvious in the writings I produced when I lived there. Compare those, Monsieur, with what I have written in my solitude, and I am sure you will find in the latter a serenity of soul that could not be merely simulated.'

Rousseau went on to explain that he had once attributed his shyness to a feeling of social inadequacy; he had been unable to show in conversation such wit as he had or 'of taking the place in the world which I thought I deserved', but once he had acquired a literary reputation, and been courted by everybody, he found his distaste for social life increased rather than diminished. The true explanation of his love of solitude, he suggested, was an 'unconquerable spirit of liberty', which made all the formal duties and obligations of polite society unbearable to him.

'And that', he went on to say,

is why intimate friendship is so precious to me. There is no longer any duty in it; one simply obeys one's own heart, and that is all. It is for the same reason that I have always been so unwilling to accept benefactions. Every service imposes its debt of gratitude... I would a hundred times rather do nothing at all than do things I do not want to do, and I have imagined a hundred times that I would be quite happy in the Bastille, since I would have to do nothing there except to stay put.

Rousseau admitted that Malesherbes might not recognize indolence in a man who had been busily writing books for the past ten years. He admitted this needed some explanation, which he could only provide by telling Malesherbes more about himself, unburdening his heart, 'painting myself without deception and without modesty'.

He asked Malesherbes to burn* the letters he proposed to write to him, but only because they were worthless, not in order to destroy evidence of past follies, for 'I do not fear to be seen as I am. I know my faults and I am very conscious of my vices, but I die full of hope in the supreme God and wholly persuaded that of all the men I have known in my life none was better than I.' In his second letter[3] Rousseau tried to explain the origins of the seemingly contradictory features of a temperament that was at the same time idle and intense:

I was very active as a child, but not in the way that other children are active. Boredom made me turn at an early age to reading. When I was six, Plutarch fell into my hands; at eight, I knew him by heart, I had read all his stories, and they made me shed buckets of tears before the age when the heart usually takes an interest in stories. That is how there came to be formed in me that love of the heroic and the romantic which has only grown stronger with time and has ended up by making me dislike everything that does not match my imagination. In my youth I thought I would meet in the world the kind of people I had come to know in books ... but I was seeking what did not exist, and little by little I lost the hope of finding what I sought.

Rousseau then told Malesherbes about the episode on the road to Vincennes in the summer of 1749, when 'a happy accident opened my eyes to what I had to do for myself and what I was to think of my fellow

---

*Malesherbes did not burn the letters, and it is unlikely that Rousseau ever wished or expected him to do so, and, as will be seen, he asked Malesherbes some months later to return them to him, at which point Malesherbes sent Rousseau copies and retained the originals. Some months after the death of Rousseau, the Marquis de Girardin, on behalf of Thérèse, asked Malesherbes to send him the originals to be published in an edition of Rousseau's *Collected Works*. By that time Malesherbes had already circulated copies of the letters, so that they came to be first published in Paris in 1779 not by Rousseau's executors but as an appendix to a rather bad poem by Jean-Antoine Roucher called *Les Mois*.[2]

men, whom I was disposed to love although I had so many reasons for hating them'. He recalled how he opened the *Mercure de France* and found the notice of a prize essay on the question of whether scientific and technical progress had improved or corrupted men's morals:

Suddenly I felt my mind dazzled by a thousand lights; a host of brilliant ideas sprang up together with such force and confusion that I was plunged into an inexpressible anxiety; I felt my head swim with a vertigo like drunkenness. A violent palpitation seized me and made me gasp for breath... I let myself drop under one of the trees of the avenue and there I spent half an hour of such agitation that when I got up I found the whole front of my jacket wet with tears I had shed unawares. Oh, Monsieur, if I could have written even a quarter of what I saw and felt under that tree, with what clarity would I have revealed all the contradictions of our social system, with what force would I have exposed all the abuses of our institutions, with what simplicity would I have shown how man is naturally good and that it is only through their institutions that men have become bad.

What he had retained of that illumination, Rousseau said he had put into his 'principal writings' – the two *Discourses* and *Émile*, which 'together form one whole'. He had been impelled to write those things and become an author 'almost in spite of myself', in order to proclaim a truth: 'if I had written simply for the sake of writing, I am sure no one would have read me'.

His belief that he had not much longer to live – 'because of an incurable ailment I have had since childhood' – gave an added urgency to his enterprise and fortified his resolution to live in a manner where his independence was assured. In Paris, he had been at the mercy of a crowd of so-called friends who wanted him to be happy in their way, not his. In his retreat he had found freedom, not complete freedom – for 'my last writings are not yet printed, and in view of the deplorable state of my poor machine of a body I do not hope to survive the publication of my collected works, but if, against my expectations, I do live to see that and finally bid farewell to the public, believe me, Monsieur, I shall be free, or else no man will ever be'.

Rousseau's third letter was dated 26 January[4] and this time he attempted to describe to Malesherbes the happiness he had found at Montmorency, although he admitted that the joy in his soul was somewhat overwhelmed by the pain in his body: 'my ills are the work of nature, but my happiness is my own'. He compared himself to the Roman courtier Similis, who declared that he had only begun to live after he had quit the court to retire to the country: 'I only began to live on 9 April 1756.'

Malesherbes may have seen nothing strange in this date, but to the reader of Rousseau's *Confessions*, where he writes of his happiness with Mme de Warens at Les Charmettes in his youth and of his miseries with Mme d'Épinay at the Hermitage – the place he entered on 9 April 1756 – the remark looks odd, but presumably Rousseau at that time had put thoughts of Mme d'Épinay and her circle out of his mind, and remembered April 1756 only as the beginning of his retirement to the country. Indeed, it was of the joys of country life that Rousseau spoke when he described to Malesherbes his present happiness: the solitary walks, the days spent 'entirely by myself or with my good and simple housekeeper, my beloved dog, my old cat, the birds of the field and the deer of the forest, with all Nature and its inconceivable Author'. He mentioned how he would wake up before the sun so as to watch it rising in his garden, and then after a morning's work and an early dinner, 'I would seek out some wild spot in the forest, where nothing revealed the hand of man or proclaimed servitude and dominion, some hiding place which I could imagine myself the first man to penetrate and where no tiresome third party could interpose himself between nature and me.' There amid the beauty of the woods, Rousseau said he would conjure up imaginary beings for his companions: 'I fashioned for myself a charming society of which I felt I myself was not unworthy.' Beyond that, he lifted his thoughts to the universe itself, to the 'incomprehensible Being who encompasses it all'. This contemplation of the infinite was not, he explained, philosophizing: it was a kind of voluptuous surrender to the power of these great thoughts, so that sometimes he would cry out in the excitement of his transports, '*Ô grand Être, Ô grand Être*,' without being able to say or think anything else. After this communion with nature, he would walk home to find a table set on his terrace, and eat a hearty supper, full of gaiety in the evening because he had been alone all day.

In the fourth of his letters,[5] Rousseau tried to defend himself against the accusation of the literary men of Paris that he was neglecting his social duties by living in solitude in the country. First, he said he considered the peasants of Montmorency more useful to society than the kind of parasitic idler whose only activity was to go six days a week to babble in an academy, so he felt better being of service occasionally to his poor neighbours in the country than he would helping amuse the petty *intrigants* of Paris. Secondly, he had been able to serve his country, Geneva, by publishing warnings against Voltaire's pernicious projects, warnings he could not have published had he actually lived in Geneva. 'In short, I have done all I could for society, as far as my strength has allowed, in working for myself, and if what I have done for society is little, the demands I have made on society have been even less.'

Rousseau admitted to Malesherbes that he had almost decided to quit his solitude as a result of the friendship that had been extended to him by M. and Mme de Luxembourg. They had approached him at a time when he was deeply depressed: 'I was dying. Without them I would almost certainly have died of melancholy. They restored me to life and it is only right that I should use my life to love them.' He had come to love them in spite of an 'aversion', as he put it, 'to those social classes which dominate others' − an 'aversion' he freely amitted to Malesherbes − 'yourself a scion of illustrious blood': 'I hate grandees; I hate their rank, their hardness, their prejudices, their pettiness, and all their vices, and I would hate them even more if I despised them less.' It was in this frame of mind, he declared, that he had first gone as one dragged to the Château de Montmorency; but the love that the Luxembourgs had lavished on him soon made him love them in return: 'My heart that does not know how to attach itself by halves gave itself up to them without reserve.' He admitted that in the heat of the enthusiasm they inspired in him, he had several times almost accepted their invitation to spend the rest of his days with them. But he had come to realize that the life of a noble household would not suit him; he would have been neither the friend nor the servant of the Luxembourgs but only their guest. He said he had dreamed a hundred times that M. de Luxembourg was not a duke, and he himself not an author, but that both were ordinary country people capable of finding simple happiness in each other's company. Even if that was an impossible dream, he could still enjoy being a guest from time to time, and at present it was enough if he could promise himself a few more of the delightful hours he had spent at the château.

Rousseau ended his letter by expressing the hope that nothing he had said would deprive him of M. de Malesherbes's goodwill. Although Malesherbes's reply has not survived, we may assume he wrote back with reassuring words.

Rousseau's illness seems to have worsened in the early weeks of 1762. In thanking[6] Duchesne for a New Year gift of a calendar, he declared, 'In the state of suffering in which Providence keeps me, my last day will be my happiest.' His friends became anxious. Rey wrote[7] from Amsterdam urging him to have another operation, and M. de Luxembourg urged[8] him to consult Frère Come once more. But nothing could make Rousseau put his trust in doctors, and he made himself even more ill by fretting over the publication of his books. His dealing with publishers were still as complicated as ever.

Rey, in sending him proofs of *The Social Contract* at the beginning of

January, complained that it was difficult to make the additions to the text
that Rousseau wanted if the copy arrived late. Rey's fellow publisher and
rival in Amsterdam, Jean Néaulme,* whose acquaintance Rousseau had
made the previous August, offered[9] to bring out Rousseau's collected
works in a luxury edition, in collaboration with Duchesne, but at the same
time Néaulme reported that Duchesne wanted to transfer the Dutch rights
of *Émile* to another publisher – evidently Rey – and he asked Rousseau if
that was what he desired.

In his reply[10] to Néaulme, Rousseau explained that while he was attached
to Rey by a long association, he would not wish Néaulme to cede his
rights to *Émile* 'for my sake' and to do so only if he was attracted by Rey's
terms. He admitted that the idea of a luxury edition of his collected
works pleased him. He had originally promised Duchesne an option, but
Duchesne's slackness in printing *Émile* had made him absolutely resolved
to have no more dealings with him. A week earlier, Rousseau had written[11]
to Duchesne protesting that when his printers sent him proofs of *Émile*
they did not return the manuscript with them: 'Must I keep on asking for
it? Really this is killing.'

When next he wrote to Rey, Rousseau mentioned his collected works
again, but said nothing about Néaulme's offer; he simply promised Rey
that he would not be forgotten in any arrangements that were made.
Rousseau was still feeling more cordial than usual towards Rey at this
time, because of Rey's spontaneous offer to settle an annuity on Thérèse
in the event of Rousseau's death.

In the *Confessions*, Rousseau writes[12] appreciatively of Rey's action:

That publisher, about whom so many hostile things were said in Paris, is
nevertheless the only one I have always had reason to praise... He often
said, when he offered me a part of his fortune, that I was responsible for
all of it. Unable to give me direct proof of his gratitude, he tried to do so
through the person of my housekeeper, on whom he settled a pension of
three hundred francs, stating in the deed that it was an acknowledgement
of the advantages I had procured him. It was settled between us without
ostentation, demonstrations or noise, and if I had not spoken of it to
anyone, nobody would ever have known anything about it.

Rousseau's actual correspondence with Rey shows that the settling of
the annuity did not proceed quite as smoothly as these words suggest, but
at least in his letter of 6 January 1762[13] he thanked Rey wholeheartedly,

---

*Jean Néaulme (1694–1780) had been a publisher and bookseller in Holland and Germany
since 1725. He was already contemplating retiring, and did so in 1763.

saying, 'it does much for my peace of mind to know that in the case of misfortune that good and honest girl will find a benefactor in you'. A week later he was angry with Rey again, protesting about his decision to entrust the correction of the proofs of *The Social Contract* to a reader in Amsterdam: 'I must tell you,' Rousseau declared,[14] 'that the idea makes me tremble. O my book, my dear book – what will become of it. . .?'

When Rey yielded and agreed to send the proofs to the author for him to correct himself, Rousseau was much relieved and wrote[15] once again to Rey in affectionate terms. His impatience had been transferred to Duchesne, for reasons he explained[16] to Lenieps:

It is true that Duchesne has taken over the printing of *Émile*. I believe he made a mistake. He ought to stick to printing almanacs and comic operas. I can tell from the way he is doing the work that it is too much for him. Besides, if he had paid me only 2,000 francs for the manuscript I would have done a very bad deal, for even if it is simply a collection of reveries it is still the work of eight years, for which Rey offered me a thousand écus [equivalent to more than 3,000 francs] and another publisher came to visit me with an offer of 200 louis [approximately 5,000 francs]. It is the last work I shall write, my dear Lenieps, and it must provide for my bread in the little time that remains for me to live.

Writing on the same day[17] to Moultou, Rousseau reported that his health was getting worse every hour and since he was in pain day and night, his imagination tormented him with black thoughts and made it difficult for him to be patient. He expressed regret over the suspicions he had entertained about Guérin being in league with Jesuits against him, and attributed those suspicions to his 'solitude' – something he had refused to admit in writing to Malesherbes. Once again he complained about the tardiness and incompetence of Duchesne in the printing of *Émile*, although he felt he had to admit at least that Duchesne was honest. Rousseau mentioned that he had transcribed what he called the 'principal part' of *Émile* – undoubtedly 'The Profession of Faith of the Savoyard Priest' – to be sent to Moultou for his approval, and he begged him to speak of it to no one other than his fellow pastor in Geneva, Roustan. In the same letter Rousseau reported that *The Social Contract* was in the press: 'it is part of a book I started ten years ago, and abandoned'.*

Ill as he was that winter, and scarcely able to muster the strength to correct the proofs of his own books, Rousseau continued to be importuned

---

*The published version of *The Social Contract* carries a note stating, 'This short treatise is an extract from a more extensive work I started in the past without considering my strength and have long since abandoned.'[18]

to write things for other people. From Dijon, Charles de Brosses, president of the provincial *parlement*, wrote[19] asking him to use his literary talents in the service of that *parlement* by drafting the remonstrances which its members wished to address to the government at Versailles. Brosses even went so far as to suggest that it was almost Rousseau's duty to do so in view of the fact that Dijon had been the first city to recognize his genius by awarding him the prize for his *Discourse on the Sciences and the Arts*. But Rousseau did not feel that this was in any way his duty; moreover he mistrusted Charles de Brosses because of his friendship and association with 'the Encyclopédistes and the Holbachians'.[20] Besides, Rousseau had no particular ideological sympathy with the campaign which the *parlement* of Dijon, together with other *parlements* in France, had for years been conducting to secure a greater share in the sovereignty of the kingdom, a campaign which Louis XV resisted with all the power he could command. It was a struggle which divided the Philosophes of the French Enlightenment into two camps,[21] those who accepted Montesquieu's theory of constitutional monarchy supporting the *parlements* against the Crown, and those who subscribed to Voltaire's theory of enlightened absolutism, supporting the Crown against the *parlements*. Rousseau favoured neither camp, and the publication of *The Social Contract* was soon to establish with his republicanism a compelling alternative to the political theories of both Montesquieu and Voltaire. He turned down the request from Brosses very brusquely – too brusquely, he afterwards admitted: 'I could have refused politely, but instead I refused harshly, and there I was wrong.'[22]

Another appeal reached Rousseau that same month, this time on behalf of victims of another *parlement*'s powers – the Protestants who were under threat of execution by the *parlements* of Toulouse. As Voltaire never ceased to assert, and Rousseau to learn to his own peril, French *parlements*, instead of fulfilling the role of bastions of freedom according to the theory of Montesquieu, were often more intolerant and despotic than the royal government at Versailles; and the religious fanaticism of the *parlementaires* at Toulouse, by no means assuaged by the blood of Calas, was again inflamed to such a degree that Rousseau's correspondent in Montauban, Jean Ribotte, implored[23] him once again to write something for publication on behalf of his co-religionists.

Even though he was considerably more sympathetic to Ribotte's purposes than to those of Charles de Brosses, Rousseau took a long time to answer his letter. When he did so, at the end of April,[24] he promised to write something if his health allowed, and he asked Ribotte to provide documentation of the Toulouse cases for him to work on: 'I shall try to put the material to good use, and although I cannot commit myself to do anything, I can assure you of my goodwill.'

Rousseau's correspondence with his lady friends was somewhat neglected in these strenuous weeks. We find his 'Julie', Mme Alissan de La Tour, reproaching[25] him for this; then him telling[26] her that he does not like receiving reproaches, and finally her saying she has no liking for quarrels, bidding[27] him 'farewell for ever'. To Mme de Verdelin Rousseau wrote a short note on 20 January[28] acknowledging belatedly a letter she had sent to Thérèse – 'who has no other secretary than me' – and telling her he was so ill that he was surprised to be still alive. No letters seem to have reached him in the first six weeks of 1762 from Mme de Luxembourg. At one point he learned she had hurt herself in a fall, but was informed on 6 February[29] by her steward La Roche that her only injury was a *callus* that would soon be better. At the same time La Roche sent Rousseau a copy of Richardson's *Pamela* on behalf of the Maréchale, together with a present of game and a catalogue of the library at the château de Montmorency, so that Rousseau could choose any book he wanted to borrow.

The Maréchale's motive for sending the *Pamela* was perhaps connected with a campaign being mounted by Diderot in Paris to boost the reputation of Richardson in order to diminish that of Rousseau's novel *Julie*; the *Journal étranger* in its January number carried an article by Diderot entitled 'Éloge de Richardson' to be followed by extracts from *Clarissa*. However, Rousseau was too busy with books still in the press to give much thought just then to *Julie* or its renown.

In Amsterdam Rey was making good progress with the printing of *The Social Contract*. Nor did he forget the pension for Thérèse. He assured Rousseau on 18 January[30] that 'Mlle Levasseur has only to draw up the deed as agreed and I will sign it. Then it will be a settled affair, and since I am pleased to do my part, all three of us will be content.' Rousseau, in his reply,[31] asked Rey to have the deed prepared in Holland, as that was the domicile of the donor.

Proofs of *The Social Contract* reached Rousseau through the intermediary of Duvoisin, the Swiss chaplain who had already scrutinized the manuscript, and these demanded his attention at the same time as the much delayed proofs of *Émile* from Duchesne, to whom Rousseau protested on 20 January[32] that he was far too ill to be able to draw up the Table of Contents that the publisher was eager to have him prepare. To Rey he gave a more detailed account[33] of his state of health. With a broken tube in the urinary canal, he was still unable to do without the use of catheters, and as for surgery (which his friends kept recommending) to remove the broken tube, he believed that his bladder was in such a bad state that such an operation would simply kill him: 'I would prefer another death to that.'

In the same letter Rousseau explained the situation concerning his collected works. He had offered them to Duchesne after he had severed his dealings with Rey; now that they were friends again, he would like Rey to have them, only it was too late to withdraw the promise from Duchesne. His sole hope was to persuade Duchesne to give up the option, or at least to share the publication with Rey, keeping the Paris edition himself and offering Rey the Amsterdam edition. As for the pension for Thérèse, Rousseau once again expressed his gratitude: 'I hope that when it is known here – and I intend to make it known as soon as it is settled – that it will alter for the better the opinion people have of you here.' Having said that, Rousseau went on to ask Rey to improve the arrangement and pay Thérèse a reduced annuity, of say, 200 francs, starting the following year instead of waiting until his death and then paying her the full annuity of 300 francs.

Evidently Rey was less than wholly pleased with this counter-proposal, and in his reply,[34] he suggested paying Thérèse an annuity of 150 francs during Rousseau's lifetime and to double it on Rousseau's death, the reason being, as he put it, 'that while she is with you she will not be in need, but without you, she will have to look after herself, which is why I shall stick to the 300 francs'.

Rey upset Rousseau again when he asked him to supply Thérèse's full name and personal details for the trust deed. Rousseau did so, describing[35] her as 'Thérèse Levasseur, spinster, daughter of François Levasseur, officer of the Mint at Orléans, aged forty-one years.' He expressed the hope that Rey did not believe, as some people did, that he had secretly married Thérèse, and that in accepting a pension for her he was indirectly taking it for himself: 'If that is what you think,' he added, ungraciously, 'then you can keep your donation, for I have always lived and shall die a bachelor'.*

Rey vigorously denied[36] having entertained such thoughts. He assured Rousseau he had never heard anyone suggest that he had secretly married Mlle Levasseur; nor had he himself any doubts at all as to Rousseau's probity. However, Rey did go on to say, less felicitously: 'There is so much corruption in people's minds today that they cannot imagine a man living with a female and not enjoying her favours.'

Finally, however, the deed was drawn up and the annuity settled on Thérèse to Rousseau's great satisfaction: 'Your liberality touches me deeply', he wrote[37] to Rey, 'and assures you of an attachment on my part which is surely owed to you together with the deep gratitude of the poor girl herself.' He said she wanted to write to him herself, and indeed ought to do so 'beginning by learning how to sign her own name'; but she

---

*He did not. He went through a form of marriage to Thérèse some four years later at Bourgoin.

was illiterate. Rousseau wrote[38] to Malesherbes to advertise Rey's act of generosity, 'something very rare among publishers': 'Seigneur Rey', as he called him, 'has granted my housekeeper an annuity of three hundred livres, and that of his own accord and in the kindest possible way.' Rousseau added that he wanted the act to be known 'because Seigneur Rey is not well spoken of in this country, although he deserves to be held in the same high esteem he enjoys in Holland'.

Rousseau must have been well aware that if Rey was held in poor esteem in France, it was largely because he himself had complained so loudly in the past about Rey's behaviour as a publisher.

While the printing of *The Social Contract* proceeded smoothly enough, that of *Émile* continued to generate problems – even over the impression which Néaulme had undertaken in Holland. When Néaulme drew attention to what he took to be mistakes that needed correction, the author replied[39] with rather less than reasonable fervour: 'What, Monsieur, can I not make mistakes when I please in my own books? Must they be written in your style and not mine? That is not right.'

Rousseau insisted that Néaulme should restore the text to the form that he, as author, had given it. Evidently Néaulme's proofreader had proposed to substitute more colloquial language for Rousseau's own, because we find Rousseau saying, 'I do not know what the "little-used words" complained of are. In writing French I do not claim to make myself understood by those who are ignorant of the language, and I do not like explaining what is already clear.'

In the same letter Rousseau informed Néaulme that Duchesne was being very secretive about his printing of *Émile*, although he had asked for, and been given, subjects for illustrations. To Duchesne himself, Rousseau complained[40] about the proofs of *Émile* being handed to a proofreader after he had corrected them himself; proofs, he insisted, should not be changed after the author himself had worked on them.

His worries about *Émile* appear to have diminished a little as his health improved in February, and he was evidently taken aback by the violence of Moultou's reaction to the 'Profession of Faith of the Savoyard Priest' which was to appear in the third volume. 'My God, I tremble for you,' Moultou wrote[41] from Geneva as soon as he had read what Rousseau had described as the 'principal part of *Émile*'. He said he did not disagree radically with the argument, but was profoundly disturbed about the effect it would have if it were published. It might well be useful in France, but it could only do harm, he urged, in Geneva and Switzerland, and even in France it was bound to be attacked from both sides, by the Catholics and sceptics alike. He dreaded what would happen to the author:

What cries, what a clamour you will excite in Geneva! How hard-pressed your friends will be to defend you! You can count on their zeal. But will they succeed? I think not. Our people are very much believers, very much attached – without fanaticism – to their religion, and that religion is your religion, bearing the seal of revelation which gives it authority for the people and leads them to virtue.

The Savoyard's denial of revelation was, warned Moultou, a heresy for which Rousseau would not be forgiven, even in France.

Rousseau refused to be alarmed by Moultou's warning; he felt wholly secure under the protection of Malesherbes. In his reply to Moultou he wrote[42] with serenity:

I am touched by your concern about my safety, but you must understand that in my present state of health it needs more candour than courage to tell truths that are good for mankind, and from now on I can defy men to do their worst to me without having much to lose... My form of prudence has always been to act so that no one can harm me without doing a wrong... To try to escape all injustice is to attempt the impossible, and must entail precautions that would never end. Besides, I have the honour of enjoying public esteem in this country, and the uprightness that people see in my writings is itself a great defence. The French are naturally humane and hospitable; what would be the point of persecuting a poor fellow who is in nobody's way and preaches only peace and virtue? So long as the author of De l'esprit lives at peace in this country, J.-J. Rousseau may hope not to be persecuted here. So calm yourself, and be assured that I am not in danger.

Rousseau's judgement of French tolerance was decidedly over-optimistic, as was proved three days after he wrote this letter, when several Protestants were tortured and put to death at Toulouse by order of the local parlement.[43] And if the author of De l'esprit – Helvétius – remained at liberty when his book was condemned by the Paris parlement it was because he had made a grovelling repudiation of his offending utterances,* something Rousseau was the last man to agree to do. But if Rousseau was over-confident about his own safety, he was still afraid that his book would be tampered with. He told Moultou that while he was resigned to the censor making cuts in the first two volumes, he was determined that they should not touch the later volumes which contained 'The Profession of

---

*Malesherbes kept his job on that occasion, but only because Teveier, the censor who had passed the book, served as a scapegoat, and took the punishment for De l'esprit being published.[44]

Faith'. He said he wholly disagreed with Moultou's suggestion that the publication of those pages would do harm in Geneva and Switzerland. He was nevertheless reinforced by Moultou's warnings in his belief that the later volumes of *Émile* should not be printed in France; even though there was no stopping the printing there of the first two. With this in mind he begged[45] Malesherbes to read the entire text of the first two volumes of *Émile* so as to be able to certify personally that there was nothing in them that could not be printed in France, and at the same time to instruct Duchesne to have the other two volumes printed in Holland.

It was a reasonable proposal, and Rousseau was not being unduly optimistic in hoping that Malesherbes would agree to it. As he explained[46] to Rey, 'all Duchesne would have to do is to print Volumes I and II in Paris and have the others set up in Holland by Néaulme'. At the same time, Rousseau revived his old allegations about the Jesuits conspiring against his book, saying he feared that if those holy fathers discovered that the last two volumes of *Émile* were to be printed elsewhere 'they will move heaven and earth to stop it'.

Malesherbes did not fall in with Rousseau's proposal; instead he chose to turn a blind eye to Duchesne's printing of the book in France. Rousseau did not like this. On 12 February,[47] he wrote an agitated letter to Duchesne saying that if he had not believed that the last two volumes of *Émile* would be printed in Holland when the contract was drawn up, he would never have signed it. As it was, he urged Duchesne at least to publish the first two volumes separately and let people assume that the last two were being printed outside France. He also urged speed: 'it is your delays that give time for public speculation and that will ruin us'.

In a letter to Mme de Luxembourg, dated 18 February 1762,[48] Rousseau explained that he wanted to have his contract with Duchesne annulled in so far as it covered the last two volumes of *Émile* and to have the manuscript returned to him: 'I would rather have the book suppressed altogether than mutilated.' He said he had learned from M. de Malesherbes that cuts were going to be made in the first two volumes even though the text had already been set up in type. He implored her to intervene once more to secure a satisfactory arrangement between himself and his publisher.

Mme de Luxembourg had in the meantime expressed[49] her continued concern about Rousseau's illness which she described as one of the 'greatest sorrows' of her life, adding that her husband was looking for a new dog to keep him company. The Maréchal himself informed[50] Rousseau about his efforts to find a dog 'to replace your poor Turc', saying the ones he had so far seen were 'too pretty' for Rousseau's taste.

Rousseau hastened to assure[51] the Luxembourgs that he did not want them to find him a new dog: 'It is not another dog I must have, but another Turc, and my Turc was unique. Losses of that kind are not replaceable. I have sworn that my present attachments of every kind shall henceforth be my last ... and as for having another dog to which I was not attached, I would rather receive it from another hand than yours.'

M. de Luxembourg had referred in his letter to Rousseau's anxieties over *Émile* being 'eased'; but they were in fact as intense as ever. His suspicions about Jesuits had only yielded to suspicions about Jansenists. These were perhaps marginally less irrational, since the Jansenists exercised considerable influence over the persecuting *parlementaires*, but, in Rousseau's case, the suspicions rested on a somewhat bizarre foundation. As he recalls in the *Confessions*,[52] they were aroused by a couple of bachelors named Ferrand and Minard, who spent their summers at Montmorency. They lived together, claimed to be cousins, did their own housework, and appeared to Rousseau to be Jansenist priests in disguise. They used sometimes to visit Rousseau for a game of chess. Because they were great gossip-mongers Rousseau called them 'the old women' and he protests that he had to put up with 'four hours of boredom for one game of chess'. One day this odd couple moved into an apartment next door to his cottage, where, as he puts it in the *Confessions*,[53]

they could hear in their bedroom everything that was said in mine or on my terrace, and from their garden it was easy to climb the wall to reach my *donjon*. This had become my study, and my table was covered with galleys and page proofs of *Émile* and *The Social Contract*. I stitched the page proofs together as soon as I received them, so that I had the volumes there before they were published. My negligence, and the confidence I had in M. Mathas, in whose grounds my cottage was situated, often made me forget to close the door at night. Finding it open in the morning would not have worried me if I had not begun to notice that my papers seemed to have been disturbed. After this I became more careful, and locked the door. However, the lock was a faulty one, and turned only half-way. As I became more attentive, I discovered my papers in even greater confusion than they were when I had left everything open. At length I missed one of my volumes for a whole day and two nights, and I did not find it until the third day, when it reappeared on my table. I never suspected M. Mathas or his nephew M. Du Moulin ... but my confidence in the 'old women' was undermined. I removed my papers to my bedroom, and stopped seeing M. Ferrand and M. Minard altogether.

Before the end of February, Rousseau had given up hope of reorganizing the publication of *Émile*, as he explained[54] to Rey: 'it is better to leave everything to fate, and let things take their course'.

Rousseau's resignation was probably the result of a visit from Malesherbes himself. He says in the *Confessions*[55] that the magistrate 'took the trouble of coming to Montmorency to calm me', although from a letter he wrote[56] at the time to Mme de Luxembourg it does not seem that he was entirely calmed, for he says there that his 'unfortunate book' still needs her protection: 'M. de Malesherbes pushed his kindness to the point of even coming here to see me. I fear the proposal to print the two last volumes in Holland will be subject every day to more obstacles, because Duchesne, alternately too lazy and too industrious at the wrong moment, has already started to print those two volumes in France. I have advised him to suspend work on them.'

Malesherbes had the reputation of the utmost probity* as well as of courage and devotion to the ideal of freedom, albeit of freedom strictly regulated by law.[58] If regarded with some contempt at Versailles because of his unkempt appearance and plain inelegant dress, his comfortable plump figure endeared him to most of the people he dealt with, not least in the literary world that he was supposed to police. It would have been wholly in keeping with this image of Malesherbes for him to have gone to Montmorency from the purest motives of goodwill and kindness towards Rousseau. Indeed Rousseau believed that to be so, and he never ceased to regard Malesherbes as his friend. Nevertheless, the evidence suggests all too plainly that Malesherbes's visit was part of a double game: on the one hand, to encourage Rousseau to accept Duchesne's decision to print *Émile* in France and, at the same time, to cover up his own part in sponsoring the enterprise.

As the date of publication approached, Malesherbes was not the only participant in the drama to become nervous. Even in Amsterdam, the city of freedom, Néaulme developed fears about *Émile*, and Rousseau had to try to persuade[59] him, as he had in writing to Moultou, that *Émile* was in no way inimical to religion: 'My book establishes in religion all that is useful for society and it does not destroy the rest. So in any well-governed state it must be a good thing for it to be published.'

As a remedy for Néaulme's anxiety about *Émile*, Rousseau advised him to sell the Dutch rights to Rey, knowing that Rey was eager to buy them, but Néaulme did not want to lose a potential *mine d'or*, and since he was, in any case, hoping to have Rousseau's collected works as well as *Émile*, he went ahead despite the dangers he apprehended.

As the printing of *The Social Contract* neared completion in Amsterdam, Rey asked Rousseau to do him a service: to approach Malesherbes with a

---

*See, for example, the elogium of 'Monsieur Guillaume' by Simon Schama in *Citizens*, where Schama claims that Malesherbes was 'virtually incapable of insincerity'.[57]

request for an import licence. Rousseau demurred. He felt he had already put Malesherbes to so much trouble over *Émile* that he could not decently seek another favour, so he suggested[60] to Rey that he should himself address a 'respectful letter' to Malesherbes in the expectation of a favourable response.

When he was told definitively that all four volumes of *Émile* would be printed in Paris, Rousseau urged[61] Duchesne to bring out the last two as soon as possible after the first, so as not to give time to 'a certain party' to act against it. He did not indicate who that 'certain party' was. In his next letter[62] he reproached Duchesne for turning aside from work to celebrate the Carnival: 'while the printers get drunk in the tavern, the publisher gets lost in the ballroom.' However it seems that Rousseau did not long remain angry with Duchesne, for we find him a week later inviting[63] him to dine at Montlouis: 'We can talk together better if we drink together.'

If he was in better spirits, it was perhaps, judging from a letter to Rey of 11 March,[64]* because he no longer believed that Duchesne would be allowed to print the last two volumes of *Émile* in France:

The first half is set up, but I will try to have its publication postponed until after that of *The Social Contract*. In the second half of *Émile* there is a section [the 'Profession of Faith'] which is the most important in the whole book and which could, if absolutely necessary, very well be published separately under another title. But I will not let that happen unless I am forced to. M. Néaulme knows nothing of this, so do not speak of it to him or to anyone.

At the same time Rousseau inquired about the pregnancy of Mme Rey. He had been invited – and agreed – to become the godfather of the child she was expecting.

A week later[65] Rousseau wrote Rey a sharp letter scolding him for opposing Néaulme's application to the Dutch authorities for a licence to publish *Émile*. He admitted that Néaulme might take advantage of the licence to usurp other writings of his, but was that not, he asked, exactly what Rey himself had done? He, as author, had given the manuscript of *Émile* to Néaulme to publish, and he begged Rey with all speed to withdraw his opposition to Néaulme's application.

Rey in his reply[66] explained that he had objected only to Néaulme receiving a licence which would allow him to publish any book by

---

*In the same letter Rousseau sent Rey instructions for the distribution of author's copies of *The Social Contract* – twelve to go to Moultou in Geneva, one to M. de Malesherbes, one each to his cousin in London Jean Rousseau and the English publisher Becket, and the rest (forty-five copies) to himself.

Rousseau other than *Émile*, to which his contract with Duchesne entitled him. By so doing, Rey insisted, he was protecting Rousseau's future writings, 'so that you – you and I – may have our hands free'.

Sometime in the spring of 1762 Rousseau ordered the first of his famous Armenian costumes. La Roche, Mme de Luxembourg's steward, found him samples of serge, wool, silk and squirrel fur from which the outfit could be made.[67] The presence of an Armenian tailor, who went regularly to visit a relation in Montmorency, gave Rousseau the idea of having a caftan made. The great advantage of this costume was that, by enabling him to dispense with breeches, it would facilitate the use of catheters and free him from spending most of his time in his bedroom with his chamber pot. He says in the *Confessions*[68] that he hesitated at first to assume such an exotic guise, but once encouraged to do so by Mme de Luxembourg, he went ahead and acquired the 'Armenian wardrobe' without, however, venturing to wear it on visits to the château, for fear of the ridicule of other guests.

On Saturday 27 March[69] both M. and Mme de Luxembourg wrote to Rousseau to tell him that they would be coming to the château the following Thursday for their Easter visit and expressing their joy at the prospect of being with him again. He had just received from Duchesne the proof of the title-page of his edition of *Émile* bearing the words 'Jean Néaulme' and 'The Hague', and promptly declared[70] to Duchesne that he was disgusted to see such words on a book printed in Paris, since it meant that 'a book by a friend of truth begins with a lie'. Moreover, he did not think anyone who saw it would really believe the book had been printed in Holland, so that it was 'a lie told to no purpose'.

When he was informed that it was standard practice to print the names of foreign publishers and places on French books to avoid trouble with the French authorities, Rousseau wrote[71] again to Duchesne, this time to assure him that he would not press his objection: 'Where it is a matter of your security I would oppose nothing you deem necessary to protect yourself.' He only advised Duchesne to make the deception more convincing by using a different type-face for Volumes III and IV, since everybody would know that Volumes I and II had been printed in France.

In the *Confessions*[72] Rousseau writes: 'The printing of *Émile* having been taken again in hand, was continued and completed smoothly, and I was struck by the fact that after the insistence on cuts in the first two volumes, the last two were passed by the censors without an objection, and the contents did not hold up the publication for a moment.'

At the time, however, Rousseau was constantly grumbling to Duchesne about delays in production. 'I would be better pleased,' he wrote at the beginning of April,[73] 'if you were less precise about money, and more

precise about the printing of the book.'* In truth, Rousseau himself was
holding things up with his own continued modifications and corrections.
As to the censor's insistence on cuts in the first two volumes, they seem
to have been fairly trivial. For example, we find Rousseau writing to
Malesherbes on 8 April[74] saying he has prepared the inserts for *Émile* 'that
you have instructed me to make'. The one thing he had left was a reference,
which the censor had questioned, to the 'passions of Angéls'; he had,
however, altered the phrase 'if there are any' to 'if they have any', thus
with one word changing an expression of doubt about the existence of
angels to an expression of doubt about the angels having passions, while
retaining the euphony of the literary style. One cannot doubt that Malesherbes appreciated the nice wit of a response that could not have come
better from Voltaire himself.

The production of *The Social Contract* proceeded on time, although this
did not stop Rousseau accusing Rey of tardiness and of further delaying
the publication of the book in Paris by sending stocks from Holland to
France by sea. 'This means,' he suggested to Rey on 4 April,[75] 'that *The
Social Contract* will not arrive before the appearance of *Émile* – or at least
a part of *Émile* – so that the two books will come out simultaneously, and
The Social Contract because of its difficult material and its appeal to a limited
number of readers will inevitably be suffocated by *Émile*.' He suggested
that Rey might be wise to postpone publication to the following winter.
Rey did not accept this idea, informing[76] Rousseau he was confident that
copies of *The Social Contract* would reach the French market by mid-May,
and indeed by mid-April[77] Rey was able to report that bales of the book
for the Paris market were on their way to M. Durend, bookseller of the
rue du Four, and that presentation copies, on superior paper, were being
sent to M. de Luxembourg and M. de Malesherbes.

Meanwhile Rousseau was busily sewing up pages of *Émile* so as to have
a copy of the book in advance of the publication. In doing so, he pricked
himself badly with the needle: 'I have hurt my right hand,' he informed
Lenieps on 18 April,[78] 'so I cannot write, but do come here.' Lenieps's
daughter had just died, and Rousseau wanted to comfort his old friend in
his grief. When Lenieps did not answer this invitation, Rousseau wrote
again:[79] 'send a word in reply to my last note I implore you; unless you
would rather bring it yourself, which would suit me much better, for after
the loss you have suffered, and I have suffered with you, the only possible
consolation one can give to a friend is to share his affliction. If you come,
you must spend a week here.'

---

*Duchesne had evidently just paid Rousseau his author's advance. Malesherbes suspected
that Mme de Luxembourg had contributed a secret subsidy to this.

Rousseau was disappointed when Lenieps failed to accept his invitation at once, and by the end of May he had to put him off: 'For the next six weeks,' he explained,[80] 'I shall be overwhelmed by the most disagreeable and troublesome business, which will leave me no time for friendship.'

Already, with the Luxembourgs at Montmorency for the Easter vacation, Rousseau had neglected his correspondence with his 'Julie', Mme Alissan, who, despite having bade him farewell for ever a few weeks earlier, had started bombarding him once more with letters. In mid-April[81] she sent him an express message reproaching him for his silence, reporting also that 'Claire' – Mme Bernadoni – was shocked 'by your indifference towards me; and has advised me no longer to expose myself to the dryness of the letters you do write me'.

Rousseau's reply[82] to this missive was as dry as could be. While he assured Mme Alissan that his heart was not insensible to the interest she took in him, he wished she would grant him the liberty of writing to her only when he felt like doing so: 'Good day, Madame, one has no need to be benevolent to give you your due; it is enough to be just; and that I shall always be with you, at least.'

In Geneva, Moultou continued to brood over what he felt to be Rousseau's gross indiscretion in publishing the 'Profession of Faith' as part of *Émile*. Once again he urged[83] the author to reconsider his decision. 'Your natural religion,' he wrote, 'is admittedly nothing other than Christianity, except that you want to demonstrate by reason what the Gospel teaches on authority. So you differ from the true Christian only in that what he believes comes from Heaven itself you believe comes from the light of reason alone.' Moultou urged Rousseau to consider the difference between an enlightened Christian such as himself and ordinary people. Ordinary people believed in Christianity only because they believed in miracles. Take away the miracles which were the basis of their faith, and they would not know what to believe. 'That is why,' Moultou continued, 'I think your book would be dangerous for Geneva, however good it might be for Paris.' Moultou also said he was afraid that the book would play into the hands of Rousseau's enemies in the city, and in this last respect his fears were to prove well-founded from the very day that copies of *Émile* – pirated copies printed in Lyons – reached Geneva.

Rousseau took some time to answer Moultou's letter, but when he did so – on 25 April[84] – he explained that the publication of *Émile* was now completely out of his hands: 'So I have resolved not to worry any more about this business, and let the book take its chance... All talk about the danger of "The Profession of Faith" is now pointless, since it is a fact that the publisher would not return *Émile* to me when I wanted to withdraw it. I hope nevertheless that you have taken an unduly pessimistic view of the effect it will have on the Genevese people's faith.' He went on to dispute Moultou's view that ordinary people were attached to religion by miracles. On the other hand, he agreed with Moultou that the book might well serve the purposes of his enemies. Indeed that was the real reason, he said, why he would never be able to come back to Geneva: 'I love my country too well to be able to see myself hated there. Better live and die in exile.' In the same letter he told Moultou that he was having him sent twelve copies of *The Social Contract*, which he wanted him to distribute;* he also asked him to deliver to the State Library a handsome edition of La Fontaine's *Fables* with 270 plates by J.-B. Oudry, which was a gift to Geneva of M. de Luxembourg.

If Rousseau had resolved to stay clear of Geneva, he was planning to visit another part of Switzerland, Yverdon in the Pays de Vaud, as he had promised Daniel Roguin. Writing to Roguin on 27 April,[85] Rousseau said he did not think it worth while bringing Thérèse with him, since he would be spending only a few weeks at Yverdon; but he would need to have another companion to give him the courage to face the discomforts of travel. We may assume that the ever-obliging François Coindet would have been happy to accompany Rousseau, but that young man had been squarely banished from Montlouis for several months. Rousseau proposed to travel to Yverdon through Pontarlier, but he forbade Roguin to quit 'his dressing-gown and his dear nieces' to come, as he offered, to the French frontier to meet him. No date was set for the visit. It was to take place sooner than either the host or the guest imagined.

To another Swiss correspondent – Vincent-Bernard Tscharner† – who sought to enrol him in the Société Économique de Berne, a newly formed academy dedicated to the ideals of the Enlightenment, Rousseau declared in a letter dated 29 April 1762 his profound scepticism as to the ability of knowledge to promote virtue:

Books are good for nothing, nor are academics and literary societies. People give no more than a sterile and vain approval to the kind of useful teaching they offer. Otherwise would not the nation that has produced Fénelon, Montesquieu and Mirabeau be the best governed and the happiest on earth? Is France any better as a result of the writings of these great men? Has a single abuse been corrected because of their precepts? No, Messieurs, do not hope to do better than they. You may interest people, but you will not make them any better or any happier.

*Rousseau wanted copies to go to Mussard, Jallabert, Perdriau senior, Gauffecourt and the State Library.

†Vincent-Bernard Tscharner (1728–78), economist and governor (*bailli*) of Aubonne in the Bernese administration.

Despite these strong words on the futility of books, Rousseau continued to spend most of his time working on, and promoting books of his own and the greater part of his correspondence was correspondence with publishers. Rey informed him on 28 April[87] that he had printed 2,500 copies of *The Social Contract* in a duodecimo edition, which he was selling to booksellers at 10 francs each. He hoped this would diminish the activities of pirate publishers although he recalled that notwithstanding the fact that he had printed 4,000 copies of the *Discourse on Inequality*, 3,000 of the *Letter to M. d'Alembert* and 4,000 of *Julie*, those three books had been pirated everywhere.

At the same time, Rey passed on the news that Néaulme was printing *Émile* in large octavo, but the fact that Néaulme was printing *Émile* in Amsterdam did not mean that Duchesne was not also printing another edition in Paris. In fact, Duchesne was printing both an octavo and a duodecimo edition, the latter being more advanced than the former. At the beginning of May[88] Rousseau expressed his dismay to Duchesne about his arrangements for putting the first two volumes of *Émile* on sale: 'I can see the consequences for the last two. But what can I do? They ought not to be printed in France. Would to God that I had been listened to!'

Rousseau's godchild was born in Amsterdam on 2 May. Although the parents had been hoping for a boy, it turned out to be a girl. In sending the news to Rousseau, Rey expressed the fear that Rousseau might be sorry not to have a godson, but Rousseau declared[89] that he was not at all disappointed: 'I learn, my dear Rey, with the greatest joy, of the happy delivery of your dear wife and the birth of my well-loved goddaughter. And what made you think I would have preferred a boy?... My preference was all for a girl, for would it not be more delightful for me to see a pretty child, as lovable as her mother, caressing and flattering her poor old godfather all day long rather than a rough, obstinate fellow storming my ears with his talk and mocking all my senilities?' He begged both Rey and his wife to give the girl two kisses each on his behalf.

In the same letter, he reported that Malesherbes had acknowledged the presentation copy of *The Social Contract* that Rey had sent him, but he warned Rey that this did not mean that they could count on an import licence for the book: 'M. de Malesherbes is good and well-disposed, but unfortunately he cannot always follow his own heart and his judgement, nor always do what he wants.'

This awareness of Malesherbes's limitations did not prevent Rousseau addressing to him on 11 May[90] what he called 'a last importunity' on the subject of *Émile*, protesting once more against the arrangement Duchesne had made. He declared that publishing the book in two parts, with the pretence that the second part had been printed in Holland, would deceive no one if the typography of the second part was identical with that of the first, which was generally known to have been printed in France:

Looking at the motto on my seal – *Vitam impendere vero* [To stake one's life for the truth] – I cannot help reflecting bitterly on the wretched necessity that Duchesne has imposed on me... For while I speak the truth when I say the book has been printed in Holland, I cannot pretend that in doing so I do not give the impression that it has been printed only in Holland and not in France. I hate the chains that society imposes on me because they make it a duty for me to be false and turn into a liar myself.

To Duchesne himself Rousseau wrote[91] in despair: 'I would make some representations to you about your plan to publish *Émile* in two parts if I thought it was any use; but if everything has been settled, my opinion will change nothing. On the other hand, it is of the utmost importance that nothing is done without the approval of Mme de Luxembourg, who realizes better than either of us what will or will not be tolerated.'

The first indication that *The Social Contract* would not be admitted to the French market reached Rey in the form of a letter[92] signed by the syndics of the bookselling trade, but undoubtedly prompted by Malesherbes himself, advising the removal of Rousseau's name from the title-page: 'The principles the book expounds,' they wrote, 'could ruin the author in France, and we cannot understand how you can have been persuaded that it would ever be tolerated here.'

Rey read this letter with dismay; 'I see,' he wrote in reply,[93] 'that M. de Malesherbes must have said that the entry of *The Social Contract* into France is impossible.' He only hoped that Malesherbes would not have the copies he had had delivered to France confiscated, although he was certain that it would be pirated by the publishers in Lyons 'within a fortnight', as indeed it was.

In the meantime, Rousseau seems to have become more confident about the fate of *Émile*, to judge from a letter he wrote to Mme de Luxembourg on 19 May:[94] 'I do not believe, Madame, that our book will appear before the holidays' – it will be noticed that he signals her share in the enterprise by calling it 'our book'. 'Duchesne assures me he counts on putting it on sale soon and you will understand that I realize what has made him so diligent.' Presumably Rousseau was referring here to Mme de Lux-embourg's personal intervention. In the same letter he asked her to take charge of distributing, from the thirty copies she would receive, one each to the Prince de Conti, the Duc de Villeroy and, if she agreed, also to the Marquis d'Armentières.*

*Louis de Conflans de St-Rémy, Marquis d'Armentières (1711–74) was an army general Rousseau had met at the château, and who, according to the *Confessions*, was one of those

Rousseau had already sent Duchesne a list* of people to whom copies of *Émile* should be sent directly from his office: Malesherbes, Guérin, Duclos, Lorenzy, the Comtesse de Boufflers, Lalive de Jully, Mme de Chenonceaux, Mme Dupin, Blondel d'Azaincourt, Carrión, d'Alembert, Watelet, Clairaut, La Condamine, Mme de Créqui, Duvoisin, Maurice-Quentin de La Tour, Lenieps, Loyseau de Mauléon, Malter the elder, d'Épinay, Bastide, Mme Alissan de La Tour, Mme Bernadoni, Voullaire, Gauffecourt, Dufour, Mallet, Father Berthier, La Poplinière and Mairan.

In this list of persons to be honoured with a presentation copy of *Émile* we see much the same assortment of scientists, writers, artists, connoisseurs and noble ladies who had been given *Julie*, although this time the gesture could be thought more flattering since *Émile* was declared to be something written for the wise whereas *Julie* was said to be fit to be read only by the corrupt. Since Rousseau had lost the services of Coindet in dismissing him from his sight, he had to supply from his own records the addresses of those intended to receive *Émile*, and he was not sure of all of them. Duclos and La Tour, he informed Duchesne, could be reached at the Louvre. Carrión at the Spanish Embassy and Duvoisin at the Dutch, Lorenzy at the Hôtel de Luxembourg, the Comtesse de Boufflers and Blondel d'Azaincourt at the rue Notre Dame de Nazareth, d'Alembert at the rue Michel-le-Comte, Mme Dupin and Mme de Chenonceaux at the rue Plastrière, Mme de Créqui at the quai des Quatre Nations, Watelet at the rue Charlot, Lalive de Jully at the Place Vendôme, Clairaut at the rue de la Verrerie, La Condamine at the cul-de-sac du Cocq, Lenieps at the rue de Savoy, Mme Alissan and Mme Bernardoni both at the rue Richelieu, M. d'Épinay at the rue St-Honoré, and Gauffecourt and Voullaire at the rue Quincampoix. Other addresses Rousseau left Duchesne to find out. At the same time he asked Duchesne to set aside the copies destined for Geneva 'until such time as I can find a means of dispatching them without great expense'. He explained that the list he had drawn up was not definitive, but consisted simply of 'names that have come to my memory'. In addition to the usual names on such lists drawn up by Rousseau there appear here the names of three bankers belonging to the Genevese colony in Paris, and Rousseau may have owed to Lenieps his acquaintance with two of them, Dufour† and Mallet,‡ but Voullaire§ was a kinsman by

'distinguished persons who did not disdain to make the very tiring climb to Montlouis to visit me'.[99]

*At the same time Rousseau instructed Duchesne to send to M. de La Roche for Mme de Luxembourg twenty copies in octavo and ten in duodecimo.

†Robert Dufour (1710–82).

‡Jacques Mallet (1724–1815).

§Antoine Voullaire (1696–1779) had married into the Berjon family, as had Jean-François Rousseau, a cousin of Rousseau's father, Isaac. Jean Berjon was Voullaire's partner in his bank.

marriage of Rousseau himself. Another new name is that of the elder Malter, who was professor of rhetoric at the Collège de Beauvais; he had the distinction of being the only educationist among the persons to whom Rousseau presented a copy of the book he described as a *Traité de l'éducation*.*

Mme de Luxembourg was able to acknowledge the delivery of her thirty copies of *Émile* on 22 May:[100] 'Here at last are the long-awaited books,' she wrote. 'M. Duchesne brought them to me this morning – first a presentation copy superbly bound in morocco and then your twenty copies.' She promised Rousseau she would do as he wished and send a copy each to her brother, M. de Villeroy, to M. d'Armentières and to the Prince de Conti. She said she had already given copies to two members of her family, the Duchesse de Montmorency† and the Duchesse de Boufflers.‡ She also proposed to give copies to Mme Du Deffand§ and Mme de Mirepoix,‖ evidently not knowing how little Rousseau cared for those two friends of hers.

Meanwhile, in Amsterdam, Néaulme seems to have reached a state of panic over *Émile* as a result of reading belatedly what he was printing in 'The Profession of Faith'. He wrote to the author on 22 May[103] saying he had undertaken to publish *Émile* with ardour and joy in his heart; he had advertised the book; he had obtained a privilege from the Dutch authorities to publish it; and now he found himself in a deplorable situation. The book would simply not be tolerated in Holland. Before he had read 'The Profession of Faith' he had been assured that Rousseau would limit his argument to a plea for natural religion; instead he was dismayed to find that Rousseau had gone on to attack revelation itself. 'Others agree with me that it will not be allowed under our laws... So I find myself faced with the harsh necessity of suspending publication and of taking steps to protect myself against danger and reprimands.'

In France the distribution of his author's copies brought Rousseau warm letters of appreciation from friends and acquaintances, but several recipients

---

*This was the original title of the book, but *Émile, ou de l'éducation* was the title he finally settled on. The manuscript which Mme de Luxembourg passed to Duchesne to print is in Geneva;[98] the copy seized by officers of the Convention during the Revolution from the house of Hérault de Séchelles is in Paris.[99]

†The widow of the Duc de Montmorency, M. de Luxembourg's son by his first wife.

‡The widow of the Duc de Boufflers, Mme de Luxembourg's son by her first husband.

§Mme Du Deffand was a close friend of Voltaire, and often spoke ill of Rousseau. In the *Confessions* he writes of her as one of the regular guests at the château who spoiled his visits there.[101]

‖The widow of the Maréchal-Duc de Mirepoix, Rousseau had first met her at Mme Dupin's salon. He describes her as 'cold, decent, and not altogether exempt from the natural *hauteur* of the House of Lorraine. She never paid me much attention.'[102] However, as will be seen, she exhibited some solicitude when Rousseau was forced to escape from France.

were shrewd enough to thank him for the book before they had read it. Duclos, for example, who already knew from what Rousseau had read aloud to him, that *Émile* contained dangerous material, explained[104] that he could not get down to reading it immediately because he was so busy working on the *Dictionary* of the French Academy and looking after a mother aged ninety-eight. Others, their curiosity pricked by rumours about 'The Profession of Faith', simply read that part alone, and wrote to congratulate the author on what he had written there; among these was Clairaut,[105] as Rousseau noted in the *Confessions*.

Alexis-Claude Clairaut was a celebrated geometer in his time, having been elected to the Academy of Sciences at the age of eighteen, and Rousseau was particularly moved by his praise of *Émile*: 'He was not afraid of expressing to me the emotion which reading the book had made him feel and he told me in clear terms how it had warmed his old soul:* and of all the people to whom I sent the book, he was the only one who declared to me squarely and freely what he thought of it.[106]

In writing this, Rousseau seems to have forgotten the frank and cordial letter[107] he received from La Condamine, who congratulated the author on having depicted in the 'Profession of Faith',† with more force than he himself could have achieved, his own feelings on the subject. He said how much he agreed with Rousseau that 'the voice of conscience, a kind of irresistible instinct, is a better guide than that proud Reason of which we feel every moment the limitations!' La Condamine begged Rousseau to allow him to visit him at Montmorency and bring a chicken for the pot.

Another correspondent who praised his book was one whose sincerity he had never any reason to doubt, Mme de Créqui. This pious friend informed[108] him after reading a hundred pages of *Émile* that it had made her realize how many things she had done wrong in bringing up her own son. At the same time she promised to come to dine with Rousseau at Montmorency, provided he did not expect her to meet him in company with the Luxembourgs: 'It is not that I dislike them, but I do not want to listen to a lot of tittle-tattle and gossip.'

In his reply[109] Rousseau declared that he was astonished that Mme de Créqui should contemplate a 'pilgrimage' to Montmorency. Anxious as he was to see her, he warned her that he was 'dying' and that even if she succeeded in restoring him to life it would hardly be for as much as a fortnight. He explained that the Luxembourgs were coming to their

---

*Clairaut, aged forty-nine, was a year younger than Rousseau. He did, however, speak in his letter of his 'old soul' being, not exactly 'warmed', but 'improved by the reading of a piece so good and so interesting as "The Profession of Faith"'. Clairaut explained that he had not read the earlier volumes of *Émile* because a friend had walked off with them.

†Like Clairaut, La Condamine admitted he had only read the third volume of *Émile*.

château the following Tuesday – he wrote on a Saturday, 29 May – and tried to persuade her that her reluctance to meet them was ill-founded. However, he promised to take her for charming walks in Montmorency if she preferred to see him alone.

Unlike Mme de Créqui, Mme Alissan de La Tour expressed[110] her thanks for *Émile* without commenting on the book, indeed adding a complaint about his sending her at the same time a copy for 'Claire' – Mme Bernadoni. She said she did not want to pass on the book to 'Claire', because that would lead to a hundred questions being asked about her correspondence with Rousseau which she did not wish to have to answer. In reply to this, Rousseau suggested[111] that Mme Alissan should present *Émile* to her friend as her own gift: 'since she has a daughter to educate, she might be pleased to have the book'. As for Mme Alissan's unwillingness to expose herself to questioning, Rousseau reminded her that there were no secrets between the Julie and Claire of his novel: 'their hearts are open to each other'.

Rousseau's eagerness to introduce Mme de Créqui and Mme Alissan to Mme de Luxembourg hardly bears out his claim in the *Confessions*[112] that he had ceased to enjoy social life at the château, and was only too happy after dining there at midday to hurry back to the simple life of Montlouis to sup in the evening with Thérèse and such plebeian neighbours as the mason Pilleu and his family 'either at their house or mine'. It is obvious from his correspondence, that Rousseau was delighted to see the Luxembourgs at Montmorency so unusually early in the season, and as it turned out, their presence there at that time proved providential for him.

In the *Confessions*[113] he laments that the publication of *Émile* did not produce the general applause that had greeted the appearance of his earlier writings: 'No book was ever more highly spoken of in private and given so little public approbation. What was said and written to me upon the subject confirmed me in my opinion that *Émile* was the best as well as the most important of the works I had written.'

This high opinion of *Émile* was not expressed by the author at the time the book came out. In writing to Dom Deschamps on 22 May,[114] Rousseau referred to the two books of his that were being published – *Émile* and *The Social Contract* – saying, 'The truth is that they are both very inferior to my other work. I do not want them judged in the light of your philosophy, and perhaps I would never have published them at all if my wretched condition of health had not forced me to scrape the barrel.'

One can hardly believe the sincerity of this assertion and Rousseau was clearly disappointed by the faint praise his work received. He was also troubled by the constraint he discerned behind most of the letters of thanks he received. In the *Confessions*[115] he recalls that everything favourable was said with an air of extraordinary mystery, as if there were a need to keep it a secret. The Comtesse de Boufflers, who declared that the author deserved a statue and the homage of mankind, ended her letter[116] by asking to have it returned to her. D'Alembert, who said the book assured my superiority and ought to place me at the head of men of letters, did not sign his letter[117] although he signed all the other letters he wrote to me.

The most ominous sign of all was that Malesherbes asked M. de Luxembourg to recover on his behalf all the letters he had written to Rousseau, and that he also asked Duchesne to return all his letters in which Rousseau was mentioned. At the time Rousseau did not realize the significance of these moves. 'I had too much confidence,' he says in the *Confessions*,[118] 'in both M. de Malesherbes and M. de Luxembourg.'

That confidence would seem reasonable enough. For had not Malesherbes been closely involved in the publication of *Émile* from the start? Was it not he who had found a French publisher for the book, supervised and corrected the drafting of the contract, twice visited the author at Montmorency to discuss the publication, and written him numerous letters on the subject? Moreover, Malesherbes had acted bravely in the past in defence of dissident writers; he had narrowly escaped dismissal for protecting Diderot's *Encyclopédie* in 1752 and 1755 and Helvétius's *De l'esprit* in 1758. However, it is clear that in the more intolerant atmosphere of 1762, Malesherbes's courage faltered and he adopted devious means to protect himself. Instead of instructing Duchesne to submit the last two volumes of *Émile* for censorship, he encouraged him to print them in France behind the pretence that they were being printed in Holland, so that he officially need know nothing about the matter. When it became clear that the deception would not work, Malesherbes decided to suppress the book and to destroy the evidence that would implicate him in its publication.

After Rousseau's death, Malesherbes in correspondence with Moultou tried to refute the suggestion that he had recovered the letters from Rousseau in order to cover up his own involvement with *Émile*; he said[119] he did not want his letters read by other people because of their private nature: 'I wrote to Rousseau several times about matters that concerned me personally and my family and I would have been upset if all that had been divulged.' It is hard to believe this story: for Malesherbes's relations with Rousseau were not such as to make it at all likely that he would have disclosed to him private and family secrets.

At what point did Malesherbes decide he would have to act against *Émile*? His position as Director of Publications was subordinate to that of

his father, Lamoignon de Malesherbes, the Chancellor, and it appears that
he discussed the book with him in the family château at Malesherbes in
the month of May. Without telling his father of his own involvement, he
warned[120] him that trouble was to be expected.

Malesherbes's first action was against *The Social Contract*, but it was not
unil 29 May[121] that Rousseau wrote to inform Rey that (as Rey had
already been told by the Paris booksellers on 13 May) '*The Social Contract*
will not be tolerated in France.' He went on to say that there was 'no
choice for us but to bow, even as republicans, to the decisions of a royal
government'. However, Rousseau argued that it did not follow from this
that his name should be removed from the title-page of a book

which I am proud to have written, and which contains nothing alien to
the sentiments of a good man and citizen, nothing I am not ready to
defend before any competent tribunal whatever. As for my person, my
conduct, my words, I know the obedience and the respect I owe to the
government and the laws of the country in which I live, and I should be
very distressed if any Frenchman were more punctilious in the observance
of his duty than I am. But as for my principles of republicanism, published
in a republic, there is in France no magistrate, no court, no *parlement*, no
minister, not even the King himself who has the right to question me
about them, and demand an account of them. If they consider the book
bad for the country, they can prohibit its entry. If they consider I am
wrong, they can refute me, that is all.

Rousseau urged Rey not to allow his friendship for him to make him
worry about his, Rousseau's, safety: 'They know and respect the law of
nations too well here,' he added optimistically, 'for them to violate that
law in an odious way against a poor invalid whose peaceful sojourn in
France is no less a credit to the government than it is to himself.'

Obviously Rousseau had not fully grasped the nature of political
developments in France, even after receiving a long letter,[122] written
ten days earlier by Ribotte from Toulouse, saying once again that the
persecution of Protestants had not ended with the execution of Jean
Calas.[123]*

In Amsterdam Néaulme had decided to go ahead and publish *Émile* but
to spread the risk by sharing the enterprise with Rey, to whom he sold
the rights of the duodecimo edition while keeping for himself the rights
to the octavo edition. Néaulme tried to explain[124] to Rousseau that a
publisher's situation was different from a writer's: 'You work for glory.

*Calas's name was only cleared three years after his execution.

We work for profit. I have been thinking, if you absolutely persist in believing that your honour depends on your book being published exactly as it is, what am I to do? I like to make money as much as anyone, but if you want to thwart me totally, I shall be of all publishers the most submissive.'

Néaulme was, however, far from submissive towards Duchesne, when he discovered that Duchesne was selling sheets of *Émile* to an unscrupulous publisher in Lyons named Jean-Marie Bruysset, who had had the effrontery to print his, Néaulme's, name and privilege on the title-page. Next time he wrote[125] to Rousseau, Néaulme said he had made up his mind to have no more dealings with Duchesne.

The date of 24 May was fixed for the publication of *Émile*, and although he knew that *The Social Contract* had been banned, Rousseau had as yet no inkling that *Émile* was also to be suppressed. He was only worried, as a result of what he had heard from Néaulme and Rey, about the pirating of it, and on 28 May[126] he wrote to the Lieutenant-General of Police, Sartine, asking him to act against the counterfeiters whose activities threatened to ruin the legitimate French publisher, Duchesne. On the same day[127] Rousseau asked Mme de Luxembourg to urge Malesherbes to intervene to protect the book from piracy, little knowing that Malesherbes had already intervened for another purpose.

Néaulme tried again[128] to shake Rousseau out of his complacency: 'You believe you have nothing to fear in proclaiming beliefs that are honourable. I fear everything, even dishonour itself.' By the time Néaulme wrote these words – 31 May – *Émile* had already been banned in Paris, and instructions issued for the confiscation of all copies, issued by the man who had organized the publication in the first place, Malesherbes.

On 1 June 1762[129] Malesherbes personally signed an order to the syndic of the Paris publishers, Charles Saillant, to seize all copies of *Émile* in the publisher's warehouse. He had, however, already sent word to Duchesne[130]* so that he could remove his stock to a convenient hiding-place. When the syndic and his assistant went to Duchesne's premises they could only find four copies of *Émile*. Even the publisher had vanished. The syndic reported[131] to Malesherbes that in the absence of Duchesne, his wife and his partner Pierre Guy had declared that the firm had already sold four or five hundred copies of the book, and that the four they surrendered were all that remained.

Rousseau himself must have known of the impending action before the end of May, since we find him sending news of it to Mme Alissan de La Tour in a letter dated 1 June.[132] Pierre Guy reported what had happened

---

*Malesherbes had once done a similar service for Diderot when forced to act against his publication, and indeed had taken the suspect materials into his own house.

in a letter to Néaulme dated 4 June,[133] in which he begged him to keep an absolute secret their arrangement to publish *Émile* jointly. Guy was clearly alarmed by the situation. Rousseau, by contrast, was still remarkably calm, for although he, too, wrote[134] to Néaulme, it was only to express his defiance:

I am very sorry about the trouble that the 'Profession of Faith' is giving you, but I must say to you, once and for all, that no interdiction, no danger, no violence, no power on earth would ever make me retract one syllable. Since you never discussed the contents of my manuscript when you negotiated the publication of it, you can have no claim against me now over the matters that embarrass you – and all the less so since the disturbing truths contained in all my other writings must have led you to expect to find more of the same kind in this work. I have neither taken you by surprise nor deceived you. I would like to help you; but I could not do it in the way you desire; and I am amazed that you should believe that a man who has taken so many steps to forestall any tampering with his works after his death, should allow it to be mutilated during his lifetime...

I have done my duty. Whether people benefit by it or not, whether they condemn me or approve of me is their business, and I would not give a fig to change their blame into praise. What is more, I defy them to do their worst. What can they do to me that Nature, and my own ill health will not achieve without their intervention?

Rousseau told Néaulme he had heard rumours that the Paris *parlement* intended to prosecute him; but, he added, 'I do not believe that such a wise and enlightened body would really do such a foolish thing.'

Malesherbes, who knew the Paris *parlement* better, had no such confidence. He was perhaps first to realize that condemnation of *Émile* would be followed by condemnation of its author and that Rousseau was in mortal danger. No doubt he wished he could rescue him, but he could not warn Rousseau, as he had warned Duchesne, without compromising himself, and that was clearly the last thing Malesherbes intended to do. There could be no question of any more letters to the author, still less of another visit to Montmorency. All Malesherbes could bring himself to do was to convey a coded message to Rousseau through intermediaries to the effect that he should leave France as soon as possible.

Unfortunately Rousseau was so stubbornly attached to his principles, so confident both of the will and the power of Malesherbes and Luxembourg to protect him, so optimistic about the wisdom of the Paris judiciary, that he continued to lead his usual life at Montlouis, unconcerned

about danger, and indeed to partake, since the Luxembourgs had returned
to their château, in such social activities there as a 'dying man' could find
the strength to enjoy.

He even invited[135] Mme Alissan to come to Montmorency and meet
Mme de Luxembourg, who, as he explained, wanted to make the acquaintance of his 'Julie'. He couched the invitation in flirtatious language:

Do I desire or fear the visit? I believe in truth that it will rob me of my
peace beforehand. And what will it be afterwards? My God, what will
you do here with those beautiful eyes that conquered a Swiss?* Will they
at least leave a Genevan undisturbed? Ah, you must pay due respect to my
ill health and my grey beard and not overwhelm me with seductive
charms. . . I have never dreaded meeting a woman as I dread meeting you.

Mme Alissan declined[136] the invitation to meet the Maréchale, and was
only alarmed at the thought of her identity being revealed to her: 'I have
a very good reason for asking this of you. Besides, my name is neither
celebrated enough nor obscure enough to serve as a recommendation.'
Without disclosing what the 'good reason' was. Mme Alissan begged
Rousseau to keep her correspondence with him a secret.

'Rest assured, Madame,' he wrote in his reply,[137]

your name will not be revealed or known. I have done only what could
be done discreetly. I will go through all your letters, starting today, and
as I do not have the courage to burn them, unless you order me to, I will
at least remove anything which might disclose or point to your identity.
Also please wait some days before you write to me again. It is said that
the *parlement* of Paris intends to arrest me. We must let them go ahead,
and not allow your letters to compromise you because of that. . .

I open up my letter to let you know that I shall remove your seal as
well and I will put your letters in a safe place, so be reassured.

At this point, Mme Alissan was clearly more worried about Rousseau
than about herself. She wrote back immediately:[138] 'For heaven's sake, put
my mind at rest about yourself. There are some horribly disturbing
rumours in circulation about you. I know that Paris is full of false news,
but when it is bad and particularly when it is bad for me, I am disposed
to believe it: and I am always afraid that any writer who publishes the
truth is sure to be sent to the penal quarries.'

On the same 7 June,[139] Rousseau wrote a long letter to Moultou,

*It is the eyes of Julie in the novel that capture the heart of her tutor, St-Preux.

begging him not to be alarmed by the rumours about him which were circulating in Paris and the provinces. According to those rumours, the Paris *parlement*, in order to justify its persecution of the Jesuits, intended to extend action against others who did not think as it did, so that 'the only man in France who believes in God, is to be the victim of these defenders of Christianity'. Rousseau added that his friends had been 'vying with each other' to make him afraid:

They offer me places of refuge on all sides, but they do not give me any good reason for accepting their offers – that is, reasons good in my own eyes. I am staying put, for your friend Jean-Jacques has not learned how to hide himself. Besides, I think they exaggerate the danger in order to shake my resolve, for I really cannot imagine by what right I, a citizen of Geneva, can be accountable to the Paris *parlement* for a book published in Holland with a privilege from the Dutch authorities.

He declared to Moultou that he would defend himself against any accusation by challenging the competence of the *parlement* in his case, and 'to say nothing but what is true'.

A curious feature of this letter is that while swearing to 'say nothing but what is true', Rousseau should refer to *Émile* as a 'book published in Holland'; and thus to utter to his most trusted friend the very half-truth he had denounced a few weeks earlier.

Rousseau had not at this time received a letter[140] from Moultou reporting that *The Social Contract* was already on sale in Geneva, despite the fact that, as he put it, the Genevese booksellers did not like doing business with Rey – 'he is a greedy man, and they are no less greedy than he.' Moultou even spoke of *The Social Contract* as a 'success' in Geneva. He made no reference to the chapter which was likeliest to provoke scandal – the one in which Christianity is criticized as being worse than futile as a civil religion. He simply expressed doubts about Rousseau's proposals for an elective aristocracy: 'Would those who dislike our democracy tolerate your aristocracy? Would they have liked that of Sparta?' As for *Émile*, Moultou said his chief concern was to denounce as pirated the edition which was coming to Geneva from Lyons. There was no indication in Moultou's letter of the storm that was brewing in Geneva against both the books and their author.

Mme de Créqui was one of several friends who urged Rousseau to go into hiding to avoid arrest, but he wrote[141] to her as he had written to Moultou: 'Jean-Jacques does not hide. Besides I cannot conceive by what right a citizen of Geneva, printing a book in Holland, with the privilege of the Dutch authorities, can be held answerable to the *parlement* of Paris.

I have paid homage to God and written only for the good of mankind. I would never refuse to suffer for such a good cause.'

Mme de Créqui was appalled at Rousseau's attitude. 'It is all too true that a warrant has been issued for your arrest,' she wrote[142] frantically on 8 May. 'In the name of God, leave! One must not judge by good intentions in these public affairs: one must act according to the circumstances. Burning your book will do no harm. But your body could not stand prison. Ask your neighbours [M. and Mme de Luxembourg]. I am sure they will agree with me. Friendship dictates what I advise. May prudence respond to it.'

At this stage, according to the *Confessions*,[143] Rousseau's 'neighbours' were less pressing than other friends, and he reproaches himself for failing to see the menacing nature of the warnings he received from so many quarters. He says he felt safe under the protection of Mme de Luxembourg, since she was herself responsible for the publication of *Émile* in France.

My tranquillity continued ... but the public and especially the *parlement* seemed irritated by my composure. The magistrates in the *parlement* were heard to say that burning books was not enough and that their authors should be burned with them, although not a word was said about burning publishers. The first time I heard that these opinions – more worthy of an inquisitor in Goa than a magistrate in Paris – were being expressed, I did not doubt that they originated in Holbach's clique, who wanted to frighten me into leaving France. I laughed at their puerile trick.

Rousseau recalls[144] that he began to take the danger more seriously when M. de Luxembourg asked him if he had written anything unfavourable about M. de Choiseul in *Émile* or *The Social Contract*. When Rousseau assured him that his only words about Choiseul were words of praise, the Maréchal remarked that he would have been wiser to have expressed himself more clearly. It was only later that Rousseau discovered that Choiseul had read his praise of him as a veiled insult* (an interpretation which Voltaire[146] encouraged in correspondence with the Minister). At the time Rousseau could not imagine he had said anything to cause offence. Moreover, as he puts it in the *Confessions*,[147] Mme de Luxembourg was too calm, too happy, too full of smiles for him to believe that anything could possibly be amiss. He says she 'watched the unfolding of events as if the fate of *Émile* had nothing to do with her'.

The one person at the château he saw as thoroughly agitated was the Comtesse de Boufflers, who 'actually told me that the Prince de Conti was taking steps to ward off the blow that was about to be aimed at me'.[148]

---

*In a letter to St-Germain of 26 February 1770[145] Rousseau says, 'I lavished praises on M. de Choiseul which he deserved too little to take literally; he felt insulted.'

The Comtesse tried to persuade Rousseau to escape to England, 'where she offered to introduce me to many of her friends, including the celebrated David Hume'. When these efforts failed, she urged him to think of the situation of Mme de Luxembourg, and argued that it was his duty to avoid being arrested in order to save his benefactress from being implicated in the affair. If he did not wish to go to England, the Comtesse even ventured to suggest that he might choose to become a prisoner in the Bastille for a while, so as to put himself outside the jurisdiction of the *parlement*. But he would not budge.

Confirmation of all the rumours reached Rousseau from Pierre Guy,[149] who reported that he had been to the office of the Procurator-General, Guillaume Joly de Fleury, and seen the draft indictment of *Émile*. This indictment was presented to the *parlement* at its session of 9 June. The Lieutenant-General of Police, Sartine, noted in a letter[150] on the subject to the Attorney-General, Omer July de Fleury: 'I hear that the author of *Émile* intends to let himself be arrested. I do not know if his protectors will allow it.'

The 'protectors' he had in mind were of course the Luxembourgs, and since, as the Comtesse de Boufflers had reminded Rousseau, his trial would inevitably compromise the Maréchale, the Luxembourgs had a motive in addition to friendly solicitude for saving Rousseau from arrest.

In the *Confessions*,[151] Rousseau recalls the days that led up to the fateful hearing in the *parlement*:

Far from being frightened and hiding myself, I went every day to the château, and in the afternoons I took my usual walk. On 8 June, the evening before the session of the *parlement*, I walked in company with two Oratorian professors, Fr. Alammani★ and Fr. Mandard.† We took a picnic with us to Champeaux, which we ate with a hearty appetite. We had forgotten to take glasses, and used stalks of rye instead, sucking up the wine from the bottle... I was never more cheerful in my life.

Rousseau's friends were far from cheerful. Coindet, who had been banished for months from Montlouis, wrote[152] to say that the trouble Rousseau was in forced him to break his pledge of silence, and offering to accompany him into exile. He recalled the journey they had once planned to the Swiss canton of Valais: 'Would this not be the time to make that journey?'

But Rousseau went to bed that night with no thoughts of travelling.

★Father Alammani was appointed Superior of the Oratory at Tours later in 1762.
†Jean-François Mandard was subsequently elected Superior-General of the Oratorian Order.

He retired early with the Bible and read the whole Book of Judges before he went to sleep. The story of the Levite of Ephraim as told there affected him so deeply that his dreams revolved around it. Then, as he recalls in the *Confessions*,[153] he was awakened by noise and a light. Thérèse entered his room carrying a candle and followed by La Roche, who said to him: 'Do not be alarmed. I come from Mme de Luxembourg. She has written you this letter and sends you another from the Prince de Conti.' In his letter the Prince de Conti explained that, despite all his efforts, the authorities were determined to act against Rousseau with the utmost severity: 'The Court demands it; the *parlement* desires it,' the Prince informed the Maréchale. 'At seven o'clock tomorrow morning the order will be issued for his arrest. Officers will be sent to him immediately to seize him. I have secured a promise, however, that he will not be pursued if he makes his escape. But if he persists in exposing himself, he will undoubtedly be taken.'

The original manuscript of the Prince's letter has not been traced, but Mme de Luxemburg's covering note is in the Rousseau archive at Neuchâtel:[154]

I send you this letter from M. le Prince de Conti. It is obvious that you have not a moment to lose in collecting all your papers and getting yourself out of the way of all the troubles that force can cause when it is not accompanied by justice. In the name of God, come here. It would be the greatest mark of friendship you could possibly offer me. La Roche will tell you my reasons for sending for you in the middle of the night.

As Rousseau continues the story in the *Confessions*,[155] La Roche told him that Mme de Luxembourg had retired to bed by two o'clock, but had declared she would not go to sleep until she had spoken to Rousseau. 'I dressed myself quickly,' he writes, 'and ran to see her. I found her for the first time agitated.' Her distress troubled him, and he says he thought less of his own predicament than of what would happen to her if he allowed himself to be arrested. He realized that he could not become a martyr to his principles without compromising her, and so, as he puts it in the *Confessions*,[156] 'I determined to sacrifice my reputation to her tranquillity.' He was only disappointed that the Maréchale did not seem to realize that in agreeing to save himself he was making a sacrifice for her sake: 'I was so shocked by her indifference that for a moment I thought of retracting my promise.'

It was just then, he says, that M. de Luxembourg entered the room accompanied by the Comtesse de Boufflers, and because they treated him as he had expected Mme de Luxembourg to treat him, there was no more hesitation on his part. The Maréchal offered to hide him somewhere in the château, but Rousseau judged it best to leave the country altogether. He thought first of Geneva, but remembering the hostility that existed there, he decided to go to Yverdon, where Roguin had assured him of a welcome. The Comtesse de Boufflers renewed her efforts to make him go to England, but Rousseau continues:[157] 'I have never loved England or the English, and the eloquence of the Comtesse, far from overcoming my reluctance, seemed to strengthen it, without my knowing why.'

Once he had made up his mind* to leave as soon as possible, Rousseau asked La Roche to go to Montlouis for his clothes and his papers – especially the letters he had filed away to document his autobiography – and bring them to the château. M. de Luxembourg offered personally to sort out any papers Rousseau chose to leave in his care. When La Roche returned with Rousseau's baggage he brought a thoroughly frightened Thérèse with him as well. 'Seeing me there,' Rousseau recalls,[159] 'she made the building resound with her cries and threw herself into my arms.'

Thérèse wanted to join him on his flight, but Rousseau explained to her that he needed her to stay behind to look after his property, since it was the practice in France when a man was arrested to register and seal his belongings and entrust them to a custodian.

'I promised her,' he continues, 'that she would join me soon, and M. de Luxembourg confirmed that promise. But I did not tell her where I was going, so that if she was questioned about it by the officers sent to arrest me, she could truthfully say she did not know where I was.'

The crucial session of the Paris *parlement* took place that morning, 9 June, under the presidency of a hostile magistrate, Maupeou. The Procurator-General and Attorney-General† together presented[160] to the Grande Chambre the indictment of *Émile*, declaring it to be subversive of religion, morals and decency, seditious, impious and sacrilegious, besides much else. The Court promptly decreed that the author should be arrested forthwith, imprisoned and interrogated at the Conciergerie, and that all copies of the book were to be seized, shredded and burned by the public executioner.

Rousseau was told that the officers of the court should have come to Montmorency to arrest him at ten o'clock in the morning, but they did not arrive until four in the afternoon, by which time he had left. M. de Luxembourg lent him his cabriolet and horses for the first stage of his

---

*After Rousseau's death Malesherbes asserted that he had urged him to escape from France when he was indicted by the *parlement*, but that he refused to go. 'The Prince de Conti warned him before I did, but Rousseau rejected his advice as well. Finally M. de Luxembourg alone persuaded him to go, and I believe he succeeded in doing so only by saying that Mme de Luxembourg would be compromised if he did not.'[158]

†The brothers Omer and Guillaume Joly de Fleury were respectively Attorney-General and Procurator-General.

journey to the frontier. The ladies of the château went to the *entresol* to bid him farewell, no doubt thoroughly excited by the drama of it all, and in some cases, sincerely distressed at his departure. Mme de Luxembourg embraced him several times with a sad look on her face, but he says in the *Confessions*[161] that he did not feel in her embrace the warmth he had felt two or three years earlier. The Comtesse de Boufflers also kissed him goodbye, saying 'many kind things', and even the usually cold and haughty Mme de Mirepoix showed a 'flicker of concern' as she bade him adieu. As for the Maréchal, Rousseau says he did not open his mouth, and was as pale as death:

He wanted absolutely to accompany me to the carriage which was waiting at the horse pond outside the château. We crossed the garden together without uttering a single word. I had a key to the park which I used to open the gate; then, instead of putting in my pocket I handed it to the Maréchal without saying a word. He took it with a surprising alacrity that I have not been able to stop myself brooding over often since that time. I have never had a moment more bitter in all my life than that parting. Our embrace was long and silent; we both had the same sense that it was to be our last.

On the road between Montmorency and La Barre Rousseau saw from his cabriolet four men in black suits in a hired carriage who saluted him as their paths crossed. He guessed that they were officers of the court sent to arrest him. He guessed correctly, as he learned later from a letter[162] from M. de Luxembourg informing him that 'the officers arrived at your house an hour after you left here: you must have met them on the road'. Rousseau was lucky. It was only because the warrant for his arrest was delayed until noon that he had time to escape. He was seen, and, he assumed, recognized as he drove through Paris – 'a traveller in an open cabriolet is not well hidden'[163] – but no one tried to stop him.

Rumours that Rousseau was under the personal protection of Malesherbes were widespread, so much so that Malesherbes felt it necessary to write the next day, 10 June,[164] to his father, the Chancellor Lamoignon, to dissociate himself from *Émile* and its author:

Father, I must take a precaution that is very important to me, and that is to warn you that people are saying that tacit permission was given for *Émile* to be published. I am well aware that the Attorney-General and the Procurator-General asserted as much in court. There is no doubt you will hear it said, but I swear and I beg you to swear to those who speak to you about it, that the assertion is false.

In the technical sense of 'tacit permission', which was something actually recorded despite its being called tacit, Malesherbes could safely say he had not given it; but the truth of the matter, as we have seen, is that he had done much more than permit its publication; he had organized it.

On the same day that the Chancellor received his son's denial of having authorized *Émile*, he received from the Attorney-General a report[165] of his officer's visit to Montmorency to arrest the author. Their quarry having fled, they were able to do no more than search the house and interrogate the housekeeper. Although their warrant instructed them to confiscate Rousseau's property, they considered his belongings to be of too little value to be worth the trouble of impounding, sealing or putting under guard. They had left the housekeeper in occupation of the cottage.

The ceremonial shredding and burning of *Émile* by the public executioner took place in Paris on 11 June, and news of this lamentable event prompted a whole series of interdictions in other countries, including the Netherlands, where, as Néaulme had feared, his privilege proved worthless, and in Geneva, where the authorities suppressed *The Social Contract* as well as *Émile* and issued yet another warrant for the arrest of the blasphemer.

On his journey to Yverdon in the Pays de Vaud, Rousseau wisely kept clear of Genevese territory, as he did of those French cities where travellers' papers were scrutinized by the local police. His first halt was at the château de Villeroy, where, with a letter from Mme de Luxembourg to her brother, the duke, he hoped to secure a letter of exemption from reporting to the Commandant of Lyons. M. de Villeroy gave him the letter, but Rousseau decided not to use it, and to avoid Lyons altogether. At Dijon he had a disagreeable experience which he does not mention in the *Confessions*, but which he described in a letter[166] to Mme de Luxembourg: being asked to state his name by the officers there, he says he took up the pen intending to write his mother's maiden name* 'but my hand trembled so much that I had to put the pen down twice, and finally "Rousseau" was the only name I could write'.

Luckily, however, Rousseau was spared disaster in this town where his name was first made famous, and he hurried on to Dôle, and then, to bypass Besançon, where he might have to face another questioning, he went on through Salins 'without being spoken to by anybody'.[167] He crossed the Jura mountains, and entered Switzerland at Pontarlier.

It was not a comfortable journey, once he had exchanged M. de Luxembourg's elegant cabriolet for hired carriages. He was painfully aware that his shabby appearance excited the contempt of the postillions, and he

*Bernard.

only made things worse by over-tipping them: 'They took me for a plebeian messenger travelling in a hired carriage for the first time in my life; from then on I was given worn-out hacks and became the butt of the postillions' mirth. I ended as I ought to have begun, by holding my tongue and being driven as it pleased them to drive me.'[168]

On the first part of his journey Rousseau's mind was tormented, he tells us in the *Confessions*, by black thoughts about people like Grimm who had wronged him in France: 'We are taught to forgive our enemies. That is undoubtedly a very fine virtue, but it does not suit me.'[169] Rousseau found relief from these feelings by thinking about vengeance in another, more exalted, context, that of the Holy Scriptures, and the story of the Levite of Ephraim he had read – and dreamed about – in his last night at Montlouis. On the road to Yverdon he decided to turn the story into a prose poem in the manner of Gessner, even though he could see that 'the pastoral style of that Swiss poet was hardly suited to so atrocious a subject'.

Presumably the ordeal of the Levite had to be atrocious to take Rousseau's mind off the atrocities he had himself endured at the hands of Grimm and others. And even by Old Testament standards the story is morbid: the Levite, travelling with a concubine he claims to be his true wife, is being entertained to dinner by an elderly man with a young daughter, when some Benjamite villagers demand that he, the Levite, be surrendered to them for their sexual gratification. The host offers them his daughter instead; but the Levite rescues the daughter and throws his beloved concubine to the mob. The Benjamites rape the girl so violently that she dies next day in the Levite's arms. He thereupon chops up her body into twelve pieces and sends one each to the twelve tribes of Israel, who are thus stirred to declare a war of vengeance on the Benjamites. Twenty-five thousand men are killed, and as Rousseau expresses it in the prose poem he wrote on the subject, 'Their land offered only a terrible emptiness covered with ashes and bones.'

But this is not the end of the story. The victors take pity on the vanquished and in order that the Benjamites may restore their numbers, the Israelites attack the tribe of Jabesh, kill all the males and deliver all the virgins to the Benjamites for forced marriages: '*Quelles noces,*' the poet exclaims, 'for these timid young maidens, whose brothers, fathers and mothers have been massacred in front of their eyes!'[170]

Despite Rousseau's acknowledgement that the subject was atrocious, he was pleased with the poem* he made out of it. It was, he thought, a triumph of art to have produced a work of aesthetic beauty out of an 'abominable' theme. Indeed, he claimed that in all his life he had 'never

---

*The work was not published until after his death; but he was eager to have it included in his collected works.[171]

written anything where a more moving tenderness of morals prevailed';[172] so that 'if the Levite of Ephraim is not the best of my works, it will always be the most cherished'.[173]

Literary critics have not shared this appreciation of the poem,[174] and it is not easy to understand why Rousseau himself thought so well of it. The academic interest of the story for him was perhaps connected with the fact that it gave Biblical confirmation to the thesis of the *Discourse of Inequality* that primitive tribal societies, after the discovery of agriculture and metallurgy and before the institution of government, experienced a 'most horrible state of war'.[175] But where is the 'tenderness of morals'?* In another text[177] Rousseau favourably compares the burning demand for vengeance by the Levite with the cool indifference of modern man, who answers crime with criminological theorizing rather than punishment. Vengeance, Rousseau evidently felt as he rattled along the stony road of exile thinking of his persecutors, is no bad thing.

The arrival of his coach on Bernese territory banished all black thoughts from his mind. He ordered the postillion to stop, climbed down, and kissed the soil of Switzerland. 'The man thought me mad. I got back in the carriage, and a few hours later I had the pure and intense pleasure of being embraced by the worthy Roguin.'[178]

From Roguin's house – a colonnaded villa beside the lake of Neuchâtel – Rousseau wrote[179] at once to M. de Luxembourg: 'At last I have set foot in this land of justice and freedom which I ought never to have left.'

His joy was not to last. Switzerland, if a land of justice and freedom for others, was not to be such a refuge for him, and he would soon be forced to leave it. His life as a 'hermit' had ended; a new life as a fugitive was about to begin.

---

*Professor Grimsley says of the poem that it proved Rousseau's 'ability to detach himself from the wickedness of the world and find consolation in the "antique simplicity" and naive innocence of a patriarchal age'.[176] But even Rousseau himself did not claim that this tale of sodomy, rape, murder, massacre and forced marriages was one of naive innocence.

LIST OF PRINCIPAL
ABBREVIATIONS USED IN
THE NOTES

Annales	*Annales de la Société Jean-Jacques Rousseau*, Geneva, 1905 –
BArs.	Bibliothèque de l'Arsenal, Paris
Besterman	Theodore Besterman, ed. *The Correspondence of Voltaire: Definitive Edition* (*The Complete Works of Voltaire*), Geneva, Banbury and Oxford, 1968–80
BL	British Library, London
BN	Bibliothèque Nationale, Paris
BPUG	Bibliothèque Publique et Universitaire, Geneva
BPUN	Bibliothèque Publique et Universitaire, Neuchâtel
CC	*Correspondance complète de J.-J. Rousseau*, ed. R.A. Leigh, Geneva, Banbury and Oxford, 1965–
CG	*Correspondance générale de J.-J. Rousseau*, ed. T. Dufour and P.P. Plan, Paris, 1924–34
Chérigny	Château de Chérigny, Chenu, Vaas, Touraine (Vicomtesse de Montmagner de Loute)
Corr. (ed. Roth)	*Correspondance de D-Diderot*, ed. G. Roth, Paris, 1955–
DI	J.-J. Rousseau, *A Discourse on Inequality*, ed. Maurice Cranston, Harmondsworth and New York, 1984
Dutch Royal Library	The Library of HM The Queen of the Netherlands, The Hague
Encyclopédie	*Encyclopédie ou Dictionnaire raisonné des sciences, des arts et des métiers*, 35 vols., Paris
Fuchs	M. Fuchs, ed. J.-J. Rousseau, *Lettre à M. d'Alembert*, Geneva and Lille, 1948
G	The 'Geneva' manuscript of Rousseau's *Confessions* (in BPUG)
Grimsley	Robert Grimsley, *Rousseau and the Religious Quest*, Oxford, 1968
Grosclaude (1960)	Pierre Grosclaude, *J.-J. Rousseau et Malesherbes*, Paris, 1960
Grosclaude (1961)	Pierre Grosclaude, *Malesherbes, Témoin et interprète de son temps*, Paris, 1961
Guillemin (1942)	Henri Guillemin: 'Les affaires de l'Ermitage', *Annales*, XXIV (1941–2)
Guillemin (1943)	Henri Guillemin, *Un homme, deux ombres*, Geneva, 1943
Hope-Mason (1979)	John Hope-Mason, *The Indispensable Rousseau*, London, 1979
J.-J.	Maurice Cranston, *Jean-Jacques, the Early Life and Work of J.-J. Rousseau*, London and New York, 1983

Jimack (1960)	P.D. Jimack, *La Genèse et la rédaction de L'Émile*, SVEC, Geneva, 1960
Jimack (1983)	P.D. Jimack, *Rousseau's Émile*, London, 1983
Masson	Pierre-Maurice Masson, ed., *La 'Profession de foi du vicaire savoyard' de Jean-Jacques Rousseau*, Fribourg and Paris, 1914
Moland	L. Moland, ed., Voltaire, *Oeuvres complètes*, Paris, 1877–85
Montbrillant	*Les Pseudo-mémoires de Mme d'Épinay: L'Histoire de Mme de Montbrillant*, ed. G. Roth, 3 vols., Paris, 1951
Musset-Pathay (1821)	V.-D. Musset-Pathay, *Histoire de la vie et des ouvrages de J.-J. Rousseau*, Paris, 1821
Musset-Pathay (1825)	V.-D. Musset-Pathay, *Oeuvres inédites de J.-J. Rousseau*, Paris, 1825
OC	*Oeuvres complètes de J.-J. Rousseau*, edited for the Bibliothèque de la Pléiade by B. Gagnebin, M. Raymond, J. Starobinski, *et al.*, 4 vols., 1959–
P	The 'Paris' manuscript of the *Confessions* (in the library of the Assemblée Nationale, Palais Bourbon, Paris)
P and P	Maurice Cranston, *Philosophers and Pamphleteers*, Oxford, 1986
Porset	Charles Porset, ed., *J.-J. Rousseau: Essai sur l'origine des langues*, Bordeaux, 1970
A. Rey (1904)	Auguste Rey, *Le Château de La Chevrette*, Paris, 1904
A. Rey (1909)	Auguste Rey, *J.-J. Rousseau dans la vallée de Montmorency*, Paris, 1909
SC	J.-J. Rousseau, *The Social Contract*, ed. Maurice Cranston, Harmondsworth and Baltimore, 1968
Schwartz	Joel Schwartz, *The Sexual Politics of J.-J. Rousseau*, Chicago and London, 1984
Soc. J.-J.R.	Archives of the Société Jean-Jacques Rousseau, Geneva (in BPUG)
Starobinski (1971)	Jean Starobinski, *Jean-Jacques Rousseau – La transparence et l'obstacle*, Paris, 1971
SVEC	*Studies on Voltaire and the Eighteenth Century*, ed. T. Besterman (1955–76) and Haydn Mason (1977–), Geneva and Oxford, 1955–
Tourneux	Maurice Tourneux, ed., *Correspondance littéraire, philosophique et critique par Grimm, Diderot, et al.*, Paris, 1877
Vallette	Gaspard Vallette, *Jean-Jacques Rousseau – Genevois*, Paris and Geneva, 1911
Wokler (1975)	Robert Wokler, 'The Influence of Diderot on Rousseau', *SVEC* (CXXXII), 1975, pp. 55–111
Wokler (1987)	Robert Wokler, *Rousseau on Society, Politics, Music and Language*, New York, 1987

NOTES

CHAPTER 1: PARIS
(pages 1–20)

1. BPUN, R286, ff.18.
2. B. de St Pierre, *Vie de Rousseau*, Paris, 1907, p.175.
3. 3.9.1759. BPUN, R302, ff.37 (*CC*, VI, 858).
4. See Prince de Ligne, *Lettres et pensées*, Paris, 1809, p.321; A. Dusaulx, *De mes rapports avec J.-J. Rousseau*, Paris, 1798, p.65; L.J. Courtois, in *Annales*, XVII (1926), p.163; Vallette, 1911, p.365.
5. See *J.-J.*, p.348.
6. To Perdriau, 20.2.1755. BPUG, unclassified (*CC*, III, 277).
7. See Leigh (*CC*, III, p.100).
8. C. Collé, *Journal et mémoires*, Paris, 1868, II, p.4.
9. 4.4.1757. BPUG, MS-Fr. 203, f.243 (*CC*, IV, 498).
10. *OC*, II, p.275.
11. 16.2.1754. Manuscript not traced (*CC*, III, 263).
12. See *J.-J.*, pp.334–5.
13. See *J.-J.*, p.333.
14. 2.1.1755. New York, Morgan Library, Heinemann Collection (*CC*, III, 268).
15. 16.12.1754. Manuscript not traced (*CC*, III, 263).
16. P, II, p.14 (*OC*, I, p.374).
17. 20.2.1755. BPUG, unclassified (*CC*, III, 277).
18. See A. Strugnell, *Diderot's Politics*, The Hague, 1973.
19. See Albert Schinz, *J.-J. Rousseau et le libraire-imprimeur, M.-M. Rey*, Geneva, 1916, pp.3–5.
20. ibid., p.15.
21. 29.5.1755. Dutch Royal Library, G16-A434, no.14 (*CC*, III, 297).
22. 20.3.1755. BN, n.a.f.1183 (*CC*, III, 283).
23. See Grosclaude (1961).
24. 2.4.1755. Dutch Royal Library, G16-A240, no.3 (*CC*, III, 287).
25. 17.4.1755. BN, n.a.f.1183 (*CC*, III, 289).
26. 10.4.1755. Dutch Royal Library, G16-A434, no.13 (*CC*, III, 288).
27. 23.3.1755. Dutch Royal Library, G16-A434, no.12 (*CC*, III, 284).
28. BN, n.a.f. 1183, f.6 (*CC*, III, 290).
29. 5.5.1755. Manuscript not traced; *CG*, II, p.184 (*CC*, III, 293).
30. BN, n.a.f. 1183, f.7 (*CC*, III, 294).
31. 29.5.1755. Dutch Royal Library, G16-A434, no.14 (*CC*, III, 297).
32. 30.3.1755. BN, Collection Rothschild, XVIII siècle (*CC*, III, 285).
33. 18.6.1755. BPUN, R301, ff.87–8 (*CC*, III, 301.
34. 29.3.1756. BPUN, R303, ff.33–4 (*CC*, III, 401).
35. 20.6.1755. BPUN, R301, ff.135–6 (*CC*, III, 303).
36. 6.7.1775. BPUN, MS R290, ff.6–7 (*CC*, III, 306).
37. P, II, p.26 (*OC*, I, p.395).
38. See *J.-J.*, pp.203–16.
39. 30.8.1755. BPUN, MS R296, ff.155–6 (*CC*, III, 317).
40. 7.9.1755. Dutch Royal Library, G16-A274 (*CC*, III, 319).
41. 20.9.1755. BPUN, MS R89, p.47 (*CC*, III, 324).
42. Besterman, XVII, D6759.
43. 20.11.1755. Wisbech Literary Institute, Townshend Collection (*CC*, III, 336).
44. ibid.
45. 2.4.1755. BPUG, MS Fr.203, ff.241–2 (*CC*, III, 286).
46. ibid.

47. BPUG, MS Fr.236, ff.16–17 (*CC*, III, 252).
48. 20.10.1755. BPUG, MS Fr.236, f.32 (*CC*, III, 329).
49. 12.12.1755. BPUG, MS Fr.236, f.36 (*CC*, III, 344).
50. 22.12.1755. BPUG, Archives Tronchin 165, ff.1–2 (*CC*, III, 353).
51. *Encyclopédie*, vol. V (1755), pp.115–16.
52. Wokler (1975), pp.77–85.
53. *OC*, III, pp.244–5.
54. *OC*, III, p.263.
55. *OC*, III, p.273.
56. BPUN, MS R89, pp.30–31 (*CC*, III, 349).
57. 26.12.1755. Rochambeau Collection (*CC*, III, 354).
58. 10.8.1755. Manuscript not traced; *CG*, II, pp.128–9 (*CC*, III, 310).
59. BPUN, MS R50 *OC*, I, p.1115).
60. See *J.-J.*, pp.165–6.
61. ibid., p.224.
62. P.-P. Plan, *J.-J. Rousseau raconté par les gazettes de son temps*, Geneva, 1912, p.13.
63. *OC*, I, p.1473.
64. 22.12.1755. BPUG, Archives Tronchin 165 (*CC*, III, 353).
65. 25.12.1755. Rochambeau Collection (*CC*, III, 354).
66. See Elisabeth Badinter's introduction to her edition of *Montbrillant* as *Contre-Confessions*, Paris, 1989.
67. 19.12.1755. (*CC*, III, 348).
68. D'Alembert, *Oeuvres posthumes*, Paris, 1799, I, p.209.
69. 27.12.1755. BPUN, MS R89, p.58 (*CC*, III, 357).
70. Paris, BArs., MS 2759, ff.81–2 (*CC*, III, 359).
71. Paris, BArs., MS 2759, ff.92–5 (*CC*, III, 368).
72. BPUG, MS Fr.30, f.55 (*CC*, III, 379).
73. 28.3.1756. BPUG, MS Supp. 1,306, ff.66–7 (*CC*, III, 400).
74. P, II, p.28 (*OC*, I, p.396).
75. ibid.
76. ibid.
77. Undated. Rochambeau Collection (*CC*, III, 381).
78. *Montbrillant*, II, p.630.
79. ibid., p.631.
80. ibid., p.632.
81. Undated. Rochambeau Collection (*CC*, III, 389).
82. *Montbrillant*, II, p.464.
83. Tourneux, III, pp.53–6 and 153–4.
84. *Mémoires de C.C. de La Billarderie-Angevilliers*, Paris, 1933, p.43.
85. Rochambeau Collection (*CC*, III, 391).
86. P, II, p.29 (*OC*, I, p.398).
87. *Montbrillant*, II, p.16).
88. P, II, p.31 (*OC*, I, p.401).
89. Rochambeau Collection (*CC*, III, 394).
90. 19.4.1756. Rochambeau Collection (*CC*, IV, 407).
91. 13.4.1756. Rochambeau Collection (*CC*, IV, 405).
92. *Montbrillant*, III, p. 17.

CHAPTER 2: THE HERMITAGE
(pages 21–54)

1. P, II, p.32 (*OC*, I, p.403).
2. *OC*, IV, p.691.
3. P, II, p.40 *OC*, I, p.417.
4. 26.1.1762. BPUN, MS R291, ff.174–9 (*CC*, X, 1654).
5. See Book VI of the *Confessions*, especially *OC*, I, pp.235–42.
6. *OC*, I, p.425.
7. A. Rey (1909), p.6.
8. P, II, p.32 (*OC*, I, p.403).
9. *Montbrillant*, III, p.18.
10. 13.4.1756. Rochambeau Collection (*CC*, IV, 405).
11. P, II, p.32 (*OC*, I, p.403).
12. ibid.
13. Rochambeau Collection (*CC*, IV, 405).

14. 19.4.1756. Rochambeau Collection (*CC*, IV, 407).
15. P, II, p.32 (*OC*, I, p.404).
16. 13.3.1756. Rochambeau Collection (*CC*, IV, 405).
17. ibid.
18. 30.5.1756. BPUG, MS Fr.206, ff.3–4 (*CC*, IV, 411).
19. See Douglas G. Creighton, *Jacques-François Deluc*, University of Mississippi, 1982, p.27.
20. 27.6.1756. BPUG, MS Fr.203, ff.22–3 (*CC*, IV, 414).
21. P, II, p.92 (*OC*, I, p.506).
22. P, II, p.104 (*OC*, I, p.526).
23. P, II, p.106 (*OC*, I, p.530).
24. *Montbrillant*, III, p.24.
25. See *J.-J.*, pp.319–20.
26. P, II, p.25 (*OC*, I, p.390).
27. P, II, p.32 (*OC*, I, p.404).
28. P, II, p.34 (*OC*, I, p.408).
29. See *OC*, III, pp.617–45). The manuscript (BPUN, MS R2) remained unpublished in his lifetime.
30. P, II, p.34 (*OC*, I, p.408).
31. *OC*, III, p.564.
32. *OC*, III, pp.601–16.
33. *OC*, III, p.589.
34. BPUN, MS R34 (see also MS R33).
35. *OC*, III, p.600.
36. Stanley Hoffman, *The State of War*, New York, 1962, p.79.
37. See François Jost, *J.-J. Rousseau, Suisse*, 2 vols., Fribourg, 1961.
38. As did a related manuscript on '*L'État de guerre*' BPUN, MS R32. Grace Roosevelt suggests a reconstruction of this manuscript in *History of Political Thought*, VIII, 2 (1987), pp.225–44.
39. P, II, p.40 (*OC*, I, p.418).
40. P, II, p.37 (*OC*, I, p.413).
41. P, II, p.38 (*OC*, I, p.414).
42. ibid.
43. *Poèmes sur le désastre de Lisbonne et sur la loi naturelle*, May 1756. Reprinted in Moland, IX.
44. Cited Paul Edwards, *Voltaire*, New York, 1989, p.69.
45. Moland, IX, p.469.
46. ibid., p.474.
47. P, II, p.46 (*OC*, I, p.429).
48. 18.8.1756. BPUN, MS R285, ff.93–100 (*CC*, IV, 424 *bis*).
49. 18.8.1756. BPUN, MS R285, ff.78–92 (*CC*, IV, 424).
50. 18.8.1756. BPUG, Archives Tronchin 165, ff.3–4 (*CC*, IV, 425).
51. *J.-J.*, pp.152–3.
52. 1.9.1756. BPUN, MS R203, ff.60–61 (*CC*, IV, 425).
53. 12.9.1756. BPUN, MS R296, ff.159–60 (*CC*, IV, 437).
54. 1.3.1764. BPUN, MS R285, f.123 (*CC*, XIX, 3174).
55. See Gauffecourt's letters to M. de Chaignon in Sion (*CC*, IV, 409, 416, 419, 445).
56. See B. Gagnebin, 'Rousseau et le Valais', *Vallesia*, xxi, pp.169–88.
57. P, II, p.44 (*OC*, I, p.426).
58. ibid.
59. P, II, p.44 (*OC*, I, p.427).
60. P, II, p.45 (*OC*, I, p.427).
61. P, II, pp.46–7 (*OC*, I, p.430).
62. *OC*, II, pp.38–9.
63. Besterman, XXIII, D9622.
64. *OC*, II, p.409.
65. *OC*, II, p.444.
66. *OC*, II, p.609. See also Hope-Mason (1979), p.140.
67. *OC*, II, p.19.
68. *OC*, II, p.5.
69. See Tony Tanner, '*Julie* and "La maison paternelle"', *Daedelus*, vol.105, 1, p.37.
70. P, II, p.45 (*OC*, I, p.428).
71. André Morellet, *Mémoires*, Paris, 1821, I, pp.102–3.
72. P, II, p.50 (*OC*, I, p.436).
73. *OC*, I, p.1479.
74. BPUN, MS R311, ff.1–2 (*CC*, IV, 415).
75. P, II, p.37 (*OC*, I, p.412).
76. ibid.
77. Rochambeau Collection (*CC*, IV, 429).
78. 26.8.1756. BPUN, MS R311, ff.5–6 (*CC*, IV, 430).

79. 10.9.1756(?). Rochambeau Collection (*CC*, IV, 435).
80. 14.9.1756. Rochambeau Collection (*CC*, IV, 440).
81. *OC*, I, p.467. See also A. Rey (1904), p.79.
82. P.H.S. Piguet, *Mélanges de littérature*, Lausanne, 1816, pp.255–8.
83. P, II, p.48 (*OC*, I, p.433).
84. 14.9.1756. Rochambeau Collection (*CC*, IV, 440).
85. 13.10.1756. BPUN, MS R311, ff.11–12 (*CC*, IV, 446).
86. P, II, p.434 (*OC*, I, p.434).
87. BPUN, MS R89, pp.115–6 (*CC*, IV, 446).
88. P, II, p.48 (*OC*, I, p.433).
89. P, II, p.46 (*OC*, I, p.428).
90. ibid.
91. BPUN, MS R89, p.116 (*CC*, IV, 446).
92. BPUN, MS R311, f.12 (*CC*, IV, 446).
93. 2.11.1756. BPUN, MS R311, ff.12–13 (*CC*, IV, 448).
94. 23.11.1756. BPUN, MS R33, ff.14–15 (*CC*, IV, 449).
95. P, II, p.36 (*OC*, I, p.411).
96. Rochambeau Collection (*CC*, IV, 450).
97. ibid.
98. BPUG, Archives Tronchin, 204, p.29.
99. P, II, p.50 (*OC*, I, p.437).
100. 25.11.1756(?). Rochambeau Collection (*CC*, IV, 455).
101. 1.12.1756. Rochambeau Collection (*CC*, IV, 455).
102. P, II, p.41 (*OC*, I, p.420).
103. P, II, p.42 (*OC*, I, p.421).
104. Rochambeau Collection (*CC*, IV, 455).
105. See *J.-J.*, pp.215–16.
106. 9.12.1756(?). Rochambeau Collection (*CC*, IV, 458).
107. 25.12.1756. Library of Congress Manuscript Collection, Washington, DC (*CC*, IV, 461).
108. 13.12.1756. BPUN, MS R311, ff.16–17 (*CC*, IV, 459).
109. 20.12.1757(?). Rochambeau Collection (*CC*, IV, 460).
110. 29.12.1756. Morgan Library, New York (*CC*, IV, 463).
111. 4.1.1757. Rochambeau Collection (*CC*, IV, 464).
112. 17.1.1757(?). Rochambeau Collection (*CC*, IV, 468).
113. 14.2.1757. Bodleian Library, Oxford, Curzon Collection (*CC*, IV, 473).
114. 25.1.1757. BPUG, Archives Tronchin 165 (*CC*, IV, 470).
115. 16.2.1757. Rochambeau Collection (*CC*, IV, 474).
116. 21.2.1757. BPUG, Archives Tronchin 204 (*CC*, IV, 475).
117. 17.2.1757. BPUG, Archives Tronchin 165 (*CC*, IV, 476).
118. P, II, p.69 (*OC*, I, p.468).
119. BPUG, Archives Tronchin 165, ff.7–8.
120. 21.2.1757. BPUG, Archives Tronchin 204, p.69.
121. 14.2.1757. Bodleian Library, Oxford, Curzon Collection (*CC*, IV, 473).
122. P, II, p.36 (*OC*, I, p.411).
123. Rousseau's letter cannot be traced. Its contents may be inferred from Diderot's reply, which seems to confirm what Rousseau says in the *Confessions*.
124. P, II, p.62 (*OC*, I, p.455).
125. 10.5.1757. BPUN, MS R293, ff.40–41 (*CC*, IV, 479).
126. P, II, p.62 (*OC*, I, p.456).
127. P, II, p.64 (*OC*, I, p.461).
128. P, II, p.62 (*OC*, I, p.456).
129. 14.3.1759. BPUN, MS R293, ff.42–3 (*CC*, IV, 482).
130. P, II, p.62 (*OC*, I, p.457).
131. 13.3.1757. Rochambeau Collection (*CC*, IV, 481).
132. 14.3.1757. BPUN, MS R293, ff.42–3 (*CC*, IV, 482).
133. 16.3.1757. BPUN, MS R314, ff.3–6 (*CC*, IV, 483). Her letter appears in a distorted form in *Montbrillant*, III, pp.46–7.

134. 16.3.1757. Rochambeau Collection (*CC*, IV, 485).
135. 16.3.1757. BPUN, MS R89, pp.135–7 (*CC*, IV, 484).
136. 16.3.1757. Rochambeau Collection (*CC*, IV, 485).
137. 16.3.1757. BPUN, MS R314, ff.7–8 (*CC*, IV, 487).
138. 17.3.1757. Rochambeau Collection (*CC*, IV, 488).
139. 21.3.1757. BPUN, MS R293, ff.44–5 (*CC*, IV, 491).
140. 26.3.1757. Rochambeau Collection (*CC*, IV, 494).
141. 23.3.1757. BPUN, MS R89, ff.141–3 (*CC*, IV, 493).
142. BPUN, MS R311, ff.18–19 (*CC*, IV, 496).
143. P, II, p.64 (*OC*, I, p.460).
144. ibid.
145. BPUG, MS Fr.203, ff.243–4 (*CC*, IV, 498).
146. Rochambeau Collection (*CC*, IV, 503).

CHAPTER 3: SOPHIE
(pages 55–103)

1. P, II, p.52 (*OC*, I, p.439).
2. ibid.
3. ibid.
4. BPUN, MS R89, p.177 (*CC*, IV, 533).
5. BPUN, MS R7851, (*OC*, II, pp.1224–31).
6. P, II, p.52 (*OC*, I, p.440).
7. P, II, p.52 (*OC*, I, p.440).
8. *Montbrillant*, III, p.96.
9. Rochambeau Collection (*CC*, IV, 466.
10. P, II, p.48 (*OC*, I, p.432).
11. 10.1.1757(?). BPUN, MS R314, ff.36–7 (*CC*, IV, 465).
12. *Montbrillant*, III, p.96.
13. ibid., p.108.
14. Cited *P and P*, p.13.
15. A. Rey (1909), p.29.
16. *Montbrillant*, III, p.84.
17. ibid.
18. P, II, p.51 (*OC*, I, p.438).
19. P, II, p.51 (*OC*, I, p.439).
20. ibid.
21. *OC*, II, p.73.
22. 22.5.1757. BPUN, MS R314, ff.38–9 (*CC*, IV, 505).
23. P, II, p.52 (*OC*, I, p.440).
24. ibid.
25. 29.5.1757. Rochambeau Collection (*CC*, IV, 507).
26. P, II, p.53 (*OC*, I, p.441).
27. ibid.
28. P, II, p.53 (*OC*, I, p.442).
29. ibid.
30. P, II, p.54 (*OC*, I, p.443).
31. P, II, p.55 (*OC*, I, p.443–4).
32. *Chosen Letters*, ed. F.V. Barry, London, 1931, pp.124–6.
33. P, II, p.55 (*OC*, I, p.444).
34. BPUN, MS R89, p.175 (*CC*, IV, 533).
35. P, II, p.55 (*OC*, I, p.444).
36. Quoted in H. Buffenoir, *La Comtesse d'Houdetot*, Paris, 1905, p.271.
37. BPUN, MS R89, p.173 (*CC*, IV, 533). See also Guillemin (1942), p.68.
38. A. Rey (1909), pp.49–52; Ritter, in *Annales*, III, pp.213–17; Courtois, in *Annales*, XV, p.91; M. Josephson, *J.-J. Rousseau*, 1932, p.221.
39. *Montbrillant*, III, pp.42–3.
40. P, II, p.56 (*OC*, I, p.446).
41. BPUN, MS R89, p.155 (*CC*, IV, 509).
42. 10.10.1757(?). BPUN, MS R89, pp.173–8 (*CC*, IV, 533).
43. P, II, p.56 (*OC*, I, p.445).
44. P, II, p.55 (*OC*, I, p.445).
45. P, II, p.56 (*OC*, I, p.445).
46. P, II, p.100 (*OC*, I, p.195).
47. P, II, p.56 (*OC*, I, p.445).
48. ibid.
49. See David Buchanan, *The Treasure of Auchinleck: the Story of the Boswell Papers*, London, 1971, pp.334–41. Our knowledge of Boswell's entries in his journal for the days covering his adventures with Thérèse is unfortunately

entirely dependent on the re-collection of Colonel Isham who read them before those pages were destroyed.

50. BPUN, MS R89, p.177 (*CC*, IV, 533).
51. P, II, p.57 (*OC*, I, p.447).
52. ibid.
53. P, II, p.57 (*OC*, I, p.447).
54. P, II, p.58 (*OC*, I, p.449).
55. *Montbrillant*, III, pp.115–16.
56. ibid., p.147.
57. P, II, p.58 (*OC*, I, p.449).
58. See *Annales*, XXIX (1941–2), pp.117–19.
59. This enlarged edition, 224 pages instead of 198, was published '*A Genève, de mon imprimerie*' in 1759.
60. *Montbrillant*, III, p.123.
61. ibid., p.125.
62. ibid., p.128.
63. ibid., p.132.
64. ibid., p.147.
65. ibid., pp.91–2.
66. *CC*, II, 196.
67. *CC*, XIV, 2395.
68. *Montbrillant*, III, p.148.
69. 12.7.1757. Paris, Bibliothèque Mazarine, MSS Berneaud 4450 (*CC*, IV, 510).
70. *Montbrillant*, III, pp.151–2.
71. Tourneux, XVI, p.219.
72. Undated. BPUN, MS R314, f.15 (*CC*, IV, 511).
73. P, II, p.65 (*OC*, I, pp.462–3).
74. *Montbrillant*, III, p.161.
75. BPUN, MS R311, ff.21–2 (*CC*, IV, 512).
76. BPUG, MS Fr.288, ff.22–3 and BPUN, MS R94.
77. *OC*, IV, pp.1077–118.
78. P, II, p.66 (*OC*, I, p.463).
79. ibid.
80. St-Marc Girardin, *Jean-Jacques Rousseau*, Paris, 1875, pp.246 and 275.
81. Charles Brifaut, *Souvenirs*, Paris, I, pp.109–11. See also Leigh (*CC*, V, pp.273–6).
82. *Montbrillant*, III, p.151.

83. See *J.-J.*, pp.274–5.
84. 11.8.1757. BPUN, MS R314, f.16 (*CC*, IV, 513).
85. 12.8.1757. Rochambeau Collection (*CC*, IV, 514).
86. BPUN, MS R314, f.16 (*CC*, IV, 513).
87. 12.8.1757. Rochambeau Collection (*CC*, IV, 514).
88. 16.8.1757. Rochambeau Collection (*CC*, IV, 515).
89. P, II, p.57 (*OC*, I, pp.447–8).
90. P, II, p.58 (*OC*, I, p.449).
91. For the date see Guillemin (1942), pp.154–7 and Leigh (*CC*, IV, p.244).
92. BPUN, MS R314, f.12 (*CC*, IV, 520).
93. BPUN, MS R89, p.158 (*CC*, IV, 521).
94. BPUN, MS R314, f.13 (*CC*, IV, 522).
95. 31.8.1757(?). BPUN, MS R89, pp.159–60 (*CC*, IV, 523).
96. BPUN, MS R314, f.14 (*CC*, IV, 524).
97. P, II, p.61 (*OC*, I, p.453).
98. *Montbrillant*, III, p.184.
99. ibid., p.186.
100. ibid., p.187.
101. 6.9.1757(?). Rochambeau Collection (*CC*, IV, 525).
102. *Montbrillant*, III, p.188.
103. 15.9.1757. BPUN, MS R285, ff.43–4 (*CC*, IV, 527).
104. P, II, p.66 (*OC*, I, p.464).
105. ibid.
106. Leigh (*CC*, IV, pp.236–7).
107. P, II, p.67 (*OC*, I, p.464).
108. The work is also highly praised by Julien Tiersot, *Les Maîtres de musique: J.-J. Rousseau*, Paris, 1912, p.224.
109. P, II, p.67 (*OC*, I, p.465).
110. P, II, p.67 (*OC*, I, p.466).
111. ibid.
112. P, II, p.68 (*OC*, I, p.467).
113. P, II, p.69 (*OC*, I, p.469).
114. 26.9.1757(?). BPUN, MS R314, ff.18–20 (*CC*, IV, 529).

115. P, II, p.71 (*OC*, I, p.472).
116. 29.9.1757. BPUN, MS R314, ff.42–3 (*CC*, IV, 530).
117. Chérigny Archives (*CC*, IV, 531).
118. 10.10.1757. BPUN, MS R89, pp.173–8. (*CC*, IV, 533). Rousseau wrote some ten years later on the text of this letter: '*Cette lettre n'a point été envoyée.*'
119. 14.8.1757. Chérigny Archives (*CC*, IV, 535).
120. 15.8.1757. BPUN, MS R314, ff.44–5.
121. See her letter to Rousseau of 22.10.1757. BPUN, MS R314, f.48 (*CC*, IV, 541).
122. Tourneux, XVI, p.219.
123. BPUN, MS R314, ff.114–15 (*CC*, IV, 534).
124. 24.10.1757. BPUN, MS R89, p.185 (*CC*, IV, 543).
125. *Montbrillant*, III, p.108.
126. The letter dated 3 November 1757 (BPUN, MS R89, pp.246–7 [*CC*, IV, 562]).
127. See Gabriel Brizard (Paris, BArs., MSS Brizard 6099, f.179).
128. *CC*, IV, 293.
129. *OC*, I, p.1503.
130. *Montbrillant*, III, pp.259–68.
131. See Guillemin (1943), p.196.
132. 20.10.1757. BPUN, MS R311, f.28 (*CC*, IV, 540).
133. P, II, p.71 (*OC*, I, p.471).
134. P, II, p.73 (*OC*, I, p.475).
135. ibid.
136. 23.10.1757(?). BPUN, MS R293, ff.46–7 (*CC*, IV, 542).
137. P, II, p.73 (*OC*, I, p.476).
138. ibid.
139. See Leigh (*CC*, IV, p.294).
140. P, II, p.74 (*OC*, I, p.477).
141. 24.10.1757. BPUN, MS R89, p.180 (*CC*, IV, 544).
142. P, II, p.74 (*OC*, I, p.478).
143. See his note on his copy of his letter (BPUN, MS R89, p.180).
144. P, II, p.75 (*OC*, I, p.478).
145. See Leigh (*CC*, IV, p.293).
146. 26.20.1757. BPUN, MS R89, pp.189–93 (*CC*, IV, 545).
147. *OC*, I, p.1138.
148. BPUN, MS R314, ff.49–52 (*CC*, IV, 546).
149. BPUN, MS R89, pp.189–93 (*CC*, IV, 545). See also Guillemin (1942), p.217.
150. P, II, p.75 (*OC*, I, pp.478–9).
151. 28.10.1757. BPUN, MS R n.a., no.23, ff.43–4 (*CC*, IV, 547).
152. 28.10.1757. BPUN, MS R413, f.126 (*CC*, IV, 549).
153. P, II, p.78 (*OC*, I, p.483).
154. 29.10.1757. BPUN, MS R89, p.194 (*CC*, IV, 550).
155. 29.10.1757. Chérigny Archives (*CC*, IV, 552).
156. 31.10.1757. Chérigny Archives (*CC*, IV, 554).
157. 31.10.1757. *Montbrillant*, III, pp.243–4 (*CC*, IV, 555).
158. BPUN, MS R89, p.200 (*CC*, IV, 556).
159. The original manuscript of Grimm's letter was returned to him and has disappeared.
160. 1.11.1757. BPUN, MS R314, ff.53–5 (*CC*, IV, 558).
161. 1.11.1757. BPUN, MS R89, p.201 (*CC*, IV, 557).
162. 2.11.1757. BPUN, MS R324, ff.56–7 (*CC*, IV, 559).
163. 2.11.1757. Chérigny Archives (*CC*, IV, 560).
164. 3.11.1757. BPUN, MS R314, ff.58–9 (*CC*, IV, 561).
165. 2.11.1757. BPUN, MS R89, p.201 (*CC*, IV, 560).
166. 3.11.1757. BPUN, MS R89, pp.246–7 (*CC*, IV, 562).
167. 4.11.1757. Chérigny Archives (*CC*, IV, 563).
168. 7.11.1757. BPUG, MS R203, f.24 (*CC*, IV, 566).
169. 5.11.1757. BPUN, MS R314, ff.60–1 (*CC*, IV, 565).
170. 7.11.1757. BPUN, MS R314, ff.62–3 (*CC*, IV, 567).

171. 14.11.1757(?). BPUN, MS R89, pp.226–7 (CC, IV, 574).
172. 13.11.1757. Chérigny Archives (CC, IV, 573).
173. 10.11.1757. Chérigny Archives (CC, IV, 569).
174. 10.11.1757. BPUN, MS R314, ff.64–5 (CC, IV, 570).
175. 13.11.1757. BPUN, MS R314, ff.66–7 (CC, IV, 572).
176. BPUN, MS R314, ff.72–5 (CC, IV, 576).
177. 17.11.1757. Chérigny Archives (CC, IV, 577).
178. 19.11.1757. BPUN, MS R314, ff.68–9 (CC, IV, 578).
179. 21.11.1757. BPUN, MS R314, ff.116–19 (CC, IV, 579). This was in effect a reply to Rousseau's letter to him of 28 October.
180. BPUN, MS R314, f.21 (CC, IV, 571).
181. BPUN, MS R89, p.218 (CC, IV, 580).
182. 23.11.1757. Chérigny Archives (CC, IV, 581).
183. Manuscript not traced; CG, III, pp.33–5 (CC, IV, 587).
184. 27.11.1757. BPUN, MS R314, ff.70–71 (CC, IV, 582).
185. 30.11.1757. Chérigny Archives (CC, IV, 583).
186. 2.12.1757. BPUN, MS R314, ff.74–5 (CC, IV, 586).
187. Montbrillant, III, p.257.
188. Manuscript not traced; CG, III, pp.219–21 (CC, IV, 587).
189. BPUN, MS R314, ff.76–7 (CC, IV, 588).
190. BPUN, MS R314, ff.22–3 (CC, IV, 585).
191. 10.12.1757. Chérigny Archives (CC, IV, 589).
192. BPUN, MS R314, ff.78–9 (CC, IV, 590).
193. P, II, pp.79–80 (OC, I, p.486).
194. Paris, BN, n.a.f.24938, ff.424–8 (Tourneux, XVI, pp.219–22).
195. The letter appears in Montbrillant, III, pp.257–8, with the date 5 December 1757. Diderot and Grimm had each a share in writing the book, and this letter has every appearance of having been concocted between them.

CHAPTER 4: MONTLOUIS
(pages 104–31)

1. P, II, p.80 (OC, I, pp.487–8).
2. Montbrillant, III, p.321.
3. P, II, pp.80–81 (OC, I, p.487).
4. 17.12.1757. BPUN, MS R89, p.225 (CC, IV, 591).
5. P, II, p.83 (OC, I, p.501).
6. The originals of these letters have not, however, been traced.
7. 17.12.1757. Chérigny Archives (CC, IV, 592).
8. P, II, p.82 (OC, I, p.489).
9. ibid.
10. Encyclopédie, VII, p.578.
11. ibid.
12. Fuchs, p.12.
13. ibid., p.17.
14. ibid., p.163.
15. ibid., p.27.
16. ibid., p.33.
17. ibid., p.34.
18. ibid., p.43.
19. ibid.
20. ibid., p.35.
21. ibid., p.46.
22. ibid., p.47.
23. ibid., p.51.
24. ibid., p.60.
25. ibid., p.68.
26. ibid., p.101.
27. ibid., p.121.
28. ibid., p.165.
29. ibid., p.106.
30. ibid., p.108.
31. ibid., p.176.
32. See J.-J., p.269.
33. Fuchs, p.82.
34. ibid., p.182.
35. ibid., p.146.
36. ibid., p.179.

37. 20.12.1757. BPUN, MS R314, ff.80–81 (*CC*, IV, 593).

38. 26.12.1757. Chérigny Archives (*CC*, IV, 595).

39. 1.1.1758(?). BPUN, MS R311, ff.29–30 (*CC*, IV, 597).

40. 26.12.1757. Chérigny Archives (*CC*, IV, 595).

41. Reported in the chronicle *Les Nouvelles à la main* (*OC*, I, p.1445).

42. BPUN, MS R314, ff.82–3 (*CC*, IV, 598).

43. BPUN, MS R314, ff.84–5 (*CC*, V, 600).

44. 5.1.1758(?). BPUN, MS R90, pp.12–13 (*CC*, V, 601).

45. Wisbech Literary Institute, Townshend Collection (*CC*, V, 602).

46. 7.1.1758. BPUN, MS R314, ff.86–7 (*CC*, V, 603).

47. 9.1.1758. BPUN, MS R314, ff.88–9 (*CC*, V, 604).

48. 10.1.1758. BPUN, MS R314, 90–91 (*CC*, V, 606).

49. 10.1.1758. Chérigny Archives (*CC*, V, 607).

50. 11.1.1758. Chérigny Archives (*CC*, V, 608).

51. 15.1.1758. Chérigny Archives (*CC*, V, 609).

52. See A.M. Wilson, *Diderot*, New York, 1972, pp.288–90.

53. 13.2.1758. Chérigny Archives (*CC*, V, 614).

54. 28.1.1758. BPUN, MS R314, ff.92–3 (*CC*, V, 612).

55. 13.2.1758. BPUN, MS R314, ff.94–5 (*CC*, V, 613).

56. 13.2.1758. Chérigny Archives (*CC*, V, 614).

57. *Corr.*, ed. Roth, II, pp.37–40.

58. 14.2.1758. BPUG, MS Fr.203, ff.30–31 (*CC*, V, 615).

59. BPUN, MS R89, pp.260–61 (*CC*, V, pp.37–8).

60. P, II, pp.82–3 (*OC*, I, pp.490–91).

61. Vol. III, pp.346–7.

62. 20.2.1758. Rochambeau Collection (*CC*, V, 618).

63. P, II, p.83 (*OC*, I, p.491).

64. BPUG, MS Supp. 1036, ff.68–9 (*CC*, V, 616).

65. *OC*, I, p.1016.

66. *OC*, IV, p.1082.

67. *OC*, IV, p.1084.

68. *OC*, IV, p.1102.

69. *OC*, IV, p.1113.

70. ibid.

71. ibid.

72. *OC*, IV, p.1114.

73. See Ronald Grimsley, ed., *Rousseau's Religious Writings*, Oxford, 1970, p.53.

74. *OC*, IV, p.1111.

75. *OC*, IV, pp.565–635. See also Masson, pp.479–99.

76. BPUN, MS R314, ff.98–9 (*CC*, V, 619).

77. 22.2.1758. BPUG, MS Fr.240 (*CC*, V, 620). This letter, bound with the manuscript copy of *Julie* which Rousseau made for Sophie, is in the same Geneva library under the same shelf mark.

78. 22.2.1758. BPUN, MS R311, ff.33–4 (*CC*, V, 621).

79. 28.2.1758. BPUN, MS R311, f.35 (*CC*, V, 622).

80. 2.3.1758. BPUN, MS R90, pp. 1–3 (*CC*, V, 624).

81. BArs, MS 6099, f.180.

82. *OC*, I, pp.1221–3. The declaration is headed: '*Reconnaissance et Obligation*'.

83. 15.3.1758. BPUG, MS Fr.236, f.42 (*CC*, V, 627).

84. 29.3.1758. BPUN, MS R n.a., no.1 (*CC*, V, 636).

85. BPUN, MS R311, ff.36–7 (*CC*, V, 628).

86. 10.5.1758. Manuscript not traced; Musset-Pathay (1925), I, pp.36–7 (*CC*, V, 640).

87. Dutch Royal Library, G 16-A 434, no.16 (*CC*, V, 626).

88. 15.4.1758. Dutch Royal Library, G 16–A434, no.17 (*CC*, V, 638).

89. J. Dusaulx, *De mes rapports avec J.-J. Rousseau*, Paris, 1798, p.102.

90. 25.3.1758. BPUG, MS Fr.203, ff.245–6 (*CC*, V, 634).
91. BPUN, MS R314, ff.102–3 (*CC*, V, 630).
92. 23.3.1758. Chérigny Archives (*CC*, V, 631).
93. 24.3.1758. BPUN, MS R314, ff.104–5 (*CC*, V, 632).
94. 25.3.1758. BPUN, MS R90, pp.3–5 (*CC*, V, 653).
95. BPUN, MS R314, ff.106–7 (*CC*, V, 639).
96. Tourneux, XVI, pp.219–22.
97. ibid.
98. See Guillemin (1942), pp.73–83.
99. Tourneux, XVI, pp.219–22.

CHAPTER 5: AN EVEN AND
TRANQUIL LIFE
(pages 132–57)

1. P, II, p.86 (*OC*, I, pp.496–7).
2. P, II, pp.90–91 (*OC*, I, p.503).
3. In G the text reads 'freedom' ('*la liberté*') rather than 'society' ('*la société*'), as in P. This must be a mistake of transcription.
4. Casanova, *Histoire de ma vie*, Paris, 1960, III, pp.220–21.
5. 11.5.1758. BPUG, MS Fr.203, ff.34–5 (*CC*, V, 642).
6. 14.5.1758. Dutch Royal Library, G16-A434, no.18 (*CC*, V, 645).
7. BPUN, MS R n.a. (*CC*, V, 646).
8. 31.5.1758. Dutch Royal Library, G16-A434, no.19 (*CC*, V, 649).
9. 31.5.1758. BPUG, MS Fr.203, ff.38–9 (*CC*, V, 650).
10. 6.6.1758. BPUN, MS R320, ff.3–4 (*CC*, V, 652).
11. 12.6.1758. BPUN, MS R320, f.7 (*CC*, V, 654).
12. Dutch Royal Library, G16-A434, no.20 (*CC*, V, 655).
13. This is dated in the printed version 'Montmorency 20 March 1758'.
14. Fuchs, p.9.
15. ibid.
16. P, II, p.87 (*OC*, I, p.497).
17. ibid.
18. 27.7.1758. BN, n.a.f. 1183, ff.16–17 (*CC*, V, 674).
19. 27.6.1758. BPUG, unclassified (*CC*, V, 660).
20. 23.7.1758. Dutch Royal Library, G16-A434, no.22 (*CC*, V, 675).
21. 4.7.1758. BPUG, MS Fr.203, ff.249–50 (*CC*, V, 664).
22. BPUN, MS R314, ff.120–21 (*CC*, V, 658).
23. 1.9.1758. BN, n.a.f.1183, ff.42–3 (*CC*, V, 685).
24. 4.9.1758. BPUN, MS R320, f.17 (*CC*, V, 687).
25. 29.9.1758. Besterman, XIX, D7842.
26. Besterman, XIX, D7864.
27. 6.9.1758. Dutch Royal Library, G16-A434, no.29 (*CC*, V, 688).
28. 4.9.1758. BPUN, MS R320, f.17 (*CC*, V, 687).
29. 13.9.1758. Dutch Royal Library, G16-A434, no.30 (*CC*, V, 691).
30. 26.9.1758. BPUG, MS Fr.203, ff.40–41 (*CC*, V, 696).
31. 4.10.1758. BPUG, MS Fr.203, ff.155–6 (*CC*, V, 698).
32. 4.10.1758. BPUG, MS Fr.204, f.200 (*CC*, V, 697).
33. 5.10.1758. BPUN, MS R291, f.14 (*CC*, V, 699).
34. See Grosclaude (1961), pp.120–27.
35. 22.10.1758. BPUG, MS Fr.203, ff.253–4 (*CC*, V, 715).
36. His annotated copy of the book is in the Bibliothèque Nationale, Paris (reserve R895).
37. For Rousseau's notes on *De l'esprit*, see *OC*, IV, pp.1119–30.
38. 29.10.1758. BPUN, MS R311, ff.39–40 (*CC*, V, 720).
39. 8.10.1758. BPUG, MS Fr.203, ff.215–16 (*CC*, V, 702).
40. 6.10.1758. BPUG, MS Fr.203, ff.251–2 (*CC*, V, 701).
41. See *J.-J.*, p.330.
42. ibid., p.331.
43. ibid., p.329.

44. ibid., pp.328–45.

45. ibid., pp.19–23.

46. For an account of Rousseau in the company of Donzel, see Leigh (*CC*, III, pp.330–31).

47. BPUN, MS R314, ff.122–3 (*CC*, V, 704).

48. 10.10.1758. BPUN, MS R314, ff.124–5 (*CC*, V, 705).

49. 11.10.1758. BPUN, MS R314, f.125 verso (*CC*, V, 706).

50. P, II, p.88 (*OC*, I, p.499).

51. 26.10.1758. BPUN, MS R313, ff.1–2 (*CC*, V, 718).

52. P, II, p.88 (*OC*, I, pp.499–500).

53. 11.10.1758. BPUN, MS R293, ff.135–8 (*CC*, V, 708).

54. P, II, p.88 (*OC*, I, p.500).

55. ibid.

56. P, II, p.89 (*OC*, I, p.500).

57. P, II, p.89 (*OC*, I, p.502).

58. P, II, p.89 (*OC*, I, p.501).

59. P, II, p.90 (*OC*, I, p.502).

60. See *J.-J.*, pp.249–50.

61. 11.10.1758. BPUN, MS R292, ff.155–6 (*CC*, V, 707).

62. BPUG, MS Fr.206, ff.7–8 (*CC*, V, 717).

63. BPUN, MS R311, ff.39–40 (*CC*, V, 720).

64. See Leigh (*CC*, V, pp.292–3).

65. 8.11.1758. BPUG, MS Fr.206, ff.9–10 (*CC*, V, 730).

66. 10.11.1758(?). BPUN, MS R319, ff.1–2 (*CC*, V, 733).

67. 3.11.1758. MS R303, ff.62–3 (*CC*, V, 734).

68. 15.11.1758. BPUN, MS R302, ff.35–6 (*CC*, V, 737).

69. 23.11.1758. BPUN, MS R303, ff.86–7 (*CC*, V, 742).

70. 26.11.1758. BPUG, Archives Tronchin 165, ff.9–10 (*CC*, V, 743).

71. 2.11.1758. BPUG, Soc. J.-J.R., MS R25 (*CC*, V, 747).

72. Section 398a-6.

73. Besterman, XIX, D7925.

74. 3.10.1758. Besterman, XIX, D7887.

75. 16.12.1758. See Leigh (*CC*, V, pp.255–6).

76. January 1759. BPUN, MS R292, ff.157–8 (*CC*, VI, 764).

77. 15.1.1759. Manuscript not traced (*CC*, VI, 765).

78. ibid.

79. 20.1.1759. BPUN, MS R292, ff.159–60 (*CC*, VI, 767).

80. 5.1.1759. BPUN, MS R292, ff. 3–4 (*CC*, VI, 758).

81. 20.6.1759. BPUG, Archives Tronchin 291, no.29 (*CC*, VI, 835).

82. 6.1.1759. Manuscript in private collection (*CC*, XLIX, 760bis).

83. Besterman, XXVII, D11760.

84. 9.1.1759. BPUG (*CC*, VI, 761).

85. BPUN, MS R294, ff.68–9 (*CC*, VI, 769).

86. 9.2.1759. BPUG, MS Fr.238, ff. 8–9 (*CC*, VI, 772).

87. 5.4.1759. BPUN, MS R291, ff.40–43 (*CC*, VI, 795).

88. See the *Mercure de France*, October 1759.

89. 11.2.1759. BPUN, MS R90, pp.50–52 (*CC*, VI, 774). The petition was accompanied by a letter dated 11.2.1759. (BPUN, Ms R90, p.49 [*CC*, VI, 773]).

90. 13.2.1759. Manuscript not traced; *CG*, IV, pp.178–9 (*CC*, VI, 777).

91. P, II, p.90 (*OC*, I, p.503).

92. 5.4.1759. BPUN, MS R291, ff.40–43 (*CC*, VI, 795).

93. See P, I, p.173 (*OC*, I, p.333).

94. 22.2.1759. Dutch Royal Library, G16-A434, no.32 (*CC*, VI, 785).

95. 27.2.1759. BPUN, MS R320, ff.26–7 (*CC*, VI, 786).

96. 14.3.1759. Dutch Royal Library, G16-A434, no.33 (*CC*, VI, 788).

97. Fuchs, p.74.

98. 20.3.1759. BPUN, MS R320, f.28 (*CC*, VI, 791).

99. This MS is now in the Heinemann Collection at the Morgan Library, New York.

100. For Diderot's opinion of Boucher's paintings, see *Oeuvres*

esthétiques de Diderot, ed. P. Vernière, Paris, 1965, pp.449–67.

101. 13.4.1759(?). BPUG, MS Fr.203, ff.63–4 (CC, VI, 797).
102. BPUN, MS R320, ff.29–30 (CC, VI, 798).
103. See Rousseau's letter to Vernes of 6 January 1759 (BPUN, MS R290 [CC, VI, 760]).
104. BPUN, MS R n.a.3 (CC, VI, 768).
105. P, II, p.94 (OC, I, pp.507–9).
106. P, II, p.94 (OC, I, pp.508–9).
107. P, II, p.94 (OC, I, p.509).
108. P, II, p.95 (OC, I, p.510).
109. P, II, p.90 (OC, I, p.503).
110. P, II, p.91 (OC, I, p.504).
111. ibid.
112. P, II, p.91 (OC, I, p.505).
113. P, II, p.93 (OC, I, p.507).
114. 13.4.1759(?). BPUG, MS Fr.203, ff.63–4 (CC, VI, 797).

CHAPTER 6: AT THE
CHÂTEAU
(pages 158–74)

1. P, II, p.100 (OC, I, p.518).
2. P, II, p.100 (OC, I, p.519).
3. ibid.
4. H. Buffenoir, La Maréchale de Luxembourg, Paris, 1910, p.15.
5. P, II, p.100 (OC, I, p.519).
6. Tourneux, V, p.92.
7. Corr., ed. Roth, II, p.154.
8. P, II, p.101 (OC, I, p.521).
9. BPUN, MS R90, pp.56–7 (CC, VI, 803).
10. 1.5.1759. BPUN, MS R318, ff. 1–2 (CC, VI, 804).
11. 25.1757(?). Dutch Royal Library, G16-A434, no.34 (CC, VI, 805).
12. Palais Bourbon, P7074, ff.9–10 (CC, VI, 808).
13. 9.5.1759. BPUN, MS R318, ff.92–3 (CC, VI, 812).
14. 6.5.1759. BPUN, MS R n.a.21 (CC, VI, 809).
15. 7.5.1757. BPUG, Soc. J.-J.R., MS R168 (CC, VI, 810).
16. 3.7.1759. BL, Add.MSS 40.690, ff.15–16 (CC, VI, 839).
17. P, II, pp.101–2 (OC, I, p.521).
18. 27.5.1759. BPUN, MS R90, pp.62–3 (CC, VI, 821).
19. 4.6.1759. BPUN, MS R318, ff. 3–4 (CC, VI, 826).
20. BPUG, Archives Tronchin 165, ff.11–12 (CC, VI, 792).
21. 17.4.1759. BPUN, MS R303, ff.64–5 (CC, VI, 794).
22. 28.4.1759. BPUG, Archives Tronchin 165, ff.13–14 (CC, VI, 801).
23. 7.5.1759. BPUN, MS R303, ff.66–7 (CC, VI, 811).
24. 16.5.1759. Besterman D8303.
25. 17.5.1759. BPUG, Archives Tronchin 165, f.14 (CC, VI, 815).
26. 30.5.1759. BPUG, Archives Tronchin 165, ff.15–16 (CC, VI, 823).
27. 6.6.1759. BPUN, MS R303, ff.68–9 (CC, VI, 828).
28. 23.6.1759. BPUG, Archives Tronchin 165, ff.17–19 (CC, VI, 837).
29. 4.5.1759. Besterman D8266.
30. 6.2.1759. BPUN, MS R291, ff.106–7 (CC, VI, 771).
31. 14.5.1759. BPUN, MS R320, f.31 (CC, VI, 814).
32. 1.6.1759. Dutch Royal Library, G16-A434, no.35 (CC, VI, 824).
33. BPUG, MS Fr.203, ff.157–8 (CC, VI, 831).
34. H. Buffenoir, Les Portraits de Jean-Jacques Rousseau, Paris, 1913, pl.14.
35. ibid., p.95.
36. ibid., p.94.
37. 21.6.1759. Dutch Royal Library, G16-A434, no.36 (CC, VI, 836).
38. 8.6.1759. Palais Bourbon, P7074, ff.11–12 (CC, VI, 829).
39. P, II, p.101 (OC, I, pp.520–21).
40. 9.6.1759. BPUN, MS R318, ff.94–5 (CC, VI, 830).
41. P, II, p.102 (OC, I, pp.522–3).
42. W. Cole, A Journal of my Journey to Paris, London, 1831, p.64.
43. P, II, p.120 (OC, I, p.557).

44. ibid.
45. 29.4.1759. BPUN, MS R309, ff.99–100 (*CC*, VI, 802).
46. 14.6.1759. BPUG, MS Fr.203, ff.255–6 (*CC*, VI, 833).
47. 2.7.1759. BPUG, Archives Tronchin 204, pp.252–3 (*CC*, VI, 838).
48. 23.7.1759. BPUN, MS R303, ff.70–71 (*CC*, VI, 844).
49. 25.7.1759. BPUN, MS R303, f.11 (*CC*, VI, 845).
50. 3.7.1759. BL, Add. MSS 40.690, ff.15–16 (*CC*, VI, 839).
51. 2.12.1759. BPUG, MS Fr.206, ff.14–15 (*CC*, VI, 902).
52. 14.7.1759 BPUN, MS R311, ff.47–8 (*CC*, VI, 843).
53. 24.10.1759. BPUN, MS R311, ff.51–2 (*CC*, VI, 874).
54. 10.11.1759. Manuscript not traced; Musset-Pathay (1821), II, pp.481–4 (*CC*, VI, 884).
55. 12.12.1759. BPUN, MS R311, f.53 (*CC*, VI, 907).
56. P, II, p.116 (*OC*, I, p.549).
57. ibid.
58. P, II, p.106 (*OC*, I, p.531).
59. BPUN, MS R318, ff.9–10 (*CC*, VI, 866).
60. P, II, p.106 (*OC*, I, p.531).
61. Dutch Royal Library, G16-A434, no.37 (*CC*, VI, 846).
62. 11.8.1759(?). BPUN, MS R318, ff.98–9 (*CC*, VI, 847).
63. 13.8.1759. Palais Bourbon, P7074, ff.13–14 (*CC*, VI, 849).
64. P, II, p.105 (*OC*, I, p.528).
65. 18.8.1759. Manuscript seen by Leigh in private collection, London (*CC*, VI, 852).

CHAPTER 7: *ÉMILE*
(pages 175–98)

1. *OC*, III, p.783.
2. See Jimack (1960), p.91.
3. *OC*, IV, p.245. See also *OC*, IV, pp.935–6 and *OC*, I, p.934.
4. Translated by Pierre Coste as *De l'éducation des enfants*, Paris, 1693.
5. *OC*, III, p.24.
6. Cited Jimack (1983), p.47.
7. *OC*, IV, p.287.
8. *OC*, IV, p.936.
9. *OC*, IV, p.288.
10. *OC*, IV, p.390.
11. *OC*, IV, p.260.
12. *OC*, IV, p.282.
13. *OC*, IV, p.267.
14. *Julie* (*OC*, II, p.538).
15. See *OC*, IV, p.1369.
16. *OC*, IV, p.310.
17. *OC*, IV, p.267.
18. BPUG, MS Favre, f.53.
19. See *OC*, IV, pp.417 and 1385.
20. *OC*, IV, p.1451.
21. See *OC*, IV, p.1378.
22. *OC*, IV, pp.392–3.
23. *OC*, IV, p.287.
24. See Jimack (1960), p.163.
25. *OC*, IV, p.352.
26. *OC*, IV, p.330.
27. Garnier – Flammarion edn, pp.196–7.
28. See William H. Blanchard, *Rousseau and the Spirit of Revolt*, Ann Arbor, 1967, pp.147–70.
29. *OC*, IV, p.814.
30. *OC*, IV, p.271.
31. *OC*, IV, p.277.
32. *OC*, IV, p.377.
33. *OC*, IV, p.945.
34. Cited Jimack (1983), p.57. See also Jimack (1960), pp.88–94.
35. *OC*, IV, p.480.
36. *OC*, IV, p.493.
37. *OC*, IV, pp.489–90.
38. *OC*, IV, p.497.
39. *OC*, IV, p.499.
40. *OC*, IV, p.503.
41. *OC*, IV, p.520.
42. *OC*, IV, pp.526–7.
43. *OC*, IV, p.528.
44. *OC*, IV, p.538.
45. *OC*, IV, p.543.
46. *OC*, IV, p.554.
47. BPUG, MS Favre, f.53v.
48. *OC*, IV, p.641.

49. *OC*, IV, p.644.
50. ibid.
51. *OC*, IV, p.657.
52. *OC*, IV, p.677.
53. *OC*, IV, p.746.
54. *OC*, III, p.168.
55. See Schwartz, p.25.
56. *OC*, III, p.158.
57. See Schwartz, pp.41–73.
58. *OC*, IV, p.694.
59. *OC*, IV, p.696.
60. *OC*, IV, p.649.
61. *OC*, IV, p.744.
62. *OC*, IV, p.743.
63. Schwartz, p.65.
64. *OC*, III, p.119.
65. *OC*, IV, p.703.
66. *OC*, IV, p.708.
67. ibid.
68. *OC*, IV, p.711.
69. *OC*, IV, p.710.
70. *OC*, IV, p.721.
71. *OC*, IV, p.737.
72. *OC*, IV, p.814.
73. *OC*, IV, p.833.
74. *OC*, IV, p.867.
75. *OC*, IV, p.868.
76. *OC*, IV, p.917.
77. *OC*, IV, pp.565–635.
78. *OC*, IV, p.634.
79. BPUN, MS R18, f.32.
80. *OC*, I, p.435.
81. *OC*, I, pp.1025–6.
82. *OC*, IV, p.575.
83. ibid.
84. *OC*, IV, pp.576–7.
85. *OC*, IV, pp.580–81.
86. *OC*, IV, p.1073.
87. *OC*, IV, p.590.
88. *OC*, IV, p.603.
89. *OC*, IV, p.594.
90. *OC*, IV, p.595.
91. Jimack (1983), p.43.
92. Masson, p.397.
93. *OC*, IV, p.605.
94. *OC*, IV, p.626.
95. Grimsley, p.73.
96. Jimack (1983), p.43.
97. Grimsley, p.83.
98. Masson, p.356.

99. *OC*, IV, p.607.
100. *OC*, III, p.735.
101. *OC*, IV, p.1286.
102. Masson, pp.412–13.
103. *OC*, IV, p.620.
104. *OC*, IV, p.607.
105. Grimsley, p.80.
106. See *J.-J.*, p.62.
107. *OC*, IV, p.627.
108. Grimsley, p.81.

CHAPTER 8: MONTLOUIS RESTORED
(pages 199–246)

1. P, II, p.104 (*OC*, I, p.526).
2. P, II, p.104 (*OC*, I, p.527).
3. 31.8.1759. Palais Bourbon, P7074, ff.67–8 (*CC*, VI, 877).
4. BPUN, MS R90, p.73 (*CC*, VI, 854).
5. BPUN, MS R318, ff.7–8 (*CC*, VI, 856).
6. 3.9.1759. BPUN, MS R318, ff.100–101 (*CC*, VI, 857).
7. 5.9.1759. Dutch Royal Library, G16-A434, no.38 (*CC*, VI, 859).
8. 13.8.1759. BPUN, MS R320, ff.34–5 (*CC*, VI, 848).
9. 20.10.1759. Dutch Royal Library, G16-A434, no.40 (*CC*, VI, 873).
10. 13.10.1759. BPUN, MS R320, ff.36–7 (*CC*, VI, 871).
11. 20.10.1759. Dutch Royal Library, G16-A434, no.40 (*CC*, VI, 873).
12. 27.10.1759. BPUN, MS R320, ff.38–9 (*CC*, VI, 875).
13. 29.10.1759. Palais Bourbon, P7074, ff.15–16 (*CC*, VI, 877).
14. The copy of *Julie* that Rousseau made for Mme de Luxembourg is in the Palais Bourbon, Paris; the one for Mme d'Houdetot in the Bibliothèque Publique et Universitaire, Geneva; and the master copy for Rey in the Morgan Library, New York.

15. 6.11.1759. BPUN, MS R318, ff.102–3 (*CC*, VI, 879).
16. 7.11.1759. Palais Bourbon, P7074, ff.67–8 (*CC*, VI, 880).
17. 8.11.1759. BPUN, MS R90, p.90 (*CC*, VI, 882).
18. 15.11.1759. Palais Bourbon, P7074, ff.21–2 (*CC*, VI, 887).
19. 17.11.1759. BPUN, MS R318 (*CC*, VI, 890).
20. 19.11.1759. BPUN, MS R318, ff.104–5 (*CC*, VI, 894).
21. 9.11.1759. BPUG MS Fr.203, ff.67–8 (*CC*, VI, 883).
22. 18.11.1759. BPUG, MS Fr.203, ff.257–8 (*CC*, VI, 891).
23. P, II, p.105 (*OC*, I, p.528).
24. P, II, p.105 (*OC*, I, p.529).
25. ibid.
26. Notably the pastel by Lefèvre (in the Château de Carrouges).
27. BPUG, Soc. *J.-J.R.*, MS R105 (*CC*, VI, 892).
28. 15.11.1759. BPUN, MS R322, ff.175–6 (*CC*, VI, 888).
29. P, II, p.96 (*OC*, I, p.512).
30. ibid.
31. Malesherbes to Moultou, 17.3.1782 (see Leigh, *CC*, VI, p.197).
32. 20.11.1759. BPUN, MS R322, ff.7–8 (*CC*, VI, 895).
33. 47.1759. BPUG, Soc. *J.-J.R.*, MS R105 (*CC*, VI, 903).
34. 21.12.1759. BPUG, MS R105 (*CC*, VI, 912).
35. 29.12.1759. BPUN, MS R318, ff.16–17 (*CC*, VI, 917).
36. 2.12.1759. BPUG, MS Fr.206, ff.14–15 (*CC*, VI, 902).
37. 17.12.1759. BPUG, MS Fr.206, 15, and Houghton Library, Harvard College, Cambridge, Mass. (*CC*, VI, 910).
38. 7.12.1759. BPUG, MS Fr.206 CC, VI, 909).
39. ee J.-L. Courtois, in *Annales*, XVII (1926), pp.152–63.
40. See *J.-J.*, p.344.
41. P. Usteri and E. Ritter, eds., Cor-

respondance de Rousseau et Usteri, Geneva, 1911, p.134.
42. 29.1.1760. BPUN, MS R289, ff.3–4 (*CC*, VII, 933).
43. Undated. BPUG, MS Fr.279, no.10 (*CC*, VI, 911).
44. 16.1.1760. Palais Bourbon, P7074, ff.23–4 (*CC*, VII, 924).
45. 28.1.1760. BPUN, MS R318, ff.108–9 (*CC*, VII, 932).
46. BPUN, MS R320, f.40 (*CC*, VI, 915).
47. Morgan Library, New York (inserted in the MS of *Julie* at p.140).
48. In the published text it occurs in letter No.50 from Julie to St-Preux (*OC*, II, pp.138–9).
49. BPUG, Soc. *J.-J.R.*, MS R105 (*CC*, VII, 923).
50. 16.1.1760. BPUN, MS R322, ff.13–15 (*CC*, VII, 926).
51. 24.1.1760(?). BPUG, Soc. *J.-J.R.*, MS R105 (*CC*, VII, 930).
52. 2.2.1760. BPUN, MS R90, p.108 (*CC*, VII, 936).
53. 9.2.1760. BPUN, MS R318, ff.18–19 (*CC*, VII, 941).
54. 9.2.1760. BPUG, MS Fr.203, ff.259–60 (*CC*, VII, 940).
55. 15.2.1760(?). BPUN, MS R303, ff.72–3 (*CC*, VII, 942).
56. 4.2.1760. BPUG, Soc. *J.-J.R.*, MS R105 (*CC*, VII, 938).
57. 7.2.1760(?). BPUN, MS R322, ff.9–10 (*CC*, VII, 939).
58. 5.3.1760. BPUG, Soc. *J.-J.R.*, MS R105 (*CC*, VII, 951).
59. 12.3.1760. BPUG, Soc. *J.-J.R.*, MS R105 (*CC*, VII, 957).
60. 5.5.1760. BPUN, MS R322, ff.179–80 (*CC*, VII, 950). The visit was planned for 18 March.
61. BPUN, MS R311, ff.54–5 (*CC*, VII, 947).
62. 3.5.1760. BPUN, MS R311, ff.56–7 (*CC*, VII, 980).
63. *Annales*, XVII (1926), p.163.
64. 3.5.1760. BPUN, MS R311, ff.56–7 (*CC*, VII, 980).

65. *OC*, II, p.1147.
66. 7.3.1760(?). BPUN, MS R318, ff.110–11 (*CC*, VII, 924).
67. 16.3.1760. BPUN, MS R318, ff.20–21 (*CC*, VII, 961).
68. 18.3.1760. BPUN, MS R90, pp.157–8 (*CC*, VII, 962).
69. 22.3.1760. BPUN, MS R318, ff.22–3 (*CC*, VII, 964).
70. 2.12.1759. BPUN, MS R90, p.85 (*CC*, VI, 898).
71. P, II, p.107 (*OC*, I, p.532).
72. ibid.
73. P, II, p.108 (*OC*, I, p.534).
74. 1.8.1760. BPUN, MS R318, ff.118–19 (*CC*, VII, 1074).
75. 1.2.1760. BPUN, MS R320, f.41 (*CC*, VII, 935).
76. 28.2.1760. BPUN, MS R320, f.42 (*CC*, VII, 945).
77. 6.3.1760. Dutch Royal Library, G16-A434, no.43 (*CC*, VII, 952).
78. 6.3.1760. BPUN, MS R284, ff.98–9 (*CC*, VII, 953).
79. 10.3.1760. Rosanbo Archives (*CC*, VII, 956).
80. 10.4.1760. Dutch Royal Library, G16-A454, no.44 (*CC*, VII, 968).
81. 7.4.1760. BPUN, MS R320, f.44 (*CC*, VII, 967).
82. 17.4.1760. Dutch Royal Library, G16-A434, no.45 (*CC*, VII, 969).
83. 24.4.1760. Dutch Royal Library, G16-A434, no.46 (*CC*, VII, 973).
84. 19.4.1760. Rosanbo Archives (*CC*, VII, 972).
85. 24.4.1760. BPUN, MS R320, ff.46–7 (*CC*, VII, 974).
86. BPUN, MS R320, f.50 (*CC*, VII, 979).
87. 8.5.1760. Dutch Royal Library, G16-A434, no.47 (*CC*, VII, 981).
88. 10.5.1760. BPUN, MS R320, f.52 (*CC*, VII, 983).
89. 11.5.1760. Dutch Royal Library, G16-A434, no.48 (*CC*, VII, 984).
90. 18.5.1760. BPUN, MS R284, ff.100–101 (*CC*, VII, 990).
91. 18.5.1760. Dutch Royal Library, G16-A434, no.49 (*CC*, VII, 992).
92. BPUN, MS R90, p.139 (*CC*, VII, 991).
93. See also *OC*, II, p.749.
94. *OC*, II, p.759. For the significance of the word '*supplément*' for Rousseau, see J. Starobinski, 1971, p.214.
95. P, II, p.103 (*OC*, I, p.524).
96. P, II, p.103 (*OC*, I, p.525).
97. ibid.
98. BPUN, MS R318, ff.26–7 (*CC*, VII, 1002).
99. BPUG, MS Fr.203, ff.50–51 (*CC*, VII, 1004).
100. P, II, p.104 (*OC*, I, p.256).
101. ibid.
102. 29.5.1760 (*CC*, VII, 1006).
103. See *J.-J.R.*, p.175
104. 31.5.1760. BPUN, MS R292, ff.90–91 (*CC*, VII, 1007).
105. P, II, p.93 (*OC*, I, p.508).
106. 21.5.1760. BPUN, MS R90, p.133 (*CC*, VII, 995).
107. 24.5.1760. Stockholm, Riksarkivet (*CC*, VII, 998).
108. P, II, p.110 (*OC*, I, p.537).
109. See Daniel Delafarge, *L'Affaire de l'Abbé Morellet en 1760*, Paris, 1912.
110. Grosclaude (1961), p.158.
111. P, II, p.110 (*OC*, I, p.537).
112. 22.5.1760. Dutch Royal Library, G16-A434, no.50 (*CC*, VII, 996).
113. 25.5.1760. Dutch Royal Library, G16-A434, no.51 (*CC*, VII, 999).
114. 22.5.1760. BPUN, MS R320, ff.56–7 (*CC*, VII, 997).
115. 28.5.1760. Dutch Royal Library, G16-A434, no.52 (*CC*, VII, 1003).
116. 26.5.1760. BPUN, MS R320, ff.58–9 (*CC*, VII, 1000).
117. 1.6.1760. BPUN, MS R320, ff.61–2 (*CC*, VII, 1009).
118. 15.6.1760. Dutch Royal Library, G16-A434, no.54 (*CC*, VII, 1015).
119. 15.6.1760(?). Manuscript not traced (*CC*, VII, 1016).
120. 17.6.1760. BPUN, MS R90, pp.137–8 (*CC*, VII, 1019).
121. P, II, p.111 (*OC*, I, p.540).

122. *OC*, I, p.1533.
123. Besterman, XXI, D9064.
124. 17.6.1760. BPUN, MS R90, pp.136–7 (*CC*, VII, 1021).
125. See Leigh, in *SVEC*, XXX (1964), pp.247–309.
126. See Rousseau to Malesherbes, 22.6.1760. BN, n.a.f.1183, f.49 (*CC*, VII, 1030).
127. BN, n.a.f.1183, f.48.
128. 30.6.1760. BPUN, MS R294, ff.25–6 (*CC*, VII, 1041).
129. 26.6.1760. BPUN, MS R292, ff.35–6 (*CC*, VII, 1036).
130. P, II, p.91 (*OC*, I, p.505).
131. ibid.
132. P, II, p.113 (*OC*, I, p.543).
133. See E.C. Mossner, *The Life of David Hume*, London, 1980, p.457.
134. See P, II, p.110 (*OC*, I, p.537).
135. 30.6.1760. BPUN, MS R90, p.149 (*CC*, VII, 1039).
136. BPUN, MS R318, ff.114–15 (*CC*, VII, 1060).
137. 28.7.1760. BPUN, MS R318, ff.116–17 (*CC*, VII, 1068).
138. 1.8.1760. BPUN, MS R292, ff. 3–4 (*CC*, VII, 1075).
139. 4.8.1760. BPUN, MS R295, ff.142–3 (*CC*, VII, 1077).
140. 6.8.1760. Palais Bourbon, P7074, ff.19–20 (*CC*, VII, 1078).
141. 1.8.1760. BPUN, MS R318, ff.118–19 (*CC*, VII, 1074).
142. P, II, p.111 (*OC*, I, p.539).
143. Besterman, XXI, D8982.
144. *Mémoires*, Paris, 1821, I, p.100.
145. BPUN, MS R318, ff.120–21 (*CC*, VII, 1062).
146. 28.7.1760. Palais Bourbon, P7074, ff.65–6 (*CC*, VII, 1066).
147. 28.7.1760. BPUN, MS R318, ff.116–17 (*CC*, VII, 1068).
148. 31.7.1760. BPUN, MS R318, ff.30–31 (*CC*, VII, 1073).
149. 1.8.1760. BPUN, MS R318, ff.118–19 (*CC*, VII, 1074).
150. 16.6.1760. BPUN, MS R320, ff.67–8 (*CC*, VII, 1018).
151. 22.6.1760. Dutch Royal Library, G16-A434, no.55 (*CC*, VII, 1027).
152. 29.6.1760. Dutch Royal Library, G16-A434, no.56 (*CC*, VII, 1037).
153. 6.7.1760. Dutch Royal Library, G16-A434, no.57 (*CC*, VII, 1046).
154. 17.7.1760. BPUN, MS R320, ff.74–5 (*CC*, VII, 1057).
155. 24.7.1760. Dutch Royal Library, G16-A434, no.59 (*CC*, VII, 1061).
156. 31.7.1760. BPUN, MS R320, f.78 (*CC*, VII, 1072).
157. 21.8.1760. BPUN, MS R320, f.81 (*CC*, VII, 1086).
158. 25.8.1760. BPUN, MS R320, f.82 (*CC*, VII, 1090).
159. 7.9.1769. Dutch Royal Library, G16-A434, no.63 (*CC*, VII, 1098).
160. BPUN, MS R308, ff.111–12 (*CC*, VII, 1011).
161. BPUN, MS R308, ff.113–14 (*CC*, VII, 1038).
162. 20.7.1760. BPUN, MS R90, p.156 (*CC*, VII, 1059).
163. 19.7.1760. BPUN, MS R318, ff.122–3 (*CC*, VII, 1058).
164. 12.8.1760. BPUN, MS R n.a.I, no.14 (*CC*, VII, 1080).
165. 13.8.1760. BPUN, MS R311, ff.76–7 (*CC*, VII, 1081).
166. 25.8.1760. BPUG, MS Fr.203, ff.169–70 (*CC*, VII, 1089).
167. 27.8.1760. BPUG, MS Fr.203, ff.174–75 (*CC*, VII, 1091).
168. 19.9.1760. BPUG, MS Fr.203, ff.54–5 (*CC*, VII, 1103).
169. P, II, p.95 (*OC*, I, pp.510–11).
170. 25.9.1760. BPUN, MS R314, ff.28–9 (*CC*, VII, 1106).
171. Undated. BPUN, MS R90, p.158 (*CC*, VII, 1110).
172. P, II, p.113 (*OC*, I, pp.542–3).
173. 7.10.1760. BPUN, MS R90, pp.159–60 (*CC*, VII, 1116).
174. P, II, p.113 (*OC*, I, p.543).
175. 6.10.1760. Palais Bourbon, P7074, ff.29–30 (*CC*, VII, 1114).
176. 7.10.1760. BPUN, MS R90, f.160 (*CC*, VII, 1116).

177. 18.10.1760. BPUN, MS R308, ff.117–18 (*CC*, VII, 1127).
178. 26.10.1760. Palais Bourbon, P7074, ff.51–2 (*CC*, VII, 1129).
179. 1.11.1760. BPUN, MS R308, ff.121–2 (*CC*, VII, 1138).
180. 31.10.1760. Palais Bourbon, P7074, ff.31–2 (*CC*, VII, 1136).
181. 1.11.1760. BPUN, MS R308, ff.119–20 (*CC*, VII, 1139).
182. 3.11.1760. Palais Bourbon, P7074, ff.33–4 (*CC*, VII, 1142).
183. 2.11.1760. BPUN, MS R308, ff.1–2 (*CC*, VII, 1141).
184. 6.11.1760. BPUN, MS R308, ff.3–4 (*CC*, VII, 1155).
185. 12.9.1760. BPUN, MS R320, ff.86–7 (*CC*, VII, 1100).
186. 14.9.1760. Dutch Royal Library, G16-D434, no.64 (*CC*, VII, 1101).
187. 21.9.1760. Manuscript not traced (*CC*, VII, 1104).
188. 29.9.1760. BPUN, MS R320, ff.92–3 (*CC*, VII, 1109).
189. 2.10.1760. BPUN, MS R320, f.94 (*CC*, VII, 1112).
190. 5.10.1760. Dutch Royal Library, G16-A434, no.65 (*CC*, VII, 1113).
191. BPUN, MS R320, ff.95–6 (*CC*, VII, 1115).
192. 22.10.1760. Rosanbo Archives (*CC*, VII, 1126).
193. 29.10.1760. BPUN, MS R295, ff.3–4 (*CC*, VII, 1133).
194. 5.11.1760. BPUN, MS R284, ff.102–5 (*CC*, VII, 1152).
195. Grosclaude (1960), pp.88–9.
196. BPUN, MS R n.a. (*CC*, VII, 1134).
197. Palais Bourbon, P7074, ff.31–2 (*CC*, VII, 1136).
198. 5.11.1760(?). BPUG, MS Fr.203, ff.195–6 (*CC*, VII, 1151).
199. 11.11.1760(?). BPUG, MS Fr.203, f.58 (*CC*, VII, 1159).
200. 7.12.1760(?). BPUG, MS Fr.203, ff.193–4 (*CC*, VII, 1183).
201. P, II, p.103 (*OC*, I, p.525).
202. See Mme de Verdelin to Rousseau, 3.11.1760. BPUN, MS R322, ff.1–2 (*CC*, VII, 1144).
203. 5.11.1760. BPUN, MS R322, ff.17–18 (*CC*, VII, 1149).
204. 5.11.1760. BPUN, MS R90, p.169 (*CC*, VII, 1150).
205. 8.11.1760. BPUN, MS R322, ff.19–20 (*CC*, VII, 1156).
206. P, II, p.106 (*OC*, I, p.530).
207. 13.11.1760(?). BPUN, MS R322, ff.5–6 (*CC*, VII, 1161).
208. 24.11.1760. BPUN, MS R322, ff.21–2 (*CC*, VII, 1172).
209. P, II, p.106 (*OC*, I, p.530).
210. Undated. BPUG, MS Fr.203, ff.27–8 (*CC*, VII, 1207).
211. P, II, p.93 (*OC*, I, p.508).
212. 13.11.1760. BPUN, MS R295, ff.5–6 (*CC*, VII, 1161).
213. 17.11.1760. BPUN, MS R248, ff.106–7 (*CC*, VII, 1164).
214. *OC*, II, p.282.
215. 20.12.1760. BPUN, MS R292, ff.107–8 (*CC*, VII, 1198).
216. See Rousseau's 'Distribution', BPUG, MS Fr.203, f.190.
217. See *J.-J.*, pp.161–2.
218. BPUN, MS R293, ff.57–8 (*CC*, VII, 1131).
219. 10.11.1760(?). BPUN, MS R293, ff.59–60 (*CC*, VII, 1158).
220. 17.11.1760(?). BPUN, MS R293, ff.61–2 (*CC*, VII, 1165).
221. 19.11.1760. BPUN, MS R90, p.171 (*CC*, VII, 1166).
222. *OC*, II, pp.5–6.
223. 19.11.1760. BPUN, MS R90, p.171 (*CC*, VII, 1166).
224. P, II, p.50 (*OC*, I, pp.435–6).
225. 22.11.1760(?). BPUN, MS R293, ff.63–4 (*CC*, VII, 1170).
226. 26.11.1760. BPUN, MS R283, ff.127–8 (*CC*, VII, 1174).
227. Rey to Rousseau, 24.11.1760. BPUN, MS R320, ff.112 (*CC*, VII, 1173).
228. BPUN, MS R298, f.42 (*CC*, VII, 1177).
229. BPUN, MS R308, ff.125–6 (*CC*, VII, 1181).

230. 12.12.1760. Palais Bourbon, P7074, ff.37–8 (*CC*, VII, 1190).
231. 1.12.1760(?). BPUN, MS R293, ff.65–6 (*CC*, VII, 1179).
232. 20.12.1760(?). BPUN, MS R293, ff.69–70 (*CC*, VII, 1199).
233. BPUG, MS Fr.206, 23rd letter (*CC*, VII, 1191).
234. 12.12.1760. Palais Bourbon, P7074, ff.37–8 (*CC*, VII, 1190).
235. Munich, Bayerische Staatsbibliothek (*CC*, VII, 1201).
236. 19.11.1760. BPUN, MS R294, ff.27–8 (*CC*, VII, 1167).
237. 21.12.1760. Munich, Bayerische Staatsbibliothek (*CC*, VII, 1201).
238. 24.12.1760. Rosanbo Archives (*CC*, VII, 1204).
239. 26.12.1760. BPUN, MS R320, ff.115–16 (*CC*, VII, 1209).
240. 31.12.1760. BPUN, MS R320, ff.117–18 (*CC*, VII, 1212).
241. 28.12.1760. BPUG, Soc. J.-J.R., MS R105 (*CC*, VII, 1210).
242. Rey to Rousseau, 20.12.1760. BPUN, MS R320, f.113 (*CC*, VII, 1200).
243. BPUN, MS R308, ff.127–8 (*CC*, VII, 1202).
244. 18.12.1760. BPUN, MS R314, ff.110–11 (*CC*, VII, 1197).
245. 8.12.1760. BPUN, MS R314, ff.108–9 (*CC*, VII, 1186).
246. 18.12.1760. BPUG, Soc. J.-J.R., MS R105 (*CC*, VII, 1195).
247. 28.12.1760. BPUG, Soc. J.-J.R., MS R105 (*CC*, VII, 1210).
248. 11.12.1760. BPUG, MS Fr.206, 23rd letter (*CC*, VII, 1191).
249. *OC*, IV, p.262.

CHAPTER 9: THE YEAR OF
JULIE
(pages 247–77)

1. BPUN, MS R318, ff.36–7 (*CC*, VIII, 1217).
2. BPUN, MS R320, ff.121–2 (*CC*, VIII, 1221).
3. BPUG, MS Fr.203, ff.190 and 192 (*CC*, VIII, 1226).
4. BPUN, MS R296, f.163 (*CC*, VII, 943).
5. *CC*, VIII, p.17.
6. BPUN, MS R311, ff.78–9 (*CC*, VIII, 1288).
7. P, II, p.46 (*OC*, I, p.428).
8. 25.1.1761. BPUN, MS R309, ff.1–2 (*CC*, VIII, 1231).
9. 19.1.1761. BPUG, MS Fr.203, ff.197–8 (*CC*, VIII, 1223).
10. 25.1.1761. BPUN, MS R309, ff.1–2 (*CC*, VIII, 1231).
11. 25.1.1761. BPUG, MS Fr.203, f.167 (*CC*, VIII, 1232).
12. 25.1.1761. BPUG, MS Fr.203, ff.213–15 (*CC*, VIII, 1233).
13. 26.1.1761. BPUG, MS Fr.303, ff.211–12 (*CC*, VIII, 1235).
14. 26.1.1761. BPUN, MS R295, ff.7–8 (*CC*, VIII, 1237).
15. 28.1.1761. BPUN, MS R284, ff.108–9 (*CC*, VIII, 1239).
16. 28.1.1761. BPUN, MS R284, ff.110–11 (*CC*, VIII, 1240).
17. 29.1.1761. BPUN, MS R295, ff.9–10 (*CC*, VIII, 1242).
18. 30.1.1761. BPUG, MS Fr.203, ff.209–10 (*CC*, VIII, 1245).
19. 30.1.1761. BPUN, MS R284, ff.110–11 (*CC*, VIII, p.1244).
20. BPUN, MS R284, ff.112–13 (*CC*, VIII, 1273).
21. 2.1.1761. Manuscript not traced. *CG*, V, pp.310–15 (*CC*, VIII, 1215).
22. Moultou sent this information to Coindet in a letter dated 14 January 1761 (BPUN, MS R119, ff.1–2 [*CC*, VIII, 1219]).
23. 21.1.1761. BPUN, MS R322, ff.181–2 (*CC*, VIII, 1228).
24. 26.1.1761. BPUG, Soc. J.-J.R., MS R105 (*CC*, VIII, 1236).
25. 30.1.1761. Manuscript not traced. *CG*, V, pp.347–8 (*CC*, VIII, 1246).
26. 23.1.1761. BPUN, MS R318, ff.128–9 (*CC*, VIII, 1230).

27. BPUN, MS R308, ff.131–2 (*CC*, VIII, 1241).
28. 3.2.1761. BPUN, MS R294, ff.70–71 (*CC*, VIII, 1255).
29. 2.3.1761. BPUN, MS R322, ff.183–4 (*CC*, VIII, 1317).
30. 11.2.1761. BPUN, MS R308, ff.5–6 (*CC*, VIII, 1281).
31. 14.2.1761. BPUN, MS R292, ff.43–4 (*CC*, VIII, 1290).
32. P, II, p.111 (*OC*, I, p.545).
33. 18.2.1761. BPUN, MS R318, ff.130–31 (*CC*, VIII, 1301).
34. 10.2.1761. BPUN MS R292, ff.5–6 *CC*, VIII, 1276).
35. 15.2.1761. BPUN, MS R19, f.4 (*CC*, VIII, 1291).
36. 16.2.1761. Palais Bourbon, P7074, ff.43–4 (*CC*, VIII, 1294).
37. 7.2.1761. BPUG, MS Fr.206, no.25, f.19 (*CC*, VIII, 1266).
38. BPUN, MS R308, ff.131–2 (*CC*, VIII, 1241).
39. 7.2.1761. BPUG, MS Fr.206, no.25, f.19 (*CC*, VIII, 1266 *bis*).
40. Besterman, D9622.
41. 9.2.1761. Montmorency, Musée Rousseau (*CC*, VIII, 1269).
42. See *J.-J.*, p.288.
43. The manuscript has not been traced. Rey reproduced the text in his own second edition of the novel.
44. 9.2.1761. BPUG, MS Fr.203, ff.203–4 (*CC*, VIII, 1268).
45. 11.2.1761. BPUG, MS Fr.203, ff.199–200 (*CC*, VIII, 1280).
46. 13.2.1761. BPUG, MS Fr.203, ff.59–60 (*CC*, VIII, 1286).
47. P, II, p.116 (*OC*, I, p.548).
48. BPUN, MS R292, ff.23–4 (*CC*, VIII, 1284).
49. Manuscript not traced; *CG*, VI, pp.14–16 (*CC*, VIII, 1285).
50. 25.2.1761. Manuscript not traced; *CG*, VI, pp.86–7 (*CC*, VIII, 1321).
51. P, II, p.116 (*OC*, I, pp.548–9).
52. The manuscript is now in Neuchâtel.
53. *OC*, III, pp.1540–43.
54. 20.1.1761. BPUN, MS R293, ff.71–2 (*CC*, VIII, 1227).
55. Dutch Royal Library, G16-A434, no.66 (*CC*, VIII, 1300).
56. 25.2.1761. BPUN, MS R320, ff.124–5 (*CC*, VIII, 1324).
57. 10.2.1761. BPUN, MS R298, ff.92–3 (*CC*, VIII, 1278).
58. 3.2.1761. BPUN, MS R322, f.26 (*CC*, VIII, 1258). The writer of this letter was probably Diane, Marquise de Polignac, but may have been Marie-Louise, also Marquise de Polignac, or Françoise-Élisabeth, Comtesse de Polignac.
59. P, II, p.111 (*OC*, I, pp.545–6).
60. ibid.
61. 31.1.1761. BPUN, MS R292, ff.165–6 (*CC*, VIII, 1249).
62. 5.2.1761. BPUN, MS R n.a., ff.105–6 (*CC*, VIII, 1262).
63. 6.2.1761. BPUN, MS R292, ff.167–8 (*CC*, VIII, 1265).
64. 31.1.1761. BPUN, MS R301, ff.102–3 (*CC*, VIII, 1250).
65. 3.2.1761. BPUN, MS R293, ff.141–2 (*CC*, VIII, 1256).
66. Besterman, D9575.
67. Geneva, Registres du Petit Conseil, 21.1.1761.
68. ibid.
69. Suggested by Leigh to be J.L. Buisson (*CC*, VIII, p.88).
70. 11.2.1761. BPUN, MS R301, ff.38–9 (*CC*, VIII, 1282).
71. *CC*, IV, 499.
72. 19.2.1761. BPUN, MS R303, ff.14–15 (*CC*, VIII, 1305).
73. Geneva, Registres du Petit Conseil, 13.2.1761.
74. 27.2.1761. BPUN, MS R321, ff.1–2 (*CC*, VIII, 1329).
75. P, II, p.115 (*OC*, I, p.548).
76. ibid. See also the *Second Preface* (*OC*, II, pp.9–30).
77. P, II, p.115 (*OC*, I, p.547).
78. 27.2.1761. BPUN, MS R292, ff.56–63 (*CC*, VIII, 1331).
79. 3.3.1761(?). BPUN, MS R283, ff.33–8 (*CC*, VIII, 1336).

80. *OC*, IV, p.194.

81. 30.1.1761(?). BPUN, MS R284, f.110 (*CC*, VIII, 1244).

82. BPUN, MS R295, ff.11–20 (*CC*, VIII, 1298).

83. 19.2.1761. BPUN, MS R291, f.188 (*CC*, VIII, 1304).

84. 19.2.1761. BPUN, MS R284, ff.114–15 (*CC*, VIII, 1303).

85. 25.2.1761(?). BPUG, MS Fr.203, ff.71–2 (*CC*, VIII, 1323).

86. 21.2.1761. BPUN, MS R298, ff.43–4 (*CC*, VIII, 1309).

87. 22.2.1761. BPUN, MS R297, ff.70–71 (*CC*, VIII, 1314).

88. 24.2.1761(?). BPUN, MS R n.a.8, ff.3–4 (*CC*, VIII, 1319).

89. 5.3.1761. BPUN, MS R297, ff.70–72 (*CC*, VIII, 1340).

90. 9.3.1761. BPUN, MS R n.a.8, ff.1–2 (*CC*, VIII, 1347).

91. 2.3.1761. BPUN, MS R320, ff.126–7 (*CC*, VIII, 1335).

92. 4.3.1761. BPUG, MS Fr.203, ff.201–2 (*CC*, VIII, 1338).

93. 5.3.1761. BPUN, MS R309, ff. 3–4 (*CC*, VIII, 1339).

94. 10.3.1761(?). Manuscript not traced; Musset-Pathay (1825), pp.49–61 (*CC*, VIII, 1350).

95. Grosclaude (1960), p.104.

96. 16.2.1761. BPUN, MS R292, ff.160–70 (*CC*, VIII, 1295).

97. 25.2.1761. Manuscript not traced; *CG*, VI, p.52 (*CC*, VIII, 1322).

98. 4.3.1761. BPUG, MS Fr.203, ff.201–2 (*CC*, VIII, 1338).

99. Translated into French in *La Semaine littéraire*, Geneva, 15.7.1922 (*CC*, VIII, pp.359–62).

100. 16.2.1761. BPUN, MS R302, ff.29–30 (*CC*, VIII, 1297).

101. 16.2.1761. BPUN, MS R292, ff.25–6 (*CC*, VIII, 1296).

102. 16.2.1761. BPUG, MS Fr.203, ff.207–8 (*CC*, VIII, 1299).

103. Sunday, 22 February 1761.

104. *Extrait du Projet de paix perpétuelle*, Paris, 1761, p.v. (*OC*, III, p.154).

105. See *Annales*, XVII, 1926, pp.147–63.

106. P, II, p.43 (*OC*, I, pp.423–4).

107. Favre cites '*vous verrez bientôt une révolution*' as Rousseau's exact words (*Annales*, XVII, p.160).

108. 27.2.1761(?). BPUG, MS Fr.203, ff.71–2 (*CC*, VIII, 1330).

109. 26.2.1761. BPUN, MS R318, ff.132–3 (*CC*, VIII, 1325).

110. 26.2.1761. Palais Bourbon, P7074, ff.17–18 (*CC*, VIII, 1326).

111. P, II, p.116 (*OC*, I, p.549).

112. ibid.

113. P, II, p.118 (*OC*, I, p.553).

114. ibid.

115. *La Muse limonadière*, vol. II, p.278.

116. 9.3.1761. BPUN, MS R292, ff.50–51 (*CC*, VIII, 1348).

117. BPUN, MS R292, ff.47–8 (*CC*, VIII, 1332).

118. 12.3.1761. BPUN, MS R19, f.6 recto (*CC*, VIII, 1355).

119. 7.3.1761. BPUN, MS R319, ff.5–7 (*CC*, VIII, 1344).

120. See especially Chapter XI, 'De la mort du corps politique', and Chapter XII (*OC*, III, pp.424–6; *SC*, pp.134–7).

CHAPTER 10: CENSORSHIP
(pages 278–30)

1. *Lettres à M. de Voltaire sur La Nouvelle Héloïse*, Geneva, 1761, 25 pages in octavo.

2. See Henri Gouhier, *Rousseau et Voltaire*, Paris, 1983, pp.160–65.

3. 9.3.1761. Dutch Royal Library, Art. II, no.129 (*CC*, VIII, 1349).

4. BN, n.a.f.24330, ff.28–9 (*CC*, VIII, 1373).

5. 9.4.1761. Dutch Royal Library, Art. II, no.129 (*CC*, VIII, 1391).

6. 11.3.1761. BPUN, MS R295, ff.59–62 (*CC*, VIII, 1354).

7. 20.4.1761. BPUN, MS R297, ff.129–30 (*CC*, VIII, 1396).

8. 22.4.1761(?). Poitiers, Bibliothèque de la Ville, MS Fr.201, p.7 (*CC*, VIII, 1398).
9. 8.5.1761. Poitiers, Bibliothèque de la Ville, MS Fr.199, ff.37–8 (*CC*, VIII, 1407).
10. 15.5.1761(?). Poitiers, Bibliothèque de la Ville, MS Fr.201, pp.9–11 (*CC*, VIII, 1412).
11. P, II, p.122 (*OC*, I, pp.560–61).
12. 11.4.1761. BPUN, MS R318, ff.134–5 (*CC*, VIII, 1393).
13. P, II, p.129 (*OC*, I, p.573).
14. P, II, p.119 (*OC*, I, p.554).
15. 15.3.1761(?). BPUN, MS R308, ff.15–18 (*CC*, VIII, 1371).
16. 21.3.1761. BPUN, MS R308, ff.19–20 (*CC*, VIII, 1375).
17. 22.3.1761(?). BPUN, MS R308, ff.21–2 (*CC*, VIII, 1377).
18. 4.6.1761(?). BPUN, MS R308, ff.7–8 (*CC*, IX, 1425).
19. P, II, p.120 (*OC*, I, p.555).
20. 12.3.1761. BPUN, MS R293, ff.75–6 (*CC*, VIII, 1357).
21. 29.3.1761. BPUN, MS R311, ff.80–81 (*CC*, VIII, 1383).
22. 23.4.1761. BPUG, MS Fr.206, ff.19–20 (*CC*, VIII, 1400).
23. BPUN, MS R318, ff.38–9 (*CC*, VIII, 1408).
24. 12.5.1761. BPUN, MS R318, ff.136–7 (*CC*, VIII, 1410).
25. 18.5.1761. Palais Bourbon, P7074, ff.61–2 (*CC*, VIII, 1413).
26. 22.5.1761(?). BPUG, MS Fr.203, ff.179–80 (*CC*, VIII, 1416).
27. BPUN, MS R318, ff.40–41 (*CC*, VIII, 1415).
28. P, II, p.117 (*OC*, I, p.550).
29. ibid.
30. P, II, pp.117–18 (*OC*, I, pp.551–2).
31. 24.5.1761. BPUN, MS R308, ff.139–40 (*CC*, VIII, 1417).
32. 28.5.1761. BPUN, MS R299, f.95 (*CC*, VIII, 1421).
33. 26.5.1761. BPUN, MS R303, ff.74–5 (*CC*, VIII, 1419).
34. 24.6.1761. BPUG, MS Fr.203, ff.261–2 (*CC*, IX, 1436).
35. 29.5.1761. BPUN, MS R289, ff.5–6 (*CC*, VIII, 1423).
36. 13.6.1761. BPUN, MS R319, ff.10–12 (*CC*, IX, 1431).
37. Manuscript not traced; CG, VI, pp.140–44 (*CC*, IX, 1429).
38. 20.6.1761. BPUN, MS R318, ff.127 *bis*–127 *ter* (*CC*, IX, 1433).
39. 26.6.1761. Manuscript not traced; CG, VI, p.145 (*CC*, IX, 1439).
40. 12.6.1761. Manuscript not traced; CG, VI, pp.146–9 (*CC*, IX, 1430).
41. P, II, p.121 (*OC*, I, p.557).
42. 7.8.1761. BPUN, MS R318, ff.142–3 (*CC*, IX, 1470).
43. 10.8.1761. Palais Bourbon, P7074, ff.39–40 (*CC*, IX, 1472).
44. P, II, p.121 (*OC*, I, p.558).
45. ibid.
46. Published in December 1764. Reproduced, with Rousseau's annotations, in CG, XII, pp.365–82.
47. P, II, p.129 (*OC*, I, p.572).
48. 20.6.1761. BPUN, MS R318, ff.127 *bis*–127 *ter* (*CC*, IX, 1433).
49. 20.6.1761(?). Manuscript not traced; Leigh reproduces a copy conserved at the Landesbibliothek, Gotha (*CC*, IX, 1434).
50. 23.6.1761(?). BPUN, MS R298, ff.90–91 (*CC*, IX, 1435).
51. 18.6.1761. BPUG, MS Fr.232 (*CC*, IX, 1432).
52. 25.6.1761. BPUN, MS R283, ff.118–19 (*CC*, IX, 1437).
53. 15.7.1761. Poitiers, Bibliothèque de la Ville, MS Fr.201, pp.16–19 (*CC*, IX, 1449).
54. 12.8.1761. Poitiers, Bibliothèque de la Ville, MS Fr.199, ff.27–8 (*CC*, IX, 1476).
55. 27.8.1761(?). Poitiers, Bibliothèque de la Ville, MS Fr.201, pp.21–4 (*CC*, IX, 1480).
56. 12.9.1761. Poitiers, Bibliothèque de la Ville, MS Fr.199, ff.33–4 (*CC*, IX, 1490).
57. 17.10.1761. Poitiers, Bibliothèque de la Ville, MS Fr.199, ff.31–2 (*CC*, IX, 1510).

58. 25.6.1761. Palais Bourbon, P7074, ff.3–4 (*CC*, IX, 1438).
59. Undated. BN, MS Fr.22073 (*CC*, IX, 1441).
60. 1.6.1761. BPUN, MS R320, ff.128–9 (*CC*, IX, 1424).
61. 9.8.1761. Dutch Royal Library, G16-A434, no.67 (*CC*, IX, 1471).
62. 17.8.1761. BPUN, MS R320, ff.130–31 (*CC*, IX, 1477).
63. 18.7.1761. BPUN, MS R318, ff.42–3 (*CC*, IX, 1453).
64. P, II, p.120 (*OC*, I, p.556).
65. ibid.
66. 20.7.1761. Palais Bourbon, P7074, ff.41–2 (*CC*, IX, 1454).
67. 18.7.1761. BPUN, MS R318, ff.140–41 (*CC*, IX, 1452).
68. 25.6.1761. BPUN, MS R295, ff.134–5 (*CC*, IX, 1460).
69. Undated. BPUN, MS R284, f.178 (*CC*, IX, 1464).
70. P, II, p.100 (*OC*, I, p.519).
71. 6.6.1761. BPUN, MS R297, ff.95–6 (*CC*, IX, 1427).
72. Palais Bourbon, P7074, ff.41–2 (*CC*, IX, 1454).
73. 24.7.1761. BPUN, MS R289, ff.7–8 (*CC*, IX, 1458).
74. 3.8.1761. BPUN, MS R302, ff.19–20 (*CC*, IX, 1468).
75. 22.7.1761. Manuscript not traced; *CG*, VI, pp.170–71 (*CC*, IX, 1457).
76. BPUN, MS R318, ff.138–9 (*CC*, IX, 1474).
77. P, II, p.122 (*OC*, I, p.559).
78. 20.8.1761. Geneva, private collection (*CC*, IX, 1478).
79. *Eloisa, or A Series of Original Letters, Collected and Published by J.J. Rousseau*, translated from the French by William Kenrick, London, R. Griffiths and T. Becket and P.A. de Hondt, 1761.
80. 21.8.1761. Nancy, Bibliothèque de la Ville, Collection Soyer-Willemet (*CC*, IX, 1479).
81. 28.8.1761. Palais Bourbon, P7074, ff.63–4 (*CC*, IX, 1481).
82. 29.9.1761. BPUN, MS R308, ff.13–14 (*CC*, IX, 1484).
83. BN, n.a.f.1183, f.53 (*CC*, IX, 1486).
84. 4.9.1761. Chaalis, Musée André, Fonds Rousseau A54.
85. 2.9.1761. Dutch Royal Library, G16-A434, no.68 (*CC*, IX, 1488).
86. BN, n.a.f.1183, f.53 (*CC*, IX, 1486).
87. 6.9.1761. BPUN, MS R300, ff.72–3 (*CC*, IX, 1489).
88. 13.9.1761. Geneva, private collection (*CC*, IX, 1492).
89. 14.9.1761. Leningrad, State Library (*CC*, IX, 1493).
90. 25.9.1761. BN, n.a.f.1183, f.55 (*CC*, IX, 1495).
91. See *J.-J.*, pp.289–91.
92. 18.11.1761. BPUN, MS R295 (*CC*, IX, 1552).
93. The essay, edited by Du Peyrou, was first published in a volume of *Traités sur la musique*, Geneva, 1781.
94. Porset, p.12.
95. 20.10.1671. BPUN, MS R284, ff.49–50 (*CC*, IX, 1514).
96. 22.10.1671. Palais Bourbon, P7074 (*CC*, IX, 1518).
97. 3.11.1761. BPUN, MS R284, f.51 (*CC*, IX, 1532).
98. 18.11.1761. BPUN, MS R318, ff.144–5 (*CC*, IX, 1551).
99. 1.12.1761. Palais Bourbon, P7074, ff.57–8 (*CC*, IX, 1575).
100. 28.9.1761. BPUN, MS R288, ff.1–2 (*CC*, IX, 1496).
101. 29.9.1761. BPUN, MS R288, ff.3–4 (*CC*, IX, 1497).
102. 21.10.1761. BPUN, MS R285, ff.149–50 (*CC*, IX, 1515).
103. Leigh suggests that this letter was addressed to the Baron de Bormes, who pestered Rousseau with several silly letters (*CC*, IX, p.193).
104. 30.9.1761. BPUN, MS R296, ff.3–4 (*CC*, IX, 1498).
105. 24.10.1761. BPUN, MS R291, f.102 (*CC*, IX, 1521).

106. Haydn Mason, *Voltaire*, London, 1981, p.98.
107. See Besterman, XXIV, D10080.
108. See Jacques van den Heuvel, *L'Affaire Calas*, Paris, 1975, p.9.
109. Haydn Mason, *Voltaire*, London, 1981, p.98.
110. 22.10.1761. BPUN, MS R320, f.183 (*CC*, IX, 1519).
111. P, II, p.22 (*OC*, I, p.559).
112. 30.10.1761. BPUN, MS R n.a.I, 33 (*CC*, IX, 1529).
113. Manuscript not traced; Musset-Pathay (1825), pp.75–6 (*CC*, IX, 1535).
114. 7.11.1761. Dutch Royal Library, G16-A434, no.70 (*CC*, IX, 1534).

CHAPTER 11: TWO SOCIAL CONTRACTS
(pages 302–22)

1. See J.W. Gough, *The Social Contract*, Oxford, 1957.
2. *OC*, III, p.176; *DI*, p.120.
3. ibid.
4. *OC*, III, p.177; *DI*, p.121.
5. ibid.
6. *OC*, III, p.171; *DI*, p.116.
7. *OC*, III, p.169; *DI*, p.114.
8. *OC*, III, p.170; *DI*,114.
9. *OC*, III, p.158; *DI*, p.103.
10. *OC*, III, p.203; *DI*, p.149.
11. See *J.-J.*, pp.244–5.
12. Wokler (1987), p.232.
13. *OC*, III, p.351; *SC*, p.49.
14. *OC*, III, p.364; *SC*, p.65.
15. *OC*, III, p.365; *SC*, p.65.
16. *OC*, III, p.360; *SC*, p.60.
17. *OC*, III, p.430; *SC*, p.141.
18. Ed. J.N. Figgis and R.V. Laurence, London, 1959, p.16.
19. See, for example, James Miller in *Rousseau, Dreamer of Democracy*, New Haven, 1984.
20. *OC*, III, p.406; *SC*, p.114.
21. *OC*, III, p.112; *DI*, p.60.
22. *OC*, III, p.384; *SC*, p.87.
23. Book I, chapter II, S4.
24. *OC*, III, p.406; *SC*, p.115.
25. ibid.
26. *OC*, III, p.364; *SC*, p.64.
27. *OC*, III, p.440; *SC*, p.153.
28. *Émile*, Paris, 1924, p.270.
29. *OC*, IV, p.598.
30. *OC*, III, p.466; *SC*, pp.183–4.
31. *OC*, III, p.467; *SC*, p.184.
32. *OC*, III, p.810.
33. *OC*, III, p.421; *SC*, p.131.
34. *OC*, III, p.808.
35. *OC*, III, pp.421–3; *SC*, pp.131–4.
36. *OC*, III, p.809.
37. *CC*, V, p.242.
38. *OC*, III, pp.841–2.
39. 24.11.1761. BPUN, MS R299, ff.100–101 (*CC*, IX, 1562).
40. P, II, p.123 (*OC*, I, p.560).
41. 12.12.1761. BPUN, MS R289, ff.9–12 (*CC*, IX, 1583).
42. 5.11.1761. BPUN, MS R288, ff.25–7 (*CC*, IX, 1533).
43. 10.11.1761. BPUN, MS R288, ff.28–31 (*CC*, IX, 1536).
44. 14.11.1761. BPUN, MS R288, ff.32–3 (*CC*, IX, 1538).
45. 18.11.1761. BPUN, MS R288, f.36 (*CC*, IX, 1550).
46. 16.11.1761. BPUN, MS R288, ff.34–5 (*CC*, IX, 1545).
47. 14.11.1761. BPUN, MS R321, ff.2–4 (*CC*, IX, 1541).
48. 12.12.1761. Dutch Royal Library, G16-A279 (*CC*, IX, 1582).
49. 15.11.1761. BPUN, MS R320, ff.134–5 (*CC*, IX, 1543).
50. 16.11.1761. Manuscript not traced; Musset-Pathay (1825), I, p.77 (*CC*, IX, 1546).
51. 18.11.1761. BN, n.a.f.1183, ff.57–8 (*CC*, IX, 1548).
52. Father Hemet and Father Coppier (see *J.-J.*, p.120).
53. P, I, p.126 (*OC*, I, p.242).
54. P, II, p.126 (*OC*, I, p.566).
55. ibid.
56. Grosclaude (1961), p.83.
57. 20.11.1761. BN, n.a.f.1183, f.60 (*CC*, IX, 1554).

58. 21.11.1761. Yale University Library (*CC*, IX, 1556).
59. 22.11.1761. BPUN, MS R295, ff.27–8 (*CC*, IX, 1558).
60. 24.11.1761. BPUN, MS R295, ff.29–30 (*CC*, IX, 1563).
61. 29.11.1761. BN, n.a.f.1183, ff.62–3 (*CC*, IX, 1567).
62. 30.11.1761. BN, n.a.f.1183, ff.64–5 (*CC*, IX, 1571).
63. 30.11.1761. BN, n.a.f.1183, f.66 (*CC*, IX, 1572).
64. 7.12.1761. BPUN, MS R295, ff.33–4 (*CC*, IX, 1578).
65. 8.12.1761. BN, n.a.f.1183, ff.69–70 (*CC*, IX, 1580).
66. BPUN, MS R289, ff.9–12 (*CC*, IX, 1583).
67. 13.11.1761. BN, n.a.f.1183, f.71 (*CC*, IX, p.1586) and Palais Bourbon, P7074, ff.49–50 (*CC*, IX, 1587).
68. 14.12.1761. BPUN, MS R295, ff.35–6 (*CC*, IX, 1588).
69. 15.12.1761. BPUN, MS R318, ff.146–9 (*CC*, IX, 1589).
70. 15.12.1761. BPUN, MS R308, ff.23–4 (*CC*, IX, 1590).
71. 16.12.1761. BPUN, MS R295, ff.37–44 (*CC*, IX, 1591).
72. 18.12.1761. BPUN, MS R295, ff.45–6 (*CC*, IX, 1594).
73. BPUN, MS R320, f.138 (*CC*, IX, 1600).
74. 23.12.1761. Palais Bourbon, P7074, ff.47–8 (*CC*, IX, 1605).
75. 24.12.1761. Palais Bourbon, P7074, ff.59–60 (*CC*, IX, 1606).
76. 25.12.1761. BPUG, Soc. J.-J.R., MS R105 (*CC*, IX, 1609).
77. 25.12.1761. BPUN, MS R295, ff.47–8 (*CC*, IX, 1610).
78. 25.12.1761. Paris, BN, n.a.f.1183, f.73 (*CC*, IX, 1611).
79. 23.12.1761. The manuscript of this letter, in private hands, was seen by Leigh (*CC*, IX, 1602).
80. 9.12.1761. BPUN, MS R297, ff.5–7 (*CC*, IX, 1581).

81. 28.12.1761. BPUN, MS Rn.a.b. (*CC*, IX, 1615).
82. P, II, p.124 (*OC*, I, p.564).

CHAPTER 12: BANISHMENT
(pages 323–62)

1. 4.1.1762. BPUN, MS R291, ff.156–61 (*CC*, X, 1622).
2. See also Grosclaude, 1960, pp.36–7.
3. 12.1.1762. BPUN, MS R291, ff.162–7 (*CC*, X, 1633).
4. BPUN, MS R291, ff.168–73 (*CC*, X, 1650).
5. 28.1.1762. MS R291, ff.174–9 (*CC*, X, 1654).
6. 1.1.1762. Manuscript not traced; Musset-Pathey (1825), I, p.83 (*CC*, X, 1620).
7. 11.1.1762. BPUN, MS R320, f.145 (*CC*, X, 1632).
8. 10.1.1762. BPUN, MS R318, ff.30–31 (*CC*, X, 1630).
9. 4.1.1762. BPUN, MS R310, ff.106–7 (*CC*, X, 1624).
10. 13.1.1762. Dutch Royal Library, 121, D9–16 (*CC*, X, 1635).
11. 6.1.1762. Manuscript not traced (*CC*, X, 1626). See Leigh's notes in *CC*, X, pp.16–17 and *Annales*, XXXIV, pp.31–81.
12. P, II, p.123 (*OC*, I, p.561).
13. Dutch Royal Library, G16-A434, no.74 (*CC*, X, 1625).
14. 13.1.1762. Dutch Royal Library, G16-A434, no.76 (*CC*, X, 1634).
15. 17.1.1763. BPUG, Soc. J.-J.R. (*CC*, X, 1639).
16. 18.1.1762. BPUG, MS Fr.206, ff.22–3 (*CC*, X, 1640).
17. 18.1.1762. BPUN, MS R289, ff.13–14 (*CC*, X, 1641).
18. *OC*, III, p.349.
19. 3.1.1762. BPUN, MS R292, ff.52–3 (*CC*, X, 1621).
20. *Confessions*, P, II, p.124 (*OC*, I, p.565).
21. See *P and P*, pp.1–8.

22. *Confessions*, P, II, p.124 (*OC*, I, p.565).

23. 26.3.1762. BPUN, MS R296, ff.11–12 (*CC*, X, 1723).

24. 27.4.1762. BPUN, MS R291, f.103 (*CC*, X, 1753).

25. 9.1.1762. BPUN, MS R288, ff.60–61 (*CC*, X, 1629).

26. 3.1.1762. BPUN, MS R288, ff.72–3 (*CC*, X, 1660).

27. 2.2.1762. BPUN, MS R288, ff.74–5 (*CC*, X, 1662).

28. BPUG, Soc. J.-J.R., MS R105 (*CC*, X, 1644).

29. BPUN, MS R318, ff.170–71 (*CC*, X, 1667).

30. BPUN, MS R320, f.146 (*CC*, X, 1642).

31. 18.2.1762. Dutch Royal Library, G16-A434, no.80 (*CC*, X, 1672); Leigh corrects the date to 11.2.1762.

32. Besançon, Bibliothèque Municipale, MS1442 (*CC*, X, 1643).

33. 23.1.1762. Dutch Royal Library, G16-A434, no.77 (*CC*, X, 1648).

34. 1.2.1762. BPUN, MS R300, ff.149–50 (*CC*, X, 1661).

35. 25.2.1762. Dutch Royal Library, G16-A434, no.82 (*CC*, X, 1694).

36. 3.3.1762. BPUN, MS R320, f.159 (*CC*, X, 1700).

37. 9.5.1762. Dutch Royal Library, G16-A434, no.90 (*CC*, X, 1767).

38. 7.5.1762. BPUN, MS R284, ff.118–19 (*CC*, X, 1765).

39. 29.1.1762. Leyden, University Library, BPL246 (*CC*, X, 1657).

40. 29.1.1762. Manuscript not traced; *CG*, VII, p.80 (*CC*, X, 1656).

41. 3.2.1762. BPUN, MS R319, ff.16–17 (*CC*, X, 1663).

42. 16.2.1762. BPUN, MS R289, ff.15–16 (*CC*, X, 1680).

43. Ribotte informed Rousseau of this in a letter dated 21 February 1762 (BPUN, MS R296, ff.9–10; *CC*, X, 1687).

44. See Didier Ozanam, *La Disgrâce d'un premier commis*, Paris, 1956.

45. 8.2.1762. BPUN, MS R284, ff.116–17 (*CC*, X, 1668).

46. 11.2.1762. Dutch Royal Library, G16-A434, no.80 (*CC*, X, 1672).

47. BPUG, Dossier Morrison (*CC*, X, 1674).

48. Palais Bourbon, P7074, ff.73–4 (*CC*, X, 1682).

49. 13.2.1762(?). BPUN, MS R318, ff.150–51 (*CC*, X, 1676).

50. 18.2.1762. BPUN, MS R318, ff.52–3 (*CC*, X, 1683).

51. 19.2.1762. Palais Bourbon, P7074, ff.75–6 (*CC*, X, 1686).

52. P, II, p.93 (*OC*, I, p.507).

53. P, II, p.128 (*OC*, I, pp.570–71).

54. 25.2.1762. Dutch Royal Library, G16-A434, no.82 (*CC*, X, 1694).

55. P, II, p.127 (*OC*, I, p.568).

56. 19.2.1762. Palais Bourbon, P7074, ff.75–6 (*CC*, X, 1686).

57. Simon Schama, *Citizens: a Chronicle of the French Revolution*, London and New York, 1989, p.98.

58. Grosclaude (1961), pp.63–80.

59. 22.2.1762(?). Manuscript not traced; J. Néaulme, *Projet ... pour ... le véritable Émile*, Amsterdam, 1763, p.8 (*CC*, X, 1688).

60. 28.2.1762. Dutch Royal Library, G16-A434, no.83 (*CC*, X, 1696).

61. 4.3.1762. Manuscript not traced; Musset-Pathay (1825), I, pp.87–8 (*CC*, X, 1701).

62. 7.3.1762. Manuscript not traced; Musset-Pathay (1825), I, pp.88–9 (*CC*, X, 1704).

63. 14.3.1762. BPUG, Papiers Duchesne no.13 (*CC*, X, 1710).

64. Dutch Royal Library, G16-A434, no.84 (*CC*, X, 1707).

65. 18.3.1762. Dutch Royal Library, G16-A434, no.86 (*CC*, X, 1715).

66. 25.3.1762. BPUN, MS R320, ff.166–7 (*CC*, X, 1721).

67. See La Roche to Rousseau, April(?), 1762. Palais Bourbon, P7074 (*CC*, X, 1740).

68. *Confessions*, P, II, p.144 (*OC*, I, p.600).

69. BPUN, MS R318, ff.152–3 and 54–5 (*CC*, X, 1724 and 1725).

70. 26.3.1762. Manuscript not traced; Musset-Pathay (1825), I, pp.94–5 (*CC*, X, 1722).

71. 28.3.1762.BPUN, MS R, Nouvelles additions 9, f.28 (*CC*, X, 1726).

72. P, II, pp.127–8 (*OC*, I, p.570).

73. 2.4.1762. Bordeaux, Municipal Archives, Roullet Collection, MSS133 (*CC*, X, 1728).

74. BN, n.a.f.21196, ff.152–3 (*CC*, X, 1735).

75. Dutch Royal Library, G16-A434, no.88 (*CC*, X, 1731).

76. 12.4.1762. BPUN, MS R320, ff.170–71 (*CC*, X, 1739).

77. 15.4.1762. BPUN, MS R320, f.172 (*CC*, X, 1741).

78. BPUG, MS Fr.206, f.33 (*CC*, X, 1744).

79. 24.4.1762. BPUG, MS Fr.206, f.23 (*CC*, X, 1749).

80. 29.5.1762. BPUG, Soc. J.-J.R., MS R59 (*CC*, X, 1808).

81. 21.4.1762. BPUN, MS R288, ff.86–7 (*CC*, X, 1745).

82. 24.4.1762. BPUN, MS R288, ff.88–9 (*CC*, X, 1748).

83. 15.3.1762. BPUN, MS R319, ff.18–19 (*CC*, X, 1713).

84. BPUN, MS R289, ff.17–18 (*CC*, X, 1752).

85. BPUN, MS Rn.a. I, no.41 (*CC*, X, 1754).

86. Berne, Burgerbibliothek, Fellenberg Collection (*CC*, X, 1761).

87. BPUN, MS R320, ff.173–4 (*CC*, X, 1756).

88. 2.5.1762. Manuscript not traced; Musset-Pathay (1825), I, pp.97–8 (*CC*, X, 1762).

89. 9.5.1762. Dutch Royal Library, G16-A434, no.90 (*CC*, X, 1767).

90. Rosanbo Archives (*CC*, X, 1768).

91. 12.5.1762. Manuscript not traced; Musset-Pathay (1825), I, pp.98–9 (*CC*, X, 1769).

92. 12.5.1762. Jean Dessaint and Charles Saillant to M.-M. Rey. BPUN, MS R320, f.180 (*CC*, X, 1772).

93. 18.5.1762, Rey to Dessaint and Saillant. BPUN, MS R320, f.179 (*CC*, X, 1777).

94. Palais Bourbon, P7074, ff.78–9 (*CC*, X, 1778).

95. P, II, p.104 (*OC*, I, p.527).

96. 16.5.1762. Manuscript not traced; *CG*, VII, pp.219–20 (*CC*, X, 1776).

97. BPUN, MS R296, ff.163 (*CC*, VII, 943).

98. BPUG, MS Fr.205.

99. Palais Bourbon, P1427–39; see B. Gagnebin (*OC*, IV, pp.1853–6).

100. BPUN, MS R318, ff.154–5 (*CC*, X, 1786).

101. *Confessions*, P, II, p.120 (*OC*, I, p.555).

102. *Confessions*, P, II, p.138 (*OC*, I, p.583).

103. BPUN, MS R310, ff.110–11 (*CC*, X, 1789).

104. BPUN, MS R293, ff.77–8 (*CC*, X, 1794).

105. 24.5.1762. BPUN, MS R292, ff.145–6 (*CC*, X, 1795).

106. *Confessions*, P, II, p.130 (*OC*, I, p.574).

107. 24.5.1762. BPUN, MS R294, ff.72–3 (*CC*, X, 1796).

108. 25.5.1762. BPUN, MS R292, ff.171–2 (*CC*, X, 1799).

109. 29.5.1762. BPUG, Soc. J.-J.R., MS R88 (*CC*, X, 1807).

110. 27.5.1762. BPUN, MS R288, ff.96–7 (*CC*, X, 1803).

111. 29.17.1762. BPUN, MS R288, ff.98–9 (*CC*, X, 1811).

112. P, II, p.105 (*OC*, I, pp.527–8).

113. P, II.

114. Poitiers, Bibliothèque de la Ville, MS Fr.199, ff.29–30 (*CC*, X, 1785).

115. P, II, p.129 (*OC*, p.573).

116. This letter has not been traced.

117. This letter has not been traced.

118. P, II, p.129 (*OC*, I, p.573).
119. Grosclaude (1960), p.100.
120. ibid., p.43.
121. Dutch Royal Library, G16-A434, no.91 (*CC*, X, 1809).
122. 19.5.1762. BPUN, MS R296, ff.13–21 (*CC*, X, 1782).
123. See Haydn Mason, *Voltaire*, London, 1981, pp.98–9.
124. 24.5.1762. BPUN, MS R310, ff.112–13 (*CC*, X, 1798).
125. 26.5.1762. BPUN, MS R310, ff.114–15 (*CC*, X, 1802).
126. Palais Bourbon, P7074, ff.81–2 (*CC*, X, 1805).
127. 28.5.1762. Palais Bourbon, P7074, ff.71–2 (*CC*, X, 1806).
128. 31.5.1762. BPUN, MS R310, ff.116–17 (*CC*, X, 1814).
129. Rosanbo Archives (*CC*, X, 1820).
130. Grosclaude (1960), p.41.
131. 2.6.1762. Rosanbo Archives (*CC*, XI, 1825).
132. BPUN, MS R288, ff.102–3 (*CC*, XI, 1816).
133. BPUN, MS R310, f.1 (*CC*, XI, 1829).
134. 5.6.1762. Leyden, University Library, BPL246 (*CC*, XI, 1830).
135. 4.6.1762. BPUN, MS R288, ff.104–5 (*CC*, XI, 1827).
136. 5.6.1762. BPUN, MS R288, ff.106–7 (*CC*, XI, 1831).
137. 7.6.1762. BPUN, MS R288, ff.108–9 (*CC*, XI, 1836).
138. 7.6.1762. BPUN, MS R288, ff.110–11 (*CC*, XI, 1839).
139. BPUN, MS R289, ff.21–2 (*CC*, XI, 1835).
140. 5.6.1762. BPUN, MS R319, ff.22–3 (*CC*, XI, 1832).
141. 7.6.1762. Manuscript not traced; *CG*, VII, pp.282–3 (*CC*, XI, 1837).
142. BPUN, MS R292, ff.175–6 (*CC*, XI, 1844).
143. P, II, pp.131–2 (*OC*, I, pp.575–7).
144. P, II, p.131 (*OC*, I, p.577).
145. BPUN, MS R285, ff.34–42R (*CC*, XXXVII, 6673).
146. See *OC*, I, p.1721.
147. P, II, p.131 (*OC*, I, p.577).
148. ibid.
149. P, II, p.132 (*OC*, I, p.579).
150. 8.6.1762. BN, MS Fleury 576, f.210 (*CC*, XI, 1846).
151. P, II, p.132 (*OC*, I, p.379).
152. 14.6.1762. BPUN, MS R309, ff.5–6 (*CC*, XI, 1862).
153. P, II, p.133 (*OC*, I, p.580).
154. 8.6.1762. BPUN, MS R318, ff.156–7 (*CC*, XI, 1843).
155. P, II, p.133 (*OC*, I, p.580).
156. ibid.
157. P, II, p.134 (*OC*, I, p.582).
158. Grosclaude (1960), p.45.
159. P, II, p.134 (*OC*, I, p.582).
160. *Arrest de la Cour de Parlement qui condamne un imprimé ayant pour titre Émile, ou de l'éducation*, Paris, 1762.
161. P, II, p.135 (*OC*, I, p.583).
162. 23.6.1762. BPUN, MS R318, ff.60–61 (*CC*, XI, 1905).
163. P, II, p.135 (*OC*, I, p.584).
164. BN, MS Fr.22145, ff.2–3 (*CC*, XI, 1855).
165. BPUN, MS R119, ff.5–6 (*CC*, XI, pp.272–4).
166. 17.6.1762. Palais Bourbon, P7074, ff.83–4 (*CC*, XI, 1882).
167. P, II, p.137 (*OC*, I, p.587).
168. P, II, p.135 (*OC*, I, p.585).
169. P, II, p.136 (*OC*, I, p.586).
170. *OC*, II, p.1221.
171. See *CC*, XXIII, 3921.
172. P, II, p.136 (*OC*, I, p.586).
173. ibid.
174. See Jean-Louis Lecercle, *Rousseau et l'art du roman*, Paris, 1969.
175. See Aubrey Rosenberg, 'Rousseau's *Lévite d'Éphraim* and the Golden Age', *The Australian Journal of French Studies*, Vol. XV (1978).
176. Grimsley, 1968, p.25.
177. Porset, p.33.
178. P, II, p.137 (*OC*, I, p.587).
179. 15.6.1762. BPUN, MS R91, f.2R (*CC*, XI, 1872).

INDEX

Rousseau, Jean-Jacques: returns from Geneva, 1; enjoys literary life of Paris, 2; chooses M.-M. Rey as publisher, 5; the *Discourse on Inequality* politely received in Geneva, 7; Voltaire's reaction, 9; R.'s *Économie politique* in Diderot's *Encyclopédie*, 11; R.'s friendship with Mme d'Épinay, 14; defends Palissot against wrath of Stanislas, 15; Mme d'Épinay offers R. the Hermitage, 16; R. first refuses, then accepts, 19; Holbach *et al.* warn R. against rustic solitude, 20; joyful installation at the Hermitage with Thérèse and her mother, 21; R. works on St-Pierre's *Project for Peace*, 25; defends Providence against Voltaire's mockery, 29; *Candide* is Voltaire's reply, 30; R. writes novel, *Julie*, to express yearnings for ideal love, 33; Deleyre makes friends with R. while Diderot and others neglect him,